# Investment Management Regulation

Fifth Edition

# Investment Management Regulation

**Fifth Edition**

Tamar Frankel
Professor of Law
Boston University School of Law

Kenneth E. Burdon, Esq.

Fathom Publishing Company
Anchorage, Alaska

ISBN 978-1-888215-60-1
Library of Congress Control Number: 2015949684

Fathom Publishing Company
P.O. Box 200448
Anchorage, Alaska 99520-0448
Telephone 907-272-3305
Fax 907-272-3305

www.teachmutualfunds.com

Printed in the United States of America

To Ray and my children, Anat and Michael

—Tamar

To Jen and my boys, Jackson and Kieran

—Kenneth

## Acknowledgements

Our many thanks to J. Colin Sullivan, Associate General Counsel, Yale University Investments Office, for his significant contribution to this manuscript. Many thanks to Bill Hecker for his dedicated research and to Eldwin Charlie Nichols, Esq. for his work on this edition.

## About Kenneth E. Burdon

Kenneth E. Burdon is an investment management attorney at Skadden, Arps, Slate, Meagher & Flom LLP. He represents public and private investment funds, investment advisers, financial services companies and other financial institutions in connection with the structuring and distribution of investment products, and in a variety of regulatory, compliance, corporate, governance, operational and transactional matters. Mr. Burdon received his J.D., *summa cum laude,* from Boston University School of Law, and was an Editor of the Boston University Law Review. The views and opinions expressed in this book are Mr. Burdon's alone, and such views and opinions are not necessarily those of Skadden, Arps, Slate, Meagher & Flom LLP or any one or more of its clients.

## A Note on Footnotes and Quotation Formats

There are two types of footnotes in this casebook: those prepared by the authors and those that are part of reproduced original documents. All footnotes are consecutively numbered on each page (1, 2, 3, etc.). Footnotes for excerpts of original documents are designated by an asterisk following the consecutive number. Please note that the excerpt footnotes are not designated by the numbers appearing in the original document.

The text prepared by the authors is set in ITC Stone Serif Standard typeface. Blocks of excerpted text and the accompanying footnotes are set in ITC Stone Sans Serif typeface and are indented.

## *Summary Table of Contents*

## *Table of Contents*

# Chapter 1

## *The Financial System*

### A. The Nature of the Financial System and the Place of Investment Companies and Investment Advisers in the System[1]

Asset managers are part of the financial system. Therefore, an overview of the financial system, its purpose, structure, functions, problems, and regulation, is critical to gaining an understanding of the purpose for regulating asset managers and investment companies and how that regulation is designed to fit the unique role asset managers and investment companies play in the financial system.

One of the main functions of a financial system in a capitalist society is to transfer money from savers (who postpone consumption) to borrowers (who will, hopefully, put the money into the most productive use). In planned economies, the government distributes capital assets. In capitalist systems, the government plays only a secondary and indirect role, and private sector intermediaries play the main role in allocating capital assets. Savers transfer their money to borrowers and receive the borrowers' obligations to repay the money under certain conditions. The terms of the obligations differ greatly. One model is debt: an obligation to repay the face amount of the obligation plus a return. Another model is equity: an obligation to pay a share of the obligor's assets on liquidation plus a share of the profits, after all debts are paid. The variations on these models seem to be infinite.

There are two types of private sector intermediaries that help transfer money from savers to borrowers. One type is securities markets — such as the New York Stock Exchange or NASDAQ and the various underwriters, brokers and dealers who use these markets. The other type is institutions — such as banks and insurance companies. In market intermediation, the savers buy the borrowers' (i.e., the issuers') obligations. In institutional intermediation, the institutions buy the borrowers' obligations. The savers buy the institutions' obligations.

Why do we need institutions? Why not transfer all the borrowers' obligations to buyers-investors through the markets? The answer is that markets arise only if certain conditions are met: standardized documents,

1. These materials are derived from Tamar Frankel & Mark Fagan, Law and the Financial System (2009).

in sufficient numbers, with sufficient information about the borrowers, available intermediaries, and trust in the system (i.e., absence of antitrust concerns and manipulation). If I wish to borrow $20,300.45, these conditions cannot be met in the market. The cost of finding a saver interested in my obligation is very high. If I wish to lend this amount to be repaid on demand, the chances for creating a market for such a loan are also very slim. The cost of finding someone who would borrow my money on these conditions is very high.

This is where institutional intermediaries come in. They issue their own obligations on terms acceptable to savers and lend the proceeds of the sale of their obligations to borrowers on terms acceptable to borrowers. Some institutions, such as banks, live off the difference between the price they pay to savers for their obligations that they sell (e.g., bank accounts), and the price they charge borrowers to whom they lend — this is the "spread." As compared to individual lenders, institutional lenders have a lower risk from default of their borrowers because they have better information about borrowers and because they can diversify their loan portfolios and thus reduce their overall risk.

The initial reasons for the rise of the different financial institutions were not necessarily intermediation. For example, one important reason for the rise of investment companies was their offer to provide expert and trustworthy investment management. Some investment companies started to meet the need for such management of foreign investments that were out of investors' control and reach. Some companies arose by renowned private trustees, who offered their services not only to select individuals but also to the public. Some investment companies were designed to meet the needs of small savers-investors for diversification because these investors did not have sufficient funds to create diversified portfolios on their own.

In sum, investment companies meet the demand for affordable expert and reliable management, and sometimes for diversification. To perform their functions, investment companies issue their obligations to the savers and buy the borrowers' obligations (whether equity or debt); hence they intermediate.

Regardless of the initial reasons for their creation, all types of financial institutions (banks, insurance companies, investment companies, pension funds, thrifts, credit unions) ended up sharing one fundamental feature. All these institutions intermediate between savers and borrowers. These institutions raise funds by issuing their own obligations to savers, and provide these funds to borrowers by acquiring the borrowers' obligations.

Thus, each institution (banks, investment companies, savings and loan associations and insurance companies) started with a different mission, and each continues to provide the services for which they were initially designed: expert management and special types of investments by investment companies, safekeeping of deposits by banks, and pooling and distribution of risks by insurance companies. At the same time the main function of each of the species of financial institutions has remained intermediation.

In 1933, Congress separated commercial banking from investment banking (e.g., underwriting and trading in the securities markets). As investors' trust in the markets rose and the memories of the 1929 crash and losses faded, markets developed and became more attractive to investors, and both insurance companies and banks sought to participate in market activities. In 1996, Congress eliminated the division of banking from investment banking. Consequently, some banks have accumulated directly and through holding companies various financial intermediaries. Among them are the ones that interest us: investment advisers and investment companies.

Investment banking, also named "underwriting," involves the initial offering of obligations by issuers to investors in the market. The market for this offering is called a "primary market." Underwriters offer potential investors the obligations of the issuers, and the issue is successful if all the securities offered are purchased by investors at the offering price (or higher). However, a primary market presents a problem to investors and lenders who need or wish to recoup their money before the payment under the obligations is due. This is especially important to savers that invested in an enterprise, which in fact promises them their money back only by relatively small dividends. The rest of the investors' main investment can be paid only upon the liquidation or sale of the enterprise or repurchase of its shares by the enterprise.

What if the investors' money was used to build factories and other enterprises that cannot be, and should not be, liquidated so long as the enterprise maintains an operating business? To offer investors liquidity — the ability to receive their money back when they need it or want it — a second, "secondary market" is usually available. In a secondary market, *investors trade with each other* in the borrowers' or issuers' obligations. The more investors are interested in trading particular obligations, the more "liquid" the obligations will be. The issuer-borrower does not receive any of these payments. However, rightly or wrongly, market prices of the issuers' shares may indicate the market judgment about the issuer's financial well-being and success.

Thus, markets offer issuers (borrowers) and investors (savers) a mechanism for transferring money from the borrowers' obligations to investors, and a second mechanism for liquidating ("liquefying" and converting into cash) these obligations by transferring and trading in these obligations.

Investment companies (mutual funds) offer an intermediation model that is similar to institutional, as well as to market, intermediaries. Yet, unlike banks, theoretically, mutual funds cannot fail. That is because mutual funds promise investors a pro rata share of whatever assets the funds hold (minus fees and costs of administration). Not more and not less. The funds' liabilities and their assets are balanced. The investors as a whole bear the entire risk of the funds' investments. However, after the 2007-8 financial crisis, and the enactment of the Dodd-Frank Wall Street Reform and Consumer Protection Act ("Dodd-Frank"), questions arose: Could an investment fund possibly be "too big to fail"[1] or

---

1. Financial Times, *available at* http://lexicon.ft.com/Term?term=too-big-to-fail. This term is most often used to denote banks and firms that would substantially damage the financial system and the rest of the economy should they "fail", i.e., go

could a mutual fund and/or any asset management company expose the financial system to unacceptable systemic risk? These questions were discussed in connection with systemic risk-impact posed by intermediaries,, such as large banks and insurance companies. Dodd-Frank[1] created the Financial Stability Oversight Council ("FSOC" or "the Council") and vested in the Council authority to designate non-bank financial institutions as Systemically Important Financial Institutions ("SIFIs"). Such a designation would subject the non-bank financial institution to heightened prudential standards and to supervision by the Federal Reserve.

Section 113 of the Dodd-Frank Act[2] authorizes the FSOC to designate regulated investment funds, specifically mutual funds, as SIFIs.[3] On May 20, 2014, the Financial Services Committee ("the Committee") of the U.S. House of Representatives held a hearing entitled *"Examining the Dangers of the FSOC's Designation Process and its Impact on the U.S. Financial System."* The memorandum to Members of the Committee on Financial Services outlines the circumstances under which the FSOC may designate a non-bank financial institution as a SIFI as follows[4]:

---

bankrupt. The logic is therefore that these organizations would receive a "bailout" of some kind from the government — at the very least, protecting creditors against losses and perhaps also enabling management to stay in place (and, in some cases, the full payment of wages and bonuses). The term has been used in the United States since at least the 1980s, when it arose in the context of the conservatorship extended to Continental Illinois. The definitive book on the history and analytics of the topic is Too Big To Fail, by Gary H. Stern & Ron J. Feldman (Brookings Institution Press 2003). Andrew Ross Sorkin's more recent book with the same title provides a blow-by-blow account of how big US banks were rescued in fall 2008 after the collapse of Lehman Brothers (Andrew Ross Sorkin, Too Big to Fail (2009)). The Dodd-Frank legislation of 2010 was argued, by its proponents, to have "ended too big to fail", for example, by extending FDIC-style resolution to all financial institutions — even the largest and most dangerous).

1. Pub. L. No. 111-203.

2. Dodd-Frank Wall Street Reform and Consumer Protection Act, Pub. L. No. 111-203, §113(a)(1), 124 Stat. 1376, 1398 (2010) (*codified at* 12 U.S.C. § 5323(a)(1)). Section 113(a)(1) of the Dodd-Frank Act states: "The Council, on a nondelegable basis and by a vote of not fewer than 2/3 of the voting members then serving, including an affirmative vote by the Chairperson, may determine that a U.S. nonbank financial company shall be supervised by the Board of Governors and shall be subject to prudential standards, in accordance with this title, if the Council determines that material financial distress at the U.S. nonbank financial company, or the nature, scope, size, scale, concentration, interconnectedness, or mix of the activities of the U.S. nonbank financial company, could pose a threat to the financial stability of the United States."

3. The FSOC is chaired by the Treasury Secretary and its voting members are the heads of the federal financial regulatory agencies and an "independent member having insurance expertise." Under the Dodd-Frank Act, bank holding companies with more than $50 billion in assets are automatically deemed SIFIs and subject to the Federal Reserve's heightened prudential supervision. *Examining the Dangers of the FSOC's Designation Process and its Impact of the U.S. Financial System:* Hearing on H.R. 4387 Before the H. Comm. On Fin. Serv. 113 Cong. (memorandum to Members of the Comm. on Fin. Serv. from FSC Comm. Maj. Staff).

4. *Id.*

> The FSOC may designate a non-bank financial institution as a SIFI if two-thirds of its voting Members — including its Chairman — find that the firm "could pose a threat to the financial stability of the United States." In making its decision, the FSOC may consider several factors, including the firm's leverage, its off-balance sheet exposures, its relationship with other financial institutions, the firm's size and "interconnectedness," the firm's reliance on short-term funding, and "any other factors the [FSOC] deems appropriate...Once a firm is designated, it is subject to heightened prudential standards and supervision by the Federal Reserve, in addition to supervision by the firm's primary regulator. These prudential standards may include risk-based capital requirements; leverage limits; liquidity requirements; resolution plan and credit exposure report requirements; concentration limits; a contingent capital requirement; enhanced public disclosures; short-term debt limits; and overall risk management requirements.

During the congressional hearing, members of the Financial Services Industry, representing various interests, testified about the dangers of designating mutual funds as SIFIs. An opponent of the FSOC's designation authority described the difference between the risk created by a large bank and an investment fund as follows:

> Banks take deposits; the resulting obligations are bank indebtedness. Mutual funds take investments; the investor's equity in the fund is a contractual right to a pro rata participation in the investment fund's gains and losses. Investment fund managers are in an agency relationship to their investors. They have a fiduciary obligation to their funds — with the corollary that their judgment as fiduciaries could be at odds with what an outside prudential regulator might require. Banks, unburdened by fiduciary obligations to their depositors (they act as principals), face no such potential conflict of interest.[1] . . .
>
> The Fed, as our central bank and the nation's lender of last resort, is concerned with overall maintenance of a stable banking system. It is a prudential regulator concerned with the safety and soundness of the banking system and, by extension, our larger financial system. Accordingly, the Fed's core concern is with capital adequacy — whether the banking system, in which leverage is inherent, is adequately capitalized and sufficiently liquid to meet its obligations as they come due. The SEC, by contrast, functions more like an umpire of the U.S. capital markets, with a professed goal of using both its rulemaking and enforcement authority to keep those markets free and fair. The Fed, then, is in the capital assurance business, while the SEC is overwhelmingly focused on the actions and activities of participants in U.S. capital markets. For the SEC, the liquidity of risk taking entities is generally the issue, rather than their capitalization. Contrast the Fed, which regulates to preferred outcomes — after all,

1. Examining the Dangers of the FSOC's Designation Process and Its Impact on the U.S. Financial System: Hearing on H.R. 4387 Before the H. Comm. on Fin. Serv. 113 Cong. 60-69 (2014) (statement of Paul S. Atkins, CEO, Patomak Global Partners).

> central bankers are central planners. The SEC tends to train its regulatory focus on activities, setting outer limits on what capital markets participants may do and enforcing those limits as necessary — again, the capital markets' umpire at work.[1]

The chairman and CEO of the Vanguard Group, Inc., one of the world's largest mutual fund complexes,[2] contrasted asset managers and banks. He, too, questioned the Federal Reserve's expertise in regulating the capital markets, and noted fundamental differences between asset managers and banks, stating:

> 1. **In asset management, managers act as agents, not as principals.** A fund and its investors, not the fund manager, bear the risk of the fund's investments. Acting as agent, a fund manager manages the fund's portfolio pursuant to a written contract and in accord with the fund's investment objectives and policies as described in the fund's prospectus. Fund management fees compensate the manager for managing the fund as a fiduciary and agent and for providing ongoing services that the fund needs to operate. The manager does not own the fund's assets and it may not use those assets to benefit itself or any other fund. Investment gains and losses experienced by a fund are solely attributable to that fund and its investors.
> 2. **In asset management, there is no need for capital requirements or '"loss absorption."** Fund investors understand that portfolio results, positive or negative, belong to them alone and accept the risk that their investments may lose value. Unlike with bank deposits, the risk of loss is inherent in an investment, including an investment in a fund.
> 3. **In asset management, there is no need for government bailouts.** The concept of public bailouts is inapposite to funds and their managers. If a fund's manager went bankrupt, the manager would have no access to the fund's assets, assets of any other funds it manages, or other client assets. There would be no expectation of government intervention to prop up the manager. The fund's board of directors would simply hire another asset management company to manage the fund. In the case of funds themselves, investors are not promised gains on their investment, or even a return of the principal amount they invested. As noted above, fund investors and the broader marketplace understand that all investment results — gains and losses, no matter how big or small — belong to the fund's investors on a pro rata basis. Indeed, many funds had sharp declines in value during the financial crisis (most have since recovered that lost value). But there was never any suggestion,

1. *Id.*
2. Examining the Dangers of the FSOC's Designation Process and Its Impact on the U.S. Financial System: Hearing on H.R. 4387 Before the H. Comm. on Fin. Serv. 113 Cong. 73-87 (2014) (statement of F. William McNabb III, Chairman and CEO of The Vanguard Group, Inc.)

expectation or need for the government to step in and "rescue" a fund.

4. **In asset management, there is no need for resolution planning.** As noted above, a fund's board of directors has the ability to replace the fund's manager. And in the event of a fund closure, federal and state laws already provide a clear process for a fund to make a pro rata distribution to its investors and wind up its affairs under the oversight of the fund's board of directors. Funds thus have no need for bank-like "resolution planning," and regulators have no need for additional authority to protect against a fund's "disorderly failure."

Because markets and institutions offer different intermediation models, different regulatory regimes apply to each model. To simplify the analysis, markets are treated in this Book as one prototype, and so are institutions, even though there are different markets and different institutions. Markets and institutions vary in ways that affect their benefits, drawbacks, and strengths; they differ by volume, nature, and size of transactions, the savers and borrowers they serve, and the regulations that govern them institutions also vary. Even so, the basic differences between them remain: Markets and institutions emerge in different circumstances and each represents a particular mix of benefits, costs, and risks.[1]

---

**Problem**

It is the fall of 2008. Lehman Brothers has just gone bankrupt. The financial markets are in a panic. The value of portfolio securities owned by major open-end investment companies, that is, investment companies that offer redeemable shares and that have to redeem their shares within 7 days of demand, has fallen drastically. Banks are failing and being acquired in hastily arranged deals. Securities are trading at depressed prices. A new client comes to consult with you. This client seeks an opportunity to establish a business designed to profit from this chaotic environment. What type of intermediary would you advise your client to establish and why?

---

## B. The Investment Management Profession

### 1. Glance at History

Even though some would call investment advice and investment management an industry, we prefer to address these services as a profession. Investment advice and management are expert services, similar to the service of a lawyer or medical doctor.

Investment management services are ancient. In the past, investment advice and management services were rendered to one large property owner or his family. Trusted servants managed the estates of absentee

1. These materials are derived from Tamar Frankel, Securitization: Structured Financing, Financial Asset Pools, and Asset-Backed Securities (Ann Taylor Schwing ed., 2d ed. 2005).

owners. A recent predecessor of today's adviser and money manager is the Boston trustee.[1] In his investments, he was guided by the trust principle of preserving capital, a principle which limited his investment choices.

"Mass-produced" investment management services to the public are relatively new, having appeared in the late 1800s. In fact, in 1897, "during a period of rapid economic development and increasingly frequent securities offerings, an editorial in *The Nation* called for persons with expertise and independence to advise the public on the merits of the securities offered to investors."[2] The appearance of the advisory profession was triggered by the availability of financial assets — securities traded in the markets which enabled small investors to participate in the economic growth of the United States both for better (gains) and for worse (losses).

In the 1920s, as investors sought investment advice from reputable persons, the Boston Trustee became an adviser to the small investors. Free of trust law constraints, he invested in stocks and speculated in the markets. The Boston Trustee viewed himself as a professional, and, like the professionals of that period, did not advertise his services and avoided commercial pursuits. Boston trustees offered advice only, and referred clients to particular brokers, from whom they may or may not have received referral fees.

Thus, the first cousin of the investment adviser is the broker-dealer. Although both advisers and brokers provide investment advice, the broker-dealer gives "free" advice and is paid for executing securities transactions or selling the securities. The broker's advice can be viewed as sales talk aimed at enhancing trading in the securities. Although the broker is required by current law to give clients "suitable advice," the broker need not seek to maximize the client's benefits nor avoid conflicts of interests. As we will see in later discussions, legal issues arise with combined sales and advice functions. The governing law for a sales relationship is contract; the governing law for a professional relationship is fiduciary law. The two do not always match.

## 2. Types of Financial Services

Financial services to individuals or specific identifiable groups can be divided into a number of subjects and may result in somewhat different regulation. While all advisers are fiduciaries to their clients, the degree to which the advisers have control over the clients and their assets, and the degree to which the individual clients have control over their own assets, may determine the extent to which the law will interfere to balance the disparity of such control.

First, what subject matter does the advice involve? Advice may involve only securities. Alternatively, advice may involve a more comprehensive subject matter concerning the overall financial planning for the client. That would cover a variety of investments, insurance, and investments

1. The Boston trustee is a prototype of a lawyer who was named as trustee for wealthy individuals, and managed their assets after their death for the benefit of their families and other beneficiaries.

2. 1 Tamar Frankel & Ann Taylor Schwing, The Regulation of Money Managers §§ 1-5 (2001 & Supp. 2015).

in real estate as well as securities. It also involves the overall investment portfolio of the client, that is, the amounts allocated to each of these investments. Further, in order to design a financial plan the planner must receive extensive information about the client's overall finances, family relationships and health situation, to name a few. This information is usually given in confidence and is similar to the information received by lawyers and medical doctors. It should not be used except for the purpose for which it was given. Hence, with respect to such information, the adviser is a fiduciary.

Second, what is the extent of the adviser's discretion? One type of advice can be non-discretionary. The investment decision of whether to invest and in what to invest is left to the client. The second type of advice is discretionary. The advice is then implemented by the adviser, at the adviser's discretion. The adviser determines the structure of the client's portfolio and the nature and amount of each investment. Usually, the adviser's discretion is limited by general or more specific guidelines that are typically provided in the agreement for investment management services between the adviser and the adviser's client.[1] These investment guidelines are in addition to the terms and conditions advisers are required to include in agreements for advisory services.[2] Thus, the distinction between nondiscretionary and discretionary managers is one of degree rather than only of kind, yet each presents problems of different magnitudes and different laws may apply to them.

Third, is the advice "personalized" or "mass-produced"? This question involves the degree in which the design of the investment addresses the client's needs. One type of personalized advice and management is designed solely for the needs of one investor, his family, or his business. The other type of investment service is "mass-produced." It offers shares in a ready-made portfolio with certain characteristics. Investors are offered shares in that portfolio. They do not have a direct contract with the adviser. The adviser's agreement is with the pool of investors' money. The pooled "mass-produced" portfolio is useful to small investors. That is because unless individuals (or families) are very wealthy, they cannot afford "personalized" advice and do not have the money for a well-structured portfolio. Discretionary managers

1. *See* Thomas P. Lemke & Gerald T. Lins, Regulation of Investment Advisers § 2:5, at 250 (2015). For example, an agreement for investment management services will typically provide investment guidelines; i.e., instructions or restrictions on management of the account. The guidelines are often in the form of a schedule or exhibit and "are used with equity, fixed income, and other types of investment strategies." In addition, due to the high risk involved with certain investments, investment guidelines usually address (i) "the permissibility of investing in foreign securities"; (ii) "use of derivatives (e.g., futures or swaps)"; (iii) "purchase of illiquid securities"; (iv) "credit quality of eligible account securities, particularly high-yield securities"; (v) "expected duration/ average maturity for the account"; and (vi) "categories of ineligible securities (e.g., tobacco stocks, etc.)." "In some cases, [the guidelines might] address socially responsible investing issues.

2. *See generally* Advisers Act, § 205, 15 U.S.C. § 80b-5; *see also* Advisers Act § 215(a) and (b), 15 U.S.C. § 80b-15(a), (b), which renders voidable an agreement for advisory services if it violates the Advisers Act; Investment Advisers Act Rel. No. 58 (Apr. 10, 1951); McEldowney Financial Services, SEC No-Action Letter, 1986 WL 67330, Fed. Sec. L. Rep. (CCH) ¶78,373 (Oct. 17, 1986).

offer their services to such small investors by pooling small investors' money to create and manage large securities portfolios. Investors buy shares or other types of participation in these portfolios. Pooling brings benefits to both investors and their managers. For the managers, pooling reduces management costs by standardizing advice, eliminating personal requirements of particular investors, and increasing the managers' fees measured as a percentage of the assets under management.

For investors, pooling reduces management expenses through economies of scale, and provides highly qualified and specialized services at a fraction of the price. In addition, investors obtain diversification of risks, which they might not be able to achieve on their own investments.

### 3. The On-Going Problems Managers Pose for Investors, the Markets, and the Economy

The benefits that investment advisers, investment companies, and the stock markets bring to investors pose problems for investors as well. For example, advisers with full discretionary powers and control over investors' funds, as is the case of advisers to investment companies, pose substantial risk of mismanagement of assets. The Investment Company Act of 1940 addresses these risks.

The regulation of investment companies, like the regulation of banks and insurance companies, is far more substantive and intrusive than that of issuers and market intermediaries under the Securities Act of 1933 and the Securities Exchange Act of 1934. While the Securities Act of 1933 and the Securities Exchange Act of 1934 regulate the sale and trade in securities, the Investment Company Act of 1940 and the Investment Advisers Act of 1940 regulate fiduciaries in the performance of their services. The Securities Act of 1933 and the Securities Exchange Act of 1934 aim at protecting investors against fraud in connection with the sale of securities and trading in securities; the Investment Company Act of 1940 and the Investment Advisers Act of 1940 aim at protecting investors against mismanagement of the money they entrusted to other people for management.

The need for this type of regulation is evidenced by abuses that occurred during the 1920s, when public investors lost a substantial portion of their investments.

The problem was discussed in John Galbraith's The Great Crash, 1929.[1] The "investment trust" became prominent in the 1920s. It enabled investors to invest in the securities of companies by investing in the trust. Investment trusts in England and Scotland enabled small investors to buy stock in an investment company, which invested in numerous operating companies. Small investors were able to spread their risk, and benefit from trust management's greater knowledge of investments.

Originally the American investment trusts were true trusts, in which investors purchased an interest in securities deposited with a trust company and the trusts were subject to trust law. However, soon "[t]he investment trust became, in fact, an investment corporation." The trusts issued securities and invested in securities which they managed. To protect management

1. John Kenneth Galbraith, The Great Crash, 1929, 46-65 (1988).

from dissatisfied investors' claims, the trusts sold investors non-voting securities or required investors to assign their voting rights to voting trusts, controlled by the managers of the trusts. Most investment trusts refused to disclose the identity of the securities they held, because this information might have affected the market demand for these securities.

"Dishonesty, inattention, inability, and greed were some of shortcomings of the new financial industry. Investment trusts were generally sponsored by other financial firms. The sponsor of a trust generally managed the trust for a fee. The sponsor might also receive commissions for transactions in its own securities. An investment bank sponsor firm could help its own business by providing a market for securities it 'manufactured.' In addition, sponsors received stock or warrants in the trust, which they could sell or exercise at a profit as the shares generally sold at a premium."[1] That is, they sold at a higher price than the value of the securities which the these trusts held.

> The public was enthusiastic about the trusts; the Chairman of the National Democratic Committee touted an investment trust plan for the poor in a major magazine. Investors were willing to pay a premium for shares in the investment trusts over the value of the portfolio securities because of the supposed "financial genius" of the managers.
>
> Investment trusts also leveraged their investments by issuing bonds and preferred stock. When the portfolio securities increased in value, the increase was generally concentrated on the common stock, as the bonds and preferred stock generally had fixed returns. The value of the common stock rose further when the stock was held by another leveraged trust. Companies used their capital gains from leverage to establish additional trusts. One company was able to control resources valued at over a billion dollars from a $500 initial purchase. However, leverage worked in the other direction as well, when poor portfolio securities experienced enormous losses.[2]

### 4. The Regulators' Study of the 1920s Investment Management Industry[3]

In the wake of the stock market crash in 1929 and the creation of the Securities and Exchange Commission, Congress commissioned the SEC to study investment trusts and work with the industry to propose a regulatory framework. Robert E. Healy, the SEC Commissioner who supervised the agency's investment-trust study, described the losses of the public that invested in these investment trusts. For example, the vice president and research director of General Motors lost most of his investment and admitted that "[h]e did not know that investment companies were not subject to supervision as were life-insurance companies and banks" and, although he was director of General Motors, he "did not understand investments." Commenting on the losses of the American public in these institutions, Mr.

1. *Id.*
2. *Id.*
3. Investment Trust Study, Investment Company Act of 1940 and Investment Advisers Act of 1940, H.R. Rep. No. 76-2639, at 6-10.

Healy stated that the investments of the trusts had made "comparatively little original contribution of capital to industry" and that security holders lost 90 percent of their net capital contribution.

Discussing the national public interest in investment trusts and investment companies, Mr. Healy stated that investment companies can potentially control or influence other firms and influence the securities markets. The losses were not only caused by the "decline in security values" but also by "selfish, and in some cases unscrupulous, mismanagement," facilitated by the fact that the companies' assets, mainly cash and marketable securities, are liquid and easily "looted." Mr. Healy noted some of the problems involved:

(1) The trusts could be operated with little capital, and run by fraudsters;

(2) They could be controlled by devices including "special voting stocks, long-term management, and underwriting contracts, voting trusts, and the pyramiding of investment companies;"

(3) Brokers, security dealers, and investment bankers could use controlled companies to benefit their own firms;

(4) Management and other "insiders" benefited from discrimination in the distribution and repurchase of investment company securities on more favorable terms than other shareholders;

(5) In companies that offered redeemable securities, the pricing of the securities sold and redeemed resulted in dilution of shareholder equity and sometimes was used for insider profits;

(6) The companies had complex capital structures, and the interests of shareholders in bonds and preferred stocks were not adequately protected;

(7) Periodic payment plans (installment sale of investment company securities) involved unfair sales practices;

(8) There were abuses in asset management: (a) the promoters and managers could set and change investment policies without shareholder approval; (b) management control was changed without shareholder approval — for example, control of the trusts was sold to "looters" or other investment companies in unfair reorganizations; (c) insiders engaged in self-dealing with the investment companies, e.g., selling securities to the companies at unfair prices, or borrowing from the companies; and (d) investors lacked adequate financial disclosure.

Mr. Healy noted that the Securities Act of 1933 and the Securities Exchange Act of 1934 did not provide adequate investor protection because these statutes generally require only disclosure and did not apply to most investment companies.

### 5. Congressional Response: The Investment Company Act of 1940

Section 1 of the Investment Company Act of 1940 provides as follows:[1]

> (a) Upon the basis of facts disclosed by the record and reports of the Securities and Exchange Commission made pursuant to section

1. 15 U.S.C. § 80a-1.

79z-4 of this title, and facts otherwise disclosed and ascertained, it is found that investment companies are affected with a national public interest in that, among other things--

(1) The securities issued by such companies, which constitute a substantial part of all securities publicly offered, are distributed, purchased, paid for, exchanged, transferred, redeemed, and repurchased by use of the mails and means and instrumentalities of interstate commerce, and in the case of the numerous companies which issue redeemable securities this process of distribution and redemption is continuous;

(2) The principal activities of such companies--investing, reinvesting, and trading in securities--are conducted by use of the mails and means and instrumentalities of interstate commerce, including the facilities of national securities exchanges, and constitute a substantial part of all transactions effected in the securities markets of the Nation;

(3) Such companies customarily invest and trade in securities issued by, and may dominate and control or otherwise affect the policies and management of, companies engaged in business in interstate commerce;

(4) Such companies are media for the investment in the national economy of a substantial part of the national savings and may have a vital effect upon the flow of such savings into the capital markets; and

(5) The activities of such companies, extending over many States, their use of the instrumentalities of interstate commerce and the wide geographic distribution of their security holders, make difficult, if not impossible, effective State regulation of such companies in the interest of investors.

(b) Upon the basis of facts disclosed by the record and reports of the Securities and Exchange Commission made pursuant to section 79z-4 of this title, and facts otherwise disclosed and ascertained, it is declared that the national public interest and the interest of investors are adversely affected--

(1) When investors purchase, pay for, exchange, receive dividends upon, vote, refrain from voting, sell, or surrender securities issued by investment companies without adequate, accurate, and explicit information, fairly presented, concerning the character of such securities and the circumstances, policies, and financial responsibility of such companies and their management;

(2) When investment companies are organized, operated, managed, or their portfolio securities are selected, in the interest of directors, officers, investment advisers, depositors, or other affiliated persons thereof, in the interest of underwriters, brokers, or dealers, in the interest of special classes of their security holders, or in the interest of other investment companies or

persons engaged in other lines of business, rather than in the interest of all classes of such companies' security holders;

(3) When investment companies issue securities containing inequitable or discriminatory provisions, or fail to protect the preferences and privileges of the holders of their outstanding securities;

(4) When the control of investment companies is unduly concentrated through pyramiding or inequitable methods of control, or is inequitably distributed, or when investment companies are managed by irresponsible persons;

(5) When investment companies, in keeping their accounts, in maintaining reserves, and in computing their earnings and the asset value of their outstanding securities, employ unsound or misleading methods, or are not subjected to adequate independent scrutiny;

(6) When investment companies are reorganized, become inactive, or change the character of their business, or when the control or management thereof is transferred, without the consent of their security holders;

(7) When investment companies by excessive borrowing and the issuance of excessive amounts of senior securities increase unduly the speculative character of their junior securities; or

(8) When investment companies operate without adequate assets or reserves.

It is hereby declared that the policy and purposes of this subtitle, in accordance with which the provisions of this subtitle shall be interpreted, are to mitigate and, so far as is feasible, to eliminate the conditions enumerated in this section which adversely affect the national public interest and the interest of investors.

---

## Discussion Topic

An excerpt from the Securities and Exchange Commission's study states: "The Securities Act of 1933 and the Securities Exchange Act of 1934 have not acted as deterrents to the continuous occurrence of abuses in the organization and operation of investment companies." In this connection, consider that the 1933 and 1934 Acts require the offering of securities to be accompanied by disclosure, and require issuers to provide information about their condition on an on-going basis. However, the government does not generally regulate the issuers' activities (except in relation to particular aspects of their business, such as the emission of toxic fumes). The government does not dictate how a company like General Motors should be organized, to what extent it should be leveraged, how it should price its products, or how it should organize the sales force to distribute its products. What is the justification for doing so with respect to investment companies?

---

### 6. The Responses of the Markets to the Problems Posed by Investment Companies: How Did Investment Company Structures Reflect the Investors' Choices? What Was the Congressional Reaction?

Sections 4 and 5 of the 1940 Act classify investment companies into the following categories: face amount certificate companies, unit investment trusts, and management companies. Management companies are further divided into open-end and closed-end companies. The regulatory structure of the 1940 Act is based on these classifications. Some regulations apply to all types of investment companies and some regulations apply to one type or one feature of investment companies. We will not deal with face amount certificate companies because they do not exist today. The classification of investment companies distinguishes investment companies by a number of features, as described below:

- **Management's discretion.** Unit investment trusts vest nearly no discretion in the trustee that holds their assets to manage the portfolios while the managers of management companies exercise substantial discretion to trade in their portfolio companies.
- **Redeeming Investment Company Shares.** Open-end management companies and unit investment trusts offer redeemable securities while closed-end investment companies offer non-redeemable securities.
- **Diversification.** Companies may not hold out their portfolios as diversified unless they comply with certain diversification standards set forth in section 5(b) of the 1940 Act. Thus, this feature depicts a class of companies that advertise their portfolio as diversified and defines for all such companies what diversification means. This standardized definition reduces investors' costs of comparing companies that hold themselves as diversified. The following table demonstrates the features of each type of investment company:

| | Management | Redemption Rights |
|---|---|---|
| Closed-End Companies | Yes | No |
| Open-End Companies | Yes | Yes |
| Unit Investment Trusts | No | Yes |

Each type of investment company may be either diversified or non-diversified.

- **Internal Versus External Management.** A distinguishing feature among management companies is internal as opposed to external management. Most investment companies are managed under a contract by an adviser. The adviser or its parent holding company is often publicly owned. One fund complex, named Vanguard, which is the largest in 2015, is managed and serviced by a unit, whose shares are owned by the investment companies which it services. These two models have their historical sources. The internally managed funds are the offspring of the Boston Trustee, who aimed to serve small investors efficiently. This adviser would pool these clients' funds to manage them together, and create an investment company. Externally managed funds were historically the offspring of an adviser who aimed at attracting investors' money to manage, as well as sell the shares for commissions. Today, the external model is far more prevalent.

Where did Congress get these models of investment companies? The Act reflects the types of companies that the Commission's staff found in the markets and reported in its Study of 1938. Why did the markets design these types of investment companies? And even if the markets did, why were these types of companies incorporated into the 1940 Act, and why was the regulatory structure founded on this classification?

One possible answer relates to investors' levels of benefits and risks from the management and redemption features of mutual funds. Unit investment trusts vest no management discretion in their trustees. It may demonstrate investors' lack of trust, and exposes the trustees to lower risk from mismanagement. Management companies (open-end and closed-end investment companies) offer investors the benefits from expert management, demonstrate greater investor trust in the managers and expose investors to higher risks from mismanagement.

Further, unit investment trusts and open-end investment companies offer investors redeemable securities. This feature benefits investors by creating liquidity, regardless of market volatility, and offering a "clout" over managers. It allows investors not only to liquidate their own securities, as they would if they sold them in the markets, but also to force liquidation of the portfolio of the investment company itself, and thereby reduce the manager's fees or even put the existence of the investment company in jeopardy. However, redemption requires such companies to operate in a way that would enable them to liquidate their portfolios to pay shareholders, and establish an accurate net asset value of their portfolio to price redemption and purchase prices. Otherwise, a low redemption price would injure the redeeming shareholders and a high redemption price would injure the remaining shareholders.

In contrast, closed-end investment companies do not provide redemption to shareholders. These shareholders must rely on liquidity in the secondary market (such as the New York Stock Exchange) and may obtain prices that are below the net asset value of the underlying portfolio when selling or purchasing closed-end investment company shares in a secondary market.

Thus, while the 1940 Act maintained the market place models of investment companies, the 1940 Act also addresses the problems posed by mismanagement and redemption.

---

## Discussion Topics

a. What are the distinctive features of each type of an investment company and how does this feature reflect investors' risks from disloyal management?

b. Are there any different costs and benefits involved in these structures? If so, then to whom?

c. Why are open-end funds today's prevailing form of mutual funds?

---

## C. The Pattern of Investment Management Regulation

### 1. Federal Statutes: The Investment Company Act and the Investment Advisers Act

Where do we find the law regulating investment advisers and investment companies? We start our search with the federal Acts of 1940 — the Investment Company Act of 1940 and the Investment Advisers Act of 1940.[1] We refer to the a Investment Company Act of 1940 in this book as either "the 1940 Act" or "the Investment Company Act," and to the Investment Advisers Act of 1940 as either "the Advisers Act" or "the Investment Advisers Act." These Acts have been amended and adjusted by the Commission for seventy-five years. Therefore, these Acts must be read with their administrative and judicial gloss, including the Commission's exemptive orders and rules, and the thousands of no-action letters issued by the Division of Investment Management.[2]

The courts have had an impact on the development and interpretation of the Acts, but to a far lesser extent than their impact on the other Federal securities laws. Similarly, there is extensive scholarship in this area, by practitioners with a scholarly bent and scholars as well. Yet, the source of the richest and most scholarly material on the two Acts is the Commission and its Releases. They are worth reading carefully.

#### a. The Substance of the Regulation

Investment advisers are regulated by the Investment Advisers Act of 1940 or by state securities laws. If an adviser manages investment company assets, the Investment Company Act will govern important aspects of the adviser's conduct, in addition to the Investment Advisers Act of 1940. The main goals and corresponding substantive regulation of mutual funds are:

First, to provide better disclosure regarding the investment companies, Sections 7, 8 and 24 of the Investment Company Act require registration not only of the securities of the companies but also of the companies themselves. Registration also helps trigger the application of the Investment Company Act.

Second, to prevent managers from changing the level of risk of the companies' assets, Sections 8 and 13 of the Investment Company Act require companies to describe their fundamental investment policies in their registration statements, and require a vote of the majority of the outstanding securities to change the policies.

Third, to prevent conflict of interest transactions by insiders, Sections 17(a)-(f) and Section 10(f) of the Investment Company Act restrict or prohibit such transactions except by the Commission's exemption. Thus,

---

1. For discussion of the history of the Investment Company Act, *see* Alfred Jaretzki, Jr., *The Investment Company Act of 1940,* 26 Wash. U. L.Q. 303 (1941); Walter P. North, *A Brief History of Federal Investment Company Legislation,* 44 Notre Dame L. Rev. 677 (1969); Comment, *Investment Company Act of 1940,* 50 Yale L.J. 440 (1941).

2. Within the Commission, the Division that is primarily responsible for administering the Investment Company Act and the Advisers Act is the Division of Investment Management.

the Investment Company Act adapts fiduciary law to the environment of investment companies.

Fourth, to strengthen the control over investment managers, Sections 10 and 16 of the Investment Company Act create a special governance structure vesting special powers in disinterested directors. Section 36(b) of the Investment Company Act imposes on insiders fiduciary duties regarding the fees they may charge to the investment companies. In addition, Section 9 of the Investment Company Act disqualifies persons who have been convicted of securities-related wrongs or very serious crimes, or are subject to injunctions, from serving as insiders of investment companies.

Fifth, to prevent embezzlement of investment company assets, Section 36 of the Investment Company Act makes conversion of these assets a federal offense and Sections 17(f) and (g) impose protective measures relating to safekeeping of investment company assets.

Sixth, to ensure that investment companies that promise to redeem their shares will meet their promises, Section 2(a)(32) defines redemption, Section 2(a)(41) defines valuation of securities, and Sections 22(c) and (e) of the Investment Company Act regulate the timing and pricing of redemptions.

Seventh, to limit over-leveraged complex financial structures that pose high risk and confusion to investors, Section 18 of the Investment Company Act regulates the financial structure of investment companies.

Eighth, to prohibit Ponzi schemes and fraudulent sales practices, and limit the sales loads which shareholders pay to brokers, Sections 9 and 22 of the Investment Company Act regulate the communication of the advisers to the investment companies' shareholders.

Ninth, to prevent fly-by-night operators from creating investment companies, Section 14(a) of the Investment Company Act requires promoters to invest seed money in the companies.

---

## Discussion Topics

Many of the 1940 Act provisions are analogous to banking and insurance regulation. Like banks and insurance companies, investment companies are subject to strict regulation aimed at preventing embezzlement of their assets, and maintaining the safe custody of, and proper accounting for, their assets. There are, however, two fundamental differences which separate investment companies and put them in a category all by themselves. These differences are reflected in their regulation.

1. First, unlike other institutional intermediaries (banking, insurance, pension management) investment companies are not covered by any government insurance. Nonetheless, holding other people's money raises temptation in all relationships between investors and fiduciaries (people who hold other peoples' money) to take risks for which the investors and not the fiduciaries must pay. Therefore, concerns about conflicts of interest, safety of assets, and accurate accounting, appear in the regulation of all these institutions. What are the consequences of these differences for the investors, the managers, and the markets?

2. Second, today most investment companies (open-end investment companies) are "transparent," because they may not offer more than one class of securities, each representing a pro rata share of their assets, as required in the 1940 Act. Therefore, investors bear the risks of the institutions' assets but not the risks of institutional structure. Banks and insurance companies are not transparent, and indeed cannot be transparent if they are to perform their other functions.

   What are the consequences of this transparency? Should investors in investment companies be told what securities their companies hold? Should the companies' managers be free to change the nature of the investments? Should the investors be told how the investment companies are structured? Should the investors decide the structures? Do all investors have the same preferences?

---

### b. Exemptive Authority, General and Particular Procedures Applicable to Requests for Exemptions; Sections 6(c), (d), (e) and Sections 9(c), 10(f), 17(b), 23(c)(3)[1]

The Investment Company Act is long in part because it is highly detailed. Yet with all its detail, the Act does not carve the industry in granite. The Act provides flexibility by vesting in the Commission broad exemptive powers. Section 6(c) of the Act authorizes the Commission to exempt "any person, security or transaction, or any class or classes of persons, securities, or transactions, from any provisions of the Act or of any rule or regulation thereunder by rule regulation or order," if and to the extent that such exemption is "necessary or appropriate in the public interest and consistent with the protection of investors and the purposes fairly intended by the policy and the provisions of the" Act. Section 6(e) authorizes the Commission to apply certain provisions of the Act to otherwise exempt companies.

In addition to these broad exemptive powers, the Act provides the Commission with the power to exempt from particular sections of the Act. Sections 6(d), 9(c), 10(f), 15(f), 17(b) and 17(e) authorize the Commission to exempt from these particular sections, under somewhat different guidelines than those in section 6(c). In addition, sections 2(a)(9), 2(a)(19), 3(b)(2) and 12(g) authorize the Commission to issue declaratory orders regarding the existence or non-existence of a state of affairs, such as control under section 2(a)(9).

Through these exemptive powers, the Commission has enabled the industry to develop money market funds, variable insurance products, and new forms of fund structures that were not allowed before, all without extensive congressional amendments to the Act, but all subject to conditions designed to ensure investor protection. For example, exchange-traded funds (ETFs), which are immensely popular investment vehicles, in 2015 operate pursuant to exemptive relief obtained from the Commission.

---

1. These materials are derived with few changes from 1 Tamar Frankel & Ann Taylor Schwing, The Regulation of Money Managers, §§ 2-1 to -67 (2001 & Supp. 2015).

As we shall see, not all of these exemptions and conditions successfully protected investors, but then, neither do conditions under the law.

The status of the Commission's exemptive orders as precedent is quite interesting. On the one hand, an exemptive order applies only to the party applicants and no one can use the exemption as a precedential authority, even if the circumstances are identical. On the other hand, when another party applies for an exemptive order under similar circumstances the Commission might be hard pressed to deny the order unless there are good reasons for doing so. Otherwise, the Commission's denial could be deemed arbitrary. Nonetheless, a party in similar circumstances cannot rely on an exemptive order as precedent, but must apply for an exemption. The exemptive process is costly and takes time even if the request is routine.

After a number of such exemptive orders, when the Commission acquires sufficient experience about the issues involved in the exemption, it may promulgate an exemptive rule. The rule may differ in some respects from the individual exemptions, responding to the general application of the rule and to the public's comments in the rule-making process. While the Commission often seeks to do this to reduce the administrative burden of granting exemptive relief and to encourage less costly competition in the market, in recent years the rule-making process has not moved very swiftly.

Under Section 38(a), the effect of an exemption is to protect those to whom it is addressed, who relied on it in good faith. Although the courts have supervisory powers over the Commission, they do not have primary jurisdiction over the subject matter of exemptions. A court may not exercise its own judgment as to whether the exemption should have been granted. The court may only interfere if the process or reasoning of the Commission is faulty. It is not clear that a court will hear a request to avoid an exemption on the ground that the application for exemption was fraudulent. For the court to interfere there must be a very strong prima facie case to this end. Exemptions may also be based on interpretations of the statute. If a later court decision or staff decision or the Commission changes the interpretation, outstanding exemptions retain full effect, but new ones will not be granted. In this sense, exemptions can be overruled.

The Commission has developed guidelines that it follows in determining whether to exempt from the Act and under what conditions. Exemptions can be granted on the basis of changes in the environment or in the industry, or alternative protections that reduce the concerns on which the prohibitions in the Act are based.[1] However, these guidelines are not free from controversy.

### c. SEC Staff No-Action Letters and Other Forms of Guidance Provided by the SEC

No-action letters mean that the Commission staff would not recommend enforcement action to the Commission in the particular case, based on the facts presented by the applicant. Essentially, the letters represent the staff's prosecutorial discretion. The staff states that it will not recommend that

1. 1 Tamar Frankel & Ann Taylor Schwing, The Regulation of Money Managers, §§ 2-1 to -67 (2001 & Supp. 2015).

the Commission allocate resources to prosecute on the facts as presented. No-action letters are subject to reconsideration by the staff and are not regarded as precedents binding on the Commission.

Practicing attorneys and academics view no-action letters as a source of law. Also, the Division of Investment Management generally permits third parties to rely on no-action or interpretive letters to the extent that the third party's facts and circumstances are substantially similar to those described in the underlying request for a no-action or interpretive letter.[1] The type of a no-action letter will determine how strongly it may serve as precedent. A no-action letter expressing the staff's interpretation of the law would constitute a weighty precedent on the legal issues to which the courts are likely to defer and the Commission would respect, at least until it is overruled in some formal way. Other similarly situated parties need not seek no-action letters on the same issue unless the staff expressly states that a particular letter may not be relied upon by third parties. A no-action letter that disagrees with the applicant's legal interpretation, and emphasizes its application to the facts of one particular case, is far weaker as reliable precedent.

No-action letters can be viewed today as the administrative common law of the Investment Company Act. The staff spends substantial amounts of time in designing the jurisprudence of the letters and assuring their consistency with other letters and with the policies of the Commission and the law.

No-action letters are beneficial to the SEC, its staff, the public and the investment management community. They provide SEC with information about proposed transactions in the market place. They alert the staff to possible legal barriers to novel transactions, and to possible problems that they might pose for investors. The letters help avoid or reduce enforcement by the SEC and litigation by regulated parties. No-action letters assist the public by publishing the staff's interpretation of the securities laws. In addition, the letters assist businesses in determining the applicability of the Advisers Act or the Investment Company Act to unique transactions, by providing a cost-efficient option to determine the application of the Advisers Act or the Investment Company Act while avoiding costly expenditure and risk.[2]

Recently, the staff provided guidance letters to the Investment Company Institute by expressing its concerns about certain issues. These letters help inform the industry about the staff's concerns, and often elicit the industry's response by voluntary self-enforcement or self-studies that provide information to the staff.

---

1. *See* Informal Guidance Program for Small Entities, Investment Company Act Rel. No. 22587 (Mar. 27, 1997), n. 20. In some instances, the staff of the Commission will expressly state in a no-action letter that third parties may not rely on it; in these cases, the no-action letter must be treated as more akin to an exemptive order — in that each market participant must obtain its own no-action letter in order to take advantage of the staff's enforcement position.
2. 1 Tamar Frankel & Ann Taylor Schwing, The Regulation of Money Managers, §§ 2-1 to -67 (2001 & Supp. 2015).

In addition, the Commission's website at www.SEC.gov provides useful and relevant information to attorneys, advisers and the public seeking guidance on the staff's interpretation of various Advisers Act and Investment Company Act issues. The Commission's website provides access to staff no-action letters organized topically, as well as staff guidance through Investment Management Guidance Updates[1] ("IM Guidance Updates"). IM Guidance Updates are publications that summarize the staff's views regarding various requirements of the federal securities laws. IM Guidance Updates are generally issued as a result of emerging industry trends, based on the staff's discussions with industry participants, reviews of registrant disclosures, and no-action letters.[2] The staff provides Investment Management information updates, which offers attorneys, advisers and the public updates to items such as forms, responds to frequently asked questions, issues concerning technology or program launches.

Further, the Commission publishes "concept" releases, soliciting public views on securities issues in order to better evaluate the need for future rulemaking.[3] The Commission provides guidance on topics of general interest to the business and investment communities by issuing "interpretive" releases, in which the Commission publishes its views and interpretation of the federal securities laws and Commission regulations. Interpretive releases (like concept releases) are not considered precedential law, but provide useful guidance regarding the position of the SEC staff. The "Regulatory Actions" web page includes interpretive releases from 1995 to the present. In addition, the Commission occasionally issues "policy statements" clarifying its position on a particular matter. These policy statements typically include inter-agency statements.

---

## Discussion Topics

a. What are the main differences between no-action letters and exemptions? What are the advantages and disadvantages of the two approaches for the clients-advisers and managers of mutual funds and for the government regulators? If the no-action process is available, when would it ever be appropriate to deal with a matter solely under an opinion of counsel?

b. What are the limitations that the SEC should impose on itself in exercising its Section 6(c) exemptive powers?

c. Can the SEC impose any conditions in awarding exemptions?

d. Can parties sue the SEC for **not** awarding an exemption?

---

1. *See generally* U.S. Sec. & Exch. Comm'n, Guidance Updates, http://www.sec.gov/investment/imguidance-updates.html.
2. *E.g.,* Cybersecurity Guidance, IM Guidance Update, No. 2015-02 (Apr. 2015), *available at* http://www.sec.gov/investment/im-guidance-2015-02.pdf.
3. The Regulatory Actions section of the Commission's website includes concept releases dating back to 1994 *available at* U.S. Sec. & Exch. Comm'n, Regulatory Actions, http://www.sec.gov/rules.shtml.

Problem

Please read Rule 486 under the Securities Act of 1933. Assume you are an SEC staff attorney in the Division of Investment Management and that you have been asked to review a request for no-action relief to rely on this rule applicable to closed-end funds for a fund that does not fall squarely within the description of the types of closed-end funds permitted to rely on the rule. What are the pros and cons of granting such no-action relief? Would you allow it to be generally applicable if you granted it, or would you make it fund-specific? Would you instead require the fund to seek an exemptive order?

---

### d. Rulemaking

Under the Investment Company Act, there are three sources for the SEC's rulemaking power: section 6(c) creating its general exemptive powers; other, specific sections granting the SEC rulemaking power, such as sections 10(f) and 17(b); and section 38(a) authorizing the SEC by rule to prescribe forms for reports and applications, procedures, and definitions. The Advisers Act provides the SEC a general rulemaking power in section 211(a), and a rulemaking power under its general exemptive powers in section 206A. The securities industry and other interested persons and organizations may participate in the promulgation of rules through comments and consultations and appearance in hearings on proposed rules.

### e. Registration Statement Comments

Another way in which the staff of the Commission creates what amounts to Investment Company Act "common law" is by the comment process on registration statements for investment companies. In order to establish an investment company, the investment company and the securities it issues must be registered with the Commission, and the Commission must declare the investment company's registration statement effective. Prior to declaring a registration statement effective, the staff of the Commission will comment on the initial draft of the filed registration statement and will not declare the registration statement effective until these comments are resolved to the staff's satisfaction. These comment letters (and issuers' response letters) are eventually made public, but often on a substantial lag. Arguably, in recent years, the Commission's staff has increasingly used the comment process in a manner that some consider is making administrative common law to implement the staff's interpretive views of the Investment Company Act. Others might consider the process as helping applicants understand the staff's interpretations and giving the applicants an opportunity to test these interpretations in the courts.

### f. Enforcement Authority Under the Investment Advisers Act and the Investment Company Act

The Investment Advisers Act

Generally, the Commission has broad authority to initiate enforcement actions when a violation of the securities laws has occurred, is occurring, or is about to occur.[1] The Advisers Act provides the Commission with enforcement authority to bring administrative sanctions, to initiate civil injunctions and for criminal prosecution. Section 203 of the Advisers Act sets forth the Commission's administrative sanctions.[2] Section 203(e) authorizes the Commission to discipline an adviser if it finds that the adviser or a person associated with the adviser.

(1) Made a false statement in an application for registration or SEC report;

(2) Has been convicted of certain felonies or misdemeanors within 10 years preceding the filing of any application for registration or thereafter;

(3) Has been convicted of any crime (not described in (2)) punishable by imprisonment for one or more years within 10 years preceding the filing of any application for registration or thereafter;[3]

(4) Has been enjoined by a court from engaging in activity in the financial services industry;

(5) Has violated the federal securities laws or related statutes;

(6) Has aided and abetted a violation of the federal securities laws or related statutes or has failed to reasonably supervise someone who commits a violation of such laws;

(7) Has been barred or suspended by the SEC from associating with an investment adviser; or

(8) Has been found by a foreign financial regulatory authority to have engaged in certain conduct.

Section 203(f) grants the Commission authority to discipline persons associated with an investment adviser, if the Commission finds that the associated person engaged in the acts proscribed by Section 203(e).[4] One of the broadest disciplinary powers enacted as part of Sections 203(e) and (f) is the power of the Commission to bring failure-to-supervise[5] actions against advisers and to seek sanctions for an adviser's failure to supervise. Sanctions for failure to supervise brought against advisers have substantially increased since 1986.[6] In addition, until 2003 cases for failure-to-supervise had been brought only against registered advisers. In December of 2003,

1. *See* Exchange Act § 21(d)(1), 15 U.S.C. § 78u(d)(1) (authorizing SEC enforcement actions in the federal district court).

2. *See* 15 U.S.C. § 80b-3 (Section 203, Investment Advisers Act).

3. *See* Morgan, Lewis & Bockius LLP, SEC No-Action Letter (Aug. 1, 2002).

4. *See* 15 U.S.C. § 80b-3(f). Section 203(f) was adopted as part of the 1970 Amendments to the Advisers Act.

5. The provision in the Investment Advisers Act for failure to supervise parallels § 15(b) of the Securities Exchange Act, 15 U.S.C. § 78*o*(b), which applies to broker-dealers.

6. *See* In re Shearson Lehman Brothers, Inc., Stein Roe & Farnham, Exchange Act Rel. No. 23640; Investment Advisers Act Rel. No. 1038 (Sept. 24, 1986) (substantial weaknesses in adviser's internal controls that allowed one of its employees to allocate trades to brokers in a manner inconsistent with an adviser's fiduciary duty).

the Commission brought a failure-to-supervise case against an employee of an unregistered adviser.[1]

Section 203(e) provides the Commission with a number of options in its determination of whether to take disciplinary action against an adviser or a person associated with an adviser. With respect to advisers, section 203(e) provides the following options: censure, impose limitations on the firm's activities, suspend for up to one year, or revoke the firm's registration.[2] In 1990, Federal securities laws were amended by the Securities Enforcement Remedies and Penny Stock Reform Act (the "Remedies Act"),[3] under which the Commission's areas of adjudication and remedies were broadened.[4] Before the passage of the Remedies Act, the Commission's options for prosecuting such violations were limited to initiating an injunctive action in federal court[5] or, if the misleading item appeared in a report required to be filed with the Commission, bringing an administrative action under section 15(c)(4) of the Exchange Act.[6] The 15(c)(4) administrative remedy, however, was arguably limited to requiring the registrant to correct its filing.[7]

The Remedies Act provided additional administrative remedies with respect to investment advisers.[8] Section 203(i) authorizes the Commission to impose monetary penalties in proceedings instituted pursuant to section 203(e) or (f). Section 203(j) authorizes the SEC to enter disgorgement orders in its administrative proceedings,[9] and section 203(k) subjects investment

1. In re Robert T. Littell & Wilfred Meckel, Investment Advisers Act Rel. No. 2203 (Dec. 15, 2003)(Commission action against a principal of an unregistered adviser). In relation to the action, an SEC official was quoted saying "[w]hether registered or unregistered, employees of investment advisers and hedge funds they advise can and will be subject to enforcement action if they fail to act appropriately to protect investors." SEC Brings First Failure to Supervise Action Against Principal of an Unregistered Investment Adviser to a Hedge Fund; Also Charges Hedge Fund Director of Investments With Fraud, SEC Press Rel. 2003-172 (Dec. 15, 2003).
2. *See* 15 U.S.C. § 80b-3(e) (§ 203(e) of the Investment Advisers Act).
3. *See* section 20(d) of the Securities Act, 15 U.S.C. § 77t(d) (2006); section 21(d)(3) of the Exchange Act, 15 U.S.C. § 78u(d)(3)(2006); *see also* Pub. L. No. 101-429, 104 Stat. 931.
4. *Id.*
5. *See* 104 Stat. at 931 (enacted "[t]o amend the Federal securities laws in order to provide additional enforcement remedies for violations of those laws").
6. *See* 15 U.S.C. § 78*o*(c)(4) (authorizing administrative action when reporting company "has failed to comply" with disclosure requirements to compel the issuer to bring itself into compliance).
7. On the operation of section 15(c)(4) actions, *see generally* William R. McLucas & Laurie Romanowich, SEC Enforcement Proceedings Under Section 15(c)(4) of the Securities Exchange Act of 1934, 41 Bus. Law. 145 (1985). Section 15(c)(4) is virtually non-existent as a result of the Commission receiving authority for cease-and-desist enforcement actions in the Remedies Act legislation.
8. *See generally* 15 U.S.C. § 80b-3.
9. "Disgorgement" refers to depriving the violator of his or her "ill-gotten gain" obtained as a result of the violation; however, as matter of policy the Commission will typically seek to distribute disgorged amounts to injured parties. Disgorgement forces a defendant to account for all profits reaped through the securities law violations even if it exceeds actual damages to victims. *See SEC v. Cavanaugh*, 445 F.3d 117 (2d Cir. 2006); *SEC v. Huffman*, 996 F.2d 800 (5th Cir. 1993).

advisers, and persons associated with them, to permanent and temporary cease and desist orders.[1]

### The Investment Company Act

Sections 8, 9 and 41 of the Investment Company Act grant the Commission oversight and authority to bring disciplinary proceedings against investment companies and persons associated with them.[2] Section 8 governs the registration requirements for investment companies and authorizes the Commission to prescribe the form of, withhold, suspend or revoke the registration of an investment company.[3] Section 9 makes it unlawful for certain persons to act as affiliated persons or as a principal underwriter for a registered investment company.[4] In addition, Section 9(b) authorizes the Commission, under certain circumstances, to prohibit any person from serving as an investment adviser for a registered investment company permanently or for a period of time.[5] Section 41 of the Act vests in the Commission authority to conduct public hearings concerning the matters listed above.[6]

### g. Settlement Agreements

Historically, most of enforcement actions brought by the Commission were settled with the defendants, who neither admitted nor denied liability. Most settlements were negotiated before the filing of the enforcement action and announced contemporaneously with the public announcement of the proceeding. Court cases settlements have become less frequent with the passage of the Remedies Act in 1990, which expanded the Commission's authority to impose administrative sanctions and to seek more severe sanctions in civil injunctive actions against regulated individuals and entities.[7]

Since at least 2003, the Commission has added conditions to settlement agreements. These conditions require some defendants to personally pay all or some of the penalties, rather than using insurance or corporate

1. *See* 15 U.S.C. § 80b-3(k).
2. *See* 15 U.S.C. §§ 80a-8, 80a-9, 80a-41.
3. 15 U.S.C. § 80a-8.
4. 15 U.S.C. § 80a-9.
5. 15 U.S.C. § 80a-9(b).
6. 15 U.S.C. § 80a-41.
7. *See* Securities Enforcement Remedies and Penny Stock Reform Act of 1990, Pub. L. No. 101-429, 104 Stat. 931 (1990). The Dodd-Frank Act eliminated the constraint on the SEC's administrative reach, i.e., the imposition of monetary penalties against regulated individuals and entities. Under the Dodd-Frank Act, the Commission was authorized in cease-and-desist proceedings to impose monetary penalties against any person, including any public company. *See* Dodd-Frank Wall Street Reform and Consumer Protection Act, § 929P, Pub. L. No. 111-203, 124 Stat. 1376, 1862-64 (2010) (amending securities acts). The harsher tone of the Commission's position on sanctions was captured in a statement made by former Chairman Breeden early in his administration. Reportedly he told the staff that he wanted an alleged securities violator to be left "naked, homeless, and without wheels." Kevin G. Salwen & Laurie P. Cohen, *Getting Tough: SEC Under Breeden Takes a Harder Line on Securities Crime*, Wall St. J. May 10, 1990, at A1.

indemnification, to cover the costs of settlement.[1] "It is the Commission's unwritten policy to require, as a condition to settling claims, that the settling party agree not to seek or accept indemnification or reimbursement from any source (including a D & O insurance policy) for any penalties or other amounts paid in settlement of the SEC action. The Commission's policy applies only to monetary penalties not to disgorgement or defense costs."[2]

On June 18, 2013, Securities and Exchange Commission Chairman Mary Jo White announced that the Commission would require parties in civil cases to admit liability as a condition of resolving securities-related charges in certain cases.[3] This announcement was a departure from the Commission's prior policy, which permitted parties to settle SEC enforcement actions without an admission of wrongdoing.[4]

Chairman White's announcement came at the heels of increased criticism of the SEC's approval of "neither admit nor deny" settlement agreements.[5] The Commission's policy of allowing defendants to neither admit nor deny liability was put to the test in *SEC v. Citigroup Global Markets Inc.*[6] In the Citigroup case, the district court rejected a proposed settlement to which the parties had agreed because the parties had not provided sufficient evidence for the court to determine whether the settlement was fair, reasonable or in the public interest.[7] Ultimately, the Second Circuit Court of Appeals sided with the Commission "ruling that while a district court must review a proposed SEC consent decree, the scope of that review is limited."

---

<u>**Discussion Topics**</u>

a. In your opinion, what should be the Commission's policy regarding settlements? Can you create a model to determine what the optimal policy should be? What principles and guidelines would you establish to create this model?

b. Can you propose a model for the defendants to determine what their optimal strategy should be?

c. How should the settlement terms be monitored and enforced?

---

### h. The Wells Notice

The SEC starts a judicial process against any party by sending the party a Wells Notice: a notice that it intends to begin enforcement proceedings against the recipient, noting that the staff believes that a violation has

1. Gregory S. Wright et al., The Securities Enforcement Manual § 14 (2d ed. 2007).
2. *Id.*
3. Securities and Exchange Commission: Wall Street Journal CFO Network Conference, C-SPAN (Jun. 25, 2013), www.c-spanvideo.org/program/313430-10.
4. *Id.*
5. *Id.*
6. 827 F. Supp. 2d 328 (S.D.N.Y. 2011).
7. *Id.*

occurred. This notice is not required by law but has been the practice of the SEC. The notice was established as a practice by the SEC in 1972, when the SEC Chairman appointed a committee to review and evaluate the SEC's enforcement policies and practices. The committee was chaired by John Wells, and hence the notice acquired his name. The Wells Committee proposed:[8]

> Except where the nature of the case precludes, a prospective defendant or respondent should be notified of the substance of the staff charges and probable recommendations in advance of the submission of the staff memorandum to the Commission recommending the commencement of an enforcement action and be accorded an opportunity to submit a written statement to the staff to be forwarded to the Commission together with the staff memorandum.

Usually, the notice is sent after investigation. Therefore, it is not a surprise to the recipient. The recipient may respond with a Wells Submission. There are reasons for the recipients to avoid such a submission because it might disclose information and arguments that could be used against it in trial as well as in civil litigation. On the other hand, it is sometimes useful to respond, for example, if: "there is a clear error in the facts," although that may be rare, or if "there is a clear and compelling policy argument against the commencement of enforcement proceedings, or when the Staff is misinterpreting the law or the facts."[9]

Therefore a Wells Submission can be a valuable tool for the defendant. It provides the prospective defendant an opportunity to speak to the decision maker and to have his or her position on the substance of the matter heard before a decision is made to commence proceedings. At the same time responding to a Wells Notice can ultimately harm a prospective defendant's position at the hearing and in later negotiations. It is therefore extremely important for a prospective respondent or defendant to analyze the pros and cons with their attorney before making the submission.[10]

### 2. Other Laws Applicable to Investment Management

#### a. State Laws

When the Investment Company Act and the Advisers Act do not apply to a particular issue, state laws apply. As in other situations, state laws are the residual laws. In addition, the Constitution limits the reach of federal laws. Thus, there have arisen issues on whether and to what extent the Investment Company Act and the Advisers Act apply to a particular situation. The other side of the coin is also open to arguments: to what extent do state laws continue to apply when the federal law regulates an issue. That is, to what extent do federal laws preempt state laws.

Under state laws, investment managers, investment advisers, directors, officers and trustees, are fiduciaries. All owe a duty of loyalty, prohibiting them from using their power over the investors' property for a purpose

---

8. Mark J. Astarita, *The Wells Notice in SEC and NASD Investigations: Could It Possibly Be a Good Thing?* (2010), *available at* http//www.seclaw.com/docs/wellsnotice.htm.
9. *Id.*
10. *Id.*

other than for performing their services. Hence, they must use the entrusted power for the sole benefit of investors. Their duty of loyalty differs in strictness, depending on the nature of the fiduciaries and on the degree of discretion and power they have over the investors' property. The strictness of the duty of loyalty also depends on the extent to which the investors can monitor the fiduciaries and protect themselves against abuse of power.[1]

The duty of loyalty is strengthened by legal duties. For example, fiduciaries must segregate the investors' money and securities from their own. Segregation protects investors from the claims of the creditors of the fiduciaries by giving the creditors notice that the fiduciaries do not own the assets. Segregation may also have a psychological effect reminding fiduciaries that they do not own the assets.

Fiduciaries must use their vested power solely for the purpose for which they received the power (usually for the benefit of the investors). After all, the only purpose of entrusting a manager with investors' money and securities is to facilitate the performance of the managers' services by giving them ready access to the property. If fiduciaries deal with the investors' property both for themselves and for the investors, the fiduciaries occupy both sides of the negotiating table. The law assumes that they will be more generous to themselves than to the investors whom they serve, helping themselves to investors' property in the process.

Law allows conflicts of interests only if the beneficiaries consent to transactions in conflict of interest provided the investors receive the full information about the transactions and can then make a decision. In addition, independent corporate directors may consent to conflict of interest transactions on behalf of the shareholders. In light of the problems and losses that arose in the 1920s, Congress passed the Investment Company Act and the Advisers Act. Thus, there is no federal requirement that investment companies would be organized in a certain way. However, even though investment companies may be organized in any legal form, or even be an individual, the Investment Company Act is superimposed on applicable organizational laws.

The Investment Company Act prohibits affiliated persons from engaging in conflicts of interest in sections 10(f), 17(a) to (f), 35, and 36. In addition, the Act expands the group of persons subject to the prohibition on conflicts far beyond the traditional family of fiduciaries, by defining the term "affiliates" very broadly[2] and imposing the prohibitions not only on affiliates but also on affiliates of affiliates, and affiliates of some non-affiliates.[3]

In addition to state law relating to fiduciaries and corporations, state securities laws (i.e., "Blue Sky Laws") have historically played a role in regulating investment management. In 1996, the National Securities Markets Improvement Act was signed into law. This Act detailed the involvement of state securities regulators with respect to the investment

1. *See generally* Tamar Frankel, Fiduciary Law (2010) (Oxford University Press).
2. *See* section 2(a)(3), 2(a)(9), 15 U.S.C. §§ 80a-2(a)(3), -2(a)(9).
3. *See, e.g.,* section 17(a), 15 U.S.C. § 80a-17(a).

management business. First, the Act contains important exemptions from state regulation for any security issued by an investment company registered under the Investment Company Act. Before this Act, state regulators generally reviewed fund prospectuses even though the documents were reviewed by the SEC. The cost of the dual regulation was high, while most investment companies acted nationally and globally rather than within state boundaries.

Second, the Act alters the federal-state regulatory balance with respect to investment advisers by regulating registration requirements for investment advisers. In 2010, Congress amended section 203(b)(3) of the Advisers Act. That section previously exempted advisers to less than 15 clients from the registration requirements of the Advisers Act. Judicial interpretation of the term "client" has included entities with thousands of investors (in other words, the entity is the "client" — not the investors in the entity). That allowed advisers to hedge funds and private funds not subject to the Investment Company Act (such as private equity funds or venture capital funds) to escape regulation as registered investment advisers under the Advisers Act. Congress, in the Dodd-Frank Wall Street Reform and Consumer Protection Act of 2010, amended section 203(b)(3) to overrule the impact of these decisions and expand the registration requirement under the Advisers Act to apply to most advisers to hedge funds and other private funds that were, prior to the enactment of the Dodd-Frank Act, excluded from the requirement to register as investment advisers under the Advisers Act. This subject will be explored later.

### b. Tax

Tax is a regulatory component that no lawyer can afford to overlook in any area, including investment management. It should be noted that the Internal Revenue Code in Subchapter M allows for pass-through treatment of most registered investment companies. That means that registered investment companies' taxable income is not taxed on the company level but only on the investor's level. However, the Code imposes substantial conditions to attain this pass-through status, such as registration under the 1940 Act, diversification of the investment companies' portfolios, and annual distribution of most income of the companies.

The tax provisions are also motivated by other policies. The pass-through benefits are subject to a number of conditions. One condition requires that the investment company will be diversified. Consequently, such investment companies cannot acquire control of portfolio companies without losing their tax advantage. Second, the investment companies must distribute 90% of their capital gains and profits at the end of each year. Thus, the shareholders must pay taxes sometimes on gains that they do not realize. Thus, the results of attempting to render the large pooled funds a mirror of large individual investments produce consequences that are not always anticipated or desirable.[1]

1. Mark J. Roe, *Political Elements in the Creation of a Mutual Fund Industry,* 139 U. Pa. L. Rev. 1469 (1991).

On Dec. 22, 2010, President Obama signed legislation modifying and updating federal tax code provisions pertaining to SEC-regulated investment companies in order to make them better conform to, and interact with, other aspects of the tax code and applicable federal securities laws.[1] The Regulated Investment Company Modernization Act, HR 4337, would "reduce the burden arising from amended year-end tax information statements, improve a mutual fund's ability to meet its distribution requirements, create remedies for inadvertent mutual fund qualification failures, improve the tax treatment of investing in a fund-of-funds structure, and update the tax treatment of fund capital losses."[2]

### c. Self Regulatory Organizations (SROs)[3]

Some self-regulatory organizations are organized by their members. That is especially so if the members of the organization deal with each other and require rules that facilitate their smooth relationships and the reputation of their business or profession. Broker-dealers had created such an organization before the establishment of the Securities and Exchange Commission. Since the government budget is insufficient to actively and closely regulate thousands of brokers and investment advisers, self-regulatory organizations were granted regulatory powers subject to the Commission's supervision. For brokers, a self-regulatory organization (formerly NASD and currently entitled FINRA) has operated for a long time, subject to the supervision of the Securities and Exchange Commission. One reason may be that the brokers deal with each other. Advisers have not been inclined to organize self-regulatory organizations, perhaps because they do not deal with each other, as brokers do, and perhaps because their styles of operation and client relationships do not lend themselves to a uniform form.

There are advantages and disadvantages to self-regulation. The reduced cost of government regulation is offset by the cost of added regulatory layers and while regulation by the more expert personnel may present an advantage, this advantage may be reduced by added conflicts with the law's objectives and a lower protection of investors' interests. Nonetheless, there is a general agreement that FINRA (a combined organization of the New York Stock Exchange and the former National Association of Securities Dealers) has been successful in achieving the goals of divergent groups and the public interest.

The Dodd-Frank Act authorizes the imposition of fiduciary duties on broker-dealers in dealing with individual investors, and required the Securities and Exchange Commission to further examine the unification of the regulation of brokers and advisers. Whether the current and future

1. Jim Hamilton, Jim Hamilton's World of Securities Regulation, Dec. 22, 2010 President Signs Legislation Modernizing Federal Tax Code Treatment of SEC-Regulated Investment Companies, *available at* http://jimhamiltonblogspot.com/2010/12/ president-signslegislationmodernizing.html.

2. *Id.*

3. *See* Tamar Frankel, Should Funds and Investment Advisers Establish a Self-Regulatory Organization? In The Financial Services Revolution, Understanding the Changing Role of Banks, Mutual Funds, and Insurance Companies (Clifford E. Kirsch ed. 1997).

SRO of the broker-dealer will regulate advisers who are not broker-dealers, or whether those who are advisers must be subject to an additional and separate SRO, remains to be seen. What has been heatedly debated since 2009 and remains unresolved in 2015 is whether and to what extent broker-dealers should be subject to Advisers Act fiduciary standards when they give advice with respect to the securities that they recommend to trade for clients. We return to this subject in the context of the Investment Advisers Act of 1940.

---

## Discussion Topics

a. In addition to the laws discussed above, the Employee Retirement Income Security Act of 1974 ("ERISA") and the Commodity Exchange Act ("CEA") often apply to advisory activities. For instance, when advisers provide services to retirement funds that are regulated under ERISA, they must take care to follow the prohibitions and regulatory requirements of that Act. When advisers use the futures markets, such activity may be subject to regulation under the CEA. Yet they do not self-regulate. Please list the way in which you would advise financial advisers to heed the various regulations.

c. In light of the materials that you have read, has federal law absorbed the principles of fiduciary law as a whole or did it limit and pre-empt state fiduciary law principles? In the second case, federal claims of breach of fiduciary duties would apply only if the federal law speaks specifically on an issue. In the first case, breach of fiduciary law applies as a matter of federal law even if the law does not address the issue specifically. Which approach do you prefer?

---

# Chapter 2

## *The Investment Advisers Act*

### A. The Investment Advisers Act: History, Outline, and Definition of Advisers

### 1. The Advisers Act: History and Outline

Even though attention was primarily focused on investment companies in 1940, Congress recognized problems related to investment advisers that were not managing investment companies. Advisers can have an impact on the securities markets, and Congress discovered advisers' abuses of clients other than investment companies. Therefore, in addition to the Investment Company Act, Congress passed the Advisers Act.

During its first 20 years, the Advisers Act was little more than a census of investment advisers, required to register. Today, this Act has far more "teeth." It imposes a broad requirement of disclosure to clients and requirements concerning permitted contractual arrangements. Advisers must maintain detailed records and have duties concerning the custody of their clients' funds. An anti-fraud section applies to registered as well as unregistered investment advisers, and the SEC has the authority to examine advisers. Registered advisers are required to appoint a chief compliance officer and establish a compliance program. Thus, the regulation of advisers has increasingly become stricter and the trend seems to continue.

Both the Advisers Act and the Investment Company Act are based on the principle that investment advisers are fiduciaries of their clients. The services they render are personal and may not be transferred without the clients' consent and many conflicts of interest between clients and advisers must be avoided in some situations, and in other situations fully disclosed and subject to clients' consent. In addition, some advisers that engage in other functions are subject to regulation under other laws, for example, broker-dealers regulation.[1]

In October 1996, the Advisers Act was amended to divide the jurisdiction over advisers between the SEC and the States. In that year, there were about 22,000 registered investment advisers, who held about $10.6 trillion

1. The original section 203(b)(2) of the Advisers Act exempted investment advisers of investment companies from registration under the Advisers Act. This exemption was deleted in 1970.

under management. Approximately 6,000 of these advisers managed approximately 95% of these assets. These advisers remained subject to the exclusive regulation of the SEC. Most of the rest, managing about 5% of the U.S. managed assets, were to be regulated exclusively by the States, with some exception. The division of regulatory authority was justified on the grounds of efficiency, avoidance of duplicative and contradictory regulation, and division of regulation: States would regulate local advisers and the SEC would regulate advisers conducting interstate and international business.

As of July 21, 2011, mid-sized investment advisers, i.e., those advising or managing assets up to $100 million (or higher amount set by the SEC), may not register with the SEC unless they advise a registered investment company or business development company.

A further discussion of the history of the Advisers Act is provided in *SEC v. Capital Gains Research Bureau* which is examined later in this Chapter. Now we turn to the definition of an investment adviser.

## 2. The General Definition of Adviser

"Investment adviser" is defined in Section 202(a)(11) of the Advisers Act as "any person who, (1) for compensation, engages in the (2) business of advising others, either directly or through publications or writings, (3) as to the value of securities or (4) as to the advisability of investing in, purchasing, or selling securities, or who, (1) for compensation and (2) as part of a regular business, issues or promulgates analyses or reports concerning securities." The SEC staff has elaborated on these various elements of the definition of "investment adviser" from time to time, including as set forth below.[1]

> Section 202(a)(11) of the Advisers Act defines the term "investment adviser" to mean. . .
>
> any person who, for compensation, engages in the business of advising others, either directly or through publications or writings, as to the value of securities or as to the advisability of investing in, purchasing, or selling securities, or who, for compensation and as part of a regular business, issues or promulgates analyses or reports concerning securities. . . .
>
> As a general matter, if the activities of any person providing integrated advisory services satisfy the elements of the definition, the person would be an investment adviser within the meaning of the Advisers Act, unless entitled to rely on one of the exclusions from the definition of investment adviser in clauses (A) to (F) of Section 202(a)(11). . . .
>
> 1. Advice or Analyses Concerning Securities
>
> It would seem apparent that a person who gives advice or makes recommendations or issues reports or analyses with respect to specific securities is an investment adviser under Section 202(a)(11), assuming the other elements of the definition of investment adviser are

---

1. Applicability of the Investment Advisers Act to Financial Planners, Pension Consultants, and Other Persons Who Provide Investment Advisory Services as a Component of Other Financial Services, Investment Advisers Act Rel. No. 1092 (Oct. 8, 1987) (footnotes omitted).

met, i.e., that such services are performed as a part of a business and for compensation. . . . The staff believes that a person who provides advice, or issues or promulgates reports or analyses, which concern securities, but which do not relate to specific securities, generally is an investment adviser under Section 202(a)(11), assuming the services are performed as part of a business and for compensation. The staff has interpreted the definition of investment adviser to include persons who advise clients concerning the relative advantages and disadvantages of investing in securities in general as compared to other investments. A person who, in the course of developing a financial program for a client, advises a client as to the desirability of investing in, purchasing or selling securities, as opposed to, or in relation to, any non-securities investment or financial vehicle would also be "advising" others within the meaning of Section 202(a)(11). Similarly, a person who advises employee benefit plans on funding plan benefits by investing in, purchasing, or selling securities, as opposed to, or in addition to, insurance products, real estate not involving securities, or other funding media, would be "advising" others within the meaning of Section 202(a)(11). A person providing advice to a client as to the selection or retention of an investment manager or managers also, under certain circumstances, would be deemed to be "advising" others within the meaning of Section 202(a)(11).

2. The "Business" Standard

Under Section 202(a)(11), an investment adviser is one who, for compensation, (1) engages in the business of advising others as to the value of securities or as to the advisability of investing in, purchasing, or selling securities, or, alternatively, (2) issues or promulgates reports or analyses concerning securities as part of a regular business. Each of these two alternatives in the statutory definition of investment adviser contains a business test — one involves "engaging in the business" of advising others while the other involves issuing reports about securities as "part of a regular business." While the "business" standards established under Section 202(a)(11) are phrased somewhat differently, it is the staff's opinion that they should be interpreted in the same manner. In both cases, the determination to be made is whether the degree of the person's advisory activities constitutes being "in the business" of an investment adviser. The giving of advice need not constitute the principal business activity or any particular portion of the business activities of a person in order for the person to be an investment adviser under Section 202(a)(11). The giving of advice need only be done on such a basis that it constitutes a business activity occurring with some regularity. The frequency of the activity is a factor, but is not determinative. . . .

The staff considers a person to be "in the business" of providing advice if the person: (i) holds himself out as an investment adviser or as one who provides investment advice, (ii) receives any separate or additional compensation that represents a clearly definable charge for providing advice about securities, regardless of whether the compensation is separate from or included within any overall compensation, or receives transaction-based compensation if the client implements the investment advice, or (iii) on anything other than rare, isolated and non-periodic instances, provides specific investment advice. For the purposes of (iii) above, "specific investment advice" includes a recommendation, analysis or report about specific securities or specific categories of securities (e.g., industrial development bonds, mutual funds, or medical technology stocks). It includes a recommendation that a client allocate certain percentages of his assets to life insurance, high yielding bonds, and mutual funds or particular types of mutual funds such as growth stock funds or money market funds. However, specific investment advice does not include advice limited to a general recommendation to allocate assets in securities, life insurance, and tangible assets.

In applying the foregoing tests, the staff may consider other financial services activities offered to clients. For example, if a financial planner structures his planning so as to give only generic, non-specific investment advice as a financial planner, but then gives specific securities advice in his capacity as a registered representative of a dealer or as agent of an insurance company, the person would not be able to assert that he was not "in the business" of giving investment advice. . . . In the staff's view, it is necessary to consider these other financial services activities. Section 208(d) of the Advisers Act makes it illegal for someone to do indirectly under the Advisers Act what cannot be done directly. . . .

3. Compensation

The definition of investment adviser applies to persons who give investment advice for compensation. This compensation element is satisfied by the receipt of any economic benefit, whether in the form of an advisory fee or some other fee relating to the total services rendered, commissions, or some combination of the foregoing. It is not necessary that a person who provides investment advisory and other services to a client charge a separate fee for the investment advisory portion of the total services. The compensation element is satisfied if a single fee is charged for a number of different services, including investment advice or the issuing of reports or analyses concerning securities within the meaning of the Advisers Act. As discussed above, however, the fact that no separate fee is charged for the investment advisory portion of the service could be relevant to whether the person is "in the business" of giving investment advice.

It is not necessary that an adviser's compensation be paid directly by the person receiving investment advisory services, but only that the investment adviser receives compensation from some source for his services. Accordingly, a person providing a variety of services to a client, including investment advisory services, for which the person receives any economic benefit, for example, by receipt of a single fee or commissions upon the sale to the client of insurance products or investments, would be performing such advisory services "for compensation" within the meaning of Section 202(a)(11) of the Advisers Act.

> B. Exclusions From Definition of Investment Adviser
>
> Clauses (A) to (E) of Section 202(a)(11) of the Advisers Act set forth limited exclusions from the definition of investment adviser available to certain persons. Whether an exclusion from the definition of investment adviser is available to any financial planner, pension consultant or other person providing investment advisory services within the meaning of Section 202(a)(11), depends upon the relevant facts and circumstances.
>
> A person relying on an exclusion from the definition of investment adviser must meet all of the requirements of the exclusion. The staff's view is that the exclusion contained in Section 202(a)(11)(B) is not available, for example, to a lawyer or accountant who holds himself out to the public as providing financial planning, pension consulting, or other financial advisory services. In such a case it would appear that the performance of investment advisory services by the person would not be incidental to his practice as a lawyer or accountant. Similarly, the exclusion for brokers or dealers contained in Section 202(a)(11)(C) would not be available to a broker or dealer, or associated person of a broker or dealer, acting within the scope of the business of a broker or dealer, if the person receives any special compensation for providing investment advisory services. Moreover, the exclusion from the definition of investment adviser contained in Section 202(a)(11)(C) is only available to an associated person of a broker or dealer or "registered representative" who provides investment advisory services to clients within the scope of the person's employment with the broker or dealer. For example, if a registered representative provides advice independent of, or separate from, his broker or dealer employer such as by establishing a separate financial planning practice, then he could not rely on the exclusion because his investment advisory activities would not be subject to control by his broker or dealer employer. Similarly, the exclusion would be unavailable if he provides advice without the knowledge and approval of his employer because in that capacity his advisory activities would, by definition, be outside the control of his employer. . . .

The Advisers Act provides a broad definition of an adviser and then excludes from the definition advisers who are either regulated by other laws or those that are unlikely to commit the type of violations that the Advisers Act addresses, such as teachers and publishers of newspapers of general circulation. In addition, the definition excludes brokers who do not receive compensation for advice, but may receive compensation for related services. Questions regarding the status of financial planners, whose numbers mushroomed during the past thirty years, prompted the SEC staff to outline its views regarding the definition of an investment adviser, part of which is reproduced below.

In 1987, the SEC staff published a Staff interpretative position concerning financial planners:[1]

---

1. Applicability of the Investment Advisers Act to Financial Planners, Pension Consultants, and Other Persons Who Provide Investment Advisory Services as a

Financial planning typically involves providing a variety of services, principally advisory in nature, to individuals or families regarding the management of their financial resources based upon an analysis of individual client needs. Generally, financial planning services involve preparing a financial program for a client based on the client's financial circumstances and objectives. This information normally would cover present and anticipated assets and liabilities, including insurance, savings, investments, and anticipated retirement or other employee benefits. The program developed for the client usually includes general recommendations for a course of activity, or specific actions, to be taken by the client. For example, recommendations may be made that the client obtain insurance or revise existing coverage, establish an individual retirement account, increase or decrease funds held in savings accounts, or invest funds in securities. A financial planner may develop tax or estate plans for clients or refer clients to an accountant or attorney for these services.

The provider of such financial planning services in most cases assists the client in implementing the recommended program by, among other things, making specific recommendations to carry out the general recommendations of the program, or by selling the client insurance products, securities, or other investments. The financial planner may also review the client's program periodically and recommend revisions. Persons providing such financial planning services use various compensation arrangements. Some financial planners charge clients an overall fee for developing an individual client program while others charge clients an hourly fee. In some instances financial planners are compensated, in whole or in part, by commissions on the sale to the client of insurance products, interests in real estate, securities (such as common stocks, bonds, limited partnership interests, and mutual funds), or other investments.

A second common form of service relating to financial matters is provided by "pension consultants" who typically offer, in addition to administrative services, a variety of advisory services to employee benefit plans and their fiduciaries based upon an analysis of the needs of the plan. These advisory services may include advice as to the types of funding media available to provide plan benefits, general recommendations as to what portion of plan assets should be invested in various investment media, including securities, and, in some cases, recommendations regarding investment in specific securities or other investments. Pension consultants may also assist plan fiduciaries in determining plan investment objectives and policies and in designing funding media for the plan. They may also provide general or specific advice to plan fiduciaries as to the selection or retention of persons to manage the assets of the plan. Persons providing these services to plans are customarily compensated for their services through fees paid by the plan, its sponsor, or other persons;

---

Component of Other Financial Services, Investment Advisers Act Rel. No. 1092 (Oct. 8, 1987) (footnotes omitted).

> by means of sales commissions on the sale of insurance products or investments to the plan; or through a combination of fees and commissions. . . . [Also] financial planners, pension consultants, sports or entertainment representatives or other persons providing financial advisory services, may be investment advisers within the meaning of the Advisers Act, state adviser laws, or both. . . .

---

**Discussion Topics**

a. How did the SEC define financial planning? How different or similar is planning from investment advice? For a broker-dealer or an insurance broker, is there any benefit to giving free financial planning service? What is the cost and benefit for an insurance agent in becoming a financial planner?

b. Why should the SEC seek to regulate advisers who give only general, as opposed to specific, advice about securities? What about advisers who only give advice as to the selection of advisers?

c. Why does the SEC require that a registered representative may rely on the broker-dealer exclusion only if she gives advice within the scope of her employment with the broker-dealer? Does this mean that before recommending a stock to a client a registered representative must get clearance from the broker-dealer or risk falling under the Advisers Act?

---

## B. The Exclusion of Publishers from the Definition of an Investment Adviser

The Investment Advisers Act excludes the following entities from the definition of adviser: (1) banks and bank holding companies; (2) lawyers, accountants, engineers and teachers; (3) broker-dealers; and (4) publishers and authors. With respect to this last category, the Supreme Court examined the line dividing newspapers from advisory letters in the following case.[1]

On May 11, 1981, the Securities and Exchange Commission revoked the registration of petitioner Christopher Lowe's Lowe Management Corporation. Lowe and his company continued to publish two investment newsletters and offered a stock-chart service. In 1982, the SEC filed suit, claiming that Lowe was violating § 203(c) of the Investment Advisers Act of 1940, which prohibits unregistered advisers from providing guidance "as to the advisability of investing in, purchasing, or selling securities."

The Advisers Act provides an exception from the definition of an adviser to "the publisher of any bona fide newspaper, news magazine or business or financial publication of general and regular circulation." The majority of the Supreme Court justices acknowledged that this restriction reflects a First Amendment concern, but avoided the constitutional issue in this case by interpreting the Advisers Act exception of "publisher" from the definition of an investment adviser, and placing Lowe's publications

1. *Lowe v. SEC,* 472 U.S. 181 (1985).

within the statutory exception. The Court emphasized the distinction between providing personalized financial advice, which is not included in the exception, and disseminating impersonal "disinterested commentary," which is what the exception was designed to exclude.

The Court ruled that the publications in question met the two criteria the Advisers Act laid out for qualifying for the exception. First, the publications were bona fide because they were "genuine" rather than merely a guise for disseminating personal advice. Second, the publications were "of general and regular circulation" despite their sporadic release because the newsletters were not "timed to specific market activity or to events affecting . . . the securities industry." Justice White concurred with the result but based his analysis on a constitutional, rather than statutory, ground. Justice White argued that it would be a violation of the First Amendment to prohibit unregistered individuals from providing impersonal financial advice through publications. In his opinion, the legislative history demonstrated that the Advisers Act was in fact intended to apply to publishers like the Lowe, and that the majority of the Court erred in avoiding the constitutional issue by construing the statute's exception in an overly broad way. Justice White distinguished between regulating professional standards and regulating speech, and argued that the Advisers Act in this case regulated speech and thus violated the First Amendment.

---

## Discussion Topics

a. How did the majority of the court interpret the Advisers Act? Did the majority resort to the constitutional aspects of the issue?

b. Is the *Wall Street Journal* included in the publisher's exclusion if it contains information about issuers and securities? What about a column that describes the facts of a particular publicly held company?

c. What policy considerations argue for and against subjecting a publication such as *Money* magazine to the Investment Advisers Act? If *Money* magazine published a special edition for senior citizens, would it be personalized enough to require registration under the Advisers Act?

d. Did the Court resolve the constitutional issue of the Advisers Act? How would you have resolved the issue?

e. Congress has used the term "personalized" in authorizing the imposition of a fiduciary duty on broker-dealers that give personalized advice to individual investors, their family and business. Does *Lowe* have any relevance to this term?

f. How do you evaluate the business model of large investment banks and banks? Assume that this model is efficient and highly profitable for the institutions. Should it be nonetheless restricted by regulation or legislation?

g. In Title VII of the Dodd-Frank Act, Congress created a new class of clients engaging in derivative transactions — named "special entities" — to whom dealers owe a duty to act in their best interest under certain circumstances, such as when a dealer acts as an adviser to any special entity in connection with a "swap" transaction. These special entities include pension plans, governmental plans (e.g., state teacher and public worker retirement plans), and endowments. What makes these entities more vulnerable than other institutional investors to overreaching by their dealer counter-parties when the dealer both acts as an adviser and benefits from the transaction as a counter-party?[1]

h. Why should investors be relieved of the burden of studying and becoming more knowledgeable about financial instruments and their investments and savings?

i. In the context of structuring a trade — e.g., designing a portfolio and identifying parties on both sides of the trades (both long and short) — what role should the dealer play as an "adviser"? Does this role change when parties on both sides of the trade (the investors) specifically request to enter into the trade (i.e., they desire a specific exposure)? Do such transactions present conflicts that the dealer-adviser cannot overcome by disclosure? Does the nature of the conflict change if, instead of structuring a trade, the investment adviser establishes a fund, solicits contributions from third party investors, and takes a position contrary to the fund's strategy (i.e., the adviser "bets" against the fund)?[2]

---

The *Lowe* decision was revisited and somewhat clarified in *SEC v. Gun Soo Oh Park*.[3] The SEC brought an action against Yun Soo Oh Park, a.k.a. Tokyo Joe, and related entities, alleging that Park violated SEC rules, and Park moved to dismiss. In or around July 1998, Park created a website through which he offered investment advice. One part of the site was open to the general public while the other part was accessible only to paying members. Park updated his website daily with trading tips and stock recommendations. The SEC claimed that Park used the site illegally to manipulate the price of stocks he was selling by advising readers to buy that stock, and "to tout the stock of a certain company in exchange for receipt of stock or other compensation from that company." The SEC alleged, among other charges, violations of § 206(1) of the Advisers Act.

Park argued that, like the Petitioner in *Lowe*, his advice was not personalized and, therefore, he was not an investment adviser under the

1. *See SEC v. Larry P. Langford*, Litigation Rel. No. 20545 (Apr. 30, 2008) and *SEC v. Charles E. LeCroy*, Litigation Rel. No. 21280 (Nov. 4, 2009) (charging Alabama local government officials and J.P. Morgan employees with undisclosed payments made to obtain municipal bond offering and swap agreement business from Jefferson County, Alabama).

2. *See Deutsche Bank Also 'Victimized' Goldman 'Victim,'* The Atlantic (Apr. 26, 2010), *available at* http://www.theatlantic.com/business/archive/2010/04/deutsche-bank-also-victimized-goldman-victim/39471/; *see also* The SEC Charges Goldman Sachs with Fraud in Connection with the Structuring and Marketing of a Synthetic CDO, Litigation Rel. No. 21489 (Apr. 16, 2010) *available at* http://www.sec.gov/litigation/litreleases/2010/lr21489.htm; *A Wall Street Scapegoat Goes Down*, The New York Times (Aug. 2, 2013) *available at* http://takingnote.blogs.nytimes.com/2013/08/02/another-scapegoat-goes-down/?ref=fabricetourre&_r=0.

3. *SEC v. Gun Soo Oh Park*, 99 F. Supp. 2d 889 (N.D. Ill. 2000).

Advisers Act. The Court distinguished this case from *Lowe*, noting that the Petitioner in *Lowe* fell into the publishers' exception from the definition of investment advisers. The impersonal nature of the advice merely helped to demonstrate that the Petitioner fit into this exception rather than establish that impersonal advice by itself demonstrated the exclusion of the Petitioner from the definition of an investment adviser. In this case, for Park to qualify for this exception, he must show that his online advice was both bona fide and "of general and regular circulation." The SEC alleged that Park's financial advice met neither of these criteria. The advice was not bona fide because it was not disinterested; Park was making recommendations that furthered his own personal interests. Further, the advice was not of general and regular circulation because Park timed his advice to "specific market activity."

The Court considered Park's First Amendment challenge to the Advisers Act because, unlike the *Lowe* case, Park's activities did not meet the exception to the definition of investment adviser. The Court noted that Park was an investment adviser if his advice was of a personalized nature, and that he did not challenge the constitutionality of the registration requirement for advisers providing personal advice. Because Park did not meet the publishers' exception and was considered an investment adviser under the Advisers Act, the Court did not discuss the constitutionality of requiring registration for individuals providing impersonal financial advice.

---

<u>Discussion Topics</u>

a. Two clients ask you for advice: They wish to publish a book on investment management. Will they fall within the definition of an adviser under the Advisers Act?

b. Suppose the authors include chapters of the book on their website?

c. Suppose they also offer to answer the readers' questions?

d. Suppose the authors are asked by reporters for their opinions on certain pending cases before the courts concerning investment advice?

e. Please outline your advice to the authors by listing the elements of the definition of investment adviser as outlined in the *Lowe* and *Park* cases.

f. In *Lowe*, Justice Stevens used the word "personalized" advice. The Dodd-Frank legislation, which seeks to impose fiduciary duties on broker-dealers, similar to those of investment advisers, used the same word "personalized." What in your opinion are the main characteristics of "personalized" advice, as compared or contrasted with "non-personalized" advice?

---

## C. The Exclusion of Broker-Dealers from the Definition of an Investment Adviser

### 1. The Status of Broker-Dealers Under the Advisers Act

The Investment Advisers Act excludes broker-dealers from the definition of an adviser under certain conditions. Section 202(a)(11)(C) excludes from the definition "any broker or dealer whose performance of such services [i.e., investment advice] is solely incidental to the conduct of his business as a broker or dealer and who receives no special compensation therefor."

Bernard L. Madoff was charged with securities fraud for perpetrating a Ponzi scheme on his firm's advisory clients. In 2009 he pled guilty to violations of the Securities Act, Exchange Act, and Advisers Act, and was sentenced to prison.[1] Prior to the discovery of this Ponzi scheme, the SEC staff had examined the institutional trading activities of Madoff's brokerage business, BLM. These activities were described as follows at the time, and provides an example of how the SEC staff would likely continue to view issues relating to the broker-dealer exemption, although the particular rule referenced has since been vacated by the D.C. Circuit (as described in the next subsection): [2]

> In BLM's institutional trading business, the customers, predominantly large hedge funds, open brokerage accounts at BLM and give BLM and its principal, [Madoff], discretionary authority over the accounts. The limitations on that authority are set forth in [account documents]. BLM then trades the assets in these accounts pursuant to its proprietary trading strategy, which is a form of split strike forward conversion. The strategy has three aspects: (1) a computer program that creates and monitors potential baskets of equities; (2) Madoff's market timing judgment; (3) a hedge consisting of a collar of S&P100 index options. The computer program constantly searches for baskets of about 50 equities from the S&P100 index whose historical performance would strongly correlate to the performance of the index as a whole. Once a potential basket is available, Madoff, based on his own judgment of market conditions — and possibly other data that we have not yet learned about — decides whether to "execute the strategy", i.e., whether to purchase the basket and to put in place the corresponding hedge. If Madoff decides to execute the strategy then BLM purchases the basket of equities and also purchases and sells the options for the hedge. The positions then remain unchanged until the earlier of two events: (1) a signal from the BLM computer program that the correlation between the performance of the basket and the entire index is no longer sufficient; (2) Madoff's decision that it is time to sell. Once the positions are sold, customer assets remain invested in cash until the next time that Madoff decides to execute the strategy. The customers take no part in any of the trading decisions and only learn of the trades that occurred in their accounts after the fact, when BLM sends them trade confirmations and account statements.
>
> . . . It does appear to us . . . that BLM's institutional trading business

1. *See, e.g.,* Ofc. of Investigations, U.S. Sec. & Exch. Comm'n, Investigation of Failure of the SEC to Uncover Bernard Madoff's Ponzi Scheme (Public Version) 1 (Aug. 31, 2009), *available at* http://www.sec.gov/news/studies/2009/oig-509.pdf.

2. Memorandum of Simona Suh, Certain Hedge Fund Trading Practices, NY-7563-A (Apr. 10, 2006), *available at* http://www.sec.gov/news/studies/2009/oig-509/exhibit-0344.pdf (edited); *see also* Tamar Frankel, The Ponzi Scheme Puzzle (2012) (Oxford University Press).

is actually investment advisory business and that BLM should be registered with the Commission as an investment adviser.

Madoff insists that BLM is not an investment adviser because: (1) BLM does not charge any performance or asset-based fees, but only charges a "commission equivalent" of 4 cents per share on equity trades and a commission of $1 per contract on option trades; (2) BLM's investment discretion is limited to timing and price of transactions by the terms of the two [account] documents. These two documents are drafted by BLM, without any input from the customers; BLM simply presents these documents to the customers who accept them without any adjustments or negotiation. (In fact, a BLM officer testified that BLM would not be able to implement its trading strategy if different trading parameters had to apply to different customer accounts.) Based on the Advisers Act Rule 202(a)(11)-1, it appears to us that Madoff's position is without merit and, because none of the exemptions from registration apply, BLM is violating section 203 of the Advisers Act by failing to register as an investment adviser. Our preliminary analysis of these issues is set forth in greater detail below. It is not clear to us, however, whether BLM was an investment adviser prior to the 2005 adoption of Rule 202(a)(11)-1, under the staff's views stated in 1978 Releases IA-626 and IA-6401. . . .

A. Is BLM an investment adviser?

Yes. Section 202(a)(11) of the Advisers Act defines an "investment adviser" as "any person who, for compensation, engages in the business of advising others, either directly or through publications or writings, as to the value of securities or as to the advisability of investing in, purchasing, or selling securities, or who, for compensation and as part of a regular business, issues or promulgates an analysis or reports concerning securities." 15 U.S.C. § 80b-2(a)(11).

Excluded from this definition are, among other categories of persons not applicable here, (1) Brokers or dealers whose performance of advisory services is "solely incidental" to the conduct of their business as brokers or dealers and who receive "no special compensation" for such services; and (2) persons designated as exempt by the Commission rules. 15 U.S.C. § 80b-2(a)(11)(C) & (E). Rule 202(a)(11)-1(b) promulgated under this Section, 17 C.F.R. § 275.202(a)(11)-1(b), provides that a broker or a dealer "provides advice that is not solely incidental to the conduct of its business as a broker or dealer within the meaning of section 202(a)(11)(C) of the Advisers Act" if that broker or dealer, among other things. "[e]xercises investment discretion . . . over any customer accounts." For the purposes of this provision, a person has "investment discretion" over an account if that person "is authorized to determine what securities or other property shall be purchased or sold by or for the account" or "makes investment decisions as to what securities or other property shall be purchased or sold by or for the account even though some other person may have responsibility for such investment decisions." Section 3(a)(35) of the Exchange Act, 15 U.S.C. § 78c(a)(35). The term "investment discretion" "does not include investment discretion granted by a customer on a temporary or limited basis." Rule 202(a)(11)-1(d) of the Advisers Act, 17 C.F.R. § 275.202(a)(11)-1(d). On adopting Rule 202(a)(11)-1, the Commission explained the exception for "temporary or limited" discretion as follows:

> In such cases, the customer is granting discretion primarily for execution purposes and is not seeking to obtain discretionary supervisory services. Such discretion must be limited to a transaction or series of transactions and not extended to setting investment objectives or policies for the customer. For example, we would view a broker-dealer's discretion to be temporary or limited within the meaning of rule 202(a)(11)-1(d) when the broker-dealer is given discretion:
>
> - As to the price at which or the time to execute an order given by a customer for the purchase or sale of a definite amount or quantity of a specified security;
> - On an isolated or infrequent basis, to purchase or sell a security or type of security when a customer is unavailable for a limited period of time not to exceed a few months;
> - As to cash management, such as to exchange a position in a money market fund for another money market fund or cash equivalent;
> - To purchase or sell securities to satisfy margin requirements;
> - To sell specific bonds and purchase similar bonds in order to permit a customer to take a tax loss on the original position;
> - To purchase a bond with a specified credit rating and maturity; and
> - To purchase or sell a security or type of security limited by specific parameters established by the customer.
>
> Certain Broker-Dealers Deemed Not To Be Investment Advisers, Release No. 34-51523, IA-2376, 2005 WL 849053 (Apr. 12, 2005).

Here, BLM acts as an investment adviser to the institutional accounts. First, BLM for compensation engages in the business of advising others about the value of securities and the advisability of investing in them. The institutional clients pay BLM compensation in the form of commission equivalent of 4 cents per share on equities and commission of at most $1 per contract on options. In exchange for this compensation, BLM (specifically, Bernard Madoff) decides when BLM's institutional clients should purchase and sell the baskets of equities created by BLM's proprietary software and the corresponding options, and also selects the strike prices for the options. Second, BLM's advisory services are not incidental to the conduct of BLM's business as a broker-dealer because BLM has the discretion over the institutional clients' accounts. Although account documents impose certain limitations on BLM's discretion, these limitations clearly do not rise to the level of limitations contemplated by [Advisers] Act Rule 202(a)(11)-1(d), where "the customer is granting discretion primarily for execution purposes and is not seeking to obtain discretionary supervisory services." . . .

## 2. Broker-Dealers' Changing Practices and the Legal Developments

As of the beginning of the mid-1990s, broker-dealers began to charge asset-based fees or fixed fees in addition to commissions for executing transactions. This new fees-structure could be viewed as special fees for advice that would require broker-dealers to register as advisers, even though the fees related only to their broker-dealer services. Therefore, in April 12, 2005 the SEC adopted a rule that excluded broker-dealers from the applicability of the Advisers Act, subject to certain conditions, notwithstanding their asset-based fees.[1] After the passage of the rule, the Financial Planning Association sued the SEC seeking a judicial decision that the SEC has exceeded its authority and striking down the rule. The D.C. Circuit agreed with the Financial Planning Association.[2] It held that section 202(a)(11)(F), which allows the Commission to add to the definition of an investment adviser, "does not lend itself to alternative meanings [of the text of the section]; to conclude otherwise would undermine Congress's purpose in enacting the IAA-to protect consumers and honest investment advisers and to establish fiduciary standards and require full disclosure of all conflicts of interests of 'investment advisers,' broadly defined." Therefore, the Commission may use subsection (F) only with respect to situations that are not covered by the rest of section 202(a)(11).

### a. The Investor Protection Act of 2009

As we discuss later, investment advisers are subject to a fiduciary duty in dealing with clients — in other words, an investment adviser must put the interests of its client first, above all else, and scrupulously avoid and disclose any conflicts of interest. On the other hand, under current law broker-dealers are subject to a "suitability" standard, which, in effect, means that recommendations broker-dealers make to their clients must be only "suitable" for the client in light of the client's risk tolerance, financial position, investment objectives and the like.

In July 2009, the Obama Administration delivered to Congress the proposed Investor Protection Act of 2009.[3] The press release noted:

> Continuing its push to establish new rules of the road and make the financial system more fair for consumers and investors, the Administration today delivered proposed legislation to strengthen the SEC's authority to protect investors. The legislation outlines steps to establish consistent standards for all those who provide investment advice about securities, to improve the timing and the quality of disclosures, and to require accountability from securities professionals. The legislation would also establish a permanent Investor Advisory Committee to keep the voice of investors present at the

1. Certain Broker-Dealers Deemed Not To Be Investment Advisers, Investment Advisers Act Rel. No. 2376 (Apr. 12, 2005).

2. *Financial Planning Association v. SEC,* 482 F.3d 481 (D.C. Cir. 2007).

3. Press Release, U.S. Dep't of the Treas., Fact Sheet: Administration's Regulatory Reform Agenda Moves Forward: Legislation for Strengthening Investor Protection (Jul. 10, 2009), *available at* http://www.treas.gov/press/releases/tg205.htm; Investor Protection Act of 2009, H.R. 3817, 111th Cong. (as introduced in House, Oct. 15, 2009).

> SEC. . . . Under current law, different standards apply for broker-dealers and investment advisers — even though many investors rely on the investment advice of broker-dealers in the same manner as an investment adviser. The Administration's legislation would give the SEC authority to require a fiduciary duty for any broker, dealer, or investment adviser who gives investment advice about securities, aligning the standards based on activity, instead of based on legal distinctions that are no longer meaningful. In addition, the SEC would be empowered to examine and ban forms of compensation that encourage financial intermediaries to steer investors into products that are profitable to the intermediary, but are not in the investors' best interest.

The amendments were generally adopted in the Dodd-Frank Wall Street Reform and Consumer Protection Act.[1]

### b. The Congressional Mandate[2]

> Congress given to the Securities and Exchange Commission ("Commission") some serious homework in the Dodd-Frank Wall Street Reform and Consumer Protection Act ("Dodd-Frank Act").[3*]
>
> First, the Commission is required to study the standards of care for brokers, dealers, and advisers and consider the elimination of the broker exclusion from the Advisers Act of 1940 ("Advisers Act").[4*]
>
> In addition, the Commission must evaluate the impact of imposing on brokers the duties of the Advisers Act.[5*] That imposition would include the duty of loyalty, acting for the best interests of the clients,

1. Dodd-Frank Wall Street Reform and Consumer Protection Act, Pub. L. No. 111-203, § 913(g)(2), 2010 U.S.C.C.A.N. (124 Stat.) 1376, 1828-29 *codified at* 15 U.S.C. § 80b-11(g) (empowering SEC to require brokers, dealers, and investment advisers advising retail customers to "act in the best interest of the customer" and meet a standard at least equal to that for investment advisers under Advisers Act section 206(1)-(2)); *id.* § 913(g)(1), 2010 U.S.C.C.A.N. (124 Stat.) at 1828 *codified at* 15 U.S.C. § 78*o*(k)(1) (empowering SEC to require broker or dealer advising retail customer to meet the standard for an investment adviser under section 211 of the Advisers Act).

2. Tamar Frankel, *Papers on a Fiduciary Duty for Broker-Dealers: The Regulation of Brokers, Dealers, Advisers, and Financial Planners*, 30 Rev. Banking & Fin. L. 123 (2010).

3*. Dodd-Frank Wall Street Reform and Consumer Protection Act, Pub. L. No. 111-203, 124 Stat. 1376 (2010).

4*. *Id.* at § 913(b)(1)-(2) ("The Commission shall conduct a study to evaluate . . . the effectiveness of existing legal or regulatory standards of care for brokers, dealers, [and] investment advisers . . . [and] whether there are legal or regulatory gaps, shortcomings, or overlaps in legal or regulatory standards in the protection of retail customers relating to the standards of care for brokers, dealers, investment advisers."). The SEC staff study recommended a uniform fiduciary standard. SEC, Study on Investment Advisers and Broker-Dealers As Required by Section 913 of the Dodd-Frank Wall Street Reform and Consumer Protection Act (2011), http://www.sec.gov/news/studies/2011/913studyfinal.pdf.

5*. *Id.* at §§ 913(c)(9)-(9)(A) (stating that the Commission "shall consider" the "potential impact of imposing upon brokers, dealers, and persons associated with brokers or dealers . . . the standard of care applied under the Investment Advisers Act of 1940").

and avoiding conflicts of interest.[1*] In today's financial world there are individual brokers, broker-dealers, advisers, and financial planners, as well as large groups and networks of brokers, dealers, advisers, financial planners, underwriters, creators of securitized assets, managers of "dark exchanges," and traders for their own account.

Second, Congress authorized the Commission to establish a fiduciary duty for brokers in providing retail clients with personalized investment advice.[2*] Congress authorized the Commission to promulgate "additional rules, where appropriate, regarding sales practices, conflicts of interest, and compensation schemes" with respect to brokers, "when providing personalized investment advice about securities to a retail customers (and such other customers as the Commission may by rule provide)."[3*] The standard of conduct the Dodd-Frank Act requires for such brokers with respect to such customers "shall be the same as the standard of conduct applicable to an investment adviser under section 211 of the Advisers Act of 1940."[4*] I believe and will argue that it is crucial to impose such rules not only on brokers, etc. who advise "retail customers," but also on brokers, etc., who advise institutional investors, even though these investors are what we call "sophisticated."

Third, the Commission should establish rules that impose on brokers a duty to disclose to investors the terms of their relationships with investors, including conflicts of interest.[5*] The clients' consent after appropriate disclosure may relieve brokers, etc. from the prohibition on conflict of interest.[6*]

Fourth, Congress provided guidelines for the Commission's enforcement.[7*] This provision raises a number of questions. Does enforcement include [the brokers' self-regulatory organization] FINRA's enforcement on the one hand and state regulation of

1.* *Id.* at § 913(g)(1) (stating that the Commission may promulgate rules to establish a fiduciary standard for broker-dealers, including requirements to "act in the best interest of the customer without regard to the financial or other interest of the broker, dealer, or investment adviser providing the advice[, that] . . . any material conflicts of interest shall be disclosed[, and that the] . . . standard of conduct shall be no less stringent than the standard applicable to investment advisers under section 206(1) and (2) of this Act when providing personalized investment advice about securities. . . .").

2*. *Id.* at § 913(f)-(g) (providing the Commission with rulemaking authority to "establish a fiduciary standard for brokers and dealers").

3*. *Id.* at § 913(g)(1).

4*. *Id.*

5*. *Id.* ("The Commission may promulgate rules to provide that the standard of conduct for all brokers, dealers, and investment advisers . . . [and] . . . [i]n accordance with such rules, any material conflicts of interest shall be disclosed and may be consented to by the customer.").

6*. *Id.* ("[A]ny material conflicts of interest shall be disclosed and may be consented to by customers.").

7*. *Id.* at § 913(h) (defining the Commission's enforcement "with respect to violations of the standard of conduct applicable to a broker or dealer providing personalized investment advice about securities to a retail customer. . . .").

investment advisers (large and small) on the other hand? Will FINRA's rules and the Commission's rules preempt state laws? Currently, there are two entities that regulate brokers: FINRA and the Commission as its supervisor. There are two entities that regulate advisers: the Commission and the states (over advisers that advise small amounts). Would brokers and advisers be subject to the advisers' regime or would small advisers be subject to the brokers' regime?

#### c. Who are Fiduciaries?

A fiduciary may be defined as a person (or institution) that provides a service which requires expertise and is socially important. Moreover, the service cannot be performed without the clients' entrustment of property or power or both. A broker cannot perform his services without entrustment of the clients' money and/or securities. Entrusted property and power are given to the fiduciary for the sole purpose of performing his duties. In addition, a fiduciary's services involve discretion; the services cannot be guided by itemized directives. Brokers' clients bear a number of risks: one risk is misappropriation of entrusted property and power — this risk is counteracted by the duty of loyalty. The other, although a lesser risk, is that fiduciaries will not perform their job well, as promised — this is the duty of care. Tight controls and even monitoring of fiduciaries can undermine the utility of the service. The cost of preventing abuse of entrustment may exceed the benefits from the relationships. Therefore, the purpose of the law is to induce entrustors to enter into relationships with fiduciaries by reducing their risk.

There is no doubt that brokers are agents, and therefore, fiduciaries. The question is with respect to what are they fiduciaries. Arguably, brokers are fiduciaries with respect to the money and power that are entrusted to them for the purpose of securities trading. Brokers who manage "sweep accounts" are fiduciaries with respect to the management of the accounts as well. Brokers are deemed agents, acting for their clients in market transactions.[1] Arguably, when brokers present themselves and act as advisers, they are fiduciaries with respect to their advice.

What if brokers have conflicts of interest with those of their clients? Suppose the brokers recommend to clients securities the sale of which gives the brokers higher commissions? In such a case, the law allows brokers, as it allowed any fiduciary, to fully disclose the conflicting interests and enable the clients to consent to the conflicts or deny consent. Congress

1. *Nelson v. Sherwood,* 687 F.2d 278, 282 (9th Cir. 1982) ("Agency is the fiduciary relation which results from the joint manifestation of consent by one person that another shall act on his behalf and subject to his control, and of consent by that other so to act.") (citing *Grace Line, Inc. v. Todd Shipyards Corp.,* 500 F.2d 361 (9th Cir. 1974); *see id.* at 282 ("The agent acts for or on behalf of the principal and subject to his control, and his acts are those of the principal.") (citing *NLRB v. United Brotherhood of Carpenters,* 531 F.2d 424 (9th Cir. 1976)); Restatement (Second) of Agency § 1(1) (1958) ("Agency is the fiduciary relation which results from the manifestation of consent by one person to another that the other shall act on his behalf and subject to his control, and consent by the other so to act."); Restatement (Third) of Agency § 1.01 (2006) ("[T]he agent shall act on the principal's behalf. . . ."); *see generally* Tamar Frankel, Fiduciary Law (2011) (Oxford University Press).

empowered the Commission to promulgate rules that impose on brokers a duty to disclose to investors the "terms of the investors' relationships" with the brokers and advisers "(including conflicts of interest)."[1] If the investors understand the conflicts of interest and are not dependent on the adviser, the investors may rely on the advisers or bid them goodbye. Otherwise, advisers' advice may not involve conflicting interests. Much depends on how these conflicting interests are disclosed. An effective disclosure must be in writing, short, clear, and highlight the danger of the conflict to the client. The brokers must bear the burden of the client's understanding of the conflict.

The fiduciary's duty to disclose (account) may be viewed as the reversal of the contract principle of *caveat emptor.* The law governing the distribution of securities presents a hybrid. The issuer or the brokers provide information about the proposed security and the client must decide whether to buy. However, attempts to educate investors in evaluating the offered securities have not been fully successful. Investors do not examine and often cannot understand the nature of the security that is being offered. Perhaps educating brokers and their registered representatives to give client advice for the clients' sole interests may be more successful.

In the context of fiduciary law, if fiduciary duties are default rules, then disclosure of the nature of the conflicts and the clients' consent to the conflicts change the prohibitions applicable to fiduciaries. In this context, congressional requirements would allow disclosing brokers to maintain their conflict of interest, provided the clients understand and consent.

Under the Advisers Act, "investment advice" includes advice as to the advisability or the desirability "of investing in, purchasing or selling securities."[2] "[I]t is sufficient that advice is generally concerned with investments in securities" and not "on particular securities."[3] Moreover, "an insurance agent who refers potential clients to an adviser for a fixed fee per client may be an adviser if the agent introduces the two [, as] [a]n introduction to an adviser implies advice that securities investment is desirable. . . ."[4]

Currently, registered representatives of a broker-dealer "need not register as advisers for distributing materials describing a subscription bookkeeping system that monitors all assets of a particular subscriber, assisting potential subscribers in preparing financial input data, and receiving compensation from the operator of the services. . . ."[5] In fact, it is "the exercise of discretion

1. Dodd-Frank Wall Street Reform and Consumer Protection Act, Pub. L. No. 111-203, §913(g)(1), 124 Stat. 1376, 1828-29 (2010) (*codified at* 15 U.S.C. § 80b-11(g)(1)) ("The Commission may promulgate rules [establishing a broker-dealer fiduciary standard, and] . . . [i]n accordance with such rules, any material conflicts of interest shall be disclosed and may be consented to by the customer.").
2. 15 U.S.C. § 80b-2(a)(11) (2012).
3. 1 Tamar Frankel & Ann Taylor Schwing, The Regulation of Money Managers, § 3.06 (2001 & Supp. 2015).
4. *Id.*
5. *Id.*

by the adviser that gives rise to opportunity for abuse and consequently to fiduciary duties. . . ."[1]

How will these definitions relate to brokers? If they speak, orally or in writing, or through other communication means, and if they suggest, note, or render clients to notice specific securities, they are advisers. Thus, brokers who list thousands of mutual fund shares for clients "free" and receive benefits from those managed funds that were placed at the top would have been within the definition of an adviser.[2]

An agreement that requires clients to sign should be held ineffective if the document allows the broker to change the terms of the agreement and the customer consents in advance to these changes, especially if the customer is required to follow and be aware of the changes. It is an incredible document that presumably no one in his right mind would sign, and yet it seems that customers sign it. We doubt whether educating the customers not to sign any of such "disclosure" documents would be effective. Customers either trust or mistrust!

The question remains: should fiduciary duties be imposed on brokers' advice to institutional sophisticated investors? Congress granted the Commission discretion to impose fiduciary duties on brokers who serve other than retail clients.[3] It may be crucial to impose fiduciary duties on all brokers regardless of whether their clients are what we call sophisticated, and even if they manage millions of dollars of investors' money, or the citizens' money, and even if they are themselves fiduciaries.

---

## Discussion Topics

a. Are there reasons for imposing fiduciary duties on institutional brokers, etc.? If yes, is the reason their size, or the size of the American people's securities investments?

b. Should fiduciary duties of brokers, etc., be imposed towards institutional customers or wealthy individuals or sophisticated individuals and institutions? Please note the example of the Deutsche Bank debacle. This large bank engages in hedge fund activities. Yet, it bought from

1. *Id.* The definition of an adviser covers advice on any securities, except exempt securities specified in section 202(a)(11)(E). In the opinion of the staff, it probably includes advice concerning investments in certificates of time deposits, which are exempt from registration under the Securities Act registration requirements.

2. Charles Schwab Corp. Managed Accounts, *available at* http://www.aboutschwab.com/about/ facts/managed-accounts.html (stating, for example, that "[m]ore than 14,500 funds are available in . . . [Charles Schwab's] Mutual Fund Marketplace, including more than 11,000 with no loads or transaction fees.").

3. Dodd-Frank Wall Street Reform and Consumer Protection Act, Pub. L. No. 111-203, § 913(f), 124 Stat. 1376, 1827 (2010) ("The Commission may commence a rulemaking, as necessary or appropriate in the public interest and for the protection of retail customers (and such other customers as the Commission may by rule provide), to address the legal or regulatory standards of care for brokers, dealers, investment advisers, persons associated with brokers or dealers, and persons associated with investment advisers. . . .").

Goldman Sachs, as broker, a financial asset created by Goldman Sachs — the securitization expert and originator — which asset contained "junk" for which Goldman Sachs the expert was paid, and against which Goldman Sachs the trader placed a bet that it would fail. Goldman Sachs manages "dark exchanges," yet according to its "business model" it may, and indeed must, trade on the information that it gathers from all these activities. Nonetheless, it claims not to be a fiduciary of its clients. They are, after all, sophisticated. Yet, this German bank has adopted the Goldman Sachs business model as well.

c. Should we consider culture in this decision?[1] Should we consider technology?[2] Should we consider anything else? How would our conclusions be implemented?

d. Who should write the rules, and enforce them? How should the rules be enforced? The Commission, FINRA? State legislatures and courts? A combination of the above?

e. Congress empowered the SEC to unify the rules regulating brokers, etc. and advisers. Is that feasible? Is it desirable?

f. How do you evaluate the business model of large investment banks and banks? Assume that this model is efficient and highly profitable for the institutions. Should it be nonetheless restricted?

g. What role, if any should culture play in this issue? If so, how should it be enforced?

h. Why should investors be relieved of the burden of studying and becoming more knowledgeable about financial instruments and their investments and savings?

i. If a person meets the definition of adviser, except that, viewed in isolation with respect to a particular advice, the definition is not satisfied because the persons did not receive compensation, should such person fall outside of the SEC's regulation? What if a person engaged in an investment advisory business has been convicted of securities fraud, but there is no evidence that he received compensation for his advice, e.g., the fraud resulted in no profits?

j. Similar to the question above, if a person or an entity receives advice from an adviser, but the adviser receives no compensation for providing such advice, should the adviser treat such person as a client?

---

1. Cass R. Sunstein, *Group Judgments: Deliberation, Statistical Means, and Information Markets,* 80 N.Y.U. L. Rev. 962, 1023 (2005) ("[T]he great advantage of the price signal is that it aggregates both the information and the tastes of numerous people, producing judgments that incorporate more material than could possibly be assembled by any central planner, even one who insists on deliberation with and among experts . . . their aggregate judgments are likely to be right. . . .").
2. Tom Lauricella & Jenny Strasburg, *SEC Probes Cancelled Trades: Regulators Looking Into Role "Quote Stuffing" May Have Played in Flash Crash,* Wall St. J., Sept. 2, 2010, at A1 (defining "quote stuffing" as "trading in which unusually large numbers of orders to buy or sell stocks are placed in a fraction of a second, only to be canceled almost immediately").

## D. The Relationship of Federal and State Law

### 1. Dividing the Burden of Enforcement

Before the 1996 Investment Advisers Supervision Coordination Act, Section 222 of the Advisers Act preserved the "jurisdiction of the securities commissioner (or any agency or officer performing like functions) of any State over any security or any person insofar as it does not conflict with the provisions of [the Act] or the rules and regulations thereunder." The 1996 Act introduced new section 203A to the Advisers Act dividing regulatory responsibilities for investment advisers between the States and the SEC.[1]

This scheme divides advisers into those (1) who manage $100 million or more in client assets or (2) who advise mutual funds or business development companies or (3) who manage $25 million or more in client assets and whose state does not register and examine investment advisers or (4) whose state has not enacted a statute regulating investment advisers. These four groups must register with the SEC and be subject to its regulation. In practice, New York is the only state that regulates investment advisers, but does not examine them; thus, investment advisers with their principal office and place of business in New York must generally register with the SEC at the $25 million assets under management threshold. Additionally, in practice, Wyoming is the only state that has not enacted a statute regulating investment advisers; thus, investment advisers with their principal office and place of business in Wyoming must generally register with the SEC regardless of their assets under management. The rest of the advisers not falling within category (1) or category (2), above, may not be registered with the SEC and are subject to state regulation, except that mid-sized advisers (between $25-100 million in assets under management) may elect to register with the SEC if they would otherwise be required to register in 15 states. The SEC is authorized to determine that certain state-covered investment advisers should be permitted to register with the SEC, if denying SEC registration would be "unfair, a burden on interstate commerce, or otherwise inconsistent with the purposes of this section."[2]

Because advisers did not organize a SRO, Congress has resolved the burden on the SEC by dividing the regulation of advisers between the SEC and the states. Under the new Section 203A(b), states may not require registration, licensing or qualification of an SEC regulated adviser. However, states continue to have the authority to investigate and bring enforcement actions with respect to fraudulent or deceitful actions committed by an SEC registered adviser or its associated persons. States have the authority to require the licensing, registration, or qualification of an "investment adviser representative" of an SEC-registered adviser who has a "place of business" in the state. The SEC has authority to pursue fraud with respect to state registered advisers.

---

1. Senate Report of the Committee on Banking, Housing and Urban Affairs, to accompany S. 1815, S. Rep. No. 293, 104th Cong. 20 (Jun. 26, 1996).
2. *Id.* at 21.

## 2. Exemptions — Venture Capital Funds, Private Funds, Foreign Private Advisers

The Dodd-Frank Act exempts from the registration requirement (i) an investment adviser that acts as adviser solely to venture capital funds[1] and (ii) an adviser solely to private funds, which adviser has less than $150 million of assets under management in the United States,[2] in addition to a limited exemption for foreign private advisers.[3] However, the SEC may require venture capital fund and mid-size private fund advisers to maintain records and provide reports as determined by the SEC.[4]

## 3. Fiduciary Duties of Advisers Under State and Federal Law

### a. Section 206 of the Advisers Act: The Anti-Fraud Provision

Section 206 of the Advisers Act is an anti-fraud provision applicable to advisers, whether registered or unregistered. In the case that follows, the Supreme Court noted that the standard applicable to the anti-fraud provision is a fiduciary standard. This fiduciary standard will guide an adviser throughout its course of conduct. In addition, the SEC has established a series of rules pursuant to Section 206, which provide a specific framework applying to adviser advertising; custody of client funds; and payment for client solicitation, among other topics (such as proxy voting, "pay-to-play" and disclosure obligations relative to investors in private funds). The following is a summary of the decision in *SEC v. Capital Gains Research Bureau, Inc.*[5]

In the *Capital Gains* case, the Supreme Court addressed the question of whether "scalping" without disclosure to clients was a "fraud or deceit" on clients under section 206. Scalping is the purchase of a security by an adviser for its own account shortly before the adviser recommends the security to clients, and then selling the security after its market price rises (at least in part because of the purchase of the securities by advisees as a result of the adviser's advice). The lower court denied the SEC an injunction requiring the adviser to disclose its trade, noting that there was no evidence of misstatements or poor advice, nor that the adviser recommended the securities for the purpose of artificially increasing the market price.

The Supreme Court reversed. It reviewed the history of the Advisers Act and noted congressional concern that "advice to a client might in some way be tinged with [an adviser's] pecuniary interest [whether consciously or] subconsciously motivated," specifically noting concern about advisers trading for their own account in securities in which their clients invested. The Court noted the adoption of the common law of fraud to a fiduciary relationship, in which a fiduciary has a duty of "utmost good faith, and

1. 15 U.S.C. § 80b-3(*l*); 17 C.F.R. § 275.203(*l*)-1 (2015) (implementing exemption by defining "venture capital fund").
2. 15 U.S.C. § 80b-3(m)(1); 17 C.F.R. § 275.203(m)-1 (2015) (implementing exemption).
3. 15 U.S.C. § 80b-3(b)(3); 17 C.F.R. § 275.202(a)(30)-1 (2015) (implementing exemption).
4. 15 U.S.C. § 80b-3(*l*); 15 U.S.C. § 80b-3(m)(2).
5. *Securities and Exchange Commission v. Capital Gains Research Bureau, Inc.*, 375 U.S. 180 (1963).

full and fair disclosure of all material facts" and an obligation "to employ reasonable care to avoid misleading" its clients.

Therefore, the Court found a duty by the adviser to disclose its own trading and the possibility of a conflict. The Court noted that an adviser may have two motivations to recommend a security: its potential for long-run price increase (benefiting the client) and its potential for short-run price increase (benefiting the adviser), and stated that disclosure is necessary for the client to properly evaluate these motivations.

### b. Fiduciary Law Principles: Section 36(b) Relating to Sales of Investment Companies' Shares — The "Give Ups"

In *Moses v. Burgin,*[1] a fund shareholder brought an action against the fund, its adviser, and certain fund directors, claiming breaches of fiduciary duty under section 36 of the Investment Company Act and the common law.

During the relevant period, the New York Stock Exchange required all brokers to charge clients a fixed commission percentage for executing clients' transactions. Brokers competing for business for fund portfolio transactions were offering to "give up" some of their commissions to brokers who were designated by the adviser. Those who received the "give-ups" were usually brokers who sold fund shares.

The adviser benefited from the give-ups to the selling brokers that increased the fund's assets. The adviser's fees depended on the size of the fund portfolio. Therefore, the court concluded that because the adviser benefited from the give-ups and did not disclose the possibility to the fund's unaffiliated directors, the adviser was liable under section 36. One of the defendant's arguments was that the fund was not allowed to receive rebates of the commissions charged for portfolio transactions because, at that time, the New York Stock Exchange imposed fixed commissions on the transactions and did not allow rebates. Therefore, the fund had to pay the full commission, notwithstanding any benefit to the defendant adviser. Therefore, the defendant argued, the rebate could be paid to the other (transaction performing) brokers for the benefit of the adviser.

---

### Discussion Topics

a. What harm, if any, was alleged by the SEC in the *Capital Gains* case? What did the SEC gain in bringing the case? Is the answer that the SEC simply wanted to force disclosure of the practice? In this connection, consider the remarks of Justice Harlan in his dissent: "[There is no dishonest dealing] revealed in the present case. It is apparent that the Court is able to achieve the result reached today only by construing these provisions of the Investment Advisers Act as it might a pure conflict of interest statute . . . something which this particular legislation does not purport to be."

1. *Moses v. Burgin,* 445 F.2d 369 (1st Cir.), *cert. denied,* 404 U.S. 994 (1971).

b. If the SEC's concern in *Capital Gains* was personal trading by the adviser or influence on the board of directors, why didn't it seek to ban or impose substantive restrictions on this activity?

c. Compare *Capital Gains* trading to insider trading. Would an investment adviser avoid potential conflict even if it has disclosed its trading adequately?

d. Suppose a publisher asserting protection under *Lowe* receives substantial payments from the companies about which it writes, as well as payments from the subscribers. What is the status of the publisher? Does disclosure about the payments by the publisher affect your determination about its status?

e. In this situation, should there be a duty on the adviser to recoup the rebate and then transfer it to the fund? The defendants may argue that such an arrangement violates the rules of the Exchange. How, if at all, can this argument be answered?

---

## E. Registration and Disclosure Requirements

### 1. Adviser Registration: Form ADV

An adviser applying for SEC registration must complete Form ADV.[1] Form ADV has four parts. Part 1A is used by the SEC "to process registrations and manage its regulatory and examination programs."[2] Part 1B is required for state-registered advisers.[3] Parts 2A and 2B set out the requirements for the required brochure for clients and the brochure supplement if required.[4]

### 2. The Information Items[5]

Part 1A disclosures include: (1) identifying information about the adviser, (2) information to determine eligibility for SEC registration, (3) form of organization, (4) successions, (5) information about the advisory business (including employees, clients, compensation arrangements, regulatory assets under management, and advisory activities), (6) other business activities, (7) financial industry affiliations, and whether the adviser is

1. 17 C.F.R. § 275.203-1(a) (2015); Form ADV, *available at* http://www.sec.gov/about/forms/formadv.pdf (links to parts of form). The Form must be updated, at least annually or more frequently if required by the Instructions. 17 C.F.R. § 275.204-1(a) (2015). The adviser may not represent or imply that it is "sponsored, recommended, or approved" by the United States or the SEC. 15 U.S.C. § 80b-3.

2. U.S. Sec. & Exch. Comm'n, Form ADV, *available at* http://www.sec.gov/answers/formadv.htm.

3. Form ADV, Part 1B, *available at* http://www.nasaa.org/wp-content/uploads/2012/10/Form-ADV-Part-1B.pdf.

4. 17 C.F.R. § 275.204-3(a) (2015) (generally requiring delivery of brochure/supplement(s) with information required by Part 2); 17 C.F.R. § 275.204-3(b) (2015) (delivery requirements, including requiring delivery before or at time of advisory contract and annual updates if there are material changes). An adviser that offers substantially different services may prepare separate brochures for different clients. Form ADV, Part 2A, Instruction 10, at 2, *available at* http://www.sec.gov/about/forms/formadv-part2.pdf.

5. This material is derived from Clifford E. Kirsch, *Investment Adviser Regulation: A Step-By-Step Guide to Compliance and the Law* § 4 (PLI 2010) (Lexis).

adviser to a private fund, (8) participation or interest in client transactions (including investment or brokerage discretion), (9) custody, (10) disciplinary information, (11) information to determine "small business" status, and (12) owners and executive officers.[1]

Part 2 sets out the minimum required disclosure for the brochure and supplement(s).[2] The disclosures must be in narrative format and plain English.[3] Additional disclosure may be required to meet the adviser's disclosure obligations as a fiduciary.[4]

Part 2A disclosures include: (1) a cover page with identifying information, (2) material changes from the last update, (3) a table of contents, (4) a description of the advisory business, (5) fees and compensation; (6) performance-based fees, and possible conflicts from side-by-side management, (7) types of clients, (8) methods of analysis, investment strategies, and risk of loss, (9) legal or disciplinary events material to a client's evaluation of the advisory business or the integrity of its management, (10) other financial industry activities and affiliations, (11) the adviser's code of ethics, participation or interest in client transactions, and personal trading, (12) brokerage practices, (13) disclosures regarding any periodic review of client accounts, (14) client referrals and other compensation, (15) custody, (16) investment discretion, (17) policies regarding voting of client securities, (18) financial information, and (19) requirements for state-registered advisers.[5] Item 4 of Part 2A disclosures include a description of the advisory firm, the types of services offered, whether/how it tailors its services to the individual needs of clients, disclosures about wrap fee programs, and the amount of client assets manages on a discretionary and a non-discretionary basis.[6]

Item 5 requires disclosures regarding fees and commissions, including possible conflicts of interests from a supervised person accepting compensation from the sale of securities.[7] Item 6 requires disclosure of performance-based fees and conflicts of interest from side-by-side management of performance-based fee accounts and other accounts.[8]

---

1. Form ADV, Part 1A, *available at* http://www.sec.gov/about/forms/formadv-part1a.pdf.
2. Form ADV, Part 2, General Instructions, at 1, *available at* http://www.sec.gov/about/forms/formadv-part2.pdf.
3. *Id.*, General Instructions 1-2, at 1.
4. *Id.*, General Instruction 3, at 1-2 (noting that adviser must make full disclosure of all material facts relating to advisory relationship and all material conflicts of interest that could affect relationship).
5. Form ADV, Part 2A, *available at* http://www.sec.gov/about/forms/formadv-part2.pdf. An adviser that sponsors a wrap fee program must deliver a special brochure to wrap fee clients. *Id.*, Part 2A, app. A. An adviser may, but is not required to, include a summary of the brochure. Form ADV, Part 2A, Instruction 8, at 2, *available at* http://www.sec.gov/about/forms/formadv-part2.pdf. Disclosure is required for a new firm and for a "separately identifiable department or division of a bank." *Id.*, Instructions 14-15, at 3.
6. *Id.*, Item 4, at 1-2.
7. *Id.*, Item 5, at 2-3.
8. *Id.*, Item 6, at 3.

Item 7 requires a description of the types of clients the adviser generally advises (e.g., individuals, trusts, investment companies, pension plans) and any requirements for opening/maintaining an account (e.g., minimum account size).[1]

Item 8 requires disclosure of the adviser's methods of analysis and investment strategies, including the risks or costs involved, including risks involving a particular type of security.[2]

Item 18 requires certain disclosures regarding financial information. It generally requires a balance sheet for the most recent fiscal year, if the adviser requires or solicits prepayment of more than $1,200 in fees per client, six months or more in advance.[3] It also generally requires disclosure of "any financial condition that is reasonably likely to impair your ability to meet contractual commitments to clients," if the adviser has discretionary authority or custody of client funds or securities, or requires or solicits prepayment of more than $1,200 in fees per client, six months or more in advance.[4] "[A] determination about what constitutes financial condition reasonably likely to impair an adviser's ability to meet contractual commitments is inherently factual in nature but will generally include insolvency or bankruptcy."[5]Part 2B sets out the disclosures for the brochure supplement, which must generally be provided with respect to any supervised person of the adviser who provides advice to the client.[6] Part 2B disclosures include: (1) a cover page, (2) the supervised person's educational background and business experience, (3) legal or disciplinary events material to a client's evaluation of the supervised person, (4) the supervised person's other business activities, (5) additional compensation from someone not a client to the supervised person for advisory services, (6) supervision of the supervised person, and (7) requirements for state-registered advisers.[7]

---

## Discussion Topics

a. How is Form ADV similar to a prospectus? How is it different from a prospectus?

b. What effect does this disclosure have? On whom? Do you believe that clients read it? If they do not, who does? Is this disclosure costly? To whom?

---

1. *Id.*, Item 7, at 3.
2. *Id.*, Item 8, at 3.
3. *Id.*, Item 18.A, at 9.
4. *Id.*, Item 18.B, at 9. For a state-registered adviser, the threshold for the balance sheet and financial information requirements is $500. *Id.*, Item 18.B, Note, at 9.
5. Amendments to Form ADV, Investment Advisers Act Rel. No. 3060 (Jul. 28, 2010), 75 Fed. Reg. 49,234, 49,245 n.177 (Aug. 12, 2010). Item 18 also requires disclosure regarding any bankruptcy petition during the past ten years. Form ADV, Part 2A, Item 18.C., at 9, *available at* http://www.sec.gov/about/forms/formadv-part2.pdf.
6. 17 C.F.R. § 275.204-3(b)(3) (2015).
7. Form ADV, Part 2B, *available at* http://www.sec.gov/about/forms/formadv-part2.pdf.

## F. Regulation of Advisers

### 1. Referrals and Advertising[1]

### a. Referrals and Paid Solicitors

Many advisers rely on referrals from brokers, insurance agents, and financial planners as sources of clients. Parties providing referrals, commonly known as "solicitors," are typically paid a cash fee by the adviser. However, compensation may take the form of non-cash arrangements or reciprocal referrals by the adviser to referring brokers.

Referrals raise two issues. First, if the adviser pays the solicitors, what are the safeguards against conflicts of interest? Second, does the solicitor have to register as an investment adviser under the Investment Advisers Act and state law as a result of its solicitation activities?

The SEC had considered prohibiting advisers from making cash payments to solicitors on the ground that such arrangements created unacceptable conflicts of interest by the solicitor. Yet, rather than a full prohibition, Rule 206(4)-3 addresses only cash payments. However, since similar conflicts may arise in non-cash payment situations, the rule to apply the rule's guidelines should apply to such circumstances as well.

Rule 206(4)-3 applies to registered investment advisers, and notes that cash referral fees may be paid only to solicitors who are not subject to certain "bad actor" disqualifications. Further, cash payment must be made pursuant to a written agreement between the solicitor and the investment adviser. The written agreement should be kept as part of the adviser's records according to the Rule 204 recordkeeping, which is subjected to examination by the SEC.

An adviser may pay a cash referral fee in three situations, each of which is dealt differently under the law: (1) arrangements with parties unaffiliated with the adviser ("third party arrangements"); (2) arrangements with affiliates of the adviser; and (3) when a party solicits clients for impersonal advisory services, such as general written materials. Not surprisingly, lawyers often deal with third party and affiliated solicitation arrangements; rarely with impersonal advisory services.

---

**Discussion Topics**

a. What problems can arise when an adviser pays cash to a broker who refers his clients to the adviser? Does it matter that the broker receives brokerage business rather than cash payments?

b. Lawyers, dentists, and other professionals refer to each other clients/ patients who need service in the area of their colleagues' expertise. Is that wrong? If not, what is the difference between the brokers and advisers who engage in the same practice?

---

1. *See* Clifford E. Kirsch, Investment Adviser Regulation, A Step-by-Step Guide to Compliance and the Law at 4-1 to 4-3 (1998) (edited).

## Problem

Read Rule 206(4)-3 under the Advisers Act. Note how paragraph (a)(2)(ii) of the rule defines affiliated solicitor arrangements: "a solicitor . . . Who is (A) a partner, officer, director or employee of such investment adviser or (B) a partner, officer, director or employee of a person which controls, is controlled by, or is under common control with such investment adviser." According to the rule, an affiliated solicitor needs to disclose only his, her or its status as a partner, officer, director or employee of the investment adviser or control affiliate of the investment adviser, and any affiliation between the investment adviser and such control affiliate, at the time of the solicitation or referral. The solicitor need not follow the elaborate disclosures the rule requires of third party (i.e., non-affiliated) solicitors.

Assume you are an associate at a law firm. You have completed research at the request of your supervising partner that indicates the following. First, the SEC staff generally takes the position that a 25% or greater equity stake in a company gives rise to control under the Advisers Act. Second, the affiliated solicitor definition was originally proposed to only cover employees of an adviser, and the SEC stated the following rationale with respect to expanding the scope of the affiliated solicitor provision in the final enacted rule: "there is little basis for assuming that potential clients will be any less aware of the inherent bias when an employee recommends an adviser who is a person associated with his employer than when he recommends the advisory services of his own employer . . . as long as a client is aware that the recommended adviser is the solicitor's employer or a close affiliate of the solicitor's employer, there appears to be little need to require the imposition of additional disclosure and recordkeeping requirements."

Prepare a memorandum for your supervising partner explaining the differences between what the rule requires of affiliated solicitors versus third party solicitors.

Your supervising partner tells you that the firm has a client who is an investment adviser. The adviser is owned 27% by a broker-dealer firm. The employees of the broker-dealer firm act as solicitors for the adviser. Your supervising partner explains that there is broad public and media awareness of the close business and economic relationship between your client and the broker-dealer firm. Your supervising partner also explains, however, that the SEC has issued an order declaring that the broker-dealer firm does not control your client, the investment adviser. Your client wishes to keep treating the broker-dealer's employees as affiliated solicitors notwithstanding this SEC order of non-control. Based on your research described above, construct an argument for use in an exemptive request to be submitted to the SEC that would seek to permit your client to continue relying on the affiliated solicitor provision. Outline this argument in a memorandum to your supervising partner.

---

### b. Advertising and Antifraud Provisions

Rule 206(4)-1 defines "fraudulent, deceptive, or manipulative" advertising.

"Advertisement" is defined to include: "any notice, circular, letter or other written communication addressed to more than one person, or any notice or other announcement in any publication or by radio or television, which offers: (1) any analyses, reports or publication concerning securities, or which is to be used in making any determinations as to when to buy or sell any security or which security to buy or sell, or (2) any graph, chart, formula or other device to be used in making any determination as to when to buy or sell any security, or which security to buy or sell, or (3) any other investment advisory service with regard to securities. . . ."

Advertising is a fraudulent, deceptive or manipulative act if it:

(1) refers directly or indirectly, to any testimonial concerning the adviser or advice,

(2) refers to past specific recommendations of such adviser which would have been profitable, unless the ad sets out or offers to furnish a list of all recommendations,

(3) represents that any device (e.g. graph, chart, formula or other device) offered can, in and of itself, be used to determine which securities to buy or sell, or represents that such device will assist in such decision, without prominently disclosing the limits of the device,

(4) contains any statement to the effect than any report, analysis or other service will be furnished for free, unless such item is furnished entirely free and without condition or obligation of any sort, or

(5) contains any untrue statement of a material fact, or which is otherwise false or misleading.

#### Testimonials

Rule 206(4)-1(a)(1) provides that an adviser's advertisement may not contain a testimonial, that is, generally any statement of a customer's experience with, or endorsement of, an adviser.[1] For example, a written statement from a satisfied advisory client is a testimonial. Additionally, the explosion of social media use raises tricky issues regarding this prohibition, which the SEC staff has sought to address in industry guidance.[2]

#### Past Specific Recommendations

Rule 206(4)-1(a)(2) makes unlawful an advertisement which refers to successful securities recommendations an adviser has made in the past without referring to the unsuccessful recommendations the adviser has made during the same period. The rule does permit an advertisement to include or offer to furnish a list of all recommendations made by the adviser within the immediately preceding period of at least one year, accompanied by the following disclosures:

---

1. *See, e.g.,* Cambiar Investors, Inc., SEC No-Action Letter (Aug. 28, 1997).
2. Guidance on the Testimonial Rule and Social Media, IM Guidance Update No. 2014-04 (Mar. 2014).

(1) the name of each such security recommended;
(2) the date and nature of each recommendation;
(3) the market price of the security recommended at the time;
(4) the price at which the recommendation was to be acted upon;
(5) the market price of each such security as of the most recent practicable date; and
(6) a legend stating that "it should not be assumed that recommendations made in the future will be profitable or will equal the performance of the securities in this list."[1]

**Automatic Selection Devices**

An advertisement may not include a representation that a "graph, chart, formula or other device" may be used in making securities investment decisions securities, unless the limitations and difficulties with respect to the uses of such devices are promptly displayed.

An advertisement may not include any statement to the effect that any report, analysis, or other service will be furnished free or without charge unless this is in fact the case (i.e., there are no conditions or obligations attached).

**Catch-all Category**

Rule 206(4)-1(a)(5), the catch-all provision, prohibits the use of any advertisement which "contains any untrue statement of a material fact, or which is otherwise false or misleading."

The SEC staff has provided guidance with respect to this category by suggesting that an adviser take into account the following factors in evaluating advertisements: "(1) the form and content of an advertisement, (2) the implications or inferences arising out of the advertisement in its total context, and (3) the sophistication of the prospective client."[2]

*In the Matter of Patricia Owen-Michel*[3] is an example of the SEC's view on the definition of "advertising." Patricia Owen-Michel was President and Chief Executive Officer of Securities Research & Management, Inc. ("SRM"), a registered investment adviser from June 1978 until it voluntarily withdrew its registration in May 1995.

SRM used a computer model to select stocks. It provided prospective clients with a promotional package including (i) a newspaper article with a client's quotes; (ii) newspaper articles quoting SRM principals' statements about performance; and (iii) charts and graphs with hypothetical performance applied retroactively.

SRM offered the STAR program, an asset allocation program, which would permit SRM to switch assets invested in some types of funds (e.g., United States equities and precious metals) to other types of funds (e.g.,

1. Clifford E. Kirsch, Investment Adviser Regulation, A Step-by-Step Guide to Compliance and the Law at 4-1 to 4-3 (1998).
2. *See, e.g.,* Investment Company Institute, SEC No-Action Letter (Sept. 23, 1988).
3. Investment Advisers Act Rel. No. 1584; Administrative Proceeding File No. 3-9107 (Sept. 27, 1996).

bonds and international equities). Clients could participate in one of three portfolios ("Conservative," "Moderate," "Aggressive").

The promotional package included "Portfolio Charts" for each portfolio, with performance results from a "pro-forma study of asset allocation" from a ten-year prior period, with purported quarterly and annual returns including average annual net returns.

> The Portfolio Charts failed to disclose, among other things:
>
> (a) that SRM only began offering its STAR program after the performance period covered by the Portfolio Charts, i.e., the advertised performance results do not represent the results of actual trading using client assets, but were achieved by means of the retroactive application of a model designed with the benefit of hindsight;[1*]
>
> (b) all material economic and market factors that might have had an impact on SRM's decision-making when using the STAR model to actually manage clients' money;
>
> (c) whether the advertised performance reflects the deduction of advisory fees, brokerage or other commissions, mutual fund exchange fees, and any other expenses that a client would have paid; and
>
> (d) the potential for loss as well as for profit. . . .

The SEC found as follows:

> From at least July 1994 to May 1995, Respondent willfully aided and abetted and caused violations of Section 206(4) of the Advisers Act and Rule 206(4)-1(a)(1) promulgated thereunder, in that she, as President and Chief Executive Officer of SRM, aided and abetted and caused SRM, by use of the mails or any means or instrumentality of interstate commerce, directly or indirectly, to engage in any act, practice, or course of business which was fraudulent, deceptive, or manipulative by, directly or indirectly, publishing, circulating or distributing advertisements which referred, directly or indirectly, to any testimonial of any kind concerning SRM or concerning any advice, analysis, report or other service rendered by SRM. . . .
>
> From at least July 1994 to May 1995, Respondent willfully aided and abetted and caused violations of Section 206(4) of the Advisers Act and Rule 206(4)-1(a)(5) promulgated thereunder, in that she, as President and Chief Executive Officer of SRM, aided and abetted and caused SRM, by use of the mails or any means or instrumentality of interstate commerce, directly or indirectly to engage in any act, practice, or course of business which was fraudulent, deceptive, or

1*. Each of the Portfolio Charts stated, in small type, that "because markets are influenced by a variety of changing conditions, future performance based upon prior results, or proforma analysis, cannot be guaranteed." This disclosure is insufficient to dispel the misleading suggestion of the advertisement that the advertised performance results represented the results of actual trading. *Cf.* Jesse Rosenblum, Investment Advisers Act Rel. No. 913 (May 17, 1984) (investment adviser's advertisement containing materially misleading statements "not cured by the disclaimers buried in the [smaller print] text" of the advertisement).

manipulative by, directly or indirectly, publishing, circulating or distributing any advertisement which contained any untrue statement of a material fact, or which was otherwise false and misleading. . . .

---

**Discussion Topics**

a. What precisely were the offending passages in SRM's advertising?

b. How was section 206(4) interpreted to impose liability on the President of SRM?

c. Compare and contrast the restrictions on adviser advertising with that of lawyer advertising.

---

### 2. Advisers' Fees

Investment adviser compensation structures vary. To some extent they reflect the adviser's services. For example, financial planners can be compensated (i) by a fixed fee, (ii) by commissions from the trading which they recommend, and which they performed as brokers or (iii) by a combination of the two, or, if they manage the clients' assets (iv) by a percentage of the managed client assets.

The Advisers Act does not regulate the structure of advisory fees, with one significant exception. Section 205(a) prohibits the charge of performance fees. Also, certain requirements apply to the disclosure of fees.

Performance fees can be viewed as unfair to clients when advisers' fees are linked to the results of their recommendations. In such cases, the advisers gain when the clients gain, but do not lose proportionally when the clients lose. In addition, this fee structure gives advisers incentives to invest or recommend investments in more risky assets. In 1940, section 205 of the Advisers Act prohibited any fees calculated "on the bases of a share of capital gains upon or capital appreciation of the funds or any portion of the funds of the client." At that time, advisers to investment companies were exempt from the Advisers Act. Therefore, they could continue to charge performance fees.

In 1970, Congress applied the Advisers Act to advisers of investment companies. As to performance fees, the industry and the SEC reached a compromise. Clients other than investment companies and those with contracts relating to assets of less than $1 million cannot be charged performance fees. Registered investment companies and clients with contracts relating to assets of more than $1 million may be charged performance fees on condition that these fees increase or decrease according to clients' portfolio performance measured against "the investment record of an appropriate index of securities prices or such other measure of investment performance" as the SEC may specify. This is referred to as a "fulcrum fee."

Additionally, Rule 205-3 allows advisers to charge performance fees provided that the client has $1,000,000 under management or is a client whom the adviser has reasonable grounds to believe has a net worth of at least $2 million dollars, or is a "qualified purchaser" under the Investment Company Act or one of certain persons affiliated with the adviser. In the case of a private investment company, registered investment company, or business development company, each equity owner is generally considered a client for purposes of this rule.[1]

---

**Discussion Topics**

a. Do you agree that performance fees are potentially unfair or dangerous to advisory clients — especially those of more modest means? Compare performance fees to contingent fees lawyers charge in litigation. Compare performance fees to executive compensation by stock options and deferred vesting of company shares.

b. May an adviser promise to repay compensation in the event of "unsatisfactory" recommendations to the client? Can he promise "satisfaction or your money back"? Can he receive "gratuities" related to capital gains?

---

### 3. Advisers' Relationships with Brokers: Regulation of "Soft Dollars" and Section 28(e) of the Securities Exchange Act of 1934

#### a. The Advisers' Interests and Incentives

Advisers to investment companies and other pooled assets for management are usually interested in selling shares in the managed asset pools. These sales involve organizations and individuals whose main function is the sale of securities — that is, broker-dealers. Advisers who are paid a percentage of the assets under management can increase these assets by performance as well as by sales. Yet, causing a rise in assets under management by performance can be far more limited and uncertain than increasing assets under management by sales. Therefore, advisers are very interested in selling the securities issued by the pool that they manage. In fact, even if the value of the securities falls, the overall value of the pool's securities may rise due to aggressive sales, thus increasing the advisory fees. In addition, advisers to open-end funds, namely funds that offer redeemable securities, are doubly interested in sales of the funds' securities to avoid "net redemptions." That is, to avoid a situation in which the amount of redemption exceeds the amount of sales. In such a case, the funds may have to sell portfolio securities to meet redemption requirements. These sales may not be at the appropriate time or appropriate amount, and advisers seek to avoid such situations. The Investment Company Act of 1940 helps avoid net redemptions. For example, section 18(e) of the Act, that otherwise prohibits an open-end investment company from issuing more than one class of securities, permits such a company to borrow only short-term from a bank under certain conditions, and sections 15(b) and 22(d) recognize the importance of principal underwriters to open-end investment companies.

1. 17 C.F.R. § 275.205-3 (2015).

### b. The Interests of Broker-Dealers

Broker-dealers engage in trading small and large amounts of securities. Trading in small, as compared to large, amounts of securities requires different skills, costs, and contacts. It also brings to brokers different revenues. Large brokerage houses are interested in trading large numbers of securities, as underwriters in the primary markets, or brokers in the secondary markets. Such transactions require expertise and contacts (e.g., avoiding depressing market prices while offering a large number of securities at the same time). Brokerage firms that trade for small clients may invest the brokers' efforts differently to contact many potential buyers and entice them to trade.

The interests of advisers and the two types of brokers have led to different incentives. While large brokerage firms are interested in executing trades in portfolio transactions of institutional investors, the institutional investors and investment advisers to such institutional investors (including investment companies) are interested in selling the securities in the managed pools as much as; if not more than; the trading of portfolio securities.

Not surprisingly, these different incentives were demonstrated in 1975 when Congress eliminated the rule of the New York Stock Exchange that required brokers to charge their customers fixed commissions. Thereafter, an adviser may, or indeed should, negotiate with broker-dealers, seeking lower commissions for its clients, both individuals and investment companies, and receiving the best execution of the trades.

Yet, brokers may be reluctant to lower their regular commission to a particular client for many reasons, for example, to avoid pressure by other clients to provide the same discount. In fact, broker-dealers have reestablished to some extent a fixed commission for institutional traders. Rebates are negotiated and sometimes made in kind (by "soft" dollars) rather than in cash. So long as the full benefit of the rebate inures to the adviser's client, the adviser meets its fiduciary obligations to its client. However, if the broker pays the rebate by covering obligations or costs that should be borne by the adviser or by someone other than the client, or if the "in-kind" rebate benefits the adviser, then the arrangement constitutes a potential violation of the adviser's fiduciary duties. The rebate becomes a "kick-back" to the adviser. The issue arose because historically large brokerage houses used to send to valuable clients (including advisers to investment companies) research reports concerning companies in which the clients were interested. When the 1975 law was changed from fixed commission rates that did not involve negotiations, to require advisers to negotiate the commission rates, the status of these research reports surfaced. May the large brokerage firms continue to send such reports to advisers without creating a problem for both parties? Barring a statutory provision, an adviser's acceptance of soft dollars could constitute a breach of the adviser's fiduciary duty. In addition, because some transactions require more than the minimal commissions, firms were concerned that law would require them to charge the same fee for all transactions.

To meet these concerns, Section 28(e) of the Securities Exchange Act of 1934 provided advisers with a safe harbor when they pay on behalf of their clients more than the lowest available brokerage commission and when they receive valuable research from the brokers. When the limits of this safe harbor have been called into question, the SEC has provided guidance as to the permissible types of rebates under Section 28(e).

One issue which section 28(e) poses is the interpretation of the word "research." What and how much does research cover? Another issue relates to advisers' conflict of interest. It is one thing to pay more for executing a trade that requires more effort and expertise than other trades. Yet it is another to allow high payment for trades as a result of the adviser's conflict of interest. If an adviser received benefits as "research," how does one prevent the adviser from overlooking poor execution of the brokers who pay most by "research"?

Throughout the years "research" has developed into a large "soft dollars market." Note that payment by soft dollars is not efficient. Similar to barter, it involves higher costs than payment in currency. Such payment is also far more difficult to evaluate in terms of currency. But standards developed with time to value about $2 of brokerage commissions for each soft dollar of benefits and services that constitutes "research."

Hence, brokers and many advisers keep accounts of the benefits given by the brokers to the advisers. In large organizations, soft dollars are not usually negotiated by the traders. The organizations have established guidelines on how and when soft dollar services will be rendered for expected future commission business.[1]

Soft dollars have been criticized for a number of reasons. First, as mentioned, they are inefficient. However, D. Bruce Johnsen[2] focused on "agency costs" in the language of the economists, that is, — conflicts of interest, and concluded that soft dollars are efficient, being "a vehicle that allows managers and brokers to align incentives and thereby reduce agency costs to the benefit of fund investors." Therefore, there is no need for stricter regulation in this area, let alone a prohibition of the practice.

Second, soft dollars cost investors more than had investors paid in cash.[3] Research suggests that mutual fund managers do not reduce explicit fees when research is financed by soft dollars. A large portion of commissions seem to be for services other than trade execution.[4]

The following questions have remained unanswered: Do broker-dealers change the advisers' way of doing business? If so, to what extent and in what direction? Do the advisers balance their interests with the clients' interests better than before?

---

1. Office of Compliance, Inspections and Examinations, U.S. Securities & Exchange Commission, Inspection Report on the Soft Dollar Practices of Broker-Dealers, Investment Advisers and Mutual Funds (Sept. 22, 1998), *available at* http://www.sec.gov/news/ studies/softdolr.htm.

2. D. Bruce Johnsen, *Property Rights to Investment Research: The Agency Costs of Soft Dollar Brokerage,* 11 Yale J. Reg. 75 (1994).

3. Miles Livingston & Edward S. O'Neal, *Mutual Fund Brokerage Commissions,* 19 J. Fin. Res. 273 (1996).

4. *Id.* Brokerage commissions are correlated positively with fund turnover and expense ratio. The correlation with expense ratio suggests that soft dollars are used to pay for nonexecution costs that should be paid from the management fee.

---

**Discussion Topics**

a. What other explanations are there for the soft dollar market?

b. Do you agree that soft dollars practice does not present problems?

---

### c. The Evolution of "Research" Under Section 28(e)

In 1986, the SEC issued an interpretative release regarding the scope of "research" under section 28(e).[1] The SEC describes Section 28(e) as "provid[ing] a safe harbor to money managers who use the commission dollars of the advised accounts to obtain investment research and brokerage services, provided that all of the conditions in the section are met."[2] The safe harbor protects "a person who exercises investment discretion with respect to an account," and allows that person to "hav[e] caused an account to pay more than the lowest available commission if that person determines in good faith that the amount of the commission is reasonable in relation to the value of the brokerage and research services provided."[3] Violations of Section 28(e) may violate federal securities laws and may amount to a breach of fiduciary duty.

On May 1, 1975, fixed commission rates were abolished. As a result, money managers and brokers worried that if they paid more than the lowest commission rate for services such as research, they would be at risk of allegations that they breached their fiduciary duty, as by purchasing research the money manager would be "relieved of the obligation to produce the research himself or to purchase it with his own money."[4] Section 28(e) was added to explicitly allow money managers to purchase research services when evaluating the price of brokerage services, as Congress acknowledged that these "soft dollar" arrangements are important.

In 1976, the SEC issued an interpretive release regarding section 28(e), stating that its safe harbor provision did not cover "products and services which are readily and customarily available and offered to the general public on a commercial basis."[5] The SEC later determined that this standard was "difficult to apply and unduly restrictive in some circumstances, and that uncertainty about the standard may have impeded money managers from obtaining, for commission dollars, goods and services they believe are important to the making of investment decisions."[6] This release describes the SEC's revised standard for section 28(e).

The SEC defines "research" as whether "it provides lawful and appropriate assistance to the money manager in the performance of his investment decision-making responsibilities. . . . What constitutes lawful and

---

1. Brokerage and Research Services, Exchange Act Rel. No. 23170 (Apr. 23,1986).
2. *Id.*
3. *Id.*
4. *Id.*
5. *Id.*
6. *Id.*

appropriate assistance in any particular case will depend on the nature of the relationships between the various parties involved and is not susceptible to hard and fast rules. Of course, section 28(e) continues to require the money manager to make a good faith determination that the value of research and brokerage services is reasonable in relation to the amount of commissions paid. The legislative history of section 28(e) makes clear that the burden of proof in demonstrating this determination rests on the money manager."[1]

Research "may integrate such diverse functions as trading, execution, accounting, recordkeeping and other administrative matters, such as measuring the performance of accounts."[2] The SEC's standard requires that uses for research and for other functions be separated, stating, "The Commission recognizes that the task of properly allocating the research and non-research properties of certain goods and services provided to fiduciaries may be complex. The Commission believes the standard will be satisfied where a fiduciary can demonstrate a good faith attempt, under all the circumstances, to allocate the anticipated uses of a product."[3]

---

**Discussion Topics**

a. What problems did the abolition of fixed commissions raise and to whom?

b. What problems do soft dollar payments raise and to whom?

c. How does the standard set forth in the SEC's 1986 release change the 1976 standard? What was "loosened" in the interpretation and what principles applied to the justifications?

d. Does section 28(e) apply to investment advisers who have no influence over portfolio transactions, such as advisers who publish advisory letters? May such advisers obtain benefits from broker-dealers who execute orders in securities that these advisers recommend? Never? Under some conditions?

e. Is a seminar providing research information given in Hawaii during the winter for Boston advisers permissible under section 28(e)?

f. What is the theoretical basis for prohibiting advisers from gaining? What are the brokers' incentives to give "soft dollars" to advisers, apart from the desire to obtain brokerage business?

---

### 4. Exemptions for Private Fund Advisers, Foreign Private Advisers and Family Offices

The original section 203(b) of the Advisers Act exempted from registration advisers who had less than 15 clients and who did not publicly present themselves as advisers. The issue arose with respect to the nature of the "clients." If the clients could be entities whose veil was not pieced, advisers

1. *Id.*
2. *Id.*
3. *Id.*

could establish 14 such entities who would sell their securities to hundreds of investors in private offerings. With the introduction of Section 3(c)(7) to the Investment Company Act exempting private investment companies from the Investment Company Act, advisers designed their structures in a way to avoid registration under the Advisers Act. The issue of whether the "client" was one of the 14 entities or the shareholders of the entities was resolved by the courts in favor counting the entities as one client. Hence, hedge fund advisers were not required to be registered with the SEC. This, of course, did not exempt them from the antifraud provisions of the Advisers Act.

The Private Fund Investment Advisers Registration Act of 2010 eliminated the exemption for advisers with fewer than 15 clients under section 203(b) of the Investment Advisers Act.[1] However, the Act requires the SEC to provide an exemption for an adviser to private funds that "acts solely as an adviser to private funds" and "has assets under management in the United States of less than $150,000,000,"[2] as well as a limited exemption for foreign private advisers.[3]

A "foreign private adviser" is defined as an adviser that (A) has no United States place of business, (B) has no more than 15 United States clients and investors (in total) in private funds it advises, (C) has aggregate assets under management attributable to United States clients and investors of less than $25 million (or such higher amount set by the SEC), and neither (i) "holds itself out generally to the public in the United States as an investment adviser" nor (ii) advises an investment company or business development company.[4]

"Private fund" is defined as "an issuer that would be an investment company, as defined in section 3 of the Investment Company Act of 1940 (15 U.S.C. 80a-3), but for section 3(c)(1) or 3(c)(7) of that Act"; that is, small investment companies and investment companies for qualified purchasers.[5] The Act authorizes the SEC to adopt appropriate recordkeeping and reporting requirements for such advisers.[6] In addition, in adopting regulations for advisers to "mid-sized" private funds, the SEC must consider the funds' "size, governance, and investment strategy ... to determine whether they pose systemic risk," and must adopt registration and examination procedures for advisers to such funds appropriate to the funds' level of systemic risk.[7]

---

1. Dodd-Frank Wall Street Reform and Consumer Protection Act, Pub. L. No. 111-203 (2010), § 403(2), amending 15 U.S.C. § 80b-3(b)(3) (effective Jul. 21, 2011).
2. Pub. L. No. 111-203, § 408, *codified at* 15 U.S.C. § 80b-3(m)(1) (effective Jul. 21,2011).
3. Dodd-Frank Wall Street Reform and Consumer Protection Act, Pub. L. No. 111-203 (2010), § 403(2), *amending* 15 U.S.C. § 80b-3(b)(3) (effective Jul. 21, 2011).
4. *Id.* § 402(a), *codified at* 15 U.S.C. § 80b-2(a)(30) (effective Jul. 21, 2011).
5. *Id.* § 402(a), *codified at* 15 U.S.C. § 80b-2(a)(29) (effective Jul. 21, 2011); 15 U.S.C. § *80a*-3(c)(1), (7). These different types of private funds are discussed in Chapter 4 of this text.
6. Pub. L. No. 111-203, § 408, *codified at* 15 U.S.C. § 80b-3(m)(2) (effective Jul. 21, 2011).
7. Pub. L. No. 111-203, § 408, *codified at* 15 U.S.C. § 80b-3(n) (effective Jul. 21, 2011).

A family office is a firm set up to manage the money of a single family.[1] The Private Fund Investment Advisers Registration Act of 2010 excepts from registration any family office, as defined by the SEC.[2] The Act requires the SEC to provide for an exemption that (1) is consistent with SEC exemptive policy[3] and the grandfathering provisions of the Act; (2) "recognizes the range of organizational, management, and employment structures and arrangements employed by family offices;" and (3) does not exclude from the exemption a person not registered or required to be registered on January 1, 2010 solely because it advises (and was engaged on January 1, 2010) the following entities: (A) certain officers, directors, or employees of the office who invested with the office before January 1, 2010; (B) a company owned exclusively and controlled by the family, "or as the Commission may prescribe by rule;" and (C) certain registered advisers that advise the family office and invest in the respective transactions on the same terms as the family office.[4]

A family office that qualifies for the exemption solely under the grandfathering provisions is subject to the antifraud provisions of the Advisers Act.[5]

### 5. Principal and Agency Transactions

Section 206(3) of the Advisers Act views advisers as fiduciaries. Therefore, advisers are prohibited from acting in conflicts of interest with those of their clients. The Act lists the situations in which such conflicts exist. These fall into transactions in which advisers act as principals trading with their clients for the advisers' own accounts (principal transactions or transactions as principals); and transactions in which advisers act as brokers on behalf of clients, as well as the other party to the securities transaction (agency cross-transactions). In both cases, advisers are required to disclose their conflicts of interest to their clients and receive the clients' consent before effecting the transactions. This regulation is discussed in the following excerpt; note, however, that this excerpt comes from a 1945 SEC release and the statutory text of Section 206 of the Investment Advisers Act quoted below has since been amended to apply to all advisers, whether registered or unregistered under the Advisers Act, and the following should be understood to apply to unregistered advisers as well.[6]

> Section 206 of the Investment Advisers Act of 1940 provides:
>
> It shall be unlawful for any investment adviser registered

---

1. *See, e.g.*, Brody Mullins, *Family Trusts Lobby to Avoid New Rules*, Wall St. J., Oct. 21, 2009, at A4, LEXIS, News Library, WSJ File.
2. Dodd-Frank Wall Street Reform and Consumer Protection Act, Pub. L. No. 111-203 (2010), § 409(a), *codified at* 15 U.S.C. § 80b-2(a)(11)(G) (effective Jul. 21, 2011); 17 C.F.R. § 275.202(a)(11)(G)-1 (2015) (implementing exemption).
3. *See e.g.*, Woodcock Fin. Mgmt. Co., LLC, Investment Advisers Act Rel. Nos. 2772 (Aug. 26, 2008) (notice) and 2787 (Sept. 24, 2008) (order). (firm represented among other conditions that firm would offer services only to family clients and would not hold self out to public as investment adviser, and firm would be owned by family members).
4. Pub. L. No. 111-203, at § 409(b) (effective Jul. 21, 2011).
5. *Id.* at § 409(c) (effective Jul. 21, 2011).
6. Investment Advisers Act Rel. No. 40 (Feb. 5, 1945).

> under section 203, by use of the mails or any means or instrumentality of interstate commerce, directly or indirectly . . .
>
> (3) acting as principal for his own account, knowingly to sell any security to or purchase any security from a client, or acting as broker for a person other than such client, knowingly to effect any sale or purchase of any security for the account of such client, without disclosing to such client in writing before the completion of such transaction the capacity in which he is acting and obtaining the consent of the client to such transaction. The prohibitions of this paragraph (3) shall not apply to any transaction with a customer of a broker or dealer if such broker or dealer is not acting as an investment adviser in relation to such transaction. . . .

An investment adviser is a fiduciary. . . . It follows that an investment adviser may not effect a transaction as principal with a client unless he obtains the client's consent to the transaction after fully disclosing any adverse interest he may have, together with any other information in his possession which the client should possess in order to determine whether he should enter into the transaction. The disclosure should include, as a minimum, (a) the capacity in which the investment adviser proposes to act, (b) the cost to the adviser of any security which he proposes to sell to his client (or, if he proposes to buy a security from his client and knows or is reasonably certain of the price at which it is to be resold, a statement of that price), and (c) the best price at which the transaction could be effected by or for the client elsewhere if such price is more advantageous to the client than the actual purchase or sale price. Moreover, any disclosure of the cost to the investment adviser (or the price he expects to receive on resale) should be so phrased that its full import is obvious to the client. The disclosure should include a statement of the total amount of the cost or resale price (or the total profit) in dollars and cents; it would not suffice, in my opinion, merely to express a formula by which those amounts may be computed, or to limit the disclosure to a percentage figure or to a maximum number of points or dollars per share or bond.

---

## Discussion Topics

a. Is disclosure an effective resolution to conflicts of interest practiced by an adviser?

b. It has been shown that fiduciaries and trusted persons who disclose their conflicts feel far more freedom to act in conflict of interest than those that do not disclose their conflicts. If that is so, what is the value of the disclosure?

c. Agency cross-transactions are transactions where the adviser is acting as investment adviser in relation to a transaction in which such investment adviser or an affiliate acts as broker for both an advisory client and for another person on the other side of the transaction. The SEC has adopted a nonexclusive safe harbor rule permitting advisers to effect agency cross-transactions in compliance with section 206(3) and Investment Advisers Act Release No. 40. Rule 206(3)-2 permits such transactions based upon a client's prospective, blanket approval subject to advance and ongoing disclosure requirements. Should the SEC staff permit the same sort of flexibility with respect to principal transactions?

---

## 6. Duty to Supervise

Section 203(e) of the Advisers Act provides that the Commission may sanction an adviser or associated person who has aided or abetted a violation of the securities laws, "or has failed reasonably to supervise, with a view to preventing violations of the provisions of such statutes, rules, and regulations, another person who commits such a violation, if such other person is subject to his supervision." The statute provides a defense if the adviser established procedures, and a system for their application, which would "reasonably be expected to prevent and detect, insofar as possible" such a violation, and the adviser "reasonably discharged the duties and obligations" required by the procedure and system "without reasonable cause to believe that such procedures and system were not being complied with."

In *In re Western Asset Management Co*[1] the SEC imposed sanctions against advisers Western Asset Management Co. ("WAM"), the subadviser, and Legg Mason Fund Adviser, Inc. ("LM Fund Adviser"), the adviser, for failure to supervise a portfolio manager employed by WAM that defrauded the fund and the advisers by inflating the pricing of securities the fund held by concealing from them financial problems with the issuers. The SEC found that the adviser "failed to have adequate policies and procedures to respond adequately to indications that the portfolio manager was overstating the value of one of the fund's securities" and that WAM "failed to have adequate policies and procedures designed to prevent securities violations by the portfolio manager."

LM Fund Adviser knew of irregularities regarding the securities. First, it knew of stale pricing (i.e., not changed daily) of some of the securities despite the issuers' recent defaults on interest payments. The portfolio manager said that the issuers were able to make the interest payments but were using their cash to "'grow the business." Second, LM Fund Adviser knew of a proposed roll up transaction in which a shell company would issue securities to the fund in exchange for the problem securities and the shell company would be managed by the broker-dealer that sold the portfolio manager the securities. Third, LM Fund Adviser became aware of more stale pricing, from a fund accounting manager noting the stale pricing, and suggesting some of the problem securities may have to be priced by the fund board.

The SEC found that "WAM was a supervisor of the Portfolio Manager" and that "WAM failed reasonably to supervise the Portfolio Manager with a view

1. Investment Advisers Act Rel. No. 1980 (Sept. 28, 2001) (footnotes omitted).

to preventing and detecting her violations of the federal securities laws." In particular the SEC also stated that "WAM, moreover, had not established or implemented adequate procedures regarding the purchase, monitoring and pricing of such private placement securities." First, WAM policy required that agreements to purchase private placement securities required approval by officers. This policy was distributed only once, by e-mail, and had no procedures regarding its enforcement. Second, WAM policy required that the portfolio manager monitor the securities for defaults. However, there was no policy or procedure to monitor the portfolio manager in this regard. Third, the funds had policies governing valuation. However, WAM did not have adequate policies or procedures to ensure that such policies were complied with.

"LM Fund Adviser did not adequately follow-up and review these irregularities and had not established or implemented procedures for such follow-up and review." It did not do an independent investigation, and only obtained confirmation about the pricing from the portfolio manager and the involved broker-dealer. "In these circumstances, LM Fund Adviser became a supervisor of the Portfolio Manager."

---

## Discussion Topics

a. How could the defendants have prevented the losses to the funds and their investors?

b. In the *Legg Mason* case, the SEC imposed sanctions on an adviser for failure to supervise an employee of a sub-adviser, in comparison to previous cases involving direct employer-employee relationships.[1] It is not clear whether Congress intended this duty to extend to supervision of an employee who is not in a control relationship (e.g., an employer/employee relationship) with the adviser. However, *Legg Mason* and subsequent comments by SEC staff suggest that the duty extends to a sub-adviser and its employees, even if the sub-adviser is not affiliated with the adviser.[2]

c. Is this duty justified? How will an adviser monitor and control a sub-adviser's personnel? Is it enough for an adviser to impose a strict duty on the sub-adviser to comply with the law? Impose added payments on the sub-adviser? Retain the power to terminate the relationship? Any other?

---

1. *In re Western Asset Mgmt. Co.,* Investment Advisers Act Rel. No. 1980 (Sept. 28, 2001).
2. Bibb L. Strench & Thomas R. Phillips, *Adviser Duty to Supervise Extends to Non-Employees, Investment Law.,* Jan. 2002, at 1 (citing Paul F. Roye, Keynote Address American Law Institute — American Bar Association Conference on Investment Management Regulation (Oct. 11, 2001); Stephen M. Cutler, Remarks Before Investment Company Institute, Securities Law Developments Conference (Dec. 6, 2001)).

### 7. The Requirement for a Code of Ethics and a Compliance Program

The following requirement is closely related to the corporate governance of advisers which are organized as institutions. That is because a code of ethics imposes on advisers duties with respect to their personnel. The subject is also related to the duties of advisers generally. In that respect, it belongs to this chapter. We may therefore revisit the subject when we consider corporate governance of advisers but discuss the same topic here as well. Chapter 10 further discusses the code of ethics requirement.

In 2004 the SEC adopted Rule 204A-1 under the Advisers Act requiring every registered adviser to adopt and enforce a code of ethics applicable to the adviser's personnel.[1]

The code should include, at a minimum, a standard (or standards) of business conduct that the adviser requires of its supervised persons, which standard must reflect its fiduciary obligations and those of the adviser's supervised persons. Other provisions must generally require (1) supervisory persons to comply with applicable federal securities laws; (2) access persons to report to the adviser, quarterly, and the adviser to review, access persons' personal securities transactions and holdings; (3) supervisory persons to report code violations promptly to the chief compliance officer (or to another designated person provided the chief compliance officer also receives reports); and (4) the adviser to provide supervisory persons with a copy of the code, and the supervised persons to provide the adviser written acknowledgement of receipt.

An access person is generally defined as a supervised person (1) with access to nonpublic information regarding any clients' purchase or sale of securities, or nonpublic information regarding the portfolio holdings of any reportable fund, or (2) involved in making securities recommendations to clients, or who has access to such recommendations that are nonpublic. If providing investment advice is the adviser's primary business, all of its directors, officers and partners are presumed access persons.

The following is the SEC's rationale for requiring investment advisers to adopt codes of ethics.[2] Do you believe the benefits described outweigh the administrative burdens?

> The Commission is adopting new rule 204A-1 under the Advisers Act to require registered investment advisers to adopt codes of ethics. The rule requires an adviser's code of ethics to set forth standards of conduct and require compliance with federal securities laws. Codes of ethics must also address personal trading: they must require advisers' personnel to report their personal securities holdings and transactions, including those in affiliated mutual funds, and must require personnel to obtain pre-approval of certain investments. The Commission is amending the Advisers Act recordkeeping rule to require advisers to keep copies of their codes of ethics and records relating to the code. The Commission is also amending the

---

1. Investment Adviser Codes of Ethics, Investment Advisers Act Rel. No. 2256 (Jul. 2, 2004) (codified as amended at 17 C.F.R. § 275.204A-1 (2015)).
2. *Id.*

client disclosure requirements under Part II of Form ADV to require advisers to describe their codes of ethics to clients . . . [and to enforce the code].

[The purpose of the Code is] to prevent fraud by reinforcing fiduciary principles that must govern the conduct of advisory firms and their personnel. The proposal was part of a package of regulatory initiatives with which we have responded to a number of recent enforcement actions against advisers or their personnel alleging violations of their fiduciary obligations to clients, including mutual fund clients.

Advisers' codes would be required to contain provisions reminding employees of their obligations to clients as well as provisions requiring reporting of personal securities transactions and holdings. In order to ensure that advisers' employees are made aware of their firms' standards, advisers would have to obtain (and keep) a written acknowledgement from each supervised person confirming that he or she received a copy of the code of ethics and any amendments. While the code of ethics would have to contain certain minimum provisions, our proposal left advisers with substantial flexibility to design individualized codes that would best fit the structure, size and nature of their advisory businesses. . . .

[The Code should] set forth a standard of business conduct that the adviser requires of all its supervised persons. The rule does not require the adviser to adopt a particular standard, but the standard chosen must reflect the adviser's fiduciary obligations and those of its supervised persons, and must require compliance with the federal securities laws.

This provision . . . establishes only a minimum requirement. Advisers are free to set higher standards for their employees, such as those established by professional or trade groups. Of course, any other code adopted for use must meet the minimum requirements of the rule, or be supplemented to meet the minimum requirements.

[Advisers were urged to] take great care and thought in preparing their codes of ethics, which should be more than a compliance manual. Rather, a code of ethics should set out ideals for ethical conduct premised on fundamental [principles] of openness, integrity, honesty and trust. A good code of ethics should effectively convey to employees the value the advisory firm places on ethical conduct, and should challenge employees to live up not only to the letter of the law, but also to the ideals of the organization. . . .

[One objective of the Code is to rein in insider trading. But it would be] impractical to segregate employees, particularly in smaller firms that have limited office space. . . . [Therefore the SEC did not require a provision in the Code but reminded] advisers that they must maintain and enforce policies and procedures to prevent the misuse of material nonpublic information [e.g.,] misuse of material nonpublic information about the adviser's securities recommendations, and client securities holdings and transactions. Advisers' duty of care also requires that they safeguard this sensitive information. Advisers should carefully consider how to control dissemination of sensitive information both within their organizations and outside them.

C. Personal Securities Trading

Each adviser's code of ethics must require an adviser's "access persons" to periodically report their personal securities transactions and holdings to the adviser's chief compliance officer or other designated persons. The code of ethics must also require the adviser to review those reports. Reviewing these reports will allow advisers as well as the Commission's examination staff to identify improper trades or patterns of trading by access persons. The reports are modeled largely on those required by rule 17j-1 under the Company Act.

1. Personal Trading Procedures

As discussed in more detail below, while rule 204A-1 requires advisers' codes of ethics to contain provisions requiring access persons to report securities transactions and holdings, it does not require advisers to adopt many of the detailed prophylactic measures common to many codes. . . . Advisory firms that have already adopted codes of ethics, however, commonly include many of the following elements, or address the following issues, which we believe that all advisers should consider in crafting their own procedures for employees' personal securities trading.

- Prior written approval before access persons can place a personal securities transaction ("pre-clearance").
- Maintenance of lists of issuers of securities that the advisory firm is analyzing or recommending for client transactions, and prohibitions on personal trading in securities of those issuers.
- Maintenance of "restricted lists" of issuers about which the advisory firm has inside information, and prohibitions on any trading (personal or for clients) in securities of those issuers.
- "Blackout periods" when client securities trades are being placed or recommendations are being made and access persons are not permitted to place personal securities transactions.
- Reminders that investment opportunities must be offered first to clients before the adviser or its employees may act on them, and procedures to implement this principle.
- Prohibitions or restrictions on "short-swing" trading and market timing.
- Requirements to trade only through certain brokers, or limitations on the number of brokerage accounts permitted.
- Requirements to provide the adviser with duplicate trade confirmations and account statements.
- Procedures for assigning new securities analyses to employees whose personal holdings do not present apparent conflicts of interest.

2. "Access Persons" Subject to the Reporting Requirements

Under rule 204A-1, the adviser's code must require certain

supervised persons, called "access persons," to report their personal securities transactions and holdings. An access person is a supervised person who has access to nonpublic information regarding clients' purchase or sale of securities, is involved in making securities recommendations to clients or who has access to such recommendations that are nonpublic. A supervised person who has access to nonpublic information regarding the portfolio holdings of affiliated mutual funds is also an access person.

We are adopting the definition of "access person" as proposed. Some commenters suggested that we adopt a narrower definition covering only those employees who actually obtained nonpublic information, the approach rule 17j-1 takes for mutual fund advisers. Others suggested that all advisory employees be covered. Our approach takes the middle course. It treats as access persons employees who are in a position to exploit information about client securities transactions or holdings, and thus provides the adviser with a tool to protect its clients.

Access persons will include portfolio management personnel and, in some organizations, client service representatives who communicate investment advice to clients. These employees have information about investment recommendations whose effect may not yet be felt in the marketplace; as such, they may be in a position to take advantage of their inside knowledge. Administrative, technical, and clerical personnel may also be access persons if their functions or duties give them access to nonpublic information.

Organizations in which employees have broad responsibilities, and where information barriers are few, may see a larger percentage of their staff subject to the reporting requirements. In contrast, organizations that keep strict controls on sensitive information may have fewer access persons.

In many advisory firms, directors, officers and partners will also be access persons. Rule 204A-1, as proposed, contains a presumption that, if the firm's primary business is providing investment advice, then all of its directors, officers and partners are access persons. Commenters supported this approach rather than rule 17j-1's special rules and revenue-based test for advisory firms "primarily engaged" in a business other than advising funds or advisory clients.

3. Initial and Annual Holdings Reports

The code of ethics must require a complete report of each access person's securities holdings, at the time the person becomes an access person and at least once a year thereafter. . . .

4. Quarterly Transaction Reports

The code of ethics must require quarterly reports of all personal securities transactions by access persons, which are due no later than 30 days after the close of the calendar quarter. . . .

5. Exceptions From Reporting Requirements

Rule 204A-1 permits three exceptions to personal securities reporting. No reports are required:

- With respect to transactions effected pursuant to an automatic investment plan.
- With respect to securities held in accounts over which the access person had no direct or indirect influence or control.
- In the case of an advisory firm that has only one access person, so long as the firm maintains records of the holdings and transactions that rule 204A-1 would otherwise require be reported.

6. Reportable Securities

Access persons must submit holdings and transaction reports for "reportable securities" in which the access person has, or acquires, any direct or indirect beneficial ownership. An access person is presumed to be a beneficial owner of securities that are held by his or her immediate family members sharing the access person's household.

Rule 204A-1 treats all securities as reportable securities, with five exceptions designed to exclude securities that appear to present little opportunity for the type of improper trading that the access person reports are designed to uncover:

- Transactions and holdings in direct obligations of the Government of the United States.
- Money market instruments — bankers' acceptances, bank certificates of deposit, commercial paper, repurchase agreements and other high quality short-term debt instruments.
- Shares of money market funds.
- Transactions and holdings in shares of other types of mutual funds, unless the adviser or a control affiliate acts as the investment adviser or principal underwriter for the fund.
- Transactions in units of a unit investment trust if the unit investment trust is invested exclusively in unaffiliated mutual funds.

The rule thus requires access persons to report shares of mutual funds advised by the access person's employer or an affiliate, and is designed to help advisers (and our examiners) identify abusive trading by personnel with access to information about a mutual fund's portfolio.

D. Initial Public Offerings and Private Placements

The code of ethics must require that access persons obtain the adviser's approval before investing in an initial public offering ("IPO") or private placement. Most individuals rarely have the opportunity to invest in these types of securities; an access person's IPO or private placement purchase therefore raises questions as to whether the employee is misappropriating an investment opportunity that should first be offered to eligible clients, or whether a portfolio manager is receiving a personal benefit for directing client business or

> brokerage. Advisory firms with only one access person would not be required to have that access person pre-clear these investments. We are adopting this provision as proposed.
>
> E. Reporting Violations
>
> Under rule 204A-1, each adviser's code of ethics must require prompt internal reporting of any violations of the code. Violations must be reported to the adviser's chief compliance officer. . . .
>
> F. Educating Employees about the Code of Ethics
>
> Under rule 204A-1, an adviser's code of ethics must require the adviser to provide each supervised person with a copy of the code of ethics and any amendments. . . .

---

**Discussion Topics**

a. How different is a Code of Ethics from a statute or regulation?

b. Why did the SEC choose to require advisers to impose a Code of Ethics rather than impose the same substantive requirements by rule?

c. Should an adviser prohibit employees involved in portfolio management and analysis from buying and selling stocks or other securities for their own account? Can such a prohibition be enforced in light of the fact that such persons usually think and talk about stocks and securities during most of their waking hours?

d. If so, what kind of rules should the adviser impose? Should the rules be similar when applied to the traders, who receive information not only on the purchase but also on the sell orders?

e. What sanctions can the SEC impose on violations of a Code of Ethics? Suppose an adviser did not require its employees to read the Code of Ethics? Or suppose the employees read the Code but violated its requirements and the adviser did not discover the violations? Or what if the adviser discovered the violations and did nothing about it?

---

### 8. Advisory Services to State and Local Governments — "Pay-to-Play" Concerns

The issue of pay-to-play and lobbying has been around for quite a while. In July 2010, the SEC refocused on the political activities of advisers as this excerpt demonstrates.[1]

> The Securities and Exchange Commission is adopting a new rule under the Investment Advisers Act of 1940 that prohibits an investment adviser from providing advisory services for compensation to a government client for two years after the adviser or certain of its executives or employees make a contribution to certain elected

1. Political Contributions by Certain Investment Advisers, Investment Advisers Act Rel. No. 3043 (Jul. 1, 2010), 75 Fed. Reg. 41,018 (Jul. 14, 2010) codified as amended at 17 C.F.R. § 275.206(4)-5 (2015)).

officials or candidates. The new rule also prohibits an adviser from providing or agreeing to provide, directly or indirectly, payment to any third party for a solicitation of advisory business from any government entity on behalf of such adviser, unless such third parties are registered broker-dealers or registered investment advisers, in each case themselves subject to pay to play restrictions. Additionally, the new rule prevents an adviser from soliciting from others, or coordinating, contributions to certain elected officials or candidates or payments to political parties where the adviser is providing or seeking government business. The Commission also is adopting rule amendments that require a registered adviser to maintain certain records of the political contributions made by the adviser or certain of its executives or employees. The new rule and rule amendments address "pay to play" practices by investment advisers.

---

**Discussion Topics**

a. What is wrong with "pay-to-play?"

b. If something is wrong with pay-to-play, has the SEC's rule addressed it?

---

### 9. Compliance Program and Compliance Officers[1]

Rule 206(4)-7 under the Advisers Act requires registered investment advisers to adopt a compliance program. Registered advisers must adopt and implement written policies and procedures reasonably designed to prevent violation by the advisers and its supervised persons of the Advisers Act and the rules thereunder. Advisers must review no less frequently than annually the adequacy of these policies and procedures and the effectiveness of their implementation. Importantly, advisers must also designate a chief compliance officer who is responsible for administering these policies and procedures.

In recent years, the SEC has increasingly brought enforcement actions against advisers on violations of the required compliance program rule. Additionally, in 2015, the SEC chair, Mary Jo White, instituted a policy of prosecuting "broken windows" violations — in other words, pursue violations no matter how small, in order to deter more serious violations. Do you believe this is an appropriate approach for the SEC? What effect do you think it has had, or will it have on the financial services and on the willingness of qualified personnel to service as compliance officers?

Consider also the following:[2]

---

1. Compliance Programs of Investment Companies and Investment Advisers, Investment Advisers Act Rel. No. 2204, Investment Company Act Rel. No. 26299 (Dec. 17, 2003), 68 Fed. Reg. 74,714 (Dec. 24, 2003), (codified at 17 C.F.R. § 275.206(4)-7 (2015)); *see also* Frederick L. White, *New SEC Rule 206(4)-7 — Compliance Programs for Investment Advisers,* Investment Law., Mar. 2004, at 1, 9.

2. Tamar Frankel, *The Jurisprudence of the Securities and Exchange Commission New Rule 206(4)-7* (2004).

> In March 2004, the Securities and Exchange Commission passed Rule 206(4)-7 (the Rule). The Rule has introduced a number of significant changes into the compliance area of investment advisers. . . . First; the Rule shifts the burden of detail compliance to the advisers. Second, the Rule is far more "micromanaging" of the advisers' compliance mechanisms than in the past. Third, the Rule reduces the burden of the Securities and Exchange Commission's staff in enforcing the Rule. Fourth, the Rule creates additional duties, the violations of which are not dependent on existing violations of the law. In fact, the Rule creates a new layer of required actions and prohibited inactions before any violations occur. Fifth, compliance duties apply not only to future violations but also to previous violations of the law, before the passage of the Rule. Thus, the 'jurisprudence' of the Securities and Exchange Commission has changed. . . . The Rule also imposes costs on honest advisers, who have not been caught in the frenzy of the 1990s. . . . However, the Rule provides protection from dishonesty not only to investors but also to other advisers. Competition on shady transactions can be chilled . . . by the consumers . . . [or] by self-limitation of most members of the profession . . . [or by] law. The law in this case can prohibit the activities but also prohibit aiding and abetting the activities. Thus law can create a broad enforcement group.

How does this discussion relate to the design of the congressional acts and the Commission's interpretation and rules?

---

## Discussion Topic

You are a disinterested director of about 100 investment companies managed by Huge Investment Adviser, HIA. Suppose that the adviser has no compliance officer on its staff:

1. What questions would you ask HIA related to legal compliance by HIA's personnel?

2. If the answer is that the advisers take good care of the personnel and they have been honest people, generally, would that answer satisfy you?

3. If HIA agrees that it needs a compliance officer, what would be the conditions and procedures that you would require HIA to establish for the compliance office? Who should determine the officer's salary, access to the board, vulnerability to dismissal? Are these relevant questions?

---

## Problem

Assume you are counsel to the independent directors of a large fund complex. The adviser to the funds has just informed the board that it intends to layoff its entire compliance staff, including its Chief Compliance Officer (CCO), and hire a third party company that provides outsourced compliance services to service the adviser's compliance needs. These services would include providing an individual to serve as the adviser's CCO on an outsourced basis. The independent directors report to you that the adviser, in response to their inquiries, has told them that this new outsourced CCO would spend approximately 1 or 2 days per week on the adviser's matters, and the reminder of his professional time would be spent acting in his capacity as an outsourced CCO to approximately 5 other registered advisers. The adviser has also asserted that it is taking this action because it would be more cost effective and improve the adviser's profitability. The independent directors want your advice as to how to react to this decision by the adviser. Explain to them the pros and cons of having the adviser's compliance function outsourced from a regulatory and fiduciary perspective. Pay particular attention to the potential risks and conflicts of interest this decision may create.

# Chapter 3

## What is an Investment Company?

### A. Introduction to the Basic Definition

Section 3 of the Investment Company Act defines an investment company. The definition is crucial for any corporate and securities lawyer because a client company may become an investment company inadvertently, and if it does not register under the Act and comply with its provisions, it may suffer serious consequences. For example, failure to register could result in court avoidance of its contracts. If such a company issued and sold its securities to the market and the price of these securities fell, the buyers may be able to recoup their original payment for the securities under section 46(b) of the Investment Company Act. The adviser may find itself to be a guarantor of the securities that were issued. If the price of the securities rose, that would be fine. If the price fell, the adviser will have to return the money received to the investors.

The definition of an investment company in section 3 is very broad. In fact, it embraces all institutional and some market intermediaries, as well as operating holding companies. That is why Congress excluded from the definition typical holding companies that operate non-investment company business through subsidiaries (section 3(b)), as well as various financial institutional intermediaries, e.g., banks and insurance companies (section 3(c)). However, if a company is not excluded, it is included. Some of the inclusions may be unanticipated and surprising, as we shall see.

Section 3(a) contains three definitions of investment companies, each of which catches a different type of company in the net of the Act. Sections 3(a)(1)(A) and 3(a)(1)(C) are widely applied today, while the type of investment company defined in 3(a)(1)(B) — a face amount certificate company — was prevalent in the 1920s and 1930s, but is virtually extinct today.

Please read section 3(a) of the 1940 Act. Note that all three definitions in section 3(a) share a common factor. An investment company under each definition must be "an issuer," defined in section 2(a)(22) of the Act. An issuer is a person that issues securities or has securities outstanding. The first component of the definition of an issuer, "person," is defined in section 2(a)(28) of the Act as an individual and a company, and "company" is defined in section 2(a)(8). The second component, "securities," is defined in section 2(a)(36) of the Act. The next two sections focus on these components.

## B. Who is an Issuer?

### 1. Who is a Person? What is a Company?

The definition of a "company" played a crucial part in the case of Prudential that follows. This case involves an issuer of a hybrid product: an insurance contract that could be a security as well. The difficult and interesting questions arise in relationship to hybrid financial arrangements that are subject to two regulatory systems. The following is the judicial analysis of the concept of "company."[1]

In the *Prudential* case, the Third Circuit decided the question of whether the Investment Company Act applies to variable insurance contracts sold to the public by an insurance company (Prudential). Under the contracts, investors will make monthly payments to a Variable Contract Account to be invested in securities during the "pay-in" period of the contract; annuity holders are then credited with "units" for their proportionate interests in the fund, which units will fluctuate in value depending on investment performance of the securities. During the "pay-out" period, the investors will receive cash as annuity payments. Note that insurance companies used "separate accounts" for various types of contracts, such as contracts paid in foreign currency.

Although Prudential, as an *insurance company*, is excluded from the applicability of the Investment Company Act, the SEC took the position that the *fund* from which the annuities would be paid is a separate investment company. Under the Act, a "company" is defined as "a trust, a fund, or any organized group of persons whether incorporated or not." Prudential argued, first that the definition includes only "identifiable business entities with some sort of internal organization," and, second, that the plan is not an "organized group of persons," a common-law trust, or a mutual fund or similar entity. The court rejected the arguments, noting that the legislative history shows that Congress used general terms to include such plans regardless of legal form. The court noted that the investor is investing in a segregated fund, not in the insurance company.

Prudential also argued that the plan should be exempt, as insurance companies were exempted, on the basis of "adequate state regulation." However, the Supreme Court rejected this argument in a previous opinion which held that "variable annuities are 'securities' and involve considerations of investment not present in the conventional contract of insurance." Therefore, state regulation of insurance is immaterial. The Court noted that the specific exemption of funds which are established by banks indicates that Congress viewed such funds as separate from banks. Further, the safeguards of the Investment Company Act should not be excluded merely because the plan is managed by an insurance company.

---

1. *Prudential Insurance Co. v. SEC,* 326 F.2d 383 (3d Cir. 1964).

---

## Discussion Topics

a. Why did Prudential set up the Variable Contract Account in connection with the sale of its variable annuity contracts? Were these accounts different from the usual separate accounts established by insurance companies? Do you think that the insurance regulators allowed the insurance companies to set up these kinds of accounts?

b. What should the Court in *Prudential* have examined in determining whether someone is an issuer under the Investment Company Act? How important is the fact that the insurance company was making certain obligations under the annuity contract? How important was a pro rata sharing of the investment experience among the contract holders?

c. As a matter of policy, should the SEC regulate separate accounts as investment companies? What policy arguments were advanced by the SEC in *Prudential*? What investor protections provided by the Investment Company Act of 1940 were needed?

d. Insurance companies establish and maintain separate accounts for many reasons. In addition to funding variable contracts, some insurers create separate accounts to fund certain types of fixed insurance contracts. These separate accounts are accounting tools that help insurance companies match assets and liabilities. When should these types of separate accounts be treated as investment companies? This issue has not been free from controversy.

e. The *Prudential* case refers to the Alexander Fund, which was the name of a managed fund in which the money of numerous investors was commingled. These investors employed Wallace Alexander as their agent to invest their money. Was an issuer created? What if Alexander did not pool the money of his principals?

---

### 2. What is an Issuer and What is a Security?

An "issuer" is a person who issues a "security." The term "security" is defined in section 2(a)(36) of the Act. Note that in all three definitions of an investment company the term "security" appears twice. An investment company is the *issuer* of securities and an *investor* in securities. If the company does not issue securities, it is not an investment company. If it does not invest in securities, it is not an investment company. Therefore, in the investment company area the same question arises: what is a security? To be sure, it is often clear that an entity is issuing a security. For example, when a person pays for a share issued by a mutual fund, a security is involved. More difficult interpretative questions arise in unique arrangements, for example with the emergence of computer technology and the repackaging of financial products. Assume that mortgages and other financial assets are pooled and transferred to an entity. If that entity issues securities to investors, are those securities?

The definition of a security in the Act is very extensive. It defines security by its form, by the general view of the instrument and by the intent of one party to pay another party for its promise to repay a greater amount. The *Howey* case interprets the term "investment contract." It has been on the books for decades, and is still a major guide to the definition of the term under the Securities Act, which guides the interpretation of the same term security in the Investment Company Act.

Rule 3a-4 under the Investment Company Act addresses the dividing line between issuing securities and giving investment advice. Rule 3a-4 is a safe harbor that is used to structure advisory services known as "wrap fee programs." As advisers seek to operate more efficiently and service more clients, they move from managing the assets of each customer, which reflect personalized customized services, to pooling customers' assets and issuing standardized securities. At some point they become issuers of securities and fall within the definition of investment companies in section 3(a). In Rule 3a-4, the SEC sought to draw the line between investment advice and the issuance of securities, thus providing advisers with a safe harbor to develop advisory programs with economical fee structures for certain types of clients.[1] Rule 3a-4 and wrap fee programs are discussed in more detail later in this chapter.

## a. What is an Investment Contract?

The definition of a security includes an "investment contract." The following case deals with this part of the definition.[2]

The Howey Company (Howey) owns citrus grove developments and offers land sales contracts to investors. A second company sells service contracts for the land and is accountable for an allocation of the net profits. The investors are generally not knowledgeable about citrus trees and are attracted by the expectation of profits.

The Securities Act of 1933 defines "security" in part as a "certificate of interest or participation in any profit-sharing agreement," "investment contract," and "in general, any interest or instrument commonly known as a 'security.'" The question is whether the transactions constitute an "investment contract" or only a sale contract and service contract.

The Supreme Court noted that although the Securities Act does not define "investment contract", the term has been broadly construed by state courts for purposes of state securities laws and "economic reality" was emphasized over form. Therefore, the Court adopted a broad definition, defining "investment contract" as "a contract, transaction or scheme whereby a person invests his money in a common enterprise and is led to expect profits solely from the efforts of the promoter or a third party, it being immaterial whether the shares in the enterprise are evidenced by formal certificates or by nominal interests in the physical assets employed in the enterprise."

---

1. We discuss later in this chapter the issue of whether a company is investing in securities.
2. *SEC v. W. J. Howey Co.*, 328 U.S. 293 (1946).

The Court found the transactions to be investment contracts, noting that the companies were "offering an opportunity to contribute money and to share in the profits of a large citrus fruit enterprise managed and partly owned by respondents" and that investors "have no desire to occupy the land or to develop it themselves; they are attracted solely by the prospects of a return on their investment."

### b. Viatical Settlements and Life Settlements

The *Siporin v. Carrington* case discusses two new innovative financial transactions and the application of the *Howey* case to these contracts.[1]

A viatical settlement is an investment contract pursuant to which an investor acquires an interest in the life insurance policy of a terminally ill person. It is the sale of a terminally ill person's life insurance policy at a discount and provides the terminally ill person (viator) with a portion of the death benefit while he or she is still living. Ultimately the purchase will yield a profit to the purchaser upon the viator's death that is equal to the difference between the death benefit paid by the insurer and the purchaser's total investment in the viatical settlement. A purchaser's profit realization on a viatical settlement investment depends on the price paid for the policy and the amount of time that passes between the policy's purchase and the viator's death.

To determine whether the settlements were a "security" under Arizona law, the court referred to the definition of "security" under the Securities Act and the *Howey* test. It defined an "investment security" as "whenever a person (1) invests money (2) in a common enterprise (3) with an expectation of profits from the efforts of others, and when such third-party efforts are 'the undeniably significant ones, those essential managerial efforts which affect the failure or success of the enterprise. . . .'"

In applying the test, the court noted the seller's efforts, including selection of life insurance policies, involving estimation of life expectancies, in turn involving obtaining and evaluating other data. The court especially noted that the seller determined the value of the death benefit and the likelihood that it would be paid in full, involving factors including the financial condition of the insurer. The seller also negotiated the price of the policy and marketed interests in the policy, and continued to monitor the policy. Therefore, the court found the arrangement to be an investment contract and a security.

The court declined to apply the rule in another viatical settlement case, in which a federal court distinguished between the seller's pre-purchase services (before sale of the interests) and post-purchase services, and held that the investments were not securities on the basis that the seller's post-purchase efforts were largely ministerial. The Arizona court noted the importance of the seller's pre-purchase efforts, the importance of pre-purchase efforts with other investments that are securities under state law, and the policy of the state securities law.

1. *Siporin v. Carrington,* 23 P.3d 92 (Ariz. Ct. App. 2001).

---

Discussion Topics

a. Are there any problems with viatical securities?

b. Who gains and who loses in these arrangements?

c. Who cannot protect himself from possible losses and needs government protection?

---

### c. The Classification of Notes

Notes are another type of financial instrument that defy clear classification. Notes can be used in commercial transactions, in which case they are not marketable instruments but rather contractual. However, they may also be securities if they are mass produced and tradable. The staff of the Commission has treated notes as securities on the basis of another condition. The following[1] is an example of this distinction.

The SEC staff addressed the "security" status of promissory notes held by a financial institution as evidence of loans under the 1940 Act. The staff rejected the argument that the notes are not securities. First, the staff declined to use a fixed test to determine whether promissory notes are securities, but instead followed consideration of facts and circumstances. Therefore, the fact that courts have found notes not to be securities in particular cases was not determinative. Second, the financial institution relied on a Supreme Court case holding that a certificate of deposit was not a security under the Securities Act and the Securities Exchange Act. Therefore the holding did not apply to the 1940 Act. The policy of the 1940 Act is "the regulation of the management of a portfolio of securities rather than the issuance or trading of such securities." Under the 1940 Act, the "commercial" or "investment" character of the instrument is not relevant. Further, the Court rejected an argument that under the "risk capital" test, the instruments are not securities because the notes are short-term and therefore presented little risk. The court noted that the 1940 Act definition specifically includes short-term paper.

---

Discussion Topics

a. Why should the exemptions under the Securities Act of 1933 not apply to the definition of securities issued by investment companies? What are the purposes of the Securities Act as compared to those of the Investment Company Act? What dangers to investors does the Investment Company Act seek to address?

b. Should the status of an entity as an investment company be based on the riskiness of the securities that the entity issues or holds? Is a company that invests in bank CDs or insurance company guaranteed investment

1. Bank of America Canada, SEC No-Action Letter (Jul. 25, 1983).

contracts an investment company? Even if the securities are exempt from registration under the Securities Act?

c. Would an entity that invests in and holds gold be considered an investment company? What about an entity that invests in stamp collections? Or a company that invests in gold mining companies? Are gold, stamps and securities of gold-mining companies equally convertible into cash? Is this relevant to making a determination of whether the entity that invests and holds them is an investment company? What about an entity that invests in securities of companies that have no market and are totally illiquid?

---

The viaticals described above are a hybrid of insurance and securities and contract. The following discussion deals with another hybrid, akin to contract and perhaps brokerage as well as investment management. The following is the SEC exemption from the Investment Company Act for such a hybrid subject to conditions. These conditions illuminate the SEC's view of the missing features of a security.

**d. The Status of "Wrap-Fee Arrangements"[1]**

In 1997, the SEC adopted rule 3a-4 under the Investment Company Act. The rule was designed to provide "a nonexclusive safe harbor from the definition of investment company for certain investment advisory programs," used to offer portfolio management services to clients investing relatively small sums.

The rule responded to the increasing number of investment advisory programs created to provide professional portfolio management services to a large number of clients, usually investing a relatively small amount of money. A sponsor monitors the account's management and administers these programs, which offer a range of services. Some of the programs provide portfolio management. Others provide advice regarding selection of an investment adviser. One type of service is called a "wrap fee program," in which "the client typically is provided with portfolio management, execution of transactions, asset allocation, and administrative services for a single fee based on the size of the account."[2] This type of program became more popular in the mid-1990s. These investment advisory programs may cross the line and fall within the definition of an investment company.

The Commission explained that "[t]he rule's provisions have the effect of ensuring that clients in a program relying on the rule receive individualized treatment. . . . Moreover, if an advisory program were operated by an investment adviser registered under the Advisers Act, clients of the program would receive the protections of that Act. The safe harbor thus is designed to provide an exemption for certain investment advisory programs without undermining the protection of investors who participate

1. Status of Investment Advisory Programs Under the Investment Company Act of 1940, Investment Company Act Rel. No. 22579, 62 F.R. 15098; Investment Advisers Act Rel. No. 1623 (Mar. 31, 1997) (codified at 17 C.F.R. § 270.3a-4 (2015)).
2. *Id.* at 15100.

in those programs. . . ."[1] The rule is designed to ensure each client receives individualized treatment, described below.

First, rule 3a-4 required that "a client's account must be managed on the basis of the client's financial situation, investment objectives and instructions."[2] Clients may have similar securities in their accounts, and portfolio managers may effect transactions for clients without separate determinations for each client. Second, the Advisers Act imposes a duty on investment advisers to provide only suitable investment advice; that is, the adviser must make a reasonable determination that the investment advice provided is suitable for the client based on the client's financial situation and investment objectives. The adviser also must contact clients and solicit information from them regarding finances, investment goals, and restrictions on the management of the account initially and at least annually; must write to the client at least quarterly to inform him that the adviser or designated person should be informed of any changes in the client's finances, goals and restrictions; and the adviser or plan sponsor must be reasonably available to consult with the client. All these requirements are designed to ensure that the advisers and managers have the clients' current data, and that the clients have reasonable access to the managers of their account, or other staff members who are "sufficiently knowledgeable to discuss and explain investment decisions that were made."[3]

All programs relying on the rule's safe harbor "must include a requirement that each client have the ability to impose reasonable restrictions on the management of [his or her] account." This provision does not require that the program allow clients to direct the adviser to buy or sell specific securities in the client's account. Whether a client's restriction is reasonable depends on an analysis of the facts. Relevant factors include whether the restriction is "clearly inconsistent with the portfolio manager's stated investment strategy or philosophy or the client's stated investment objective . . . difficulty in complying with the restriction, the specificity of the restriction and the number of other restrictions imposed by the client."[4]

If a program's staff concludes a client's proposed restrictions are unreasonable, the client should be notified and given an opportunity to restate the restriction. If the client insists on an unreasonable restriction, the program may remove or refuse to accept the client.

The program must provide each client with a quarterly statement listing all activity in the client's account during the previous quarter. During the notice and comment period of this rule, the SEC asked for feedback on a proposed rule that did not specify a minimum size for client accounts in a program. There is no requirement that clients' accounts will be of a particular size, in order to ensure individualized investment management. However, "the Commission will consider a relatively large minimum

1. *Id.* at 15101.
2. *Id.* at 15102.
3. *Id.* at 15104.
4. *Id.*

account size as evidence that individualized treatment is being provided to clients of the program. . . ."[1]

---

Discussion Topics

a. The number of wrap fee programs has grown since 1999. What accounts for this popularity? How different are these arrangements from the commingled fund described in the *Prudential* case?

b. What elements in rule 3a-4 exclude advisers from the definition of "issuers"? How different is the program from an investment company? Can an investment company meet the elements in the rule? What additional conditions would you impose to ensure that a wrap fee client receives individualized treatment?

c. What element in the definition of a security is missing when an adviser provides customized investment advice to one client? What policy reasons are there for classifying an adviser as an issuer if his advice is not customized? What are the policy reasons for requiring an issuer to provide offeree investors with a prospectus?

---

### e. The Distinction Between a Security and Advisory and Information Services

Chapter 1 discussed how Boston trustees have moved to organize mutual funds, a movement which paralleled the industrial revolution. The Boston trustees provided expert advice and management to wealthy individuals in three aspects. The trustees determined the need of the particular individuals, then designed a portfolio strategy for the particular individuals, and then chose the securities that would fit the portfolio strategy. Mutual funds eliminated the individual advice stage, and offered instead a particular defined strategy, selection of securities to fit the strategy, and expert management for the portfolio securities. Thus, mutual fund advisers offered two of the three types of services which were made on an impersonal basis. Investors had to determine their needs and the type of mutual funds that would meet these needs. Because investors were not expert in designing investment strategies, mutual fund managers increased the diversity of their offerings and with certain limitations offered diversified portfolios of diversified mutual fund shares. Some mutual funds offered to automatically change the composition of the investors' portfolios upon the investors reaching certain ages. Presumably, upon retirement, for example, investors would need a less volatile portfolio and a larger assured income. However, such an automatic change does not take into account market changes. An automatic sale of stock and the purchase of bonds during the year 2008 could cause investors an enormous amount of losses.

With the development of sophisticated computer programs, some advisers offered software, which investors could use to design their

1. *Id.* at 15106.

own investments. In 2000, a new generation of such software led to an investment vehicle, which was new to the mutual fund service industry and to Congress.

At the outset "Folios" offer investors the choice of following one or more portfolios among a number of securities portfolios. The choice of portfolio designs is limited to ready-made portfolios. However, investors may change the composition of the portfolio which they chose by adding or reducing stocks. Then the sponsor of the Folio provides investors with software into which investors may input their personal data. The software provides investors with information about the consequences *to each of the investors* of the changes they may make, including tax consequences. Thus, after investors choose prepared portfolios, they can customize and personalize them.

Investors open a brokerage account with the sponsor and execute their transactions through the sponsor. The sponsor's fees are fixed. The sponsor pools the investors' orders and thereby achieves economies of scales for investors in their purchasing and selling their portfolios' stocks. However, the indicia of ownership over the portfolios remain with the investors. In addition, sponsors periodically update their ready-made portfolios and promote the performance of these portfolios.

A list of the sponsor's services includes: providing the software and executing the investors' orders, either to purchase the portfolios as they are offered or the purchase of personalized portfolios, for a fixed fee. The assumption is that, like the sponsor of Folio, the sponsor of such offering will be registered as a broker-dealer.

On March 28, 2001, the Investment Company Institute, the mutual funds' trade association, filed with the SEC a proposed interpretative rule under which Folio and other offerings of this vintage will be deemed investment companies and the sponsors — sponsors of investment companies and advisers to investment companies. The SEC responded to this petition in August 23, 2001.[1]

"In the Commission's view, the programs described in the Petition do not at this time appear to raise interpretive issues that warrant the Commission undertaking a rulemaking."[2] The Commission noted that in the case of "Folio" the management of the investors' portfolios remains with the investors. Even though the investments start with model portfolios, the investors can change the portfolios' composition.

> In other words, the investor does not hold an undivided interest in a pool of securities; rather the investor is the direct beneficial owner of each of the securities included in the portfolio. Each investor has all of the rights of ownership with respect to such securities, including the right to vote, receive dividends and receive confirmations, proxy statements and other documents required by law to

1. U.S. Sec. & Exch. Comm'n, Letter in Response to Petition for Rulemaking from Investment Company Institute, *available at* http://www.sec.gov/rules/other/ltrresp4-442.htm (Aug. 23, 2001).
2. *Id.*

> be provided to security holders. Each investor also has the right to withdraw or pledge his or her securities and to receive the cash value of the securities at any time.[1]

The Commission noted that the sponsors of portfolio investment programs generally have registered as broker-dealers under the Securities Exchange Act of 1934, and may be subject to the Advisers Act, if it renders advice, yet it will follow the "Folios" development. The petition was denied and as of September 2015, the Commission has not changed its position.

### C. Definition of Investment Company by the Nature of its Business and by the Nature of its Assets, Presentation to the Public and its Main Business: Section 3(a)(1)(A); Section 3(a)(1)(C) and Section 3(b)

In addition to the requirements that an entity be an issuer, Section 3(a) of the 1940 Act establishes two alternative tests to determine whether an entity is deemed an investment company. One test, in section 3(a)(1)(A), focuses on the intent of the sponsors, the company's business and how the company holds itself out to the public. It defines an investment company as an issuer that "is or holds itself out as being engaged primarily, or proposes to engage primarily, in the business of investing, reinvesting, or trading in securities."

Section 3(a)(1)(C) focuses almost entirely on the composition of the company's assets. It defines an investment company as an issuer that is "engaged or proposes to engage in the business of investing, reinvesting, owning, holding, or trading in securities, and owns or proposes to acquire investment securities having a value exceeding 40 per centum of the value of such issuer's total assets (exclusive of Government securities and cash items) on an unconsolidated basis."[2]

"Investment securities" are securities which the company holds as a non-controlling, passive investor. Thus, the term excludes securities of companies that are majority-owned subsidiaries. The assumption is that a company with majority-owned subsidiaries is a holding company, actively managing a business rather than an investment company managing a portfolio as a passive investor, unless the subsidiaries are investment companies (in which case the exclusion does not apply).

In addition, the term "investment securities" excludes government securities and cash. That is because cash and cash items do not help distinguish between operating companies and investment companies. Government securities are deemed to be acceptable under all circumstances.

The following materials discuss the slippery area between operating a business and the service of investment management.

#### 1. When Does an Operating Company Become an Investment Company?

The factors that determine whether a company is or proposes to be engaged in the investment management business is discussed in the following case.

---

1. *Id.*
2. Investment Company Act of 1940, Section 3(a)(1)(C), 15 U.S.C. § 80a-3(a)(1)(C).

Most importantly, it demonstrates the gray area. The first question is: when does an operating company slide into becoming an investment company? Reality does not always follow one applicable section or another. Therefore, in addition to sections 3(a)(1)(A) and 3(a)(1)(C), we consider the exclusion of operating business from the definition of an investment company under section 3(b).[1] This exclusion provides a signal to the distinction between a holding company that is an operating company and that which is an investment company.

Fifth Avenue Coach Lines (Fifth) operated municipal transit systems. New York City acquired the company's bus lines by condemnation. For several years the company had no business except litigating its claims against the city. After receiving a condemnation award, the company invested in companies in various industries which sustained losses. It had little cash left.

The District Court found that Fifth had become an investment company under the predecessor of section 3(a)(1)(A) of the 1940 Act. Fifth argued that it was "seeking ventures in which to purchase control for the purpose of operating companies." The Court found that while that may have been its intention, the company was not successful in gaining control of any company and that "the only business that it can fairly be found to be primarily engaged in was the business of investing in securities."

The Second Circuit referred to the SEC's 1941 study of investment companies. In its study, the SEC distinguished between "companies includ[ing] those with holdings primarily in wholly-owned or non-wholly-owned subsidiaries (defined as companies owned 50% or more)," whose business is deemed to be that of their subsidiaries, and "companies with investments primarily in diversified securities or corporations in which they have working control (defined as ownership of 10% to 50% of the outstanding voting power)," deemed to be part of the investment company industry. Where the line between management of subsidiaries and control of companies blurs, the report suggests factors including "the degree of integration or non-integration of the company and its affiliates, the volume of trading by the company in its portfolio securities, the frequency of shifts in portfolio securities, and the representations made to the public or its shareholders regarding the nature of its business."

The Court affirmed the District Court decision.

---

## Discussion Topic

a. What led to the conversion of Fifth Avenue from an operating company into an investment company under section 3(a)(1)(A)?

---

1. *SEC v. Fifth Avenue Coach Lines, Inc.*, 435 F.2d 510 (1970).

## 2. Excluding Operating Companies Whose Assets May Be Investment Securities?

Section 3(b) of the Investment Company Act provides:

> Notwithstanding paragraph (1)(C) of subsection (a), none of the following persons is an investment company within the meaning of this title: Any issuer primarily engaged, directly or through a wholly-owned subsidiary or subsidiaries, in a business or businesses other than that of investing, reinvesting, owning, holding, or trading in securities.

Please note that section 3(b) does not exclude companies that are subject to section 3(a)(1)(A) but excludes only companies subject to section 3(a)(1)(C).

The case described below deals with the definition of an investment company, and the exclusion of operating companies' different types of assets.[1]

Presto, a maker of consumer goods and ammunitions, formerly made its own products but later contracted most of its production to other firms and had 62% of its physical and operating assets in financial instruments and cash. The SEC and the District Court found the firm to be an investment company under the 40% test of section 3(a)(1)(C). The Circuit Court reversed. The Court touched on many aspects of this section.

First, the Court addressed the definition of "Government securities and cash items." The Court held that "municipal bonds" do not strictly fit the definition, although they may be "Government securities" for purposes of the definition of "diversified company" in section 5(b)(1). The definitional clause states "unless the context otherwise requires" and for this purpose investors would be interested in securities' economic attributes (i.e., tax advantages).

Second, the Court addressed the argument that Presto's holding of "variable-rate demand notes" should be deemed cash items. Although "cash items" is not defined in the Act, the Court looked to Rule 3a-1 under the Act and found that the notes were not cash items because the notes involved investment intent (i.e., higher return and attendant risk).

Since Presto met the 40% trigger in section 3(a)(1)(C), it is an investment company unless an exception to the definition applies to it. Presto attempted to rely on the section 3(b)(1) exception. The Court found the term "primarily" in the statute unhelpful to Presto. A significant amount of its assets was invested in securities.

Then the Court turned to the holding in the *Tonopah* case, in which the SEC provided a list of factors to determine whether a company that sells its operating assets and chooses not to distribute the proceeds is an "inadvertent investment company."

The *Tonopah* factors are: "the company's history, the way the company represents itself to the investing public today, the activities of its officers and directors, the nature of its assets, and the sources of its income." Applying

1. *SEC v. National Presto Industries, Inc.,* 486 F.3d 405 (7th Cir. 2007).

these factors, the Court found that all but the nature of the assets favor Presto.

First, the company's history is that of an operating enterprise, even though it has changed from being a manufacturer to acting as a seller of products made by others.

Second, the company represents itself to the investing public as an operating company, according to its website, annual reports, and "publicity," and the price of its stock depends on its operating income rather than its investment income.

Third, the officers/directors factor favors Presto as most of their activity is managing Presto's operating company activities rather than managing its investment portfolios.

Fourth, the net asset test favors the SEC, because over 60% of net assets are investment securities. However, the Court rejected an argument that this factor should be the principal factor to determine the company's status A firm (such as Presto) could have high earnings and low book-value assets. In addition, if it were the most important consideration, the section 3(b)(1) exemption would in effect have no meaning except to restate the 40% test in section 3(a)(1)(C) as 50%.

Fifth, the last factor, source of income, favors Presto. Over 90% of gross income, and currently at least 60% of net income, is from operating activities.

Therefore, the Court held that the firm was not an investment company.

---

## Discussion Topics

a. What was the problem in this case? Did the SEC and the management of the corporation deal with the issues correctly and rationally?

b. How did the lawyers in this case approach the issue? Would you have approached it differently? Why did the SEC lawyers insist on an exemption of the corporation?

c. Did the judge deal with this issue correctly? What do you think is the judge's philosophy concerning the regulators and the substance of regulatory Act?

d. How did the Court interpret section 3(a)(1)(C)? What element of section 3(a)(1)(c) did the court pay attention to? How did the Court reach the decision under section 3(b)?

e. Attitudes apart, was the decision correct? What should the SEC do or suggest that Congress should do in the future?

---

## Problem

Assume you are an associate at a large law firm. You are staffed on XYZ Company's initial public offering and your firm is issuer's counsel (i.e., you are representing XYZ Company). XYZ Company is a holding company that, through its subsidiaries, is engaged in the business of manufacturing and marketing guns and butter. In every IPO, issuer's counsel must deliver an opinion to the underwriters opining, among other things, that after the issuance of the company's securities the company will not be an investment company, as defined in the Investment Company Act. You have been tasked with completing the diligence necessary for your firm to render this opinion and completing the relevant analysis under the Investment Company Act. Please draft (1) a due diligence questionnaire for XYZ Company's CFO designed to elicit the factual information you need as part of your analysis, (2) a document request list seeking those documents you believe you need to review as part of your analysis and (3) a certificate to be executed by XYZ Company's CFO that will serve as your firm's backup that XYZ Company does not fall within the definition of "investment company" under the Investment Company Act.

# Chapter 4

## *Companies Excluded from the Definition of an Investment Company and from the Investment Company Act*

### A. Introduction

Section 3(a) of the 1940 Act is very broad. It includes operating companies as well as many financial intermediaries, such as banks, insurance companies, pension funds, and mortgage bankers. All these entities issue their own obligations and invest the proceeds in the obligations of others, and these obligations usually include securities. Yet, these institutions operate and are regulated differently. Hence, section 3(c) of the Act excepts such companies from the definition of an investment company under the Act.

One exclusion from the definition of an investment company applies to holding companies. These are companies that hold all or most of the securities issued by other companies, and issue their own securities to the public. The assumption is that if the holding company holds and controls operating companies it is not an investment company. Thus, section 3(a)(1)(C) excludes from the definition of an investment company those companies that hold a certain percentage of their assets in securities of other companies. Section 3(b) provides an additional exclusion to holding companies of operating companies that might fall under the definition of an investment company notwithstanding. The 1940 Act definition could apply to holding companies, that is, companies that issue securities to the public and invest in securities of subsidiaries through which they operate a business. Yet, Congress did not intend the 1940 Act to apply to all of these institutions and companies. Hence, section 3(b) of the Act contains an exception from the definition of an investment company. Specific exclusions apply also to institutions that are subject to alternative regulation, that is, banks, savings and loan associations, insurance companies (section 3(c)(3)), pension funds (section 3(c)(11)), brokers (section 3(c)(2)) and bank holding companies (section 3(c)(6)).

Further exclusions apply to investment companies that seem to be sufficiently controlled by their investors, such as "private investment companies" with a limited number of investors (section 3(c)(1)), and companies whose investors are sophisticated (section 3(c)(7)), or charitable organizations whose investors are strongly motivated to donate rather than to invest for their own benefit (section 3(c)(10)). Finally, there are exclusions for institutions that were not an important part of the financial system when the Investment Company Act was enacted, such as mortgage bankers and industrial banks (sections 3(c)(4), 3(c)(5)), and oil and gas financing arrangements (section 3(c)(9)). This Chapter focuses on the main exceptions to the definition of an investment company.

## B. Exceptions for Operating Companies

### 1. Section 3(b)

Operating companies (OCs) present a clear contrast to investment companies. Generally, OCs focus on appreciation and income from their operations or the operations of their subsidiaries while investment companies focus on the appreciation and income from their securities portfolios. The directors and officers of an OC are responsible for the business of the enterprises or that of the subsidiaries; the directors and officers of an investment company are responsible for the management of the securities portfolios of the company. We briefly touched on the exceptions for OCs in the previous chapter, and the following discusses these exceptions in more depth.

As noted in the previous chapter, section 3(b) provides:

> Notwithstanding paragraph (1)(C) of subsection (a), none of the following persons is an investment company within the meaning of this title:
>
> (1) Any issuer primarily engaged, directly or through a wholly-owned subsidiary or subsidiaries, in a business or businesses other than that of investing, reinvesting, owning, holding, or trading in securities.
>
> (2) Any issuer which the Commission, upon application by such issuer, finds and by order declares to be primarily engaged in a business or businesses other than that of investing, reinvesting, owning, holding, or trading in securities either directly or (A) through majority-owned subsidiaries or (B) through controlled companies conducting similar types of businesses. The filing of an application under this paragraph in good faith by an issuer other than a registered investment company shall exempt the applicant for a period of sixty days from all provisions of this title applicable to investment companies as such. For cause shown, the Commission by order may extend such period of exemption for an additional period or periods. Whenever the Commission, upon its own motion or upon application, finds that the circumstances which gave rise to the issuance of an order granting an application under this paragraph no longer exist, the Commission shall by order revoke such order.
>
> (3) Any issuer all the outstanding securities of which (other than short-term paper and directors' qualifying shares) are directly or indirectly owned by a company excepted from the definition of investment company by paragraph (1) or (2) of this subsection.[1]

1. Investment Company Act, Section 3(b), 15 U.S.C. § 80a-3(b).

## a. Operating Companies that Have Financial Assets

One type of operating company that is excepted from the definition of an investment company is the holding company that operates a non-investment business through subsidiaries. The status of such a company became less clear with the trend of holding companies to diversify, and sell and purchase companies more often than in the past. Also, holding companies often enter into joint ventures and acquire less than 100% of the venture's shares. If such companies engage in acquiring portfolio companies for the purpose of selling the shares of these portfolio companies, and if the companies' public investors expect their profits from these sales, then these companies resemble an investment company. The legislative history of the 1940 Act suggests that such companies, called "special situation" companies, were to be included in the definition of an investment company under Section 3(a)(1)(A). The SEC reiterated that special situation companies are deemed investment companies for purposes of the Investment Company Act.

The following materials outline the criteria that the SEC has been applying to distinguish operating companies from investment companies. *ICOS Corporation*[1] points to the changes that have occurred in the technological and business environment. The *ICOS* release refers to *Tonopah Mining Co. of Nevada,* which set forth a five-factor analysis for determining an issuer's primary business, and an adjustment that the SEC made in this case in order to recognize the unique situation presented by research and development companies. In addition, the SEC passed Rules 3a-1[2] and 3a-8 excepting from the Investment Company Act certain companies (Rule 3a-8 in particular addressing certain types of research and development companies) that have more than 40 percent of their assets invested in investment securities.

ICOS is a biotechnology company that raises capital through stock offerings to fund drug research and development and invests it in short-term government and commercial debt instruments. ICOS sought an exemptive order under section 3(b)(2).

Applying *Tonopah,* discussed in the previous chapter, the SEC used *five* factors to determine ICOS' primary business: (1) "the company's historical development;" (2) "its public representations of policy;" (3) "the activities of its officers and directors;" (4) "the nature of its present assets," and (5) "the source of its present income," and "accorded the fourth and fifth factors the most weight."

The SEC stated, "Under a strict application of the *Tonopah* analysis, an issuer generally is deemed to be engaged primarily in the business of investing in securities if most of its assets are securities and most of its income is derived from such securities."

Under this strict analysis, ICOS would be deemed to be engaged primarily in investing in securities. However, the focus on present income and assets may not be appropriate to research and development companies. First,

---

1. ICOS Corp., Investment Company Act Rel. No. 19334 (Mar. 16, 1993).
2. Rule 3a-1 was adopted in 1981. *See* Certain Prima Facie Investment Companies, Investment Company Act Rel. No. 11551 (Jan. 14, 1981).

they need capital to fund development of products that do not currently produce income. They must raise capital when it is feasible and invest it in liquid assets. Second, they use their capital for "intellectual capital," i.e., retention of professionals, which does not appear on balance sheets.

Therefore, for bona fide research and development companies, the SEC adopted three new factors instead of the present income and assets factors: (1) reduction of principal, (2) nature of expenses, and (3) preservation of capital.

Under the reduction of principal test, the SEC considers whether a company uses securities and cash to finance research and development, i.e., if its research and development expenses exceed its gross investment income.

Under the nature of expenses test, the SEC considers whether a substantial portion of its expenses are research and development expenses, and whether its gross investment expenses are de minimis.

Under the preservation of capital test, the SEC considers whether the investment in securities is consistent with preservation of assets to finance operations, i.e., whether substantially all its securities have limited credit risk, as opposed to investments in equity or speculative debt.

If these new requirements are met, the remaining historical factors (historical development, public representations of policy, activities of officers and directors) are also examined.

Pursuant to this analysis, the SEC granted an exemptive order to ICOS.

---

<u>Discussion Topics</u>

a. How was ICOS similar to an investment company? How was it different?

b. Why was the test articulated in *Tonopah* unsuitable for research and development companies? How did the SEC refine the *Tonopah* analysis with respect to such companies? What potential abuse may result from the SEC's refinement?

c. If ICOS fell under section 3(a)(1)(A), could it take advantage of section 3(b)(2)? Why not?

d. Was the SEC's action in excepting ICOS from the Act a proper exercise of agency authority? Is this the type of determination that should be made by Congress?

---

### b. Case Study: The Yahoo Case

In *Yahoo! Inc.*[1] Yahoo!, a "global internet new media company," applied for an exemption under section 3(b)(2) and a temporary order pursuant to the subsection. Yahoo! argued that the forty percent test of section 3(a)(1)(C), which has been interpreted to exclude intangible assets, underestimated

1. *In the Matter of Yahoo! Inc.* (no release no. in original) (Feb. 11, 2000).

the firm's non-investment company assets as Yahoo!, like other technology firms, had a relatively high concentration of intangible assets. Second, Yahoo! argued that it must hold "Cash Management Investments" because it needs sufficient cash to compete in the industry, and "Strategic Investments" in firms that complement or enhance its business. In addition, much of the value of its assets was attributable to wholly- and majority-owned subsidiaries and controlled companies. One of Yahoo!'s interests was not a majority-interest and could be considered an "investment security" even though Yahoo! controlled its operations. The firm's operating income as its advertising revenue fluctuates and it incurs "substantial non-recurring costs in connection with its numerous acquisitions." Yahoo! noted that the SEC has allowed applicants to substitute a revenue test for the income test, and that investment income has been "a small portion of its gross revenues."

The SEC granted a temporary order[1] and later granted an exemption.[2]

The exemption was granted on the conditions that Yahoo! use "its accumulated cash and Cash Management Investments for bona fide business purposes" and not invest or trade in these investments for "short-term speculative purposes."[3]

c. **Case Study:** *Daxor*[4]

In a case that is facially similar to that of *Yahoo!,* the Commission reached a different conclusion. After issuing a cease and desist order pursuant to section 9(f) of the Investment Company Act, the Commission concluded as follows.

*Daxor* was founded to engage in biotechnology services, but in recent years had focused on the developing, and marketing, of a new medical device. In finding Daxor to be an investment company, the SEC noted that Daxtor's assets consisted almost entirely investment securities, which generated almost all the company's income. This income was also far more than its research and development expenses.

In addition, the company's investment policy and strategy put its capital at risk. Its investment portfolio, managed by the CEO, was invested entirely in equity securities and was actively traded. The percentage of net investment income derived from the sale of securities and options transactions as compared to dividend income had increased, and the investment policy had been modified to allow more speculative investments. Portfolio turnover was responsible for much of the company's cash flow, and the company financed its investment activity through borrowing.

The SEC also noted that *Daxor* raised capital for development of the device yet did not finance the development by liquidating marketable securities; besides the device has not been commercially successful.

1. Yahoo! Inc., Investment Company Act Rel. No. 24377 (Apr. 5, 2000).
2. Yahoo! Inc., Investment Company Act Rel. No. 24459 (May 18, 2000) (application), Yahoo! Inc., Investment Company Act Rel. No. 24494 (Jun. 13, 2000) (exemption).
3. Yahoo! Inc., Investment Company Act Rel. No. 24494 (Jun. 13, 2000).
4. In the Matter of Daxor Corp., Investment Company Act Rel. No. 29417 (Sept. 17, 2010) (footnotes omitted).

## 2. SEC rules

The SEC has passed rules to codify exemptive positions it had taken in approving section 3(b)(2) applications. One example is the following statement, made in connection with the proposal (and later adoption) of Rule 3a-1 under the Investment Company Act, which applies generally to companies that may fail the statutory 40% test in Section 3(a)(1)(C).[1]

> Although Congress and the Commission in 1940 believed that section [3(a)(1)(C)] would effectively exclude most ordinary holding and industrial companies from the Act's prohibitions and regulatory provisions, section 3(b) (1) . . . and section 3(b)(2) were added to further ensure their exclusion. Section 3(b)(1) of the Act provides, generally, that any issuer which is primarily engaged, either directly or through wholly-owned subsidiaries, in a business other than that of investing, reinvesting, owning, holding or trading in securities is excluded from the definition of the term "investment company," although that issuer otherwise would be an investment company as defined in section 3(a)(1)(C) of the Act. Section 3(b)(2) of the Act provides, generally, that any issuer which the Commission finds, and by order declares to be, primarily engaged — directly, or through majority-owned subsidiaries, or through controlled companies conducting similar types of businesses, — in a business other than that of investing, reinvesting, owning, holding or trading in securities is excluded from the Act, although the issuer otherwise would be an investment company as defined in section 3(a)(1)(C) of the Act.
>
> It should be noted that certain operational differences exist between section 3(b)(1) and section 3(b)(2). Section 3(b)(1) is self-operating, while section 3(b) (2) requires a Commission order. Additionally, section 3(b)(1) applies only to companies operating either directly or through wholly-owned subsidiaries, while section 3(b)(2) applies additionally to companies operating through majority-owned subsidiaries and certain controlled companies. These differences ensure that "special situation investment companies" are not excluded from the Act's definition of investment company. Special situation investment companies are companies which secure control of other companies primarily for the purpose of making a profit in the sale of the controlled company's securities. Accordingly, they are considered to be investment companies for purposes of the Act.
>
> Critical to a determination of whether a company is excluded from the definition of investment company by section 3(b)(1) or 3(b)(2) is whether the company is "primarily engaged" in a non-investment company business. The determination of a company's primary engagement is a factual issue concerning the nature of its

1. Certain Prima Facie Investment Companies, Investment Company Act Rel. No. 10937 (Nov. 13, 1979) (footnotes omitted). The Rule was adopted in January 1981. *See* Certain Prima Facie Investment Companies, Investment Company Act Rel. No. 11551 (Jan. 14, 1981), 46 Fed. Reg. 6879 (Jan. 22, 1981) (current version at 17 C.F.R. § 270.3a-1 (2015)).

business. Relevant criteria for resolving this issue are: (1) the company's historical development, (2) its public representation of policy, (3) the activity of its officers and directors, (4) the nature of its present assets, and (5) the sources of its present income. Of these factors, most significant are the character of a company's assets (as evidenced by the percentage of the company's assets invested in investment securities), and the sources of the company's present income (as evidenced by the percentage of the company's income derived from investment securities.) In such an analysis, securities of controlled companies through which a holding company engages in a business other than an investment company business effectively are not considered to be investment securities.

Since determining a company's primary engagement involves considering many factors, no specific guidelines can be established for concluding in all conceivable circumstances whether a company is an investment company. As a general rule, however, if a company has no more than 45 percent of its assets invested in — and derives no more that 45 percent of its income from — investment securities, it is primarily engaged in a business other than being an investment company. Accordingly, it would not appear necessary or appropriate in the public interest for the Commission to regulate such a company under the Act.

II. Discussion

The Commission proposes to adopt rule 3a-1 under the Act which, under specified circumstances, would exclude certain prima facie investment companies from regulation under the Act. The proposed rule is not intended to exclude from the Act all companies which could qualify upon application to the Commission for receipt of an order pursuant to section 3(b)(2) of the Act. Rather, it would exclude only those companies whose asset composition and sources of income would provide conclusive evidence that such companies are not investment companies for purposes of section 3(a)(3) [sic] [of] the Act. In such circumstances, there would be no need for the Commission to conduct a formal inquiry into other facts and circumstances which may more fully characterize a particular company's business. However, companies which do not meet the proposed rule's standards nonetheless may be found, pursuant to the application process, not to be investment companies upon the Commission's determining that the attendant facts and circumstances warrant such a finding.

The proposed rule would apply to companies which are investment companies solely by virtue of the definition stated in section 3(a)(3) [sic] of the Act, only for that period during which they comply with the rule's standards. Companies meeting the statutory definition of the term "investment company" set forth in sections 3(a)(1) or 3(a)(2) of the Act as well as special situation investment companies would not be excluded from the Act's definition of "investment company" by the rule.

> The exemptive relief which would be provided by proposed rule 3a-1 would be conditioned on the company's having no more than 45 percent of the value (as defined in section 2(a)(41)(A) of the Act) of its total assets (exclusive of Government securities and cash items) consisting of, and receiving no more than 45 percent of its net income after taxes from, securities other than: (1) Government securities; (2) securities issued by employees' securities companies; (3) securities issued by majority-owned subsidiaries of the issuer (other than subsidiaries relying on the exclusion from the definition of investment company in section 3(b)(3) of the Act [15 U.S.C. 80a-3(b)(3)]) which are not investment companies; and (4) securities issued by certain controlled companies through which an issuer engages in a non-investment company business.
>
> These asset and income percentages are to be determined on an unconsolidated basis, except that the issuer shall consolidate its financial statements with any wholly-owned subsidiaries. . . .

In June 2003, the SEC adopted rule 3a-8, which updates and codifies the terms of the *ICOS* order. The SEC stated that the rule provides a nonexclusive safe harbor and that companies could still use the factors in the *ICOS* order.[1]

The rule provides an exemption for a company that meets the following requirements:

> (1) Its research and development expenses for the last four fiscal quarters combined are a "substantial percentage" of its total expense. . . .
>
> (2) Its net income derived from "investments in securities" for the last four fiscal quarters combined does not exceed twice its research and development expenses. . . .
>
> (3) Its expenses for investment advisory and management activities, investment research and custody, for the last four fiscal quarters combined, do not exceed five percent of its total expenses. . . .
>
> (4) Its investments in securities are "capital preservation investments," except that: (i) no more than 10 percent of its total assets may consist of other investments, or . . . 25 percent provided that at least 75 percent of these other investments are "investments made pursuant to a collaborative research and development arrangement";
>
> (5) It does not hold itself out as being engaged in the business of investing, reinvesting, or trading in securities, and is not a special situation investment company;
>
> (6) It is primarily engaged (directly or through subsidiaries or companies it controls primarily) in a business or businesses other

1. Certain Research and Development Companies, Investment Company Act Rel. No. 25835 (Nov. 26, 2002); Certain Research and Development Companies, Investment Company Act Rel. No. 26077 (Jun. 16, 2003) (current version at 17 C.F.R. § 270.3a-8 (2015)).

than investing, reinvesting, owning, holding, or trading in securities, as evidenced by (i) the activities of its officers, directors, and employees . . . (iii) its historical development, and (iv) an appropriate resolution of its board of directors (or person(s) performing similar functions), which resolution or action has been appropriately recorded . . . and

(7) Its board of directors (or person(s) performing similar functions) has adopted a written investment policy with respect to its capital preservation investments.[1]

Rule 3a-2 excludes certain "transient investment companies" from regulation under the Act for up to one year. The SEC recognized that an issuer may be considered an investment company under the Act "as a result of an unusual business occurrence," including:

(1) a "start-up" company's investing its offering proceeds in securities while arranging to purchase operating assets;

(2) a company's selling a large operating division and investing the proceeds in securities pending acquisition of additional operating assets; and

(3) a company's making a tender offer to stockholders of a non-investment company, and failing to obtain a majority of the target company's stock.[2]

The issuer must "ha[ve] a bona fide intent . . . to be engaged primarily, by the termination of such period of time, in a business other than that of investing, reinvesting, owning, holding or trading in securities."[3]

The intent must be evidenced by the issuer's business activities and an appropriate resolution of the board of directors (or other appropriate person or persons) and recorded contemporaneously in its minutes or comparable documents. The one-year period begins on the earlier of (1) the date the issuer owns securities and/or cash valued at over 50 percent of the value of its total assets on a consolidated or unconsolidated basis or (2) the date it owns or proposes to acquire investment securities (defined under the Act) valued at over 40 percent of its total assets (excluding Government securities and cash items) on an unconsolidated basis. An issuer may rely on the rule only once in a three-year period.

Section 3(b)(3) excepts from the definition of investment company in section 3(a)(1)(C) "[a]ny issuer all the outstanding securities of which (other than short-term paper and directors' qualifying shares) are directly or indirectly owned by a company excepted from the definition of investment company by [section 3(b)(1) or 3(b)(2)]." Rule 3a-3 exempts from regulation under the Act certain investment companies owned by companies other

1. Rules and Regulations Promulgated under the Investment Company Act, Rule 3a-8, 17 C.F.R. § 270.3a-8 (2015).

2. Transient Investment Companies, Investment Company Act Rel. No. 10943 (Nov. 16, 1979) (footnotes omitted). The Rule was adopted in 1981. *See* Transient Investment Companies, Investment Company Act Rel. No. 11552 (Jan. 14, 1981), 46 Fed. Reg. 6882 (Jan. 22, 1981) (current version at 17 C.F.R. § 270.3a-2 (2015)).

3. Rules and Regulations Promulgated under the Investment Company Act, Rule 3a-2, 17 C.F.R. § 270.3a-2 (2015).

than investment companies. The Rule was adopted to exempt a subsidiary that is a small business investment company that would not qualify under section 3(b)(3) because it issued debt obligations to the Small Business Administration.[1]

---

**Discussion Topics**

a. What was the SEC's rationale for promulgating exemptive rule 3a-1? What were the elements that the SEC considered essential to determining whether an investment company exists?

b. Given the background presented so far with respect to sections 3(a) and 3(b), consider the following: Years ago, the du Pont family members determined to keep control over E.I. du Pont de Nemours and Company (the "Du Pont Company"). The family also wished to enable its members to liquidate their holding without at the same time reducing the family's control over the Du Pont Company. This was achieved by establishing Christiana Securities Company. A controlling block of Du Pont stock was transferred to Christiana and a substantial block of the stock of Christiana was issued to the family members. The stock representing a minority of Christiana was sold to the public and traded on the New York Stock Exchange. Christiana merely held the Du Pont stock and distributed the income from the stock to its shareholders. Christiana neither bought nor sold other securities. Was Christiana an investment company? If so, how would you classify it? Should it be an investment company?

---

## C. Venture Capital Companies and Business Development Companies: Sections 2(a)(48), and 54 through 63

Venture capital companies help start up new, often small, businesses. Many such businesses fail because their owners, who could be very creative in inventing their products, have little experience in managing their companies or marketing the products. Therefore, venture capital companies offer not only financing but also assistance in management and marketing. Often these venture capital companies take over the control of these small companies to ensure that they are operated on a sound business basis that minimizes risk. Although many ventures may fail, successful ventures eventually distribute their shares to the public at a far higher price than the price at which the shares were initially sold to the venture capital company and the other promoters. In addition, venture capital companies obtain options and warrants to acquire a substantial number of shares of the companies that they finance at low prices — their value at time of issuance. When these companies make a public offering, the venture capitalists receive the difference between the price of the shares at issuance and the public offering price.

1. Certain Investment Companies Owned by Companies Which Are Not Investment Companies, Investment Company Act Rel. No. 11553 (Jan. 14, 1981), 46 Fed. Reg. 6884 (Jan. 22, 1981) (current version at 17 C.F.R. § 270.3a-3 (2015)).

## C. Venture Capital Companies

Because the mode of operation of venture capital companies cannot meet the limitations of the 1940 Act (for example, the issuance of options and warrants and dealings with their controlled companies, and especially dealings by affiliated persons with the controlled companies), and because of the difficulties in determining that such companies fall with section 3(b), most such venture capital companies rely on some exclusion from the definition of an investment company under the Act, such as the exclusions in sections 3(c)(1) and 3(c)(7) (which we examine below), offering their securities in private placements to sophisticated investors, rather than in public offerings.

Also of note, in 1980 Congress provided "business development companies" (defined in section 2(a)(48) of the Act) tailor-made exemptions from the strictures of the 1940 Act in sections 54 through 63 of the 1940 Act. From the industry's point of view, the business development company exemptions did not go far enough. Congress, however, was concerned that further expansion of the exemptions would expose public investors to risks of unacceptable conflict of interest transactions. Thus, notwithstanding these exemptions, only a few publicly held business development companies were established initially, though in recent years many publicly held business development companies have been established as a means of offering private equity-style investing in a publicly-offered investment product. In 2013 Congress proposed legislation that would relax the restrictions on business development companies.[1] However, the Congressional Budget Office estimated that the legislation would reduce revenues by shifting income from taxable C corporations.[2] As of May 2014 it appeared that the legislation would be delayed or would not pass.[3] However, in November 2015, the House Financial Services Committee passed similar legislation, and full House and Senate votes may continue the process into 2016.[4]

---

### Discussion Topics

a. What distinguishes a special situation company from (i) an investment company or (ii) a holding company that falls within section 3(b) of the 1940 Act?

b. In *Entrepreneurial Assistance Group, Inc.*,[5] the SEC no action letter states that "[i]f EAG intends to control companies for the purpose of increasing the value of their securities for profitable resale at some future date, its

---

1. Small Business Credit Availability Act, H.R. 1800, 113th Cong. (2013).
2. Cong. Budget Ofc., Cost Estimate: H.R. 1800, Small Business Credit Availability Act (rev. Jun. 30, 2014), *available at* http://www.cbo.gov/sites/default/files/cbofiles/attachments/hr1800revised.pdf.
3. *Fitch: Unfavorable Tax Estimate May Halt BDC Leverage Limit Rise*, Business Wire, May 7, 2014, LEXIS, News Library, Curnws File.
4. Lynn Adler, BDCs Step Closer to New Legislation, More Leverage, REUTERS, Nov. 19, 2015, *available at http://www.reuters.com/article/2015/11/19/us-bdc-legislation-idUSKCN0T82DW20151119?feedType=RSS&feedName=PersonalFinance#eA4tp2q9FzMOjmMQ.97*; Small Business Credit Availability Act, H.R. 3868, 114th Cong. (2015).
5. Entrepreneurial Assistance Group, Inc., Corres. (Jun. 16, 1973).

primary business could be found to be investing in securities. . . ." Is the SEC position reasonable? Aren't all acquisitions of securities by operating companies done with a view to profitable resale?

c. How would you advise an operating company client that planned to borrow substantial amounts of cash in order to attempt to take over of a number of other companies? Would the type of business in which the client operating company engages matter? Would it matter how much money the client planned to borrow? What other factors would you consider?

d. What steps would you take as counsel in making sure that your client, a company seeking to take over another company, is not deemed an investment company? How would you distinguish such a company from a company that is buying securities of other companies in order to extract greenmail or to sell the securities on the market when market prices rose in anticipation of a takeover?

e. Warren Buffett, one of the most successful investors in this country, and one of the world's richest, is the controlling shareholder of Berkshire Hathaway.[1] Berkshire Hathaway is a former textile company that Buffett purchased in 1962. Although the mills were no great success, shutting down in 1985, they provided enough capital for Buffett to purchase two insurance companies in 1967. The insurance companies flourished under a philosophy of indifference to the volume of insurance that they had as long as the price made sense. Thus, when the insurance business became extremely competitive, and prices fell, Buffett supported management's policy to limit the insurance underwriting, and even cease issuing policies when prices were too low.

More importantly, however, the insurance companies provided excellent investment vehicles. Buffett was one of the first investors to take advantage of the "float" (the cash funds of the premiums that are not immediately needed to pay claims).[2] These funds are invested by insurance companies to cover future insurance costs and to generate profits. Buffett, in contrast to the insurance industry at the time, invested these funds aggressively. Berkshire now owns several insurance companies, and companies in other industries including candy, furniture, manufacturing, and a newspaper.

Berkshire Hathaway purchases controlling blocks of shares, usually around 80 to 90 percent, in companies that have an earnings potential. Buffett's intention is not to sell the shares when their price rises but to profit from the companies' operation. In this sense, Berkshire resembles a holding company. In contrast to a holding company, however, Berkshire does not manage the portfolio companies. In fact, Buffett often stipulates in the purchase agreement that current management will continue to operate the company. When Berkshire contemplates buying a company, its management is considered as an asset or a liability. If a company's management is a liability, Berkshire will not buy the company. Buffett's philosophy is that if

1. Robert G. Hagstrom, Jr., The Warren Buffett Way: Investment Strategies of the World's Greatest Investor (1994); Roger Lowenstein, Buffett: The Making of an American Capitalist (1995).
2. Roger Lowenstein, Buffett: The Making of an American Capitalist 135 (1995).

he does not like the way a business is run, there is no reason to buy it. In this regard, Berkshire resembles an investment company.

The question then is: which of Berkshire's features should be given greater weight? If Berkshire's philosophy of retaining the shares of its controlled companies, regardless of rising share prices and profiting from operations, is paramount, then Berkshire should be deemed a holding company. If, however, Berkshire's unwillingness to manage the companies in which it holds a controlling position is paramount, then perhaps it is an investment company.

Arguably, Berkshire manages its controlled companies by allowing the existing management free rein. Berkshire buys companies that either do well or have the potential to do well. If a holding company buys a company that is doing well, it is reasonable for the holding company to leave well enough alone, and not change management. It should not be assumed that Berkshire (Buffett, for all practical purposes) would remain passive if the management of one of the controlled companies showed incompetence, or engaged in objectionable activities. Therefore, arguably, Berkshire is managing its controlled companies in a "hands-off" management style. In addition, it can be argued that Berkshire manages the companies directly. When Berkshire buys a company, it considers management as an asset, although management is not bought literally. Therefore, Berkshire, in a sense, acquires the management. Arguably, there should be no difference between Berkshire replacing the existing management with one it acquired separately, and using the management of the acquired corporation.

Is Warren Buffett's Berkshire Hathaway an investment company? Should the SEC regulate Berkshire Hathaway? What theory could the SEC use to do so?

---

## D. Private Investment Companies

### 1. Section 3(c)(1)

Section 3(c)(1) was designed to exclude from the definition of an investment company "private investment companies." These are companies whose outstanding securities (other than short-term commercial paper) are beneficially owned by not more than 100 persons, and which do not make or presently propose to make a public offering of their securities. The main rationale for the section is that 100 or fewer investors could have access to, and could exert control over, the investment manager. Thus, self-help in this case is adequate to protect investors from the dangers that the Act was designed to prevent.

Initially, private investment companies covered by section 3(c)(1) were mainly investment clubs, and these are still proliferating in this country. In addition, promoters may use section 3(c)(1) to offer hedge funds and "offshore" funds, which use investment techniques and financial structures that are impermissible under the 1940 Act.

To prevent circumventing the 100 beneficial owners limit, section 3(c)(1)(A) provides an attribution rule. The existing attribution rule provides that if an entity which is, or but for the exception provided by section 3(c)(1) or section 3(c)(7) (discussed below) would be, an investment company owns 10% or more of the voting securities of a section 3(c)(1) fund, the number of this entity's shareholders will be attributed to the number of section 3(c)(1) fund shareholders. Otherwise, beneficial ownership by an entity is deemed to be beneficial ownership of the 3(c)(1) company by one person. This attribution rule raises complex issues, such as the meaning of "voting securities" defined in section 2(a)(42) of the Act. Additionally, a section 3(c)(1) company cannot be making or propose to make a public offering of its securities.

---

## Discussion Topics

a. Suppose a company that has 500 shareholders holds half of the debt securities of a Fund. Suppose Fund seeks to rely on section 3(c)(1). Does the company holding the debt securities count as one shareholder or would its shareholders be counted as shareholders of the Fund? What would the rationale be for viewing such a large holding as voting securities, even if the debt securities do not entitle the holders to voting rights?

b. Should a company with 98 security holders be permitted to register under the Act to take advantage of the tax treatment offered to "regulated investment companies" under the Internal Revenue Code? In other words, is reliance on section 3(c)(1) mandatory? Should it be?

c. Suppose your client sponsored a section 3(c)(1) company, Best of All Worlds, and discovered that 180 investors are interested in buying the shares. May the client establish another section 3(c)(1) company, Best of All Worlds II? See Reg. D under the Securities Act of 1933, 17 C.F.R. §§ 230.501-508 (2015), especially section 502(a) of Reg. D, and the list of factors regarding integration of offerings. Note also that the SEC staff has addressed the unique issues posed by integration of section 3(c)(1) company offerings in various no action letters, and other factors the SEC staff looks at in determining whether to integrate section 3(c)(1) company offerings include (1) whether the entities share the same investment objectives, investment portfolios and portfolio risk/return characteristics, and (2) whether two funds are intended for distinct groups of investors. The SEC staff has stated that it will generally require integration if a reasonable purchaser qualified to invest in both offerings would view an interest in one offering as not materially different from another. Moreover, the SEC staff has also taken the position that, although spacing offerings more than 6 months apart may provide a safe harbor under Regulation D for Securities Act purposes, it would not necessarily preclude integration under section 3(c)(1) of the 1940 Act.

d. As a matter of policy, how stringent should the provisions be in section 3(c)(1) against making a public offering? May the sponsor of a 3(c)(1) company advertise the existence of such a company on the Internet? May a publishing company offer a directory of 3(c)(1) companies on the Internet? Consider the application of the JOBS Act and Rule 506(c) under Securities Act Regulation D, which remove the prohibition on general solicitation and general advertising when conducting private offerings. We discuss these issues later in this section.

---

## 2. Section 3(c)(7)

In the National Securities Markets Improvement Act of 1996, Congress enacted section 3(c)(7), which created a new type of a private fund that is excluded from the definition of an investment company. This fund may have an unlimited number of investors, provided these investors meet certain financial tests. Section 3(c)(7) reads as follows:[1]

> (c) Notwithstanding subsection (a) none of the following persons is an investment company within the meaning of this title: . . . (7)(A) Any issuer, all the outstanding securities of which . . . are owned exclusively by persons who, at the time of acquisition of such securities, are qualified purchasers, and which is not making and does not at that time propose to make a public offering of such securities. Securities that are owned by persons who received the securities for a qualified purchaser such as gift or bequest, or in a case in which the transfer was caused by legal separation, divorce, death, or other involuntary event shall be deemed to be owned by a qualified purchaser, subject to such rules, regulations, and orders as the Commission may prescribe as necessary or appropriate in the public interest or for the protection of investors. . . .
>
> (D) An issuer that is excepted under this paragraph shall nonetheless be deemed to be an investment company for the purposes of the limitations set forth in subparagraphs (A)(i) and (B)(i) of section 12(d)(1) relating to the purchase or other acquisition by such issuer of any security issued by any registered investment company and the sale of any security issued by any registered open-end investment company to any such issuer.
>
> (E) For purposes of determining compliance with this paragraph and paragraph [3(c)](1), an issuer that is otherwise excepted under this paragraph and an issuer that is otherwise excepted under paragraph [3(c)](1) shall not be treated by the Commission as being a single issuer for purposes of determining whether the outstanding securities of the issuer excepted under paragraph [3(c)](1) are beneficially owned by not more than 100 persons or whether the outstanding securities of the issuer excepted under this paragraph are owned by persons that are not qualified purchasers. Nothing in this subparagraph shall be construed to establish that a person is a bona fide qualified purchaser for the purposes of this paragraph or bona fide beneficial owner for the purposes of paragraph [3(c)](1).

The amendments also add section 2(a)(51) that defines "qualified purchaser."

> (A) 'Qualified purchaser' means –

---

1. Investment Company Act, Section 3(c)(7), 15 U.S.C. § 80a-3(c)(7).

(i) any natural person . . . who owns not less than $5,000,000 in investments, as defined by the Commission;

(ii) any company that owns not less than $5,000,000 in investments and that is owned directly or indirectly by or for 2 or more natural persons who are related as siblings or spouses (including former spouse), or direct lineal descendants by birth or adoption, spouses of such persons, the estates of such persons, or foundations, charitable organizations, or trusts established by or for the benefit of such persons;

(iii) any trust that is not covered by clause (ii) and that was not formed for the specific purpose of acquiring the securities offered, as to which the trustee or other person authorized to make decisions with respect to the trust, and each settlor or other person who has contributed assets to the trust, is a person described in clauses (i), (ii) or (iv); or

(iv) any person, acting for its own account or the account of other qualified purchasers, who in the aggregate owns and invests on a discretionary basis, not less than $25,000,000 in investments.

(B) The Commission may adopt such rules and regulations applicable to the persons and trusts specified in clauses (i) through (iv) . . . as it determines are necessary or appropriate in the public interest or for the protection of investors.[1]

Congress required the SEC to define the term "investments" for purposes of the qualified purchaser definition. In 1997, the SEC noted in a release as follows:[2]

> The 1996 Act added new section 3(c)(7) of the Investment Company Act to create an alternative exclusion for investment companies that sell their securities solely to investors who are "qualified purchasers." As is the case for a Section 3(c)(1) Fund, a Section 3(c)(7) Fund cannot make, or propose to make, a public offering of its securities.[3*]

1. Investment Company Act, Section 2(a)(51) 15 U.S.C. § 80a-2(a)(51).

2. Privately Offered Investment Companies, Investment Company Act Rel. No. 22597 (Apr. 3, 1997).

3*. Section 3(c)(7) of the Act. While the legislative history of the 1996 Act does not explicitly discuss the limitations of section 3(c)(7) on public offerings by Section 3(c)(7) Funds, the limitation appears to reflect Congress's concerns that unsophisticated individuals should not be inadvertently drawn into a Section 3(c)(7) Fund. See The Investment Company Act Amendments of 1995: Hearing on H.R. 1495 before the Subcomm. on Telecommunications and Finance of the Comm. on Commerce, House of Representatives, 104th Cong., 1st Sess. 53 (1995) (hereinafter House Hearings) (testimony of Matthew P. Fink, President, Investment Company Institute, urging that section 3(c)(7) include a public offering limitation). Section 3(c)(1)'s limitation on public offerings has been interpreted to permit "transactions by an issuer not involving any public offering" under section 4(2) of the Securities Act of 1933 ("Securities Act") [15 U.S.C. 77d(2)]. See, e.g., Engelberger

> New section 2(a)(51)(A) of the Investment Company Act defines the term qualified purchaser as (i) any natural person who owns not less than $5 million in investments (as defined by the Commission), (ii) a family-owned company ("Family Company") that owns not less than $5 million in investments, (iii) certain trusts, and (iv) any other person (e.g., an institutional investor) that owns and invests on a discretionary basis not less than $25 million in investments.

The SEC then went on to define "investment" broadly "to include not only securities (other than controlling interests in certain issuers)," but also "real estate, futures contracts, physical commodities, and cash and cash equivalents held for investment purposes . . . and that the nature of the asset should indicate that its holder has the investment experience and sophistication necessary to evaluate the risks of investing in unregulated investment pools."

Both sections 3(c)(1) and section 3(c)(7) require a determination that an entity is not engaged in a public offering. In a no-action letter addressed to Lamp Technologies, Inc.,[1] the staff of the SEC addressed this requirement.

Lamp intended to set up a web site with information about private funds excluded under section 3(c)(1) or 3(c)(7) and privately offered under Regulation D of the Securities Act. The information would include both descriptive information (e.g., offering memoranda) and performance information.

To obtain a password granting access to the website information, a potential investor would have to (i) complete a questionnaire to allow Lamp to determine that the investor is an "accredited investor" under Regulation D, and (ii) pay a subscription fee. A subscriber would also have to agree generally not to invest in a posted fund for 30 days following qualification. These restrictions were designed to ensure that a subscriber does not join to invest in a particular fund.

The SEC has stated that private offering materials in a website without limiting access would not be consistent with the prohibition in Rule 502(c) of Regulation D on general solicitation and general advertising in connection with private offerings. However, in an earlier no-action letter, the staff noted that posting a notice of a private offering on a web site would be permissible with appropriate pre-qualification and password-protection procedures. Therefore, based on the limited access, the posting of private fund information might not be deemed a "public offering."

More recently, the JOBS Act directed the SEC to remove the prohibition on general solicitation in private offerings. "General solicitation" or "general advertising" generally means advertisements, articles, notices or other communications published in any newspaper, magazine, or similar media or broadcast over television or radio, and any seminar or meeting whose attendees have been invited by any general solicitation or general

---

Partnerships (Dec. 7, 1981). The Commission believes that section 3(c)(7)'s public offering limitation should be interpreted in the same manner as the limitation in section 3(c)(1).

1. Lamp Technologies, Inc., SEC No-Action Letter (May 29, 1997).

advertising. "General solicitation" would include, for example, advertising on a publicly accessible website.

The SEC implemented this Congressional directive by revising Rule 506(c) under Securities Act Regulation D, which now operates to remove the prohibition on general solicitation and general advertising when conducting private offerings pursuant to Rule 506 of Regulation D, and imposes various obligations on issuers using general solicitations and general advertising in private offerings. As part of this rulemaking, the SEC expressed its view that the text of the JOBS Act operates to permit 3(c)(1) and 3(c)(7) funds to conduct offerings pursuant to Rule 506 using general solicitation and general advertising, and that such offerings would continue not to be "public offerings" for purposes of the requirements of section 3(c)(1) and 3(c)(7) of the 1940 Act. Issuers retain the ability to conduct private offerings in the traditional manner without general solicitation and general advertising.

One other issue to note is that 3(c)(1) and 3(c)(7) funds often charge performance fees. Section 3(c)(7) funds may charge performance fees as a result of Section 205(b)(4) of the Investment Advisers Act, which exempts advisers' contracts with such funds from the general performance fee prohibition. Section 3(c)(1) funds may charge performance fees only if all of the fund's investors are "qualified clients," which are described in more detail in Chapter 2 and generally include investors with (i) $1 million in assets under management with the adviser or (ii) a net worth of at least $2 million (excluding the value of the investor's primary residence).[1]

### 3. Hedge Funds

Section 3(c)(1) and 3(c)(7) have been extensively used by funds entitled "hedge funds." In 1997, hedge funds offered very high returns to sophisticated investors. Hedge funds flourished. "In the nine years to Dec. 31, 1996, the typical US hedge fund returned a net gain of 18% a year to investors. That performance easily beats the Standard & Poor's 500 index (16.5% a year over the same period) and it leaves the average US equity mutual fund (13.9%) trailing in the dust."[2] Although some funds have crashed, "over the long haul, many funds have posted eye-popping results. The lucky investor who put US$ 100,000 into Soros's Quantum Fund when it was launched in 1969 would be worth US$ 314 million today. Less affluent investors have pressed for an opportunity to invest in these hedge funds."[3] The problem for most would-be investors is the large sums of money required to invest. "Most hedge funds require a minimum investment of US$ 250,000 to US$ 500,000. . . . Still, with stock markets at record highs, now may be the time to take a close look at hedge funds — especially since there are ways around the big up-front investment that most funds require. . . ."[4] However, in 2008, hedge funds performed poorly,

1. Order Approving Adjustment for Inflation of the Dollar Amount Tests in Rule 205-3 Under the Investment Advisers Act of 1940, Investment Advisers Act Rel. No. 3236 (Jul. 12, 2011), 76 Fed. Reg. 41,838 (Jul. 15, 2011) (current version at 17 C.F.R. § 275.205-3(d)(1) (2015)).

2. Andrew Poon, *How the Rich Get Richer,* Canadian Bus., Nov. 14, 1997, at 95.

3. *Id.*

4. *Id.*

having overextended their leverage. Moreover, in 2010, a number of hedge funds have been suspected and sued for trading on insider information. Thus, perhaps not all performance was legitimate.

In 2003, the Chairman of the SEC listed a number of issues that hedge funds have raised. First, they have become numerous (almost 5700) and managed approximately $600 billion as compared to $50 million in 1990. The Chairman noted a number of concerns. First, there were problems with marketing techniques and conflicts of interest. Investors in hedge funds take higher risks in various ways. They commit their money for longer periods because they have no right to redeem their shares nor an available liquid secondary market for their shares. The funds are not required to hold diversified portfolios and are not subject to leverage limits. Generally, they have no board of directors. They charge in addition to a percentage of the assets, a percentage of performance (usually 20%).

Yet, the regulation of hedge funds has not been strict. In addition to exemptions from the Investment Company Act, they enjoyed exemption from some of the regulation of the Securities Act of 1933 because they offer their securities only in private placements. Investors in these funds are presumed to be able to fend for themselves.

In 2003, the SEC noticed that "investment advisers to registered investment companies increasingly are offering hedge fund investments to their clients."[1] They have responded to the demand of investors as well as to the demand of their portfolio managers. Managers who have had a large stake in such hedge funds may have been tempted to favor these funds over registered investment companies. Valuation of the securities may also have posed conflicts of interest because hedge funds were not subject to the rules concerning valuation. Hedge funds may have evaluated their portfolio shares by including their future value rather than their current market value, subject to antifraud provisions. Ultimately, it may have been impossible for an investor to know the actual value of a hedge fund's portfolio securities.

During 2003, the SEC focused on the "retailization" of hedge funds. Such as the establishment of funds that invest in hedge funds. "Registered investment companies that invest all, or substantially all, of their assets in an underlying pool of hedge funds are another means of increased availability of hedge funds to public investors. . . . The Commission's Division of Investment Management has seen a boom in these funds. In the summer of 2002, the first fund of hedge funds became eligible to sell its securities to the public. Subsequently, there have been 17 other funds of hedge funds cleared for the public market. All of these funds currently are subject to fund-specific minimum investment requirements of at least $25,000. But, there is currently no federal requirement for a minimum investment, and it is possible that funds might seek to lower this requirement making these types of funds available to a greater number of investors with even less capital. These possibilities also implicate the need to focus on suitability

1. Testimony Concerning Investor Protection Implication of Hedge Funds, William H. Donaldson, Before the Senate Committee on Banking, Housing, and Urban Affairs (Apr. 10, 2003).

determinations and sales practices of those marketing hedge funds."[1] These funds enable "investors to invest indirectly in the very hedge funds in which they likely may not otherwise invest directly under the current law."[2] These types of funds have continued to proliferate.

Further, hedge funds use "prime brokers." These brokers are full-service broker-dealers that often serve active market traders. Prime brokerage involves a prime broker, who clears and finances the trades performed by an executing broker and acts as custodian, offers margin loans and provides risk management. Customers, such as hedge funds, prefer a prime brokerage arrangement. In addition, it seems that prime brokers connect hedge fund managers with potential customers.

Finally, there have been complaints about stock market price manipulations by short selling. It seemed that in 2003 hedge fund fraud had increased, such as making misleading statements, manipulating markets, misappropriating assets, insider trading, and reporting false valuation and performance of securities. The SEC lacked sufficient information about the details and was concerned about the impact of hedge funds on the markets and lack of transparency.

---

## Problem

Assume you are in-house counsel at a registered investment adviser. To date, you have only managed separate accounts (in other words, no pooled investment funds). Your CEO comes to you and explains that he believes the firm's investment strategy could be attractive to many more investors and that he would like to explore establishing a pooled investment fund. He views breaking into the fund management business as a substantial growth opportunity and asks you to formulate a proposal for the basic regulatory infrastructure the firm should establish. His only "rule of the road" is that he does not want to manage investment companies registered under the Investment Company Act. He believes that it would be too costly to set up the regulatory and compliance infrastructure to run 1940 Act-registered funds and have the business be profitable within his established time horizon. Draft your CEO a memo explaining the pros, cons and similarities of establishing a business around 3(c)(1) funds versus 3(c)(7) funds. Pay particular attention to the manner in which these funds can be offered, investor qualifications and limits and the initial and on-going diligence necessary to remain in compliance with these two 1940 Act exclusions.

---

## E. Banks and Savings and Loan Associations: Section 3(c)(3)

Section 3(c)(3) excludes from the applicability of the Investment Company Act a number of institutional intermediaries. These include banks and common trust funds, which are vehicles established by banks for investment purposes. While the exclusion for banks is straightforward, the

1. *Id.*
2. *Id.*

exclusion for common trust funds is less obvious and, given their similarity to mutual funds, has raised public policy considerations.

From 1933 to 1999, the Glass-Steagall Act prohibited banks from engaging in investment banking activities. They were, however, allowed to continue to manage personal trusts as they have done in the past and to pool the assets of small such trusts. Those trust funds were excluded from the definition of an investment company for a number of reasons. First, trust departments were subject to strict trust laws. Second, trust departments that attempted to advertise their investment acumen met the resistance of the Securities and Exchange Commission. While the Comptroller of the Currency, that regulated the banks' trust activities, strove to expand their services and their profits, free of the regulation of investment companies, the SEC raised objections to this expansion.[3] In 1999, however the Gramm-Leach-Bliley Act virtually eliminated the prohibition. Banks are currently engaged in the advisory function to mutual funds. Since that date, banks have been converting some trust departments or expanding them to include the advisory services of mutual funds. Other banks have invested the trust funds in investment companies which they created.

---

**Discussion Topics**

a. Why do banks establish common trust funds?

b. The Comptroller's regulation of common trust funds prohibits banks from engaging in conflicts of interest transactions, similar to trust law. Banks are subject to substantial regulation with respect to their safety and soundness, and costly federal insurance by the FDIC. Is the application of the 1940 Act to common trust funds necessary? What if the common trust funds are used as a vehicle for general investment by the public?

c. How different is a position of a trustee from that of a manager of a mutual fund? If you managed a bank and looked for profitable business, which business would be more attractive, trust department business or mutual fund business? Under what conditions would each of them prosper? Note that banks are currently converting their trust vehicles to investment companies, presumably because mutual fund shares are more attractive to investors. Why is that so?

d. Should a mutual fund that issues shares sold by a bank be able to rely on Section 3(c)(3)?

e. Now that banks may engage in the mutual fund management services, what would banks consider to determine whether to convert common trust funds into mutual funds or conduct both businesses?

---

3. Testimony of Richard C. Breeden, Chairman, U.S. Securities and Exchange Commission, Concerning Proposed Revisions to Rules Governing Bank Common Trust Funds Before the Subcomm. on Telecommunications and Finance of the Comm. on Energy and Commerce, 101st Cong. (1990).

## F. Insurance Companies: Section 3(c)(3)

As discussed in Chapter 1, life insurance companies share much with investment companies because they invest in financial assets, including securities. However, unlike investment companies, insurance companies bear the risk of such investment rather than the insured; and the insurance regulators regulate such investments.

In addition to life insurance that covers the risks of premature death, life insurance companies also issue annuities that cover the risks of longevity (i.e., the risk that a person would use all his savings before he dies and remain without financial means). In one way, this dual coverage of risks helps insurance companies diversify their business.

Annuities can be purchased with a lump sum or by installments. In the latter case, there is a pay-in period and a pay-out period. During the pay-in period the annuitant makes periodic payments to the insurance company. These payments are invested and reinvested. In conventional annuities, the insurance company is the debtor and promises a fixed rate of interest. In contrast, variable annuities, which we study later, offer a rate tied to the securities market. Upon retirement or on a particular date, the insurance company begins to make periodic payments to the annuitant, while continuing to invest and reinvest the remaining funds.

Because both life insurance and annuities constitute long-term obligations by the insurance company, the focus of insurance regulation is on the safety and soundness of the insurance company's business, thus indirectly ensuring that the company would meet its obligations to policyholders and annuitants. This focus is different from that of the 1940 Act, which provides investors with protection against excessive charges and fees and conflict of interest transactions of investment companies' affiliates.

Rule 3a-6 excepts foreign banks and foreign insurance companies from the definition of an investment company. "The primary effect of the rule is to permit foreign banks and insurance companies, and related entities, to sell their securities in the United States without registering as investment companies."[1]

---

### Discussion Topic

Recall our discussion of the *Prudential* case in Chapter 3 and specifically that the separate account established by Prudential was not qualified to rely on the insurance company exclusion provided in Section 3(c)(3). What justifies treating insurance company separate accounts and bank common trusts differently for purposes of Section 3(c)(3)?

---

1. Exception from the Definition of Investment Company for Foreign Banks and Foreign Insurance Companies, Investment Company Act Rel. No. 18381 (Oct. 29, 1991) (current version at 17 C.F.R. § 270.3a-6 (2015)).

## G. Financing, Factoring, and Real Estate Companies: Section 3(c)(5)[1]

Under section 3(c)(5), the following persons are excluded from the definition of investment company:[2]

> Any person who is not engaged in the business of issuing redeemable securities, face-amount certificates of the installment type or periodic payment plan certificates, and who is primarily engaged in one or more of the following businesses: (A) Purchasing or otherwise acquiring notes, drafts, acceptances, open accounts receivable, and other obligations representing part or all of the sales price of merchandise, insurance, and services; (B) making loans to manufacturers, wholesalers, and retailers of, and to prospective purchasers of, specified merchandise, insurance and services; and (C) purchasing or otherwise acquiring mortgages and other liens on and interest in real estate.

The conditions in this section reflect the dual nature of investment companies. The section limits: (1) the type of securities which the company may offer as an investment, and (2) the type of businesses in which the company may engage as an investor.

In 1970, Congress excluded from the section companies that issue redeemable securities. The 1969 Senate Report noted that some companies which purported to be primarily engaged in factoring, discounting, and real estate business had actively sought out unsophisticated investors by issuing redeemable securities and were perceived as, and acted in fact as, open-end investment companies.

An investment company is excepted from the definition only if it is primarily engaged in one or more of the enumerated businesses. The first business, in subsection (A), is financing of consumer purchases — namely, "[p]urchasing or otherwise acquiring notes, drafts, acceptances, open accounts receivable, and other obligations representing part or all of the sales price of merchandise, insurance, or services." A company which purchases from banks negotiable debt instruments representing loans to purchase cattle feed and other farm products, and thereby becomes the primary party to which payment is made, is not required to register under the Act. Credit unions are excluded from the definition of an investment company under this subsection.

The second qualifying business, in subsection (B), is "making loans to manufacturers, wholesalers, and retailers of, and to prospective purchasers of, specified merchandise, insurance and services." In the opinion of the staff, a company proposing to make commercial loans which would be secured by the borrowers' accounts receivable (not to be collected or serviced by the lending company) qualified for the exception in section 3(c)(5)(B), as long as not more than 35 percent of its assets were invested in equity interests of its borrowers, and provided its prospectus disclosed this limitation. The 35 percent limit was probably designed to ensure that the

---

1. Derived from 1 Tamar Frankel & Ann Taylor Schwing, The Regulation of Money Managers, §§ 6-151 to -157 (2001 & Supp. 2015) (footnotes omitted).
2. Investment Company Act, Section 3(c)(5), 15 U.S.C. § 80a-3(c)(5).

company does not invest more than 40 percent of its assets in "investment securities" in section 3(a)(1)(C).

The third qualifying business, in subsection (C), is "purchasing or otherwise acquiring mortgages and other liens on and interest in real estate." Initially, the staff interpreted the phrase not to include the purchase of securities of companies engaged in real estate. Thereafter, it relaxed the exclusion: first, to GNMA, FNMA, and other government mortgage-backed securities, and then further to other financial assets.

Additionally, rule 3a-5 exempts certain finance subsidiaries of United States and foreign private issuers from the definition of an investment company. The Rule defines a "finance subsidiary" as a corporation "[a]ll of whose securities other than debt securities or non-voting preferred stock meeting [certain requirements] or directors' qualifying shares are owned by its parent company or a company controlled by its parent company" and whose "primary purpose . . . is to finance the business operations of its parent company or companies controlled by its parent company." The SEC stated that "it is appropriate to exempt a finance subsidiary from all provisions of the Act where neither its structure nor its mode of operation resembles that of an investment company" and that this is the case when the above conditions are met.[1]

---

<u>Discussion Topic</u>

What are the policy reasons for limiting section 3(c)(5) to companies that are not issuing redeemable securities? In your opinion, is the following a redeemable security?

> (1) A security granting investors the right of redemption three years after issuance, at net book value or fair market value of the assets according to the audited financial statements, whichever is less.
>
> (2) A debt obligation which grants an investor the right, at its option, to receive the value of his contribution and income is very similar to a redeemable security, notwithstanding a provision that a portion of the corporate income will be excluded from the repurchase price.[2]

---

## H. Charitable Corporations: Section 3(c)(10)[3]

Section 3(c)(10) of the 1940 Act excludes from the definition of an investment company: "Any company organized and operated exclusively for religious, educational, benevolent, fraternal, charitable, or reformatory

1. Exemption from the Definition of Investment Company for Certain Finance Subsidiaries of United States and Foreign Private Issuers, Investment Company Act Rel. No. 14275 (Dec. 14, 1984) (current version at 17 C.F.R. § 270.3a-5 (2015)).

2. *See* G.A.B.E., Inc., Corres. (1974), CCH [1973-1974 Trans. Binder] Fed. Sec. L. Rep. ¶ 79,740; *see also* Huntoon, Paige & Co., Corres. (1973), CCH [1973-1976 Trans. Binder] Mut. Funds Guide ¶ 9948.

3. 1 Tamar Frankel & Ann Taylor Schwing, The Regulation of Money Managers, §§ 6-183 to -192 (2001 & Supp. 2015).

purposes . . . no part of the net earnings of which inures to the benefit of any private shareholder or individual."[1] The 1933 Act exempts securities of these companies from registration: "Any security issued by a person organized and operated exclusively for religious, educational, benevolent, fraternal, charitable, or reformatory purposes and not for pecuniary profit, and no part of the net earnings of which inures to the benefit of any person, private stockholder, or individual."[2]

Very little was said in the legislative history about these companies except that the Act excepts "eleemosynary institutions." Presumably, the exception rests on the social desirability of charitable institutions and the belief that without the profit motive there is little likelihood of abuse.

The Philanthropy Protection Act of 1995 expanded the exception. The amendment was driven by a then-pending case regarding a donation to a charitable foundation that assumed management responsibilities for the money received and agreed to pay the donor a monthly sum until her death, at which point the foundation would keep the remainder. The foundation probably commingled the donor's funds with those of other donors to reduce management costs, creating a charitable income fund. More importantly, the foundation accepts nowadays donation that promise donor some financial benefits, thus edging towards a security.

The amendment excepts "[a]ny company organized and operated exclusively for religious, educational, benevolent, fraternal, charitable, or reformatory purposes . . . which is or maintains" one of certain collective investment funds that invest and reinvest in certain assets, generally including property transferred by a donor who retains a life estate in the donated property, or donations of money in return for charitable gift annuities.[3]

---

## Discussion Topics

a. Is the regulation of charitable trusts necessary to protect elderly persons who may be manipulated?

b. Does it matter that the other beneficiaries are charitable organizations?

---

## I. Pension Plans: Section 3(c)(11)

The 1940 Act excludes from the definition of an investment company an employee's pension, stock bonus, or profit sharing trust meeting certain Internal Revenue Code provisions, collective trust funds maintained by banks that consist of such assets, or any insurance company separate account the assets of which are derived by contributions made pursuant to certain provisions of the Code.

1. Investment Company Act, Section 3(c)(10)(A)(i), 15 U.S.C. § 80a-3(c)(10)(A)(i).
2. Securities Act of 1933, Section 3(a)(4), 15 U.S.C. § 77c(a)(4).
3. Investment Company Act, Section 3(c)(10)(A)(ii)-(b), 15 U.S.C. § 80a-3(c)(10)(A)(ii)-(b); *see* 1 Tamar Frankel & Ann Taylor Schwing, The Regulation of Money Managers, §§ 6-187 to -192 (2001 & Supp. 2015).

When the Investment Company Act was enacted, the typical pension plan was a defined benefit plan. Such a plan was established by an employer for its employees and assured employees of fixed retirement income for life. The investment risks and gains of such plans were borne by the employers. The exclusion of these plans and vehicles from the definition of an investment company was based on the assumption that the plans' terms and managements were negotiated at arm's length. The benefits for the employers and the employees coincided. Therefore, the protections of the 1940 Act were not needed.

However, it transpired that the employers did not fund their obligations. If the employers became bankrupt, the employees stood in line after other, more secure creditors. The Employee Retirement Income Security Act of 1974 ("ERISA") imposed on employers the duty to fund their obligations (and even established a government backup to partially protect the plan). Then the model of pension plans changed dramatically. Currently employers typically offer employees "defined contribution" plans instead of defined benefit plans. The employers often contribute to the pension of the employees (e.g., through a 401(k) "match"), but the investment risk falls on the employees. Banks, investment companies and insurance companies are increasingly targeting the pension markets which have become enormous. Should these pools of money be excluded under section 3(c)(11)?

Consider the conclusions of the staff of the SEC's Division of Investment Management.[1]

> ERISA and, to a lesser extent, the Comptroller's rules provide important safeguards to ensure that plan participants will receive the benefits at retirement that they both expect and need. Nonetheless, participants increasingly are expected to rely on the investment performance of their individual accounts to provide their retirement benefits. Further, a growing number of plans are requiring that the participants, themselves, decide how to invest their individual accounts.
>
> For many pension plan participants, choosing where to invest their retirement plan assets will be the most important investment decision they will ever make. Participants need to be furnished complete information about their investment options, both concerning initial investment decisions (i.e., prospectuses) and reallocations (i.e., prospectuses and shareholder reports). To provide employees with adequate information about their investment decisions, legislation is needed to (1) amend section 3(a)(2) of the Securities Act to remove the exception for interests in collective trust funds and separate accounts in which participant-directed defined contribution plans invest, and (2) amend the federal securities laws to require delivery of prospectuses for the underlying investment vehicles, including investment companies, to plan participants who direct their investments. Further, to provide employees with adequate information

1. Division of Investment Management, U.S. Securities and Exchange Commission, Protecting Investors: A Half Century of Investment Company Regulation 178-179 (1992).

to enable them to monitor their investments' performance, the Exchange Act and the rules under the Investment Company Act should be amended to ensure that all plan participants receive semi-annual and annual shareholder reports issued by the pooled investment vehicles in which they invest.

We do not recommend that Investment Company Act regulation (other than the shareholder reporting provisions) be imposed on collective trust funds and separate accounts in which employee benefit plans invest. The participants in these plans are sufficiently protected by other regulatory schemes, and the additional benefits to be derived by imposing Investment Company Act regulation are outweighed by the costs.

Since 1974 pension plans have been regulated by the Department of Labor, under ERISA. ERISA, together with its body of regulation and associated issues, is expansive and remains outside the boundaries of our topics.

# Chapter 5

## *Financial Institutions That Do Not Fall Squarely Under the 1940 Act: Special Purpose Corporations*

This chapter deals with three types of financial institutions that are very similar to investment companies: they issue securities and invest in financial instruments that could include securities. Yet the regulatory scheme of the 1940 Act does not fit them well. Chapter 4 covered institutional intermediaries that section 3 of the 1940 Act excludes from the definition of an investment company. The rationale for those exclusions focused on the differences between the operations of investment companies and those of the other institutions (e.g., banks), as well as the alternative regulation to which the excluded institutions are subject.

In this chapter we discuss the exclusions of three other institutions: Special Purpose Vehicles (SPVs) that are part of the securitization process, offshore funds, and commodity pools. Their exclusion from regulation as investment companies is based more on extraneous functions: where they operate, their different purposes and the different types of their underlying assets.

An on-going policy issue that arises with respect to investment pools is whether all these pools should be subject to the same regulatory regime. In fact, many of the financial obligations that these pools issue may be offered to investors by the same investment manager and managed in a very similar fashion. For example, mutual funds and offshore funds may be managed in almost an identical way. Nonetheless, the reach of United States law is limited in the case of off-shore funds. In a world of close international interaction, the limited reach of United States law involves a policy issue. We start with a discussion of a financial innovation that has developed to create a true avalanche: securitization. Included in the process of securitization is a piece that constitutes an investment company. This part was exempted and regulated differently than investment companies.

### A. Pools that Are Used to Securitize Financial Assets: Special Purpose Vehicles (SPVs)

Securitization of financial assets involves the creation of pools to hold financial assets, and the pools' issuance of securities, backed by income from the assets that the pools hold. To understand such pools and their status under the 1940 Act, it is important to review the context in which these pools have arisen, that is, the process of securitization.

## 1. Introduction[1]

What is securitization? Securitization is a form of intermediation — a channel through which savers transfer money to borrowers and receive the borrowers' payments under the borrowers' obligations. The process helps convert illiquid loans into tradable securities backed by these loans. That is why the securities are called "asset-backed securities" and the process is called "securitization." The process of securitization starts with the creation of an entity designed to receive the illiquid loans (a "Pool"), and this entity issues standardized obligations that can be traded in the markets. Here, we focus on pooling.

## 2. Pooling

Pooling is used to securitize numerous small and different loans.[2] The steps leading to securitization are as follows:

- Lenders, such as banks, thrifts, mortgage bankers, or manufacturers, and servicers make loans to borrowers and receive the borrowers' obligations to repay the loans.
- Lenders sell the loan-obligations either by selling loans wholesale to "originators" that would securitize the loans, or by securitizing the loans themselves.
- A legal entity (a Special Purpose Vehicle (SPV)), is created. The SPV can be organized in any legal form. The SPV's sole business is to hold the loans and issue marketable, standardized securities, in sufficient numbers and suitable denominations to create a market in them for investors. In addition, the SPV is used to protect the assets it holds from third parties' claims, including claims of the loan sellers-creditors. The limited purpose of the SPV reduces the costs of monitoring the safety of its assets (the loans) and limits the risks of including other businesses with these loans. It provides a pass-through tax treatment, usually in the form of a limited partnership or a trust, or pursuant to special laws that allow such tax treatment. Arguably, it lowers the cost of rating the SPV's securities. However, as we shall see, it did not.
- The loans are transferred to the Pool.
- Someone services the loans in the Pool's portfolio — collects money from the borrowers, invests the money short-term, as required, and distributes it to the investors on maturity dates. The servicer could be the lender or the originator of the loans who retained the servicing business, or another entity that bought the servicing rights from the originator.

---

1. This material has been extrapolated from Tamar Frankel, Securitization: Structured Financing, Financial Asset Pools, and Asset-Backed Securities (Ann Taylor Schwing ed., 2d ed. 2005).
2. The term "loans" is used broadly to mean financial assets, including debts, such as credit card receivables, and ownership claims, such as shares of stock or partnership agreements.

- The credit risk and other risks posed by the SPV's assets or securities are directly or indirectly (fully or partially) underwritten by third parties — the U.S. Government, the originating lenders, or sponsors, banks, or insurance companies. These parties, alone or in combination, offer "credit enhancement" to the SPV or to the investors in Pool securities directly. Usually, the SPV's securities are rated by a rating agency.
- The SPV issues its securities to investors. The price that investors pay for the securities is then paid to the person or entity that transferred the loans to the SPV, minus expenses. As borrowers repay their loans, the money is distributed to the investors.
- Broker-dealers develop secondary markets for SPV securities. Thus, investors obtain the liquidity that they value and for which they are willing to forego some return.

### 3. Highlights of Securitization

The most important element of securitization is the combination of the first and final stages of the process that results in the transformation of illiquid loans that cannot be traded in the markets. The loans, as such, cannot be traded in the markets because the form, amounts, and terms of the loans do not meet the conditions necessary to create in them efficient active markets. Traded instruments are standardized and offered in a sufficient number and in denominations that would attract trading investors. Not all borrowers can or will provide such instruments. Because loans lack these necessary attributes, markets in them rarely develop.

When the conditions necessary for creating markets are absent, institutional intermediaries enter the picture and bridge the gap between the parties. Institutions usually raise money by issuing their own obligations on terms acceptable to savers, and then use the proceeds to make loans on terms acceptable to borrowers.

Some borrowers can raise funds both by issuing securities and by borrowing from institutions, and some investors can invest both by purchasing securities and by lending to borrowers, directly or through institutions (e.g., bank deposits). But not all have the luxury of choice. Most small borrowers and investors cannot use the markets, but must resort to institutional intermediaries.

For over fifty years, the financial system in this country consisted basically of two intermediation channels: financial institutions and securities markets. The channels were kept more or less separate, and banks functioned as the primary institutional lenders. Since the early 1970s, however, the securities market channel has been widening considerably, and the separation between the two channels is being blurred. Paving the way to securitization was a movement to substitute securities for loans and increase the shares of market intermediation. Large borrowers chose to raise more funds by issuing securities (e.g., commercial paper or "junk bonds") and less by bank loans. Similarly, large investors chose to invest more funds in securities and less in bank deposits.

Securitization has emerged as a new intermediation system. It separates the traditional functions that institutions used to perform, and allows new actors to engage in selected functions. Securitization also combines institutional and market intermediation or converts one into the other to take advantage of both forms.

In addition, securitization can be viewed as an efficient way of marketing loans or other financial obligations. For example, manufacturers who offer credit to customers may wish to receive cash immediately to operate, and invest in, their businesses. Arguably, small manufacturers may raise funds cheaper by selling the accounts receivable of their large customers with a better credit rating than the manufacturer's own. Depository institutions, such as banks, may need to convert illiquid assets into cash to pay off short-term obligations. In many cases, institutions are motivated to sell their financial assets because of accounting and regulatory pressures. Most of the banks' liabilities are short-term, such as demand deposits and savings accounts that depositors can withdraw on short notice.

The law and the regulators require, however, that a certain percentage of bank liabilities consist of "capital," that is, long-term obligations and equity. Banks can raise capital in two ways. One is by issuing stock or long-term bonds; the other is by reducing the assets and paying off some of the short-term liabilities. In both cases, the capital, as compared to the short-term liabilities, will rise.

Before the 1970s, banks that needed to raise capital were successful in issuing stock or long-term bonds; but in the 1970s, capital became prohibitively expensive for the banks. They began to increase their capital by selling their assets, that is, the loans they held, including illiquid loans. The need to sell illiquid loans created an incentive to securitize and convert the loans into liquid securities. Because investors value liquidity, they are willing to forego a return. Therefore, securitizing the loans reduced the cost of capital for the sellers. Generally, pressures to securitize produced incentives to make the process more efficient for the sellers' net benefit.

In addition, securitization can be described as a tool for separating the traditional functions of institutional intermediaries, such as banks, and allowing other actors to perform some of these functions. In the past, banks made loans, held them and serviced them to maturity or failure. Securitization enabled banks and other lenders to make loans and sell them rather than hold and service them. The process has opened the doors to non-traditional and unregulated lenders. Further, because making loans and securitizing the loans are separate activities, the promoters of the process need not be lenders. Wholesale markets for large and small loans have expanded dramatically, allowing promoters to buy and securitize loans made by others.

### a. Benefits and Disadvantages, Winners and Losers

Many commentators believe that securitization has injured the banks. Short-term, banks could sell their assets and raise their capital, but in the long run they increased the risk level of their assets for two reasons. First, they sold their best loans, exposing them to enormous competition for borrowers, weakening the banks' position as the primary lenders in the country, and enticing the banks to become sellers of loans rather than only lenders.

Second, because the banks could make long-term loans but sell them and experience only short-term risks, they began to produce high-risk loans which they securitized and sold. Thus, securitization enabled the banks to create high-risk loans for the markets but lower risk for themselves.

The years of 2000 to 2008 have demonstrated the problems that securitization poses. Banks and other lenders offered loans on enticing terms for some years (to be greatly increased later). The borrowers were not necessarily credit worthy. An army of mortgage brokers enticed such persons to borrow and buy homes they could not afford, or mortgage their homes and use the loans for travel, cars, and luxuries they could not otherwise afford. Home prices rose and with the price — the amount of the loans. Banks began to draw their profits not from the loans (long-term) but from the sale of the loans (short-term and continuous).

However, banks had to keep an inventory and made implied promises to buy back loans. There developed an enormous market in such securitized loans and with it the offer of insurance by organizations that did not have the funds to meet their obligations, if such obligations matured. Thus, lenders produced loans by borrowers who could not pay their loans, and insurance companies provided security that they could not meet and the price of the collateral — the homes — was overpriced. In addition, rating agencies failed to rate the loans accurately. When this bubble burst, it affected the banks, the borrowers, the market for homes, and hence, the financial system and the economy. To prevent large banks from failing, the United States government bailed them out by the billions, and even though some of the loans were repaid, the government's deficit has risen close to the ceiling.

Another disadvantage of securitization for borrowers is that they can no longer renegotiate the loan agreements with the lenders. Because the loans are sold, the servicers, which may not be the original lenders, have no authority to amend the terms of the loans. If interest rates fall, and the borrowers wish to take advantage of these lower rates, they can only refinance their loans: prepay the current loans and borrow again on better terms. If refinancing is more costly than amending the existing loan agreements, the borrowers may not benefit as much as in the past.

---

**Discussion Topics**

a. Outline the advantages and disadvantages of securitization.

b. How could the disadvantages be controlled while maintaining the advantages?

c. Where is the turning point from the good to the bad?

---

### b. The Status of SPVs: Exclusion from the Applicability of the Investment Company Act

Even though SPVs are similar to investment companies because they issue securities and invest in loans that could be classified as securities, SPVs could not function if the Investment Company Act applied to them in full. Therefore, the SEC granted exemptions to such entities, and, in 1992, adopted rule 3a-7 which excluded SPVs from the applicability of the Act, subject to certain conditions.

A summary of the SEC's statement is as follows:[1]

> The Securities and Exchange Commission is adopting a new rule, rule 3a-7 under the Investment Company Act of 1940 (the "Act"), to exclude issuers that pool income-producing assets and issue securities backed by those assets ("structured financing") from the definition of "investment company." The rule permits structured financings to offer their securities publicly in the United States without registering under the Act and complying with the Act's substantive requirements. Rule 3a-7 removes an unnecessary and unintended barrier to the use of structured financings in all sectors of the economy, including the small business sector.
>
> Structured finance is a technique whereby income-producing assets, in most cases, illiquid, are pooled and converted into capital market instruments. In a typical financing, a sponsor transfers a pool of assets to a limited purpose entity, which in turn issues non-redeemable debt obligations or equity securities with debt-like characteristics ("fixed-income securities"). Payment on the securities depends primarily on the cash flows generated by the pooled assets. Issuers that have more assets or that expect to receive more income than needed to make full payment on the fixed-income securities also may sell interests in the residual cash flow.
>
> A servicer, which often is the sponsor or an affiliate of the sponsor, is the primary administrator of the pool, collecting payments on the underlying assets when due and ensuring that funds are available so that investors are paid in a timely manner. In most cases, an independent trustee, usually a large commercial bank, monitors the issuer's fulfillment of its obligations.
>
> Since its inception in the 1970s, structured finance has grown tremendously, becoming one of the dominant means of capital formation in the United States. Nevertheless, the growth and development of this market has been constrained in some degree by the Act.
>
> Structured financings fall within the definition of investment company under section 3(a), but cannot operate under the Act's requirements. Many private sector sponsored financings have avoided regulation under the Act by relying on section 3(c)(5), which generally excepts from the definition of investment company any person who

1. Exclusion from the Definition of Investment Company for Structured Financings, Investment Company Act Rel. No. 19105 (Nov. 19, 1992) (footnotes omitted) (current version at 17 C.F.R. § 270.3a-7 (2015)).

> is not engaged in the business of issuing redeemable securities and who is primarily engaged in one of the finance businesses enumerated in the section. In addition, the Commission has issued more than 125 orders exempting other structured financings, primarily those involving mortgage related assets, from the Act. Financings that cannot rely on section 3(c)(5) or obtain an exemption must sell their securities in private placements in reliance on section 3(c)(1), the "private" investment company exception, or outside the United States.
>
> As a practical matter, the Act treats similar types of structured financings very differently, depending solely on the assets securitized. Some sectors of the economy, including small business, generally are unable to use structured financings as sources of capital, and many United States investors are denied the opportunity to purchase sound capital market instruments. . . .

Rule 3a-7, under the Investment Company Act, excludes from the definition of investment company (and therefore from the application of the 1940 Act) an issuer engaged in the business of acquiring and holding eligible assets and who does not issue redeemable securities.

The issuer must issue fixed income self-liquidating securities or other securities that entitle their holders to receive payments that depend primarily on the cash flow from the eligible assets. Fixed income securities that are rated at the time of sale in one of the four highest long-term or equivalent short-term categories by at least one nationally recognized rating agency may be sold without restriction.

Other fixed income securities may be sold only to certain accredited investors as defined in the Securities Act. All other securities may be sold only to qualified institutional buyers as defined in rule 144A under the Securities Act and to persons (other than any rating organization rating the issuer's securities) involved in the organization or operation of the issuer or an affiliate (as defined in rule 405 under the Securities Act) of such a person. The rule also sets forth other conditions relating to the acquisition and disposition of eligible assets and the independence of the trustee holding the assets. The non-redemption feature in rule 3a-7 was designed to prevent investors from confusing pools with mutual funds.

Thus, rule 3a-7[1] excludes from the definition of an investment company SPVs subject to the following conditions: (i) management of the SPV's portfolios is restricted, (ii) SPV assets must be held by an independent trustee, (iii) the securities issued by the SPV must not be redeemable, (iv) securities issued publicly must be limited to debt or debt-like securities, and (v) securities issued publicly must be limited to those rated in one of the four highest longer or equivalent short-term categories by a nationally recognized rating agency. Should these conditions be changed in light of the sub-prime crisis?

---

1. 1 Tamar Frankel, Securitization: Structured Financing, Financial Asset Pools, and Asset-Backed Securities § 11.31 (Ann Taylor Schwing ed., 2d ed. 2005).

Rule 3a-7's provisions highlight distinctions between investment companies and SPVs. These distinctions help avoid investors' confusion between regulated investment companies and SPVs, and, in addition, preclude regulated investment companies from finding in rule 3a-7 an escape from regulation. Therefore, these purposes ought to be kept in mind when interpreting the conditions of rule 3a-7.

An issuer of redeemable securities, as defined in section 2(a)(32) of the 1940 Act, is not qualified under rule 3a-7 because investors might confuse an SPV with open-end investment companies or unit investment trusts. In the Commission's staff opinion, the following financing program by an SPV may be issuing redeemable securities if the SPV issues two classes of securities, one of which entitles the holder, absolutely or conditionally, to withdraw portfolio securities from the program upon acquisition and presentation of a specified amount of other securities of another class. Thus, if the SPV issues Class A and Class B securities, and Class A holders acquire a specific amount of Class B securities, then Class A could withdraw some securities which the SPV holds.

The staff disagreed with the argument that '"because the decision to combine [the two classes] is the investor's and is not dictated by the terms of the offering . . . the program is [not] the 'issuee' of the combined security. . . . Although the decision to combine is the investor's, the structured financing program will define all of the rights attributable to the [two classes], and . . . the program, not the investor, is the obligor of the recombined security." The test of whether securities are not redeemable, wrote the staff, is "whether there are substantial enough restrictions on an investor's ability to withdraw portfolio securities," in light of eight factors:

> (1) whether the investor's right is conditional or absolute, (2) whether the issuer offers the matching securities for sale to investors at the same time or only at different times, (3) whether and how often the issuer sponsors activities (such as auctions and mandatory tender features) designed to facilitate an investor's ability to acquire the matching security or securities and present them for withdrawal, (4) whether the amount of portfolio securities that an investor can withdraw from the program at any time is limited or unlimited, (5) how often an investor can withdraw portfolio securities from the program, (6) whether or not there is a holding period requirement, (7) the denomination of the securities and the minimum amount needed to withdraw portfolio securities, and (8) how the withdrawal right feature is presented to investors.[1]

To qualify under rule 3a-7, the issuer must issue "fixed-income securities or other securities which entitle their holders to receive payments that depend primarily on the cash flow from eligible assets."[2]

The Rule defines "fixed income securities" as any securities that entitle the holder to receive:

---

1. Brown & Wood, Corres. (Feb. 24, 1994) (citing SuperTrust Trust for Capital Market Fund, Inc. Shares, Investment Company Act Rel. No. 17613 (July 25, 1990)) (footnotes omitted).

2. 17 C.F.R. § 270.3a-7(a)(1) (2015).

(i) A stated principal amount; or

(ii) Interest on a principal amount (which may be a notional principal amount) calculated by reference to a fixed rate or to a standard or formula which does not reference any change in the market value or fair value of eligible assets; or

(iii) Interest on a principal amount (which may be a notional principal amount) calculated by reference to auctions among holders and prospective holders, or through remarketing of the security; or

(iv) An amount equal to specified fixed or variable portions of the interest received on the assets held by the issuer; or

(v) Any combination of amounts described in paragraphs (b)(2)(i), (ii), (iii), and (iv) of this section;

*Provided that* substantially all of the payments to which the holders of such securities are entitled consist of the foregoing amounts.[1]

This definition reflects the difference between these securities and debt securities on the one hand, and equity securities on the other. Fixed-income securities also include securities whose terms (mainly interest rate) are adjusted periodically by auction in which current and any interested new holders, including the issuer, participate. Further, the issuer's qualified securities include interest only and principal only securities and securities whose value does not depend on fixed income, such as the residual interests in the issuer, so long as the payment on the issued securities is "primarily" based on the cash flow from the assets that the issuer holds and not on market price fluctuations of the assets in the portfolio. Therefore, preferred stock does not qualify for the purpose of the Rule.

Further, the fixed-income securities "sold by the issuer or any underwriter thereof" must be "rated, at the time of initial sale, in one of the four highest categories assigned long-term debt or in an equivalent short-term category (within either of which there may be sub-categories or gradations indicating relative standing) by at least one nationally recognized statistical rating organization that is not an affiliated person of the issuer or of any person involved in the organization or operation of the issuer to be sold without restriction."[2]

The rating requirements were designed to distinguish SPVs "from registered investment companies. The [SEC] wishes to emphasize that although ratings generally reflect evaluations of credit risk, the rating requirement is not intended to address investment risks associated with the credit quality of the financing."[3] The final Rule relaxed the rating requirement to qualify lower credit quality securities, and would presumably include securities backed by small business loans. Nonetheless, as compared to investment companies, this condition is costly and helps distinguish the SPV securities from those of investment companies.

1. 17 C.F.R. § 270.3a-7(b)(2) (2015).
2. 17 C.F.R. § 270.3a-7(a)(2) (2015).
3. Exclusion from the Definition of Investment Company for Structured Financings, Investment Company Act Rel. No. 19105 (Nov. 19, 1992).

Fixed-income securities that do not meet the rating requirements can be sold to certain types of "accredited investors." In addition, the issuers may sell any securities to qualified institutional buyers as defined under Securities Act Rule 144A and to persons involved in the organization or operation of the issuer or an affiliate (as defined in rule 405 under the Securities Act) of such a person, except the rating agency involved. Individuals, however, do not fall within these qualifications. In addition, the "issuer and any underwriter thereof affecting such sale" must "exercise reasonable care to ensure that such securities are sold and will be resold" only to these qualified persons, for example, by disclosing the limitations, putting legends on the certificates, and inquiring whether the securities are being purchased on behalf of or for others. Thus, presumably, the more sophisticated the investors are, the more they can evaluate the securities, and the less assurance they require from rating agencies.

The criteria for exemption under rule 3a-7 relate to the issuer's assets as well. First, the issuer's business must consist of "purchasing, or otherwise acquiring, and holding eligible assets." Eligible assets are defined to mean "financial assets, either fixed or revolving, that by their terms convert into cash within a finite time period plus any rights or other assets designed to assure the servicing or timely distribution of proceeds to security holders."[1] Eligible assets include assets that would support liquidity and offer credit enhancement for the portfolio, such as guarantees. Qualified financial assets may also include securities that might be deemed equity such as pass-through securities representing a pro rata share in a pool of mortgages. Even though the definition is not clear, eligible assets would probably include also cumulative preferred stock.

To qualify for the exemption, the issuer's (SPV's) business must consist of "purchasing, or otherwise acquiring, and holding eligible assets." The issuer may not engage, even in part, in any other business. Unlike other exceptions from the definition of an investment company, rule 3a-7 does not qualify the type of business of the issuer by the word "primarily." That means that an SPV which engages primarily in purchasing and holding eligible securities, but also engages in another business, will not be exempt. Further, the issuer is restricted from actively managing and trading in its portfolio — that is, acquiring additional assets or disposing of eligible assets that it holds. The Rule authorizes the qualified issuer to acquire additional eligible assets, or dispose of eligible assets, only if:

> (i) The assets are acquired or disposed of in accordance with the terms and conditions set forth in the agreements, indentures, or other instruments pursuant to which the issuer's securities are issued;
>
> (ii) The acquisition or disposition of the assets does not result in a downgrading in the rating of the issuer's outstanding fixed-income securities; and
>
> (iii) The assets are not acquired or disposed of for the primary

1. 17 C.F.R. § 270.3a-7(b)(1) (2015).

> purpose of recognizing gains or decreasing losses resulting from market value changes . . . .[1]

---

## Discussion Topics

a. To what extent does the provision prohibiting the sale of SPV assets preclude trading activities in the assets of the SPVs? For example, in some segments of the market the Originator is allowed to substitute the SPV's financial assets for other similar financial assets held by the issuer or repurchase an asset from the SPV issuer, subject to certain conditions. These conditions can include substitution and repurchase upon a breach of representation or warranty relating to an asset, or if the asset documentation is defective. Should such a transaction fall under the prohibition?

b. Similarly, should the substitution and repurchase of SPV defaulted or charged-off assets fall under the prohibition? What if these conditions are specified in the transaction's documents? What if they are typical to structured financing or securitization and are not typical to mutual fund securities?

c. To interpret the provisions of the rule, one might look to its main purposes, which are to distinguish between SPVs and mutual funds, and preclude SPV originators and operators from competing with regulated investment companies, so that regulated investment companies will not use this format to avoid regulation. Suppose the document that establishes the SPV impose quantitative limits on substitution and repurchases, such as a maximum of 20 percent of the collateral balance in the aggregate and 10 percent if the collateral balance for substitution and repurchase are credit related. What legal and other risks are raised in this case?

d. What about a document that establishes an SPV that allows the SPV to sell the SPV's assets either because the assets have deteriorated or because they have improved in credit quality, or as part of a discretionary sales "bucket;" for example, up to 15 percent of the value in a 12-month period?

e. Is rule 3a-7 important to securitization? If so, where does this importance lie?

f. As securitization developed, the designers of the SPV would pick part of the assets, usually of a low rating, and transfer them to another SPV, where again part of the asset would acquire a higher rating. The process would then be repeated. Thus, the structure could resemble an SPV of an SPV or an SPV. Why did the designers resort to this structure? Is this structure permissible under the Investment Company Act? Is it permissible under Rule 3a-7? How does this structure fare under section 12(d) of the Investment Company Act?

---

1. 17 C.F.R. § 270.3a-7(a)(3) (2015). This discussion is derived from 1 Tamar Frankel, Securitization: Structured Financing, Financial Asset Pools, and Asset-Backed Securities § 11.31 (Ann Taylor Schwing ed., 2d ed. 2005).

### c. Qualification for Rule 3a-7

To qualify for the exemption under Rule 3a-7, Rule 3a-7(a)(4) requires the following of several steps. First, it requires that issuers appoint unaffiliated trustees qualified under section 26(a)(1) of the Act and cause the SPV or its sponsor to enter into agreements with trustees containing provisions to the effect set forth in section 26(a)(3) of the 1940 Act. These requirements generally mean that the trustee needs to be a bank with capital, surplus, and undivided profits of at least $500,000, and that the trust indenture provide, in substance, that the trustee shall not resign until either (A) the SPV has been completely liquidated and the proceeds of the liquidation distributed to the security holders of the SPV, or (B) a successor trustee, having the qualifications described above, has been designated and has accepted such trusteeship. In the opinion of the SEC staff, the term "trustee" in Rule 3a-7(a)(4) does not include a custodian, because the rule 3a-7 specifically requires the appointment of a trustee. Rule 3a-7 does not prevent the trustee from acting as backup servicer if the primary servicer is unable to perform the functions. The requirement for appointing a trustee does not apply to securities backed by commercial paper. Because these securities are short-term, they do not involve the representation that long-term investors need. These short-term securities are not usually issued under a trust indenture.

The SEC granted an exemption from the requirement that the trustee would be unaffiliated when the trustee is affiliated with an underwriter involved with the organization of the issuer. Due to changes in the laws governing banking, most trustees providing services are affiliated with issuers through underwriters. Therefore, that requirement is disadvantageous to the asset-backed securities market and investors by requiring trustee selection by reasons other than market considerations. In addition, the affiliation would not result in a conflict of interest, because of the timing and nature of the role of the trustee and the underwriter. The underwriter's role generally ends after the security distribution. Therefore, there is no opportunity for the parties to act in concert. Further, the trustee has "virtually no discretion" in determining the choice of the securities to be held in the SPV.[1]

Second, the rule 3a-7 requires that SPVs take "reasonable steps to cause the trustee to have a perfected security interest or ownership interest valid against third parties in those eligible assets that principally generate the cash flow needed to pay the fixed-income security holders, provided that such assets otherwise required to be held by the trustee may be released to the extent needed at the time for the operation of the issuer."[2] Rule 3a-7 does not require that the security interest be taken in ancillary assets, such as the car bought with money from the securitized loan. The requirement applies only to the main assets that provide the cash flow for payment on the securities. The cash flows must be deposited periodically in a segregated account. However, the servicer may retain cash flows for some time, if a rating agency has determined that the risk to the assets is minimal.

1. Deutsche Bank Trust Co. Americas, Investment Company Act Rel. Nos. 27644 (Dec. 28, 2006) (notice) and 27673 (Jan. 23, 2007) (order).
2. 17 C.F.R. § 270.3a-7(a)(4)(ii) (2015).

Rule 3a-7 does not require the sponsor of the issuer or the trustee to keep a list of the security holders of the issuer, as the proposed rule did, because such a requirement would preclude the issuance of bearer securities, which are often issued in international transactions.

Finally, Rule 3a-7(a)(4) requires that SPVs take "actions necessary for the cash flows derived from eligible assets for the benefit of the holders of fixed-income securities to be deposited periodically in a segregated account that is maintained or controlled by the trustee consistent with the rating of the outstanding fixed-income securities."[1]

Rule 3a-7 was expected to increase the volume of securitization of various financial assets, except stock, which is outside rule 3a-7, and it did. Whether rule 3a-7 has caused these changes or met the expectations, however, is impossible to prove because any change may have occurred in the market for other causes or cumulative causes. The one effect that rule 3a-7 has had, however, is to reduce the requests for no-action letters and exemptions.

What was the effect of SPV exemptions on third parties?[2] SEC exemptive orders did not address the question of whether exempted SPVs remain investment companies for the purpose of determining the status and rights of third parties. The SEC's exemptions can be selective. The exemptions can cover the status of the SPVs as investment companies or only the activities of the SPVs. So the initial issue relates to the SPV being regulated as an entity, whether it is an investment company or not, and then the issue is whether the transactions that the SPV is involved in are exempted from the Securities Act?

Two issues have arisen with respect to SEC exemptions. One issue concerns the holding company of such an SPV. If 50% or more of the voting securities of the SPVs are held by another company ("holding company"), the securities of an exempted SPV that is an investment company will be "investment securities" within the meaning of section 3(a)(1)(C) of the 1940 Act. These securities will be counted in determining whether more than 40% of the value of the *assets of the holding company* consist of "investment securities." If they do, the holding company itself will become an investment company under section 3(a)(1)(C). A bank and an insurance company are excepted from the definition of an investment company, but other companies might not be.

The second issue that arises with respect to the status of exempted SPVs as investment companies is whether the SPVs' securities are subject to the provisions of section 12(d) of the 1940 Act. That section limits the holdings of investment companies in other investment companies' securities. Thus, if exempt SPVs are investment companies, the limitations of section 12(d) apply to investment companies that hold such SPV securities. Otherwise, they may hold investment companies' securities as well as create a pyramid of SPVs that hold *tranches* of other SPVs.

---

1. 17 C.F.R. § 270.3a-7(a)(4)(iii) (2015).

2. 1 Tamar Frankel, Securitization: Structured Financing, Financial Asset Pools, and Asset-Backed Securities § 11.32F (Ann Taylor Schwing ed., 2d ed. 2005).

## B. Offshore Funds

A financial institution that is similar to an investment company but falls outside the umbrella of the Investment Company Act is the offshore fund. American sponsors of investment companies may establish such investment companies outside the United States to seek new markets for investment programs, both institutional and retail. Also, U.S. sponsors generally offer offshore funds to their "bigger" clients in transactions that are carefully designed to avoid U.S. registration requirements.

As offshore funds expand, so do offshore financial centers. These offer administrative services, flexible financial regulation, financial secrecy laws, and limited or no taxation of foreign investors. Lack of regulation does not cause concern to sophisticated investors if these investors can protect themselves by private law such as custody and contract arrangements and by business pressures such as ability to mar the reputation of service givers.

The following material provides background for the offshore marketplace, explains how these funds are organized, and discusses various regulatory considerations.[1]

> There are a number of offshore fund jurisdictions in the world, many of which fiercely compete against one another for business. Geographically, the leading jurisdictions are grouped in two areas: Europe and the Caribbean. Although they have yet to achieve the prominence of the European and Caribbean centers, centers located in the Indian Ocean area, such as Mauritius and the Seychelles, as well as Malaysia, are expected to play an increasing role in the offshore financial services sector due to their proximity to growing Asian markets.
>
> Competition among the leading offshore centers is, to a large degree, based on the regulatory and legal structures (or lack thereof) they provide to their clients. . . . "Legitimate" jurisdictions tend to require more local contacts . . . [and] tend to be more strict when it comes to enforcing compliance with international conventions dealing with money laundering. . . .
>
> Of the European centers, Luxembourg is by far the leading center for offshore mutual funds in terms of asset value. A number of administrative and "back office" operations for U.S.-based financial institutions (not limited to fund management, and including insurance and banking) have been attracted to Dublin's International Financial Services Center because of its relatively low labor costs, high quality of the local workforce, and status of English as the principal working language. Other major European centers include the "traditional" offshore territories of the British Isles, Guernsey, Jersey, the Isle of Man and more recently-Ireland Gibraltar, Madeira, Malta and Cyprus. . . .

---

1. This is an abridged version of Robert W. Helm, *Offshore Investment Funds,* appearing in The Financial Services Revolution, Understanding the Changing Role of Banks, Mutual Funds, and Insurance Companies (Clifford E. Kirsch ed., 1997). Some footnotes have been omitted and others have been edited.

The growth of the European "domestic" offshore fund business has been greatly aided by the Directive on Undertakings for Collective Investment in Transferable Securities ("UCITS"), promulgated by the Council of the (then) European Community in 1988. . . .

While most UCITS funds are organized to be sold principally in the country of the fund sponsor,[1*] there has been a discernable trend more recently towards the development of "pan-European" products. Accession of new Member States to the EU (notably Austria, Norway, and Sweden) may hasten the development of funds sold in multiple jurisdictions.

Because of the access they potentially grant to EU countries, offshore UCITS funds have become a favorite vehicle for U.S. investment management firms to establish and market mutual funds to the European markets. Fidelity Investments, Federated Investors, Prudential Securities, Smith Barney and Merrill Lynch are among the more prominent U.S. firms which have established footholds in Europe through the use of offshore funds organized in UCITS form. . . .[2*] Many of the Caribbean jurisdictions are renowned for their secrecy laws and minimal regulations, and consequently have somewhat murkier reputations than their European counterparts.[3*]

Offshore funds are not the only investment funds that are offered and sold on a cross-border basis. A number of countries, including Germany, the U.K., Japan and Hong Kong have domestic statutes that, at least in theory, permit the approval of non-domestic funds for local offer and sale. Some U.S. firms have had success selling U.S. funds in those jurisdictions on a registered, public basis. Despite the complications imposed by tax laws and other competitive considerations, there is a fair amount of cross-border fund activity in the world today.

*Factors Influencing the Selection of an Offshore Fund Jurisdiction*

Depending on the particular investment policies and objectives to be pursued for the fund, some jurisdictions may be more attractive than others because they may permit more flexibility in the design of fund investment policies and restrictions [or restrict some investments].

Distribution considerations may be as important as investment policy considerations when establishing an offshore fund. . . . In particular, the jurisdiction's time zone should be practicable for the markets that the fund is trying to reach. This has been a factor in developing the Caribbean islands as a leading location for funds sold in Latin America, and Luxembourg for funds sold in continental Europe. It is also important to know the local rules on distribution

1*. Norma Cohen, "EU Collective Investment Scheme Laws a Failure," The Financial Times, Oct. 28, 1994. This article notes that just over one-third of funds organized under the UCITS Directive are marketed across European borders.
2*. Judy Rehak, "U.S. Fund Industry's Marketing Drive Takes Off: Investors See the Light (Refreshments)," 4 Int'l Fund Investment No. 1, at 51 (Spring 1995).
3*. Ingo Walter, The Secret Money Market 188-9 (1990).

and advertising, and how they will they affect marketing efforts, if at all.[1*]

The corporate structure of a fund is often dictated by the needs of the intended shareholders and the marketing strategy of the fund sponsor. An obvious consideration in choosing a jurisdiction is whether the local law permits the desired form of [organization: master feeder fund, or multiple investment portfolios, or minimal required shareholder approval for changes in corporate structure, no annual meetings, amendment of fund's constituent documents by the board at will, and no taxes on the issuance and redemption of shares].

If the sponsor is interested in maximum distribution flexibility, it will be necessary to establish that, under local law, funds can issue shares with respect to multiple investment portfolios (series), preferably with the ability to add new series without shareholder approval. Moreover, a fund should be able to issue separate classes of shares with respect to a single series, and to serve as the "master" fund for a master/feeder fund arrangement.

If . . . a U.S.-registered fund will be purchasing shares in an offshore fund, it may be useful if the local fund can issue securities that will not be "voting securities" as the term would be defined under the 1940 Act. This may help address issues arising under the "fund of funds" provisions of the 1940 Act, which can restrict the investment by registered investment companies in other investment companies.

The establishment of offshore vehicles, especially those targeted at the retail market, requires an elaborate coordination of the efforts of service providers based in a number of different jurisdictions. The selection of the right combination of service providers can make a project a complete success, whereas a poor selection can produce delays and frustration for all. . . . [Sponsors will also consider all tax liabilities].

Finally, there are intangible factors. These range from consideration of the integrity, strength and reputation of the local regulatory authority (and as to whether there is in fact any local regulation or control), to the work ethic and quality of the local work force, to the issue of who else does business in the jurisdiction, and whether the sponsor feels comfortable being associated with them.

*The Investment Company Act of 1940*

Section 7(d) of the 1940 Act prohibits any investment company organized outside the United States from using the U.S. mails or facilities of interstate commerce in connection with a public offering of its securities, except pursuant to a Securities and Exchange Commission (the "SEC") order. Such an order must be based on a finding that "it is both legally and practically feasible effectively to enforce the provisions of [the 1940 Act] against such company."

1*. As noted above, UCITS funds are subject to local distribution rules for each state in which they are distributed.

There is no statutory definition of "public offering" in the 1940 Act. However, the SEC Staff has historically read the "public offering" language in Section 7(d) to have the same meaning as in the Securities Act of 1933 (the "1933 Act") and in Section 3(c)(1) of the 1940 Act, the "private investment company" exception from the statute's definition of "investment company. . . ." [A]n unregistered foreign fund making a public offering of its shares outside the United States may make a private offering of its securities to U.S. residents without registering under the 1940 Act provided it has, at the end of the day, no more than 100 beneficial holders of its shares who are U.S. residents (not counting any holders of short-term paper).

Considerations arising under the 1940 Act . . . generally combine to limit the degree of permissible U.S. contact of an offshore fund. Offshore funds with U.S. sponsors or advisers generally attempt to structure as much of their activity, including fund administration and distribution efforts, offshore in a real and substantial manner. Moreover, an unregistered offshore fund will generally regulate share ownership and restrict the transfer of shares to non-U.S. persons so as to avoid potential registration issues under the 1940 Act. Consequently, such funds may be less concerned about potential extraterritorial applicability of the 1933 Act to their offerings conducted abroad than other issuers that may have U.S. underwriters or other more significant U.S. contacts. Regulation S under the 1933 Act, which sets forth certain "safe harbor" rules for securities offerings to foreign investors (and specifically is not available to investment companies "registered or required to be registered" under the 1940 Act) may nevertheless provide some guidance with respect to helping a fund sponsor determine that the fund's distribution activities are truly being conducted in "offshore transactions" as defined in the Regulation.

*Investment Advisers Act of 1940*

An offshore fund client of a U.S.-registered investment adviser, like all clients of the adviser, is entitled to a wide range of protections under the Advisers Act. The Advisers Act imposes significant fiduciary obligations and disclosure requirements on all registered advisers, and further subjects registrants to compliance with rules governing the custody of client assets, adviser advertising and the presentation of past performance information. . . .

*The Future of Offshore Funds*

Offshore funds operate in an environment of regulatory uncertainty and laxity. The actors are therefore left to rely on private law and reputation. Unless actors have created reputation in the same jurisdiction, reputation created in another jurisdiction may mislead. Different environments and laws induce different behavior.

An area of significant concern for all participants in the offshore fund and investment business is the problem of preventing the use of offshore investment products for money laundering purposes. As noted above, domestic legislation, international conventions and less formal efforts at cooperation have established minimum standards for institutional inquiry as to the source of funds and identity of potential customers of offshore firms and funds. However, these limited efforts are not sufficient to stem the vast tide of money laundering activity that occurs globally through a variety of financial media. Increasing focus on anti-money laundering initiatives may encourage the "legitimate" offshore fund business to further concentrate itself in a smaller number of better-regulated jurisdictions, while the less-regulated jurisdictions may come under increasing pressure to tighten controls over domestic institutions and to abandon their *laissez faire* approach to regulation.

Finally, there are issues of fiscal accountability and transparency, and the uneasy place occupied by offshore financial transactions in any national system of taxation. The potential use of offshore products as tax avoidance mechanisms by individual investors cloaked by laws on banking secrecy remains a difficult issue for national policy makers. It seems clear that, in general, U.S. tax policy is not offended if U.S. corporate taxpayers provide services to offshore funds. On the other hand, U.S. tax policy is offended if offshore funds or vehicles are used to avoid U.S. taxes. Proposed legislation would further restrict the ability of some U.S. taxpayers to use offshore vehicles for tax avoidance purposes.

Moreover, from the perspective of individual offshore products, there is always an element of risk that national revenue authorities may seek to disallow certain tax benefits, or disallow certain structures used for offshore products, that in their view offend national tax policy. . . . International tax advisors can only offer carefully qualified opinions as to these issues.

From time to time, there is talk within the EU about the need to modify tax policies that encourage or permit the use of offshore centers, including centers located within the EU itself. To date, these initiatives have not been successful, possibly reflecting the economic and commercial reality that leading EU financial institutions maintain offices in tax havens, not limited to Dublin and Luxembourg, and earn taxable revenue from offshore financial business. Offshore financial centers also produce employment opportunities for local residents or, in the case of Luxembourg in particular, for individuals from all over the EU. . . .

As governments grapple with these difficult issues, it is hoped that what results is not the end of the offshore investment products marketplace. Offshore funds and related investment products provide continual sources of innovation and challenge to existing regulatory systems and patterns of thought. Offshore funds offered multiple classes of shares with respect to the same investment portfolio long before any U.S. fund ever sought permission from the SEC to do so. The same is true of the master/feeder structure. Innovations in the development of offshore investment products continue to this day. A vibrant, active offshore marketplace for investment products remains important for national markets as an incubator of new fund

> structures and ideas and as a perpetual challenge to the complacency of national regulatory systems.

---

**Discussion Topics**

a. Would you invest your hard-earned money in the shares of an offshore fund? Would you invest your money in the shares of a United States regulated fund that invests in an offshore fund?

b. What are the public policy considerations regarding regulation of financial intermediaries with respect to tax avoidance and money laundering? How should regulators approach these issues?

c. Why do offshore financial centers avoid creating a fully sheltered environment for investors who seek tax avoidance and money laundering?

---

## C. Commodity Pools

Today, commodity futures contracts generally appear in the life of money managers quite frequently. Increasingly, futures contracts are entering mainstream investment management and, as they do, pools may emerge to offer small investors shares in a pool of managed futures contracts.

Pools of futures contracts are not covered by the 1940 Act because the pools do not invest in securities. However such pools are subject to alternative regulation under the Commodity Exchange Act of 1934. The following excerpt explores the regulation of such pools.[1]

> Increasingly, money managers use the futures markets to protect or enhance the value of portfolio assets. For example, hedge funds, mutual funds and pension funds use futures transactions to manage portfolio risks, effect changes in investment strategy or portfolio mix, modify portfolio durations, create synthetic bonds or other interests and for a host of other purposes. When the funds of multiple investors are pooled for investment in the futures markets, the commingled investment fund may be deemed to be a "commodity pool" subject to regulation under the Commodity Exchange Act ("CEA"), the federal statute governing the nation's futures and commodity option markets.
>
> Administered by the Commodity Futures Trading Commission ("CFTC"), an independent federal agency modeled in many respects on the Securities and Exchange Commission, the CEA is a comprehensive structure for the regulation of transactions in futures contracts and commodity options. This regulatory framework principally provides for oversight of the trading of futures contracts and commodity options on futures exchanges and of brokers and commodity professionals acting for or rendering advisory or investment management services to customers in connection with such transactions.

---

1. Susan C. Ervin, Commodity Pools: Collective Investment Funds Under the Futures Regulatory Framework (1998).

Under this framework, collective investment vehicles that engage in futures or commodity option transactions, known as "commodity pools," are subject to disclosure, reporting and record-keeping requirements, and the operator of the commodity pool must register with the CFTC. Significantly, however, given the proliferation of investment funds making use of the futures markets, commodity pools are not limited to funds that invest exclusively or even predominantly in futures or commodity options. Rather, commodity pools subject to CFTC regulation include collective investment vehicles that invest in multiple types of investment products and whose futures activities are incidental to other investment activity.

Commodity pools generally are organized as limited partnerships or limited liability companies and are offered in securities offerings subject to the Securities Act of 1933 ("1933 Act"); they may also be subject to the Investment Company Act of 1940. The regulation of commodity pools under the CEA is not fundamentally incompatible with the requirements of the 1933 Act, as both futures regulation and the 1933 Act require prospectus disclosures of material information and do not generally constrain the investment activity of the fund. The CEA differs, however, from the 1933 Act in that it does not provide as broad an exemption from regulation as that for private securities offerings; nor does it provide a correlate to the exclusion for privately offered investment vehicles that have no more than 100 beneficial owners in Section 3(c)(1) of the Investment Company Act of 1940 ("ICA") or the more recently enacted ICA Section 3(c)(7) exception for issuers whose securities are not publicly offered and are owned exclusively by qualified purchasers.

Consequently, the CEA may reach funds that escape the bulk of securities regulation, and the common assumption that hedge funds and similar private investment companies are wholly unregulated may well be inaccurate, as many such funds are active participants in the futures markets. However, although its potential application is broad, the CEA imposes few constraints upon the structure, governance, investment activity, or manner of operation of regulated funds, relying principally upon registration of the fund's operator and required disclosures to customers. Further, in administering the CEA, the CFTC has created a number of regulatory exemptions which substantially narrow the CFTC's regulation of funds sold to highly accredited purchasers and funds primarily engaged in securities transactions.

1. Basics of the CEA Regulatory Structure for Commodity, Pools Commodity Pool Definition

. . . The CEA defines a "commodity pool operator" as "any person engaged in a business that is of the nature of [a commodity pool,] investment trust, syndicate, or similar form of enterprise, and who, in connection therewith, solicits, accepts, or receives from others, funds, securities, or property, either directly or through capital contributions, the sale of stock or other forms of securities, or otherwise, for the purpose of trading in any commodity for future delivery on or subject to the rules of any contract market [futures exchange]. . . ."[1*] The [CEA's] definition of commodity pool is similarly broad, reaching "any investment trust, syndicate or similar form of enterprise operated for the purpose of trading commodity interests, [including any commodity for future delivery, security futures product, or swap.]"[2*]

The commodity pool definition has been construed to reach investment vehicles that transact in futures contracts or commodity options, whether or not those transactions represent the fund's predominant activity or even one of its principal activities. Essentially, "to the extent that a collective investment vehicle trades commodity futures and options, the vehicle is deemed to be a commodity pool."[3*] As a result, the commodity pool definition encompasses a diverse collection of vehicles ranging from funds designed purely as speculative ventures in the futures markets to funds created to serve as vehicles for investment in the securities markets.

A hedge fund, for example, might invest 90% of its assets in securities or other investments and post the other 10% of its assets as margin deposits on futures contracts. Such an entity clearly would constitute a commodity pool subject to regulation under the CEA, although it may qualify for exemption from at least some of the CFTC's requirements applicable to commodity pools. This is not an anomalous result if the actual risk/reward profile of the fund is considered. Futures transactions transfer contract rights, not assets, and the margin deposit required to be posted to engage in a futures transaction represents a performance bond, not a down-payment on the purchase price. Consequently, futures margins are established at levels that are relatively low in comparison to securities margins, often representing as little as 2 or 3% of the total value of a futures contract. As a result, a very small percentage of the assets of a fund could be deposited as margins on futures contracts that have a value equal to that of the fund's entire portfolio. Although not designed to serve as a risk measure, the futures contract value is likely to better capture the actual risk exposure on the contract than the amount of the margin deposit; however, since futures price risk is theoretically unlimited, the actual risk exposure inherent in a futures position exceeds even the contract size.

In short, a simple mathematical test comparing the percentage of a fund's assets in futures with the percentage of the fund's assets in other types of transactions does not effectively measure the relative importance of those transactions to the risk/reward profile of the fund. Such a comparison would be likely to understate, perhaps quite dramatically, the potential impact of the fund's futures

---

1*. 7 U.S.C. § 1a(11).

2*. 7 U.S.C. § 1a(10).

3*. Risks That Hedge Funds Pose to the Banking System: Hearing Before the House Comm. on Banking, Finance and Urban Affairs, 103d Cong. 144 (1994) (statement of Barbara Pedersen Holum, Acting Chairman, Commodity Futures Trading Commission).

activities upon its performance. Consequently, the CFTC has been reluctant to adopt a bright line quantitative test to determine how much margin posted to secure futures positions would give rise to the duty to operate as a commodity pool.[1*] However, in specific cases, CFTC staff have granted relief from regulation based upon factors such as the very limited nature of a fund's futures activities both in terms of the amount of the fund's assets used for that purpose and strict restrictions upon the type of futures activity, *e.g.*, for *bona fide* hedging purposes only, high levels of financial accreditation of the investors in the fund, and the small size of the pool.

The commodity pool definition also reaches funds that invest only indirectly in futures by purchasing interests in other funds that transact in the futures markets. "Fund of funds" structures are quite common and enable a fund to attain futures exposure without the administrative burdens or potentially unlimited liability of direct participation in the futures markets. These potential benefits should not, however, obscure the substance of the investment activity in question. A commodity pool is a conduit by which multiple investors may invest in futures on a collective basis and share in the resulting profits and losses; the entity performs the same function whether it invests directly in the futures markets or through ownership in another legal entity.

Thus, absent exemption, all vehicles engaging in futures transactions would be required to be operated in accordance with the CEA and CFTC regulations governing commodity pools. The principal regulatory duties that flow from status as a commodity pool are: (1) required registration of the commodity pool operator and sales agents for the fund; (2) required delivery to prospective investors of a disclosure document containing specified information concerning the fund's risks, fees and operations; (3) periodic reporting to investors; and (4) maintenance of books and records. Further, commodity pool operators are subject to statutory and regulatory anti-fraud prohibitions and are deemed to be fiduciaries in their activities involving the pool.

*Registration Requirements.* The operator of the commodity pool and salespersons ("associated persons") for the pool must register with the CFTC. This requirement precludes persons with significant criminal or civil disciplinary histories, which constitute statutory bars to registration, from operating or marketing commodity pools. Applicants for registration as a commodity pool operator, as salespersons of the pool operator, or as principals of the pool operator, must file information concerning their employment and disciplinary

1*. A CFTC staff study published in 1991 underscores the difficulty of using a margin-based quantitative definition of "commodity pool." The study indicated that for commodity pool operators with over $10 million in net assets under management, only about 8% of net assets under management was posted as margin deposits for futures transactions. Survey of Commodity Pool Operators in Futures Markets with an Analysis of Interday Position Changes (CFTC Division of Economic Analysis) (1991) at 1.

histories, together with fingerprint cards to facilitate fitness screening through the Federal Bureau of Investigation database. In the case of a commodity pool operator, a disqualification of the commodity pool operator itself or any of its principals may bar the pool operator from registration. The CPO and its associated persons generally also must pass the National Commodity Futures Examination, a proficiency examination administered by the National Futures Association, in order to become registered.

The trading advisor or advisors for the fund also must register as "commodity trading advisors," essentially the futures analogues of securities investment advisers. A commodity trading advisor is a person who, for compensation engages in the business of advising others concerning the trading of futures contracts or commodity options or the advisability of such trading or who issues analyses or reports concerning futures or commodity option transactions. The CEA has the same types of exclusions from the commodity trading advisor definition as the Investment Advisers Act of 1940 has for banks, news publishers, and the like, with the important distinction, however, that for the statutory exclusion from the commodity trading advisor definition to apply, the trading advice rendered must be solely incidental to the conduct of the excluded entity's primary business.[1*]

*Structural Restrictions.* The CFTC's regulatory framework for commodity pools relies heavily upon required disclosures as the central protection for investors and imposes no restrictions upon the investment activity in which the fund may engage or other aspects of the fund's operations. CFTC Rule 4.20, however, establishes several fundamental bulwarks against self-dealing and misuse of investor property by the commodity pool operator. First, the commodity pool operator must operate the commodity pool as a separate legal entity that is distinct from the pool operator. (Currently, the most prevalent structure for domestic commodity pools is that of the limited partnership, with the commodity pool operator serving as general partner). Second, all funds received from existing or prospective pool participants must be received in the name of the commodity pool and not that of the pool operator. Third, the property of the commodity pool may not be commingled with that of the pool operator or of any other person.

*Disclosure Duties.* Each commodity pool operator soliciting prospective investors for a pool must provide the prospective participant, and file with the CFTC, a disclosure document containing information specified in CFTC rules. The disclosure document must be provided prior to or at the time of solicitation. Required disclosures include: the principal risk factors relevant to investment in the pool; the pool's investment program; fees and expenses of operation, including the "break-even point" for the investment, that is, the trading profit required to equal all fees and expenses of the

1*. 7 U.S.C. § 1a(5) (1994).

investment; the business backgrounds of the pool operator and its principals; the historical performance results of the commodity pool, its operator and its trading advisors; conflicts of interest on the part of the pool operator and the trading advisors for the pool; and material legal proceedings against the commodity pool operator and the pool's trading advisors.

*Reporting and Recordkeeping Duties.* Commodity pool operators also must furnish pool participants with periodic account statements (monthly for pools with net assets of more than $500,000, otherwise quarterly) and annual reports, including certified financial statements. Account statements and the annual report must be prepared in accordance with generally accepted accounting principles and, in the case of the annual report, must include data for the two previous years and be filed with the CFTC. Commodity pool operators must maintain specified books and records at their main business office and make them available for inspection by the CFTC and the U.S. Department of Justice. For each pool operated, the commodity pool operator must maintain records that include, for example, an itemized daily record of each futures contract or commodity option transaction for the pool; a journal of original entry of all receipts and disbursements of money, securities and other property; general ledgers of all asset, liability, expense and income accounts; and canceled checks, bank statements, and all other records prepared or received in connection with the operation of the commodity pool. Commodity pool operators are also required to maintain and make available for inspection records concerning their own activities, including both futures-related and non-futures related activities, as well as of the futures-related activities of their principals.

*Fiduciary Obligations and Anti-fraud Prohibitions.* Commodity pool operators, their associated persons and other commodity professionals providing services to a commodity pool are deemed to be acting as fiduciaries. All activities of the commodity pool, the commodity pool operator, trading advisors for the pool, and the associated persons of the pool operator and trading advisors in connection with the commodity pool are subject to anti-fraud prohibitions of the CEA.

2. Exemptions from Regulation

*Small Pools (Rule 4.13).* As noted above, the CEA provides no wholesale exclusion from regulation for privately offered pools comparable to the "100 person" private investment company or the recently established "qualified purchaser" exceptions under the Investment Company Act of 1940. However, the CEA authorizes the CFTC to exclude from the definition of commodity pool operator, and thus from regulation as pool operators, "such persons not within the intent of the definition of the term as the Commission may specify by rule, regulation, or order." (Section 1a(4) of the CEA). The CFTC has used this authority sparingly. CFTC Rule 4.13 provides two categories of exemption for small, family-based or informal pools. It exempts from registration commodity pool operators who receive no compensation other than reimbursement for administrative expenses; operate only one pool; are not otherwise required to register with the CFTC or affiliated with a person required to register with the CFTC; and engage in no advertising for the pool. A second Rule 4.13 exemption applies to commodity pool operators who accept no more than $200,000 in aggregate gross capital contributions for all of the commodity pools they operate and who do not operate any pool which has more than 15 participants at any time.

*Registered Investment Companies and Other Specified Regulated Entities (Rule 4.5).*CFTC Rule 4.5 provides an exclusion from the commodity pool operator definition for several categories of regulated persons operating certain types of collective investment vehicles, subject to compliance with the operating criteria set forth in the rule. Qualifying entities for this purpose include registered investment companies, insurance company separate accounts, bank trust funds, and pension plans subject to Title I of the Employee Retirement Income Security Act of 1974 (ERISA).

*Pools Offered Only to Qualified Participants (Rule 4.7).* CFTC Rule 4.7 provides a sweeping exemption from disclosure, reporting and recordkeeping requirements to commodity pool operators offering a pool exclusively to persons who satisfy relatively strict financial requirements or are registered investment professionals. This exemption represents the closest analogue under the CFTC's regulatory framework to the private offering exemption from registration under the Securities Act of 1933. Qualified eligible participants fall into three general categories. The first category consists of registered futures and securities professionals, e.g., futures commission merchants (commodity brokers), securities broker-dealers, the commodity pool operator and the commodity trading advisors for the pool being offered, and commodity pool operators and commodity trading advisors who have been registered and active as such for the prior two years and who have $5,000,000 under management. The second category generally includes persons who qualify as "accredited investors" as defined in the SEC's Regulation D private offering safe harbor and who satisfy a portfolio requirement under which, at the time of purchase of the pool interest the customer must be reasonably be believed to: (1) own securities (of issuers not affiliated with the customer) or other investments with an aggregate market value of at least $2,000,000; (2) have had on deposit with a futures commission merchant at any time during the preceding six-month period at least $200,000 in exchange-specified initial margin and option premiums for commodity interest transactions; or (3) a combination of (1) and (2). The third category includes entities in which all unit owners or participants are qualified eligible participants.

The relief available under Rule 4.7 includes: (1) exemption from the specific CFTC requirements applicable to disclosure documents, *e.g.*, the specific performance history disclosures required by CFTC rules; however, any offering memorandum distributed for the pool must include all disclosures necessary to make the information contained therein not misleading; (2) permission to provide pool participants, in lieu of the prescribed account statement, a quarterly statement that indicates the net asset value of the pool as of the end of the reporting period and the change in net asset value from the end of the previous reporting period; and (3) acceptance, in lieu of the prescribed certified annual report, of an uncertified annual report which contains, at a minimum, Statements of Financial Condition and of Income (Loss). Rule 4.7 also provides an exemption from the specific recordkeeping requirements applicable to commodity pool operators generally but maintains the requirement that the pool operator maintain all account statements, annual reports and all other books and records prepared in connection with its activity as the commodity pool operator of the pool. Rule 4.7 exempt pools remain subject to the CFTC's anti-fraud rules.

*Commodity Pools Primarily Engaged in Securities Activities (Rule 4.12(b))*. CFTC Rule 4.12(b) provides narrower exemptive relief than Rule 4.7 but is likely to be available to a broader range of investment vehicles. As the rationale for Rule 4.7 relief is the substantial financial wherewithal and thus presumed financial sophistication of the pool's participants, the predicate for the Rule 4.12(b) exemption is that the fund's primary investment activity is in securities and that the fund's futures activity is limited and incidental to its securities trading activities. In this context, the securities activities of the fund predominate sufficiently that compliance with applicable securities requirements in lieu of compliance with certain CFTC requirements is considered warranted. Rule 4.12(b) relief is available to registered commodity pool operators who operate pools which: (1) are offered and sold pursuant to the Securities Act of 1933 or an exemption therefrom; (2) are generally and routinely engaged in the purchase and sale of securities and "securities derived instruments"; (3) do not commit more than ten percent of the fair market value of their assets to establish commodity futures or option positions; and (4) will trade commodity futures or options in a manner solely incidental to their securities trading.

The Rule 4.12(b) exemption permits the pool operator to: (1) use an offering memorandum prepared in accordance with the Securities Act of 1933 or relevant exemption therefrom, supplemented by certain, but not all, disclosure document information otherwise required to be included in the pool disclosure document prepared by the CFTC; (2) provide a quarterly statement that indicates the net asset value of the pool as of the end of the reporting period and the change in net asset value from the end of the previous reporting period in lieu of the prescribed account statement; (3) provide in lieu of the prescribed annual report a certified annual report which includes, at a minimum, Statements of Financial Condition and of Income (Loss); and (4) claim exemption from certain recordkeeping requirements.

*Offshore Pools*. Many U.S. fund managers operate "offshore" funds, that is, funds organized in locations outside of the United States and offered only to non-United States persons. To the extent

> that such funds engage in futures transactions and are operated by pool operators located in the United States, the CFTC's registration, disclosure, and other requirements apply. However, pursuant to delegated authority, CFTC staff have made exemptive relief available from disclosure document, account statement, annual report and certain recordkeeping requirements where: (1) the pool is organized and operated outside the United States; (2) none of the participants in the pool is a United States person; (3) no capital is committed, directly or indirectly, to the pool from United States sources; and (4) the commodity pool operator will not engage in any marketing activity with respect to United States persons. The U.S. operators of offshore funds remain subject to anti-fraud and anti-manipulation prohibitions, to certain recordkeeping requirements, and to requirements to provide information upon request of the CFTC. (See generally CFTC Advisory No. 18-96, [Current Transfer Binder] Comm. Fut. L. Rep. (CCH) 25,659 (April 11, 1996)).

Of particular note in this context is the application of CFTC Rule 4.5 to advisers to registered investment companies. Advisers to registered investment companies are subject to regulation by the CFTC, and are not excluded from such regulation under CFTC Rule 4.5, if an investment company that is advised by the investment adviser either (i) invests, directly or indirectly, more than a prescribed level of its liquidation value in CFTC-regulated futures, options and swaps or (ii) markets itself as providing investment exposure to such instruments (excluding investments for *bona fide* hedging purposes). In practice, many investment companies are able to meet these requirements, but some are not. Advisers subject to CFTC regulation with respect to investment companies are subject to additional CFTC disclosure, reporting and recordkeeping obligations, though the impact of these additional requirements is mitigated by CFTC efforts to "harmonize" the CFTC and SEC regulatory regimes for such advisers.

---

## Discussion Topics

a. Please examine the problems posed by commodity future pools; how similar or different are these problems from those posed by investment companies?

b. How different or similar is the regulation of commodity future pools from the regulation of investment companies? Why the differences?

c. As a policy matter, should all pooled collective investment vehicles be regulated in the same manner?

---

## Problem

You were asked to review a draft prospectus for a new registered investment company. The fund has the authority to engage in derivatives transactions, including buying and selling commodity futures contracts, options on such contracts and various swaps subject to CFTC jurisdiction. The fund will not, however, engage in such investments in excess of the numerical limitations contained in CFTC Rule 4.5 (excluding investments for *bona fide* hedging purposes). But, the draft prospectus does contain a variety of disclosures describing these investments and their attendant risks. This disclosure covers about five pages in the prospectus and is broadly consistent with the scope and content of similar disclosure used by other registered investment companies claiming the CFTC Rule 4.5 exclusion.

Write an email to your colleague with primary responsibility for drafting the prospectus explaining your view as to whether this disclosure constitutes marketing the fund as a commodity pool, or otherwise as a vehicle for trading in the commodity futures, commodity options, or swaps markets.

---

# Chapter 6

## *Registration and Disclosure*

### A. Registration Under the Investment Company Act

Section 8 of the Investment Company Act requires that *investment companies* register, similar to the registration of issuers under section 12 of the Securities Exchange Act of 1934. In addition, section 24(a) of the Act requires the registration of the *securities* issued by investment companies similar to the registration of securities of issuers under the Securities Act of 1933.

Who may register an investment company? Section 7(a) prohibits transactions in interstate commerce by unregistered investment companies, and section 47(b) provides that a contract made in violation of the Act is generally unenforceable. Thus, registration of the investment companies triggers the applicability of the Act. The Act applies to investment companies and their sponsors, if they should have registered but did not, in violation of the Act. Otherwise violators would be rewarded.

Section 7(d) prohibits foreign investment companies from *publicly* distributing their securities unless the SEC permits them by order to register. The SEC's discretion is limited to situations in which the Commission finds that it is both legally and practically feasible to effectively enforce the provisions of the 1940 Act against such company and that the issuance of the order is consistent with the public interest and the protection of investors.

Note that the prohibition on registration of foreign investment companies applies only to those companies that offer their securities publicly. However, the SEC staff has interpreted this limitation to further limit foreign companies to the constraints of section 3(c)(1) or section 3(c)(7) of the Act. Thus, not only should a foreign investment company avoid offering its securities publicly without SEC order, but it must also comply with the other conditions of section 3(c)(1) or section 3(c)(7). Note that statutory exceptions from the definition of an investment company, for example, of banks, apply only to companies that are supervised by U.S. regulators. Therefore, under the text of the Act, a foreign bank is subject to section 7(d) while its branch, subject to U.S. supervision, is not. The branch is excluded from the definition of an investment company under the Act. Rule 3a-6 under the Act extends the exclusion from the definition of an investment company to foreign banks and foreign insurance companies subject to regulation as such by a foreign government.

---

## Discussion Topics

a. Why did Congress restrict the registration of publicly held foreign investment companies under section 7 of the Investment Company Act?

b. Are Americans prohibited from purchasing shares of foreign investment companies when they travel abroad?

c. May Americans buy such shares by placing orders with their brokers abroad, or with their domestic brokers?

d. What about foreign investment companies that issue securities to foreign citizens who come every winter to Florida and own or rent an apartment there?

---

## B. Disclosure: The Prospectus and the Statement of Additional Information (SAI)

### 1. The Prospectus and the Statement of Additional Information (SAI)

Both investment companies and their securities register on one form, Form N-1A (Form N-2 for closed-end funds). This form serves a dual purpose by allowing a fund to register both itself under the Investment Company Act and its securities under the Securities Act. The form creates a two-part disclosure document — one document, the prospectus, which the issuer must send to investors; the other document, a statement of additional information (SAI), which the issuer must send investors upon their request. The allocation of information to these parts is not always clear. This issue has arisen in the case of *White v. Melton*[1] below.

In *White,* the investor claimed that "a critical piece of information was omitted from the . . . [p]rospectus" although it was in the SAI which was incorporated by reference in the prospectus. This piece of information pertained to a "freeze rule" relative to the sales charge. The fund's sales charge is imposed when shares are redeemed and is reduced based on the holding period. Shareholders may transfer their holdings into other funds, but if they switch back the freeze rule provides that time spent in the other fund does not count toward the reduction. However, subsequent registration statements disclosed this rule in the prospectus.

The issue was whether the "freeze rule" had to appear in the prospectus or if it was permissible to incorporate it by reference from the SAI. Form N-1A and SEC guidelines require that procedures regarding redemption of shares and charges and restrictions on redemption be included in the prospectus. However, the Form N-1A instructions only require the prospectus to "list" any special purchase plans (including exchange privileges) and the form requires a "description" of such plans in the SAI.

---

1. *White v. Melton,* 757 F. Supp. 267 (S.D.N.Y. 1991).

The Court found that the company complied with the instructions and with SEC policy as the information was "of interest only to that limited class of investors who would wish to switch their money out of the Plus Fund, switch it back in again, and redeem their shares, all before the seventh year of their investment." The Court said that the prospectus "should be as simple and direct as reasonably possible" and concluded that the rule was not a "fundamental characteristic" of the company but "the sort of 'excessive detail'" that should be in the SAI.

---

**Discussion Topics**

a. Do you agree that the law should permit the information in the SAI to be incorporated by reference into the prospectus? If so, doesn't this mean, in effect, that a person is deemed to have received information that he or she did not receive?

b. What should determine whether information belongs in the prospectus or statement of additional information? Is it that, as the court says, information belongs in the SAI if it "is of interest only to [a] limited class of investors"? Note that, as the opinion indicated, the registration statements subsequent to the February 3, 1987 prospectus included the freeze rule in the prospectus. Given the court's determination that the freeze rule was of interest to only a limited class of investors, why did the lawyers shift it to the prospectus, and should the SEC have ordered the information to be moved back to the SAI?

---

**Problem**

Prospectus disclosure practices used by open-end funds and closed-end funds differ considerably as they relate to the description of portfolio instruments and risk factors. Open-end funds often have cursory disclosure in their prospectuses and include very detailed disclosure in the SAI. Closed-end funds, on the other hand, tend to include detailed descriptions of principal portfolio instruments and risk factors in their prospectus, supplement these descriptions as necessary in the SAI, and include detailed descriptions of portfolio instruments and risk factors that are not the principal portfolio emphasis in the SAI. Your client is trying to decide how to organize the information in a new closed-end fund's prospectus. Please write a memo explaining to your client the relative benefits and drawbacks to these two different organizational approaches.

---

### 2. Efforts to Enhance the Effectiveness of Prospectus Disclosure

#### a. Prospectus Simplification and the Summary Prospectus

In spite of the court's holding in *White v. Melton,* fund legal counsel have generally chosen to include a significant amount of cautionary language in the prospectus as a legal defense against investor claims. Yet, the more generalized and complicated material prospectuses contain, the less legible they become. Therefore, in December 1996, the Commission proposed a thorough revision of Form N-1A. The SEC also proposed an innovative new short-disclosure instrument, the profile. The structure of the profile was intended to be standard and easy to read. It contained nine items arranged in the format of questions and answers. Issuers were permitted to use the profile to solicit and make sales of their shares, provided the investors receive a statutory prospectus (i.e., a prospectus meeting the requirements of section 10(a) of the Securities Act) upon confirmation of the sale. The profile could also be used as an "executive summary" or an introduction to the prospectus, or sent with the prospectus at any other time. In 2009, the SEC again adopted amendments to the registration form for investment companies and their securities designed to simplify and make information more readable and replaced the profile with a "summary prospectus."[1] The SEC announced:

> The Securities and Exchange Commission is adopting amendments to the form used by mutual funds to register under the Investment Company Act of 1940 and to offer their securities under the Securities Act of 1933 in order to enhance the disclosures that are provided to mutual fund investors. The amendments require key information to appear in plain English in a standardized order at the front of the mutual fund statutory prospectus. The Commission is also adopting rule amendments that permit a person to satisfy its mutual fund prospectus delivery obligations under section 5(b)(2) of the Securities Act by sending or giving the key information directly to investors in the form of a summary prospectus and providing the statutory prospectus on an Internet Web site. Upon an investor's request, mutual funds are also required to send the statutory prospectus to the investor. These amendments are intended to improve mutual fund disclosure by providing investors with key information in plain English in a clear and concise format, while enhancing the means of delivering more detailed information to investors. . . .

Note also that a "summary prospectus" is considered a prospectus under section 10(b) of the Securities Act and that a prospectus under Section 10(b) of the 1933 Act, unless otherwise provided by the SEC, is not subject to the liabilities under Section 11 of the 1933 Act.[2] This relieves the issuers from liabilities for abbreviated information that might not be fully informative as a prospectus should be.

---

## Discussion Topics

a. Will these proposals improve the quality of prospectus disclosure that is present in prospectuses? Why is such technical legal jargon used in the first place? Is it the fault of the drafters? Is it the fault of the SEC staff

1. Enhanced Disclosure and New Prospectus Delivery Option for Registered Open-End Management Investment Companies, Investment Company Act Rel. No. 28584 (Jan. 13, 2009), 74 Fed. Reg. 4546 (Jan. 26, 2009) (codified as amended at 17 C.F.R. § 230.498 (2015)).
2. 15 U.S.C. § 77j(b) (2012).

that reviews and comments on registration statements? Or the fault of the statute and form requirements?

b. As an investor, how important to you is the information contained in the annual and semi-annual reports? What type of periodic information would you like to receive?

c. What role should the SEC staff play in the review of disclosure documents?

---

### b. Improving Risk Disclosure

The SEC noted a problem that disclosure by investment companies posed:[1]

> Investment companies' prospectuses have been criticized as unintelligible, tedious, and legalistic. Although prospectuses remain the most complete source of information about a fund, technical and unnecessarily lengthy prospectus disclosure often obscures important information relating to a fund investment and does not serve the information needs of the majority of fund investors. As millions of Americans have turned to funds as an investment vehicle of choice investors need to be provided with clear and comprehensible information that will help them evaluate and compare fund investments.

In 1995, the Commission discussed possible improvements to investment companies' disclosure.[2] The following is an excerpt of the discussion.

> Today the SEC is continuing its efforts to enhance the information that investors in funds receive to assist them in making an informed investment decision. In recent years, the SEC has taken significant steps designed to improve the understandability and comparability of fund disclosure of performance and expenses. The SEC is now requesting comment on how to improve risk disclosure for investment companies, including ways to increase the comparability of disclosure about funds' risk levels through quantitative measures or other means.
>
> Under existing SEC rules, a fund is required to discuss in its prospectus the principal risk factors associated with investing in the fund. Funds typically describe the risks of investing in the fund by describing the risks of particular investment policies that the fund may use and investments that the fund may make. Lengthy and highly technical descriptions of permissible policies and investments that are often used in meeting existing requirements may make it difficult for investors to understand the total risk level of a fund. The SEC staff has found that funds typically provide only the most

---

1. Registration Form Used by Open-End Management Investment Companies, Investment Company Act Rel. No. 22528 (Feb. 27, 1997), 62 Fed. Reg. 10,898, 10,898-99 (Mar. 10, 1997) (footnotes omitted).
2. Improving Descriptions of Risk by Mutual Funds, and Other Investment Companies, Investment Company Act Rel. No. 20974 (Mar. 29, 1995).

general information on the risk level of the fund taken as a whole and has encouraged funds to modify their existing disclosure to enhance investor understanding of risks. . . . The SEC believes that it is now appropriate to explore whether SEC disclosure requirements should be revised in order to improve the communication of fund risks to investors and increase the likelihood that investors will readily grasp the risks of investing in a particular fund before they invest.

Several factors make it important that the SEC explore better ways of explaining fund risks to investors. First, average Americans are placing increasing reliance on funds to meet important financial needs, such as retirement and college expenses. Understanding the risks of various investment products is one of the most important ingredients in creating an overall investment strategy or portfolio to meet these financial needs. Second, new ways of describing risks may improve investor understanding of the risks associated with the use by some funds of increasingly complex instruments, such as derivatives. Third, the number and types of funds have proliferated, increasing fund investors' need for information that will help them to compare and contrast alternatives.

The importance of risk disclosure was underscored last year when some short-term government bond funds experienced losses as interest rates increased sharply. Shareholders in these funds expressed surprise at the losses, and several shareholder lawsuits were filed. Whatever the legal merits of the shareholder complaints may be, the SEC believes that these events highlight the importance of clear, concise disclosure of risks.

In this Release, the SEC requests that those submitting comments discuss the specific goals of, and various alternatives for improving, risk disclosure. Comments are requested on the relative merits of written and other presentations of risk, including quantitative or numerical measures, graphs, tables, and other pictorial representations.

The Release describes and requests comment on several specific quantitative measures of risk and risk-adjusted performance, including standard deviation, semi-variance, beta, duration, the Sharpe Ratio, the Treynor Ratio, and Jensen's Alpha. These measures of risk are potentially useful because they may give investors a tool for balancing the potential returns of a fund against the risks of the fund. For instance, if a fund has historical annual returns which are 2% above a market index, historical risk measures may provide some indication of the risks that were taken to produce the increased returns. Quantitative risk measurements may provide investors with tools to measure how funds have fared historically in the relationship between risk and return.

The Release also asks for comments addressing a number of general topics related to quantitative risk measures. These include:

* The benefits to be derived from quantitative measures versus the costs and burdens to the fund that must produce such information;

* Quantitative measures currently used by fund managers to

assess risk, and whether such internally used measures should be disclosed to investors;

* Investor understanding of quantitative measures, and means to increase that understanding;

* Standardizing the ways in which funds calculate quantitative measures to assure comparability and the validity of any underlying assumptions; and

* Availability of quantitative risk information from third party providers (e.g., the financial press and rating services).

Comments are also requested on whether funds should be required to disclose a self-assessment of their risk level, using an SEC-created standard scale or some other method. In addition, comments are requested on whether funds should describe to investors the ways or strategies that fund managers use to manage, understand, and monitor the risks of their funds. . . .

[Commentators should] define, as precisely as possible, what "risks" should be disclosed to investors. To what extent are investors concerned with the likelihood that they will lose principal, that their return will not exceed a specified benchmark (such as the Standard & Poor's ("S&P") 500), or with the variability of their returns (or the volatility of the value of their investment) over time? How should the relationship between risk and an investor's time horizon shape the disclosure that is provided to investors? For example, is the same risk information useful to an investor with an investment time horizon of less than one year and to an investor with an investment time horizon of twenty years? How can the disclosure of risk help investors answer the fundamental questions — Is this investment suitable for me? If I have diversified my investments, how does this particular fund fit into my diversification strategy?

Comments are requested on the nature of risk comparisons that are useful to investors. For example, should risk disclosure facilitate comparison among a broad range of investment options, such as between funds and other investment products? Or is it sufficient to facilitate comparisons among all funds and fund types, both equity and fixed income? Or among all equity funds, on the one hand, and all fixed income funds, on the other? Or only within groups of funds with similar investment objectives and policies, such as short-term government bond funds?

Is improved disclosure of risks equally important for equity fixed income, and balanced or asset allocation funds? Do recent derivatives-related losses by some fixed income funds, and the apparently greater use of derivatives by fixed income funds, suggest that the need for improved disclosure of risks is greater for fixed income funds? In light of the substantive limits on permitted money market fund investments, should risk disclosure requirements for money market funds be different from those applicable to other funds?

Comments are also requested on the degree of detail regarding

> fund risk that ideally would be communicated to investors. In meeting existing disclosure requirements, funds often describe the purposes of using particular types of instruments and the risks associated with each type, but typically provide only the most general information on the risk level of the fund taken as a whole. Should disclosure convey the risks of each particular type of instrument held by a fund, the risks of broader classes of instruments (for instance, derivatives as a group), the risks of the fund's portfolio as a whole, or some combination of the foregoing? Should the focus of disclosure be shifted from the characteristics of particular securities to the nature of the investment management services offered, including the objectives of a fund manager and the associated risks and rewards? Do investors need to understand separately the different types of risk, such as market, credit, legal, and operational risks, or is it the aggregate effect of different types of risk that is important to an investment decision. . . ?

More recently, the SEC has focused on the quality of risk disclosure around investment companies' use of derivatives. In particular, the SEC staff has noted:[1]

> [W]e believe that all funds that use or intend to use derivative instruments should assess the accuracy and completeness of their disclosure, including whether the disclosure is presented in an understandable manner using plain English. Further, any principal investment strategies disclosure related to derivatives should be tailored specifically to how a fund expects to be managed and should address those strategies that the fund expects to be the most important means of achieving its objectives and that it anticipates will have a significant effect on its performance. In determining the appropriate disclosure, a fund should consider the degree of economic exposure the derivatives create, in addition to the amount invested in the derivatives strategy. This disclosure also should describe the purpose that the derivatives are intended to serve in the portfolio (*e.g.*, hedging, speculation, or as a substitute for investing in conventional securities), and the extent to which derivatives are expected to be used.

The SEC staff has been particularly focused on these matters related to derivatives disclosure in recent years and often requires funds to make representations in the registration statement review process that they have considered the staff's views as described above in crafting derivatives-related disclosure.

---

## Discussion Topics

a. In your opinion, would most investors prefer to be told about risk by narrative or non-narrative means?

1. Letter from Barry Miller, Associate Director, to Karrie McMillan, General Counsel, Investment Company Institute, (Jul. 30, 2010); *see also* Division of Investment Management, IM Guidance Update No. 2013-05 (Jul. 2013).

b. Can an investor truly understand the risk of his or her fund without knowing the characteristics of the fund's portfolio investments?

c. Do you think the industry would embrace the idea of a self-assessment of its risk? What potential liability issues arise in such a case?

d. Is the evaluation of mutual fund risk better left to rating agencies? Who would pay a rating agency for providing this service?

---

## C. Electronic Delivery of Disclosure

Electronic transfer of information has already affected the regulation of securities offerings and is bound to force fundamental changes in the regulation of the securities offerings and industry. The SEC has been quick to respond to the new technology. The following release illustrates the various interpretative questions that arise when a fund delivers disclosure electronically.[1]

> General
>
> The federal securities statutes do not prescribe the medium to be used for providing information by or on behalf of issuers, or by or on behalf of third parties with respect to issuers. The Commission believes that delivery of information through an electronic medium generally could satisfy delivery or transmission obligations under the federal securities laws.
>
> The federal securities laws, among other purposes, seek to promote fair and orderly markets by requiring the disclosure of material information that enables investors to make informed investment and voting decisions. The extent to which required disclosure is made, as opposed to the medium for providing it, should be most important to the analysis of whether sufficient disclosure has occurred under the securities laws. An electronic medium would not provide an adequate means for the delivery of required disclosure, and thus not serve the statutory purposes, if the medium does not permit effective communication to investors or is practically unavailable.
>
> The Commission believes that the question of whether delivery through electronic media has been achieved is most easily examined by analogy to paper delivery procedures. The Commission would view information distributed through electronic means as satisfying the delivery or transmission requirements of the federal securities laws if such distribution results in the delivery to the intended recipients of substantially equivalent information as these recipients would have had if the information were delivered to them in paper form. As is the case with paper delivery, there should be an opportunity to retain a permanent record of the information. . . .
>
> Mutual Funds
>
> The Commission is aware that investment companies, particularly

1. Use of Electronic Media for Delivery Purposes, Investment Company Act Rel. No. 21399 (Oct. 6, 1995).

open-end investment companies ("mutual funds" or "funds") have been active in using electronic means to communicate with their shareholders and prospective investors. Given the extent to which funds have embraced the new technologies, the Commission believes that it is appropriate to include the following (guidance).

* * *

Examples

(31) A fund sends an e-mail to a recipient with a prospectus attached. The prospectus file includes an application form. The recipient fills out the form and mails it with a check to the fund.

Delivery of the prospectus may be inferred from the recipient's use of the form (provided the fund can identify it as coming from the electronically transmitted prospectus).

(32) A current prospectus is faxed to a potential investor who has requested the prospectus and provided the phone number of the fax machine.

This transmission satisfies the prospectus delivery requirements.

(33) A current prospectus and an application are faxed to a potential investor. The investor did not request the fax, but the sender knows the investor's fax machine phone number.

If the investor completes and mails in the application form included in the faxed prospectus, delivery of the electronic prospectus may be inferred.

* * *

(36) A prospectus is made available through an on-line system that allows users to access, download or print the entire prospectus and has the capacity to track which users accessed, printed or downloaded which documents.

A fund may rely upon a user's having accessed, printed or downloaded a prospectus for the fund in order to deliver supplemental sales literature or an order form for the fund or to establish delivery of the prospectus in connection with a sale of fund shares.

(37) A fund's prospectus is available through an on-line service that does not have the capacity for downloading or printing or to track retrieval by a user. Investors do not provide any consent. The fund mails or e-mails supplemental sales literature, or an application to all of the service's subscribers, without including a prospectus.

Absent other factors that would indicate delivery of the prospectus, the fund may not send the supplemental sales literature or an application in this fashion, because it is not preceded or accompanied by the prospectus for purposes of Section 2(10)(a) of the Securities Act. This would be true even if the general subscription agreement for the service contained a provision consenting to receipt of documents, because such consent would not be sufficient to give the fund reason to believe that delivery requirements relating to the prospectus will actually be satisfied.

(38) A server available through the Internet contains a fund's prospectus and application form in separate files. Users can download or print the application form without first accessing, downloading or printing the prospectus; the form includes a statement that by signing the form, the investor certifies that he or she has received the prospectus. Logistically it is significantly more burdensome to access the prospectus than the application form (e.g., the investor needs to download special software before accessing the prospectus).

The statement in the form about receipt of the prospectus would not by itself constitute electronic delivery of the prospectus, and the application form is not evidence of delivery of the prospectus, given the need to download special software before the prospectus can be viewed.

(39) A server available through the Internet contains a fund's prospectus. Users must download the prospectus to view or print it. When a user downloads the prospectus, the user receives the prospectus and an application form in separate files. It is not significantly more burdensome to access the prospectus than the application form (e.g., no additional software is necessary to read either document, although the documents may be in different formats).

If the fund can identify the application form as coming from the electronic system, electronic delivery of the prospectus can be inferred. The application form is evidence of delivery of the prospectus.

(40) A fund's prospectus and application form are available through an electronic system like that described in the preceding example, except that the investor needs to download special software before the prospectus and application form can be downloaded.

If the fund can identify the application form as coming from the electronic system, electronic delivery of the prospectus can be inferred. The application form is evidence of access to the prospectus.

* * *

(42) A fund transmits prospectuses over an electronic bulletin board. Investors provide specific consent to receipt of the prospectus through that system. The consent states that the current version of the prospectus will be made continuously available and notice of material amendments will be given by mail, e-mail, or some other manner specifically directed to investors.

The prospectus delivery requirements will be satisfied with respect to subsequent additional purchases by those investors.

(43) A fund places its prospectus on its Internet Web site and revises the electronic version whenever the prospectus is modified. The fund materially amends the prospectus and decides to send a postcard or e-mail to persons to whom the prospectus has been

> delivered through electronic means or who have consented to electronic delivery notifying them of the availability of the amended prospectus.
>
> This procedure provides for delivery of the prospectus to those who have consented and to those to whom the prospectus has been previously delivered (if the fund expects those persons to be able to receive the amended prospectus). Alternatively, the fund could choose to satisfy its prospectus delivery requirements by sending a paper copy of the amended prospectus to investors in the fund, including investors who consented to receive documents electronically.
>
> (44) A fund places its prospectus on its Internet Web site. Potential investor John Doe obtains access to the prospectus. John Doe does not purchase shares in the fund. Subsequently, the prospectus is amended.
>
> The fund does not need to provide John Doe with notice of the amendment.
>
> * * *
>
> (47) A fund sends investors upon request a CD-ROM containing its current prospectus and registration statement materials for the fund's offering.
>
> This would provide delivery to investors.
>
> (48) Prospectuses and other materials are available through a computer server that requires users to obtain a user ID and password before they can access documents on the system. The process for obtaining the ID and password requires significant information from the user and involves a delay of one day or even several days before the user can access the system. After a user accesses a prospectus, a fund sends him or her supplemental sales literature.
>
> The process provides for delivery of the prospectus. Although the system imposes burdens in the process for obtaining access to the prospectus, these burdens are part of the process of providing access to all the information, including the supplemental sales literature, and not burdens upon access to the prospectus that is delivered.
>
> (49) A prospectus is made available through an on-line system that allows users to download the entire prospectus. The system does not permit on-line viewing. An investor downloads the prospectus.
>
> Assuming downloading, this method would satisfy the delivery requirements because on-line viewing is not a prerequisite to electronic delivery. . . .

Additionally, the SEC has recently proposed various rules designed to improve investment companies' periodic reports. As part of this proposal, the SEC has proposed a new rule 30e-3 under the Investment Company Act to allow investment companies to satisfy their delivery obligations for periodic shareholder reports by posting those reports on the Internet and sending a brief notice of availability to shareholders. Importantly, these proposals relate only to periodic shareholder reports, and not to offering documents such as prospectuses; however, funds could continue to rely on the above-described guidance with respect to electronic delivery of prospectuses.[1]

---

<u>Discussion Topics</u>

a. Is it appropriate for the SEC to view electronic delivery as an alternative to paper delivery?

b. Should the SEC have used this release as a vehicle to make changes in the way information is provided to investors? For example, should the SEC have required investors to pass an on-line test demonstrating proficiency in investing before they can invest?

---

### D. Prospectus Updates

Because in 2016 most mutual funds are open-end funds, they typically sell their securities on a continuous basis to help offset redemptions and become larger, presumably in order to reduce management costs. Therefore, a current prospectus must be maintained on an on-going basis. Specifically, section 10(a)(3) of the Securities Act requires that any prospectus used more than 9 months after the registration statement's effective date must contain financial and other information as of a date not more than 16 months prior to such use. This means that a prospectus containing financial statements as of December 31, 2014 will become stale as of May 1, 2016. Prospectuses can become stale for reasons other than outdated financial statements. For example, advisory fees may change, a fundamental investment policy may be revised, or a fund may be merged into another fund. A fund generally updates its prospectus on an annual basis by filing a post-effective amendment to its registration statement that contains updated financial statements and other information. The SEC has established rules under the Securities Act that permit these annual updates to go automatically effective if the only changes being made are updating the financial statements and making other non-material changes; otherwise, these rules provide for a 60-day review period of the annual update.[2] In between annual amendments, funds typically "sticker" their prospectuses with updates that are in the form of a one or two page supplement delivered with the prospectus describing the updated information. These "stickers" are also filed with the SEC.

### E. Liability for a Misleading Prospectus

The issuer of an investment company's securities is the investment company. However, the preparation and management of these companies is in the hands of the sponsoring investment adviser. On June 13, 2011, the Supreme Court decided the issue of who can be sued for a misleading or inaccurate prospectus. The following is a summary of the Court's five

---

1. Investment Company Reporting Modernization, Investment Company Act Rel. No. 31610 (May 20, 2015).
2. 17 C.F.R. § 230.485 (2015).

to four decision in the case of *Janus Capital Group, Inc. v. First Derivative Traders.*[1]

An investment company, Janus Investment Fund ("Fund"), was advised by Janus Capital Management, LLC, ("Adviser"), a wholly owned subsidiary of a Janus holding company, Janis Capital Group, Inc. ("JCG"). First Derivative Traders ("First Derivative"), representing a class of plaintiffs who owned the publicly traded stock of JCG, filed a private action against the Adviser and JCG for making false statements in the Fund's prospectuses, in violation of Rule 10b-5. This rule makes it unlawful for "any person . . . [t]o make any untrue statement of a material fact" in connection with the purchase or sale of securities. The prospectus was filed by the Fund. The false statement, once uncovered, affected the price of JCG's stock (as a result of redemptions from the Fund, and thus decreased revenue for the Adviser in the form of an asset-based management fee). The Fund, the Adviser and JCG are separate legal entities.

The Fourth Circuit held that First Derivative sufficiently alleged that the Adviser and JCG, by participating in the writing and dissemination of the Fund's prospectuses, made the misleading statements contained in the documents and that JCG was liable as a controlling person.

The Supreme Court, by a 5 to 4 majority, held that it was the Fund who was "maker" of the misstatements in its prospectuses. The majority held that because the Fund filed the registration statement, the Adviser (and thus JCG as a control person of the Adviser) that participated in preparing it was not liable for the misstatements contained therein. The Adviser is like the speech writer that enables the speaker — the Fund — to deliver the speech. Only the speaker is liable for the misstatement.

The majority of the Supreme Court justices emphasized the importance of recognizing the acting corporate entities and allocating to each the true liability. It also noted the movement to limit the reach of federal private rights of action. Unless the private right of action is bestowed by Congress, courts will not tend to imply a private right of action from a criminal prohibition. In this case, however, the Court restated the existence of a private right of action under rule 10b-5, but noted that its reach has excluded aiders and abettors and hence the "preparer of the speech," as compared to the actual speakers.

The minority four judges viewed the issues differently. Focusing on the word "make" in rule 10b-5, the dissent noted that common English and the Court's earlier cases did not limit the scope of that word to those with "ultimate authority over a statement's content," but rather "indicate that, depending upon the circumstances, a management company, a board of trustees, individual company officers, or others, separately or together, might 'make' statements contained in a firm's prospectus — even if a board of directors has ultimate content-related responsibility." Such circumstances may exist here as the Adviser allegedly created the impression it would curb market timing and allegedly knew the statements were false and material.

1. *Janus Capital Group, Inc. v. First Derivative Traders,* 131 S. Ct. 2296; 180 L. Ed. 2d 166 (2011).

The dissent disagreed with the majority's narrow interpretation of the word "make" and disagreed that a broader interpretation would undermine the principle that rule 10b-5 does not include aiding and abetting, as the case relied on for that principle left open the possibility that secondary actors could have primary liability.

The dissent also suggested that the majority's rule may create a loophole under which managers could write a fraudulent prospectus and fool the board and no party would be liable, as the managers would not be liable as principals and did not aid or abet another primary violator.

---

**Discussion Topics:**

a. What are the implications of the Supreme Court case above for other liabilities under the Investment Company Act?

b. The judicial source of implied rights of action is state law derived from the maxim that if there is a wrong (in this case a criminal offense) there should be a remedy (which the courts should provide). Did the Supreme Court follow this principle?

---

## F. The Relationship Between the Prospectus and the SAI

The case described below, *Tabankin v. Kemper Short-term Global Income Fund,*[1] highlights the relationship between the prospectus and supplemental sales literature.

In *Tabankin,* investment company investors suffered a loss when the net asset values of the funds decreased. They brought a lawsuit for federal securities law and common law fraud. A brochure said, "If you like the idea of a conservative investment, but not conservative yields, consider an investment in Kemper Investment Portfolio Short-Term Global Income Portfolio. . . ." The prospectus said, "The objective of [the Fund] is to provide as high a level of current income as is consistent with prudent investment management. . . ." The investors alleged that the fund managers did not follow "prudent" or "conservative" investment management. Much of the fund's assets were invested in bonds denominated in weak foreign currencies, and when the countries devalued their currencies, the fund's net asset value decreased.

The Court followed the rule that "failure to disclose material information in supplemental literature is not fraud if that information is disclosed in the prospectus." Applying that rule, the Court failed to find material misrepresentations, noting that "the brochures themselves contained disclosures about risks and referred the reader to the [p]rospectus." The Court failed to find facts to show imprudent management; other statements in the prospectus clarify "prudent investment management" and the

1. *Tabankin v. Kemper Short-Term Global Income Fund,* 1994 U.S. Dist. LEXIS 965 (N.D. Ill. Jan. 31. 1994), *complaint dismissed,* 1994 U.S. Dist. LEXIS 8498 (N.D. Ill. Jun. 22, 1994) (internal citations omitted).

fund used the investment strategies in the prospectus (e.g., investment in specified foreign currencies and a cross-hedging strategy).

The Court also failed to find materiality. A material statement must "significantly alter the total mix of information available to the investor." In conjunction with the "total mix," the statements in question do not establish misrepresentation; there were clear disclosures such as "The Fund's returns and net asset value will fluctuate." "[A] general statement of the [f]und's objective" does not establish fraud "when the [p]rospectus clearly states that there is no assurance that the objective will be achieved, goes on to list specific risks associated with the particular [f]und, and the plaintiffs' loss results from those very risks."

---

## Discussion Topics

a. What caused the decline in net asset value of the fund? Was this risk adequately discussed in the brochure or the prospectus?

b. In determining whether Kemper's statements contain a misrepresentation, the court's opinion focuses on the prospectus: "[A] failure to disclose material information in supplemental literature is not fraud if that information is disclosed in the prospectus." Why? Why not require the material information to be in both places?

c. In this case, the court sets out the standard for materiality that was originally established in *Basic v. Levinson,* 485 U.S. 224 (1988). The *Basic v. Levinson* standard examined materiality with respect to shares of an issuer that was not an investment company. Should the standard of materiality with respect to mutual funds be different?

---

The adequacy of statements made in a prospectus was further discussed in *Hyperion Securities Litigation.*[1] This case is summarized below.

Investors in investment companies investing primarily in mortgage-backed securities alleged that the offering materials and "roadshows" (presentations to brokers) misrepresented the companies' investment strategy and risks. Investors brought actions for misrepresentation under the securities laws and common law fraud, and alleged that the defendants misstated the investment strategy and concealed the degree of risk. "Defendants allegedly misstated the investment strategy by purporting to design 'balanced' portfolios that would remain neutral to interest rate fluctuations, when in reality they assembled a 'biased' fund skewed in favor of rising interest rates." In addition, they allegedly concealed the risk of permanent loss of capital if interest rates declined.

The court found no material misrepresentations or omissions, as the "[investment] strategy and risks were either disclosed or truthfully represented." The prospectus discussed the "bias" and "the prospectuses

1. *In re Hyperion Securities Litigation,* 93 Civ. 7179 (MM), U.S. Dist. LEXIS 10020 (S.D.N.Y. Jul. 12, 1995).

clearly 'bespeak caution' through a mantra of caveats, disclaimers, and qualifications" regarding the risk.

Investors cannot base their claim on inferences from statements made in the road shows if "those inferences are contradicted by specific disclosures in the prospectuses." In addition, "a reasonable investor would have familiarized himself with the potential for loss disclosed in the prospectuses, rather than relying on the oral assurances of brokers who attended the roadshows."

---

**Discussion Topics**

a. The court states that "the prospectuses clearly 'bespeak caution' through a mantra of caveats, disclaimers, and qualifications." What impact do you believe this standard has on efforts of the SEC to make prospectuses more readable?

b. What weight should the court give to statements made to brokers during roadshows? Are such statements intended to reach the public?

c. Is the court correct in stating that "a reasonable investor would have familiarized himself with the potential for loss disclosed in the prospectuses, rather than relying on the oral assurances of brokers who attended the roadshows"? How effective is the disclosure to brokers, as compared to the prospectus, in influencing investors?

---

## G. Advertising

### 1. Background[1]

Section 24(a) of the 1940 Act authorizes the Commission to design the format by which investment companies' securities are registered under the Securities Act of 1933. The Securities Act has a very strict framework governing written communications (e.g., advertisements) used in the sale of securities. Written offers of securities must meet the requirements of Sections 2(a)(10), 5, and 10 of the Securities Act of 1933, unless excepted from the requirements. To be excepted from these requirements investment companies' marketing materials must fall within one of three categories. In addition, some materials can be included in "supplemental sales literature" rather than in the prospectus. This material, however, is deemed part of the prospectus.

The three kinds of advertisements that are excluded from the regulation of a prospectus are Rule 134 tombstone advertisements, Rule 482 omitting prospectuses and Rule 135a generic advertisements. Each of these categories has restrictions on the type of material that may be included.

The foundation for tombstone advertisements is Section 2(b)(10)(B) of the Securities Act which excepts certain communications from the definition of a prospectus. Pursuant to authority in Section 2(b)(10)(B), the SEC adopted

1. Adapted from Clifford E. Kirsch, Investment Adviser Regulation, A Step-by-Step Guide to Compliance and the Law 6-10 to -12 (1996).

Rule 134 under the Securities Act of 1933 which specifies the information that may be included in such ads.

In the case of investment companies, tombstone advertisements could contain a description of the company's investment objectives, policies, services, methods of operation, year of incorporation or organization, and the aggregate net asset value of all registered investment companies managed by the same adviser, as well as offers, descriptions, and explanations of any company product or service not required to be registered under the Securities Act. Such information, however, could not "relate directly to the desirability of owning or purchasing a security issued by a registered investment company." Significantly, tombstone advertisements could not contain performance data.

Until 2003, Rule 134 under the Securities Act of 1933, permitting issuers to include certain information in tombstone advertisements, applied to registered investment companies and business development companies. However, in 2003 the SEC amended Rule 482, at the same time eliminating the applicability of Rule 134 to these companies. The foregoing materials on tombstone advertisements are obsolete, to the extent they pertain to investment companies, and provide the historical description of the law.

A second type of advertisement is a "Rule 482 ad"; these advertisements are permitted pursuant to Securities Act Rule 482 which was adopted under authority the SEC has to adopt rules allowing for prospectuses which omit or summarize information. As such, a Rule 482 ad is considered a "prospectus" under the Securities Act and thus Securities Act liability attaches to the advertisements. These types of advertisements are very popular and daily newspapers are full of them.

Rule 482 permits these types of advertisements to be used once a registration statement for the fund has been filed (i.e., it can be used prior to effectiveness of the registration statement) and does not limit the content of advertisements, provided the advertisement states from whom a prospectus can be obtained, advises the investor to read it before investing and advises the investor to consider the fund's investment objectives, risks, charges and expenses carefully before investing. Rule 482 ads may include information the substance of which is not included in the fund's statutory prospectus; however, it is advisable from a liability point of view that Rule 482 ads not contain information which is inconsistent with the information in the statutory prospectus. Importantly, Rule 482 ads may show performance information and the rule requires that performance information be presented in a standardized format; nonstandardized performance may be included if such presentations are accompanied by standardized performance numbers.

The third type of advertisement is known as a "generic ad." Generic ads are permitted by Rule 135a under the 1933 Act which permits advertisements that only contain general information about investment company securities and do not mention a particular investment company. Generic ads are not as popular as tombstone ads or Rule 482 ads because they are limited to providing only very general information about investment company securities.

In addition to the three categories of advertisements discussed above, communications that are "preceded or accompanied by" a statutory prospectus are permitted to be used as marketing communications. This type of communication is referred to as "supplemental sales literature" and is excepted from the definition of a prospectus under section 2(a)(10)(a) of the Securities Act. Supplemental sales literature may include a wide range of material. Like Rule 482 ads, if they present performance information, they must do so in a standardized format; nonstandardized performance may be included if such presentations are accompanied by standardized performance numbers.

In addition to the SEC regulations governing investment company advertisements and supplemental sales literature, these communications are generally subject to FINRA rules. This is because most broker-dealers selling investment company shares are members of FINRA and therefore subject to its rules which, among other things, apply to investment company marketing material. The primary rules in this area are the FINRA Rules, particularly Rule 2210 which governs "Communications with the Public." These rules generally require that investment company marketing material be filed with FINRA's Advertising Regulation Department. This Department reviews and comments on filed material. Rule 482 ads that are filed with FINRA need not be filed with the SEC.

Section 35(d) prohibits a registered investment company from adopting a name which "the Commission finds materially deceptive or misleading." Rule 35d-1 provides that a name is "materially deceptive and misleading" if (1) it suggests guarantee or approval by the United States government; (2) it suggests investment in certain investments or industries, or certain countries or geographic regions, unless certain requirements are met; or (3) it suggests that fund distributions are tax-exempt, unless certain requirements are met.

## 2. Performance Advertising

Historically, the Commission prohibited funds from advertising their performance on the ground that, because such advertising may imply future performance, it is misleading. Because public investors continuously sought performance information, the Commission changed its position to allow such advertising as long as the performance was set forth in a standardized format.

Like any other business, a mutual fund is constantly evolving into various permutations. Determinations about when a fund's performance begins and ends are not as easy as they might appear. When a fund replaces its portfolio manager, does its performance history begin anew? When a private account converts itself to a mutual fund, should it be able to carry over its past performance? Should a portfolio manager be permitted to "take" past performance with him or her as he or she job-hops to different fund complexes? These issues are considered in a no-action letter to Philadelphia Fund[1] and in the presentation of Commissioner Issac C. Hunt.

1. Philadelphia Fund, Inc., SEC No-Action Letter (Oct. 17, 1989).

Philadelphia Fund, Inc. ("Philadelphia") was advised by Universal. Universal sold its assets to Fahnestock, formed specifically as adviser to Philadelphia and another fund, and staffed with new advisory personnel, including Baxter, who served as sole portfolio manager of Philadelphia. Fahnestock became Nesbitt pursuant to the acquisition of its parent, but maintained its corporate form and personnel and Baxter continued as sole portfolio manager. Subsequently, Philadelphia entered an advisory contract with Baxter Financial, a firm with Baxter as president and sole director and shareholder.

Philadelphia sought no-action relief from Rule 482(e) of the Securities Act and Rule 34b-1 under the 1940 Act to exclude, from prospectuses advertisements and sales literature, investment results prior to the sale to Fahnestock (i.e., prior to the periods in which Baxter served as portfolio manager).

The staff granted no-action relief, noting the funds' representations that "any advertisement or sales literature presenting performance information would (1) clearly indicate the date of inception for the particular Fund and the fact that the Fund previously operated under different management, (2) state that per share income and capital changes for the last ten fiscal years of the Fund are disclosed in its statutory prospectus, and (3) indicate that average annual total return figures for one, five, and ten year periods are available upon request."

### a. A Bit of History

The following is a summary of the remarks of Isaac C. Hunt, Jr. Commissioner, U.S. Securities and Exchange Commission in 1997.[1]

The Commissioner focused his remarks on how mutual funds advertise their past performance. He noted that the staff has granted no-action assurances, allowing a fund to use performance information of related funds in its prospectus. This assurance covered a predecessor fund, a fund managed by the same advisory firm, or a fund previously managed by the same portfolio manager. Later it granted relief to use performance information of related funds in its advertisements and sales literature.

The staff noted in these assurances that the related funds had "substantially similar investment objectives" and noted the funds' specific representations, including that each fund would:

- prominently disclose that the other account performance is not the fund's own performance, and should not be considered indicative of the past or future performance of the fund;
- prominently disclose that the other account performance should not be considered a substitute for the fund's performance;
- present other account performance information in addition to, and no more prominently than, the fund's own performance information (provided the fund has a performance history); and

1. Remarks of Isaac C. Hunt, Jr., Commissioner, U.S. Securities and Exchange Commission, 1997 Investment Adviser Conference, Investment Company Institute Washington, D.C. (Jun. 16, 1997).

- explain all material differences between the other accounts and the fund to ensure that the other account's information is not presented in a misleading manner.

The Commissioner questioned, first, whether a fund should be allowed to advertise past performance, noting the required legend stating that past performance may not reflect future returns.

Second, assuming that past performance is relevant, is the past performance of other funds relevant, and if so, which funds? One approach focuses on the advisory firm rather than the portfolio managers. Advisory firms "have strong corporate cultures and huge research departments, and there is often a firm method of stock picking that is not tied to any one individual." A second approach focuses on the individual portfolio managers, given their importance and the fact that reportedly "a true team at a fund complex is very rare."

Finally, under the portfolio manager approach, the Commissioner questioned whether a fund should be allowed to advertise its former manager's results. The Commissioner also questioned whether it would be sensible for funds in different complexes to advertise the same results.

---

<u>Discussion Topics</u>

a. Does the position of the SEC staff in *Philadelphia Fund, Inc.* allow a fund too much flexibility to "bury" past performances?

b. Should a fund be required to (instead of permitted to) reflect performance only from the time of a new portfolio manager? What about a new investment adviser?

---

### b. An Example of Wrongful Advertising[1]

The Growth Fund was originally an incubator fund not generally available to the public. The portfolio manager invested with "the goal of establishing a performance track record to be used in marketing the fund to the public." During this period, the fund attained high returns, largely attributable to investment in "hot" initial public offerings (IPOs).

The fund was opened to the public for investment by issuing its securities, and its net assets increased from $1.1 million to $110.1 million. The fund's underwriter prepared and distributed sales literature for the fund, which accurately noted the fund's return but not the impact of IPOs on performance nor their magnified impact due to the small fund size. The fund's advertisement also stated: "The Fund's adviser believes the Fund was managed substantially the same as if the Fund had opened for investment to all public investors." Similarly, the semi-annual report attributed the performance to four industry sectors and did not mention IPOs, and the investment adviser and underwriter made public statements, including

1. In re Van Kampen Investment Advisory Corp., Investment Company Act Rel. No. 23996 (Sept. 8, 1999).

"It's not as if the Growth Fund has had a bunch of hot IPOs;" and "the performance of the [Growth Fund] last year was not greatly influenced by investments in initial public offerings."

The SEC found that a statement that a large portion of the fund's return was attributable to IPOs would have been material to an investor's decision, particularly since it was questionable whether the fund could continue to experience similar performance.[1]

---

**Discussion Topic**

Did the advertising mentioned above violate Rule 482? Should Rule 482 provide that performance may be presented only when there is a reasonable basis to conclude that past performance is sustainable in the future?

---

**Problem**

You are advising a client regarding the initial public offering of a new closed-end investment company. Your client explains that closed-end funds are very "yield-centric" investments — in other words, the typical investor in a closed-end fund invests with the expectation of receiving income in the form of dividends (this is "yield"). The closed-end fund's income, which it distributes as dividends, in turn typically comes from investing in income producing securities, such as bonds or equity securities that consistently pay dividends. Your client wants to state in a rule 482 advertisement that its "target yield" is 7% annually on the IPO price of $20 per share. (Note that rule 482 ads are permitted, once a registration statement for a fund has been filed, but before the SEC has declared the registration statement effective. Therefore the rule 482 ads can be used as sales-documents for fund IPOs.) Your client further explains that this is not information that will be contained in the prospectus. You are aware that it is impossible to guarantee a particular yield to investors. Please write an email to your client explaining your recommendation concerning putting the target yield in the proposed rule 482 ad. If yes, would you condition it on anything else and what kind of disclosure would you recommend accompany it? If no, why not?

---

## H. Disclosure of Adviser Holdings and Fund Transaction Costs

### 1. History

In the 1960s and 1970s, the number of securities held by institutional investors led to concerns that these investors' dominance might create undesirable effects in the securities markets.[2] In 1968, Congress, concerned

---

1. *Id.*
2. *Institutional Investors Full Disclosure Act: Hearings Before the Subcomm. on Sec. of the S. Comm. On Banking, Hous. & Urban Affairs,* 93d Cong. 217, 218-20 (statement of Securities Industry Association).

about "the lack of adequate data respecting the increased amount of securities held and traded by institutional investors," authorized a study on the effects of these investors on the markets.[1] The SEC concluded from the study that in view of the growth of these investors in the equity markets, timely information about their holdings and transactions was necessary.[2]

Consequently, in 1975, Congress enacted section 13(f) of the Securities Exchange Act, the Institutional Investors Full Disclosure Act.[3] Section 13(f) generally requires an "institutional investment manager" with investment discretion over accounts of at least $100 million in equity securities (or such lesser amount as the SEC may determine, not less than $10 million) to file periodic reports with the SEC, including such information as the name of each issuer, the number of shares held, and their fair market value. In addition, for accounts over which the manager has investment discretion, the SEC may require similar disclosure about the securities and transactions involving the accounts, including more detailed disclosure for transactions involving at least $500,000 in exempt securities (or other amount determined by the SEC).

The SEC may exempt managers or securities from these requirements. The legislation was supported by the SEC[4] and generally supported by the Investment Company Institute.[5] The New York Stock Exchange generally supported the legislation, noting concerns from individual investors over "unfair institutional advantages."[6] However, the Exchange expressed its concerns about the burdens of duplicative reporting, noting that it had already required similar periodic disclosure for some of its members,[7] and opposed an exemption for national bank trust departments in a prior version of the legislation.[8] The version passed by Congress directed the SEC, in exercising its authority under the section, to consult with other regulators and exchanges to avoid duplicative reporting. The enacted legislation also defined "institutional investment manager" more broadly to eliminate the exemption for national bank trust departments.

In light of the concerns over the costs of investing in mutual funds, the SEC has taken an interest in the costs incurred by mutual funds in the purchase and sale of securities held in their investment portfolio. These costs are not included in a fund's expense ratio that is disclosed to fund investors and otherwise the SEC's disclosure rules contain little that requires funds to explain or to quantify their costs in trading securities. The SEC has issued a "concept" release, summarized below which invites public

1. *Id.* at 19, 20 (statement of Ray Garrett, Jr., Chairman, SEC).
2. *Id.* at 20.
3. Securities Acts Amendments of 1975, Pub. L. No. 104-29, § 10, 89 Stat. 97, 119-21 (*codified at* 15 U.S.C. § 77m(f) (2012)).
4. *Institutional Investors Full Disclosure Act: Hearings on S. 2234 and S. 2683 Before the Subcomm. on Sec. of the S. Comm. on Banking, Hous. & Urban Affairs,* 93d Cong. 19, 20 (statement of Ray Garrett, Jr., Chairman, SEC).
5. *Id.* at 108, 108-09 (statement of Robert L. Augenblick, President, Investment Company Institute).
6. *Id.* at 207, 207-08 (statement of New York Stock Exchange, Inc.).
7. *Id.* at 207, 208.
8. *Id.* at 207, 208-09.

comment on what rules could be proposed that would provide informative disclosure to shareholders.[1]

As the summary of the release below demonstrates, a fund incurs costs that are readily quantifiable (brokerage commissions) and other costs that are more difficult to measure or lend themselves to different measuring methodologies.

Transaction costs are important because they are often substantial and because of conflicts, for example, commissions "may . . . be used to pay for research or trading support functions (brokerage services) that might otherwise be paid for by the fund's investment adviser (soft dollar commissions)." Fund directors should scrutinize such costs so that they will not "include payment for services that benefit the fund's adviser at the expense of the fund."

Transaction costs are not included in the expense ratio because "they are either included as part of the cost basis of securities purchased or subtracted from the net proceeds of securities sold and ultimately are reflected as changes in the realized and unrealized gain or loss on portfolio securities in the fund's financial statements." Currently, funds (except money market funds) must disclose the portfolio turnover rate and dollar amount of brokerage commissions, which are related to transaction costs. But funds are not required to disclose actual transaction costs.

Transaction costs include "all . . . costs that are associated with trading portfolio securities" including "commissions, spreads, market impact costs and opportunity costs."

Commissions are generally "charges that a broker collects to act as agent for a customer in the process of executing and clearing a trade." They are the only transaction costs that can be measured directly and they are easily measured, i.e., they are "explicit" costs. The "spread" is the difference between the "bid" price (at which a fund sells a security to a dealer, slightly below current value) and the "asked" price (at which a fund buys a security from a dealer, slightly above current value). The spread includes an imputed commission and market impact costs, which are "the price concessions (amounts added to the purchase price or subtracted from the selling price) that are required to find the opposite side of the trade and complete the transaction." They "cannot be calculated directly" but "can be roughly estimated" by comparing the actual trade price to market process at or near the same time. Impact cost may be reduced by stretching out a trade over a long time period. The benefit of reduced impact cost may be reduced or eliminated by an increase in opportunity cost. Opportunity costs are "the cost of missed trades," i.e., the change in the market price between the time the transaction is conceived and when it is executed. The spread, market impact costs, and opportunity costs are "implicit" costs and may "greatly exceed" the explicit costs.

The SEC noted a number of proposals to quantify transaction costs. First, funds could be required to disclose commission costs to effect securities

1. Request for Comments on Measures to Improve Disclosure of Mutual Fund Transaction Costs, Investment Company Act Rel. No. 26313 (Dec. 18, 2003).

transactions. Second, they could be required to quantify and disclose all transaction costs. Third, they could quantify the "trade effect," or the combined effect of transaction gains and losses from short-term trading. It would reflect the difference between the value of the portfolio at the end of the day and the hypothetical value if no trades had been made that day.

The SEC also noted alternatives that provide additional information about the level of transaction costs. Existing disclosure requirements include portfolio turnover and the dollar amount of commissions paid. Another set of alternatives would include: (1) disclosure of transaction costs in terms of rated categories, from very high to very low, compared to an industry standard, (2) greater prominence to portfolio turnover, (3) information about average net flows in and out of funds, (4) other narrative disclosures (such as the impact of management style on portfolio turnover or the impact on transaction costs from the types of securities or their markets or the adviser's portfolio management strategies, or the expected portfolio turnover rate), (5) moving brokerage cost information to the prospectus, or disclosure of average commission rate per share, and (6) disclosure of gross returns (returns generated by the portfolio manager), which could be compared to the currently required standardized returns (returns after fees and expenses).

### 2. Transaction Costs and Soft Dollars

Consider the following description of a comment letter submitted by Fidelity Investments on the SEC's transaction cost concept release.[1]

Fidelity urges the SEC to "require investment managers to disclose the amounts of brokerage commissions they pay for investment research in reliance upon the safe harbor of Section 28(e) (the 'Safe Harbor') of the Securities and Exchange Act of 1934 (the '1934 Act')," both "in dollar terms and as a percent of funds' net assets."

"[S]oft dollar research expenses are the least transparent of fund expenses, because they are 'bundled' with payments for a distinctly separate service — the execution of securities trades — in brokerage commissions paid by investment managers to brokers."

There should be "no distinction between research prepared by an executing broker (so-called 'proprietary' research) and research by a broker uninvolved in the execution of the fund's trades (so-called 'third party' research)." "Requiring disclosure of only third party research expenses . . . would . . . provide unhealthy incentives for advisers to send trades to brokers for reasons other than achieving best execution for fund trades."

---

<u>Discussion Topics</u>

a. Is disclosure of brokerage commission costs useful to mutual fund investors in choosing among different funds in which to invest? Although a

1. Comments of David B. Jones, Senior Vice President, Product Strategy & Communications, Fidelity Management & Research Co. & Eric D. Roiter, Senior Vice President and General Counsel, Fidelity Management & Research Co. (Mar. 2, 2004), *available at* http://www.sec.gov/rules/concept/s72903/fidelity03022004.htm.

fund discloses its investment returns, and the brokerage commissions paid by the fund have a direct effect on those returns, would investors learn more about the funds by comparing their level of brokerage commissions? Could they learn more about other issues concerning the funds' performance?

b. Should the SEC adopt a rule that establishes one methodology for measuring "market impact" costs and require all mutual funds to disclose such costs to investors under such methodology? Will disclosure of market impact costs help mutual fund investors make more informed decisions in choosing among mutual funds in which to invest? Does this disclosure affect the trust of investors in the mutual fund managers?

c. Should the SEC require disclosure by mutual funds of the dollar amounts of commissions used to acquire research from brokers? Or should the SEC recommend to Congress that Section 28(e) be repealed and require that brokerage commissions be paid solely to compensate brokers for carrying out portfolio trades for a fund?

---

## I. Abusive Trading Practices

The SEC has proposed a number of rules against recurrent abusive or unfair trading practices in mutual fund shares that were uncovered in 2003. Many of these trading practices are named "market timing," a term that covers a variety of excessive, short-term trading strategies by investors who seek to take advantage of short-term market movements. However, the main issue in market timing stems from the same source: insider information. The most abusive form of market timing arises in instances where sudden price movements in underlying securities (particularly foreign securities) held in a mutual fund's portfolio are not immediately or accurately reflected in the fund's net asset value (NAV), but are disclosed to some investors, for indirect payments to the funds' advisers.

One of the first SEC actions in response to the market timing scandals was a December 2003 proposed revision to its disclosure requirements with respect to:

(i) market timing policies and procedures;
(ii) practices regarding "fair valuation" of portfolio securities; and
(iii) policies and procedures with respect to the disclosure of portfolio holdings.

This proposal was adopted in April 2004. The SEC's adopting release follows:[1]

> I. INTRODUCTION AND BACKGROUND
>
> Millions of individual American investors hold shares of open-end management investment companies ("mutual funds"), relying on these funds for their retirements, their children's educations, and their other basic financial needs. The tremendous number of mutual fund investors reflects the trust that they have placed in both funds

1. Disclosure Regarding Market Timing and Selective Disclosure of Portfolio Holdings, Investment Company Act Rel. No. 26418 (Apr. 16, 2004).

and the regulatory protections provided by the federal securities laws.

Recent scandals, however, have revealed instances where some in the mutual fund industry, and some intermediaries that sell fund shares, have violated the trust that has been placed in them and lost sight of their obligations to investors under the federal securities laws. Many of these abuses relate to "market timing," including the overriding of stated market timing policies by fund executives to benefit large investors at the expense of small investors, or to benefit the fund's investment adviser. Other abuses involve the selective disclosure by some fund managers of their funds' portfolio holdings in order to curry favor with large investors. This selective disclosure can facilitate fraud and have severe, adverse ramifications for a fund's investors if someone uses that portfolio information to trade against the fund, or otherwise uses the information in a way that would harm the fund. . . .

With respect to market timing, the amendments that the Commission is adopting will require improved disclosure in fund prospectuses of a mutual fund's risks, policies, and procedures. The amendments will:

- Require a mutual fund to describe in its prospectus the risks, if any, that frequent purchases and redemptions of fund shares may present for other shareholders;
- Require a mutual fund to state in its prospectus whether or not the fund's board of directors has adopted policies and procedures with respect to frequent purchases and redemptions of fund shares and, if the board has not adopted any such policies and procedures, state the specific basis for the view of the board that it is appropriate for the fund not to have such policies and procedures;
- Require a mutual fund to describe in its prospectus any policies and procedures for deterring frequent purchases and redemptions of fund shares, and in its Statement of Additional Information ("SAI") any arrangements to permit frequent purchases and redemptions of fund shares; and
- Require similar disclosure in prospectuses for insurance company separate accounts offering variable insurance contracts, with respect to frequent transfers among sub-accounts. . . .

With respect to selective disclosure of portfolio holdings, the amendments will require mutual funds and insurance company managed separate accounts that offer variable annuities to disclose their policies with respect to disclosure of portfolio holdings information. The amendments will:

- Require a fund to describe in its SAI any policies and procedures with respect to the disclosure of the fund's portfolio securities to any person and any ongoing arrangements to make available information about the fund's portfolio securities to any person; and

- Require a fund to state in its prospectus that a description of the policies and procedures is available in the fund's SAI, and on the fund's website, if applicable.

II. DISCUSSION

A. Disclosure Concerning Frequent Purchases and Redemptions of Fund Shares . . .

*1. Description of the Risks of Frequent Purchases and Redemptions of Fund Shares*

We are adopting, as proposed, amendments that will require a mutual fund's prospectus to describe the risks, if any, that frequent purchases and redemptions of fund shares may present for other shareholders of the fund. These risks may include, among other things, dilution in the value of fund shares held by long-term shareholders, interference with the efficient management of the fund's portfolio, and increased brokerage and administrative costs. The disclosure should be specific to the fund, taking into account its investment objectives, policies, and strategies. For example, we would generally expect a fund that invests in overseas markets to describe, among other things, the risks of time-zone arbitrage.

*2. Adoption of Policies and Procedures by Fund's Board*

We are also adopting, as proposed, amendments that require a mutual fund's prospectus to state whether the fund's board of directors has adopted policies and procedures with respect to frequent purchases and redemptions of fund shares by fund shareholders. If the fund's board of directors has not adopted any such policies and procedures, the fund's prospectus will be required to include a statement of the specific basis for the view of the board that it is appropriate for the fund not to have such policies and procedures.

*3. Description of Fund Policies and Procedures With Respect to Frequent Purchases and Redemptions*

We are adopting, with one modification, a requirement that the fund's prospectus include a description of policies and procedures adopted by the board with respect to frequent purchases and redemptions, including:

- whether or not the fund discourages frequent purchases and redemptions of fund shares by fund shareholders;
- whether or not the fund accommodates frequent purchases and redemptions of fund shares by fund shareholders; and
- any policies and procedures of the fund for deterring frequent purchases and redemptions of fund shares by fund shareholders.

The description of the mutual fund's policies and procedures, if any, for deterring frequent purchases and redemptions of fund shares by fund shareholders will be required to include any restrictions imposed by the fund to prevent or minimize such frequent purchases and redemptions, including:

- any restrictions on the volume or number of purchases,

redemptions, or exchanges that a shareholder may make within a given time period;

- any exchange fee or redemption fee;
- any costs or administrative or other fees or charges that are imposed on shareholders deemed to be engaged in frequent purchases and redemptions of fund shares, together with a description of the circumstances under which such costs, fees, or charges will be imposed;
- any minimum holding period that is imposed before an investor may make exchanges into another fund;
- any restrictions imposed on exchange or purchase requests submitted by overnight delivery, electronically, or via facsimile or telephone; and
- any right of the fund to reject, limit, delay, or impose other conditions on exchanges or purchases or to close or otherwise limit accounts based on a history of frequent purchases and redemptions of fund shares, including the circumstances under which such right will be exercised.

The amendments will require a fund's policies and procedures for deterring frequent purchases and redemptions, including any restrictions imposed to prevent or minimize such frequent purchases and redemptions, to be described with specificity. For example, a fund might state that a 2% redemption fee will be applied to all redemptions within five days after purchase or, in describing any restrictions on the volume or number of purchases, redemptions, or exchanges that a shareholder may make within a given time period, a fund might state that it prohibits more than five round-trips in and out of a particular fund per year. A fund will also be required to indicate whether each restriction applies uniformly in all cases, or whether the restriction will not be imposed under certain circumstances. If any restriction will not be imposed under certain circumstances, the fund will be required to describe with specificity the circumstances under which the restriction will not be imposed.

Commenters were divided on whether funds' policies, procedures, and restrictions on purchases and redemptions should be required to be described with specificity. Many commenters, including a number of investors and intermediaries, argued that requiring specific disclosure of a fund's policies, procedures, and restrictions is important in order to put investors on notice of what types of activities the fund considers harmful, and to encourage funds to apply their restrictions uniformly. On the other hand, several commenters from the fund industry argued that the specificity requirement could have the unintended effect of assisting investors who wished to engage in frequent purchases and redemptions, and could deprive funds of flexibility in administering their policies and procedures to deter frequent purchases and redemptions. In addition, one commenter asked for clarification that a fund may reserve the right to reject any trade for any reason, because it is not possible to identify all types of potentially abusive trading in advance.

On balance, we continue to believe that it is important that a fund's prospectus describe with specificity its policies, procedures, and restrictions with respect to frequent purchases and redemptions of fund shares. We believe that requiring specificity in this disclosure will help investors both to assess mutual funds' policies and procedures with respect to frequent purchases and redemptions, and to assess whether such policies and procedures are in line with their expectations. We agree with those commenters who argued that requiring specific disclosure may discourage funds from applying or waiving their restrictions arbitrarily. We also believe, however, that funds will be able to more effectively deter abusive market timing if they have some flexibility to address abuses as they arise. To that end, a fund may reserve the right to reject a purchase or exchange request for any reason, provided that it discloses this policy in its prospectus.

We are removing the proposed requirement that a fund describe its policies and procedures for detecting frequent purchases and redemptions of fund shares. Many commenters . . . argued that disclosure about how the fund detects frequent purchases and redemptions could . . . [harm] the fund, in that it might provide investors seeking to engage in market timing through frequent purchases and redemptions with a "road map" on how to avoid detection. Further, commenters argued that this disclosure would be of marginal utility to most investors. We agree.

In connection with removing this proposed requirement, we are adding a statement clarifying that a fund's disclosure regarding whether its restrictions to prevent or minimize frequent purchases and redemptions are uniformly applied must indicate whether each such restriction applies to trades that occur through omnibus accounts at intermediaries, such as investment advisers, broker dealers, transfer agents, third party administrators, and insurance companies. We continue to believe that investors should be informed about how a fund applies its restrictions on frequent purchases and redemptions to persons trading through omnibus accounts, which would have been addressed by the proposed disclosure regarding policies and procedures for detecting frequent purchases and redemptions. The overall effectiveness of a fund's restrictions on frequent purchases and redemptions may depend significantly on how effectively the fund can deter frequent purchases and redemptions made through such omnibus accounts. . . .

*5. Description of Arrangements Permitting Frequent Purchases and Redemptions*

We are adopting, substantially as proposed, the requirement that a mutual fund describe any arrangements with any person to permit frequent purchases and redemptions of fund shares, except that we are moving the required disclosure to the fund's SAI and requiring a cross-reference to this disclosure in the fund's prospectus. The description of arrangements to permit frequent purchases and redemptions must include the identity of the persons permitted to engage in frequent purchases and redemptions and any compensation or other consideration received by the fund, its investment adviser, or any other party pursuant to such arrangements. . . .

We believe that disclosure of the persons who have arrangements with a fund to permit frequent purchases and redemptions is necessary in order to help investors assess the risks to fund shareholders of frequent purchases and redemptions. We are, however, modifying the requirement to permit a fund that has an arrangement to permit frequent purchases and redemptions by a group of individuals, such as the participants in a defined contribution plan that meets the requirements for qualification under Section 401(k) of the Internal Revenue Code, to identify the group rather than identifying each individual group member. . . .

[A] mutual fund that enters into an arrangement with any person to permit frequent purchases and redemptions of fund shares may only do so consistent with the antifraud provisions of the federal securities laws and the fiduciary duties of the fund and its investment adviser. Disclosure provided pursuant to these amendments will not make lawful conduct that is otherwise unlawful. For example, disclosure will not render lawful an arrangement whereby an investment adviser permits frequent purchases and redemptions of a mutual fund's shares in return for consideration that benefits the adviser, such as an agreement to maintain assets in other accounts managed by the adviser. . . .

B. Disclosure of Circumstances Under Which Funds Will Use Fair Value Pricing and the Effects of Such Use

[The SEC adopted a requirement that funds (other than money market funds) disclose the circumstances under which they will use fair value pricing and the effects of such use. This reflects the requirement that funds use such pricing when market quotations are not readily available. The disclosure of circumstances should be specific to the fund.]

C. Selective Disclosure of Fund Portfolio Holdings

[The SEC adopted a requirement that funds disclose their policies and procedures regarding disclosure of portfolio securities and any ongoing arrangements to make available information about them to prevent the misuse of material, nonpublic information.]

---

## Discussion Topic

In what sense did market timing involve fraud? What benefits did the market timer have that other investors did not have? Shareholders of mutual funds are generally restricted from obtaining information about the content of the funds' portfolio before all other investors. What was the purpose of this restriction? If the prohibition applies to insiders, why should it apply to outside investors? Why did these shareholders bribe insiders to receive the information? How does this issue relate to the continuous trading of these privileged investors?

---

Another SEC proposal, made in 2004, would enhance the disclosure that a mutual fund investor receives confirming his or her transaction. It would also require a new type of document at the point-of-sale that highlights conflicts of interest that may tempt sales persons to sell one type of fund as opposed to another.[1] As of October 2015, the proposed amendments had not been adopted.

> II. Introduction
>
> The Commission is proposing new rule 15c2-2 under the Exchange Act, which would govern the obligations of brokers (including municipal securities brokers), dealers and municipal securities dealers to disclose transaction-related information in confirmations or other documents when customers buy or sell certain investment company securities and municipal fund securities. The Commission also is proposing new rule 15c2-3 under the Exchange Act, which would govern the obligation of brokers, dealers and municipal securities dealers to disclose information to investors prior to effecting transactions in those securities.
>
> The proposed new rules respond to concerns that investors in mutual fund shares, UIT interests (including certain insurance company separate accounts that issue variable insurance products) and municipal fund securities used for education savings lack adequate information about certain distribution-related costs, as well as certain distribution arrangements, that create conflicts of interest for brokers, dealers, municipal securities dealers, and their associated persons. Those costs and other distribution arrangements have evolved substantially since 1977, when the Commission adopted its general confirmation rule, rule 10b-10. We believe that disclosure of information about those costs and conflicts can help investors make better informed investment decisions.
>
> Proposed rule 15c2-2 would require specific confirmation disclosure of information about front-end and deferred sales fees ("loads") and other distribution-related costs that directly impact the returns earned by investors in mutual fund shares, UIT interests and 529 plan securities. It also would require brokers, dealers and municipal securities dealers to disclose their compensation for selling those securities, and to disclose information about revenue sharing arrangements and portfolio brokerage arrangements that create

1. Confirmation Requirements and Point of Sale Disclosure Requirements for Transactions in Certain Mutual Funds and Other Securities, and Other Confirmation Requirement Amendments, and Amendments to the Registration Form for Mutual Funds, Investment Company Act Rel. No. 26341 (Jan. 29, 2004).

conflicts of interest for them. Moreover, the proposed rule would require brokers, dealers and municipal securities dealers to inform customers about whether their salespersons or other associated persons receive extra compensation for selling certain fund shares or fund share classes.

As part of this rulemaking process, the Commission intends to withdraw a no-action letter that the Commission's Division of Market Regulation granted to the Investment Company Institute ("ICI") in 1979, related to confirmation disclosure of mutual fund sales loads and related fees. The relief granted by that letter is inconsistent with proposed rule 15c2-2, which would mandate specific disclosure of load information on customer confirmations.

To avoid redundancy with proposed new rule 15c2-2, we are also proposing to modify rule 10b-10 to exclude certain transactions in mutual fund shares and UIT interests from the rule's scope, and to make other changes consistent with proposed rule 15c2-2. In addition, we are proposing to modify rule 10b-10 to clarify, consistent with proposed rule 15c2-2, that the rule does not provide a safe harbor for activity that would violate the antifraud provisions of the federal securities laws or other legal requirements.

Because confirmation disclosure does not provide information to investors prior to transactions in securities — i.e., at the time they make investment decision — we also are proposing new rule 15c2-3 to require brokers, dealers and municipal securities dealers to provide point of sale disclosure to customers prior to effecting transactions in mutual fund shares, UIT interests and 529 plan securities. The proposed rule would enable investors to see transaction-specific information about distribution-related costs, and about remuneration arrangements that lead to conflicts of interest for their brokers, dealers or municipal securities dealers. That information would enable investors to better understand the costs and conflicts associated with investments in those securities prior to entering into transactions, which should promote better informed investment decision-making. The Commission also proposes to amend Form N-1A to require improved disclosure by mutual funds regarding sales loads and revenue sharing arrangements.

In addition, the Commission also proposes to amend rule 10b-10 to require broker-dealers to disclose whenever preferred stock can be called by the issuer. Rule 10b-10 requires similar disclosure for transactions in debt securities that are callable by the issuer. The Commission further proposes to amend rule 10b-10 to require disclosure of the date of first call for certain transactions in callable debt securities. . . .

* * *

IV. Improved Confirmation Disclosure for Transactions in Mutual Fund Shares, Unit Investment Trust Interests and 529 Plan Interests

A. Investors Need Better Disclosure about Distribution-related Costs and Conflicts

1. Types of distribution-related costs and conflicts . . .

a. Distribution-related costs

Mutual fund investors may, directly or indirectly, incur distribution-related costs that can reduce their investment returns. The type and amount of those costs often vary among funds and among share classes issued by the same fund. Some mutual funds issue share classes that impose sales fees, or loads, on investors when they purchase the fund shares ("front-end" sales loads). Mutual funds may also sell share classes with sales loads that investors must pay when they redeem fund shares ("deferred" or "back-end" sales loads). The amount of the deferred sales load, generally calculated as the lesser of a percentage of the value of the initial investment or the account's value upon redemption, typically declines each year that the investor holds the shares, and eventually disappears entirely. Some mutual funds also use their assets to pay distribution-related expenses, including compensation of broker-dealers in connection with distributing fund shares, under plans adopted pursuant to rule 12b-1 under the Investment Company Act ("12b-1 fees"). Sales loads and asset-based sales charges and service fees reduce the returns that investors earn on their mutual fund investments. Not all mutual funds are sold subject to front-end or deferred sales loads or impose asset-based sales charges and service fees.

Mutual fund principal underwriters use deferred sales loads in conjunction with rule 12b-1 fees. Usually, the deferred sales load is intended to recover amounts that the principal underwriter advances to a selling broker-dealer to compensate it for mutual fund share transactions if the customer redeems its shares before the underwriter can recover such amounts through the rule 12b-1 fee.

b. Conflicts-of-interest

As discussed in detail below, broker-dealers that sell mutual fund shares to customers may participate in distribution arrangements that create conflicts of interest for the broker-dealers as well as their personnel. Those arrangements can give broker-dealers a heightened financial incentive to sell particular funds or share classes, and therefore may lead a broker-dealer to provide some groups of funds with heightened visibility and access to the broker-dealer's sales force, or otherwise influence the way that broker-dealers and their associated persons market those funds or share classes to customers. Those arrangements therefore pose special confirmation disclosure issues. Moreover, some of those arrangements may violate NASD [now FINRA] rules, and the failure to disclose relevant information about those arrangements — regardless of whether disclosure specifically is required by the confirmation rules — also may violate the antifraud provisions of the federal securities laws.

As part of those distribution arrangements, broker-dealers that sell mutual fund shares generally earn sales fees from the fund's principal underwriter at the time of sale. Alternatively, the principal underwriter may pay the selling broker-dealer sales fees attributable to a particular sales transaction over time, for as long as the customer holds the shares purchased. The amount of those sales fees is not uniform, however, and a broker-dealer may receive a higher fee for selling a particular dollar amount of shares issued by one fund rather than shares issued by another fund, or for selling one share class rather than other share classes issued by the same fund and available to the customer.

Broker-dealers also may be paid in other ways for distributing fund shares, such as through revenue sharing payments from a fund's investment adviser. In some cases, a broker-dealer may receive payments from a fund or a fund's affiliates that are characterized as service fees, recordkeeping and transfer fees, seminar sponsorships or other types of payments that ostensibly compensate the broker-dealer for costs that it incurs as part of its mutual fund distribution activities. Broker-dealers may also be compensated for distribution through receiving commissions for portfolio transactions executed on behalf of the fund or affiliated funds, even though the broker-dealer may not necessarily execute those transactions.

These types of distribution-related arrangements may give broker-dealers heightened incentives to market the shares of particular mutual funds, or particular classes of fund shares. Those incentives may be reflected in a broker-dealers use of "preferred lists" that explicitly favor the distribution of certain funds, or they may be reflected in other ways, including incentives or instructions that the broker-dealer provides to its managers or its salespersons. Such incentives create conflicts between broker-dealers' financial interests and their agency duties to customers.

In addition to conflicts of interest at the firm level, associated persons of broker-dealers face conflicts arising from financial incentives that promote the sale of some shares or share classes — or "differential compensation." Associated persons may receive higher commissions when they sell shares of a particular fund than they would if they sold the same dollar amount of the shares of another fund. They may also receive higher commissions when they sell a particular class of shares within the same fund. Other forms of differential compensation may include a broker-dealer waiving certain fees or reimbursement of certain expenses ordinarily borne by an associated person, when the associated person sells the shares of particular mutual funds. Broker-dealers may also sponsor sales contests that provide cash compensation to representatives and managers for meeting certain sales goals. Associated persons, moreover, may receive additional fees in the years after a sale, such as fees that some funds pay to broker-dealers for providing shareholder services. Each of those types of arrangements may motivate broker-dealer personnel to promote the sale of some funds over others. The funds that are favored by those arrangements may include proprietary funds that are affiliated with the broker-dealer, or funds whose advisers pay revenue sharing to the broker-dealer. Differential compensation may give the associated person an incentive to improperly limit the range of mutual fund choices presented to customers, or may affect the associated person's recommendations. . . .

2. Current confirmation disclosure requirements for mutual funds and municipal fund securities

Rule 10b-10 under the Exchange Act requires broker-dealers to disclose specific information to their customers about securities transactions. While the rule generally directs broker-dealers to disclose the required information at or before the completion of each securities transaction, broker-dealers may also disclose the information monthly or quarterly in limited situations, such as when a customer has entered into a periodic plan for purchasing mutual fund shares. The rule requires disclosure of, among other information, the identity of the security, the number of shares purchased or sold, and the price at which the transaction was effected. When a broker-dealer acts as the customer's agent, it must also disclose the amount of the remuneration it receives from the customer. For agency transactions in which the broker-dealer also participates in the distribution of the securities, it must disclose the source and amount of remuneration that it receives from third parties.

The Commission and its staff have taken the position, with respect to mutual fund transactions, that a broker-dealer may satisfy its rule 10b-10 obligations without providing customers with a transaction-specific document that discloses information about loads or third-party remuneration, so long as the customer receives a fund prospectus that adequately discloses that information. This position had its genesis in a statement by the Commission when it adopted rule 10b-10. In response to comments related to the rule's disclosure requirement about third-party remuneration, the Commission suggested that prospectus disclosure would be an adequate substitute for confirmation disclosure, explaining:

In the case of offerings registered under the Securities Act of 1933, the final prospectus delivered to the customer should generally set forth the information required by the proviso with respect to source and amount of remuneration. . . . In such situations the information specified in the proviso need not be separately set forth in the confirmation.

In other words, the Commission was of the view that broker-dealer disclosure of third-party remuneration would be redundant if the customer received a prospectus disclosing that information.

The Commission's staff reflected that position in a 1979 letter to the Investment Company Institute, in which the Division of Market Regulation stated that it would not recommend enforcement action against broker-dealers that did not provide transaction-specific disclosure about mutual fund loads and related charges, so long as the customer received a prospectus that "disclosed the precise amount of the sales load or other charges or a formula that would enable the customer to calculate the precise amount of those fees."

The Commission later discussed how Rule 10b-10 disclosure obligations apply to mutual fund transactions in an amicus brief filed with the Second Circuit in 2000. That brief focused on the adequacy of prospectus disclosure by broker-dealers that received third-party remuneration — in the form of rule 12b-1 payments from funds and revenue sharing payments from fund investment advisers — in connection with sweeping customer funds into money market accounts. We concluded that the prospectus disclosure at issue substituted for confirmation disclosure, when the prospectuses included the information required to be disclosed by Form N-1A, including the maximum rule 12b-1 fees payable by the funds as a percentage of net assets, and noted the presence of "significant amounts" of non-rule 12b-1 payments by the funds' investment advisers. In arriving at that conclusion, we interpreted the rule 10b-10 Adopting Release as establishing the general principle that "delivery of a prospectus containing sufficient disclosure can satisfy a broker-dealer's obligations under Rule 10b-10." Recognizing that "there is no precise standard as to how much disclosure the Rule currently requires," we went on to note that the staff's 1979 letter, with its "precise amount" standard for prospectus disclosure of loads and related fees, did not apply to third-party remuneration because precision was not necessary to inform customers about conflicts of interest.

While the Commission has never directly addressed the disclosure of payments to a broker-dealer in the form of portfolio brokerage commissions, the same principles apply. Currently, if a prospectus is not delivered at or before completion of the transaction, or if the prospectus fails to disclose the fact that the fund pays portfolio brokerage commissions to broker-dealers that participate in distribution, or fails to disclose information about the degree of the resulting conflict, then the transaction confirmation must provide information about the source and amount of those payments.

In one case before the Second Circuit, we viewed the disclosures at issue as meeting the requirements of rule 10b-10, but we went on to state: "We are not saying that this is necessarily all the disclosure about these types of fees that should be required as a matter of policy." We also noted that we had directed the staff to make recommendations to us about whether to require new disclosures or to refine the existing disclosures. The Second Circuit also questioned whether the prospectus disclosure at issue adequately placed investors on notice about the receipt of those payments and any resulting conflicts of interest. The rules we propose today address those concerns.

3. Concerns about the adequacy of current disclosure practices

The disclosure rules we are proposing are designed to respond to the ways in which the mutual fund industry and its distribution practices have evolved in the years since the 1977 adoption of rule 10b-10 and the staff's 1979 letter to the ICI.

During the past quarter century, the number of mutual fund customers, the value of mutual fund investments, and the number of mutual funds all have increased exponentially. The public increasingly has placed retirement savings into mutual funds through individual retirement accounts and other retirement plans. In addition, distribution costs and broker-dealer conflicts have grown more complex. Since 1980, many funds have offered multiple share classes, including class B shares with deferred sales loads that can have the effect of obscuring the distribution costs borne by investors. Many mature funds continue to rely on rule 12b-1 fees to pay for distribution, even though those fees were intended by the Commission to be short-term tools for helping funds gather assets. The increase in the number of mutual funds has made broker-dealer "shelf space" more critical to investment companies, leading to revenue sharing and other distribution arrangements that quietly compensate broker-dealers for distribution. The growth of funds affiliated with broker-dealers has also generated special broker-dealer marketing incentives to promote the distribution of those affiliated "proprietary" funds. In addition, the development of fund "supermarkets" sponsored by broker-dealers has led to related arrangements in which a fund or its affiliates compensates broker-dealers in ways that are not generally disclosed to investors. Moreover, the introduction of highly promoted 529 plans has brought many new investors into products that themselves invest in mutual funds and that are associated with similar distribution-related costs and conflicts.

Those changes raise significant concerns about the adequacy of current disclosure practices. For example, we are concerned that some investors may misunderstand the costs associated with purchasing mutual fund shares and 529 plan securities because they lack transaction-specific confirmation and point of sale information about loads and fees.

In late 2002, in response to learning that some mutual fund investors did not receive appropriate volume discounts on the front-end sales loads they paid — commonly known as "breakpoint discounts" — NASD [now FINRA], the ICI, and the Securities Industry Association ("SIA") convened a task force to recommend industry-wide changes relating to breakpoints. The task force issued a report in July 2003 recommending, among other changes, that mutual fund confirmations include front-end sales load disclosure. The task force also recommended that the Commission staff revisit its 1979 letter to the ICI. While the task force was studying the issue, the Commission also received a rulemaking petition on behalf of a mutual fund customer asking the Commission to require broker-dealer confirmations to specifically disclose the front-end sales loads that customers incur with mutual fund transactions.

Our concerns, however, go beyond the adequacy of front-end

load disclosure. More complete disclosure also may help customers understand the costs associated with purchasing fund share classes that carry deferred sales loads, as well as the potential conflicts of interest that broker-dealers and their associated persons have in connection with the sale of those share classes. For example, when the amount invested reaches [c]ertain breakpoint discount levels, associated persons of broker-dealers generally are paid more for selling class B shares than for selling shares of other classes. Because class A shares typically carry front-end sales loads while class B shares do not, some investors may be inclined to purchase class B shares believing that they are cheaper, even though class B shares generally carry contingent deferred sales loads and higher 12b-1 fees. NASD [now FINRA] has issued an alert informing investors that, before purchasing class B shares, "you should determine whether this investment is in your interest, and not just in the interest of your broker or adviser who may receive higher commissions from the sale of Class B shares than other classes of fund shares." In fact, questions have been raised about whether class B shares *ever* would be appropriate for most investors. Recent enforcement actions have underscored how those types of compensation arrangements produce conflicts of interest that lead associated persons of broker-dealers to act against the interests of their customers.

Investors also lack information about whether their broker-dealers receive revenue sharing or other third-party remuneration to distribute particular mutual funds. Prospectus disclosure does not identify which individual broker-dealers receive revenue sharing, let alone quantify those arrangements. Yet the magnitude of revenue sharing payments — estimated in 2001 to be $ 2 billion annually — suggests that those arrangements influence the mutual fund choices that broker-dealers and their representatives present to investors. Prospectus disclosure, moreover, is not designed to inform investors about whether their particular broker-dealers are compensated in other ways for distributing fund shares, such as by receiving commissions for fund portfolio brokerage transactions.

Broker-dealer compensation practices related to proprietary funds raise additional disclosure issues. In 1994, a committee was formed at the request of the Commission's Chairman to examine securities industry compensation practices, identify actual and perceived conflicts of interest, and identify "best practices" for controlling those conflicts. The committee raised a number of concerns in its 1995 report, including concerns about the practice of offering higher payouts for selling proprietary mutual funds. It recommended that broker-dealers pay identical commissions to registered representatives for selling proprietary and non-proprietary products within a product category. While some broker-dealers followed that recommendation, its adoption has not been uniform.

In September 2003, NASD [now FINRA] requested comment on proposed rules to require member firms to disclose certain information about revenue sharing and differential compensation to customers at account opening or, if no account is established, at the time the customer first purchases shares of an investment company. Stating that those compensation arrangements could create conflicts of interest for broker-dealers and their associated persons, NASD added, "Disclosure of revenue sharing and differential cash compensation arrangements would enable investors to evaluate whether a registered representative's particular product recommendation was inappropriately influenced by these arrangements." The Commission will consider the proposal in the event that NASD submits it as a proposed rule change. We note, however, that NASD's proposal is geared to giving customers generalized access to information about revenue sharing and differential compensation at the time the customer is evaluating potential mutual fund investments. That particular focus would complement the disclosures we propose today — which would improve disclosure of transaction-specific information about distribution-related costs and arrangements that lead to conflicts of interest. Investors who have access to relevant transaction-specific information about those costs and conflicts of interest should be better prepared to scrutinize the adequacy of the investment choices presented by their broker-dealers as well as the recommendations their broker-dealers make.

B. New Rule and Proposed Amendments Regarding Cost and Conflict Disclosure

1. Proposed rule 15c2-2

To provide investors with adequate access to information regarding the costs of their investments, as well as the conflicts of interest their broker-dealers face, the Commission is proposing a new rule to require brokers, dealers and municipal securities dealers to provide their customers with certain information in connection with certain transactions in mutual fund shares . . .

[Proposed rule 15c2-2 would require enhanced disclosure concerning: (i) distribution-related costs that investors incur when purchasing those types of securities, and (ii) distribution-related arrangements that pose conflicts of interest.]

V. Point of Sale Disclosure for Transactions in Mutual Fund Shares, Unit Investment Trust Interests and 529 Plan Interests

[Proposed] rule 15c2-3 . . . would require brokers, dealers and municipal securities dealers to provide customers with specified information at the point of sale — prior to the time they purchase mutual fund Shares . . . .

C. Information Requirements

Proposed paragraph (a) would require a broker, dealer or municipal securities dealer to deliver quantitative information about distribution-related costs that the investor may bear and the dealer concession that the broker, dealer or municipal securities dealer may expect to receive in connection with the transaction, combined with qualitative information about practices that lead to conflicts of interest in connection with the transaction. This proposed scope of information is intended to give investors useful context for evaluating whether to proceed with a possible investment, while accommodating practicalities of disclosure.

Proposed paragraph (a)(1) specifically would require the broker, dealer or municipal securities dealer to inform its customer about the distribution-related costs that the customer would be expected to incur in connection with the transaction, with separate disclosure about: the amount of sales loads that would be incurred at the time of purchase; estimated asset-based sales charges and asset-based service fees paid out of fund assets in the year following the purchase if net asset value remained unchanged; and the maximum amount of any deferred sales load that would be associated with the purchase if those shares are sold within one year (other than deferred sales loads of no more than one percent that expire no later than one year after purchase, when no other sales load would be incurred on that transaction), along with a statement about how many years a deferred sales load may be in effect. Proposed paragraph (a) (1) also would require the broker, dealer or municipal securities dealer to disclose the dealer concession or other sales fees it would expect to receive in connection with the transaction. Those amounts would be disclosed by reference to the value of the purchase, or, if that value is not reasonably estimable at the time of the disclosure, by reference to a model investment of $ 10,000.

Proposed paragraphs (a)(2)(i) and (a)(2)(ii) would require the broker, dealer or municipal securities dealer to state whether it receives revenue sharing or portfolio brokerage commissions from the fund complex. Proposed paragraph (a)(2)(iii) would require the broker, dealer or municipal securities dealer to state whether it pays differential compensation in connection with transactions in the covered security, if the covered security charges a deferred sales load or is a proprietary covered security. . .

---

## Discussion Topics

a. Does it make sense to impose on mutual fund advisers these detailed requirements? How costly is it for the adviser to provide these details? How much have investors that are not part of the insider group lost because of the absence of this rule? Who pays for the protection of investors?

b. Some advisers view their activities not as servicing investors but mostly as a business. Unlike CEOs, these advisers do not only manage the funds' assets but also manage their own business. Are they similar to law firms or to inside legal counsel? Why should advisers provide details of the costs of managing their business? Why are law firms not required to do so for their clients? Would you invest your money in a mutual fund whose adviser adopts this approach and these arguments?

---

## J. Privacy of Consumer Financial Information and Use of Consumer Financial Information in Marketing Solicitations[1]

1. General

In August 2009 the SEC adopted Regulation S-AM, which generally prohibits the use of consumer information from an affiliate to make a marketing solicitation to the consumer unless initial notice and opt out requirements are met. . . . Regulation S-AM does not prohibit sharing of information, but restricts its use in marketing solicitations.

The initial notice must disclose "clearly and conspicuously" to the consumer, in writing (or electronically, if the consumer agrees), "in a concise notice," that the affiliate may use eligibility information about the consumer received from its affiliate for marketing solicitations to the consumer. In addition, the consumer should receive "a reasonable opportunity and a reasonable and simple method to 'opt out'" of receiving the solicitations and the consumer must not have opted out.

The prohibition in the regulation "applies to any broker or dealer other than a notice-registered broker or dealer, to any investment company, and to any investment adviser or transfer agent registered with the Commission." An "affiliate" of one of the above is generally defined as "any person that is related by common ownership or common control" with the party. A broker, dealer, investment company, or registered investment adviser or transfer agent is also deemed an affiliate if it 'is regulated under section 214 of the FACT Act, Public Law 108-159, 117 Stat. 1952 (2003), by a government regulator other than the Commission' and rules adopted by the regulator under that section treat the firm as an affiliate.

[The regulation defines "eligibility information" and the definition includes, e.g., information about the consumer's account history and data that contains personal identifiers. "Marketing solicitation" includes, e.g., a telemarketing call, direct mail, or e-mail, but excludes advertising directed at the general public.]

The regulation generally defines "making a marketing solicitation" as (i) a covered person receiving eligibility information from an affiliate; (ii) a covered person (A) identifying the consumer or type of consumer to receive the solicitation; (B) establishing criteria to select such consumer; or (C) deciding which products or services to market to such consumer, or tailoring the solicitation to that consumer; and (iii) as a result of the covered person's use of the information, the consumer receives the solicitation. There is a general exception for an affiliate's use of its own information and an exception for the use of eligibility information by a service provider if certain conditions are met. The regulation provides examples of making a marketing solicitation.

1. These materials are derived from 2 Tamar Frankel & Ann Taylor Schwing, The Regulation of Money Managers § 13.04 (2001 & Supp. 2015) (footnotes omitted).

The regulation includes other exceptions: (1) a pre-existing business relationship exception for a covered person using information from an affiliate to make a solicitation to a consumer with whom the person has a pre-existing business relationship,[1*] (2) an employee benefit plan exemption,[2*] (3) a service provider exception generally allowing a covered person to perform services on behalf of an affiliate, (4) a response to a consumer-initiated communication about the provider's products or services, (5) a response to a consumer's authorization or request to receive solicitations, and (6) an exception where compliance would violate state insurance laws against discrimination.

**Notice.** . . . [A] Covered Person may not use eligibility information about a consumer received from an affiliate unless three conditions are met: (i) a notice requirement must be met; (ii) the consumer must have had a reasonable opportunity and method to "opt out"; and (iii) the consumer must in fact not have opted out. [Notice must be "clearly and conspicuously disclosed to the consumer in writing or, if the consumer agrees, electronically, in a concise notice . . . ."]

In addition, the notice must be provided by (i) "an affiliate that has or has previously had a pre-existing business relationship with the consumer"; or (ii) "[a]s part of a joint notice from two or more members of an affiliated group of companies, provided that at least one of the affiliates on the joint notice has or has previously had a pre-existing business relationship with the consumer."

"Pre-existing business relationship" is in turn defined as: a relationship between a person, or a person's licensed agent, and a consumer based on: (i) A financial contract between the person and the consumer which is in force on the date on which the consumer is sent a solicitation covered by this subpart; (ii) The purchase, rental, or lease by the consumer of the person's goods or services, or a financial transaction (including holding an active account or a policy in force or having another continuing relationship) between the consumer and the person, during the 18-month period immediately preceding the date on which the consumer is sent a solicitation covered by this subpart; or (iii) An inquiry or application by the consumer regarding a product or service offered by that person during the three-month period immediately preceding the date on which the consumer is sent a solicitation covered by this subpart. . . .

[E]xamples of pre-existing business relationships and examples where no such relationship is created [include a] consumer's current brokerage account with a broker-dealer or an advisory contract with a registered investment adviser . . . .

---

1*. 17 C.F.R. § 248.121(c)(1) (2015).

2*. 17 C.F.R. § 248.121(c)(2) (2015) (exception applies "[t]o facilitate communications to an individual for whose benefit [the Covered Person] provide[s] employee benefit or other services pursuant to a contract with an employer related to and arising out of the current employment relationship or status of the individual as a participant or beneficiary of an employee benefit plan").

If a consumer owning investment company securities redeems them, there is a relationship and the 18-month period begins at redemption. An inquiry to a broker-dealer about an affiliated investment company's products or services constitutes a relationship with both companies. Similarly, if a consumer with a pre-existing business relationship with an investment company affiliated with a broker-dealer makes an inquiry to a centralized call center for both companies about the broker-dealer's products or services, there is a relationship with the broker-dealer. However, an inquiry to a centralized call center about the consumer's existing account with a broker-dealer does not establish a relationship with affiliates, nor does an inquiry only about retail locations and hours.

"**Opt Out**". A consumer's opt out generally "prohibits any affiliate covered by the opt out notice from using eligibility information received from another affiliate as described in the notice to make marketing solicitations to the consumer." If there is a continuing relationship with the Covered Person or affiliate, the notice may apply to eligibility information obtained in connection with (A) a single continuing relationship or multiple continuing relationships (including relationships established after delivery of the opt out notice), so long as the notice adequately describes the covered relationships, or (B) any other transaction with the Covered Person or affiliates as described in the notice. If there is no continuing relationship (e.g., only an isolated transaction), the notice applies only to information obtained in connection with that transaction.

A consumer may be given a "menu of alternatives" (i.e., opting out of some solicitations and not others) provided that one alternative is opting out of all solicitations from all affiliates covered by the notice. The opt out must be effective for at least five years unless revoked by the consumer in writing (or, if the consumer agrees, electronically) and a longer period may be established. The regulation sets out requirements for the opt out notice. It must be "clear, conspicuous, and concise," and must include: (i) the name of the affiliate(s) providing the notice, (ii) a list of the affiliates or types of affiliates whose use of information is covered by the notice, (iii) a description of the types of information that may be used for solicitations to the consumer, (iv) disclosure that the consumer may limit the use of information for solicitations, (v) disclosure that the election will apply for the specified period to the consumer (and, if applicable, notice that it may be renewed), (vi) if provided to consumers who may have previously opted out, disclosure that such consumer need not act again before it receives a renewal notice, and (vii) a "reasonable and simple" method to opt out. If two or more consumers jointly obtain a product or service, they may be provided one notice and any may opt out.

The regulation requires a "reasonable opportunity" [and] a "reasonable and simple" method to opt out. . . .

# Chapter 7

## *Fund Management: The Advisory Function, Fees and Contract Terms*

### A. Introduction

An adviser is a person who suggests to another a course of action or an idea to follow. Public policy encourages reliance on experts' advice.[1]

An investment adviser may give advice, which clients can choose to follow or ignore ("non-discretionary advice"). Alternatively, an investment adviser may give "discretionary advice" in which the adviser is entrusted with the power to make the investment decision, and to carry it out, subject to guidelines or restrictions and periodic reporting to the client. Advisers to investment companies are discretionary advisers as well as manager of other functions that are necessary for investment management. Thus, in the case of investment companies the adviser not only advises but also manages the investors' assets. However, investors in unit investment trusts and open-end funds have the right to redeem their shares and terminate the relationship. Investors in closed-end funds can terminate the relationship by selling their shares if a market for the shares exists (and usually it does).

The business of investment management was described in 1966 by the SEC staff as follows:[2]

> *The Management Function and Its Cost*
>
> To avail themselves of professional management and portfolio diversification, increasing numbers of Americans have been entrusting their capital to investment companies.
>
> * * *
>
> An examination of management costs in the investment company industry should begin by considering the process of portfolio management, the central factor in investment company operations. Investment company portfolio management involves a number of common elements. Although the emphasis placed on each element varies widely from company to company and from complex

1. *See* Tamar Frankel, Fiduciary Law, Ch. 1 (2010) (Oxford University Press).
2. Report of the SEC on the Public Policy Implications of Investment Company Growth, H.R. Rep. No. 89-2337 (1966).

to complex, in most respects such management is not essentially different from the management of other large portfolios of securities. [The common features include analyses of the economy and of the securities markets; analyses of particular industries; and selecting specific securities].

* * *

Non-advisory services [include] "the preparation, printing and distribution of prospectuses, shareholder reports, and proxy material, the holding of directors' or trustees' and shareholders' meetings, the issuance, transfer and cancellation of share certificates, the payment of dividend and capital gain distributions, and compliance with State and Federal regulatory requirements. . . . [as well as] brokerage services, safekeeping of the company's portfolio securities and other assets, receipt and delivery of securities bought and sold, receipt of dividend and interest income, proxy material and other communications from issuers of portfolio securities — and in the case of mutual funds, the computation, usually made once or twice daily, of offering and redemption prices for the fund's shares. . . . data processing . . . office equipment and clerical personnel [and] the services of professionals such as lawyers and accountants.

* * *

*Advisory Contracts*

The Act prohibits any person from serving as an investment adviser to a registered investment company except pursuant to a written contract. It also requires that the contract 'precisely describe the compensation to be paid thereunder.' The Act does not, however, specify or set express limitations on the type of fee arrangements that may be contained in advisory contracts. . . .

[T]he overwhelming majority of advisory contracts in the mutual fund industry provide for the payment of advisory fees solely on the basis of the market value of the funds' average net assets. The traditional formula has been a flat annual rate of 0.50 percent of the fund's average net assets. Since the publication of the Wharton Report in 1962, there has been a tendency, especially among the larger funds, to substitute scaled-down fee schedules for the traditional flat rate. Most such schedules still apply the standard 0.50 percent rate up to a breakpoint which varies from $100 million to $500 million of net assets, and apply somewhat lower rates to any portion of the fund's assets in excess of that figure.

[This fee structure] serves as a direct incentive for the investment adviser to devote its efforts to promoting the sale of the fund's shares. Since the advisory fee is based on the current market value of the fund's assets rather than on their cost, it also provides an incentive for increasing the value of the fund's portfolio through effective performance of the advisory function.

A few funds pay advisory fees on a basis related to or influenced by factors other than the market value of the funds' assets. . . . Some funds have advisory contracts which specifically relate the advisory fee to the fund's investment performance . . . based on a percentage of both investment income and net capital gains. In a few instances it is based entirely on investment income. Performance-based fee arrangements, like those based on a percentage of assets, provide strong incentives for increasing fund size through sales of shares. The larger the size of the assets managed, the greater potential for increasing the dollar amount of the fund's income and capital gains and hence the amount of the advisory fee.

*Services paid for by the advisory fee*

. . . . [Mutual funds do not have staffs or managers. These functions are "outsourced" to the adviser that established the funds in the first place, or to service providers chosen by the adviser.] In some cases, advisory fees cover all normal operating expenses of the funds, except taxes and expenses for services provided by their principal underwriters. In others, the advisory fee pays only for investment management; the fund pays an additional fee to its investment adviser, principal underwriter or to another organization designated as its 'trustee' or 'business manager' for nonadvisory services or obtains them directly from banks, broker-dealers, attorneys, accountants, and printers.* * *

*The Cost of Management: The Economies of Size*

The cost of providing investment advice to mutual funds depends on a variety of factors...It is generally recognized, however, that increases in the assets of a fund do not lead to a commensurate increase in the cost of furnishing it with investment advice and other managerial services. . . . [and] operating costs decline proportionately as the size of a trust increases. . . . The economies of size, in large measure, reflect the fact that the management of both large and small security portfolios requires much the same general economic and market forecasting, analyses of various industry groups and evaluations of particular securities. Increases in fund size are not necessarily followed by increases in the number of portfolio securities, since even a relatively small fund may be large enough to attain adequate diversification of investment risk. Indeed, in recent years there has been a tendency among many larger funds to decrease rather than increase the number of common stock holdings in their portfolios despite substantial growth through sales of fund shares. . . .

---

## Discussion Topics

a. Is the management function, as described by the 1966 SEC Staff Report, similar to the management function of the 21st century? Are the economies of scale, cited in the Public Policy Implications (PPI) study, more or less prevalent today?

b. What alternatives are there in structuring an advisory fee? What are the advantages and disadvantages to the adviser of calculating the advisory fee on a fixed percentage of the assets managed? What are the interests of the investors in one fee structure as opposed to another?

c. The PPI study notes that some mutual funds were charging performance fees based on a percentage of both investment income and net capital gains. Recall the discussion of performance fees in Chapter 2. There, we noted that as a result of the 1970 legislation, such performance fees were prohibited with some exceptions.

d. What employees do advisers have? What would advisers do to attract business and market their services? Once they attract clients, what are the functions that advisers will perform to provide the services?

e. List the types of employees that advisers would hire, including portfolio managers. What does each type of employee do? Do advisers need to hire persons to perform the functions you listed, or can they obtain these services in a different way, for example, by purchasing the services in the market? What are the pluses and minuses of hiring employees rather than buying services in the markets?

f. How do you view advisers? Do you view them as organizations that promote and service investment companies? As organizations that raise funds to manage? As service providers or product vendors? Do these views affect your perception of the problems that advisers may pose for clients, and which the law does address or should address?

g. What is the difference between a portfolio manager and an investment adviser? Should the primary focus of the Investment Company Act be on regulating investment advisers or portfolio managers? Does it matter? What does history tell us about the difference and the need for regulation?

---

## B. Structuring Advisory Services

### 1. External and Internal Advisory Services

In the Report of the SEC on the Public Policy Implications of Investment Company Growth (1966), the staff noted two forms in which advisory services may be structured, that is, externally and internally, stating:

> Like typical business enterprises elsewhere in the economy, some investment companies, especially closed end companies, are internally managed by officers and staffs employed directly by the companies. . . . [H]owever, the management function of most mutual funds is contracted out to an external investment advisory organization, the principals of which are the persons who organized and promoted the fund from its inception or the successors of such persons. In such instances, the analysts and other professional personnel on whose expertise the fund relies are employees of the adviser, not of the fund. The top decision-makers to whom these persons report are typically the full-time officials of the adviser. They may be also

officers of the fund, but even in that event they receive all or most of their remuneration from the adviser.[1]

In 1940, Congress found that both external and internal forms of advisory relationships were being used. Because investment advisory services constitute the main function of investment advisers, some advocated prohibiting investment companies to "outsource" advisory services. Nonetheless, Congress allowed external advisory structures. However, recognizing the problems stemming from such arrangements, Congress imposed on these advisers fiduciary duties, in addition to regulating their contractual arrangements with investment companies and established independent directors of the investment companies to protect investors.

Chief Executive Officers manage corporations as employees. External advisers manage mutual fund portfolios not as employees but as outside enterprises that offer management services. This structure is generally not practical for, or used by, ordinary operating companies. Ordinary operating companies generally do not "outsource" the management of their enterprises. Investment companies, whether organized as corporations or otherwise, are permitted to, and indeed do, outsource the management of their business, which is — managing their financial assets. However, the relationship of outside advisers to the mutual funds is not merely contractual. As we shall see, section 15 imposes strict limits on advisers' freedom, while it recognizes their "business-investment aspects." Note where the model of an "outsourced" mutual fund manager comes from: Its model was the investment adviser, who was far more trusted than the underwriters, and brokers-dealers, who established mutual funds in 1920s.

Although most investment companies are managed by external advisers, a number of such companies are not. The second largest fund, Vanguard, is managed internally. That is, the adviser is organized as an entity, but is owned by the various funds and services the funds at cost. This cost includes the employees' salaries.

After the year 2000, among the fifty largest fund managers, only eight remain privately held (plus investment companies--owned Vanguard). Six firms are publicly held, and the remaining thirty-five management companies are owned by giant financial conglomerates — twenty-two by banks and insurance companies, six by major brokerage firms, and seven by foreign financial institutions.[2]

---

**Discussion Topics**

a. If you were an adviser, which would be more attractive to you: an external or an internal structure? Which form would be more efficient and allow you to draw larger capital and larger profits? Do you think that one form would protect you from legal liability more than another, or is your

1. *Id.*
2. John C. Bogle, Founder and Former Chairman, The Vanguard Group, *The Mutual Fund Industry 60 Years Later: For Better or Worse?, available at* http://www.vanguard.com/ bogle_site/sp20050102.htm.

legal liability the same in both cases? What form would ensure you more control over the operation as against takeovers, or bind the clients more tightly to you and prevent them from terminating the relationship with you?

b. As an investor, which form of relationship do you prefer? Or do you care?

c. Corporate directors and officers, trustees, and partners are generally not permitted to delegate their discretionary powers to others. Why should these fiduciaries to investment companies be allowed to delegate their powers and responsibilities to an external adviser by contract?

d. What are the implications of the current ownership of external investment advisers by investment companies? What are the implications of investment advisers as businesses, seeking higher return for their investors?

---

## 2. The Advisory Contract: Section 15

As noted earlier, the 1940 Act recognized that external investment advisers occupy a special position by acting as substitutes for actively managing directors and officers of investment companies.[1] Congress permitted external management of investment companies to continue because, as the staff of the SEC stated, small companies could not afford the salaries needed for expert in-house advisers. The staff recommended "a few elementary safeguards" as to management contracts and the maintenance of the status quo.[2] These elementary safeguards could become more important with the growth of the funds.

In this connection, the 1940 Act draws on fundamental principles regulating fiduciary services:

- First, to avoid misunderstandings, section 15(a)(1) of the 1940 Act provides: "It shall be unlawful for any person to serve or act as investment adviser of a registered investment company, except pursuant to a written contract . . . ."
- Second, all advisory contracts with registered investment companies must be approved by the investment company's shareholders. In connection with the establishment of a new investment company, this can be accomplished by the investment company's sole initial shareholder, which is usually the adviser itself or an affiliate. The theory here is that investors do not have to purchase shares of the new company if they do not like the fee structure being offered. However, new advisory contracts or material changes to existing advisory contracts in respect of existing investment companies require approval by the existing public shareholder base. The SEC staff's position is that any material change to an advisory contract creates a new advisory contract that must be approved; however,

1. *Hearings on S. 3580 before a Subcomm. of the Senate Comm. on Banking and Currency*, 76th Cong. 251 (1940).
2. *Id.* at 252.

one exception to this general rule is that an adviser may reduce its advisory fee without obtaining shareholder approval.

- Third, section 15(a)(2) permits all contracts to continue in effect for a period of more than two years only if the contract's continuance is approved at least annually by the investment company's board or by a vote of the investment company's shareholders. Additionally, section 15(c) makes it unlawful for the investment company to enter into, renew, or perform an advisory contract, unless a majority of the independent members of the board of directors of the investment company approve the contract in person at a meeting called for that purpose.

Section 15(c) contains a number of procedural safeguards in connection with the approval or continuance of an advisory contract. Recognizing the importance of the duty to approve or continue an advisory contract, section 15(c) requires the independent directors to separately approve the advisory contract (or its continuance) in person. This means what it says. A quorum of the independent directors must be present, in person, and not on the phone or by any other electronic means (including, for example, video conference), and consider and approve the advisory contract. Otherwise, section 15(c)'s requirements are not satisfied. In addition, section 15(c) requires the directors to request and evaluate, and the adviser to furnish, such information as may be reasonably necessary to evaluate the terms of the advisory contract. In practice, this means the directors, or their counsel, typically send the adviser a letter with a list of information the directors desire to review, and the adviser must respond to this information request with the relevant information. The requirements of section 15(c) are in addition to those of section 15(a)(2) — in other words, an advisory contract can only be approved or continued by (1) a vote of the full board or the fund's shareholders, <u>and</u> (2) a vote of the fund's independent directors.

Another principle regarding advisory contracts reflects fiduciary relationships. It provides that advisory contracts are not assignable without the consent of the client. Recognizing the "fiduciary" nature of advisers, section 15(a)(4) provides that upon its assignment an advisory contract with an investment company will be terminated. Assignment of advisory contracts, and for that matter, all fiduciary relationships, is prohibited because these relationships are personal, entitling the investors to rely on the particular adviser and requiring the advisers to be trustworthy. Also, because investment companies hold assets that are easily embezzled, transfer to unscrupulous people could open the door to looting the assets.

"Assignment" is broadly defined in the 1940 Act to include both a transfer or hypothecation of the contract itself, as well as any change in control of the existing adviser.[1] "Control" under the 1940 Act is generally tied to a transfer of 25% or more of an adviser's voting stock.[2] Thus, with some administrative exceptions developed through the no-action letter process,[3]

1. Investment Company Act § 2(a)(4).
2. *See* Investment Company Act § 2(a)(9).
3. *See, e.g.,* Am. Century Cos., SEC No-Action Letter, 1997 WL 803129 (Dec. 23, 1997); Dean Witter, Discover & Co., SEC No-Action Letter, 1997 WL 192125

transactions where 25% or more of an adviser's voting stock changes hands will terminate the advisory contracts of any investment company clients and will require approval by the investment company's shareholders of a new advisory contract. In an attempt to mitigate the draconian aspects of these practicalities, the SEC promulgated rule 15a-4 under the 1940 Act, which provides conditions under which an investment company's board can approve an interim advisory contract pending solicitation of shareholder approval.

Automatic termination of the advisory contract, however, presents problems for the investment company shareholders. Unlike individual clients, they may have greater difficulties in hiring another adviser, and assuring continuity of management.

Automatic termination also poses problems for external advisers. These advisers are entrepreneurs, who may also have invested in the creation of investment companies and financed the costs of creating the investment companies, like other business entrepreneurs. However, others are generally free to sell the businesses that they create.

Section 15(f) is an attempt to accommodate both principles: allow advisers to "cash in" on their investment in their business while protecting investors from possible harm as a result of the transfer of the advisory contract. Under section 15(f), the assignment of the advisory contract is permissible, subject to two conditions.

First, for three years after the transaction the investment company's board must consist of 75% of independent directors — and those directors must be independent of both the predecessor adviser and the new adviser. Presumably, these directors would determine whether the assignee adviser is appropriate and acceptable.

Second, to prevent a "buyer" of the investment contract from recouping its price from the investors, no "unfair burden" may be imposed on the investment company as a result of the transaction or any express or implied terms, conditions, or understandings applicable thereto.

Section 15(f) generally defines an "unfair burden" to mean any arrangement, during the two years after the transaction, where the old or new adviser (or any interested person of either) receives or is entitled to receive any compensation directly or indirectly (i) from any person in connection with the purchase or sale of securities or other property to, from, or on behalf of the investment company, other than bona fide ordinary compensation as principal underwriter for the investment company, or (ii) from the investment company or its shareholders for other than bona fide investment advisory or other services.

---

(Apr. 18, 1997) (merger with Morgan Stanley Group, Inc. will not constitute an "assignment"); Dean Witter, Discover & Co., SEC No-Action Letter, 1993 WL 44288 (Feb. 8, 1993) (IPO & spin-off "will not trigger the requirements of Sections 15(a)(4) or 205(a)(2)").

The following case addresses a section 15(a)(4) action, and was the predicate for the enactment of section 15(f), which is a fiduciary safe harbor for an adviser seeking to sell its business.[1]

Lazard organized a fund (the "Fund"), which employed it as its investment adviser. Lazard learned that Moody's Investors Service, Inc., an investment adviser, was considering entering the mutual fund market. Lazard approached D & B, the parent of Moody's. One agreement provided that the Fund would "merge" into Moody's Capital Fund, which would employ Moody's A & D as investment adviser. Shareholder approval would constitute approval of the new advisory contract. Another agreement between Lazard and D & B would become effective on the merger date if the advisory contract were approved at that time. Under this agreement, D & B would provide Lazard D & B stock as consideration for certain undertakings.

The Fund notified its stockholders of the meeting regarding approval of the merger and adoption of the advisory contract. Stockholders were told of the agreement between Lazard and D & B but not asked to approve it. Plaintiff Rosenfeld alleged that the transactions involved a sale of Lazard's advisory office.

Subsequently, stockholders approved the merger. Plaintiff argued that the receipt of shares to Lazard was not in consideration for its undertakings, but, at least in part, a payment for Lazard's assistance in bringing about the merger and the engagement of Moody's A & D as adviser. Defendant was granted summary judgment, and this appeal followed.

At the outset, the Court stated the equity principle that a fiduciary may not sell or transfer its office for personal gain, and that Lazard, as an investment adviser, was a fiduciary.

> III.
>
> It is argued that, however all this might otherwise be, a different result is demanded because Lazard's advisory contract necessarily terminated under § 15(a) (4) of the Investment Company Act and that, pursuant to § 15(a), the stockholders of the Fund authorized a new contract with Moody's A & D, allegedly on full disclosure, an issue we will discuss below.
>
> Insofar as the argument hinges merely on the statutory nonassignability of the contract with the consequent inference that there was no advisory office that Lazard could sell or transfer, it proves too much. The same could be said of an alleged sale of corporate office or directorship or, in the absence of appropriate provisions in the dispositive instrument, of an executor's or trustee's position. The role of Lazard, an organizer of the Fund and its practical control of the proxy machinery used to recommend the approval of Moody's A & D as new adviser, made it quite as active and influential as a corporate president who recommends a successor to his board of directors, or a trustee who puts the name of a successor before a judge. Indeed, the very fact of nonassignability demonstrates that any payment made to the outgoing adviser by his successor in these

1. *Rosenfeld v. Black,* 445 F.2d 1337 (2d Cir. 1971) (some internal citations omitted).

circumstances over and above the value of any continuing services represents consideration not for lawful assignment of the contract — which is prohibited — but primarily for the use of influence in securing stockholder approval of the successor who expects to profit from the post. While it is true that the advisory contract is not conceptually an asset of the Fund, it is equally true that the expectation of profits under that contract is not an asset which, under the Act, the adviser can assign outright. Hence, if plaintiffs are correct in asserting that Lazard's few covenants were only a minor part of the consideration for D & B's payment to Lazard, Lazard and D & B must have assumed that the outgoing adviser was in a position to help effect the transfer of his office and that his efforts in so doing were worth valuable consideration.

The more serious contention is that §§ 15(a), (c) and (d) constitute a policy determination by Congress that compliance with those provisions was to be the exclusive protection to an investment company when there is a change in advisory office. We cannot accept that view on the facts of this case. In § 1(b) of the Act, after noting abuses that had been disclosed with respect to investment companies, including the management of such companies in the interest of investment advisers and the transfer of control or management without the consent of the security holders, Congress declared: "that the policy and purposes of this title, in accordance with which the provisions of this title shall be interpreted, are to mitigate and, so far as is feasible, to eliminate the conditions enumerated in this section which adversely affect the national public interest and the interest of investors."

The purpose of § 15 was to furnish the added protection of approval of a new adviser by a majority of the stockholders, not to withdraw safeguards already afforded by equity. As has been said, "Section 15(a) (4) is directed at transfers of control without shareholder consent, as distinct from profiteering on a transfer of fiduciary office. Hence, the section on its face hardly compels the conclusion that it is the exclusive antidote for such conduct."

That alone might suffice to require reversal here, since any argument that simple failure of § 15 to supplant the rule of equity leaves plaintiffs with only a state created claim would be answered by the fact that their contentions with respect to the inadequacy of the proxy statement, hereafter considered, afford a sufficient basis for pendent federal jurisdiction. However, we do not rest decision on that ground. We believe rather that the statute not merely did not withdraw safeguards equity had previously provided but impliedly incorporated them. We held in *Brown v. Bullock,* 294 F.2d 415, 421 (2 Cir. 1961), that in requiring annual approval of investment advisory contracts by directors (or, alternatively, by stockholders) Congress meant to prescribe a uniform federal standard of directorial responsibility. It is wholly consistent with that view to say that when Congress required stockholder approval of a contract with a new investment adviser, it intended that the retiring adviser's use of the proxy machinery to procure appointment of the new adviser must conform to the standards of abnegation of personal gain that equity had long imposed. When Congress, in § 15(a), required shareholder approval of any new advisory contract, it must have meant an approval uninfluenced by any improper motivations on the part of the outgoing adviser-fiduciary. If lured by the possibility of profit, the retiring adviser might recommend a successor who was less qualified or more expensive than other candidates, and who might be on the lookout for ways to recoup his "succession fee" at the expense of the Fund. . . . There is thus every reason for believing that Congress meant to adopt the established prophylactic rule. This brings us to the *Insurance Securities* case. . . . The SEC there unsuccessfully attacked a transaction whereby controlling stockholders of a service company which acted as sponsor, depositor, investment adviser and principal underwriter of an investment company sold their stock to a new controlling group at a price twenty-five times its net asset value, and the stockholders of the investment company then approved new contracts with the service company. The actual holding can be readily distinguished since the SEC was proceeding under § 36 of the Act. This authorized the Commission to bring suit for "gross misconduct or gross abuse of trust" and provided that if the court found the Commission's allegations to be established, it should enjoin the person found guilty from acting in its prior capacity either permanently or for such period as the court deemed appropriate. Words and remedies such as these were clearly addressed to highly reprehensible conduct, see *Los Angeles Trust Deed & Mortgage Exchange v. SEC,* 264 F.2d 199, 210 (9 Cir. 1959), cert. denied, 366 U.S. 919, 81 S. Ct. 1095, 6 L. Ed. 2d 241 (1961); we would not dream of suggesting, much less holding, that Lazard's actions were so culpable. However, there are passages in the opinion suggesting that in the court's view none of the excess of the price received by the controlling stockholders over the book value of their stock would be recoverable under any circumstances by stockholders of the investment company. . . . While we do not find it necessary at this time to determine whether the difference between a transaction such as that here before us and the sale of a controlling block in a corporate adviser at a price reflecting the expectation of profits under a renewed contract with the corporation which the sellers were to aid in procuring, is sufficiently substantial to warrant a different result in this latter case, we should not wish to be understood as accepting these views.

IV.

Appellees also rely on the history of the recent amendment to the Investment Company Act, 84 Stat. 1413 (1970). In the Investment Company Report, after stating that "the manager of a mutual fund is unquestionably in a fiduciary relationship to it," and that "consequently, the transfer of that relationship for a price has some elements of the sale of a fiduciary office [which was] strictly prohibited at common law because of the conflicts of interest which are involved," the Report added that "certain of the protective provisions of the

Act have had the somewhat ironical, and presumably unintended, effect of diluting the protections provided by common law principles of fiduciary responsibility." The Report continued that "by reason of the automatic termination provisions in the event of assignment and the requirement that shareholders approve the new arrangements, it can be argued, as was successfully done in *SEC v. Insurance Securities, Inc.,* that there is no sale of the fiduciary office, since that office automatically terminates and a new one is created with stockholder approval." It went on to say that "however unrealistic this conclusion may appear in the light of the ability of the retiring management to use the proxy machinery to insure the installation of its self-chosen successors, application of the strict common-law principle might well be unfair insofar as it denies to the retiring management any compensation for the elements of value in the relationship which they may have built up over the years" and "could also be harmful to the Fund, since existing management might be reluctant to surrender that relationship and to provide the Fund with new and possibly more effective management." Arguing that "there is presently no adequate remedy in the Act" since the Commission "must rely primarily at present on its authority to seek an injunction under section 36 of the act upon the ground that, in arranging the succession, management or directors have been 'guilty' of 'gross misconduct or gross abuse of trust,'" a stigma which the courts "might be extremely reluctant" to place upon businessmen "merely because the terms of succession appear unfair," it urged Congress to amend the Act to prohibit a transfer of an advisory contract or the sale of a controlling block in an adviser, "if the sale, or any express or implied understanding in connection with the sale, is likely to impose additional burdens on the investment company or to limit its freedom of future action. . . ." The bill enacted by Congress did not carry out this recommendation.

Appellees would have us draw two inferences from this episode. One is that the SEC has acceded to the view that the prohibition against receiving compensation for the sale of a fiduciary office is inapplicable to a situation where the retiring adviser of an investment company profits from influencing the designation of a successor. The passages we have quoted demonstrate that if there was any such acceptance, it was a reluctant one, believed, erroneously in our view, to be compelled by the Ninth Circuit's decision in *Insurance Securities*. That case, as we have pointed out, dealt only with the Commission's powers under § 36 as it then stood. The SEC's belief that the unamended Act did not adequately protect fund shareholders against sales of the management organization rested upon a realistic assessment of its own power under § 36 but what we deem an unjustifiably defeatist view of private equitable actions, which the Report apparently did not consider. Although we respect the SEC's interpretation of the statutes it administers, the ultimate responsibility for construction lies with the courts.

The second and even more important inference we are asked to draw is that, by failing to adopt the SEC's proposal, Congress indicated an intention to exclude all remedies other than termination of the old contract and the need for stockholder approval of the new one, even if such approval was obtained by an adviser who was realizing a profit. We have been cited to nothing in the committee reports, in the floor debates, or even in the hearings that casts light on the failure to enact the proposal, or shows that the SEC seriously pressed it. As is well known, the SEC had other, and more important, fish to fry. Congress could well have thought it had handled the problem created by the *Insurance Securities* decision by expanding the SEC's powers under § 36 so that, instead of having to allege that a defendant had been "guilty . . . of gross misconduct or gross abuse or trust," the Commission need now allege only that he has engaged or is about to engage "in any act or practice constituting a breach of fiduciary duty involving personal misconduct." While a new § 36(b) expressly declares that "the investment adviser of a registered investment company shall be deemed to have a fiduciary duty with respect to the receipt of compensation for services, or of payments of a material nature, paid by such registered investment company, or by the security holders thereof, to such investment adviser or any affiliated person of such investment advisor," the context makes plain that Congress did not mean this to be the only fiduciary duty of investment advisers.

* * *

The order granting defendants' motion for summary judgment is reversed and the cause is remanded for further proceedings not inconsistent with this opinion.

---

## Discussion Topics

a. What is the effect of a contract that does not comply with section 15(a)? See section 47(b) of the 1940 Act. Can the shareholders approve the contract retroactively?[1] Can they authorize the execution of the contract in the future? What is the effect of a contract transfer that does not conform to the conditions of section 15(f)?

b. Compare and contrast the replacement of a portfolio manager to a fund with another manager from the same advisory organization with the assignment of an advisory contract to another adviser. Which creates a greater regulatory risk?

c. The investment management service providers have been consolidating in recent years. Both investment advisers and investment companies have been merging. Combined investment advisers have increased their client base (investment companies and institutional and individual clients).

1. Investors Diversified Servs., Inc., 30 S.E.C. 273, 280 (1949) (the SEC granted exemption to enable the company to approve the contract and to remove a ban to a settlement which would permit the adviser to collect fees for the period before approval).

These mergers have attracted investors' attention, especially if the advisers enrich their managerial talent.

Consolidation among investment companies has taken place either within a fund complex or among funds that are managed by different advisers. For example, Adviser A that manages 200 funds may cause the merger of funds X and Y, or transfer the assets of fund Y to fund X and dissolve fund Y. Alternatively, Adviser A that manages fund X may merge with Adviser B which manages the assets of fund Y and merge funds X and Y into fund Z.

Do the mergers of investment companies pose different problems for investors as compared to mergers of advisers?

---

### 3. The Sub-Advisory Relationship

Advisory services can be provided through a sub-advisory structure. In this structure an adviser selects a sub-adviser to direct day-to-day management of a fund.[1] Sub-advisory contracts are likewise subject to approval by the fund's board and shareholders under section 15. Note the following response of the SEC to an application for an exemption regarding obtaining shareholder approval for sub-advisory services. Note the self-imposed conditions of the applicants. These are usually agreed upon with the SEC staff in advance.

ICMI serves as adviser for Penn Series Funds (Company), consisting of nine Funds. ICMI recommends the selection or termination of sub-advisers (Managers) to Funds' boards, monitors the Managers, and may reallocate assets among them. Managers are approved by the boards, including a majority of independent directors. This type of fund is known as a "multi-manager" fund.

The Funds requested an exemptive order from section 15(a) of the 1940 Act to allow ICMI to enter into and amend sub-advisory agreements without shareholder approval. The Funds argued that the shareholders in effect hire ICMI to manage the fund through external managers through its manager selection and monitoring. The relief would not apply to a Manager affiliated with Funds or ICMI under section 2(a)(3) except as an Affiliated Manager as described in the representations below.

The SEC granted an exemptive order subject to conditions:[2]

> Applicants agree that the order granting the requested relief will be subject to the following conditions:
>
> 1. Before any Fund may rely on the requested order the operation of the Fund in the manner described in the application will be approved by a majority of each Fund's Shareholders, or, in the case of a Future Fund whose public Shareholders purchase shares on the basis of a prospectus containing the disclosure contemplated

---

1. Penn Series Funds, Inc., Investment Company Act Rel. No. 24376 (Apr. 4, 2000).
2. Note that these types of orders to permit this flexibility in a multimanager structure are routinely granted by the SEC and this excerpt represents only one example.

by condition 2 below, by the sole initial shareholder before offering shares of any Future Fund to the public.

2. The prospectus for each Manager of Managers Fund will disclose the existence, substance and effect of any order granted pursuant to the application. In addition, each Manager of Managers Fund will hold itself out to the public as employing the "manager of managers" approach described in the application. The prospectus for each Manager of Managers Fund will prominently disclose that ICMI has ultimate responsibility to oversee the Managers and recommend their hiring, termination, and replacement.

3. Within 90 days of the hiring of any new Manager, ICMI will furnish Shareholders all information about the new Manager that would be included in a proxy statement. To meet this obligation, ICMI will provide Shareholders with an information statement meeting the requirements of Regulation 14C, Schedule 14C and Item 22 of Schedule 14A under the Securities Exchange Act of 1934.

4. ICMI will not enter into a Subadvisory Agreement with any Affiliated Manager without such agreement, including the compensation to be paid thereunder, being approved by the Shareholders of the applicable Manager of Managers Fund.

5. At all times, a majority of the Company's Board will be Independent. Directors, and the nomination of new or additional Independent Directors will be at the discretion of the then existing Independent Directors.

6. When a Manager change is proposed for a Manager of Managers Fund with an Affiliated Manager, the Company's Board, including a majority of the Independent Directors, will make a separate finding, reflected in the applicable Fund's Board minutes, that such change is in the best interests of the Fund and its Shareholders and does not involve a conflict of interest from which ICMI or the Affiliated Manager derives an inappropriate advantage.

7. ICMI will provide general management services to each Manager of Managers Fund, including overall supervisory responsibility for the general management and investment of each Manager of Managers Fund's securities portfolio, and, subject to Board review and approval, will (i) set each Manager of Managers Fund's overall investment strategies, (ii) recommend and select Managers, (iii) allocate, and when appropriate, reallocate a Manager of Managers Fund's assets among its Managers when a Fund has more than one Manager, (iv) monitor and evaluate Manager performance, and (v) implement procedures designed to ensure that the Manager complies with the Manager of Managers Fund's investment objectives, policies, and restrictions.

8. No director or officer of the Company, or director or officer of ICMI will own, directly or indirectly (other than through a pooled investment vehicle over which such person does not have control), any interest in a Manager, except for (i) ownership of interests in ICMI or any entity that controls, is controlled by or is under common

> control with ICMI; or (ii) ownership of less than 1% of the outstanding securities of any class of equity or debt of a publicly traded company that is either a Manager or an entity that controls, is controlled by, or is under common control with a Manager. . . .

---

## Discussion Topics

a. What was the purpose of the proposed structure? Why would an adviser "outsource" advisory services, rather than offer these services directly, or through its own subsidiaries? Were there business reasons for this structure? Were there legal reasons?

b. What are the reasons for requiring shareholder approval of new advisers? Does the requirement reflect the classification of the relationship under the law? Why are these reasons not as weighty in this case?

---

## C. Regulatory Response to the Potential Conflicts of Interest Posed by the Determination of the Adviser's Fees

In this section, we consider the conflicts of interest that are present in the advisory relationship and the regulatory framework that has been enacted to guard against these conflicts. The following is a summary of the 1966 SEC Report (the "PPI Report") discussion of the advisory fees and contract terms.[1] The materials are followed by two cases concerning the issue of excessive fees.[2]

Historically most funds charged 0.50% advisory fees regardless of the size of the assets under management and the consequent economies of size. Restraints by competition and disclosure did not seem to have made a difference. The staff noted the difference between the higher rates of advisory fees charged externally managed funds and the lower fees charged pension and profit-sharing plans and other non-fund investment advisory clients. The staff attributed the difference to the absence of active competition. External advisers competed by offering their services through the sale of their funds' shares. Therefore, share prices rather than the cost of services attract the investors. Fees do not seem to play the important role they actually do.

> Advisory fees, however, are the funds' principal operating expense and have become very substantial in amount. Mutual funds are unique among large purchasers of investment management services because neither cost considerations nor other competitive factors influence the funds' choice of their advisers.

* * *

---

1. Report of the SEC on the Public Policy Implications of Investment Company Growth, H.R. Rep. No. 89-2337 (1966).
2. *Krinsk v. Fund Asset Management*, 875 F.2d 404 (2d Cir. 1989); *Jones v. Harris Associates, L.P.*, 130 S. Ct. 1418, 176 L. Ed. 2d 265 (2010) (footnotes omitted).

*Advisory fees and the limitations of disclosure*

Disclosure is often termed the "keystone" of the Federal securities laws. Disclosure requirements imposed on issuers of securities help public investors to make informed investment decisions and provide them with necessary information to take legal and other action against corporate abuse. In addition, and in many respects just as important, disclosure develops and maintains conventional limitations over the relationships between corporate managements and public shareholders. It does so by making publicly available a body of information which guides investors and corporate managers themselves in appraising the propriety of particular actions, circumstances, and arrangements.

The disclosure requirements developed by the Commission in the administration of the Federal securities laws place considerable emphasis on the remuneration and other benefits received by officers, directors, controlling persons and other insiders of publicly held corporations. Congress determined at the time of the passage of the Investment Company Act that disclosure alone provides inadequate protection for investment company shareholders. . . .

Externally managed funds pay for most management services through gross fees to separate advisory organizations rather than through salaries and other remuneration to the individuals who manage their affairs. Although such fees pay for the services of those persons affiliated with investment advisers who perform the same functions as officers and employees of internally managed companies, they also pay for the services of other professional, administrative, and clerical personnel and for the office and research facilities incidental to these services. Appraisal of the fairness of the charges for the entire package of these services is far more complex than an appraisal of the reasonableness of individual executives' compensation. . . .

To the extent that disclosure has served to develop and maintain conventional limitations on the level of advisory fees charged to externally managed companies, these limitations have served mainly to keep advisory fee rates from rising above the 0.50 percent fee rate traditional in the industry. As noted, this traditional fee rate was developed at a time when mutual funds and fund complexes were only a fraction of their present size. It was itself derived from the advisory fee rates commonly charged for the more costly management services, per dollar of assets managed, provided to the much smaller portfolios of individual investment advisory clients.

*Shareholder voting rights*

The Act's safeguards with respect to advisory fees consist mainly of the provisions of the Act requiring initial approval of advisory contracts by the holders of a majority of the outstanding voting shares and annual renewal.

The requirements for initial approval of advisory contracts by shareholders, together with the disclosure requirements for proxy material soliciting their approval, have had a prophylactic effect and may well have served to discourage advisers from charging fees at rates higher than the traditional 0.50 rate. However, requirements for shareholder approval of advisory contracts cannot realistically — as experience has demonstrated — be relied upon to achieve any material departures from the traditional 0.50 percent advisory fee rate that would reflect the economies of size available from the growth of the funds.

Shareholder voting in mutual funds, as in most publicly held enterprises, is conducted almost entirely by proxy. In most instances proxies are solicited only on behalf of management. The Commission's proxy rules require that the form of the management proxy afford shareholders an opportunity to signify either their acceptance or rejection of management proposals. In addition, the rules provide shareholders with an opportunity to vote on proposals initiated by shareholders.

The shareholders' opportunity to accept or reject management and shareholder proposals can provide them with meaningful alternatives in connection with most matters for which their approval is solicited. As a practical matter, however, these alternatives do not exist in connection with shareholder approval of advisory contracts. Proxy contests initiated by competing investment advisers have taken place only in very rare instances where existing management relationships have completely broken down. The shareholders themselves cannot select a new adviser, formulate a new advisory contract or set a new advisory fee; only the fund's board of directors and the shareholders acting together can do that. The shareholders can only ratify what management proposes. Shareholder refusal to adopt or renew the contract proposed by management, however, might leave the fund without an effective advisory contract, and the Act provides that no person or organization may serve as an investment adviser to a registered investment company except pursuant to a written contract. Thus, exercise of the shareholders' right to refuse to ratify the adoption or the renewal of an advisory contract is fraught with uncertainty for — and possibly with harm to — the fund's operations. The drastic consequences that may attend the exercise of that right impair its effectiveness as a control over advisory fees.

Given sufficient shareholder understanding of and unrest over advisory fee rates, shareholders might attempt through the exercise of their voting rights to obtain a reduction in advisory fees by electing a board of directors or trustees independent of existing management and pledged to seek a reduction. The directors or trustees of most funds are elected annually by shareholders, and the Act contains provisions designed to safeguard this right.

* * *

But there is little likelihood of shareholder-initiated opposition to the management of a mutual fund. Mutual fund managers through their relationship with the dealers and salesmen who sell the funds' shares have an advantage over outsiders in the solicitation of shareholder votes that managements of most other publicly held corporations do not have. Moreover, as the Wharton Report noted, mutual fund share ownership tends to be more highly dispersed than that of other publicly held enterprises, with the dispersion being greatest in larger funds. Seldom does any individual or organized group of public shareholders own a significant portion of the outstanding shares of any of the larger funds. Should such large shareholders as there are become dissatisfied with a fund's management, they may redeem their shares at current net asset value. On the other hand, large shareholders of other types of enterprises may find it difficult to liquidate their holdings at current market prices.

In mutual funds, as in other publicly held enterprises, shareholder voting can serve as an important method of communication with management. Indications of shareholder dissatisfaction expressed in this way may play a significant role in influencing the actions of fund managers on many matters of policy. But shareholder voting rights cannot be used effectively to obtain departures from traditional fees that inadequately reflect the economies of size in the management of investment companies or with respect to other matters that affect so crucially the interests of the adviser and those who are affiliated with it.

*The role of the unaffiliated directors*

Mutual fund advisers generally are the organizers of the fund and, as such, select the fund's original board of directors. Although the fund later may grow to substantial size, because of the diffusion of share ownership and the absence of organized shareholder participation in fund affairs, the power to select the fund's directors remains with the original organizers or their successors. The adviser's discretion generally is limited only by those provisions of the Act, which require that specified percentages of the board members not be officers or employees of the fund or persons affiliated with the adviser, its principal underwriter, its regular broker, or any investment banker and their affiliates.

The unaffiliated directors are in a position to, and frequently do, perform a valuable service for the funds and their shareholders. They often bring broad perspectives from their diverse business and professional experience to the management of fund affairs, and in many instances they have sought to fulfill their responsibilities in a highly responsible and dedicated way. The Wharton Report suggested, however, that unaffiliated directors "may be of restricted value as an instrument for providing effective representation of mutual fund shareholders in dealings between the fund and its investment advisers." The unaffiliated directors usually have other occupations and necessarily cannot devote unlimited time to their directorial duties — duties for which they, like other corporate directors who are not part of full-time management, seldom receive more than minimal compensation. They also have no staff of officers and employees who work for and are compensated by the fund. In most cases, even the fund's counsel is the adviser's counsel as well. Hence the unaffiliated directors necessarily obtain most of their information about fund operations from persons who also owe allegiance to, and obtain the preponderance of their compensation from, the adviser-underwriters and who cannot be expected to look at such matters as advisory fees in a disinterested way. . . .

[In the Commission's experience] the unaffiliated directors have not been in a position to secure changes in the level of advisory fee rates in the mutual fund industry. In most instances the adviser serves as, or is closely affiliated with, the fund's principal underwriter which maintains a distributing organization for the fund's shares. The organization that has developed over a period of years to manage the fund's portfolio and to furnish it with some, and in certain cases virtually all, of the nonadvisory services necessary to its operation belongs to the adviser and not to the fund. Indeed, in some cases, all of the fund's records are maintained by the fund's adviser. Although the unaffiliated directors under State law have an unqualified right of access to these records, the adviser, as a practical matter, is in a position to seriously hamper any employment of that right which might interfere with or threaten the adviser's operation of or control over the fund.

Thus, negotiations between the unaffiliated directors and fund advisers over advisory fees would lack an essential element of arm's-length bargaining — the freedom to terminate the negotiations and to bargain with other parties for the same services. In view of the fund's dependence on its existing adviser and the fact that many shareholders may have invested in the fund on the strength of the adviser's reputation, few unaffiliated directors would feel justified in replacing the adviser with a new and untested organization simply because of difficulty in obtaining a reduction in long-established fee rates which are customary in the industry.

Moreover, even if some of the unaffiliated directors were so inclined, they might not have the power to obtain another investment adviser for the fund. In some cases, the unaffiliated directors are only a minority; in many others they constitute only a bare majority of the board of directors and would need the support of all the unaffiliated directors for this drastic step. Even with such support it is unlikely that the action of the unaffiliated directors would be uncontested.

The possibility of disrupting the fund's operations, the prospect of a bitter and expensive proxy contest, and the risk and uncertainty involved in replacing the entire fund management organization with a new and untested one, make termination of the existing advisory relationship a wholly unrealistic alternative in negotiations over advisory fees. Without such an alternative, advisory fees negotiated between advisers and the unaffiliated directors lack the essential element of arm's-length transactions and provide inadequate assurance that the fees bear a reasonable relationship to the price at which similar services could be obtained in a genuinely competitive market.

*The position of the investment adviser*

The absence of competitive pressures, the limitations of disclosure, the ineffectiveness of shareholder voting rights, and the obstacles to more effective action by the unaffiliated directors have meant that the determination whether and to what extent the economies of size realized from fund growth should be shared with the funds and their shareholders is left largely to the judgment of the adviser. As noted, some advisers voluntarily had reduced the fee rates for the funds under their management long before the publication of the Wharton Report and the institution of shareholder litigation attacking the fees as excessive. However, most advisers did not. Moreover, the ability of the managements of the publicly held fund advisory organizations to initiate reductions in advisory fee rates in the interest of fund shareholders is significantly affected by their responsibilities to the adviser's public investors.

Under these circumstances, for most funds only the pressures generated by the Wharton Report and the pendency of shareholder litigation have been sufficient to effect departures from the pattern of the flat 0.50 percent fee rate prevailing in the industry. The extent of these departures in many instances has not been substantial. The reasons for this lie in an understanding of the background and nature of the shareholder fee litigation and the circumstances under which most of the suits were terminated.

---

## Discussion Topics

a. What are the strengths and the weaknesses of the following regulatory approaches as a means to regulate advisory fees: disclosure; shareholder voting; and the actions of unaffiliated directors? How should they be made more effective? Are there alternatives or additional approaches to address the fee problem?

b. The staff's 1966 report dealt with a far less complicated environment than the one that exists in 2016. The types of expenses that often used to be separate, such as fees, administrative expenses, and shared distribution costs, are now interwoven, paid sometimes by the investment company, sometimes by the shareholders of the investment company, and sometimes by the adviser from its profits on its fees. What impact does this trend have on the level and the regulation of advisory profits? Would shareholders be better served if all the fees and expenses were bundled, and if shareholders were assessed a single fee?

c. The 1966 Report indicates that an examination of the level of advisory fees suggested inadequacies in the competitive environment of the fund industry. Consider this finding in the context of the current competitive environment. What impact should the size of fund assets and the number of competing funds have on advisory fees?

---

The PPI report led to significant revisions of the Investment Company Act. One of the more noteworthy of these revisions was the addition of Section 36(b). With respect to advisory fees, section 36(b) imposes on certain persons a fiduciary duty. In particular, section 36(b) imposes on an investment adviser to a registered investment company a fiduciary duty with respect to the receipt of compensation for services, or of payments of a material nature, paid by the investment company, or by the shareholders thereof, to the investment adviser or any affiliated person of the investment adviser. Section 36(b) contains an express private right of action.

In the next chapter were will deal with a broader exploration of the role of the Board of Directors. Here, while you read the following case,[1] consider the factors the directors should take into account in approving the advisory fees.

> Plaintiff-appellant Jeffrey Krinsk is a shareholder in the CMA Money Fund ("Fund"), which is one component of the Cash Management Account program ("CMA program"), a financial services package offered by Merrill Lynch, Pierce, Fenner & Smith Inc. ("MLPF & S"). . . . Krinsk alleges a breach of fiduciary duty in that the fees paid by the Fund and its shareholders are excessive. . . . We find no error in the district court's determination that Krinsk failed to prove that the fees are disproportionately large. Accordingly, we affirm. . . .
>
> The CMA program was introduced by MLPF & S in 1977 and has been widely imitated since that time. It consists of a bundle of financial services administered through a central asset account that combines (1) a securities trading account, (2) a savings vehicle, consisting of one of three money market funds (one of which is the Fund) or an insured savings account, (3) a VISA debit card, (4) check-writing privileges and (5) a detailed monthly statement. The focal point of the CMA program is the securities account, which generates substantial revenue for MLPF & S. The program links the securities account to the savings vehicle through a "sweep" feature that automatically transfers idle cash into the savings vehicle — credit balances of $ 1,000 or more are transferred into savings the day after receipt; balances of less than $ 1,000 are swept weekly. An initial deposit of $20,000 is required to open a CMA program account, but a minimum balance thereafter need not be maintained.
>
> The subject of this lawsuit, the Fund, is a no-load, diversified, open-ended investment company and thus subject to provisions of the Act. The Fund is the largest registered money market mutual fund, with approximately $ 19 billion in assets and over 850,000 shareholders as of January 1987. . . . Participation in the CMA program is required in order to invest in the Fund. Participants in the program, however, are not required to invest in the Fund and instead may designate one of the other savings vehicles as their primary savings account. . . .
>
> MLPF & S, the sponsor of the CMA program, is the largest

1. *Krinsk v. Fund Asset Management,* 875 F.2d 404 (2d Cir. 1989).

securities firm in the United States. It acts as a distributor for the Fund and services the individual CMA program accounts. The day-to-day management of the Fund is performed by Merrill Lynch Asset Management, Inc. ("MLAM"), which serves as investment adviser to approximately forty to fifty mutual funds as well as to institutional and individual investors. Both MLPF & S and MLAM are owned by Merrill Lynch & Co., Inc. ("ML & Co."). The Fund's investment adviser is Fund Asset Management, Inc. ("FAM"), a wholly-owned subsidiary of MLAM.

These companies — MLPF & S, MLAM, ML & Co. and FAM (collectively "Merrill Lynch") — are the defendants-appellees in this action along with the Fund. . . .

Direct compensation for services and management comes from three fees: (1) a $ 65 annual service fee paid by each CMA program participant to MLPF & S; (2) an investment advisory fee paid by the Fund to FAM based on the Fund's asset level; and (3) payments made by the Fund to MLPF & S pursuant to a 12b-1 plan, under which the payments are passed on almost entirely to the financial consultants.

Although all program participants are obliged to pay the service fee, approximately 25% of them do not invest in the Fund. The second fee, the advisory fee, is based on a schedule of declining percentages as assets increase beyond certain breakpoints: 0.5% of the average daily value of net assets under $ 500 million, 0.425% of that amount between $ 500 million and $ 1 billion, and 0.375% of that amount in excess of $ 1 billion. The third fee, paid pursuant to the 12b-1 plan, is based on a distribution each month at an annual rate of 12.5 basis points (0.125% of the Fund's assets).

The Fund is governed by a Board of Trustees, comprised of one affiliated trustee and six independent trustees. The unaffiliated trustees have joined the Board at the invitation of Merrill Lynch, and each acts as a trustee or director of one or more of Merrill Lynch's other mutual funds. The Board oversees the investments and administration of the Fund, and evaluates the advisory fee annually and the 12b-1 plan quarterly.

The investment advisory fees of the Fund have been approved by the shareholders. In July of 1984, defendants mailed to the shareholders a proxy statement, one of the principal purposes of which was to obtain shareholder approval of the continuance of the investment-advisory fee agreement. The proxy statement set forth the three-tier schedule of the Fund's advisory fee. It listed also all the other investment companies for which FAM and MLAM act as investment advisers. The list included two columns, indicating for each of the listed companies its "Rate" and "First Breakpoint." The first of the listed money market funds was Merrill Lynch's Ready Asset Trust ("RAT"), with a listed rate of 0.5% and first breakpoint at $ 500 million, the same percentage and breakpoint as the Fund. The statement failed to indicate, however, the relevant differences between the RAT and the Fund — that RAT had no service fee (as opposed to the then — $ 50 annual charge for participation in the Fund's program) and had seven break-points (as opposed to the Fund's three). Also omitted in the statement was the fact that the annual rate of the advisory fee of the RAT effectively was 0.34% as opposed to 0.38% for the Fund. . . .

DISCUSSION

1. Section 36(b)

Section 36(b) of the Act places on the investment adviser of a registered investment company a fiduciary duty with respect to the receipt of compensation for services paid by the investment company or by the securities holders. Krinsk contends that the trustees neglected this duty by taking excessive fees from the Fund. He notes that lower fees are paid by the RAT fund, which is the second largest investment company affiliated with Merrill Lynch and the only fund comparable in size to the CMA Fund. He observes that despite the Fund's enormous growth, there has been no decrease in the advisory fee rate since 1979, and the rate never has been scaled down beyond the $ 1 billion breakpoint. He highlights as well the indirect benefits that Merrill Lynch derives from the CMA program: "non-fee-based" revenues and expenses generated from other services integral to the program, such as securities trading and margin interest; and "fall-out" benefits, such as profits made by a Merrill Lynch subsidiary from trading with the Fund.

Krinsk proposes that the trustees had a duty to negotiate for the Fund the "best deal" possible. However, the standard to apply in determining whether compensation for managing a mutual fund violates the fiduciary duty imposed by section 36(b) is "whether the fee schedule represents a charge within the range of what would have been negotiated at arm's-length in the light of all of the surrounding circumstances." *Gartenberg v. Merrill Lynch Asset Management, Inc.* . . . (1983) ("*Gartenberg I*"). To violate section 36(b), "the adviser-manager must charge a fee that is so disproportionately large that it bears no reasonable relationship to the services rendered." *Id.*

The following factors are to be considered in applying this standard: (a) the nature and quality of services provided to fund shareholders; (b) the profitability of the fund to the adviser-manager; (c) fall-out benefits; (d) economies of scale; (e) comparative fee structures; and (f) the independence and conscientiousness of the trustees. . . . These factors, considered below *seriatim,* all weigh in favor of Merrill Lynch.

A. Nature and Quality of Services

Krinsk does not dispute that the services provided by Merrill Lynch have been anything but the highest quality. From 1984 to 1986, the Fund had the third best performance out of 56 prime money funds, with an annual rate of return of 8.4% as compared to the industry average of 8%. During the same years, the Fund ranked second among the nine money market funds associated with central asset accounts.

Krinsk suggests that, because the Fund invested in high-risk items that generally are more profitable, the Fund's performance should be analyzed on a "risk-adjusted" basis. According to Krinsk, the Fund's performance would be below average when adjusted to compensate for the risk. Krinsk's expert conceded, however, that neither the SEC nor the money market industry has adopted "risk adjusted performance" as an industry standard. . . .

Krinsk contends also that the Fund's performance is artificially high because the $ 65 annual CMA program fee was not included as a Fund expense when calculating the Fund's yield. The district court did not err in rejecting this argument. The fee is not paid by the Fund, but by all the participants in the program regardless of whether they invest in the Fund. Furthermore, Merrill Lynch presented evidence, apparently uncontradicted by Krinsk, that leading industry publications exclude such annual program fees in their computation of yields and expense ratios. The expert witness for Merrill Lynch also testified he knew of no money market fund that refers to such charges when reporting to the SEC the yields and expense ratios.

B. Profitability to Merrill Lynch

Krinsk claims that the Fund is highly profitable to Merrill Lynch, and more profitable than Merrill Lynch admits because costs attributed to the Fund should be attributed to the CMA program. Krinsk further suggests that "excessive profitability alone should suffice to support a finding of unreasonableness." He cites to no case in support of this proposition, however, and in fact courts "must look to all the costs and benefits associated with the Fund," *Gartenberg v. Merrill Lynch Asset Management, Inc.*, 740 F.2d 190, 194 (2d Cir. 1984) ("*Gartenberg II*").

Because the Fund is an integral part of the CMA program, it is difficult to calculate the revenues and expenses associated with the Fund apart from those associated with the other aspects of the CMA program. Merrill Lynch's accounting firm and expert at trial, Peat Marwick Mitchell & Co. ("PMM"), therefore developed a "fee-based" analysis, which subtracted fee costs from fee revenues in an effort to determine the profits derived by Merrill Lynch from the Fund. Defendants introduced at trial an additional study, which they themselves prepared, that was similar to the PMM study. Krinsk had no independent profitability study prepared, but criticized the PMM and Merrill Lynch studies. The district court accepted none of the studies in full, recognizing that "costs within the CMA program must be properly allocated in any profitability study lest the Fund subsidize the costs of Merrill Lynch's commission-generating activities," para. 93,812, at 98,908. The court therefore made its own determinations as to costs and profitability. We agree with those determinations:

*(1) 12b-1 Plan Fees*

The 12-b1 plan fees, as stated above, are monthly distributions to MLPF & S personnel based on the net assets in the Fund.

The district court treated these fees in the same way as did PMM, namely, as a wash, offset by the cost of payments to the personnel. Krinsk, however, argues that because, in his view, the plan did not achieve its stated purpose — the sale of fund shares — the fees should be counted as revenue to MLPF & S with no offsetting expenses. Since the district court found that Krinsk "failed to demonstrate that the 12b-1 payments have not contributed to the growth of the Fund" . . . and Krinsk's own expert conceded that considering the 12b-1 payments as a fee-based cost was "within the realm of reason," we cannot say that the court's treatment of those fees was "clearly erroneous," *Gartenberg II,* 740 F.2d at 192.

*(2) Other Costs*

Krinsk attacks numerous aspects of the PMM study and the district court's findings as to systems costs, overhead, declines and overrides, CMA marketing and the allocation of certain costs to the securities side as opposed to the Fund side. Determination of these matters, involving extensive analysis of factual data, is best left to the discretion of the district court, which held a two-week trial to resolve the factual questions.

*(3) Measure of Profitability*

Krinsk disputes Merrill Lynch's measure of profitability and offers instead a "return on equity" analysis utilizing a "Dupont formula." The application of the formula was flawed, however, by a speculative approach and lack of crucial figures. Krinsk offers also a "yardstick" analysis that compares the return on equity of the Fund with the return from other segments of the financial services industry, such as banks, insurance companies and companies dealing with stocks and bonds. According to this formula, the Fund reaps a lower return because its fee-based activities are relatively stable. Not accounted for in this formula, however, is the Fund's connection to the CMA program, which provides a variety of financial services. Moreover, the yardstick formula would reduce the Fund's advisory fee to a level far below that of any other mutual fund. The unreasonable result of applying this formula casts suspicion on the formula itself. We therefore cannot fault the district court for rejecting Krinsk's theories and crediting the testimony of Merrill Lynch's expert.

C. Fall-out Benefits

Krinsk argues that fall-out benefits should include all securities commission and margin revenues from CMA accounts, even if the benefits would have come to Merrill Lynch absent the existence of the Fund (or the CMA program). The district court rejected this definition as too broad. In *Gartenberg II,* a suit attacking Merrill Lynch's RAT fund, Judge Pollack characterized fall-out benefits as the "commissions received by [MLPF & S] that would not have been earned *but for* the fact that [MLPF & S] was able to solicit [RAT fund] shareholders. . . ." Krinsk urges rejection of that approach, noting that our Circuit does not require "but for" causation for costs to be offset with income from "voluntary" float benefits and free credit balances. See *Gartenberg II*, 740 F.2d at 194. However, float benefits and free credit balances are generated directly by the money market fund and cannot be characterized as fall-out revenue. . . .

D. Economies of Scale

Krinsk alleges that Merrill Lynch's expenses, in terms of a percentage of fee-based revenues, have declined as a result of the Fund's asset growth. He argues that the Fund should receive the benefit of this economy of scale. The district court noted, however, that the fact that "expenses . . . declined at a time when the Fund size grew. . . . does not establish that such decline was necessarily due to economies of scale. . . ." Rather, to show economies of scale, plaintiff bore the burden of proving that the per unit cost of performing Fund transactions decreased as the number of transactions increased. See *Gartenberg I* . . . . Krinsk offered no such evidence. Merrill Lynch, in contrast, offered evidence that the per unit costs for most money market funds generally do not decrease as a fund grows. As the Merrill Lynch view is not unreasonable . . . (per unit cost of providing shareholder services remained relatively stable), we cannot say the district erred in finding that Krinsk failed to sustain his burden of proof.

E. Comparative Expense Ratios and Advisory Fees

The district court found that the Fund's expense ratio and advisory fee are not only consistent with the industry norms, but have been among the lowest of any mutual fund in the industry. Krinsk does not dispute these findings, but instead argues that a general comparison of fees is of limited use. Indeed, we have cautioned against providing much weight to this type of comparison. See *Gartenberg I* . . . . According to Krinsk, the only viable comparison of fees would be to a fund comparable in size to the CMA Fund, and the only such fund is Merrill Lynch's RAT. That fund has an effective advisory fee that is 10% less than the CMA advisory fee. Unlike the CMA Fund, however, the RAT is a stand-alone fund, where the investors do not derive the many benefits of the central asset account.

Additionally, the district court allowed Merrill Lynch to exclude the service fee from the computation of the Fund's yield. Krinsk argues that it is inconsistent to consider benefits arising from the program components that are ancillary to the Fund to allow a higher fee, and yet not attribute that fee as a cost to the Fund. Where a money market fund is embedded in a central asset account, the apportionment of the costs and benefits is, as the district court recognized, "an art rather than a science. . . ." Since the fee under consideration is paid by nonshareholders of the Fund as well as shareholders, we are not prepared to say that the district court erred in allowing Merrill Lynch to exclude the fee from the computation of yield.

F. Trustees' Approval

The expertise of the trustees, whether they are fully informed, and the extent of care and conscientiousness with which they perform their duties are among the most important factors to be examined in evaluating the reasonableness of compensation under section 36(b). See *Gartenberg I* . . . Krinsk cannot dispute the district court's finding that the trustees were qualified and well-informed. Krinsk, however, attacks the independence and deliberations of the trustees, alleging that they did not act at arm's length, did not conclude that the 12b-1 plan would benefit shareholders before voting for it, did not consider profitability to Merrill Lynch, and were more concerned about the CMA program than the Fund of which they were the trustees. He notes, for instance, that the trustees did not fine-tune the advisory fee, as there is no breakpoint beyond $ 1 billion in the advisory fee schedule.

The evidence amply supports a finding that the trustees were independent and exercised care in their deliberations. For example, when the trustees were not satisfied with the profitability study Merrill Lynch prepared, they required the study to be redone. The trustees also did not violate their fiduciary duties in approving the 12b-1 incentive fee; in fact, the fee seems to have benefited the shareholders. As a result of the creation of competing bank funds, the CMA Fund had lost approximately 25% of its assets in 1982. The 12b-1 fee was adopted to counteract this erosion of assets. By providing an incentive for the sale of shares, the 12b-1 plan created a positive cash flow for the Fund, enabling the manager to improve the Fund's performance. That the plan has had the added effect of raising morale of MLPF & S financial consultants and consequently improving the quality of services to existing Fund shareholders is no reason to deem the plan, or the motives of the trustees, improper. *Cf. Meyer v. Oppenheimer Management Corp.* . . . Accordingly, the district court did not err in finding that the trustees were independent and that they deliberated conscientiously. . . .

---

## Discussion Topics

a. The CMA account discussed in this case has been viewed by the financial services industry as revolutionary. Joseph Nocera, in *A Piece of the Action* 155 (Simon & Schuster, 1994), stated "What was it about a cash management account that made it such a threat to the existing order? The short answer was that it took disparate elements — each of which had previously been connected to one particular segment of the financial world — and gathered them in one account."

b. What types of fees are charged to the users of a CMA account? Which of these fees are at issue in this case?

c. Are courts equipped to determine the acceptable fees that advisers may charge funds? If so, what are the criteria that courts should follow to determine the fees? Krinsk argued unsuccessfully that fund trustees had a duty to negotiate for the fund the "best deal" possible. What in your opinion is the difference between the following: fiduciary duty, "best deal," "reasonableness," "fairness," and "corporate waste" doctrines? Which criterion is preferable, and why?

d. The level of advisory fees has remained a controversial issue. Consider the following remarks made by Barry Barbash, then the Director of the SEC's Division of Investment Management, at an Investment Company Institute Conference held on December 3, 1996:[1]

> As the fund industry has grown dramatically over the past decade, advisory fees, to the surprise of many, also have risen . . .
>
> To date, the response of many in the industry to the increase in advisory fees is simply to explain it away or minimize its importance. I am not going to stand here this morning and assess the validity of the various explanations for higher fund management fees . . . I am going to suggest, however, that industry participants, from fund sponsors to independent directors and trustees, take a forward-looking approach to the level of management fees.
>
> As the Morningstar commentary to which I referred earlier noted, the recent increase in advisory fees is hard to justify and ultimately would not seem to be sustainable by an industry that, to remain competitive, must provide better returns at lower costs than other investment options. Moreover, as we all seem willing to accept, the market's performance will have to come down at some time in the future, as will fund performance. Lower performance inevitably will lead to unhappy shareholders who will redeem their shares or start to look more carefully at fees and ask whether those fees are consistent with the provisions of the securities laws. Section 36(b) suits, whether brought by shareholders or the Commission, would likely not only mar the reputation of the funds against which they are brought, but likely would also cast a shadow on the industry as a whole.

---

In the 2010 case of *Jones v. Harris,* the Supreme Court outlines what mutual fund shareholders must demonstrate to successfully bring a section 36(b) action for breach of fiduciary duties.[2]

Petitioners filed an action in a district court under section 36(b) of the Investment Company Act. The Court granted summary judgment for the adviser, holding that petitioners failed to raise an issue as to "whether the fees charged . . . were so disproportionately large that they could not have been the result of arm's-length bargaining. . . ." in view of comparisons to fees the adviser charged other clients and other advisers charged similar funds.

1. Barry P. Barbash, Keynote Address, "This Year in Funds: The Responsibilities of Prosperity," Dec. 3, 1996.
2. *Jones v. Harris Associates, L.P.,* 130 S. Ct. 1418, 176 L. Ed. 2d 265 (2010).

A Seventh Circuit panel affirmed based on a different test, "disapprov[ing] the Gartenberg approach." By analogy to trust law the court noted that "[a] fiduciary duty differs from rate regulation. A fiduciary must make full disclosure and play no tricks but is not subject to a cap on compensation. . . ." It held that the amount of an adviser's compensation would be relevant only if the compensation were "so unusual" as to give rise to an inference "that deceit must have occurred, or that the persons responsible for decision have abdicated." The panel noted that in today's market "sophisticated investors . . . move their money elsewhere" and keep fees low, said that *Gartenberg* "'relies too little on markets,'" and rejected the comparison to fees charged to other clients, as other clients require different time commitments and some costs (e.g., research) benefit multiple client categories. The Seventh Circuit denied rehearing en banc. "The dissent from the denial of rehearing argued that the panel's rejection of *Gartenberg* was based 'mainly on an economic analysis that is ripe for reexamination . . . ' Among other things, the dissent expressed concern that [the adviser] charged 'its captive funds more than twice what it charges independent funds,' and the dissent questioned whether high adviser fees actually drive investors away. . . ."

The Supreme Court granted certiorari to resolve the Circuit split.

Justice Alito delivered the opinion. The Court restated the *Gartenberg* standard as "essentially whether the fee schedule represents a charge within the range of what would have been negotiated at arm's-length in the light of all of the surrounding circumstances" and that a violation would require "a fee that is so disproportionately large that it bears no reasonable relationship to the services rendered and could not have been the product of arm's-length bargaining." This determination requires that "'all pertinent facts must be weighed'" specifically including "'the adviser-manager's cost in providing the service . . . the extent to which the adviser-manager realizes economies of scale as the fund grows larger, and the volume of orders which must be processed by the manager. . . .'"

The Court held that the *Gartenberg* court rejected the argument that "'the principal factor to be considered in evaluating a fee's fairness is the price charged by other similar advisers to funds managed by them,'" as there may be little competition, "although the [*Gartenberg*] Court did not suggest that this factor could not be 'taken into account. . . .'" Similarly the *Gartenberg* court "rejected the 'argument that the lower fees charged by investment advisers to large pension funds should be used as a criterion for determining fair advisory fees for money market funds,' since a 'pension fund does not face the myriad of daily purchases and redemptions throughout the nation which must be handled by [a money market fund]. . . .'"

Further, the Court held that *Gartenberg's* basic formulation of the statute was correct, i.e., "to face liability under § 36(b), an investment adviser must charge a fee that is so disproportionately large that it bears no reasonable relationship to the services rendered and could not have been the product of arm's length bargaining."

The Court examined the phrase "fiduciary duty" and a Supreme Court case regarding fiduciary duty in another context, and concluded that "'The essence of the test is whether or not under all the circumstances the transaction carries the earmarks of an arm's length bargain.'" The Court stated that the Investment Company Act modifies the test by placing the burden of proof on the party claiming breach. The *Gartenberg* approach reflects this and "insists that all relevant circumstances be taken into account" and "uses the range of fees that might result from arm's-length bargaining as the benchmark for reviewing challenged fees."

The Court also noted that *Gartenberg* "reflects § 36(b)'s place in the statutory scheme," as it states that "'the expertise of the independent trustees of a fund, whether they are fully informed about all facts bearing on the [investment adviser's] service and fee, and the extent of care and conscientiousness with which they perform their duties are important factors to be considered in deciding whether they and the [investment adviser] are guilty of a breach of fiduciary duty in violation of § 36(b). . . '"

The Court addressed "comparisons between the fees that an adviser charges a captive mutual fund and the fees that it charges its independent clients." "[T]he *Gartenberg* court rejected a comparison between the fees that the adviser in that case charged a money market fund and the fees that it charged a pension fund. . . . " However, the Court rejected a categorical rule regarding comparisons:

> [C]ourts may give such comparisons the weight that they merit in light of the similarities and differences between the services that the clients in question require, but courts must be wary of inapt comparisons. . . . [T]here may be significant differences between the services provided by an investment adviser to a mutual fund and those it provides to a pension fund which are attributable to the greater frequency of shareholder redemptions in a mutual fund, the higher turnover of mutual fund assets, the more burdensome regulatory and legal obligations, and higher marketing costs. . . . If the services rendered are sufficiently different that a comparison is not probative, then courts must reject such a comparison. Even if the services provided and fees charged to an independent fund are relevant, . . . the Act does not necessarily ensure fee parity between mutual funds and institutional clients . . . .
>
> By the same token, courts should not rely too heavily on comparisons with fees charged to mutual funds by other advisers. These comparisons are problematic because these fees, like those challenged, may not be the product of negotiations conducted at arm's length. . . . Finally, a court's evaluation of an investment adviser's fiduciary duty must take into account both procedure and substance. See 15 U.S.C. § 80a-35(b)(2) (requiring deference to board's consideration "as is deemed appropriate under all the circumstances") . . . Where a board's process for negotiating and reviewing investment-adviser compensation is robust, a reviewing court should afford commensurate deference to the outcome of the bargaining process. . . . Thus, if the disinterested directors considered the relevant factors, their decision to approve a particular fee agreement is entitled to considerable weight, even if a court might weigh the factors differently. . . . This is not to deny that a fee may be excessive even if it was negotiated by a board in possession of all relevant information,

> but such a determination must be based on evidence that the fee "is so disproportionately large that it bears no reasonable relationship to the services rendered and could not have been the product of arm's-length bargaining." . . .
>
> In contrast, where the board's process was deficient or the adviser withheld important information, the court must take a more rigorous look at the outcome. When an investment adviser fails to disclose material information to the board, greater scrutiny is justified because the withheld information might have hampered the board's ability to function as "an independent check upon the management." . . . . But an adviser's compliance or noncompliance with its disclosure obligations is a factor that must be considered in calibrating the degree of deference that is due a board's decision to approve an adviser's fees.
>
> It is also important to note that the standard for fiduciary breach under § 36(b) does not call for judicial second-guessing of informed board decisions. . . . "[P]otential conflicts [of interests] may justify some restraints upon the unfettered discretion of even disinterested mutual fund directors, particularly in their transactions with the investment adviser," but they do not suggest that a court may supplant the judgment of disinterested directors apprised of all relevant information, without additional evidence that the fee exceeds the arm's-length range. . . . In reviewing compensation under § 36(b), the Act does not require courts to engage in a precise calculation of fees representative of arm's-length bargaining. . . . As recounted above, Congress rejected a "reasonableness" requirement that was criticized as charging the courts with rate-setting responsibilities. . . . Congress' approach recognizes that courts are not well suited to make such precise calculations. . . .
>
> By focusing almost entirely on the element of disclosure, the Seventh Circuit panel erred . . . The Gartenberg standard, which the panel rejected, may lack sharp analytical clarity, but we believe that it accurately reflects the compromise that is embodied in § 36(b), and it has provided a workable standard for nearly three decades. The debate between the Seventh Circuit panel and the dissent from the denial of rehearing regarding today's mutual fund market is a matter for Congress, not the courts.

The Court vacated the circuit court judgment and remanded the case.

In a concurring opinion, Justice Thomas agreed with the Court's "approach" but "would not shortchange the Court's effort by describing it as affirmation of the 'Gartenberg standard. . . .'" *Gartenberg* could be read to emphasize "fairness," but subsequent cases citing it have adopted a stricter standard, deferring to fund boards and requiring a "heavy burden of proof."

It is important to understand that the analysis summarized and set forth in the foregoing cases has formed the basis for directors' deliberation process around the approval and continuance of advisory contracts for registered investment companies. The SEC has also embraced this analysis and a fund is required to disclose the factors its board considered in approving or continuing an advisory contract in its periodic shareholder reports. The applicable form requirements obligate the fund to discuss its board's consideration of the so-called "Gartenberg" factors described in the cases above.

---

**Problem**

You have just become counsel to the independent directors of a mutual fund. You are aware that the current materials relating to annual advisory contract approvals under section 15 of the Investment Company Act of 1940 include (i) comparisons with fees charged by other advisers to similar third party mutual funds, (ii) information about the adviser, its investment experience and personnel, (iii) information on how similar third party mutual funds have performed and (iv) information on brokerage commissions and soft dollars related to the fund. The adviser typically gives a general oral presentation about its profitability and whether it is realizing any economies of scale in managing the fund. The adviser is a large asset manager that manages not only other mutual funds (including mutual funds with similar strategies to the fund), but also separate accounts for retail and high net-worth individuals, hedge funds, and portions of pension funds. Please write a memo to the independent directors suggesting improvements to the written materials they receive in the advisory contract renewal process in light of the cases you have just read.

Assume that historically there has not been any written request for information from the independent directors to the adviser for information to consider in determining whether to approve the advisory contract for another year. The independent directors have asked you to draft such a written request. Please include a draft of such a request as an exhibit to your memo.

---

In 2000, the SEC examined trends in mutual fund fees, including advisory fees and expenses. Among the considerations was the charge under Rule 12b-1.[1] Rule 12b-1permits the adviser to charge an investment company a fee devoted to cover the cost of selling fund shares, subject to various conditions, including the approval of the funds' board of directors. Thus, instead of paying brokers' commissions for purchasing investment company shares once, investors are charged by the fund, annually, up to a certain percentage of the fund assets. For this charge, investors receive sale of fund shares and various other services. Consider the following report, and focus on the process by which mutual fund fees are established:[2]

> A. Background and Scope of the Report . . .
>
> The growth of the fund industry has been accompanied by a

1. 17 C.F.R. § 270.12b-1 (2015).

2. Division of Investment Management, Securities and Exchange Commission, Report on Mutual Fund Fees and Expenses (Dec. 2000), *available at* http://www.sec.gov/ news/studies/feestudy.htm (last modified Jan. 10, 2001).

debate over the appropriate level of fund fees. The focus on fund fees is important because they can have a dramatic impact on an investor's return. For example, a 1% increase in a fund's annual expenses can reduce an investor's ending account balance in that fund by 18% after twenty years.

Some commentators argue that fund fees are too high. They claim that the growth in the fund industry has produced economies of scale and that funds have not passed on to shareholders the benefits of these economies of scale in the form of reduced fees. Others contend that fund fees are not too high and that shareholders today are getting more for their money — more services . . . and greater investment opportunities . . . .

In the most recent contribution to the public dialogue, the United States General Accounting Office issued a report that provides a wide-ranging analysis of mutual fund fees and the market forces and regulatory requirements that influence those fees. The report's major conclusion is that additional disclosure could help to increase investor awareness and understanding of mutual fund fees and, thereby, promote additional competition among funds on the basis of fees. The report recommends that the Commission require that periodic account statements include additional disclosure about the portion of mutual fund fees that the investor has borne.

* * *

B. Summary of Findings and Recommendations

1. Summary of Findings

[W]e observed the following from the data that we collected:

- Overall, mutual fund expense ratios (i.e., a fund's total expenses, including rule 12b-1 fees, divided by its average net assets) have increased since the late 1970s, although they have declined in three of the last four years.
- Although fund expense ratios rose on average during the 20 years covered by our study, the overall cost of owning fund shares may not have risen if changes in sales loads are taken into consideration. (Sales loads are not taken into consideration when calculating expense ratios and have generally decreased during the period.)
- The increase in mutual fund expense ratios since the 1970s can be attributed primarily to changes in the manner that distribution and marketing charges are paid by mutual funds and their shareholders. Many funds have decreased or replaced front-end loads, which are not included in a fund's expense ratio, with ongoing rule 12b-1 fees, which are included in a fund's expense ratio. This change complicates the comparison of current expense ratios with expense ratios from earlier periods.
- Mutual funds with the largest proportion of defined contribution retirement plan assets (e.g., 401(k) plans) generally have lower expense ratios than other funds.

- Mutual fund expense ratios generally decline as the amount of fund assets increase.
- Specialty funds have higher expense ratios than equity funds, which, in turn, have higher expense ratios than bond funds. International funds have higher expense ratios than comparable domestic funds.
- Index funds and funds that are available only to institutional investors generally have lower expense ratios than other types of funds.
- In a sample of the largest 1,000 funds in 1999, funds that are part of large fund families (in terms of asset size) tend to have lower management expense ratios than funds that are part of small fund families. These findings may reflect economies for the investment adviser generally.
- In a sample of the 100 largest mutual funds, most funds have some type of fee breakpoint arrangement that automatically reduces the management fee rate as the asset-size of the individual fund or the fund family increases. Most funds in the sample with management fee breakpoints, however, have assets above the last breakpoint.

2. Summary of Recommendations

We believe that the current statutory framework's primary reliance on disclosure and procedural safeguards to determine mutual fund fees and expenses, rather than on fee caps or other regulatory intervention, is sound and operates in the manner contemplated by Congress. We believe, however, that the framework can be enhanced in certain areas. A brief summary of our recommendations follows. . . .

a. Disclosure and Investor Education

Many observers give the Commission high marks for requiring funds to disclose information about their fees in a format that is understandable to investors and that facilitates comparison with the fees charged by other funds and other investment alternatives. The Commission should, nevertheless, consider whether requiring the disclosure of additional types of fee information would facilitate investors' awareness of fund fees and investors' ability to understand their effect. For example, the General Accounting Office recommended in its report that the Commission require mutual funds and/or broker-dealers to send fund shareholders account statements that include the dollar amount of the fund's fees that each investor has indirectly paid. We recommend that, because the recommended information could be disclosed in various ways, the Commission should evaluate the most effective way of disclosing fees and expenses that investors incur, taking into account the cost and burden that various alternative means of making such disclosures would entail.

We agree with the General Accounting Office that the fund industry and the Commission should encourage fund shareholders to pay greater attention to fees and expenses. We believe that changes to mutual fund disclosure requirements have generally produced the best results when the changes are designed to meet the information needs of investors and assist them in making better investment decisions. With respect to fund fees and expenses, we believe that investors need information, in addition to information about the dollar amount of fees, that helps them to understand the fees that they pay. Moreover, they need to be able to compare the fees of their fund to the fees of other funds and other types of investments. To satisfy these broader needs, we believe that any additional required fee information, including the dollar amount of fees, should be provided in semi-annual and annual shareholder reports. One advantage of this approach is that it would enable investors to not only compare the fees of funds but also to evaluate the fee information that would be contained in the reports to shareholders alongside other key information about the fund's operating results, including management's discussion of the fund's performance.

The additional information about actual costs could be presented in a variety of ways. One possible way to present the data would be to require shareholder reports to include a table showing the cost in dollars incurred by a shareholder who invested a standardized amount (e.g., $10,000) in the fund, paid the fund's actual expenses, and earned the fund's actual return for the period. . . .

The full benefits of improved fee disclosure will not be realized without a strong investor education campaign. We recommend that the Commission continue its program (described in Section II) to improve the financial literacy of investors with respect to mutual funds and their costs. As new requirements to provide information about fund fees take effect, we recommend that the Commission develop educational materials that help investors understand how to make use of the new information, and encourage funds, brokers, and others to do so as well.

For many fund shareholders, taxes on income dividends, capital gains distributions, and gains realized when shares are redeemed have a greater impact on the growth of their investment than does the fund's expense ratio. The Commission should adopt rules that would require mutual funds to report their investment returns on an after-tax basis, similar to or as proposed in March 2000.

b. Fund Governance

We believe that the current statutory framework can be enhanced by strengthening the ability of independent directors to monitor fund fees and expenses. As described in Section II, the Commission took major action in this area in October 1999, when it proposed new rules and rule amendments designed to enhance the effectiveness of independent directors in dealing with fund management. We recommend that these proposals be adopted as soon as practicable, taking into account public comments on the proposals.

In addition to strengthening the ability of independent directors to deal with fund management, the Commission also should consider the following recommendations with respect to the regulatory framework for fees:

- The Commission should continue to emphasize that mutual fund directors must exercise vigilance in monitoring the fees and expenses of the funds that they oversee. Fund directors should, for example, attempt to ensure that an appropriate portion of the cost savings from any available economies of scale is passed along to fund shareholders. The Commission should continue to encourage efforts to educate directors about issues related to fund fees and expenses, including the types of information that they may request when they review the funds' management contracts, and the techniques that are available to evaluate the information that they receive.
- Fund directors, in addition to approving the management fee, may also approve a plan under Rule 12b-1 under the Investment Company Act to use fund assets to pay for distribution and marketing expenses. That rule is now twenty years old. The Commission should consider whether the rule needs to be modified to accommodate changes in the mutual fund industry. . . .

---

## Discussion Topics

a. What are the justifications for charging open-end investment companies any of the costs of the companies' share distribution activities? Who benefits from the distribution of investment company shares?

b. Focusing on Rule 12b-1, assume that the fund closes and does not accept any more investors, what would be the justification of charging fund shareholders the expenses of distributing fund shares?

c. If you were a director of an open-end company, what guidelines would you establish concerning the charge of rule 12b-1 fees?

---

# Chapter 8

## *Corporate Governance: Fund Directors and Shareholder Voting*

### A. Introduction

Investment companies can take any legal form their promoters choose for them: partnerships, limited partnerships, business trusts and corporations. Therefore, if a promoter decides to create a corporation under the Maryland Corporation statute, or a business trust under the Delaware Statutory Trust Act, it can do so.[1] The 1940 Act, however, superimposes on the state statutes a uniform structure. In so doing, the 1940 Act creates a federal corporate law with respect to investment companies, with the primary purpose of checking abusive management.

### 1. Popular Forms of Organization Under State Law

There are a number of organizational forms available to the promoters of investment companies, under various laws. One is corporate law, such as the Maryland statute, which has relaxed many of the corporate requirements and made its law attractive to promoters. Many open-end investment companies are organized as business trusts under a declaration of trust. The legal title to the assets of the trust is held by a trustee while the beneficial interest is divided into transferable units or shares. Business trusts may be established under the common law or under statutes, like the Delaware Statutory Trust Act, or as a Massachusetts business trust, which is a creature of the common law. Those open-end investment companies that are established as business trusts do so because the form is flexible, simple and economical in organizing and operating and sometimes presents tax advantages.

Business trusts differ from corporations in that the trustee is the legal owner of the trust property. That poses questions of liability for the trustee and for the beneficiaries-investors, if they exercise control over the operations of the trust. Massachusetts courts have minimized these liabilities through interpretations, and a Delaware statute has eliminated the liabilities by providing trustees with the same protection that is granted

1. As illustrated by the *Prudential* case in Chapter 3, investment companies can also arise without any legal form: simply as unincorporated funds owned by a group of people.

to corporate directors. Similarly, even though there are some "soft spots" with respect to the liability of investors-beneficiaries, they are minimal and have been eliminated by the Delaware statute. In addition, Massachusetts law is valuable because business trusts have withstood attack in the courts. Lastly, Maryland has recently enacted a statutory trust act that provides many of the same benefits as the Delaware Statutory Trust Act and recently some investment companies have either begun to establish themselves as Maryland trusts or have redomiciled as Maryland trusts from another jurisdiction.

## 2. Description of the Delaware Statutory Trust Act[1]

The Supreme Court has defined a business trust as "an arrangement whereby property is conveyed to trustees, in accordance with the terms of an instrument of trust, to be held and managed for the benefit of such persons as may from time to time be the holders of transferable certificates issued by the trustees showing the shares into which the beneficial interest in the property is divided." Business trusts allow promoters great flexibility in designing their organizations. The Delaware Business Trust Act addresses legal uncertainties and contains permissive provisions, allowing promoters to design their relationships with beneficiaries-investors with the characteristics of traditional trusts, business trusts, corporations, or partnerships.

In addition, the Act may allow reduction or elimination of director or management liability to shareholders. While Delaware corporation law and the Delaware Trust Code have converted director's duty of care to a default rule but maintained the duty of loyalty, the Act arguably allows promoters to eliminate both duties. However, courts may interpret the Act as limiting the ability of the promoters to obtain a waiver on the ground that the shareholders' consent, as the waiver may cover broad conflicts or embezzlement the shareholders did not anticipate. Shareholders also may not accept a waiver.

The business trust form may be risky for national or international businesses, as some states do not recognize the limited liability status of beneficiaries of business trusts, and countries with code-based legal systems, as opposed to common law, may not recognize the trust institution.

## 3. Investment Company Act Regulation of Corporate Structure: Sections 2(a)(19), 10, 16, 36(a)

Under state law, corporations are established by charters or articles of association under general corporation laws. These instruments must contain certain information outlined in the laws, and may contain other information. Some shareholders, but not necessarily all, must have voting rights. Corporations have a board of directors elected by the voting shareholders, and officers appointed by the board of directors. Corporate laws impose fiduciary duties on both directors and officers. Their activities in conflict of interest are subject to approval by disinterested directors or

1. This material is derived from Tamar Frankel, *The Delaware Business Trust Act Failure as the New Corporate Law*, 23 Cardozo L. Rev. 325 (2001) (footnotes omitted).

the courts, according to varying standards, and depending on the activities and circumstances. Corporate laws regulate corporate structural changes usually by requiring directors' and shareholders' approval.

The 1940 Act imposes on investment companies with managed portfolios (that is, open-end and closed-end investment companies) the basic features imposed by state law on corporations. On some issues, however, the 1940 Act's requirements are stricter and allow the promoter of an investment company less flexibility.

Investment companies must have a board of directors. Each share issued by such companies must have equal voting rights. Generally, directors may not serve unless they are elected by the shareholders. In connection with the establishment of a new fund, this election may be accomplished by the fund's sole initial shareholder, which is usually the adviser itself or an affiliate. Section 16(a) of the 1940 Act permits director vacancies to be filled in any legal manner so long as, after filling the vacancy, at least two-thirds of the directors then holding office have been elected by the shareholders. Additionally, if at any time less than a majority of directors were elected by shareholders, section 16(a) requires the investment company to call a special meeting to elect directors.

At least 40% of the board members must be disinterested (i.e., "independent") directors. The criteria for independence are far stricter than those established under state corporate laws. Section 2(a)(19) of the 1940 Act sets forth detailed criteria for independence, including the following highlights:

- An independent director and members of his or her "immediate family" cannot be an affiliated person of either the fund, its adviser or its principal underwriter;
- An independent director cannot have acted as legal counsel for the fund, its adviser or its principal underwriter at any time since the beginning of the last two completed fiscal years of the fund; and
- An independent director cannot knowingly have any direct or indirect beneficial interest in, or be designated as trustee, executor, or guardian of any legal interest in, any security issued by the fund's investment adviser or principal underwriter (or by a controlling person thereof) — in other words, ownership of one share of stock of the investment adviser or its controlling person disqualifies you from being an independent director.

The scope of these independence standards are further understood through the scope of relationships they cover. An "immediate family member" includes any parent, spouse of a parent, child, spouse of a child, spouse, brother, or sister, and includes step and adoptive relationships. An "affiliated person" is defined in section 2(a)(3) of the 1940 Act to include owning 5% or more of the voting stock of a company, being a director, officer, partner, copartner or employee of a company, or otherwise controlling a company (section 2(a)(19) expressly states that being a director of the investment company does not in and of itself make a person not independent). Other criteria in section 2(a)(19) focus on director relationships with broker-dealers who do business with the fund or its adviser, and on other business relationships with the fund, its adviser and its principal underwriter.

In effect, this group of independent directors functions as a board within a board. The advisory and underwriting contracts, including fees and expenses, must be approved by a majority of such directors periodically. The importance of investment company independent directors has increased during the past twenty-five years, as the independent directors have been vested with increasing responsibilities to supervise the activities of the investment adviser and the insiders in managing the investment company. These responsibilities came with SEC exemptive rules that benefitted the advisers, but required higher internal supervision by the boards of directors, and in particular the independent directors. These exemptive rules, which benefitted the advisers, required the number of the independent directors to rise from the 40% required under section 10(a) of the 1940 Act, to a majority of the board.

While corporate law allows independent directors on the board to approve conflict of interest transactions, the 1940 Act does not (with certain exceptions which we will review in Chapter 12). Only the Commission can exempt from the prohibition on conflict of interest transactions. Finally, section 36(a) of the 1940 Act extends fiduciary duties involving personal misconduct to a number of insiders of investment companies and vests in the board of directors review powers with respect to those activities.

For many years advisers to mutual funds have argued that the corporate governance structure established by the 1940 Act is too costly as well as ineffective because investors do not vote their shares. Yet attempts to adopt alternative models without such a governance structure have met with little enthusiasm, even by the advisers. Perhaps the cost of soliciting proxies and paying board members is very low relative to the assets of the funds, especially today; perhaps shareholders' franchise, as little as it is exercised, provides an inexpensive way to maintain public confidence in the integrity of investment companies and their advisers, and perhaps the dollar savings from eliminating the board and voting are not worth the risk of eroding this confidence.

Perhaps cost is not the only measure for regulating the people who manage other people's money. Perhaps a danger of investors' failing trust is important as well. Thus, cost is balanced with the other (perhaps more important) considerations. As we go through the materials, let us de-emphasize cost, although we remain aware of it. Note that the cheapest money-management for the business of management is no regulation. However, the promoters of mutual funds recognize that with no regulation and no support of investors' trust, there will be no business, at least not for long.

### 4. The Additional Provisions Imposed by the Investment Company Act

Superimposed on state law are specific requirements of the Investment Company Act. For example, one such requirement is the provision that imposes on the investment company structure a statement regarding the investment policies of the investment companies. Section 8 of the Act requires such policies to be stated in the registration statement of the companies. Section 13(a) requires that any change in the fundamental investment policies of the investment company must be approved by a majority vote of the investors. This requirement is superimposed on any form in which the investment company is organized, whether a corporation, trust or partnership.

However, a violation of this provision is not subject to a shareholder's private claims but only to claims by the SEC. Like other sections of the 1940 Act, the courts have eliminated private rights of action unless Congress has expressly provided for such an action.[1]

---

## Discussion Topics

a. How do you evaluate the cost/benefit argument with respect to the corporate structure of investment companies?

b. Are the provisions of the Investment Company Act a proper encroachment into the traditional domain of state law? Note that this issue has arisen in connection with a recent SEC rule, which has since been overturned, that entitled a 3% shareholder, that held the shares for 3 years to nominate a director to a publicly held corporation that is registered under section 12 of the Securities Act of 1934. Arguably, shareholders do not own the corporation. They produce nothing. They just provide raw materials for creative managers. A similar, but more limited argument is proposed by the advisers and managers of mutual funds. What is your opinion?

---

## Problem

You are counsel to the independent directors of a mutual fund. One of the independent directors informs you that his granddaughter has just graduated from college and has accepted a job as an entry-level employee of the mutual fund's investment adviser. Write an email to this director advising him whether his granddaughter's new job causes him to be an interested person of the fund under section 2(a)(19). Would your answer change if, instead, this director's granddaughter was instead an in-house lawyer for the adviser and in connection with that role was also vice-president and assistant secretary of the fund?

Separately, the adviser's affiliated broker-dealer has historically acted as principal underwriter for the fund. However, the adviser's parent company has decided to close down this broker-dealer and, as a result, the fund must find a third party principal underwriter. The adviser has proposed that the fund retain XYZ Securities as principal underwriter. XYZ Securities is a wholly-owned subsidiary of XYZ, Inc., a public company traded on the New York Stock Exchange. Another independent director has informed you that he owns 2 shares of XYZ, Inc. common stock through his brokerage

1. *Northstar Financial Advisors, Inc. v. Schwab Investments,* 615 F.3d 1106 (9th Cir. 2010).

account. Write an email to this director explaining whether this share ownership causes him to be an interested person of the fund under section 2(a)(19).

---

## B. Relationship Between State Law and the Investment Company Act

If federal law conflicts with state law, state law will be preempted. The question is when and how do the conflicts arise? For example, if federal law does not require annual shareholders meetings but requires only meetings for particular purposes, should Maryland law, which does not require annual meetings, apply? If federal law does not address the issue of demand on directors when shareholders sue the directors derivatively, does state law apply?

These issues were addressed by Mr. Justice Brennan in the following case of *Burks v. Lasker.*[1]

*Burks v. Lasker* presented the question of "whether the disinterested directors of an investment company may terminate a stockholders' derivative suit brought against the company's board and the adviser under the Investment Company and Investment Advisers Acts of 1940." The plaintiffs alleged breach of duties under the 1940 and Advisers Acts and the common law. The board followed the five disinterested directors' determination that the fund would not continue the litigation.

The District Court held that, under the "business judgment rule," a quorum of disinterested directors may terminate a derivative suit if in good faith they find it against the company's best interests. Their decision was upheld. The Second Circuit reversed holding that, under the 1940 Act, "disinterested directors of an investment company do not have the power to foreclose the continuation of nonfrivolous litigation brought by shareholders against majority directors for breach of their fiduciary duties."

In an opinion by Justice Brennan, the Supreme Court determined whether this issue was governed by state or federal law. First, the Court determined which law creates the cause of action. In this case it was not disputed that the causes of action were implied derivative causes of action under the 1940 Act and Advisers Act. Therefore, it was not necessary to consider the policy of federal law.

However, in this case the disputed relevant area was not covered by a "complete body of federal law." Under state law, suits on behalf of corporations are brought by the directors. The shareholders' right to bring a derivative suit is based on state law; while federal law in this area is "largely regulatory and prohibitory"; the 1940 Act "functions primarily to '[impose] controls and restrictions on the internal management of investment companies. . . .'" Therefore, the 1940 Act and Advisers Act "do not require that federal law displace state laws governing the powers of directors unless the state laws permit action prohibited by the Acts, or unless 'their application would be inconsistent with the federal policy underlying the cause of action. . . '."

1. *Burks v. Lasker,* 441 U.S. 471 (1979).

Therefore, the lower courts should have, first, determined whether state law permitted the board of directors to terminate the suit, and, second, if so, whether the particular state law applicable to the facts of the case was consistent with the policy of the federal statutes regarding the activities under consideration. The Court found state law consistent with the federal law policy, noting the concerns of Congress about "abuse inherent in the structure of investment companies" (i.e., conflicts of interest) and its policy of relying on unaffiliated directors as "independent watchdogs" rather than direct controls on conduct. The Court noted specifically the 1940 Act's requirement that a certain percentage of the directors be unaffiliated and the duties the 1940 Act imposes on unaffiliated directors.

The Court reversed and remanded for further proceedings consistent with its opinion without deciding the state law question of whether state law prohibits termination of the claim.

Justice Blackmun concurred, but suggested that "a situation could very well exist where state law conflicts with federal policy." Justice Stewart concurred in the judgment but disagreed "that there is any danger that state law will conflict with federal policy judgment," noting that "[t]he business decisions of a corporation are normally entrusted to its board of directors" and that "Congress intended disinterested directors of mutual funds to be 'independent watchdogs.'"

The following staff letter demonstrates how the SEC staff has balanced state law and the Investment Company Act.[1]

> You state that because Minnesota law does not require annual shareholders' meetings, the Minnesota funds will not hold such meetings. This statement indirectly raises the recurring question of whether Section 16(a) of the Act requires investment companies to hold shareholders' meetings to elect directors (or those persons holding equivalent positions) on an annual basis, irrespective of the requirements of applicable state law. While your letter does not request an interpretation on this issue, we would like to take this opportunity to state our views on this matter.
>
> The specific language of Section 16(a) of the Act makes clear that Congress intended the Act to require investment companies to hold an annual or special meeting to elect directors in two situations: (1) to elect the initial board of directors; and (2) to elect directors to fill existing vacancies on the board in the event that less than a majority of directors were elected by shareholders. In either case, the Act requires that a shareholders' meeting must be held, irrespective of the requirements, or lack of requirements, of applicable state law. Absent either of these situations, however, the language of Section 16(a) is ambiguous regarding whether, as a matter of federal law, investment companies must hold shareholders' meetings annually to elect directors, and the relevant legislative history is not dispositive on this question. In light of this ambiguity, the interpretive issue presented is whether (1) Congress intended the Act to require

1. John Nuveen & Co., Inc., SEC No-Action Letter (Nov. 18, 1986).

> investment companies to have annual shareholders' meetings to elect directors, notwithstanding that the specific language of the Act requires such meetings only in two situations, or (2) Congress intended applicable state law to govern the timing of shareholders' meetings to elect directors in situations other than the two-set forth in the Act. In our opinion, the latter view is preferable because it is consistent with the regulatory structure intended by Congress whereby investment companies are incorporated and operate pursuant to state law subject to certain requirements imposed by the Act. Accordingly, in situations other than the two addressed specifically in Section 16(a), we believe that applicable state law governs the timing of shareholders' meetings to elect investment company directors. . . .

In addition, it is important to note other sources of law that apply to corporate governance issues, such as exchange listing standards. For example, closed-end investment companies are typically listed on a national securities exchange such as the New York Stock Exchange. NYSE rules require these investment companies to hold annual meetings and impose more stringent requirements on board structure — i.e., section 16(a) permits a board to stagger itself in up to five classes (in other words, directors can be elected for five year terms and the term of one class must expire each year), but NYSE rules permit a board to stagger itself in only up to three classes.

---

<u>Discussion Topics</u>

a. In *Burks v. Lasker,* did the Court place too much importance on the role of independent directors as "watchdogs"? Who selects and appoints the independent directors? Is this question relevant? Specifically, did the Court take into consideration the fact that Congress delegated many decisions regarding conflicts of interest, apart from the advisory contract, to the SEC rather than the board? This limitation on director authority is in stark contrast to corporate law. Had the Court focused on section 17 of the Act and the different controls over conflicts of interest that Congress provided, would the Court have reached the same conclusion? In other words, are the arguments against the decision of the Court convincing?

b. Under the Investment Company Act, the annual approval of the advisory contract must be performed by the directors in person and cannot be delegated. Is this an encroachment of the Investment Company Act into what is typically a matter left to state law? Should state fiduciary law and its policies apply in this case? If it does, is state fiduciary law conflicting with the federal law?

---

## C. Composition of the Board: Section 10(a)

### 1. Section 10(a) of the Investment Company Act of 1940 and the SEC's Structural Changes

Section 10(a) of the 1940 Act requires that a registered investment company's board of directors may not consist of more than 60% interested persons. In other words, at least 40% of the board members must be "disinterested" — that is, independent. Section 10(a) represents a reaction to the pre-1940 situation, in which the adviser's appointee sat on the board and served the adviser's interests. This deficiency was met by the requirement for disinterested directors, who would watch out for the shareholders' interests. In fact, most boards are currently composed of a majority of disinterested directors.

Throughout the years the SEC provided exemptions by rules, listed below, and in each rule conditioned the exemption on having a majority of independent directors on the investment company's board, among other corporate governance standards. These requirements are contained in Rule 0-1(a)(7) under the 1940 Act and are known as the "Fund Governance Standards." These exemptive rules are so commonly relied on by investment companies that, as a practical matter, the Fund Governance Standards have required all funds to have a majority of independent directors. The ten exemptive rules are:

(1) Rule 10f-3 (permitting funds to purchase securities in a primary offering when an affiliated broker-dealer is a member of the underwriting syndicate);

(2) Rule 12b-1 (permitting use of fund assets to pay distribution expenses);

(3) Rule 15a-4(b)(2) (permitting fund boards to approve interim advisory contracts without shareholder approval where the adviser or a controlling person receives a benefit in connection with the assignment of the prior contract);

(4) Rule 17a-7 (permitting securities transactions between a fund and another client of the fund's investment adviser);

(5) Rule 17a-8 (permitting mergers between certain affiliated funds);

(6) Rule 17d-1(d)(7) (permitting funds and their affiliates to purchase joint liability insurance policies);

(7) Rule 17e-1 (specifying conditions under which funds may pay commissions to affiliated brokers in connection with the sale of securities on an exchange);

(8) Rule 17g-1(j) (permitting funds to maintain joint insured bonds);

(9) Rule 18f-3 (permitting open-end funds to issue multiple classes of voting stock); and

(10) Rule 23c-3 (permitting the operation of interval funds by enabling closed-end funds to repurchase their shares).

When the SEC proposed to expand these conditions to raise the minimum number of independent directors to 75% of the board, and to require boards to have a chairman who is an independent director, the proposal met with strong opposition by some members in the industry and was challenged in court. The D.C. Circuit struck down the parts of the rule requiring that 75% of the board members be independent directors and that boards have a chairman who is an independent director.[1]

Other aspects of the Fund Governance Standards that continue to stand include requiring (1) the independent directors to select and nominate other independent directors, (2) any legal counsel for the independent directors to be "independent legal counsel" (i.e., sufficiently independent of the adviser, principal underwriter and administrator of the fund), (3) the directors to engage in an annual self-assessment of their performance, (4) the independent directors to meet at least once quarterly in executive session without inside (i.e., "interested") directors present and (5) the independent directors to be authorized to hire employees and retain advisers and experts necessary to carry out their duties.

## 2. The Issue of High Compensation and Directors' Independence

One of the issues concerning fund directors' independence arose with respect to directors who earn significant compensation for serving. Those payments were related to the advisers' input, and rose with the number of the funds in the funds' complex. Thus, directors may sit on the boards of hundreds of funds in one complex and gain significant fees. This issue was discussed in a case involving a derivative action brought under Maryland law. The question was whether a demand on a fund's board of directors should be excused when the independent directors serve on multiple boards, earn significant compensation, and are therefore no longer independent. In such a case, demand can be excused, and the shareholder plaintiff could proceed with his action.

In the case of *Strougo v. Scudder, Stevens & Clark Inc.*,[2] the court held that the majority of the directors were not independent, having been paid significant fees for serving on numerous boards within the fund complex. The decision raised concern because, as the number of funds offering special investment policies grew, it was unlikely to be able to recruit the required number of qualified directors. Various state statutes have therefore negated the impact of the *Strougo* decision.

---

## Discussion Topics

a. Any legal counsel to disinterested directors of funds relying on certain widely relied-upon exemptive rules must be independent of the fund's adviser, principal underwriter and administrator. Is this an appropriate requirement? Is this a necessary requirement, without which the directors, who are not lawyers, could not make an independent and knowledgeable decision?

b. How would the adviser and his counsel relate to the disinterested directors' counsel?

1. *Chamber of Commerce v. SEC*, 443 F.3d 390 (D.C. Cir. 2006).
2. *Strougo v. Scudder, Stevens & Clark Inc.*, 964 F. Supp. 783 (S.D.N.Y. 1997).

c. How should independent directors be paid in order to best maintain their independence?

d. Should there be a limit on the length of the terms of interested directors as well as of independent directors' terms? Should there be a limit on the number of fund boards on which they should sit?

---

## D. The Role of the Board

The following is an excerpt of a presentation by Arthur Levitt, Chairman of the Securities and Exchange Commission, about board directors' responsibilities to investors.[1]

> All fund directors may be called upon to take significant action at some point. Yours is a complex job that requires enormous diligence, skill, and responsibility. You must be prepared to step in at any time; you must know what to look for; you must know when to act; and, lest we forget, you must also know when not to act. . . . But underneath all those complex questions lies a simple truth, one that has guided me without fail in both private and public sectors. I've learned over the years that you'll end up on the right side of almost any issue you'll confront in the securities industry if you make the interests of investors your guide.
>
> This formula applies even to your decision to accept a nomination. A few basic questions will give you an idea of your fellow directors' priorities and degree of commitment to investors. I don't mean any one of these should be controlling — every rule has exceptions — but they are important questions to consider. For example: How many times a year does the board meet? I don't care how talented you are, it's hard to be a good watchdog if you're only on limited patrol. The commitment of adequate time is an essential requirement for directors.
>
> What kind of people are on the board, and how did they get there? I'd be especially wary if I saw too many board members with personal or social ties to the CEO.
>
> Is the board conscientious about expenditures and sensitive to symbolism, or have its members turned imperial, demanding expensive perquisites? Are they more concerned about what they receive than what they contribute?
>
> Does the board understand where the investment company has been and where it is headed?
>
> Even more important: Do board members speak their minds, or do they march in lockstep with management? Board independence is crucial; strictly defined, it means that directors are sufficiently

---

1. Mutual Fund Directors as Investor Advocates, Remarks by Chairman Arthur Levitt, U.S. Securities and Exchange Commission, The Second Annual Symposium for Mutual Fund Trustees and Directors, Washington, D.C., Apr. 11, 1995.

removed from conflicts of interest to be able to take views without regard to management's interests.

You've heard by now of the bipartisan legislation introduced last Friday in the House by Congressmen Fields and Markey, to modernize mutual fund regulation. One provision would require that a majority of directors on investment company boards be independent -- it's about time this was written into law.

Asserting an independent voice can be made difficult by one feature of all successful organizations "team spirit." It's a wonderful thing, but it can lead people to subordinate personal judgments to those of the group. That's where fund directors play an absolutely critical role. In many cases, it falls to you to serve as the fund's conscience. We at the Commission have a sense of how thankless a task this can be; it's even harder to stand apart from the team when you're a member of it, as you are.

But stand apart you must. How else is a fund manager to know when a judgment is wrong, or a standard too low, unless someone with a clear sense of right and wrong has the courage to question it? Even one person can make a tremendous difference. Thirty years ago, it was common to curry favor with New York City policemen by offering them "gifts." One officer couldn't accept the system; his efforts succeeded in raising law enforcement standards in New York and throughout the nation.

Not every question is that clear-cut. You are in a position to define and maintain standards for your funds. I want to talk to you today about four broad areas of board activism and involvement: compliance activities; derivatives; "soft dollar" arrangements; and disclosure. I think it's useful to keep directors abreast of the SEC's agenda for the months ahead.

Compliance is the least concrete of these issues, but the most important. It underlies all the others. The Commission has been devoting a great deal of attention to all aspects of compliance. We recently consolidated all of our inspection functions within a single Office of Compliance Inspections and Examinations, to ensure that our program is as cost-efficient as possible. Directors ought to be paying at least as much attention to compliance activities as we are.

We don't expect directors to be involved with day-to-day matters, but we do expect you to ask the hard questions. What resources has a fund manager devoted to compliance activities? The mutual fund business can be a very profitable one. Isn't it incumbent upon fund managers to plow some of those profits into making funds work better, as compliance surely does? Does the compliance staff receive the full support of management? To whom do they report? When the auditors report a problem, what is the reaction of management? When SEC examiners send a deficiency letter, how quickly does management respond?

Asking these questions makes good business sense. A fund manager's financial success depends heavily on reputation. Compliance problems are suicide-they can take you off the road to prosperity and into the vicious circle of bad publicity, shareholder redemptions, further compliance problems, fewer new shareholders and so on.

And speaking of bad publicity, let's move on to derivatives. A few years ago, few people had heard the word "derivative," and most did not know what it meant. Today, "derivative" has become a household word . . . and most people still don't know what it means.

When I called upon directors more than a year ago to review derivatives policies, some people were skeptical. "That's of concern to money managers, not directors," they said. Some asserted that I was expecting too much of directors, asking them to get involved with something as technical as derivatives. But like it or not, you're already involved with something the moment it appears in your fund's portfolio.

It might be argued — though not by me — that the average American can afford to be ignorant on this esoteric subject; but in your case, when it comes to derivatives, ignorance is not bliss — it's an invitation to disaster. Consider the casualties over the last year alone: Gibson Greetings. Proctor & Gamble. Bankers Trust. Air Products. Piper Jaffray. Orange County, California. Barings PLC. All ended up on the wrong side of some pretty big bets. . . .

I do not view these as solely "a derivatives problem," as if derivatives somehow had the power to force people to invest in them. As I've said on numerous occasions, it would be a grave error to demonize derivatives and blame them for these losses. Derivatives are not inherently good or bad — they're something like electricity: dangerous if mishandled, but bearing the potential to do good. What these spectacular losses highlight for me is the importance of proper oversight and supervision. The best defense any system of investment can have against major loss is an effective risk management system and stringent internal control mechanisms.

If directors don't take the time to understand how derivatives work, how a fund is using them, how clearly they are described to shareholders, and what the exposure of shareholders is — well, if the investment portfolio begins to explode, those directors are likely to get burned along with the fund and its shareholders.

We've been working with the securities industry and our fellow regulators to establish voluntary standards for dealers' use of derivative products. Earlier this month, we announced the adoption of guidelines by the six securities dealers with the largest derivatives business. I commend these guidelines for your review-the principles discussed in them may be useful for funds as well.

The use of "soft dollars" is another issue directors would do well to stay on top of, for it also presents the potential for problems. In the typical soft-dollar arrangement, an adviser routes client brokerage orders to particular brokers and in exchange, gets research. More recently, brokers have agreed with some funds to pay for or provide certain services that funds normally would pay for directly, including custodian arrangements and transfer agent services.

The Investment Company Act requires directors to request and review all information necessary to evaluate the terms of the contract between adviser and investment company. Because they may bear upon the reasonableness of advisory fees, soft dollar arrangements must be disclosed to boards by fund managers. As directors, you need to react to this disclosure, because the practice opens the door to so many valid questions: Which broker is being used, and why not another? What is the value of services being provided? How does it benefit shareholders?

That brings us to public disclosure, an area in which directors clearly can make a difference. Your responsibility for the fund's disclosure obligations gives you an extraordinary tool with which to protect investors. Does the fund clearly describe its strategies? Are risks adequately conveyed?

As you know, the Commission has taken a special interest in cutting through some of the dense prose that has come to characterize mutual fund prospectuses. The law of unintended results has come into play: the Commission's passion for disclosure has interacted with portfolio managers' thirst for flexibility and lawyers' instinct for ironclad liability protection. The result has been prospectuses that are more redundant than revealing.

How can we expect investors to read and understand materials that even securities lawyers find daunting? Why not set a standard: If board members cannot readily understand the fund's prospectus, then it's back to the drawing board until the drafting committee gets it right.

The Commission is encouraging the industry not only to use clearer language in writing prospectuses, but also to organize information in more accessible ways. Last year, I announced that eight major fund groups had stepped forward to pilot a "profile prospectus," that is, a prospectus that includes a concise summary of salient points, for clarity and comparability. We and our state regulator colleagues now have prototypes in hand, and we hope that profile prospectuses will be in use in the very near future.* * *

Boards of directors of investment companies generally play a different role than boards of directors of operating companies. If the investment company's operations are operated by an *internal adviser* (such as a subsidiary owned by the investment company), the board supervises the management in the same way as the board of an operating company. If the operations are in the hands of an *external adviser* under contract, the board supervises the adviser; it approves the adviser's fees and performs certain other actions. The following further describes the unique role the independent directors play for investment companies.[1]

1. These materials are derived from 2 Tamar Frankel & Ann Taylor Schwing, The Regulation of Money Managers, §§ 9-69, 9-88 to -92, 9-94 to -103, 9-115, 9-117 to -119, 9-121 to -22 (2001 & Supp. 2015).

### *General Duties*

Directors are subject to a duty of *due care,* generally that of the "prudent person," requiring them to become adequately informed on matters before the board.

Directors are also subject to a duty of *loyalty,* requiring them to place the interests of the investment company over those of the directors or others, and a duty to act in *good faith.*

If there is more than one class of securities (i.e., in a closed-end company), the directors must balance the interests of the classes. In addition, if directors sit on the board of more than one investment company, they should be aware of conflicts of interest.

### *Continuous Review and Supervision*

Directors have a duty of *continuously review and supervise.* They meet to review the performance of the portfolio and adviser. They should obtain appropriate knowledge about the company, and the adviser should provide disinterested directors with financial statements. They should check whether the company's policies are being followed with respect to purchases and sales of portfolio securities, and examine the company's registration statements. They should not automatically approve the adviser's actions.

The adviser and affiliated directors must disclose possible conflicts of interest to the disinterested directors, who must scrutinize these activities. Directors should also: (1) watch for abuses such as "churning," (2) not allow the adviser to recoup promotional losses for a new company from the investment company, (3) examine the adviser's practices in placing portfolio transactions with broker-dealers, (4) ensure that the company's operations and activities conform to its stated investment objectives, (5) ensure that the shareholders' right to approve certain changes in investment policy is preserved, (6) ensure that the adviser does not improperly delegate it duties or transfer its contract, (7) examine any lending of portfolio securities, (8) supervise the adviser to ensure it performs its contract, (9) obtain information regarding the arrangement and transactions with the custodian, and (10) determine whether the adviser has an interest to prefer other clients.

### *Specific Duties and Powers*

The board has specific duties under the 1940 Act. The advisory contract between the company and its adviser must be approved by the board and a majority of the disinterested directors, pursuant to section 15(a) and 15(c). The board must also approve any underwriting contract and the bonding arrangements of officers, directors and employees having access to company assets. If there is a joint bond with investment company affiliates, the premium must be approved by the disinterested directors.

### *Approval of the Advisory Contract*

Generally, the board need not shop around for a new adviser, as long as the present adviser's services, performance, and fees are acceptable. If, however, the independent directors are convinced that the present adviser cannot offer the funds a chance for good performance, they should contact other advisers and solicit competing offers to manage the fund's portfolio, with the professional help of, for example, a management consultant firm.

### *Approval of the Underwriting Contract*

The underwriting contract, unlike the advisory contract, need only be approved by the board and not the shareholders.

With respect to a *registered open-end* investment company, section 15(b) requires a written contract with the principal underwriter, which (1) shall continue for more than two years only as approved annually by the board or shareholders, and (2) provides for termination if assigned.

In addition, section 15(c) makes it unlawful for any registered investment company with a board of directors to enter into or renew a contract whereby a person undertakes regularly to serve or act as a principal underwriter (written or oral) for the investment company unless the terms are "approved by the vote of a majority of directors, who are not parties to such contract or agreement or interested persons of any such party, cast in person at a meeting called for the purpose of voting on such approval."

### *Approval of the Contract for the Custody of Assets*

If the investment company holds its assets in the custody of a bank, the disinterested directors must also examine the custodial fees. At least annually, the board must ratify the contract with a custodian who is a member of a stock exchange, pursuant to rule 17f-1(d).

### *Approval of Bonding Arrangements*

By rule 17g-1(d), a majority of the disinterested directors of a management investment company (a closed-end or open-end company) must approve the fidelity bond that the investment company must provide pursuant to that rule, either alone or with its adviser and underwriter or other investment companies of the same fund complex.

### *Duties of the Independent Directors — Duty and Right to Seek Information*

The 1940 Act has imposed special responsibility on the independent directors to act as watchdogs over the adviser, underwriter and others who render services to the company. The independent directors generally are not involved in the day-to-day operations of the company and may not, particularly when first elected, be knowledgeable about the general nature of investment companies and the applicable laws, or about the specific characteristics of the company on whose board they sit. Therefore, the inside directors and adviser have a duty to give the outside directors and the board pertinent information to enable them to make intelligent decisions. Because investment company operations are sometimes technical and complicated, disinterested directors are under a duty to educate themselves, and insiders must inform them in these matters. This duty is either explicit in the 1940 Act or implied from other requirements in the 1940 Act or in other applicable laws.

Section 15(c) of the 1940 Act expressly imposes on the adviser a duty to inform, and on the disinterested directors to request information, before approval of the advisory contract by the disinterested directors.

Section 15(c) provides in part: "It shall be the duty of the directors of a registered investment company to request and evaluate, and the duty of an investment adviser to such company to furnish, such information as may be reasonably necessary to evaluate the terms of any contract whereby a person undertakes regularly to serve or act as investment adviser of such company." This section indicates a congressional policy that the adviser must provide information and directors must seek information in all areas in which they must act, whether singly or as a group.

Concern about the adequacy of boards' reviews of advisory contracts, especially the advisory fees (as compared to fees charged to institutional investors), led the SEC to adopt in June 2004 amendments to Forms N-1A, N-2, and N-3. These forms require reports of registered management investment companies to shareholders to "[d]iscuss in reasonable detail the material factors and the conclusions with respect thereto that formed the basis for the board's approval [of an] investment advisory contract."[1] The discussion should include: ". . . [f]actors relating to both the board's selection of the investment adviser and approval of the advisory fee and any other amounts to be paid by the Fund under the contract"[2] and "[i]f applicable, any benefits derived or to be derived by the investment adviser from the relationship with the Fund such as soft dollar arrangements by which brokers provide research to the Fund or its investment adviser in return for allocating Fund brokerage."[3]

On November 24, 2003 the SEC added disclosure requirements concerning the operations of the boards of directors, including the boards of directors of investment companies. "Specifically," stated the introduction to the amending rule, "we are adopting enhancements to existing disclosure requirements regarding the operations of board nominating committees and a new disclosure requirement concerning the means, if any, by which security holders may communicate with directors. These rules require disclosure but do not mandate any particular action by a company or its board of directors; rather, the new disclosure requirements are intended to

---

1. Disclosure Regarding Approval of Investment Advisory Contracts by Directors of Investment Companies, Investment Company Act Rel. No. 26486 (Jun. 23, 2004).
2. *Id.* These factors include, but are not limited to: "a discussion of the nature, extent, and quality of the services to be provided by the investment adviser; the investment performance of the [fund] and the investment adviser; the costs of the services to be provided and profits to be realized by the investment adviser and its affiliates from the relationship with the [fund]; the extent to which economies of scale would be realized as the [fund] grows; and whether fee levels reflect these economies of scale for the benefit of [the fund's] investors." The discussion should also indicate "whether the board relied upon comparisons of the services to be rendered and the amounts to be paid under the contract with those under other investment advisory contracts, such as contracts of the same and other investment advisers with other registered investment companies or other types of clients (e.g., pension funds and other institutional investors). If the board relied upon such comparisons, [the discussion should] describe the comparisons that were relied on and how they assisted the board in concluding that the contract should be approved." These factors should sound familiar, as they are the *Gartenberg* factors discussed in the previous chapter.
3. *Id.*

make more transparent to security holders the operation of the boards of directors of the companies in which they invest."[1]

---

## Discussion Topics

a. Please review section 15(c). Is this section sufficient to ensure that the directors receive the information they need? Who should be responsible for ensuring that the adviser brings all relevant matters to the attention of the board? What will be the directors' liability if they do not perform their duties properly?

b. Another important responsibility of the board of directors is to determine the liquidity and valuation regarding certain complex instruments (e.g., derivatives). What should be the exact contours of the board's role? Who, apart from the board, would protect the investors' interests?

c. To what extent will the "business judgment rule" under corporate law apply to the board's decision to approve the contract?

d. Is it appropriate to require the board to disclose its reasons for approving the advisory contract? If not, how would anyone know what the board's reasons were?

e. Would you be willing to become a member of an investment company's board of directors? How much material would you expect to receive and how much time would you expect to spend on preparing for the board meetings? Would your willingness depend also on the amount of money you would receive or the importance of the position you hold?

f. Is there a need for an organization that offers ways to measure the effectiveness of fund boards, and searches for mutual fund directors? If there is such a need, what is the legal status of such an organization? What problems arise from its services? If you were a director, what questions would you ask before you used its advice? If you were the adviser to the CEO of such an organization, what issues would you raise?

g. If you were an investor, would you like to know what is done with your money and how those who are your representatives take care of your interests?

h. If you are a legislator, who wishes to retain the public's trust in mutual funds, and avoid the 1929 debacle, how would you evaluate these questions and the answers?

---

## E. Shareholder Voting

A component of corporate governance is shareholder voting. Like shareholders in any company, fund shareholders have the right to vote on

1. Disclosure Regarding Nominating Committee Functions and Communications Between Security Holders and Boards of Directors, Investment Company Act Rel. No. 26262, (Nov. 24, 2003).

various matters. Under the Investment Company Act shareholder voting is required to, among other things, elect board members, implement changes to a fund's fundamental investment policies, and approve fees. Section 18(i) of the 1940 Act requires that each share of stock be voting stock and carry equal voting rights.

Like any corporation, a proxy mechanism is used when a fund is required to solicit votes of shareholders. The federal securities laws treat fund proxies like they treat proxies of the typical corporation. Section 20(a) of the 1940 Act subjects investment companies' proxy solicitations to SEC rules, and rule 20a-1 under the 1940 Act[1] applies the Securities Exchange Act proxy rules to investment companies and sets additional requirements for investment companies.

Rule 14a-8 under the Securities Exchange Act[2] governs shareholders' proposals and provides bases for a company to exclude a proposal, including relevance and a "matter relating to the company's ordinary business operations." The SEC staff has issued letters interpreting these exclusions narrowly.[3]

Additionally, fund bylaws (particularly those of closed-end funds) often contain detailed and complicated requirements and procedures for a shareholder to nominate a director or propose business outside of the requirements of rule 14a-8. These bylaws are referred to as "advance notice bylaws" and have been the subject of frequent litigation. Some fund bylaws also contain detailed director qualification requirements that are designed to identify conflicts of interests that board members, or potential board members, may have (beyond those that would make a director an "interested person" of the fund under section 2(a)(19) of the 1940 Act) and give the board an opportunity to consider the impacts of such potential conflicts and whether to waive the potential disqualification in particular instances.

---

**Discussion topic**

a. To what extent would investors be interested in controlling their funds' investment management?

b. Would that interest differ from small investors and activist investors?

---

1. 17 C.F.R. § 270.20a-1 (2015).
2. 17 C.F.R. § 240.14a-8 (2015).
3. Tamar Frankel & Ann Taylor Schwing, The Regulation of Money Managers, §§ 21-150 to 152, 21-155 to 156, 21-167 to 168 (2001 & Supp. 2015).

# Chapter 9

## *Capital Structure*

State law permits corporations to design their capital structure provided the structure is described in their charters or articles of association. In contrast, the Investment Company Act imposes limitations on the nature of the securities issued by an investment company. This Chapter examines the Investment Company Act's provisions that regulate investment companies' issuance of securities, such as stocks and bonds.

### A. Issuance of Stock: Redeemability and Sections 2(a)(32), 22(c), 22(e) and Rule 22c-1

The 1940 Act does not require investment companies to issue redeemable securities. If, however, such companies offer redeemable securities, the Act requires them to conform to standardized terms of redeemability. That is because, before the passage of the 1940 Act, companies offered redeemable securities subject to a confusing variety of conditions. Under the 1940 Act, redemption is defined, and a company that offers redeemable securities must comply with sections 22(c) and rule 22c-1 with respect to the valuation of the securities, and effect redemptions within seven days of the investor's demand (with some exceptions), as prescribed by section 22(e).

#### 1. Definition of Redeemability

Section 2(a)(32) of the Investment Company Act defines a redeemable security as "any security . . . under the terms of which the holder, upon its presentation to the issuer or to a person designated by the issuer, is entitled . . . to receive approximately his proportionate share of the issuer's current net assets, or the cash equivalent thereof."

In a no-action letter to Brown & Wood (SEC No-Action Letter, Feb. 24, 1994),[1] the SEC staff stated that whether securities are redeemable depends on the strictness of the restrictions on the investors' ability to withdraw their shares from the funds. The factors to be considered are: whether the right of withdrawal is conditional, whether the issuer offers matching securities at the same time or different times, whether and how often the issuer sponsors activities designed to facilitate the investors' ability to acquire the

1. *Citing* SuperTrust Trust for Capital Market Fund, Inc. Shares, Investment Company Act Rel. No. 17613 (Jul. 25, 1990); *see also* Donaldson, Lufkin & Jenrette Sec. Corp., SEC No-Action Letter (Sept. 23, 1994).

matching security and present them for withdrawal, whether the amount of the portfolio securities that investors can withdraw is limited, how often investors can withdraw, holding period requirements, denomination of the securities and minimum amount needed to withdraw portfolio securities, and how the withdrawal right feature is presented to investors. What is the common denominator of all these factors?

The question of whether an open-end investment company may impose expenses on redeeming shareholders arose in connection with the issue of "market timing." In this case, some investors who were either knowledgeable or acquired information about market prices were redeeming and purchasing fund shares at a furious rate, far greater than other shareholders who purchased and held investment company shares long-term. Thus, even though these trading shareholders imposed costs on those who did not trade, the definition of redemption seems to prohibit the imposition of significant charges on redeeming shareholders. The SEC resolved the issue by Rule 22c-2. The rule permits open-end investment companies to impose "a redemption fee, not to exceed two percent of the amount redeemed, to be retained by the fund. The redemption fee is intended to allow funds to recoup some of the direct and indirect costs incurred as a result of short-term trading strategies, such as market timing. The new rule also requires most funds to enter into written agreements with intermediaries (such as broker-dealers and retirement plan administrators) that hold shares on behalf of other investors, under which the intermediaries must agree to provide funds with certain shareholder identity and transaction information at the request of the fund and carry out certain instructions from the fund."[1]

---

## Discussion Topics

a. What is the effect of a provision in the articles of association of an investment company that allows for monthly redemption by shareholders? Does the provision meet the redemption definition and requirements of the Investment Company Act?

b. May investment companies redeem their shares "in kind" (*e.g.*, distribute pro rata portfolio shares to their redeeming shareholders)? Could an investment company experiencing a "run" or "net redemptions" redeem its shares in kind? How would that work? Would it affect the effects of the "run"?

c. In rule 3a-7,[2] the SEC exempted from some of the provisions of the 1940 Act certain issuers that, among other things, do not issue redeemable securities. These are entities that issue asset-backed securities. Why, in your opinion, did the SEC impose this condition? Did such a condition create difficulties for the entities that issue asset-backed securities?

---

1. Mutual Fund Redemption Fees, Investment Company Act Rel. No. 26782 (Mar. 11, 2005) (codified as amended at 17 C.F.R. § 270.22c-2 (2015)).
2. 17 C.F.R. § 270.3a-7 (2015).

## 2. Pricing Redeemable Shares

Rule 22c-1[1] requires that purchases and redemptions of redeemable shares be effected at the current net asset value per share that is *next computed* (i.e., the next price after the order is received) after the receipt of the purchase or redemption request. Determining the current net asset value involves calculating the value of a fund's underlying securities and dividing by the number of the fund's outstanding securities (i.e., the shares owned by the persons who own the mutual fund).

The importance of asset valuation in the mutual funds area cannot be exaggerated. It affects (1) the purchase and redemption price of the funds' securities; (2) the funds' and securities' performance information; (3) the comparison with other funds' performance; (4) "capital allocation decisions;" and (5) the securities' market volatility. It can "impair the correctness of financial statements" and help detect "operational flaws." Valuation can also impact a fund's credit exposure and tax treatment. There is almost no function in the investment management area that is immune to valuation.[2]

### a. Valuation

Ask a lawyer, an accountant, an economist, and the Internal Revenue Service to define the term, "value," and you may get at least four answers. For the lawyer, value is the market value. For the accountant, it is a fair value. For the economist, the value is the exit price net of expected transaction costs. For the Internal Revenue Service, it is a fair market value.

However, the lawyer's definition — market value — means the last quoted price. If there is an end-of-day quotation, that is the security's value, even if the owner could never realize the value upon sale. The elegance of this valuation lies in its simplicity. Earnings management is precluded by such a method. It is easily verifiable.

FASB defines fair value as the amount at which the investment could be exchanged in a current transaction between willing parties, other than in a forced or liquidation sale. While quoted market prices may be the best evidence of value, accountants have enough leeway to override them if circumstances warrant, such as transactions in large blocks or restricted stock. The economist looks at the security and asks, "If I disposed of the asset today, what would I receive?" While the economist's exit price theoretically might be the most truthful measure of value, it is a difficult one to verify and, because of its complexity, it is highly susceptible to earnings management.

The Internal Revenue Service determines the fair market value as the value of the highest and best use to which the property can be put. For example: on December 31 XYZ security traded 10 million shares throughout the day in minimum blocks of 10,000 shares with a bid-asked spread of $100-$110 on its principal exchange. The final trade of the day on the

1. 17 C.F.R. § 270.22c-1 (2015).
2. International Association of Financial Engineers Investor Risk Comm., Valuation Concepts for Investment Companies and Financial Institutions and their Stakeholders, Jun. 8, 2004, at 2-3.

principal exchange, however, for only 100 shares, traded at $105-$115. In a transaction after the close of trading on the principal exchange, someone sold 100 shares for $120. Our investor in question owns 10,000 shares.

Thus, while a lawyer might value the stock at $115 — the last market quotation, the accountant might accept either the last bid on the principal exchange — $105, or the midpoint of the bid-asked spread — $110, as the fair value, as long as the methodology employed by the investor was consistently applied. The economist would use a value of $100 per share — the exit price, minus an adjustment for expected transaction costs. The IRS would require the taxpayer to value the security at $120 per share — its highest and best use.

Some have argued that a volume-weighted average price represents a better estimate of market value than the last quoted price. While the exit price best represents fair value, this approach arguably approximates exit price but leaves less room for earnings management. This approach has been called "optimal value," which aligns the values calculated by the lawyer, accountant, and economist, but not with that of the IRS. The benefits to this approach are simplicity, truth, verifiability, objectivity, comparability, anti-manipulation, and consistency.

Under a realization method of accounting, gain or loss is measured as the difference between the sales proceeds, the actual fair market value, and the cost of the asset. Marking to market takes into account the difference between the fair market value at the end of the period and that at the beginning of the period. If sales proceeds is the best indicator of FMV in an actual sale, expected sales proceeds should be the best measure of FMV under a MTM regime.

### b. Valuation Under the Investment Company Act

Under the 1940 Act valuation of an asset is based on a number of guiding principles and objective, subjective and speculative evaluations.

Some suggest that valuations should follow market prices, if the markets represent the invisible hand: the price that results from many trades in arm's length transactions. Valuation may also follow established and provable facts rather than speculative future possibilities. In addition, because valuations involve the valuators, some of the principles concerning valuations aim at ensuring the valuators' qualifications and their absence of bias. Finally, because valuations are affected by the environment and by special situations of the valuated assets, there are guides that allow controlled deviations from the guidelines.[1]

Section 2(a)(41) defines value in different ways depending on the context of different sections of the 1940 Act. With respect to sections 3 (determining investment company status), 5 (determining diversification), and 12 (anti-pyramiding restrictions), (i) regarding securities owned at the end of the last preceding fiscal quarter for which market quotations are readily available, the value of the securities will be the market value at the end of each such quarter; (ii) with respect to other securities and assets owned at the end of the last preceding fiscal quarter, the value is the fair value at the

1. *Id.*

end of such quarter, as determined in good faith by the board of directors; and (iii) with respect to securities and other assets acquired after the end of the last pricing fiscal quarter, the value is the cost of those securities and other assets. Value as used elsewhere in 1940 Act (e.g., for purposes of determining a fund's net asset value) means (i) with respect to securities for which market quotations are readily available, the market value of such securities; and (ii) with respect to other securities and assets (e.g., that do not have readily available market quotations), fair value as determined in good faith by the board of directors. The board has discretion to re-evaluate in good faith even securities that have a market value.

The calculation of the value of a fund's underlying securities, especially when a portfolio contains complex financial instruments, is subject to potential abuse. In other words, the buyer or redeemer of a mutual fund share does not know the precise price at which the shares will be redeemed. The statutory approach was designed to prevent insiders from purchasing their shares at less than the net asset value or redeeming the shares at more than the net asset value. In the beginning of the twenty-first century, an attempt to circumvent this objective was uncovered. The following New York case describes the way it was done.[1] The State of New York sued a number of defendants including a hedge fund and its manager on the following facts.

> From 1999 to 2003, Canary engaged in two fraudulent schemes and benefitted to the extent of tens of millions of dollars at the expense of mutual fund investors. Both schemes involved the complicity of mutual fund management companies that violated their fiduciary duties to their customers in return for substantial fees and other income for themselves and their affiliates. . . . The first scheme was Canary's "late trading" of mutual fund shares. As described in greater detail below, the daily price of mutual fund shares is generally calculated as of 4:00 p.m. EST. Orders to buy, sell or exchange mutual fund shares placed at or before 4:00 p.m. EST on a given day receive that day's price. Conversely, orders placed after 4:00 p.m. EST are supposed to be priced using the following day's price. Canary agreed with certain financial institutions (including the Bank of America) that orders Canary placed after 4 p.m. on a given day would illegally receive that day's price (as opposed to the next day's price, which the order would have received had it been processed lawfully). This allowed Canary to capitalize on post-4:00 p.m. information while those who bought their mutual fund shares lawfully could not. . . .
>
> Late trading can be analogized to betting today on yesterday's horse races. . . . The second scheme involved "timing" of mutual funds. "Timing" is an investment technique involving short-term, "in and out" trading of mutual fund shares. The technique is designed to exploit inefficiencies in the way mutual fund companies price their shares. This practice is by no means limited to Canary. Indeed: (1) it

1. Complaint, *State v. Canary Capital Partners* (N.Y. Sup. Ct. Sept. 3, 2003), *available at* http://news.findlaw.com/nytimes/docs/nys/nyscanary90303cmp.pdf.

is widely acknowledged that timing inures to the detriment of long-term shareholders; (2) because of this detrimental effect, mutual fund prospectuses typically state that timing is monitored and the funds work to prevent it; and (3) nonetheless, in return for investments that will increase fund managers' fees, fund managers enter into undisclosed agreements to allow timing. . . .

In fact, certain mutual fund companies have employees (generally referred to as the "timing police") who are supposed to ferret out "timers" and put a stop to their short-term trading activity. Nonetheless, the mutual fund managers arranged to give Canary and other market timers a "pass" with the timing police, who would look the other way rather than attempt to shut down their short-term trading. . . . The mutual fund prospectuses created the misleading impression that mutual funds were vigilantly protecting investors against the negative effects of timing. In fact, the opposite was true: managers sold the right to time their funds to Canary and other hedge fund investors. The prospectuses were silent about these arrangements. . . . As a result of "late trading" and "timing" of mutual funds, Canary, the mutual fund companies and their intermediaries profited handsomely. The losers were unsuspecting long-term mutual fund investors. Canary's excess profits came dollar-for-dollar out of their pockets.

A. Late Trading

Canary's practice of late trading exploited the unique way in which mutual funds set their prices. Mutual funds are valued once a day, usually at 4:00 p.m. EST, when the New York market closes. The price, known as the Net Asset Value or "NAV," generally reflects the closing prices of the securities that comprise a given fund's portfolio, plus the value of any cash that the fund manager maintains for the fund. A mutual fund stands ready to buy or sell (the mutual fund industry refers to sales as "redemptions") its shares at the NAV with the public all day, any day — but unlike a stock, the price of a mutual fund does not change during the course of the day. Accordingly, orders placed at any time during the trading day up to the 4:00 p.m. cutoff get that day's NAV, but an order placed at 4:01 p.m. or thereafter receives the next day's NAV. This is the rule of "forward pricing", which became law in 1968. . . .

This system assures a level playing field for investors. Mutual fund investors do not know the exact price at which their mutual fund orders will be executed at the time they place the orders (unlike stock investors), because NAVs are calculated after the market closes. Orders placed on or before 4 p.m. on a given day are filled at the NAV determined that day while orders placed after 4 p.m. are filled at the NAV calculated the next day. Thus, all investors have the same opportunity to assemble "pre-4:00 p.m. information" before they buy or sell. And no investor has (or at least is supposed to have) the benefit of "post-4:00 information" prior to making an investment decision. The importance of this protection becomes clear when, for example, there is an event after 4:00 p.m. (like an unexpectedly positive corporate earnings announcement) that makes it highly probable that the market for the stocks in a given fund will open sharply higher the next day. Forward pricing ensures fairness: those who bought the fund during the day, before the information came out, will enjoy a gain. Those who buy shares in the fund after the announcement are not supposed to share in this profit. Their purchase order should receive the NAV set at the end of the next day, when the market will have digested the news and reflected its impact in (1) higher prices for the stock held by the fund and therefore (2) a higher NAV for the fund. . . .

An investor who has the ability to avoid forward pricing and buy at the prior NAV enjoys a significant trading edge. He or she can wait until after the market closes for significant news such as the above-earnings announcement to come out, and then buy the fund at the old, low NAV that does not reflect the impact of the new information. When the market goes up the next day, the lucky investor would be able to sell and realize an arbitrage profit based solely on the privilege of trading on the "stale" NAV. . . .

Where does the late trader's arbitrage profit come from? Dollar for dollar, it comes out of the mutual fund that the late trader buys. In essence, the late trader is being allowed into the fund after it is closed for the day to participate in a profit that would otherwise have gone completely to the fund's buy-and-hold investors. When the late trader redeems his shares and claims his profit, the mutual fund manager has either to sell stock or use cash on hand — stock and cash that used to belong to the long-term investors — to give the late trader his gain. This makes late trading basically a zero-sum game. Putting to one side the investment results of the mutual fund for the brief time that the late trader actually holds it, the late trader's gain is the long-term investors' loss. The forward pricing rule was enacted to prevent this kind of abuse. See 17 C.F.R. § 270.22c-1(a). . . .

Summary of Canary's Late Trading. Canary engaged in late trading on a daily basis from in or about March 2000 until this office began its investigation in July of 2003. It targeted dozens of mutual funds and extracted tens of millions of dollars from them. During the declining market of 2001 and 2002, it used late trading to, in effect, sell mutual fund shares short. This caused the mutual funds to overpay for their shares as the market went down, serving to magnify long-term investors' losses. . . .

Canary obtained some of its late trading "capacity" (the opportunity to engage in late trading) directly from one mutual fund manager, the Bank of America. Bank of America installed special computer equipment in Canary's office that allowed it to buy and sell Bank of America's own mutual funds — the Nations Funds — and hundreds of other mutual funds at the 4:00 p.m. price until 6:30 p.m. New York time. In return, Canary agreed to leave millions of dollars in Bank of America bond funds on a long-term basis. These parked funds are known in the trade as "sticky assets. . . ."

Canary obtained additional late trading capacity from intermediaries, including Security Trust Company ("STC"), an Arizona company providing trust administrative services (including access to mutual funds) to retirement plans. STC gave Canary the ability to trade hundreds of additional mutual funds as late as 9:00 p.m. New York time. So profitable was this opportunity that STC ultimately demanded, and received, a percentage of Canary's winnings. . . .

Mutual funds are meant to be long-term investments. They are designed for buy-and-hold investors, and are therefore the favored homes for Americans' retirement and college savings accounts. Nevertheless, quick-turnaround traders routinely try to trade in and out of certain mutual funds in order to exploit inefficiencies in the way they set their NAVs. . . . This strategy works only because some funds use "stale" prices to calculate the value of securities held in the fund's portfolio. These prices are "stale" because they do not necessarily reflect the "fair value" of such securities as of the time the NAV is calculated. . . . A similar type of timing is possible in mutual funds that contain illiquid securities such as high-yield bonds or small capitalization stocks. Here, the fact that some of the fund's securities may not have traded for hours before the New York closing time can render the fund's NAV stale, and thus open it to being timed. This is sometimes known as "liquidity arbitrage." . . .

The Effect on Long Term Shareholders...Like late trading, effective timing captures an arbitrage profit. And like late trading, the arbitrage profit from timing comes dollar-for-dollar out of the pockets of the long-term investors: the timer steps in at the last moment and takes part of the buy-and-hold investors' upside when the market goes up, so the next day's NAV is reduced for those who are still in the fund. If the timer sells short on bad days — as Canary did — the arbitrage has the effect of making the next day's NAV lower than it would otherwise have been, thus magnifying the losses that investors are experiencing in a declining market. . . .

Timing is not entirely risk free, however. For example, the timer has to keep his or her money in the target fund for at least a day, so he or she may enjoy additional gains or incur losses, depending on the market. But such gains and losses are distinct from the timer's arbitrage profit, which is essentially crystallized at the moment of purchase. . . . Besides the wealth transfer of arbitrage (called "dilution"), timers also harm their target funds in a number of other ways. They impose their transaction costs on the long-term investors. Indeed, trades necessitated by timer redemptions can also lead to realization of taxable capital gains at an undesirable time, or may result in managers having to sell stock into a falling market. Accordingly, fund managers often seek to minimize the disruptive impact of timers by keeping cash on hand to pay out the timers' profits without having to sell stock. This "strategy" does not eliminate the transfer of wealth out of the mutual fund caused by timing; it only reduces the administrative cost of those transfers. However, at the same time it can also reduce the overall performance of the fund by requiring the fund manager to keep a certain amount of the funds' assets in cash at all times, thus depriving the investors of the advantages of being fully invested in a rising market. Some fund managers even enter into special investments as an attempt to "hedge" against timing activity (instead of just refusing to allow it), thus deviating altogether from the ostensible investment strategy of their funds, and incurring further transaction costs. . . .

Tools to Combat Market Timing. Mutual fund managers are aware of the damaging effect that timers have on their funds. And while the effects on individual shareholders may be small once they are spread out over all the investors in a fund, their aggregate impact is not: for example, one recent study estimates that U.S. mutual funds lose $4 billion each year to timers. . . . While it is virtually impossible for fund managers to identify every timing trade, large movements in and out of funds — like those made by Canary — are easy for managers to spot. And mutual fund managers have tools to fight back against timers. . . . [They can] reject timers' purchases [or institute] short-term trading fees ("early redemption fees") that effectively wipe out the arbitrage that timers exploit. [The fees reimburse the affected fund] for the costs of short term trading. In addition, fund managers are required to update NAVs at the end of the day in New York when there have been market moves that might render the NAV stale. . . . It eliminates the timer's arbitrage. As fiduciaries for their investors, mutual fund managers are obliged to do their best to use these weapons to protect their customers from the dilution that timing causes.

Incentives for Allowing Market Timing. [W]hy would a mutual fund manager allow his fund to be timed? The answer lies in the way that mutual funds are organized. Typically a single management company sets up a number of mutual funds to form a family. . . . While each mutual fund is in fact its own company, as a practical matter the management company runs it. . . . The management company makes its profit from fees it charges the funds for financial advice and other services. These fees are typically a percentage of the assets in the fund, so the more assets in the family of funds, the more money the manager makes. The timer understands this perfectly, and frequently offers the manager more assets in exchange for the right to time. Fund managers have succumbed to temptation and allowed investors in the target funds to be hurt in exchange for additional money in their own pockets in the form of higher management fees. . . .

Canary found many mutual fund managers willing to take that deal. In the period from 2000 to 2003, Canary entered into agreements with dozens of mutual fund families allowing it to time many different mutual funds. Typically, Canary would agree with the fund manager on target funds to be timed — often international and equity funds offering time zone or liquidity arbitrage — and then move the timing money quickly between those funds and a resting place in a money market or similar fund in the same fund family. By

> keeping the money — often many million dollars — in the family, Canary assured the manager that he or she would collect management and other fees on the amount whether it was in the target fund, the resting fund, or moving in between. In addition, sometimes the manager would waive any applicable early redemption fees. By doing so, the manager would directly deprive the fund of money that would have partially reimbursed the fund for the impact of timing. . . .
>
> As an additional inducement for allowing the timing, fund managers often received "sticky assets." These were typically long-term investments made not in the mutual fund in which the timing activity was permitted, but in one of the fund manager's financial vehicles (e.g., a bond fund or a hedge fund run by the manager) that assured a steady flow of fees to the manager. . . .
>
> These arrangements were never disclosed to mutual fund investors. . . . Canary realized tens of millions of dollars in profits as a result of these timing arrangements.

The defendants were sued under New York laws that prohibit fraud and deception. New York sought injunction and disgorgement of profits.

### c. Establishing the Net Asset Value (NAV)

In 2001, the staff of the SEC issued the following no-action letter addressing and clarifying the issues concerning the establishment of net asset value (NAV):[1]

> The 1940 Act requires funds to calculate their net asset values ("NAVs") by using the market value of their portfolio securities when market quotations for those securities are "readily available." When market quotations for a portfolio security are not readily available, a fund must calculate its NAV by using the fair value of that security, as determined in good faith by the fund's board. . . .
>
> Funds generally calculate their NAVs by using the closing prices of portfolio securities on the exchange or market (whether foreign or domestic) on which the securities principally trade. Many foreign markets, however, operate at times that do not coincide with those of the major U.S. markets. For example, Asian markets generally operate during the evening and nighttime in the United States and close before the opening of the major U.S. markets. As a result, the closing prices of securities that principally trade on foreign exchanges or markets ("foreign securities") may be as much as 12-15 hours old by the time of the funds' NAV calculation, and may not reflect the current market values of those securities at that time. In particular, the closing prices of foreign securities may not reflect their market values at a fund's NAV calculation if an event that will affect the value of those securities ("significant event") has occurred since the closing prices were established on the foreign exchange or market, but before the fund's NAV calculation.

1. Investment Company Institute, Corres. (Apr. 30, 2001) (footnotes omitted).

B. The Failure to Determine the Fair Value of Portfolio Securities Following Significant Events May Result in Dilution

Funds may dilute the value of their shareholders' interests if they calculate their NAVs using closing prices that were established before a significant event has occurred. Dilution generally may occur, for example, if fund shares are overpriced because redeeming shareholders will receive a windfall at the expense of the shareholders that remain in the fund. Similarly, dilution may occur when a fund sells its shares at a price lower than its NAV. The risk of dilution increases when significant events occur because such events attract investors who are drawn to the possibility of arbitrage opportunities. In such situations, short-term investors may attempt to exploit the discrepancies between market prices that are no longer current, and the values of a fund's portfolio securities.

Fair value pricing can protect long-term fund investors from short-term investors who seek to take advantage of funds as a result of significant events occurring after a foreign exchange or market closes, but before the funds' NAV calculation.

* * *

The Good Faith Requirement

In [a previous letter issued in 1999] we discussed the requirement that fund boards must determine, in "good faith," the fair value of portfolio securities for which market quotations are not readily available. We stated our view that the good faith requirement is a flexible concept that can accommodate many different considerations, and that the specific actions that a board must take will vary, depending on the nature of the particular fund, the context in which the board must fair value price, and the pricing procedures adopted by the board.

Since we issued the 1999 Letter, we have been requested to provide additional guidance concerning the good faith requirement. In our view, a board acts in good faith when its fair value determination is the result of a sincere and honest assessment of the amount that the fund might reasonably expect to receive for a security upon its current sale, based upon all of the appropriate factors that are available to the fund. Furthermore, we believe that a board acts in good faith when it "continuously review[s] the appropriateness of the method used" in determining the fair value of the fund's portfolio securities. Compliance with the good faith standard generally reflects the directors' faithfulness to the duties of care and loyalty that they owe to the fund.

We believe, however, that a fund board generally would not be acting in good faith if, for example, the board knows or has reason to believe that its fair value determination does not reflect the amount that the fund might reasonably expect to receive for the security upon its current sale. In addition, a fund board generally would not be acting in good faith if it acts with reckless disregard for whether its fair value determination reflects the amount that the fund might reasonably expect to receive for the security upon its current sale. The Commission has instituted several enforcement actions against fund directors under these circumstances.

* * *

The Inappropriate Use of Fair Values when Market Quotations are Readily Available

We also wish to set forth our views on the obligation of funds to value their portfolio securities for which market quotations are readily available. In such circumstances, funds are not permitted to ignore these quotations and fair value price the securities. This would not be consistent with a fund's obligation under the 1940 Act and could result in an incorrect NAV.

We believe that funds must exercise reasonable diligence to obtain market quotations for their portfolio securities before they may properly conclude that market quotations are not readily available. If, for example, a fund obtains market quotations for a portfolio security from one source and determines that they are unreliable, the fund should diligently seek to obtain market quotations from other sources, such as other dealers or other pricing services, before concluding that market quotations are not readily available. . . .

More recently, the SEC has focused again on directors' duties with respect to valuation. In December 2012, the SEC charged eight directors of a mutual fund complex with violating their asset pricing responsibilities under the 1940 Act.[1] In settling this matter, the SEC observed:[2]

Under the securities laws, fund directors are responsible for determining the fair value of portfolio securities for which market quotations are not readily available. In addition, fund directors must determine the methodologies to be used to fair value securities and must periodically reevaluate the appropriateness of those methodologies. The Commission made clear in Accounting Series Release No. 118 (Dec. 23, 1970) and In the Matter of Seaboard Associates Inc., Investment Company Act Release No. 13890 (April 16, 1984) that while fund directors may engage others to assist them to calculate fair values of these securities, they continue to be ultimately responsible to determine fair value in good faith.

The settled order finds that the eight directors failed to satisfy these responsibilities. Specifically, the directors delegated their fair valuation responsibility to a valuation committee without providing adequate substantive guidance on how fair valuation determinations should be made. The directors then made no meaningful effort to learn how fair values were being determined. They received only

1. SEC Charges Eight Mutual Fund Directors for Failure to Properly Oversee Asset Valuation, SEC Press Rel. 2012-259 (Dec. 10, 2012); In the Matter of J. Kenneth Alderman et al., Investment Company Act Rel. No. 30300 (Dec. 10, 2012).
2. Former Mutual Fund Directors Agree to Settle Claims that They Failed to Properly Oversee Asset Valuation, SEC Press Rel. 2013-111 (Jun. 13, 2013); *see* In the Matter of J. Kenneth Alderman, Investment Company Act Rel. No. 30557 (Jun. 13, 2013).

limited information about the factors involved with the funds' fair value determinations, and obtained almost no information explaining why particular fair values were assigned to portfolio securities. The limited information provided to the directors was particularly problematic because fair valued securities comprised a significant percentage of the funds' net asset values (NAVs) -- in most cases above 60 percent.

The settled order finds that the valuation committee to whom the directors delegated the fair valuation responsibilities did not utilize reasonable procedures and often allowed the portfolio manager to arbitrarily set values. As a result, the settled order finds that the funds overstated the value of their securities as the housing market was on the brink of financial crisis in 2007.

---

## Discussion Topics

a. In the case of *Canary*, cited above, did the shareholders of the hedge fund suffer any losses? Did the bank and its shareholders suffer any losses? Who suffered losses in this case?

b. What was the true wrongful act that was uncovered by the *Canary* case? Where was the true corruption uncovered?

c. The SEC addressed the issue in part by attempting to impose the Advisers Act on hedge fund advisers. How does the registration of the advisers to hedge funds solve the problems that the case raised? Are there alternative solutions to these problems?

d. Why did the SEC choose to attempt to regulate the advisers to hedge funds instead of regulating the hedge funds themselves?

e. What are the advantages to allowing the existence of hedge funds in the first place? What if the hedge funds not only offer higher returns but also impose higher risks? Why not prohibit hedge funds in the first place?

---

### d. SEC's Reaction to Market Timing

In reaction to the market timing scandal, the SEC introduced a number of changes to the rules under the 1940 Act and passed rule 22c-2, part of which, as amended, is reproduced below:

§ 270.22c-2 Redemption fees for redeemable securities.

(a) Redemption fee. It is unlawful for any fund issuing redeemable securities, its principal underwriter, or any dealer in such securities, to redeem a redeemable security issued by the fund within seven calendar days after the security was purchased, unless it complies with the following requirements:

(1) Board determination. The fund's board of directors, including a majority of directors who are not interested persons of the fund, must either:

(i) Approve a redemption fee, in an amount (but no more than two percent of the value of shares redeemed) and on shares redeemed within a time period (but no less than seven calendar days), that in its judgment is necessary or appropriate to recoup for the fund the costs it may incur as a result of those redemptions or to otherwise eliminate or reduce so far as practicable any dilution of the value of the outstanding securities issued by the fund, the proceeds of which fee will be retained by the fund; or

(ii) Determine that imposition of a redemption fee is either not necessary or not appropriate.

(2) Shareholder information. With respect to each financial intermediary that submits orders, itself or through its agent, to purchase or redeem shares directly to the fund, its principal underwriter or transfer agent, or to a registered clearing agency, the fund (or on the fund's behalf, the principal underwriter or transfer agent) must either

(i) Enter into a shareholder information agreement with the financial intermediary (or its agent); or

(ii) Prohibit the financial intermediary from purchasing in nominee name on behalf of other persons, securities issued by the fund. For purposes of this paragraph, "purchasing" does not include the automatic reinvestment of dividends.

(3) Recordkeeping. The fund must maintain a copy of the written agreement under paragraph (a)(2)(i) that is in effect, or at any time within the past six years was in effect, in an easily accessible place.

The rule excepts the following funds, unless they elect to impose a redemption fee: money market funds; any fund that issues securities that are listed on a national securities exchange; and any fund that affirmatively permits short-term trading of its securities, if its prospectus clearly and prominently discloses that the fund permits short-term trading of its securities and that such trading may result in additional costs for the fund.

Rule 22c-2(c) contains important definitions.

(1) Financial intermediary means:

(i) Any broker, dealer, bank, or other person that holds securities of record issued by the fund, in nominee name;

(ii) A unit investment trust or fund that invests in the fund in reliance on section 12(d)(1)(E) of the Act (15 U.S.C. 80a-12(d)(1)(E)); and

(iii) In the case of a participant-directed employee benefit plan that owns the securities issued by the fund, a retirement plan's administrator under section 3(16)(A) of the Employee Retirement Income Security Act of 1974 (29 U.S.C. 1002(16)(A)) or any person that maintains the plan's participant records.

(2) Fund means an open-end management investment company that is registered or required to register under section 8 of the Act (15 U.S.C. 80a-8), and includes a separate series of such an investment company.

(3) Money market fund means an open-end management investment company that is registered under the Act and is regulated as a money market fund under § 270.2a-7.

(4) Shareholder includes a beneficial owner of securities held in nominee name, a participant in a participant-directed employee benefit plan, and a holder of interests in a fund or unit investment trust that has invested in the fund in reliance on section 12(d)(1)(E) of the Act. A shareholder does not include a fund investing pursuant to section 12(d)(1)(G) of the Act (15 U.S.C. 80a-12(d)(1)(G)), a trust established pursuant to section 529 of the Internal Revenue Code (26 U.S.C. 529), or a holder of an interest in such a trust.

---

Discussion Topics

a. The rule above has been fairly effective in preventing late trading and market timing. Can you explain why?

b. Why did the rule impose duties on broker-dealers and other intermediaries? Why did they not object to it?

c. Why did the rule not impose duties on the board of directors and advisers?

---

### 3. Payment of Redemptions: Section 22(e)

Under section 22(e) of the Investment Company Act, an investment company may not suspend redemptions or postpone the date of payment for more than 7 days after the tender of the security to the company or its agent designated for redemptions. Exceptions for this prohibition are made when 1) the New York Stock Exchange is closed; 2) an emergency exists, as defined by SEC rules; or 3) the SEC so orders.

The SEC has been very cautious in providing extensions of the 7-day time period. It has provided an extension from the 7-day requirement when a substantial portion of a fund's assets had been converted by an officer and its net asset value could not be fully and accurately ascertained because a significant portion of its net assets consisted of a claim against an employee dishonesty bond and the fund had no assurance it would be able to recover its loss under the bond.[1] In another case, an extension was provided when a fund received redemption requests relating to shareholder accounts of an 80% shareholder and redemption within the 7-day period would have

1. Sagittarius Fund, Inc., Investment Company Act Rel. No. 8489 (Sept. 9, 1974) (application); Sagittarius Fund, Inc., Investment Company Act Rel. No. 8543 (Oct. 17, 1974) (order).

reduced the net asset value of the remaining shares, harming the remaining shareholders.[1]

---

## Discussion Topics

a. Are all short-term trades (purchases followed shortly thereafter by redemptions) in mutual fund shares "unfair" to other shareholders who remain in a fund? If not, what criteria could be applied to distinguish between "unfair" and "fair" short-term trades?

b. Should the imposition of redemption fees be imposed only on "unfair" short-term trades? Or, should a shareholder who engages in any short-term trade be required to reimburse the fund for the expenses that the fund is reasonably expected to incur in satisfying a redemption including the brokerage commissions paid to sell securities from a fund's investment portfolio to generate cash to make the redemption payment to the shareholder?

c. If a shareholder who redeems after a short holding period (say, five days) is required to bear the cost of the redemption, should not a shareholder who redeems after a long holding period (say, five years) also be required to bear the costs of that redemption?

d. More broadly, why not require each fund shareholder to reimburse or pay the fund for any expense that the shareholder requires the fund to incur, including answering telephone inquiries or correspondence from the shareholder?

e. Suppose an investor demands redemption on day 1 and receives payment on day 7. Suppose the value of the shares in the fund rose between day 1 and day 7. The redemption price would be the one on day 1? The different price would work for the benefit of the investors who did not redeem their shares. Now suppose the value of the funds' shares fell. Would the redeeming investor receive the price of the shares on the day the investor demanded redemption? Suppose the shareholder who demanded redemption did not receive the value of his shares on day 7, because the company simply did not pay him on time, but delayed payment until 40 days after the date of the demand. What should the redeeming investor receive? The lower value on day 7, after the demand? The higher value on the day on which he received payment?

---

Consider the following comments in a letter by Fidelity Investments to the SEC[2] on the proposed 2% mandatory redemption fee rule:

1. OTC-100 Fund, Inc., Investment Company Act Rel. No. 16846 (Mar. 3, 1989) (application); OTC-100 Fund, Inc., Investment Company Act Rel. No. 16866 (Mar. 15, 1989) (order).

2. Comments of David B. Jones, Senior Vice President, Fidelity Management & Research Co. & Eric D. Roiter, Senior Vice President and General Counsel, Fidelity Management & Research Co. 8-9 (Jun. 4, 2004), *available at* http://www.sec.gov/rules/proposed/s71104/fidelity060404.pdf (footnote omitted).

[A] rule imposing a uniform fee on all redemptions is an overly broad measure that conflicts with the 1940 Act as the Commission and its staff have long construed that statute. The analysis of the statutory limits placed on redemption fees is set forth in the no-action letter issued to Fidelity by the staff of the Division of Investment Management in 2001. . . . We quote from the . . . no-action letter. . . .

During the legislative hearings on the [1940] Act, the Commission characterized the right of mutual fund shareholders to receive the net asset value of their shares upon redemption as 'the most important single attribute which induces purchases of the securities of open-end companies.' The Commission further stated that 'the importance of the redemption feature of open-end securities appears to the Commission beyond question.'

Congress incorporated the Commission's views into the Act by requiring that the securities of an open-end investment company be 'redeemable,' which in turn requires that fund shareholders receive approximately their proportionate share of the issuer's current net assets, or its equivalent in cash, upon redemption. The effect of these requirements, as the Commission has recognized, is that:

The imposition of any charge or fee upon the redemption of fund shares raises serious questions.... A fee payable upon redemption may take the securities issued by the fund outside the definition of a 'redeemable security.'

Because the imposition of a redemption fee by an open-end fund raises serious questions about the redeemability of the fund's shares, the Commission has adopted rules that permit funds to impose only limited redemption fees, and the staff has taken no-action positions consistent with those rules. The Commission and staff positions recognize certain principles, including that . . . .

A redemption fee may recoup or offset only limited types of administrative expenses caused by shareholder redemptions, i.e., the following expenses that are 'directly related to' processing shareholder redemption requests: (a) brokerage expenses incurred in connection with the liquidation of portfolio securities necessitated by the redemption; (b) processing or other transaction costs incident to the redemption and not covered by any administrative fee; (c) odd-lot premiums; (d) transfer taxes; (e) administration fees; (f) custodian fees; and (g) registrar and transfer-agent fees (collectively, 'Administrative Costs').

A fund may not impose a redemption fee greater than the lesser of: (a) an amount approximating, or 'reasonably related to,' the anticipated, specific Administrative Costs identified above; or (b) 2% of the net asset value of the redeemed shares, even if the fund's approximate, anticipated Administrative Costs exceed 2%."

In light of the Commission's steadfast interpretation of the 1940 Act's terms governing "redeemable securities," it is difficult to articulate the legal basis that would support adoption of a rule that would compel mutual funds not only to impose a redemption fee, but in

> doing so to disregard the administrative expenses caused by shareholder activity and instead subject all redemptions to a 2% fee. Certainly no such legal basis has been set forth to date.

Consider also the following rule amendments that the SEC proposed for comment on September 22, 2015.[1]

> Under the proposed reforms, mutual funds and ETFs would be required to implement liquidity risk management programs and enhance disclosure regarding fund liquidity and redemption practices. The proposal is designed to better ensure investors can redeem their shares and receive their assets in a timely manner.
>
> A fund's liquidity risk management program would be required to contain multiple elements, including: classification of the liquidity of fund portfolio assets based on the amount of time an asset would be able to be converted to cash without a market impact; assessment, periodic review and management of a fund's liquidity risk; establishment of a fund's three-day liquid asset minimum; and board approval and review. In addition, the proposal would codify the 15 percent limit on illiquid assets included in current Commission guidelines.
>
> The proposed reforms also would provide a framework under which mutual funds could elect to use "swing pricing" to effectively pass on the costs stemming from shareholder purchase or redemption activity to the shareholders associated with that activity. The swing pricing proposal would enable mutual funds, subject to board approval and oversight, to reflect in a fund's net asset value (NAV) costs associated with shareholders' trading activity. It is designed to protect existing shareholders from dilution associated with shareholder purchases and redemptions and would be an additional tool to help funds manage liquidity risks.

Do you think that these proposed reforms would benefit shareholders? If you were a shareholder, under what circumstances would you not want to be subject to "swing pricing"? Do you think "swing pricing" is a better alternative to manage costs related to redemption activity than the redemption fees discussed earlier? What impact do you think the proposed "three-day liquid asset minimum" would have on portfolio management and mutual fund returns? Do you believe these reforms have a sound policy basis in view of the 75-year experience the mutual fund industry has with liquidity management under the Investment Company Act?

## B. Issuance of Senior Securities (e.g., Bonds and Preferred Stock): Section 18 of the Investment Company Act

Section 18 prohibits open-end investment companies from issuing more than one class of stock (with one exception). Therefore, such funds may not

1. SEC Proposes Liquidity Management Rules for Mutual Funds and ETFs, SEC Press Rel. 2015-201 (Sept. 22, 2015); *see* Open-End Fund Liquidity Risk Management Programs; Swing Pricing; Re-Opening of Comment Period for Investment Company Reporting Modernization Release, Investment Company Act Rel. No. 31835 (Sept. 22, 2015).

issue senior securities. Open-end funds may, however, borrow from a bank. The following excerpt explains the background of section 18.[1]

> Investment company abuse of leverage was a primary concern that led to enactment of the Investment Company Act. In the Act's preamble, Congress cited excessive leverage as a major abuse that it meant to correct, declaring that the public interest and the interest of investors are adversely affected 'when investment companies by excessive borrowing and the issuance of excessive amounts of senior securities increase unduly the speculative character of their junior securities.'
>
> Section 18(f) of the Investment Company Act restricts leveraged capital structures, generally prohibiting [open-end funds] from issuing any class of "senior security." Funds may, however, borrow from banks if they maintain 300% asset coverage for all such borrowings. Section 12(a) authorizes the Commission to regulate two trading practices that may result in leverage, margin purchases and short sales.
>
> One reason for limiting investment company leverage was to prevent [the public distribution] of senior securities, which were sold as low risk investments. Investment company assets during the 1920s and 1930s consisted mostly of common stocks that did not provide the stable asset values or steady income stream necessary to support senior charges. Because the sponsors often kept all or most of the junior, voting securities for themselves, they could operate the company in their own interests. Senior securities tended to lead to speculative investment policies to the detriment of senior securityholders because the common stockholder/sponsors, who often had a relatively small investment at risk in the fund, looked to capital gains for profit. Multiple classes of senior securities and pyramiding frustrated senior securityholders' attempts to determine whether secure returns were likely.
>
> Another reason for limiting investment company leverage was to protect public common stockholders by limiting the volatility of their investments. . . . [T]he leverage of the senior-junior capital structure magnified losses suffered by common stockholders. . . . The provisions authorizing the Commission to regulate margin purchases and short sales implicate similar concerns. . . .

Section 18 has been applied to the following three situations each discussed below: 1) a fund's use of borrowed money; 2) structural issues involving different versions of the same fund; and 3) derivative investments.[2]

---

1. Mutual Funds and Derivative Instruments, Memorandum from the Division of Investment Management, U.S. Securities and Exchange Commission to Chairman Levitt (Sept. 26, 1994).
2. Richard H. Farina, John P. Freeman & James Webster, *Mutual Fund Industry: A Legal Survey,* 44 Notre Dame Law. Rev. 732, 746-748, 776-784, 803 (1969).

## 1. Use of Borrowed Money Leverage

A closed-end investment company may use senior capital (bonds, debentures, preferred stock, or bank loans) to create "leverage," which magnifies changes in the net asset value of the company's common stock. During a market upswing this works to the advantage of its common shareholders; but during a market decline it magnifies common shareholders' losses. As reflected above, open-end investment companies may only leverage by borrowing from a bank.

For example, assume that an investment company purchases $1,000,000 in portfolio securities by issuing 25,000 shares of stock with a $10 par value (total $250,000) and $750,000 in bonds. The portfolio securities increase in value by $3,000,000 to $4,000,000. The increase would be $120 per share ($3,000,000/25,000). Assume instead that the company had purchased the securities by issuing 100,000 shares of $10 par stock (total $1,000,000). The increase would be only $30/share ($3,000,000/25,000). Therefore, the more leveraged company achieves a higher increase in its value per share because it achieved he same increase in the value of its portfolio securities by issuing fewer shares.

### a. History of Leveraged Closed-End Funds

Leverage has been most commonly used by closed-end funds. In 1929, leveraged closed-end funds outnumbered open-end funds. However, as investors discovered, in a falling market leverage will magnify the decline in the company's net asset value, as the decline will be divided among fewer shares, and in a leveraged firm a smaller decline is required to eliminate the shareholders' equity value. Consequently, by 1932, the shares of most leveraged closed-end companies were "under water," and by 1966, there were only a few such companies.

At the same time as leverage was becoming popular, sponsors (e.g., underwriters, brokers, security distributors, investment counsel) created new investment companies. For example, brokers saw them as an added source of brokerage fees. Control over the companies was achieved through, e.g., stock with unequal voting rights; elimination of stockholder preemptive rights by charter; voting trusts; or long term management contracts with a management company operated by the sponsor.

U.S. & Foreign Securities Corporation (U.S. & Foreign) was a closed-end company established in 1924 by investment banker Dillon, Read & Co. (Dillon, Read). It achieved leverage and control with only a 16% capital contribution through the issuance of three classes of securities: (1) $25 million of no-par first preferred; (2) $5 million of no-par second preferred; and (3) one million shares of no-par common stock. The first preferred was sold to the public, who also received 250,000 shares of common stock as a "bonus." The second preferred, carrying with it the right to 750,000 shares of common, was sold to Dillon, Read. Therefore, Dillon, Read had 75% control with a relatively small investment.

Similarly, in 1928 Dillon, Read and U.S. & Foreign jointly organized a second investment company, U.S. & International Securities Corporation (U.S. & International), as a subsidiary of U.S. & Foreign. The public purchased a total of $50 million in first preferred, accompanied by 500,000 shares of voting common plus warrants for an additional 500,000 shares of common, exercisable at $25 per share. The entire $10 million issue of second preferred was sold to U.S. & Foreign, who also received 2,000,000 shares of voting common stock and outright control. As a result of the formation of U.S. & Foreign, and the "pyramiding" of it on U.S. & International, Dillon, Read achieved control over two companies in which the public had invested $75 million with its $5 million capital contribution.

Meanwhile, in 1924 Massachusetts Investors Trust (MIT), an open-end company, was organized as a Massachusetts trust. The sponsors maintained control through a self-perpetuating board of trustees that was given absolute power to invest the company's funds.

From 1924 to 1927, a number of investment companies were organized similarly to U.S. & Foreign or MIT, and most were sponsored by investment houses or brokerage firms.

During this period of 1927 to October 24, 1929, the number of investment companies and investment company investors greatly increased. This increase was partly due to increased awareness of the profits available through investment company sponsorship, and the availability of control with little investment. During this period, investors had little protection against managerial overreaching, and state laws were not effective.

### b. Effects of the 1929 Crash on Investment Companies

Dishonest investment company management cost investors $1.1 billion. Leveraged closed-end companies, which represented most companies and most assets managed in 1929, bore the brunt of the crash.

Non-leveraged companies took losses, but still outperformed the market. They did this primarily by repurchasing their shares from shareholders at discounts below net asset value, which improved the net asset value of the remaining shares. Such repurchases not only enabled the companies to make "paper profits," but also permitted them to peg the market price of the securities at what company management considered a proper value. However, most such transactions were undisclosed repurchases from the general public; the shareholders were not aware they were selling to the investment company, or that they were selling at discounts or that they were losing the amount of the discount.

Open-end funds did about as well as the market during the period. Congress was less motivated by the general drop in stock prices as by the $1.1 billion loss from dishonest management.

### c. General Response in Section 18 of the 1940 Act

Section 18 of the 1940 Act allows closed-end companies to obtain leverage by borrowing from a bank or by issuing debt securities and/or preferred shares subject to asset coverage requirements. These features are discussed in more detail in our discussion on closed-end funds.

Section 18 of the 1940 Act more severely restricts the use of leverage by open-end companies, presumably because of the possibility that a highly leveraged fund may face a large amount of redemptions; open-end companies may not issue senior securities and may borrow from a bank only subject to asset coverage restrictions.

## 2. Structural Issues Involving Different Versions of the Same Fund

The Commission began to consider relaxing the limitations of section 18 while addressing the underlying concerns for the prohibitions. One area in which the limitations of section 18 have been relaxed is with respect to open-end funds operating a multiple class structure. Open-end funds often seek to offer multiple classes of shares in order to offer different types of investors different options for paying for the costs of distribution. For example, one class of shares might have a distribution fee and shareholder servicing fee paid out of the fund's assets, whereas another class might have no such fees but charge an upfront sales load. The Commission granted an exemption for multi-class structures when the structures did not pose the concerns underlying the prohibition in section 18. The following release deals with the interpretation of section 18 and the consequences of holding that multi-class share structures created by open-end funds are not senior securities (note that closed-end funds are not covered by the exemption, though the SEC often grants individual exemptive orders to closed-end funds to issue multiple classes of shares).[1]

> Since 1985, the Commission has issued approximately 200 exemptive orders allowing funds to issue multiple classes of shares representing interests in the same portfolio, typically with different distribution arrangements. The orders frequently impose as many as 20 conditions designed to address various investor protection concerns.
>
> The Commission is adopting rule 18f-3 under the Investment Company Act, which will permit funds to issue multiple classes of shares . . . .
>
> Over the past few years, many fund sponsors have adopted another distribution arrangement designed to achieve many of the same business goals as the multiple class structure without the need to obtain exemptions under section 18. This 'master-feeder' arrangement comprises a two-tier structure in which one or more funds (the upper tier) invest solely in the securities of another fund (the lower tier).[2*] Although master-feeder structures are functionally similar to multiple class funds, they are viewed as not needing exemptions and have been subject to different disclosure requirements.
>
> The disclosure requirements . . . apply equally to multiple class and master-feeder funds. . . . A prospectus for a (multi) class or feeder fund will be required to include disclosure about other publicly offered classes or feeder funds not offered through the prospectus and a telephone number an investor may call to receive additional

1. Exemption for Open-End Management Investment Companies Issuing Multiple Classes of Shares; Disclosure by Multiple Class and Master-Feeder Funds; Class Voting on Distribution Plans, Investment Company Act Rel. No. 20915 (Feb. 23, 1995) (codified as amended at 17 C.F.R. § 270.18f-3 (2015)).

2*. Master-feeder funds are often referred to as "core and feeder" or "hub and spoke" funds. Signature Financial Group is the originator and patent licensor of the Hub and Spoke (registered) form of the master-feeder structure.

> information about other classes or feeder funds sold by the same bank, broker, or other financial intermediary. . . .
>
> Both the multiple class and master-feeder structures may benefit shareholders and fund sponsors. These structures may increase investor choice, result in efficiencies in the distribution of fund shares, and allow fund sponsors to tailor products more closely to different investor markets. Fund sponsors assert that multiple classes may enable funds to attract larger asset bases, permitting them to spread fixed costs over more shares, qualify for discounts in advisory fees ("breakpoints"), and otherwise experience economies of scale, resulting in lower fees and expenses. They also state that multiple classes avoid the need to create "clone" funds, which require duplicative portfolio and fund management expenses. Furthermore, fund sponsors state that a larger asset base permits greater portfolio liquidity and diversification.
>
> Master-feeder funds may achieve similar benefits of economies of scale, thus potentially lowering expenses, and also allow several different small funds access to the same management and compliance personnel. The master-feeder structure allows a fund sponsor to offer feeder funds that invest in specialized portfolios, even though the sponsor's expected asset base may not justify organizing a stand-alone fund for that market or market segment. Sponsors also use this structure to offer off-shore and other unregistered feeder funds.
>
> Investor understanding of sales and service charges in both arrangements, however, has been a subject of concern to the Commission. Some commentators have asserted that the complexity generated by these arrangements may confuse many investors, who often may not understand them or the effect that fees have upon performance. . . .

Rule 18f-3 allows an open-end fund (or class or series thereof) to issue multiple classes of voting stock, provided that certain conditions are met. Classes must differ in their arrangement for shareholder services and/or distribution of securities, and must pay the expenses of that arrangement.

Certain expenses must be allocated by class. Rule 18f-3 provides methods for allocation of income, realized gains and losses, unrealized appreciation and depreciation, and fundwide expenses. Expenses may be waived or reimbursed by the adviser, underwriter, or any other service provider.

Each class must have exclusive voting rights on any matter that relates solely to its arrangement, and separate voting rights on any matter in which the interests of one class differ from any other class. Otherwise classes must have the same rights and obligations.

Funds may offer a class with an exchange privilege for securities of another company, or a conversion feature for shares of another class, provided that conversion is based on net asset values and expenses for the target class are not higher. Funds may also allow conversions under certain circumstances when an investor is no longer eligible to own shares of a class.

Additionally, multi-class funds must have a written multi-class plan (often referred to as an "18f-3 plan") that sets forth the applicable payment arrangements related to each class and the expense allocation for each class. A majority of directors, including a majority of disinterested directors, must find that the multi-class plan "is in the best interests of each class individually and the company as a whole."

Multi-class funds must also meet disclosure requirements.

---

## Discussion Topics

a. Compare a master-feeder structure with multi-class structure. How do they differ? Why did some funds adopt one and not the other?

b. Under rule 18f-3, the board of directors must consider the plan for multi-class structure and, before approving, should determine that the "plan is in the best interests of each class individually and the fund as a whole." What does "best interests of each class" mean? How different, if at all, is it from the standard of "fair to each class?"

c. What is disclosure designed to achieve in this case? How effective would it be?

---

## 3. Leveraged Investments and Derivatives

### a. Derivatives

Derivatives ("synthetic" instruments) have appeared with the availability of fast computing technology. Instruments derived from the securitization process may be deemed derivatives. Derivatives may also represent a contract among two or more parties to pay each other amounts dependent on some independent events or measures. For example, while the U.S. government issues treasury bonds at a particular maturity date and return, one party may agree that it will pay another party the difference between the return on such government bonds, if the interest rate rises (and the value of such bonds falls), while the other party will undertake to pay the difference if the market rate falls (and the value of the bonds rises). Similar undertakings can also be linked to indexes or different market rates. These undertakings are of course made at a price.

Such derivatives provide protection for those who wish to shield their holdings from market changes, provided, of course that the institutions which provide the protection have the assets to cover their obligations. Thus, the holder of government bonds may wish to protect the value of its bonds against interest rate fluctuations by payment of a fixed amount or by foregoing the rising price of the bonds. Some derivatives can magnify losses, depending on the formula that they use.

The SEC views certain trading practices used by investment companies, including derivatives, as having embedded economic leverage and thus raising "senior security concerns." The SEC first articulated this position in a release in 1979 in which it focused on reverse repurchase agreements, firm commitment agreements and standby commitment agreements.[1] This position has expanded dramatically over the years and has been the subject of numerous no-action letters and, most recently, a concept release seeking comment on a wide variety of issues involving derivatives.[2] The guiding principles from the SEC's 1979 release are as follows:[3]

> The Commission believes that reverse repurchase agreements, firm commitment agreements, and standby commitment agreements fall within the functional meaning of the term "evidence of indebtedness" for purposes of Section 18 of the Act. Generally, included within it would be all contractual obligations to pay in the future for consideration presently received; the term would not be limited to notes or other acknowledges of debt. The Commission's views are based not so much on the conclusion that reverse repurchase agreements and firm commitment agreements, considered in isolation, are inherently securities for all purposes, but more upon the proposition that trading practices involving the use by investment companies of such agreements for speculative purposes or to accomplish leveraging fall within the legislative purposes of Section 18.
>
> The Commission has reviewed the legislative history and the Congressional intent underlying the Act. In light of the concerns discussed therein, the Commission believes that its construction of "evidence of indebtedness" in Section 2(a)(36) of the Act, for purposes of Section 18 of the Act, is reasonable because the fundamental economic nature of reverse repurchase, firm commitment, and standby commitment agreements is such that each poses a risk of loss to an investment company analogous to the danger caused by leverage, which is discussed throughout the legislative history of the Act.
>
> * * *
>
> In circumstances involving similar economic effects, such as short sales of securities by investment companies, the Division of Investment Management has determined that the issue of compliance with Section 18 will not be raised with the Commission by the Division if the investment company "covers" the senior security by establishing and maintaining certain "segregated accounts." The Commission agrees that segregated accounts, if properly created and maintained, would limit the investment company's risk of loss. . . .
>
> A segregated account freezes certain assets of the investment company and renders such assets unavailable for sale or other disposition. If an investment company continues to engage in the

1. Securities Trading Practices of Registered Investment Companies, Investment Company Act Rel. No. 10666 (Apr. 18, 1979) ("Release 10666").
2. *See* Registered Investment Company Use of Senior Securities — Select Bibliography, Staff of the SEC Division of Investment Management (last modified May 11, 2015), *available at* https://www.sec.gov/divisions/investment/seniorsecurities-bibliography.htm#P3_2015.
3. Release 10666 (footnotes omitted).

> described securities trading practices and properly segregates assets, the segregated account will function as a practical limit on the amount of leverage which the investment company may undertake and on the potential increase in the speculative character of its outstanding common stock. Additionally, such accounts will assure the availability of adequate funds to meet the obligations arising from such activities.

The following materials represent the concerns of congressional leaders and the response of the Commission to these concerns.

**b. The Study of Derivatives**

In 1994, the SEC Division of Investment Management issued a memorandum responding to Congressional concerns about investment companies' use of derivatives. The staff recommended that the Commission "should consider requiring some form of quantitative risk measure in mutual fund prospectuses and should seek public comment on this topic no later than early 1995 . . . consider reducing the ceiling on fund illiquid holdings . . . continue to evaluate liquidity and pricing issues raised by derivatives through the mutual fund inspection process [and] . . . consider issuing rules to address matters such as proper procedures for mutual fund pricing and liquidity determinations." The staff recommended a reexamination of "the leverage restrictions of the Investment Company Act of 1940 . . . to derivative instruments and should seek public comment on whether regulatory and legislative solutions are necessary to address the leverage created by mutual fund use of derivatives. [And the Commission should] recommend that congressional enhancement of the Commission's ability to obtain information required to monitor fund use of derivatives."

In March 2010, the SEC staff announced that it was conducting a review concerning derivative use by investment companies. It stated that it would review issues related to mutual funds' derivative use, including (1) consistency of market practices with the 1940 Act's "leverage, concentration and diversification" provisions, (2) adequacy of risk management procedures, (3) appropriateness of board oversight, (4) adequacy of rules for pricing and liquidity determinations, (5) adequacy of prospectus disclosure, and (6) possible reporting requirements for derivative activities.

Later in 2010, an ABA task force issued a report on investment company use of derivatives and leverage, partly to assist the SEC and its staff. The task force noted concerns regarding derivatives and made several recommendations, including: (1) a principles-based approach to the regulation of derivatives; (2) measurement of diversification through use of reference assets; (3) regulation of counter-party risk; (4) limitations on leverage; (5) determining whether a fund invests in assets consistently with its name through use of reference assets; (6) enhanced disclosure of how derivatives affect investment results; and (7) board oversight regarding derivatives rather than micromanagement.

In 2011, the SEC built on the ABA task force report and issued a concept release seeking feedback on a wide variety of issues related to investment companies' use of derivatives.[1] The release sought comment on fund use of derivatives, and the application of the 1940 Act's provisions regarding leverage, diversification, concentration, exposure to certain securities-related issuers, valuation, and related matters. As of October 2015 the SEC has not released revised or updated guidance on investment companies' derivatives use. However, the SEC has recently proposed additional periodic reporting requirements for investment companies relating to their use of derivatives,[2] and the SEC staff has continued to express its views on various derivatives related disclosure and compliance issues though the registration statement comment process.

### c. Derivative Investments by Investment Companies

As described above, certain trading practices raise issues under section 18 of the 1940 Act, which generally prohibits or limits the issuance of a "senior security" depending on the type of the investment company. Certain portfolio trading practices, including some involving derivative securities (such as swaps, futures, forwards and options), create leverage and could be deemed to create senior securities. This is particularly problematic for open-end funds seeking to use these trading strategies, since section 18(f) generally prohibits open-end funds from issuing senior securities except for bank debt.

However, the SEC and its staff have allowed companies to overcome the prohibition by "covering" the obligations resulting from the use of these trading practices by placing liquid assets in a segregated account, or earmarking such assets on the fund's books and records, to limit leverage and avoid creating a senior security.[3] Similarly, holding an economically offsetting position is considered sufficient "cover" for a leveraged portfolio transaction, such as a derivative. For example, if a fund writes (sells) a call option, but holds the security underlying the call in its portfolio, the written option is "covered" by the offsetting portfolio position and no segregated account is necessary.

The SEC staff addressed the question of what assets qualify for a segregated account or for earmarking on the fund's books and records.[4]

> The purposes behind the segregated account requirement are twofold. First, requiring the maintenance of a segregated account places a practical limit on the amount of leverage that a fund may undertake and on the potential increase in the speculative character of its outstanding shares. Second, the accounts assure the availability of adequate funds to meet the obligations arising from the transactions in which leverage is created.
>
> Regarding the first purpose set forth above, the type of asset placed in the segregated account would have no effect on the maximum

1. Use of Derivatives by Investment Companies Under the Investment Company Act of 1940, Investment Company Act Rel. No. 29776 (Aug. 31, 2011).
2. Investment Company Reporting Modernization, Investment Company Act Rel. No. 31610 (May 20, 2015).
3. *See* Release 10666.
4. Merrill Lynch Asset Mgmt., L.P., SEC No-Action Letter (Jul. 2, 1996).

> amount of leverage that a fund can assume. Similarly, the second purpose of the segregated account — the assurance of the availability of adequate funds — will be satisfied so long as only liquid assets are maintained in the segregated account, and the value of those assets is marked to the market daily.
>
> We believe that it would be consistent with the language and policy of Section 18(f) and Release 10666 to permit a Fund to place any asset, including equity securities and non-investment grade debt, in a segregated account, so long as the asset is liquid and marked to the market daily.

Additionally, as mentioned in the earlier Chapter on fund disclosure, the SEC staff has been active in providing guidance about the scope and content of funds' disclosures in prospectuses and shareholder reports regarding the use of derivatives.

### d. Dealing Effectively with Derivatives

The following is an excerpt of a statement by Andrew J. Donohue, the former Director of the Investment Management Division of the SEC, before the American Bar Association Spring Meeting in Vancouver, Canada on April 17, 2009.[1]

He observed that since 1994 "investment companies . . . have increased their investment in derivatives" and offer more investment opportunities. Derivative investments must comply with the 1940 Act's constraints, such as the requirements of Section 35(d), i.e., disclosure concerning the funds' names, compliance with the funds' investment objectives and policies stated in the registration statement, compliance with the purposes of Section 18 regarding trading practices involving derivatives and leverage, i.e., coverage of the fund's position with segregated assets or an offsetting hedge, and stringent diversification and liquidity standards.

[The speaker's concerns are:]

> Funds should have a means to deal effectively with derivatives outside of disclosure; a fund's approach to leverage should address both implicit and explicit leverage; and a fund should address diversification from investment exposures taken on versus the amount of money invested. . . .
>
> [S]hould the application of '40 Act leverage restrictions to derivatives held by investment companies be re-examined? Is the thirty year patchwork of stated Commission policy and staff positions regarding investment companies' use of derivatives sufficient or is regulatory and/or legislative action necessary to address the leverage created by investment companies' use of derivatives? If you believe action is necessary, what do you recommend? Do existing rules sufficiently address matters such as the proper procedure for investment company pricing and liquidity determinations of derivatives holdings? Are investment company boards exercising meaningful

1. http://www.sec.gov/news/speech/2009/spch041709ajd.htm.

oversight of funds' use of derivatives, including risk management, proper accounting and internal controls?

---

**Discussion Topics**

a. Are futures and options securities covered by the 1940 Act? If so, are they "senior securities" under section 18 of the Act? What would have been the consequences if these instruments were deemed not to be securities?

b. Is the SEC correct in reading section 18 of the 1940 Act to limit an investment company's ability to sell puts and calls?

c. How does the SEC distinguish between the sale of a call and the purchase of a call?

d. Should the SEC regulate to limit the use of derivatives, especially by investment companies that represent themselves to be conservative?

e. Should the SEC be concerned about market losses to mutual fund investors? Does its mandate cover such concerns? Are there other mechanisms that the SEC can use to meet its legitimate concerns? Note the recent debate on whether risk disclosure can be improved by using quantifiable and standardized risk measures in a graphic form rather than by words. Since risk measures differ and some are very complex, how would you communicate these measures to investors?

f. In July 1996, Fidelity, the largest fund complex, announced its intention to establish an insurance company for the purpose of insuring certain market losses caused by certain types of instruments. The insurance company would be owned by funds that Fidelity advises. Critics argued that the insurance is merely an advertising ploy, that the insurance would offer a competitive advantage to Fidelity against its smaller competitors, or that the insurance would relieve the adviser from pressure to shore up money market funds that "broke the dollar." Other fund complexes and an insurance company followed Fidelity with announcements that they will offer similar insurance coverage.

---

**Problem**

Assume you are in-house counsel at a mutual fund. Your fund is what is commonly known as a "liquid alt" fund — in other words, it uses hedge fund-like strategies in a registered fund format. Part of the strategy of your fund involves significant use of derivatives — in particular credit default swaps. In a credit default swap, the "protection buyer" pays the "protection seller" a stream of payments, and the "protection seller" commits to pay to the "protection buyer" the principal amount of a debt obligation if the debtor defaults. The fund is both a protection buyer and a protection seller of credit default swaps. The CEO of the mutual fund wants a refresher on the legal issues associated with how to address the leverage inherent in this derivative. Write a memo to your CEO addressing the following topics:

1. If the fund is a protection buyer, what should its segregation or coverage obligation be?
2. If the fund is a protection seller, what should its segregation or coverage obligation be?

# Chapter 10

## *The Investment Company as Investor*

### A. Introduction

This Chapter deals with three issues involving investment companies. First, what are the securities in which investment companies may invest? With a few exceptions in section 12, the 1940 Act does not regulate an investment company's investments. It requires disclosure of the investment policies that the investment company will follow and limits changes to these investment policies. Section 12, however, limits investments in broker-dealers, underwriters, investment advisers, insurance companies, and other investment companies. Numerous exemptions by the Commission have relaxed these restrictions. The second issue covered by this Chapter deals with the regulation of investment companies as investors in their own portfolios. The third issue focuses on investment companies' role in the boardroom of their portfolio companies and their voting of their portfolio companies' shares.

The last part of this Chapter covers two investing-related topics: the first topic involves issues concerning the safekeeping of investments; the second topic relates to Regulation FD, which imposes limits on portfolio managers and other securities professionals with respect to non-public information. Please note that later, in Chapter 12 of this Book, we deal with conflicts of interest by investment company personnel and with internal controls that advisers must impose on their organizations.

### B. Restrictions on Investments of Investment Companies: Section 12

### 1. Investments in Broker-Dealers, Underwriters, and Advisers

### a. Section 12(d)(3)

Section 12(d)(3) of the 1940 Act prohibits investment companies and companies that are controlled by investment companies from purchasing or acquiring any securities issued by or any other interest in the business of any broker, dealer or a person engaged in underwriting, or in an investment adviser. The prohibitions in section 12(d)(3) apply to investments in broker-dealers, underwriters and investment advisers regardless of whether they are affiliated with the investment company.

Why did Congress select these particular businesses for prohibition? After all, there are numerous other risky investments on which the 1940 Act puts no limit. Further, the prohibition on acquisition of an investment adviser's shares may seem surprising given that this business is not necessarily risky.

Legislative history suggests two reasons for this prohibition. First, the prohibition was intended to protect investment companies from specific risky financial investments. Broker-dealers and underwriting businesses were considered risky, mainly because historically they were organized as partnerships. Investments in these partnerships would subject investment companies to unlimited liabilities, as partners. In addition, such partnership interests would likely be illiquid.

Second, the prohibition was intended to restrict reciprocal practices between investment companies and members of the securities industry. These practices would result in the use of investment companies' assets to finance members of the securities industry and the use of investment companies' portfolio transactions and sale of investment companies' shares to benefit members of the securities industry. Arguably, the restrictions in section 12(d)(3) reflected memories of the substantial losses that investment companies sustained in the past, presumably the result of their support of underwriters and broker-dealers that created investment companies to finance their own operations. As you read the materials, consider whether the limitations in section 12(d)(3) are justified today.

The Commission has granted a number of exemptions by orders and by rules, based on a number of reasons. First, the Commission has emphasized the new environment. Many operating companies, such as General Electric, Sears, Roebuck, and General Motors have owned and controlled financial intermediaries such as broker-dealers. American Express owns a very large adviser, IDS, that operates investment companies. A prohibition would harm investment companies by preventing them from investing in these companies. In addition, most securities-related businesses are now organized as corporations and not as general partnerships.

In rule 12d3-1,[1] the Commission distinguishes between investments in issuers that derive more than 15% of their income from securities business and issuers that derive 15% or less of their income from securities business. While rule 12d3-1 imposes no limitation on investments in an issuer that derives 15% or less of its income from securities business (provided that the investment company does not control the issuer after the acquisition), it limits the acquisition of issuers that derive more than 15% of their income from securities business. After the acquisition of securities of an issuer that derives more than 15% of its income from securities business, the investment company may not: (1) own more than five percent of the issuer's equity securities (if acquiring equity securities); (2) own more than ten percent of the issuer's debt securities (if acquiring debt securities); and (3) invest more than five percent of its total assets in the issuer. Importantly, whereas section 12(d)(3) prohibits investment companies and companies that are controlled by investment companies from purchasing or acquiring any securities issued by "or any other interest in" a securities related-issuer, rule 12d3-1 exempts only acquisitions of "securities" of a securities-related issuer.

1. 17 C.F.R. § 270.12d3-1 (2015).

In addition, rule 12d3-1 does not exempt the acquisition of: (1) a general partnership interest; (2) a security issued by the investment company's promoter, principal underwriter, or any affiliated person of such promoter or principal underwriter; or (3) a security issued by the investment company's investment adviser, or an affiliated person of the adviser (other than a security issued by a subadviser or an affiliated person of a subadviser of the investment company, provided that (i) the subadviser or affiliate is not in certain prohibited relationships with the investment company and (ii) the advisory contracts of the subadviser and any subadviser advising the portion of the investment company purchasing the securities include certain restrictions).

Section 12(d)(3) seems to prohibit investment companies from investing in repurchase agreements (agreements whereby the fund purchases securities from a counter-party subject to an agreement by the counter-party to repurchase those securities in the future at an agreed upon price — conceptualize it as a loan collateralized by the underlying securities), because many such agreements are offered by brokers and could be viewed as an "interest in" the broker and thus prohibited by section 12(d)(3) and not subject to exemption by rule 12d3-1. The SEC, however, in effect permits investment companies to "look through" repurchase agreements to the underlying securities for purposes of compliance with section 12(d)(3) provided certain requirements with respect to collateralization are met[1], and has made rule 12d3-1 available even if these "look through" requirements are not met.[2]

The SEC has recently focused on a host of issues involving investment companies' use of derivatives. One issue that arises is how to treat derivative transactions for purposes of section 12(d)(3) and rule 12d3-1. The SEC observed the following in a 2011 concept release seeking comment on a variety of derivatives-related issues:[3]

> When a fund invests in an OTC [over-the-counter] derivative, the fund receives the obligation of its counter-party to perform under the contract. If the counter-party is a securities-related issuer, a fund's acquisition of that obligation may constitute an acquisition of a security or another interest in a securities-related issuer within the scope of section 12(d)(3) of the Investment Company Act. As noted above, in the case of exchange-traded derivatives that are cleared, the issuer of the derivative typically is the clearinghouse. In a no-action letter, the staff did not object to the assertion that, in acquiring an exchange-traded option, a fund generally would not appear to be acquiring securities issued by, or an interest in, a securities-related issuer. In the case of OTC derivatives, if a fund's counter-party is a securities-related issuer, the fund's transaction with

1. 17 C.F.R. § 270.5b-3 (2015).
2. Treatment of Repurchase Agreements and Refunded Securities as an Acquisition of the Underlying Securities, Investment Company Act Rel. No. 25058 (Jul. 5, 2001).
3. Use of Derivatives by Investment Companies Under the Investment Company Act of 1940, Investment Company Act Rel. No. 29776 (Aug. 31, 2011) (footnotes omitted).

the counter-party may represent the acquisition of a security issued by, or an interest in, that issuer.

If an OTC derivative with a securities-related issuer as the counter-party is a security issued by that counter-party, then the fund may be able to rely on rule 12d3-1 to engage in the transaction. If such a derivative is not a security issued by the counter-party, but the transaction may be deemed to be the fund's acquisition of "an interest in" a securities-related issuer (the counter-party), then rule 12d3-1 would not be available because it exempts only acquisitions of securities, and the transaction would be prohibited under the Investment Company Act. There is no bright-line test distinguishing transactions that may or may not constitute a fund's acquisition of an "interest in" a securities-related issuer. . . .

The issue of whether an OTC derivative transaction is prohibited under the Investment Company Act as an impermissible acquisition of a security issued by, or an interest in, a securities-related issuer, also may require analysis of a fund's exposure to a reference asset underlying the derivative. If the derivative transaction is based upon the price or value of securities issued by, or interests in, a securities-related issuer, the fund's relationship to the issuer of the reference asset may raise both of the concerns underlying section 12(d)(3) — the fund's exposure to the risks of that securities-related issuer and the potential for reciprocal practices.

---

## Discussion Topics

a. Could the policy of Section 12(d)(3) have been effectuated by simply prohibiting an investment company from investing in shares of a broker-dealer which effects trades for the investment company?

b. Are there other types of reciprocal practices besides brokerage about which the Investment Company Act should be concerned? For example, what potential conflicts exist when a fund complex serves as a funding vehicle for a company's 401K plan?

c. Does section 12(d)(3) allow investment companies to buy put options from broker-dealers ? If not, why not?

---

### b. The Commission Staff's Approach

The following no-action letter demonstrates the Commission staff's approach to the prohibition of section 12(d)(3).[1] This no-action letter was requested by Calvert Social Index Fund ("Fund") regarding the Fund's proposed investment in securities issued by Comerica Inc. ("Parent"). Parent was an affiliated person of World Asset Management L.L.C., which was the Fund's investment subadviser ("Subadviser").

1. Calvert Social Index Fund, SEC No-Action Letter (Sept. 4, 2001).

The Fund is an index fund whose investment objective is to match the performance of an Index created by the Calvert Entities, subsidiaries of Calvert, the parent of the investment adviser. Subadviser's decisions are "nonvolitional" in that it must invest in securities in the Index in approximately the same proportion as the Index. Parent is included in the Index and the Fund does not currently invest in Parent because of the restrictions of section 12(d)(3). Fund also cannot rely on rule 12d3-1 because Parent is an affiliate of Subadviser.

The SEC noted a previous no-action letter regarding section 12(d)(3):

> On several occasions, we have agreed not to recommend enforcement action to the Commission under Section 12(d)(3) against index funds that sought to purchase securities issued by certain affiliated persons of the funds' investment advisers or principal underwriters that were directly or indirectly engaged in a securities-related business. In Victory, our position was based on the facts and representations that:
>
> (i) the fund's investment objective was to match the investment performance of an unaffiliated, broad-based index;
>
> (ii) the fund would purchase securities issued by an affiliated person of the fund's investment adviser and maintain its position in such securities only in the approximate percentage that the affiliated person was represented in the index; and
>
> (iii) any purchase of securities issued by the affiliated person would be in compliance with Rule 12d3-1(a) and (b).
>
> We explained in Victory that the non-volitional nature of the index fund's purchases reduced the likelihood that the selection of the fund's portfolio securities would be made in the interest of the fund's investment adviser or principal underwriter, rather than in the interest of the fund's shareholders.
>
> We also stated in Victory that we would no longer respond to requests for no-action relief in this area unless they present novel or unusual issues. Your letter, however, presents a novel issue because, unlike Victory, the Fund's investment objective is to match the investment performance of an affiliated Index. The Fund and the Index may be "affiliates" of each other because they may be under the common control of Calvert.

The staff granted no-action relief, noting the applicant's representations:

> (i) the Fund's investment objective is to match the investment performance of the Index;
>
> (ii) the Fund will purchase securities issued by the Parent and maintain its position in such securities only in the approximate percentage that the Parent is represented in the Index, subject to the limitations: (x) set forth in Rule 12d3-1(a) and (b); and (y) that during any period that the Fund is investing in a representative sample of the Index, the Fund will not make any additional Investment in securities issued by the Parent;

(iii) neither the Subadviser nor any of its affiliates are, will be, or have ever been involved in the creation or maintenance of the Index nor have they ever influenced the composition of the Index;

(iv) the relationship between the Subadviser and the Parent has not been and will not be a factor in determining the composition of the Index;

(v) the Calvert Entities did not create the Index for the purpose of including the Parent in it; and

(vi) none of the Calvert Entities is an affiliated person, or an affiliated person of an affiliated person, of the Subadviser or any of its affiliates and neither the Subadviser nor the Parent is an affiliated person, or an affiliated person of an affiliated person, of the Calvert Entities or any of their affiliates.

---

**Discussion Topics**

a. In a previous no-action letter, the staff noted that it would no longer respond to requests for such letters on this subject. Why in your opinion did the staff make this statement? And why, notwithstanding the statement, did the staff respond to the request of the Fund?

b. How do the conditions of the previous letter compare with the conditions in the Fund's letter reproduced above? What is the difference between the two types of conditions?

---

### 2. Investments in Insurance Companies: Section 12(d)(2)[1]

In 1940, the SEC, and both the securities industry and the insurance industry, agreed that it was undesirable for investment companies to own and control insurance companies. Management may be tempted to convert investments of insurance reserves to investments for profits, and thereby endanger the financial stability of insurance companies. Depending on who is dominant, insurance or investment companies may "dump" worthless securities on each other. . . . Section 12(d)(2) makes it "unlawful for any registered investment company and any company or companies controlled by such registered investment company to purchase or otherwise acquire any security . . . issued by any insurance company . . . if such registered company and any company or companies controlled by it own in the aggregate, or as a result of such purchase or acquisition will own in the aggregate, more than 10 per centum of the total outstanding voting stock of such insurance company.

1. Tamar Frankel & Ann Taylor Schwing, The Regulation of Money Managers, §§ 22-60 to –61 (2001 & Supp. 2015).

### 3. Investments in Other Investment Companies: Section 12(d)(1)

#### a. The Nature and Rationale of Restricting Investments in Other Investment Companies

With certain exceptions, section 12(d)(1) of the 1940 Act restricts investment companies from investing in the securities of other investment companies, some of which were relaxed by Congress in 1996.

The basic rule of section 12(d)(1) is set forth in section 12(d)(1)(A). Generally, a registered investment company cannot own more than 3% of the outstanding voting stock of another registered investment company, cannot invest more than 5% of the value of its total assets in another registered investment company and cannot investment more than 10% of the value of its total assets in all other registered investment companies. The restriction on owning more than 3% of the outstanding voting stock of a registered investment company also applies to private investment companies, such as hedge funds, that rely on section 3(c)(1) or section 3(c)(7) of the 1940 Act to avoid registration. Section 12(d)(1)(B) generally prohibits an open-end fund from selling its shares to another investment company if that investment company would own more than 3% of the open-end fund's voting stock, or if that investment company, together with all other investment companies, would own more than 10% of the open-end fund's voting stock. This prohibition also applies to the open-end fund's principal underwriter and any registered broker-dealer. Section 12(d)(1)(C) generally limits other investment companies, together with all other investment companies sharing the same investment adviser, from collectively owning more than 10% of the outstanding voting stock of a closed-end fund.

Section 12(d)(1) contains various statutory exemptions to these basic rules, and the SEC has further expanded the scope of these exemptions through rulemakings. Section 12(d)(1)(E) generally permits arrangements where an investment company (the "acquiring company") can own another investment company (the "acquired company") if (1) the acquired company's securities are the only investment securities owned by the acquiring company and (2) arrangements are made for "pass through" or "echo" voting (i.e., voting rights in the acquired company are passed through to the acquiring company's shareholders, or the acquiring company votes its shares in the acquired company in the same proportion as the vote of all other holders of acquired company securities). One important impact of section 12(d)(1)(E) is that it permits "master-feeder" structures, which are discussed further later in this chapter.

Section 12(d)(1)(F) and rule 12d1-3 generally relax the restrictions of section 12(d)(1) by permitting an acquiring company to acquire up to 3% of an acquired company's voting stock so long as the 3% is calculated by aggregating the holdings of the acquiring company with all of the acquiring company's affiliated persons (e.g., the investment adviser, officers and directors of the fund and other funds sharing the same, or affiliated, investment advisers). Other conditions of this exemption from the general restrictions of section 12(d)(1) include limits on the sales load that can be charged and a requirement for the acquiring fund to use "pass through" or "echo" voting with respect to voting rights in the acquired fund. Section 12(d)(1)(G) and rule 12d1-2 generally permit "affiliated fund of funds" arrangements where an open-end fund can purchase other open-end funds in the same group of investment companies, subject to various conditions. This exemption permits fund managers to offer products that pursue their investment objectives by investing in other funds managed by the same adviser.

The reasons for the restrictions found in section 12(d)(1) are described in the following application for exemption. Note that relief is requested from section 12(d)(1) as well as from section 17(a) which prohibits affiliates from selling and purchasing property to and from their affiliated investment companies, and section 17(d) which prohibits joint or joint and several transactions among investment companies and their affiliates.[1] Note that this application for exemption was one of the precursors to section 12(d)(1)(G), described above.

The Spectrum Fund proposed to invest in certain Price Funds ("Underlying Funds"). It was designed to provide investors (primarily retirement fund investors) diversification through two portfolios: the Growth Fund and the Income Fund. The Growth Fund would invest in common stock funds; the Income Fund, in bond funds; and both portfolios, in an equity income fund and a money market fund. The Portfolios would invest in the Underlying Funds according to predetermined percentage ranges which may be changed only by shareholder vote.

The Spectrum Fund would be charged no advisory fee but would bear part of the advisory fees and expenses of the Underlying Funds. However, the Spectrum Fund, by attracting additional assets to the Underlying Funds, would reduce their expense ratios. The Underlying Funds' boards would determine whether their benefits from the Spectrum Fund are greater than the expenses of the Spectrum Fund. If so, the Spectrum Fund would not be charged for services. The Spectrum Fund also asserted that the retirement plan shareholders would realize savings by incurring only one annual fiduciary fee per Portfolio, instead of a higher number of fees based on the number of Underlying Funds in which they would have invested.

The applicants noted the policy of section 12(d)(1):

> Section 12(d)(1) is intended to prevent the pyramiding of investment companies, the layering of fees, and undue organizational complexities. Applicants represent that none of the negative effects associated with fund holding companies are present with respect to the proposed arrangement and that the Spectrum Fund will provide the benefits of diversification and account cost savings to small and retirement-oriented investors. Spectrum Fund shareholders will not be subject to two advisory fees, distribution costs, directly or indirectly, or a sales load. Applicants represent that concerns under Section 12(d)(1) regarding the largely illusory value of diversification and "wash transactions" that achieve no investment purpose

1. T. Rowe Price Spectrum Fund Inc., Investment Company Act Rel. No. 17198 (Oct. 31, 1989).

are answered by the differing investment objectives of the two portfolios and monitoring of "wash transactions." Wash transactions will be monitored on a periodic basis, including the use of a computer assisted program. In addition, where such transactions indicate that a particular asset class (e.g., small cap stocks or high dividend paying stocks) held by the Growth or Income Fund is over-represented, holdings of that asset class will be reduced. Congress' concern about concentration of control and undue influence will be minimized because the Spectrum Fund will "mirror" vote its shares in each Underlying Fund, has agreed to limitations on its redemption rights, and will not acquire more than fifteen percent in the aggregate of any Underlying Fund. Finally, the inherent conflicts of interest are mitigated by separate, independent boards of directors for the Spectrum Fund and the Underlying Funds.

Applicants agreed to the following conditions:

1. Shares of the Spectrum Fund will be offered and sold (including sales by exchange or transfers between the Portfolios) only to individuals investing through tax-advantaged retirement accounts organized under the provisions of the Internal Revenue Code (and distributions therefrom) and to individuals investing through other accounts established for long-term investment purposes (collectively, "Long-Term Investors"), in both cases subject to an aggregate $ 30,000 investment limit during any one calendar year. Appropriate procedures and controls will be instituted to ensure the Spectrum Fund is limited to such Long-Term Investors.

2. Spectrum Fund will operate under a fundamental investment policy of allocating its assets to specified Underlying Funds according to a schedule of percentage ranges; changes in either an Underlying Fund or a percentage range must be submitted to shareholders for approval. Except for temporary investments in a money market fund for defensive purposes, the difference between the upper limit and the lower limit may not be greater than 15%.

3. No Portfolio of Spectrum Fund will purchase or otherwise acquire shares of any Underlying Fund if, as a result of such purchase, Spectrum Fund would own in the aggregate more than 15% of the outstanding securities of any Underlying Fund. Spectrum Fund's holdings in that Underlying Fund may temporarily exceed this 15% limitation under the standards set forth in Section 5(c) of the 1940 Act.

4. Redemptions from any Underlying Fund by Spectrum Fund will be limited to 1% of the Underlying Fund's assets in any period of less than 30 days, except where necessary to meet Spectrum Fund shareholder redemption requests.

5. Exchanges into and out of any Portfolio of Spectrum Fund will be limited to two "round trips" per year. A "round trip" is one exchange into and one exchange out of a Portfolio.

6. A majority of Spectrum Fund's directors will not be "interested persons," as defined in Section 2(a)(19) of the 1940 Act

(the "Independent Directors"). Further, none of the Independent Directors will be directors of any Underlying Fund.

7. Spectrum Fund will vote its shares in each Underlying Fund in proportion to the vote of all other holders of the securities of each respective Underlying Fund.

8. Spectrum Fund will not offer any Portfolio in addition to the Growth Portfolio and Income Portfolio without first filing an amended application for and being granted further exemptive relief under Section 6(c) of the 1940 Act.

9. Neither Spectrum Fund nor any Underlying Fund will establish a distribution plan under Rule 12b-1 of the 1940 Act or sell its shares with a sales load. Spectrum Fund will not be charged an advisory fee by Price Associates or Price-Fleming or any affiliated person.

10. The Board of Directors, including a majority of the Independent Directors, will establish procedures to monitor "wash transactions" among the Underlying Funds, and will take appropriate action to keep wash transactions at a de minimis level.

11. The Directors of Spectrum Fund will cause a report to be filed with the Division of Investment Management within 60 days of the close of each of Spectrum Fund's first two fiscal years, summarizing the actual expenses involved in the operation of Spectrum Fund.

### b. Hub and Spoke Funds of Funds (or, "Master-Feeder Funds")

In the following excerpt, a certain type of mutual fund structure called the "hub and spoke" or "master-feeder" is examined with a view to the applicability of section 12(d)(1) to such an arrangement.[1]

Section 12(d)(1) of the 1940 Act restricts the ability of one investment company to invest in another investment company or companies. As adopted in 1940, the section was intended to prevent one investment company from buying control of other investment companies and creating complicated pyramidal structures. In 1966, because of the emergence of the "fund of funds," the Commission recommended amendments to strengthen the restrictions of section 12(d)(1) to prevent such abuses as the unnecessary layering of costs, undue influence by the fund holding company over its underlying funds, and the threat of large scale redemptions of the securities of the underlying investment companies.

Despite this concern over fund holding companies, Congress has twice refused to prohibit ownership of the securities of one investment company by another. The original draft of section 12(d)(1) flatly prohibited an investment company from acquiring any securities of another investment company. . . . Because fund holding companies were not a significant problem in 1940, however, Congress permitted limited investment in other companies in order to permit

1. Letter of Richard C. Breeden, Chairman, Securities and Exchange Commission, to The Honorable John D. Dingell, Chairman, House Committee on Energy and Commerce, (Apr. 15, 1992).

investment companies to take advantage of good business opportunities. . . . During reconsideration of the 1940 Act following publication of the PPI study in 1966, a flat prohibition on funds of funds was again proposed. . . . Again, however, the final version of the amended section 12(d)(1) did not include such a flat prohibition.

When section 12(d)(1) was amended in 1970, however, Congress added section 12(d)(1)(E) to preserve the existing exception for unit investment trusts, and to extend that exception to similar vehicles not organized in trust form. Section 12(d)(1)(E) in effect permits an acquiring investment company (e.g., the spoke) to own the shares of another investment company (e.g., the hub) so long as those shares are the only investment securities owned by the acquiring investment company.

Thus, although Congress probably did not envision the hub-and-spoke structure, it is expressly permitted by section 12(d)(1)(E) of the 1940 Act. Because the Division believes that the major abuses at which section 12(d)(1) was aimed are either not present in these arrangements or have been addressed during our review of hub-and-spoke registrations, it has not challenged hub-and-spoke registrants' reliance on section 12(d)(1)(E).

1. Duplication of Fees and Expenses

Layering of expenses in a hub-and-spoke arrangement is minimal. Portfolio management and related functions are consolidated at the hub level. The investment adviser's fees, and the expenses of portfolio securities transactions and custodial services are paid out of the hub fund's assets. Some transfer agent fees are also paid at this level, but they are low because the few shareholders (i.e., the spokes) bunch their purchase and redemption orders. Because the hub fund sells its shares only to the spokes, its distribution costs are minimal or non-existent.

Marketing and distribution take place at the spoke level. The distributions expenses that spoke funds incur are usually paid for by front-end or differed [sic] sales loads and/or rule 12b-1 fees. Most transfer agency fees are incurred at the spoke level as well. Because the spoke invests only in securities issued by the hub fund, it pays no investment advisory fees. In addition, because the spoke's only assets are shares of the hub fund, maintained on a book-entry system, its custodial and accounting expenses are minimal.

Thus, investors pay for advisory services and portfolio transactions at the hub level and for distribution and most transfer agency fees at the spoke level. Because two funds are involved, some layering of fees appears unavoidable; each fund bears its own custodial fees, expenses of preparing and mailing reports to shareholders; expenses of shareholder meeting; and any other costs of administering the fund. Nevertheless, the aggregate of these expenses appears to be less than the cost of establishing and operating an individual fund, rather than a spoke, because of the inefficiencies of operation and the cost of advisory services for each fund.

Accordingly, even if section 12(d)(1)(E) did not permit hub-and-spoke arrangements, these arrangements would comport with the policy of section 12(d)(1) with respect to layering of fees. Section 12(d)(1) limits, but does not prohibit, duplication of expenses. Furthermore, unlike the complicated pyramidal structures addressed in section 12(d)(1), a hub-and-spoke is a fairly simple two tier arrangement, capable of being understood by investors. The Division has therefore addressed the risk of undue layering of expenses by requiring clear disclosure of all expenses in the spoke fund's prospectus.

2. Risk of Large Scale Redemptions

The Commission's 1966 PPI Report also identified the threat of large-scale redemptions as another potential abuse associated with a fund of funds. After evaluating the likelihood and the magnitude of this risk, however, the Division has concluded that it is not appreciably greater in hub-and-spoke arrangements than in traditional mutual funds.

Many mutual funds have large investors whose redemptions may affect the expense ratio of the fund. In some cases these large shareholders are individuals; more frequently they are institutions -- for example, bank trustees who maintain omnibus accounts with a mutual fund on behalf of a number of beneficial owners. The value of these accounts may amount to a large percentage of the fund's assets. It is true that the departure of a very large spoke could cause some per share increase in expenses for the remaining shareholders. A large redemption could also cause a hub to lose the advantage of reduced advisory fees because its assets would fall below certain "break points." Again, however, the risk that break points will be lost by redemption of a few large shareholders (or by a large number of small shareholders) is present in a single tier mutual fund.

Indeed, the hub-and-spoke structure may reduce the risks associated with large scale redemptions. A large shareholder in a traditional, single tier mutual fund can redeem its shares unilaterally at any time without notice to the fund. In contrast, investment in a hub fund is an investment policy of a spoke fund. Before the spoke may deviate from this policy and redeem its shares in the hub it needs, at a minimum, approval of its board of directors, and possibly its shareholders. Obtaining this approval might prevent, and would certainly slow, large scale redemptions. Thus, even if a large redemption was approved, the additional time required for the approval, and the advance notice that the hub likely would receive, should permit the hub to manage its portfolio in anticipation of the redemption in such a way as to reduce any disruption affecting the other shareholders of the hub.

The Division believes that the possibility of large scale redemptions requires prospectus disclosure that the economies of scale expected from the hub-and-spoke structure may not be achieved. Because the probability of such redemptions is slight and because

> the impact would likely be minimal, however, greater disclosure is not necessary. . . .

---

## Discussion Topics

a. What are the justifications for prohibiting "fund of funds?" What are the justifications for the exceptions from the prohibitions?

b. Consider the amendments introduced by Congress in October 1996. The Senate Report regarding fund of funds states as follows:

> In 1970, the Investment Company Act was amended to restrict fund of funds arrangements — where one investment company invests in another investment company. The restrictions were made in response to concerns that these types of arrangements resulted in excessive layering of fees and abuses of control arising from the concentration of voting power in the acquiring fund.
>
> A new type of fund of fund, involving a fund that invests in other funds belonging to the same group or "family" of funds, has become a popular way for investors to diversify a fund investment through a single, professionally managed portfolio. The SEC has granted individual exemptions from the investment Company Act's restrictions to several similar fund of funds arrangements, [including T. Rowe Price which is excerpted above] subject to certain conditions that address the concerns underlying the statutory restrictions. S. 1815 enables fund of funds arrangements involving a group of investment companies to be offered without obtaining prior exemptive relief from the Commission. The bill also gives the SEC authority to adopt rules to fill any gaps in investor's protection or to address any abuses arising in connection with this new fund-of funds exemption.[1]

What policy reasons justify Congress limiting to affiliated funds the flexibility provided to establish fund of funds? What arguments would you offer to the SEC in support of an exemption under Section 12(d)(1)(J) to permit an unaffiliated fund of funds arrangement?

c. How does a fund of funds differ from a wrap fee arrangement?

---

### 4. The Regulation of Investment Companies as Investors in Their Own Portfolios[2]

As noted, under section 22(e) open-end investment companies may not suspend their shareholders' redemption rights or postpone the date of payment for more than seven days after the tender of such security to the mutual fund. The Investment Company Act does not impose upon open-end investment companies any duty to keep some of their assets liquid in order to meet redemption demands by their shareholders. Yet, such

1. S. Rep. No. 104-293, at 7 (1996).
2. This material is derived from Clifford E. Kirsch, Investment Adviser Regulation, A Step-by-Step Guide to Compliance and the Law 10-9 to -11 (1998).

companies should have enough cash to meet potential redemption demand. The Commission and its staff, however, have imposed such requirements indirectly. Thus, in 1992, the staff recommended amending the Investment Company Act to require that open-end investment companies maintain liquidity in their portfolios:[1]

> The Act, however, was not amended but the Guidelines to Form N-1A were revised to permit open-end mutual funds to increase from 10% to 15% the amount of illiquid investments they may hold.[2*] The SEC views an investment as illiquid if it cannot be sold in the ordinary course of business within seven days at approximately the value at which the mutual fund has valued the investment on its books.[3*] Restricted securities, that is unregistered securities, are generally treated as illiquid, subject to several exceptions.[4*]

---

## Problem

Assume you are a lawyer at a law firm. Your client, a large asset manager, asks for your help in working through the various legal issues involved in structuring a registered fund that invests part of its assets in hedge funds and/or private equity funds. All of the hedge funds and private equity funds would rely on the exclusion from the definition of investment company found in section 3(c)(1) or 3(c)(7) of the 1940 Act. Also, you learn that there is no reliable secondary market for hedge fund or private equity fund interests and that these funds offer to redeem their interests (usually limited partnership or LLC interests) at their net asset value no more frequently than quarterly. Please write your client a memo analyzing the following issues:

(1) What limits, if any, would section 12(d)(1)(A) impose on the fund's investments in these hedge funds and/or private equity funds?

(2) If the fund were structured as an open-end fund, would the SEC staff's interpretations regarding portfolio liquidity requirements impose any limits on the fund's investments in these hedge funds and/or private equity funds?

---

1. Protecting Investors: A Half Century of Investment Company Regulation, Division of Investment Management, United States Securities and Exchange Commission (May 1992). Note that, as described in the previous Chapter, the SEC has proposed to codify these positions regarding open-end fund liquidity requirements via rulemaking. *See* Open-End Fund Liquidity Risk Management Programs; Swing Pricing; Re-Opening of Comment Period for Investment Company Reporting Modernization Release, Investment Company Act Rel. No. 31835 (Sept. 22, 2015).

2*. The revision was intended to permit investment companies more flexibility to make investments in the illiquid securities of small businesses, remove unnecessary barriers to capital formation and provide small businesses with better access to capital markets.

3*. Inv. Co. Act Rel. No. 14983 (March 12, 1986).

4*. Restricted securities are defined in Rule 144(a)(3) of the Securities Act of 1933.

## 5. Diversification[1]

### a. Diversification Under the Investment Company Act

Investment companies may be described as diversified or undiversified. The Investment Company does not require diversification, although Chapter M of the Internal Revenue Code, which allows for a pass-through tax treatment of investment companies, does impose this requirement. In any event, under the Investment Company Act, if a company describes itself as diversified, then it must follow a certain structure. Thus, the term has achieved a standardized meaning under the Act. Section 5(b)(1) of the Act provides that the portfolio of an open-end investment company that describes itself as "diversified" must have the following structure. At least seventy-five percent of the fund's assets must consist of "cash and cash items (including receivable), Government securities, securities of other investment companies, and other securities" and may not include in the 75 percent basket securities of a single issuer accounting for more than 5 percent of the fund's assets or constituting more than 10 percent of the issuer's voting securities. The 25 percent basket of the fund's assets need not follow the restrictions.

### b. Diversification Under the Internal Revenue Act

Section 851 of the Internal Revenue Code also comes into play with respect to a fund's portfolio holdings. The portfolio of a "regulated investment company" must be diversified as follows: At least 50 percent of the value of the total assets of the company must be represented by (1) cash and cash items (including receivables), government securities, and securities of other regulated investment companies, and (2) other securities generally limited (for purposes of this calculation) in respect of any one issuer to 5 percent of the value of the total assets of the company and to 10 percent of the outstanding voting securities of the issuer.

If the Commission certifies that the company "is principally engaged in the furnishing of capital to other corporations which are principally engaged in the development or exploitation of inventions, technological improvements, new processes, or products not previously generally available," the company is allowed to include a larger amount of securities in respect of an issuer for the 50 percent test. In addition, not more than 25 percent of the value of the total assets may be invested in the securities (other than government securities or the securities of other regulated investment companies) of any one issuer, or of two or more issuers which the company controls and which are determined, under Treasury regulations, to be engaged in the same or similar trades or businesses or related trades or businesses.

---

1. This material is derived from CLIFFORD E. KIRSCH, INVESTMENT ADVISER REGULATION, A STEP-BY-STEP GUIDE TO COMPLIANCE AND THE LAW 10-11 (1998).

### c. Investment Policies and Industry Concentration

Recall Galbraith's comments about the investment trusts of the 1920s that acted as "corporations." He meant that the managers of investment trusts were free to invest and change their investments. One day a trust could be invested in government securities — conservative investments — and the next day its investments could be sold and the money invested in a start-up with a cloudy future. In contrast, trusts usually direct the trustee to invest in a particular way and in the past trustees could invest only in "legal investments" specified in the statutes. Congress took a middle road. Investment discretion was left to the managers but the investment policies had to be established at the outset in the registration statement of the investment company. That investment policy was left to the promoters of the companies. However, section 13 provides that any changes in "fundamental investment policies" of the company as described in its registration statements were subject to the majority vote of the shareholders. Thus, the assumption is that the investors would know what they are buying and have a say in any changes.

Section 8(b)(1) of the 1940 Act requires a recitation of the fund's policy of concentrating investments in a particular industry or group of industries. The 1940 Act does not define what it means to "concentrate" in an industry, though the SEC staff has taken the position that a fund is concentrated in a particular industry if it invests more than 25 percent of the value of its total assets in an industry.[1] In addition, Section 35(d) prohibits a registered investment company from adopting a name which "the Commission finds materially deceptive or misleading." Rule 35d-1 provides that a name is "materially deceptive and misleading" if it suggests investment in certain investments or industries, or certain countries or geographic regions, unless certain requirements are met. The company must have adopted a policy to invest, under normal circumstances, at least 80 per cent of the value of its assets in the investments, industry, industries, country, countries, region, or regions suggested. In addition, the policy must be a fundamental policy under section 8(b)(3) or the company must have adopted an appropriate policy to provide shareholders at least 60 days notice before any change in the policy.

The following is a no-action letter that describes an issue relating to the investment policy of an investment company.[2] As critical background, the SEC believes that funds may not reserve the freedom of action to switch from concentration to non-concentration in an industry.

The First Australia Fund ("Fund") requested no-action relief from section 8(b)(1). The Fund invested primarily in securities of Australian firms included in an index ("Index") maintained by the Australian Stock Exchange. The Fund was actively managed and was not an index fund. At the time the Fund requested relief, the Fund invested no more than 25 percent of its total assets in any one industry. However, at the time the Fund requested relief, at least one industry represented nearly 25 percent of the Index.

---

1. Guidelines for the Preparation of Form N-8B-1, Investment Company Act Rel. No. 7221 (Jun. 9, 1972).
2. First Australia Fund, Inc., SEC No-Action Letter (Jul. 29, 1999).

> The Fund proposes to implement a new concentration policy to permit it to invest up to 35% of its total assets in the equity securities of issuers in a particular industry or any one group of industries if, at the time of investment, that industry represents 20% or more of the Index. This would allow the Fund to continue to overweight or underweight a particular industry, with a maximum investment of 35% in any one industry, consistent with the Fund's investment policies and objectives.

The staff granted no-action relief:

> Section 8(b)(1) permits a fund to implement a concentration policy that allows for some degree of discretion, provided that the circumstances under which the manager may exercise its discretion to change the fund's concentration status are described, to the extent practicable, in the fund's registration statement. To satisfy this standard, we believe that a fund must clearly describe, in as much detail as is practicable, the circumstances under which the fund may concentrate its investments. You state that the Fund's proposed concentration policy describes, insofar as practicable, the extent to which the Fund intends to concentrate in an industry by setting clear, objective limitations on the manager's ability to freely concentrate in an industry.
>
> We agree. Our conclusion is based specifically on your representations that: (1) the Fund's principal investment objective is to invest primarily in equity securities of Australian companies that are included in the Index; (2) the Index is established and maintained by an unaffiliated third party and is widely recognized; (3) an industry must represent more than 20% of the Index before the manager may invest more than 25% of the Fund's total assets in that industry; and (4) the manager cannot invest more than 35% of the Fund's total assets in that industry. We believe that, under these circumstances, the Fund's proposed concentration policy is consistent with Section 8(b)(1) of the Act.

---

## Discussion Topics

a. As adviser to a client that embarks on designing an open-end fund, how would you outline the diversification requirements to meet the provisions of both the Investment Company Act and the Internal Revenue Code?

b. Does the Investment Company Act require diversification? If not, why not? Why is its directive sufficient to induce most managers of open-end investment companies to diversify their portfolios?

c. Is the diversification in the Internal Revenue Code aimed at protection of investors or at some other public policy?

---

## C. The Role of the Investment Company in the Portfolio Company's Board Room

Academics have long advocated greater involvement of investment companies and other institutional investors in the corporate governance of their portfolio companies. The advisers of mutual funds and other institutional investors rejected the call for such activity. The SEC entered the fray in 2003 with the adoption of a rule requiring certain steps that a fund needs to take with respect to proxy voting. After the crash of 2008, it passed a rule that allowed a three-year shareholder that holds 3% of the company's shares to nominate a director to the company's board. In 2011, this rule was vacated by the D.C. Circuit, holding, among other reasons, that "the Commission failed adequately to consider the rule's effect upon efficiency, competition, and capital formation."[1] If such a rule gains legality, it will open the door to the wider participation of institutional investors in corporate governance. Moreover, it might reduce the emphasis and self-image of investment companies' advisers as traders and balance it with the image of, and emphasis on, long-term investors. The following are excerpts of two opposing views about advisers' involvement in corporate governance and a discussion of the 2003 rule regarding the voting disclosure by investment advisers and investment companies.

### 1. The Arguments for Involvement of Investment Companies' Advisers[2]

> Mutual funds have huge financial resources. . . . Yet despite their size, mutual funds rarely participate in corporate governance. They are intermediaries, channeling funds from disparate individuals into investments. They gather and process information about industrial investments that the funds' owners cannot easily gather and process. They do the paperwork that individuals begrudge. They provide diversification, which is what many investors want. Yet they are not intermediaries that invest in concentrated holdings and that enter the corporate boardroom to represent their shareholder beneficiaries, which is what some investors might want. Voices are heard complaining that institutional investors do not become actively involved in monitoring, or supporting, the managements of their portfolio companies. Yet mutual funds usually stay far from the scene of corporate governance; only rarely can they be found inside the corporate boardroom.
>
> In the 1930s some mutual funds began to act as monitoring intermediaries. They underwrote securities, became active players in bankruptcy reorganizations, and participated in management. The Revenue Act of 1936, followed up by the Investment Company Act of 1940, forced the funds to stop. Why?
>
> Odder still is the timing of the cut-off of mutual funds from corporate governance. In the early 1930s Berle and Means publicized their finding that with the atomization of shareholdings, power was

1. *Bus. Roundtable v. SEC,* 647 F.3d 1144 (D.C. Cir. 2011).

2. Mark J. Roe, *Political Elements in the Creation of a Mutual Fund Industry,* 139 U. Pa. L. Rev. 1469 (1991).

shifting from shareholders to managers in the large public company. Mutual funds could concentrate shareholders' power. The manager of a mutual fund could have been a conduit of shareholder power. The mutual fund would have the potential power and motivation to check the activities of management. But within a few years, tax rules and the 1940 Act raised the cost of (or outright prohibited) close mutual fund involvement with their portfolio companies.

The prohibitions and restrictions were not oversights, nor were their consequences unintended. Key players in the Administration and Congress wanted to prevent mutual fund (and other banker) control of industrial companies. Explanations for severance can be seen in (a) popular opinion mistrustful of large financial institutions, (b) public-spirited rules intended to foster stable mutual funds for the average investor, (c) the accidents of tax doctrine, and (d) a glimmer of an interest group story of some political actors favoring local managers over Wall Street.

Opinion polls show the popular mind has mistrusted large financial institutions with accumulated power and has always been wary of Wall Street controlling industrial America. Politicians responded to this mistrust by enacting rules restricting the power of private financial institutions. . . .

A pattern can be seen in the history of American corporate finance. Institutions that can influence industry are restrained from growing too big. If they do grow anyway, their portfolios are forcibly fragmented. If the fragmented institutions attempt to link themselves together to control industry, law prohibits those links. For banks, insurance companies, pension funds, and mutual funds, the story is the same. . . . What's more, there is a pattern of politics behind these prohibitions. In this article, I examine one of these financial institutions, the mutual fund.

I. THE 1940 ACT RESTRICTIONS

Mutual funds pool the investment funds of hundreds of investors, thereby enabling the investors both to diversify and to buy the investment expertise of the fund's managers. . . .

A. Power of Control

Congress was suspicious of mutual funds with the power to control industrial companies. . . . Holding companies rather than mutual funds were organized for control. And this control was denigrated. . . .

Only unscrupulous financiers mixed investment with control . . . .

The SEC declared in its proposed bill that "the national public interest . . . [is] adversely affected . . . when investment companies [have] great size . . . [and] have excessive influence on the national economy. . . ." The SEC conceded that mutual funds had the expertise, motivation and financial muscle to ameliorate the informational and organizational problems of scattered shareholders. . . . Nevertheless, the disadvantages of investment companies with the power to control outweighed the advantages. The SEC wanted mutual fund directors and employees off the boards of all portfolio companies; they wanted a Glass-Steagall-type severance. They also wanted to bar any fund from exceeding $ 150 million in assets. Eventually the SEC had to compromise with the mutual fund industry, but they still achieved a great deal of severance.

B. Diversification

First, under the Investment Company Act of 1940, a mutual fund cannot advertise itself as "diversified" if it owns in the regulated part of its portfolio more than 10% of the voting stock of any company. Three-quarters of the portfolio is subject to this fragmentation rule, even if that influential block of stock is only a small portion of the fund's entire portfolio. The SEC wanted that restriction to disable mutual fund control of portfolio companies. Some mutual funds might have competed as monitors by owning large blocks of stock. That prospect was cut-off for diversified investment companies. Today, virtually all mutual funds call themselves diversified: they do not control public firms.

* * *

By requiring some standard of fragmentation if the fund chooses to call itself diversified, the 1940 Act helps make sure investors get what they were promised. But this crude standard only justifies the 5% restriction (the mutual fund may not invest more than 5% of its regulated assets in any single company). The 10% restriction (the mutual fund may not buy more than 10% of a portfolio company's voting stock) is unnecessary for true diversification. . . . To be sure, the rule has disclosure benefits. And even a modern definition of diversification would require some fragmentation. . . . Although the 1940 Act definition prevents a large diversified fund from taking large chunks of portfolio companies' stock, the rule is only a nuisance, not a show-stopper: the fund could decline to call itself diversified and this part of 1940 Act wouldn't bite. But as shall be seen, the large block would trigger other 1940 Act nuisances; the 1940 Act, and other rules, make it difficult to network medium-sized blocks held by several different financial institutions, and tax rules that roughly track the diversification definition would still apply, and be more than a nuisance. . . .

C. Networks and Affiliates

But for that limited portion of the portfolio that may be concentrated, other restrictions apply. . . . But if the mutual fund owned 5% of a portfolio company's stock and networked with a group of institutions owning 5% of the stock of the portfolio company, all would become 1940 Act affiliates. The 1940 Act prohibits the mutual fund lacking an SEC exemption from acting jointly with an affiliated financial institution to join a portfolio company's board of directors, or otherwise jointly assert influence. . . . Each mutual fund in a constellation of separate mutual funds with a common advisor might take 4.9% of the portfolio company's stock. The common advisor to the funds could then wield a large block of stock. But I understand that while some mutual fund complexes have multiple holdings in several different mutual funds, they usually avoid having the aggregate ownership of the complex reach 10%, perhaps because of fear of entering legal gray areas.

The 1940 Act prohibits cross-ownership. . . . Moreover, if the mutual fund wished to act jointly with an affiliate to exercise control, it would need prior SEC approval. We can imagine an incipient network of institutional investors: An investment bank, an insurance company, or a commercial bank might become the investment adviser to a mutual fund. The adviser might take the 4.9% of the stock that the mutual fund holds, and combine that with a similar-sized holding of the investment bank, affiliated mutual funds, the insurance company, the commercial bank's trust department, or the bank's holding company. That combined block might be large enough to be influential, getting a representative into the boardroom. . . .

II. ORIGINS IN THE 1936 REVENUE ACT.

A. Subchapter M of the Internal Revenue Code.

If a mutual fund were to deploy most of its portfolio in large influential blocks, it would be taxed unfavorably on its entire portfolio, because the Tax Code allows only diversified mutual funds to pass income through, untaxed to the conduit mutual fund. The 1936 Revenue Act's notion of diversification, like the 1940 Act's notion, is not that found in modern textbooks on corporate finance; mutual funds have to have their investments in companies constituting no more than 5% of the portfolio and constituting no more than 10% of the portfolio company's outstanding stock. Later, in 1942, the Tax Code was amended to allow half of the portfolio to be more concentrated; for that other half, no more than 25% of the fund's assets can go into a single company's stock. . . .

III. THE POLITICAL ROOTS OF DISARMING MUTUAL FUNDS

The American public opinion has always been mistrustful of accumulations of economic power; mechanisms such as mutual funds that would control industry are unpopular. . . . American politics has usually opted for fragmentation of financial power. A standard move in public choice analysis is to find an interest group that has "bought" the legislation at the expense of a diffuse and disorganized citizenry. In the financial regulation of banks and takeovers, legal commentators have seen strong elements of this interest group approach. But I believe this approach is less useful in understanding the 1940 Act. Mutual funds just were not financially important enough in the 1930s to evoke much interest group intervention. Rather, politicians were operating at the symbolic level. They were creating a mutual fund industry. Through regulation and taxation, politicians created a framework for mutual funds based on their concept of what a legitimate mutual fund ought to be. Thereafter, mutual funds had to grow up within that framework. . . .

Anti-Wall Street pressures were not the only reason for mutual fund regulation; populist pressure cannot explain everything. Surely some mutual funds wanted to regularize their industry, making it attractive to the average saver by reducing the risks of banker wheeling and dealing. And Congress wanted to protect investors, fearing that unsophisticated investors would invest in mutual funds expecting diversification but be unable to evaluate the portfolio. The SEC testified that a mutual fund's only positive function was to provide diversification; any extension risked thievery.

Keeping mutual fund managers out of controlling positions kept them free of conflicts of interest. . . . Key senators wanted regulation that would eliminate mutual fund looting at any cost, irrespective of whether the looting amounted to 1% or 30% of fund assets. . . . Senators also wanted to protect individual investors in mutual funds from the machinations of insider-manipulators. Denying financiers power to control industry was thought to reduce their ability to manipulate the controlled business. Financiers would control companies to issue unneeded, overpriced securities that would be dumped into controlled mutual funds, solely to generate fees for the financiers.

The mutual fund industry didn't strongly oppose all of the restrictions, in fact it preferred some elements. It wanted to sell its product and needed a code of conduct to certify the industry to the public. To make money off of the unsophisticated, the mutual fund industry didn't need complex relations with portfolio companies; authority to use a heavy load was enough. Although resale price maintenance has been illegal in antitrust (but attacked as not necessarily good policy), the mutual fund industry had federally-mandated noncompetition among dealers: the advisor sets the load, dealers cannot cut it. Price competition among mutual fund dealers is a criminal offense. These elements can be seen as part of the political payoff to the mutual fund industry for the operating restrictions. And, as I note below, one type of mutual fund — the Massachusetts trust — preferred that Congress require all mutual funds to use a structure that the Massachusetts trust had already adopted. . . .

One reason to block control was to block cartelization. A mutual fund could be the means by which an investment banker controlled several companies in a single industry, as Morgan did. That control could be used to promote and police a cartel. Louis Brandeis is often cited as setting the tone and providing a plan for action. "The dominant element in our financial oligarchy is the investment banker. Associated banks, trust companies and life insurance companies are his tools. . . ." Woodrow Wilson also believed small groups of people in large corporations made autocratic decisions, concentrating in their own hands the "resources, the choices, the opportunities, in brief, the power of thousands. . . ." The anti-cartel theory can be seen even today in subchapter M. Congress liberalized the portfolio fragmentation requirements in 1942, at the behest of the mutual fund industry. But it was quite careful to stymie mutual fund control of industry. . . . If monitoring by mutual funds were functionally possible, this tax rule would be a barrier. Monitoring requires specialized staff, with industry knowledge. If the fund cannot concentrate its influential blocks in a single industry, or its vertically related parts, assembling a staff would be difficult or impossible.

The post-1942 structure of Subchapter M produces odd results. If the mutual fund keeps its entire portfolio fragmented, it can put its entire portfolio into a single industry. A few mutual funds do this — Fidelity's "Select" funds come to mind. Shareholders of these funds get little diversification. Because the fund managers are exclusively investing in a single industry, they might acquire enough expertise so that they can second-guess some portfolio company managers every now and then. Functionally, the fund might get enough expertise to feel comfortable with a few influential positions. After all, the shareholders are not getting much diversification from the fund anyway: its portfolio is all in one industry. But the fund managers cannot put more than 25% of its assets into control blocks in a single industry; the fund cannot concentrate investments in a single industry without a tax penalty.

From a modern perspective, one would have expected managers to have been ardent supporters of the fragmentation of mutual funds. Corporate managers want independence from their shareholders. Certainly one can readily find managerial support for anti-takeover legislation, and managers benefitted from financial fragmentation. But the evidence does not show direct, powerful lobbying, or even testifying by managers in 1936 or 1940. Perhaps managers did not exert their influence because in the 1930s mutual funds were small players in the financial world, and the political action then was mostly symbolic. But that does not mean we should dismiss the managerial public choice story completely. At least some politicians who promoted the 1940 Act appealed to managerial freedom from Wall Street control, and there is evidence that the 1936 and 1940 Act fragmentation provisions had survival strength because they did not threaten managers. ...Floor debates during the securities legislation of the 1930s show the House of Representatives applauding calls to limit the power of bankers. . . .

IV. POLITICS AND ECONOMICS.

I am seeking a political story to partly explain the fragmented ownership of the large public corporation in the United States. Politics produced financial fragmentation and financial fragmentation partly produced the large public corporation. The critical political elements are Federalism, interest groups and popular ideology, leavened by the public interest. Populism tended to weaken financial institutions. While populism could not itself weaken all of them, when there were plausible public-regarding benefits to fragmentation, or when an important interest group favored fragmentation, the result has usually been to fragment finance. . . . [P]opular ideology and some public-interest views, leavened by some lukewarm interest group action, [led to] fragmented mutual funds.

But perhaps there is an overriding economic story, conceivably an efficiency one, to explain the political story. Why have Germany and Japan had much more powerful financial institutions that can heavily influence and indeed sometimes control industry? Several hypotheses are possible. The accidents of history may have led different systems to evolve in different countries. Perhaps the Japanese and German systems are inefficient, or just different but no better and no worse. Perhaps they lag an advanced American financial system, although we must wonder why they have caught up or surpassed us in industry but lag in finance. Or perhaps countries with a feudal past and a recent acquisition of democracy more willingly tolerate the hierarchical implications of industry influence and control by financial institutions. To the extent this is so, then we should now expect to see political pressure in Germany and Japan to reduce the power of their financial institutions.

But there is another possibility, a "meta" economic explanation for the political result: perhaps American and Japanese political and financial institutions responded to the underlying economics in each nation. Could the relative scarcity of managerial talent and capital explain the varying institutional arrangements?

Capital and resources have been relatively abundant in America, while skilled labor, perhaps including skilled managers, have been relatively scarce. Post-World War II Japan lacked capital and resources, but had a relative abundance of skilled and disciplined managers and workers. Did the relatively scarce resource in the United States — managerial talent — lead to contracts that favored managers at the expense of the abundant resource — capital? Those favorable contracts could include managerial autonomy from capital. These contracts were written, this story would go, but written in the political environment. In Japan and Germany, with capital scarce, the arrangements would favor capital.

This economic "meta"-story could help explain why contracts favoring managers would arise in the United States more than in Germany or Japan. But it wouldn't explain why these contracts would be written by Congress, instead of privately by each company and its managers. Here is one possibility: political pressure always arises to fragment finance, but politicians in an environment where capital is relatively more scarce resist this legislation. Why? Some politicians are reluctant because of the public interest; those managers who want autonomy may not seek the legislation vociferously, since with capital scarce other forms of private financial control will emerge anyway; institutions with capital resist the restrictions more strongly than they otherwise would. When capital is plentiful, the forces of fragmenting don't face these impediments.

What prediction would we make if capital became relatively more scarce in America and less scarce in Germany and Japan, a reversal occurring during the last decade? We should expect pressure, both financial and political, in Germany and Japan to change the relationships between capital and managers. Japanese and German managers would become more free from capital; and American financial institutions would develop more muscle. The first seems to be happening; the second possibility is generating talk.

V. SOME POLICY IMPLICATIONS.

My main purpose here has been to understand how politics and the 1930s conception of the proper role of mutual funds led to regulation and taxation that prohibited mutual funds from becoming important players in corporate governance. But this story has potential prescriptive implications. The SEC is now reviewing whether it should seek amendment to the 1940 Act. The SEC should consider corporate governance as well as investor protection as it rethinks mutual fund regulation.

Because I am dubious about the monitoring or informational potential of more powerful financial institutions, I am uncertain about what prescriptions are in order. True, Japan and Germany have had different relationships between financial institutions and industrial companies, and have not been irredeemably hobbled by these differences. But we cannot yet tell whether the German and Japanese arrangements were inefficient (although they couldn't have been debilitatingly so) or efficient only in the context of German and Japanese history, culture, and ability to systematically produce good regulation and good regulators.

In Germany investment companies play an important role in corporate governance. Banks aggregate the vote of stock they own directly, stock owned by investment companies that the bank controls, and stock owned by individuals but deposited with the bank as custodian. They aggregate these votes — frequently amounting to 40% of the vote in many companies — to elect directors of portfolio companies, directors not beholden to the portfolio companies' managers. This activity would be barred in the United States by the Glass-Steagall Act and would face serious, probably prohibitive obstacles under the 1940 Act because of the likelihood of conflicts of interest. How and whether this conflict is avoided in Germany is unclear.

A common misconception about German and Japanese banks is that their influence in industry comes only from control of credit. In Germany control over credit is a secondary factor; in Japan control over credit (which is weakening as a securities market for debt arises) may have been primary; but banks there control large blocks of stock as well. This misconception is understandable. Americans are so inured to banks being separated from commerce that credit intuitively seems to be the means of bank influence. But German banks enter the boardroom not through the usual advantage of a bank — control over credit — but through control of the proxy machinery.

Even if we thought that greater involvement of financial institutions would be salutary, we should be cautious. . . .

In the governance of small firms financiers play important roles, despite that the entrepreneur is better informed about the business. The financier there — called then a venture capitalist — appears to

> be functional. Such financiers know enough to avoid managing the enterprise, to only ask questions and put operating managers on a budget. Yet financiers disappear from the boardroom when the enterprise goes public. Perhaps financiers usually disappear from the boardroom because their involvement would be dysfunctional. But although they cannot always be dysfunctional, it is nearly always so that their involvement is legally restricted, as is the involvement of a mutual fund or its investment advisor. . . .
>
> CONCLUSION
>
> Elements of a "traditional" public choice story — of interest groups buying favorable legislation — are present. But surprisingly the interest group story does not drive the legislation. The ideology of fragmentation seems paramount. Key actors — FDR, Douglas, Brandeis, and Wilson — thought that Wall Street control of industry was bad. . . . Rather than an interest group story, we should think of the politics of mutual funds in the 1930s as creating mutual funds. Without tax exemption, the funds could not survive. Politicians allowed tax exemption consistent with their conception of what a mutual fund should be and should not be. It should not control industry; it should not have concentrated investments; it should not be entangled in financial alliances that could create conflicts of interest. Politicians created a framework for mutual funds to grow, a framework that made it difficult or impossible for mutual funds to actively affect portfolio companies. . . . Obviously, some goals must be traded off against others. . . . These laws reduce the agency costs in the intermediary, but are unhelpful in reducing the agency costs in the portfolio company, or in integrating industry with capital, by facilitating the flow of soft and proprietary information from the industrial company to capital intermediaries that take large stock positions and sit on the boards of portfolio companies. Perhaps that is the right trade-off to make. But it isn't obvious that it is the only plausible way to trade-off goals; it is not the trade-off made in other countries.

## 2. Voting on Behalf of Investment Companies but Keeping the Record Secret[1]

Over $6 trillion worth of corporate securities are owned and traded by mutual funds. The funds are managed by advisers as fiduciaries, for the benefit of the funds' shareholders. Among their functions, advisers vote thousands of portfolio companies' securities. Fidelity, the largest U.S. fund complex, votes the shares of nearly 4,600 domestic and foreign corporations. This is no small task, and is quite costly. On September 20, 2002 the Securities and Exchange Commission proposed a rule requiring mutual funds to disclose their record of voting their portfolio shares. On its face, the proposal is quite innocuous. What can be wrong with the claim that investors of mutual funds have a "right to know" how their assets

---

1. Letter by Tamar Frankel, Professor of Law, Boston University School of Law, to Securities and Exchange Commission, Mutual Funds as Shareholders of Corporate America: Should Funds Be Required to Disclose Their Voting Record? (2002).

— the shares in the funds' portfolios — are voted? What harm could any disclosure ever do? Yet, in fact, publication of the voting record can be harmful to mutual fund investors. The proposal raised very serious issues.

> Disclosure of one fact alone -- a vote for management -- can harm investors by creating misleading impressions, marring effective relationships between fund advisers and portfolio companies' management, and politicizing the funds investors' voting power. Publicity pressures can divert the attention of fund advisers from the objective of high performance to serving other objectives, such as higher salaries for corporate employees or increased power for their unions -- without the permission of all the funds' investors. . . . Fund advisers are known to follow the "Wall Street Rule," selling the securities of poorly managed corporations rather than reform the corporations by replacing their weak management or intervening in their operations. Fund advisers choose corporations that satisfy performance and investment policies' objectives.
>
> Advisers cannot hold stock to vote it in the annual meeting. Indeed, they must cast their ballots on the trading floor. Then the advisers vote for the management. Fund advisers vote against corporate management by selling, and not by voting. Besides, advisers' sales are a very powerful signal, far more powerful than the vote. And if the signal is ambiguous, management usually receives the explanation. Therefore their support of the management of portfolio companies -- the ones they chose -- leads to a misleading impression that the advisers consistently support all corporate managements. Without the selling record and considerations of the portfolio designs the simple voting number is highly misleading. The Wall Street Rule does not apply to index funds. . . . The funds have portfolios adjusted to reflect the markets, and advisers have no choice. Fund shareholders have indirectly ordered the advisers to vote for management. Voting for the management of portfolio companies is not blind and automatic. Mutual fund advisers watch not only the ticker tape, but also follow the operations of their portfolio companies. The advisers study the "fundamentals" of portfolio companies, receive in-depth reports about them, and then decide to invest, hold or sell. But when the voting record shows that advisers mostly support management, the fact can give a very wrong impression that the advisers are the lackeys of corporate management.
>
> Voting for management does not mean that advisers benefited themselves in conflict to the interests of fund investors. But a voting record in support of corporate management can be used to imply just that, and do a good job of casting a shadow of suspicion on the advisers. Yet voting for management will not necessarily mean conflict because excellent performance could also justify such vote of support. The solution to concerns about conflicts of interest is not disclosure of the voting record but disclosure of specific, explicit conflicts. . . . In fact, very few conflicts of interests escape the restrictions under the Investment Company Act of 1940, which casts a net tighter than any law regulating any other financial institution in

> the United States. But an impression of a voting record is difficult to counteract and undo by describing the complicated and comprehensive provisions of sections 2(a)(19) and 17 of the Investment Company Act of 1940. The sections are precise, but far from "plain English." In the battle of communication, the effective and sometimes draconian provisions of the federal law are sure to lose against a single number of proxies voted for management.
>
> Disclosure of the voting record can mar an effective informal monitoring of corporate...The adversarial models of labor-management relationship and court proceedings do not suit the advisers-management relationship, where both parties are independent yet likely to continuously interact. . . . The publicity of voting records may politicize the advisers' voting decisions. . . . As important as social or political objectives are, the voting power of some investors should not pressure advisers into voting for policies that do not command consensus of all investors. Advisers in a one-to-one relationship with clients can privately account for their voting and receive directions from clients. But fund advisers must publicize their vote. Publicity may have consequences other than informing the shareholders. Client shareholders cannot and would not direct advisers on how they should vote over 4,500 times a year.
>
> Exposing fund managers to political pressures can hurt investors both in their pockets and in their convictions. . . . The implicit purpose of fund advisers is to maximize investors' wealth. It is assumed that this objective is understood and agreed upon by all shareholders. . . . Activists have pressured mutual fund advisers to act aggressively on issues, such as treatment of the workforce, corporate responsibility to the communities, protection of the environment, ethics, refraining from trading with certain countries (e.g., South Africa when it practiced apartheid, and perhaps currently -- Israel for its treatment of the Palestinians). Pension funds have been the most socially active. Yet, as some activist funds have discovered, even a search for candidate directors is fraught with political strife, and it is unclear that fund advisers are experts in replacing and choosing management.
>
> Not only are social or political objectives outside the advisers' expertise, but allowing or pressing advisers to choose social objectives and mix with wealth maximization offers them far broader discretion. That is not expedient unless the shareholders could control and supervise the advisers. With millions of small investors, supervision is unlikely. . . . Mutual funds can establish criteria on which their representatives will vote, and the harms of publishing the voting record can be avoided. . . .

In 2003, the Commission passed a rule regarding voting disclosure by investment advisers.[1] It requires an adviser with voting authority over client securities to:

---

1. Proxy Voting By Investment Advisers, Investment Advisers Act Rel. No. 2106 (Jan. 31, 2003) (codified at 17 C.F.R. § 275.206(4)-6.

> (a) Adopt and implement written policies and procedures that are reasonably designed to ensure that you vote client securities in the best interest of clients, which procedures must include how you address material conflicts that may arise between your interests and those of your clients;
>
> (b) Disclose to clients how they may obtain information from you about how you voted with respect to their securities; and
>
> (c) Describe to clients your proxy voting policies and procedures and, upon request, furnish a copy of the policies and procedures to the requesting client.

In a companion release[1], the SEC passed a rule requiring certain disclosures by investment companies regarding proxy voting. A management investment company must generally disclose its policies and procedures for voting portfolio securities in its registration statement, and must file with the SEC and disclose to shareholders (on its website or upon request) its record of voting proxies relating to portfolio securities by filing Form N-PX.

In the companion release, the SEC explained the policy for proxy voting disclosure by investment companies:

> As of September 2002, mutual funds held $ 2.0 trillion in publicly traded U.S. corporate equity, representing approximately 18% of all publicly traded U.S. corporate equity. This represents a dramatic increase from only 7.4% at the end of 1992. Millions of individual American investors, in turn, hold shares of equity mutual funds, relying on these funds -- and the value of the corporate securities in which they invest -- to fund their retirements, their children's educations, and their other basic financial needs. Yet, despite the enormous influence of mutual funds in the capital markets and their huge impact on the financial fortunes of American investors, funds have been reluctant to disclose how they exercise their proxy voting power with respect to portfolio securities. We believe that the time has come to increase the transparency of proxy voting by mutual funds. This increased transparency will enable fund shareholders to monitor their funds' involvement in the governance activities of portfolio companies, which may have a dramatic impact on shareholder value.
>
> Mutual funds are formed as corporations or business trusts under state law and, as in the case of other corporations and trusts, must be operated for the benefit of their shareholders. Because a mutual fund is the beneficial owner of its portfolio securities, the fund's board of directors, acting on the fund's behalf, has the right and the obligation to vote proxies relating to the fund's portfolio securities. As a practical matter, however, the board typically delegates this function to the fund's investment adviser as part of the adviser's general management of fund assets, subject to the board's continuing oversight.

1. Disclosure of Proxy Voting Policies and Proxy Voting Records by Registered Management Investment Companies, Investment Company Act Rel. No. 25922 (Jan. 31, 2003) (codified at 17 C.F.R. § 270.30b1-4 (2015)).

The investment adviser to a mutual fund is a fiduciary that owes the fund a duty of "utmost good faith, and full and fair disclosure." This fiduciary duty extends to all functions undertaken on the fund's behalf, including the voting of proxies relating to the fund's portfolio securities. An investment adviser voting proxies on behalf of a fund, therefore, must do so in a manner consistent with the best interests of the fund and its shareholders.

Traditionally, mutual funds have been viewed as largely passive investors, reluctant to challenge corporate management on issues such as corporate governance. Funds have often followed the so-called "Wall Street rule," according to which an investor should either vote as management recommends or, if dissatisfied with management, sell the stock. In recent years, however, some funds, along with other institutional investors, have become more assertive in exercising their proxy voting responsibilities. The increased assertiveness by mutual funds in the voting of proxies may have a number of causes. In some instances, funds have come to hold such large positions in a particular portfolio company that they cannot easily sell the company's stock if the company's management is performing poorly. The investment policies of index funds typically do not permit them to sell poorly performing investments, and thus these funds may become active in corporate governance in order to maximize value for their shareholders.

Recent corporate scandals have created renewed investor interest in issues of corporate governance and have underscored the need for mutual funds and other institutional investors to focus on corporate governance. The increased equity holdings and accompanying voting power of mutual funds place them in a position to have enormous influence on corporate accountability. As major shareholders, mutual funds may play a vital role in monitoring the stewardship of the companies in which they invest.

Moreover, in some situations the interests of a mutual fund's shareholders may conflict with those of its investment adviser with respect to proxy voting. This may occur, for example, when a fund's adviser also manages or seeks to manage the retirement plan assets of a company whose securities are held by the fund. In these situations, a fund's adviser may have an incentive to support management recommendations to further its business interests.

Yet, in spite of the substantial institutional voting power held by mutual funds, the increasing importance of the exercise of that power to fund shareholders, and the potential for conflicts of interest with respect to the exercise of fund proxy voting power, limited information is available regarding how funds vote their proxies. At present, the Commission's rules do not require mutual funds to disclose either their proxy voting policies and procedures or their proxy voting records. Several mutual fund complexes voluntarily provide information to investors, often on their websites, about the policies and procedures that they use to determine how to vote proxies and, in some cases, their actual proxy voting decisions. The Internet

> provides a medium for these funds to make information about their proxy voting available to shareholders quickly and in a cost-effective manner. We applaud these voluntary efforts of mutual funds to disclose proxy voting information to shareholders.
>
> We believe, however, that the time has now arrived for the Commission to require mutual funds to disclose their proxy voting policies and procedures, and their actual voting records. Investors in mutual funds have a fundamental right to know how the fund casts proxy votes on shareholders' behalf. . . .
>
> Proxy voting decisions by funds can play an important role in maximizing the value of the funds' investments, thereby having an enormous impact on the financial livelihood of millions of Americans. Further, shedding light on mutual fund proxy voting could illuminate potential conflicts of interest and discourage voting that is inconsistent with fund shareholders' best interests. Finally, requiring greater transparency of proxy voting by funds may encourage funds to become more engaged in corporate governance of issuers held in their portfolios, which may benefit all investors and not just fund shareholders.

The next two excerpts examine the role of an institutional intermediary as a corporate activist. As you read the following article, compare and contrast the role in corporate governance of mutual funds and public pension plans.

> Policies and politics v. investments and returns[1]
>
> John Goss is convinced that tobacco stocks are sound investments. He is equally certain that public pension plans can't, by dumping the tobacco stocks they own, do anything to loosen the grip cigarettes have on their massive consumer base.
>
> Nevertheless, the 76-year-old Mr. Goss lent an ear to fellow retired Vermont schoolteachers and found their sentiment loud and practically uniform: Vermont teachers' pension money has no business supporting tobacco makers.
>
> So against his own convictions, Mr. Goss, a longtime trustee of the Vermont State Teachers' Retirement System, asked the $840 million pension system's board to reconsider its recent vote on divesting tobacco stocks. The board had deadlocked 3-to-3 on that June 4 vote. But the second time around, Mr. Goss changed his "no" vote to "yes" and the motion carried. The pension plan now is in the process of unloading $10 million of tobacco stocks.
>
> To Mr. Goss, a 28-year veteran of the board that directs the teachers' retirement system, changing his vote was a measure of accountability. He was voting the minds of the 10,000 active and 3,000 retired Vermont teachers he represents — not his own mind.
>
> "I voted what I considered was my fiduciary obligation," says Mr. Goss, a former football, basketball and track three-sport coach. He

1. David Franecki, *Pension Trustees Pressed to Quit Tobacco,* Wall St. J., Jul. 7, 1997, at B10B.

spent 40 years as an English teacher, school administrator and guidance counselor in three Vermont communities. "Educators," he says, "tend to agree that tobacco is not good."

Mr. Goss is among a small but powerful group of state workers, both active and retired, who oversee billions in public pension dollars. Board members typically come from varying backgrounds, and often have little or no professional investment experience. Yet they are called on to weigh multimillion-dollar investment decisions fraught with social, political and moral ramifications. Currently many of those overseers are being asked if it's prudent for public workers' retirement money to help support America's tobacco giants.

Public pension systems in Florida and Maryland have voted to dump their tobacco shares. Others in New York, Texas and Washington have either capped their tobacco investments or are considering unloading them. Florida's May 28 decision to sell its $800 million of tobacco stocks has lent credence to the divestment argument and could kindle similar actions across the U.S. says Doug Cogan, director of the tobacco information service of the Investor Responsibility Research Center, an independent firm that researches corporate governance and public-policy issues relating to investments.

"These trustees wear two hats," says Mr. Cogan. "One is to represent their constituents, and the other is to be a fiduciary and look after the investments of their constituents. And sometimes those two roles come into conflict."

Mr. Goss maintains that his duty to pick the most profitable investments for Vermont's pension system was overridden by the overwhelming opinions of his constituents. He sees no conflict between his decision and a "prudent-investor" rule embraced by many public pension plans that rejects so-called social investing and binds investment officials to invest "solely in the interests of beneficiaries." The rule is rooted in the Employee Retirement Income Security Act, a 1974 law that established guidelines for the management of private pension funds. Public pension funds aren't bound by Erisa, but many still follow its key provisions.

Others contend that political influences inevitably surround tobacco divestment debates and distort the sole responsibility of retirement boards — improving the bottom line. They argue that pension fiduciaries like Mr. Goss can become political tools of a tobacco backlash aimed at punishing tobacco companies any way possible.

Tobacco investments are being attacked on more than just the social front, too. The viability of tobacco as an investment increasingly is being questioned, in light of world-wide litigation concerns and calls for stricter regulation of the industry.

Larry Chase, a Vermont teacher and pension board member who voted both times to keep the tobacco stocks, says the board is guilty of social investing. "It's a way to make political hay," says Mr. Chase, a 54-year-old science teacher at South Burlington High School. "It's pretty en vogue to beat up on tobacco."

Indeed, both Republican State Treasurer James Douglas and Vermont's Democrat Gov. Howard Dean weighed in on the side of divestment. When the teachers' pension board deadlocked in its first vote, the three state government representatives voted to divest and the three trustees representing teachers voted to keep tobacco stocks.

Mr. Chase contends the tobacco divestment movement in Vermont is "the brainchild" of the state treasurer. Mr. Douglas, who sits on the boards of all three of Vermont's pension systems, has been vocal about his desire to rid them of tobacco stocks. "I think investing public funds in tobacco companies is contrary to the values of most Vermonters and is clearly contradictory to the message that the state is sending in other forums," says Mr. Douglas.

No public support for tobacco has been evident in Vermont, which is one of about 40 states suing tobacco companies to recover Medicaid costs of treating smoking-related illnesses. "I think the folks who wanted to stay with our tobacco shares felt pretty lonely," says Mr. Douglas.

The effects of a pension plan unloading its tobacco stocks are debatable. The $10 million sale by the Vermont State Teachers' Retirement System will easily find its way back into the market, considering that some 174 million shares of Philip Morris Cos. stock alone changed hands in June.

Mr. Chase fears that by dumping tobacco stocks, which have soared in value in recent years, investment returns will take a hit that taxpayers will have to pay for through bigger contributions to the pension system. Vermont, like many states. [sic] depends on a combination of asset growth, state taxes and employee contributions to fund pensions for state workers.

Mr. Chase is also concerned that the state has no real criteria for considering social-investment questions. For instance, if tobacco companies aren't prudent investments, what about producers of alcoholic beverages or gambling stocks?

For his part, Mr. Goss says the most solid affirmation of his decision to rid Vermont's pension system of tobacco stocks came from his daughter, who is a teacher and mother of two young children.

"When the first vote came out, she called me and said she appreciated me voting my mind," says Mr. Goss. "At the second one, she said 'Dad, I'm glad you did it.'"

---

## Discussion Topic

Would Mr. Goss' actions with respect to tobacco stocks be permissible if he were a mutual fund portfolio manager?

---

SEC Commissioner Paul R. Carey discussed how investment advisers vote the securities in their funds' portfolios: [1]

> Mutual funds own approximately 3 trillion dollars in common stocks. With a total market capitalization of 17 trillion dollars, funds — or more accurately, their investment advisers — control a significant percentage of voting stock in this country.
>
> The mutual fund governance question is obvious: How should investment advisers exercise this voting power?
>
> In theory, and under the law, the answer is clear. Advisers are fiduciaries. As fiduciaries, advisers must act in the best interest of their beneficiaries. Thus, when voting portfolio securities, a fund adviser must act in the best interest of the fund, and not in its own interest.
>
> However, in practice, in deciding how to vote portfolio company shares, how effectively are advisers carrying out their responsibilities as fiduciaries? What are funds and advisers doing to promote responsible proxy voting? Industry participants are focusing more attention on these issues, as well. In fact, in a recent speech, John Bogle, the founder of the Vanguard Group, questioned whether fund advisers were living "up to their responsibility of corporate citizenship. . . ."
>
> Prior to casting a single vote, fund advisers could, and many do, use their influence as large shareholders to highlight certain management practices that may not increase shareholder value. Consistent with their fiduciary duties, fund advisers may discuss with management their views on key issues that affect shareholder value, such as: setting executive compensation levels; repricing stock options; and managing earnings through inappropriate accounting practices.
>
> Opening lines of communication with portfolio company management to discuss these types of issues can often prove very beneficial to fund shareholders. . . .
>
> [For example,] [w]hen Michael Price was the portfolio manager of the Mutual Series Funds, he often advocated for change in the companies in which his funds held large positions.
>
> This type of active role, however, seems to be the exception rather than the rule. Some fund advisers approach these corporate governance issues simply by voting proxies according to the recommendations of proxy consultants. Many other fund advisers "vote with their feet" by selling if they are dissatisfied with company management, rather than trying to work with company management to increase shareholder value. . . .
>
> Should fund advisers do more?
>
> Sometimes, fund advisers may not do more because they have concluded that doing more is not in the best interest of the fund. Clearly, fund advisers must engage in a cost/benefit analysis, and weigh the costs of possible courses of action against the potential

1. (Dec. 9, 1999), *available at* http://www.sec.gov/news/speech/speecharchive/1999/spch335.htm (last modified Dec. 10, 1999) (footnotes omitted).

> benefits to the fund. In some cases, the costs of engaging company management on an issue may outweigh the potential benefits that may accrue to the fund. Fund advisers should not expend resources if they have no reasonable expectation that doing so will provide a net benefit to the fund. For example, if a fund holds only a small position in a company, a decision to not engage management in discussions, or to switch rather than fight, may be appropriate — particularly if the issue involved would not significantly affect the value of the fund's holdings.
>
> Unfortunately, sometimes, fund advisers may not do more, because, to do more, might conflict with the interests of the adviser. A fund adviser could have an economic interest to vote the fund's shares to please company management, even if such a vote might not be in the best interests of the fund. This could be because a fund adviser might manage — or hope to manage — the retirement plan of a company whose stock is owned by the fund. If the fund adviser wants the pension business of XYZ Company, or it wants to continue to manage XYZ's pension business, it might think twice before voting against the recommendation of XYZ's management — even if voting against the recommendation could increase the value of the funds' holdings. Clearly, this result is contrary to a fund advisers' fiduciary duty to the fund and its shareholders. . . .

## D. Custody of Investment Company Assets: Section 17(f)

### 1. Regulation of Custodians

Like banks and insurance companies, and like fiduciaries generally, investment companies are legally required to put their clients' funds in safe custody, and sometimes segregate clients' funds from the adviser's own funds and earmark them. Sections 17(f) and 26(a) (applying to unit investment trusts) of the Investment Company Act deal with this topic. Section 17(g) of the 1940 Act requires that employees who have access to the investment company's funds should be covered by a fidelity bond. Under section 17(f) the trustee or custodian should be a bank (as defined in section 2(a)(5) of the 1940 Act) that has an aggregate capital, surplus, and undivided profits of an amount of not less than $500,000. The section also regulates the terms upon which the custodian shall serve.

Section 17(f) designates the qualifications of a custodian, for example, the requirement that the custodian be a bank having a certain amount of capital and surplus. The section does not address the issues of a custodian that is an affiliated person of the investment company or its adviser. However, the section does allow for self-custody by the investment company and for custody by broker-dealers. These permissible arrangements are offered to facilitate an efficient and cost-effective trading in the investment company's portfolio. Custody of fund assets other than with a bank, as described above, is accompanied by conditions to reduce the possibility of misappropriation of fund assets. These conditions are contained in various rules adopted under section 17(f). Additionally, custody with an affiliated person of the fund or its adviser is generally viewed as "self-custody" and such arrangements also must take care to not run afoul of the prohibition in section 17(d) regarding "joint transactions" with affiliates (discussed in further detail later in this book).

---

**Discussion Topics**

a. Investment companies are usually established by entrepreneurs. Some establish unit investment trusts by accumulating a portfolio of securities, depositing the portfolio with a trustee in exchange for securities representing a pro rata share of the portfolio, and selling these securities. Some entrepreneurs establish closed-end or open-end investment companies, and invest the "seed money" necessary to start these companies of at least $100,000, as required in section 14(a). What is the status of such entrepreneurs as custodians? Note the definition of a promoter and depositor in sections 2(a)(30) and 26(a) respectively. May a promoter or depositor serve as a custodian?

b. Section 17(f) is situated in a section that deals with conflicts of interests with affiliates of investment companies. Should section 17(f) be interpreted as restricting affiliates only to hold the funds' assets? Or should the section be interpreted more broadly to cover safety of the assets of investment companies?

---

### 2. Foreign Custodians: Rule 17f-5

When investment companies began to invest in foreign securities, it was not feasible to require custody of such securities in U.S. banks. Hence, the SEC promulgated rule 17f-5 to allow custody of such securities with foreign custodians. In 1997,[1] the SEC amended the rule, highlighting the problems regarding foreign custody of investment company assets.

The amendments are designed to "give management investment companies greater flexibility in their foreign custody arrangements by (i) permitting fund boards of directors to delegate their responsibilities to select and monitor foreign custodians, and (ii) expanding the class of eligible foreign custodians." Before the amendments, the rule required the board of directors to determine whether a particular foreign custody arrangement was in the "best interests" of the fund and its shareholders. The amendments permit fund directors to play a more traditional oversight role with respect to the custody of fund assets overseas. Directors may delegate their duties to select a foreign custodian and monitor a fund's foreign custody arrangements to the fund's investment adviser, officers, or a U.S. or foreign bank, and are no longer required to approve foreign custody arrangements annually. Thus, the amended rule replaced this standard with a more "focused determination:" whether the foreign custodian will maintain fund assets with "reasonable care based on standards applicable to custodians in the particular foreign market," after considering all factors

1. Custody of Investment Company Assets Outside the United States, Investment Company Act Rel. Nos. 21259 (Jul. 27, 1995) (proposed); and 22658 (May 12, 1997) (adopted) (codified as amended at 17 C.F.R. § 270.17f-5 (2015)).

relevant to the safekeeping of fund assets, including the custodian's financial strength, its practices and procedures, and internal controls.

The amended rule eliminates the requirement that the board consider "prevailing country risks," i.e., risks associated with investment in a particular country rather than placing assets with a particular custodian, because these country risks are investment risks appropriately considered by a fund's board or investment adviser when deciding whether the fund should invest in a particular country, rather than custodial risks to be addressed in rule 17f-5.

The amended rule also eliminates the requirement that foreign custodians meet specific capital requirements. Instead, the foreign custodian would be selected based on its ability to maintain fund assets with "reasonable care as evidenced by the custodian's financial strength and other relevant factors."

### 3. Bonding of Persons Having Access to Investment Company Assets

Section 17(g) of the 1940 Act requires that persons having access to an investment company's assets be covered by a fidelity bond. A number of questions arose in connection with this section. In a drive for savings, the personnel of the adviser and the personnel of the investment company, as well as of affiliated companies, should be covered by the same fidelity bond. That joint coverage raises issues under section 17(d) and rule 17d-1. The SEC permits such joint arrangements under conditions that ensured the equal treatment of investment companies and their affiliates. A second issue involves the supervision and monitoring of the board of directors over such bonding arrangement. Rule 17g-1(d)[1] requires that a majority of the disinterested directors approve the fidelity bond at least once a year, and determine that the bond is in a reasonable form after considering all the relevant factors, such as the value of the aggregate fund assets, the type and terms of the bond and arrangements made for the custody and safety of the fund's assets, and the nature of the fund's securities portfolio.

Rule 17g-1 also regulates the minimum amount of a single bond and other terms of the bond and requires the fund to report to the SEC any claims made on the bond, and any shortfall that the bond did not cover. There are very few cases in which such bonds have been activated. The Investment Company Institute established an insurance company under its auspices to provide the industry with an alternative to private insurance companies, providing competition that reduced the premiums on the fidelity bonds.

## E. Personal Investment Activities of Investment Company Personnel: Section 17(j)

Section 17(j) of the 1940 Act prohibits fraudulent, deceptive or manipulative acts or practices in the purchase or sale of a security held or to be acquired by a registered investment company by (1) an affiliated person of, or principal underwriter for, a registered investment company or (2) an affiliated person of an investment adviser of, or principal underwriter for, a registered investment company. This section authorizes the SEC to define such acts and prescribe means to prohibit such acts and specifically

1. 17 C.F.R. § 270.17g-1(d) (2015).

authorizes the requirement of codes of ethics by registered investment companies and investment advisers of, and principal underwriters for, such investment companies. Rule 17j-1 thus prohibits (1) an affiliated person of, or principal underwriter for, a registered investment company, or an affiliated person of an investment adviser of, or principal underwriter for, a registered investment company, to engage in such acts or practices.[1]

Rule 17j-1 also (1) generally requires a registered investment company and an investment adviser of, or principal underwriter for, such company, to adopt a code of ethics to prevent such conduct by its access persons; (2) requires such access persons to report their personal securities transactions to their organizations; and (3) requires the above organizations to comply with certain recordkeeping requirements. An "access person" is generally defined in rule 17j-1 to include (a) the officers and directors of a fund or its investment adviser, and (b) employees of the fund or its investment adviser (or other such officers and directors, including those of companies in a control relationship with the fund or adviser) who, in connection with their regular functions or duties, make, participate in, or obtain information regarding, the purchase or sale of securities by a fund, or whose functions relate to the making of any recommendations with respect to such purchases or sales (a standard similar to that set forth in (b) is applied to officers and directors of a fund's principal underwriter).

The SEC noted that "no single set of guidelines would be appropriate for all funds" and therefore codes of ethics need not contain specific restrictions or prohibitions. In addition, rule 17j-1 does not restrict the nature or timing of personal securities transactions.[2]

In 1995, the SEC noted concerns following recent developments, including the termination of a well-known portfolio manager for failure to report personal trading, and a large fund complex amending its personal trading rules in response to certain practices. Following a report by the Investment Management Division, the SEC proposed amendments to the rule 17j-1.[3] The amendments were adopted in 1999. The amendments (1) enhance board oversight by providing that the board (including a majority of independent directors) approve the fund's code of ethics and that of any investment adviser or principal underwriter; (2) require additional monitoring by requiring initial and annual holdings reports from access persons and compliance personnel review of personal trading; and (3) require disclosure of the fund's personal investment policies in the fund's registration statement.[4]

---

1. 17 C.F.R. § 270.17j-1 (2015).
2. Personal Investment Activities of Investment Company Personnel and Codes of Ethics of Investment Companies and Their Investment Advisers and Principal Underwriters, Investment Company Act Rel. No. 21341 (Sept. 8, 1995).
3. Personal Investment Activities of Investment Company Personnel and Codes of Ethics of Investment Companies and Their Investment Advisers and Principal Underwriters, Investment Company Act Rel. No. 21341 (Sept. 8, 1995) (codified as amended at 17 C.F.R. § 270.17j-1 (2015)).
4. Personal Investment Activities of Investment Company Personnel, and Codes of Ethics of Investment Companies and Their Investment Advisers and Principal Underwriters, Investment Company Act Rel. No. 23958, Investment Advisers Act

The last chapter in this book is devoted to issues concerning ethics. The issue of Codes of Ethics that advisers are required to establish belongs both to that chapter as well as to this chapter. The required substance of the Code mandated that this requirement be inserted here. The nature of law-mandated ethical behavior belongs to the last chapter, especially because of the importance of the subject. On the issue of ethical conduct, consider the introduction to the last chapter.

In 2004 the SEC adopted Rule 204A-1 under the Advisers Act requiring every registered adviser to adopt and enforce a code of ethics applicable to the adviser's personnel.[1] Often, advisers to registered investment companies adopt one policy that covers both 17j-1 and 204A-1 since these rules have significant overlap.

The code must include, at a minimum, a standard (or standards) of business conduct that the adviser requires of its supervised persons, which standard must reflect its fiduciary obligations and those of its supervised persons. Other provisions must generally require (1) supervisory persons to comply with applicable federal securities laws; (2) access persons to report to the adviser, quarterly, and the adviser to review, access persons' personal securities transactions and holdings; (3) supervisory persons to report code violations promptly to the chief compliance officer (or to another designated person provided the chief compliance officer also receives reports); and (4) the adviser to provide supervisory persons with a copy of the code, and the supervised persons to provide the adviser written acknowledgement of receipt.

An access person is generally defined in rule 204A-1 as a supervised person (1) with access to nonpublic information regarding any clients' purchase or sale of securities, or nonpublic information regarding the portfolio holdings of any reportable fund, or (2) involved in making securities recommendations to clients, or who has access to such recommendations that are nonpublic. If providing investment advice is the adviser's primary business, all of its directors, officers and partners are presumed access persons.

There are three exceptions to the reporting requirements: (i) securities held in accounts over which the access person had no direct or indirect influence or control; (ii) transactions effected pursuant to an automatic investment plan; and (iii) a report which would duplicate information contained in broker trade confirmations or account statements that are held in the adviser's records provided that it receives the confirmations or statements no later than 30 days after the end of the applicable quarter.

Pre-approval of certain investments is required. The code of ethics must require access persons to obtain pre-approval before acquiring a security in an initial public offering or limited offering. Pre-approval is not required for an adviser with only one access person provided that the adviser maintains its required records of its holdings and transactions.

---

Rel. No. 1815 (Aug. 20, 1999) (as corrected Mar. 6, 2000), 64 Fed. Reg. 46,821 (Aug. 27, 1999) (codified as amended at 17 C.F.R. § 270.17j-1 (2015)).

1. Investment Adviser Codes of Ethics, Investment Advisers Act Rel. No. 2256 (Jul. 2, 2004) (codified as amended at 17 C.F.R. § 275.204A-1 (2015)).

Access persons must report with respect to "reportable securities." "Reportable securities" do not include: (i) direct obligations of the United States government; (ii) bankers' acceptances, bank certificates of deposit, commercial paper and high quality short-term debt instruments (including repurchase agreements); (iii) shares of money market funds; (iv) shares of open-end funds other than reportable funds (i.e., shares of open-end funds other than a fund for which the adviser serves as an investment adviser or a fund whose investment adviser or principal underwriter controls, is controlled by, or is under common control with, the adviser); or (v) shares of unit investment trusts invested exclusively in open-end funds other than reportable funds.[1]

The SEC emphasized that the code of ethics requirement sets only a minimum requirement:

> Rule 204A-1 requires each adviser's code of ethics to set forth a standard of business conduct that the adviser requires of all its supervised persons. The rule does not require the adviser to adopt a particular standard, but the standard chosen must reflect the adviser's fiduciary obligations and those of its supervised persons, and must require compliance with the federal securities laws.
>
> This provision . . . establishes only a minimum requirement. Advisers are free to set higher standards for their employees, such as those established by professional or trade groups. Of course, any other code adopted for use must meet the minimum requirements of the rule, or be supplemented to meet the minimum requirements.
>
> We urge advisers to take great care and thought in preparing their codes of ethics, which should be more than a compliance manual. Rather, a code of ethics should set out ideals for ethical conduct premised on fundamental principals of openness, integrity, honesty and trust. A good code of ethics should effectively convey to employees the value the advisory firm places on ethical conduct, and should challenge employees to live up not only to the letter of the law, but also to the ideals of the organization.[2]

The SEC also listed elements advisory firms commonly include in codes of ethics and that advisers should consider:

- Prior written approval before access persons can place a personal securities transaction ("pre-clearance").
- Maintenance of lists of issuers of securities that the advisory firm is analyzing or recommending for client transactions, and prohibitions on personal trading in securities of those issuers.
- Maintenance of "restricted lists" of issuers about which the advisory firm has inside information, and prohibitions on any trading (personal or for clients) in securities of those issuers.

1. Investment Adviser Codes of Ethics, Investment Advisers Act Rel. No. 2256 (Jul. 2, 2004) (codified as amended at 17 C.F.R. § 275.204A-1 (2015)).
2. *Id.*

- "Blackout periods" when client securities trades are being placed or recommendations are being made and access persons are not permitted to place personal securities transactions.
- Reminders that investment opportunities must be offered first to clients before the adviser or its employees may act on them, and procedures to implement this principle.
- Prohibitions or restrictions on "short-swing" trading and market timing. Requirements to trade only through certain brokers, or limitations on the number of brokerage accounts permitted.
- Requirements to provide the adviser with duplicate trade confirmations and account statements.
- Procedures for assigning new securities analyses to employees whose personal holdings do not present apparent conflicts of interest.

---

## Discussion Topics

a. How different is a code of ethics from a statute or regulation?

b. Why did the SEC choose to require advisers to impose a Code of Ethics rather than impose the same requirements as a rule?

c. Should an adviser prohibit employees involved in portfolio management and analysis from buying and selling stocks or other securities for their own account? Can such a prohibition be enforced in light of the fact that such persons usually think and talk about stocks and securities during most of their waking hours?

If so, what kind of rules should the adviser impose? Should the rules be similar when applied to the traders, who receive information not only on the purchase but also on the sell orders?

d. What sanctions can the SEC impose on violations of a Code of Ethics? Suppose an adviser did not require its employees to read the Code of Ethics? Or suppose the employees read the Code but violated its requirements and the adviser did not discover the violations? Or what if the adviser discovered the violations and did nothing about it?

---

The *Speaker* case illustrates issues related to a portfolio manager's personal trading activities.[1]

Speaker was a portfolio manager for investment adviser Janus and an officer for a mutual fund it advises. Speaker, in his capacity as portfolio manager, was contacted by a broker-dealer who offered the opportunity to purchase certain securities at a certain price. He rejected the offer on behalf of the fund. Later he learned of a bid by another broker-dealer for the securities at a higher price. He personally purchased the securities and sold them at a profit without disclosure to the fund or its consent. He purchased

1. In the Matter of Ronald V. Speaker, Investment Company Act Rel. No. 22461 (Jan. 13, 1997) (some footnotes omitted).

and sold the securities through a private trading account he maintained through the adviser at a bank, where he was authorized to use the adviser's institutional clearing account to settle his personal trades.

The SEC first found that Speaker, as a portfolio manager, was a fiduciary, and, as such, "under the highest obligation to avoid conflicts of interest with their clients by disclosing personal trading practices that may affect their recommendations." Investors seeking an adviser's advice should be aware of such conflicts to properly evaluate "whether an adviser is serving 'two masters' or only one." Therefore, "personal investments by managers require particularly careful scrutiny."

The SEC found violations of sections 206(1) and 206(2) of the Advisers Act, section 17(j) of the 1940 Act and Rule 17j-1(a) thereunder, and section 10(b) of the Exchange Act and Rule 10b-5 thereunder.

The SEC also discussed Janus' supervision of Speaker. Janus' compliance department reviewed the trades "primarily for conflicts with trading activity by the fund" but "took no further action." "Janus had no mechanism for disclosing the trades to the fund and obtaining the prior consent of the fund, or of a disinterested Janus employee authorized to waive this opportunity on the fund's behalf." Therefore, "Janus failed reasonably to supervise Speaker within the meaning of Section 203(e)(5) of the Advisers Act."

## F. Portfolio Managers' Access to Information

Regulation FD (Fair Disclosure)[1] generally prohibits the selective disclosure of material nonpublic information by issuers. While this impacts portfolio managers' access to information, it also impacts the dissemination of information by closed-end funds, which themselves are subject to Regulation FD as issuers.

When an issuer (or any person acting on its behalf) discloses material nonpublic information regarding the issuer or its securities to one of certain persons (generally a broker, dealer, investment adviser, investment company, or holder of the issuer's securities "under circumstances in which it is reasonably foreseeable that the person will purchase or sell the issuer's securities on the basis of the information"), the issuer must make public disclosure of the information: simultaneously, for intentional disclosure, or promptly, for non-intentional disclosure. Public disclosure is made through a filing on Form 8-K or "through another method (or combination of methods) of disclosure that is reasonably designed to provide broad, non-exclusionary distribution of the information to the public."

The SEC discussed the policy of Regulation FD in its adopting release:[2]

> [W]e have become increasingly concerned about the selective disclosure of material information by issuers. As reflected in recent publicized reports, many issuers are disclosing important nonpublic information, such as advance warnings of earnings results, to securities analysts or selected institutional investors or both, before making

1. 17 C.F.R. § 243 (2015).
2. Selective Disclosure and Insider Trading, Investment Company Act Rel. No. 24599 (Aug. 15, 2000).

full disclosure of the same information to the general public. Where this has happened, those who were privy to the information beforehand were able to make a profit or avoid a loss at the expense of those kept in the dark.

We believe that the practice of selective disclosure leads to a loss of investor confidence in the integrity of our capital markets. Investors who see a security's price change dramatically and only later are given access to the information responsible for that move rightly question whether they are on a level playing field with market insiders.

Issuer selective disclosure bears a close resemblance in this regard to ordinary "tipping" and insider trading. In both cases, a privileged few gain an informational edge -- and the ability to use that edge to profit -- from their superior access to corporate insiders, rather than from their skill, acumen, or diligence. Likewise, selective disclosure has an adverse impact on market integrity that is similar to the adverse impact from illegal insider trading: investors lose confidence in the fairness of the markets when they know that other participants may exploit "unreadable informational advantages" derived not from hard work or insights, but from their access to corporate insiders. The economic effects of the two practices are essentially the same. Yet, as a result of judicial interpretations, tipping and insider trading can be severely punished under the antifraud provisions of the federal securities laws, whereas the status of issuer selective disclosure has been considerably less clear.

Regulation FD is also designed to address another threat to the integrity of our markets: the potential for corporate management to treat material information as a commodity to be used to gain or maintain favor with particular analysts or investors. . . . [I]n the absence of a prohibition on selective disclosure, analysts may feel pressured to report favorably about a company or otherwise slant their analysis in order to have continued access to selectively disclosed information. We are concerned, in this regard, with reports that analysts who publish negative views of an issuer are sometimes excluded by that issuer from calls and meetings to which other analysts are invited.

. . . [T]echnological developments have made it much easier for issuers to disseminate information broadly. Whereas issuers once may have had to rely on analysts to serve as information intermediaries, issuers now can use a variety of methods to communicate directly with the market. In addition to press releases, these methods include, among others, Internet webcasting and teleconferencing. Accordingly, technological limitations no longer provide an excuse for abiding the threats to market integrity that selective disclosure represents.

To address the problem of selective disclosure, we proposed Regulation FD. It targets the practice by establishing new requirements for full and fair disclosure by public companies.

The SEC noted the following concern about the effects of Regulation FD on issuer communications:

> One frequently expressed concern was that Regulation FD would not lead to broader dissemination of information, but would in fact have a "chilling effect" on the disclosure of information by issuers. In the view of these commenters, issuers would find it so difficult to determine when a disclosure of information would be "material" (and therefore subject to the regulation) that, rather than face potential liability and other consequences of violating Regulation FD, they would cease informal communications with the outside world altogether. Some of these commenters therefore recommended that the Commission not adopt any mandatory rule prohibiting selective disclosure, like Regulation FD, but instead pursue voluntary means of addressing the problem, such as interpretive guidance, or the promotion of a "blue ribbon" panel to develop best practices for issuer disclosure. Other commenters recommended various ways that Regulation FD could be made narrower or more well-defined, in order to ameliorate some of the concerns about chilling. Other commenters, however, took issue with the supposition that issuer disclosures would be chilled. As some commenters stated, the marketplace simply would not allow issuers to cease communications with analysts and security holders.
>
> We have considered these views carefully. . . . [W]e are mindful of the concerns about chilling issuer disclosure; we agree that the market is best served by more, not less, disclosure of information by issuers. Because any potential "chill" is most likely to arise -- if at all -- from the fear of legal liability, we included in proposed Regulation FD significant safeguards against inappropriate liability. Most notably, we stated that the regulation would not provide a basis for private liability, and provided that in Commission enforcement actions under Regulation FD we would need to prove knowing or reckless conduct.

The following excerpt is the Investment Company Institute's comment letter on the Regulation FD proposal.[1]

> Proposed Regulation FD is intended to curtail the selective disclosure of material nonpublic information to certain marketplace participants. The proposed rule would mandate that if an issuer discloses material nonpublic information to any person outside the company, the issuer must simultaneously disseminate that information publicly. (In the case of inadvertent disclosure, such dissemination would have to occur "promptly.") The Proposing Release notes that the Commission is "troubled by the many recent reports of selective disclosure and the potential impact of this practice on market integrity." The Commission infers from this reported conduct that many market participants view the Supreme Court's decision in *Dirks v.*

1. Investment Company Institute, Re: Proposed Rules Relating to Selective Disclosure and Insider Trading (Apr. 27, 2000), *available at* http://www.ici.org/policy/comments/ci.00_SEC_REGFD_COM.print.

*Securities and Exchange Commission* "as affording considerable protection to insiders who make selective disclosures to analysts, and to the analysts (and their clients) who receive selectively disclosed information. . . ."Proposed Regulation FD would be the Commission's first attempt to regulate the rich and varied informal dialogue that takes place between public companies and the marketplace. These informal communications — analyst conference calls, investor conferences, and "one-on-one" meetings with management of issuers — are an integral part of the information provided to the marketplace. The contacts are important to both sides of the discussion. For market participants, including mutual fund portfolio managers, these communications represent a fundamental aspect of research. At the same time, issuers that participate actively in these informal contacts experience less volatility in their stock price and lower costs of capital.

These informal contacts require issuers to strike a difficult balance between responding to requests for information on a "real time" basis and not selectively disclosing important information to certain analysts. To the Commission's credit, the Proposing Release frames proposed Regulation FD with this concern in mind. The enforcement remedy is limited to knowing violations of the rule and there is a provision for corrective releases in response to inadvertent disclosures.

The Institute's single greatest concern with proposed Regulation FD centers on its exclusive reliance on the term "materiality," one of the most amorphous concepts in the securities laws. Under the proposed rule, information must be disseminated broadly if it is "material," that is, if "there is a substantial likelihood that a reasonable person would consider it important." This is a difficult, subjective analysis. Indeed, in Staff Accounting Bulletin No. 99, issued last August, the staff cautioned that while traditional quantitative measures may form part of the analysis, qualitative considerations must be weighed carefully as well. SAB No. 99 notes, for example, that "the demonstrated volatility of the price of a registrant's securities in response to certain types of disclosures may provide guidance as to whether investors regard quantitatively small misstatements as material."

An unqualified reference to materiality is inadequate in the context of informal communications between issuers and the marketplace. These materiality judgments are different from those made while preparing periodic reports, registration statements and other situations in which the issuer controls the content and the timing of the communication. Analyst conference calls and one-on-one meetings require managers who are not lawyers to make difficult materiality judgments literally "on their feet." The Institute is concerned that the uncertainty of this analysis and the constant risk of after-the-fact assessments could chill valuable marketplace contacts. Corporate managers might regularly choose to err on the side of saying too little that is useful or responsive to analysts' legitimate inquiries. Additionally, we fear that less information could increase marketplace volatility.

In light of these concerns, we suggest certain modifications to the substance of proposed Regulation FD, as discussed below. We also suggest that the Commission reaffirm the core principles of the "mosaic theory. . . ."

A. Scope of Proposed Regulation FD

The Institute believes that the proposed rule should be limited as a remedy for certain isolated abuses rather than clouding all informal contacts with regulatory uncertainty. In this regard, we recommend that proposed Regulation FD specify and be limited to the type of information that is most prone to selective disclosure abuses. When government regulates speech, courts require that this regulation precisely impose the minimum restriction necessary to implement the policy. Making the vague materiality standard the guiding principle for Regulation FD is inconsistent with this approach. Therefore, the Institute suggests that proposed Regulation FD be limited to those types of information that are especially likely to have a significant impact on the price of an issuer's securities. In this regard, the rule's "definitions" section should include a list of such types of information. We recommend that the list include the following:

[The ICI's recommendations included such items as filing for bankruptcy, defaulting on loan covenants or senior securities, and hiring and termination of the CEO, CFO, or COO].

This list is derived, in part, from Form 8-K filing requirements, recent proposed amendments to that form, and guidance provided by exchanges.

Much of the imprecision in proposed Regulation FD would be eliminated if this list were constituted as one that is exclusive. In that event, Regulation FD clearly would identify information that typically should be disseminated broadly before it is addressed with any one segment of the market. In the absence of such a delineation in the rule, the Institute fears that proposed Regulation FD would invite too much uncertainty. If this uncertainty is not curtailed, it could have the unintended effect of decreasing the real-time continuous flow of information and increasing marketplace volatility.

B. The Mosaic Theory

The Institute urges the Commission, in its release adopting Regulation FD, to reaffirm the core principles of the "mosaic theory" as applicable to all research efforts. The Commission has long recognized that skilled securities analysts ferret through nonpublic information (itself not material) "to form a 'mosaic' which is only material after the bits and pieces are assembled into one picture." While this principle has been developed primarily in matters involving "sell side" analysts who publish research on behalf of their broker-dealer employers, it applies equally to "buy side" analysts, including those analysts and portfolio managers for advisers to investment companies.

The Proposing Release makes only a passing reference to the important role of sell side analysts and does not acknowledge expressly the existence of buy side analysts. The Commission's adopting release should underscore that proposed Regulation FD neither limits appropriate market research nor the capacity to benefit from such research. In certain instances, members of the Commission have suggested that recipients of selectively disclosed information should be constrained from trading on the basis of that information. Indeed, the Commission has initiated proceedings related to the use of selectively disclosed material information.

The Institute is concerned that the interests of a broad cross-section of investors would be impaired if, for example, concerns about the scope of Regulation FD caused issuers to curtail individual meetings or conversations with fund investment personnel who have made substantial investments in their companies. The potential adverse impact of this rulemaking exercise would be mitigated if the adopting release includes a statement affirming that the Commission recognizes an inherent right to invest based on a prescient analysis.

---

## Discussion Topic

A portfolio manager of a health care fund learns from her contact at one of the fund's portfolio companies that the FDA is going to give expedited review to the company's request for approval of a new product. How is this information required to be handled pursuant to Regulation FD?

---

# Chapter 11

## *Distribution of Investment Company Shares*

Having examined the Investment Company Act's regulation of advisory services and fees, let us turn to the Act's regulation of the sale of fund shares. This Chapter deals with the regulation of the payments that investors are charged on redemptions and fund shares' distribution (sales loads) and the advisers' payments to the broker-dealers and other distributors of fund shares. The Chapter ends with the regulation of retail price maintenance, buying fund shares on margin, and exchange of fund shares.

Even though these functions differ from investment management and even though they offer different benefits to investors, all these services have one "side effect" — they all cost investors. They are also related, in terms of the advisers' incentives, to some conflicts of interest, the involvement of the boards of directors and the Commission. Thus, to some extent this Chapter deals not only with the distribution of funds' securities but also with the distribution cost to investors, the benefits to the sales force and to advisers. We are bound to revisit it in these different contexts.

### A. Regulation of Sales Loads; Different Methods of Paying for Distribution

A sales load is the money that investors pay in order to buy investment company shares. The law focused on sales loads because investors do not always calculate the effect of the load on the returns of their investment returns. Before the Investment Company Act was passed, investors paid the salespersons a commission. This commission was usually deducted from the initial payment that the investor paid for the shares. Therefore, an investor who bought shares for $100, and paid a sales load of $8, received only an investment of $92. This type of payment is called "a front-end sales load." To attract investors, new types of loads have emerged: contingent deferred sales load, deferred sales loads, and rule 12b-1 fees.

#### 1. The Forms of Payments

The following release describes the various forms of these payments and the issues that they raise.[1] It should be noted, however, that rule 6c-1

1. Proposed Exemptions for Certain Registered Open-End Management Investment Companies to Impose Deferred Sales Loads, Investment Company Act Rel. No. 16619 (Nov. 2, 1988).

was not passed; however, the SEC subsequently passed a rule, Rule 6c-10, permitting the contingent deferred sales loads described in the following release.

> Background
>
> Mutual funds [especially funds that issue redeemable securities] engage in a continuous public offering of redeemable securities. Until [about 1988 most sales loans were front end loans] . . . expressed as a percentage of the public offering price of the shares. . . . [The number of no load funds has grown in the 1970s and with it competition.] This increased competition from no-load funds and a perceived resistance among mutual fund investors to products that charge front-end sales loads have prompted load funds to develop alternative methods of distribution financing, such as the imposition of sales loads payable other than at the time of purchase.
>
> The practice of imposing deferred sales loads originated with separate accounts. In 1979, one such account was granted exemptions from several provisions of the Act to permit the imposition of a "contingent deferred sales load" ("CDSL") on variable annuity contracts issued by that account. The CDSLs were to be paid when all or part of a shareholder's interest in the separate account was either redeemed from the account or converted to an annuity. Exemptions were sought because the provisions of the Act do not specifically address situations where investment companies, whether separate accounts or mutual funds, charge sales loads payable other than at the time of purchase. [After the Commission granted a number of specific exemptions it codified the exemptions in 1983 in rule 6c-8].
>
> * * *
>
> Following the adoption of rule 6c-8, the Division of Investment Management ("Division") began to receive applications for exemptions from mutual funds and certain related persons ("Applicants") to permit deduction of deferred sales loads upon redemption of fund shares. . . .
>
> The majority of Applicants have been funds and related persons that use a combination of a CDSL and a distribution plan, adopted in accordance with rule 12b-1 under the Act (commonly, and herein, referred to as a "12b-1 plan"), as a substitute for charging investors a front-end sales load. [Rule 12b-1 permits the advisers to charge the funds a certain percentage of the funds' assets subject to processes and limitations and use the money to pay for fund shares' distribution]. Typically, a fund's principal underwriter initially pays the sales and promotional expenses associated with the sale of fund shares, including any sales commissions paid to persons that sell the shares. The principal underwriter then recovers the amounts expended through payments under the fund's 12b-1 plan. However, because 12b-1 plans provide that annual payments for distribution may not exceed a specified percentage of the fund's average net assets, or some similar ceiling, it may be several years before the principal underwriter can recover fully the amounts expended on the fund's

behalf. According to Applicants, this delay in payment raises the possibility that a shareholder will redeem fund shares before the payments under the fund's 12b-1 plan have reimbursed fully the principal underwriter for expenses incurred in connection with the sale of those shares. Thus, Applicants have sought to impose on each redeeming shareholder a CDSL designed to approximate the amount of unreimbursed expenses.

Applicants generally have represented that no CDSL will be imposed upon the redemption of shares purchased through the reinvestment of dividends or capital gains distributions. In addition, in calculating the amount of a CDSL due upon redemption, shares not subject to any CDSL generally will be redeemed first. After all such shares have been redeemed, the remaining shares will be redeemed in the order purchased.

Applicants routinely have sought exemptions from sections 2(a)(32), 2(a)(35), 22(c) and 22(d) of the Act, and from rule 22c-1 under the Act, to the extent necessary to permit a CDSL. [These exemptions are necessary, as discussed below]. . . .

Section 2(a)(32) of the Act defines the term "redeemable security" to be a security that, upon its presentation to the issuer or to a person designated by the issuer, entitles the shareholder to receive approximately his proportionate share of the issuer's current net assets, or the cash equivalent of those assets. Because the imposition of a CDSL would cause a redeeming shareholder to receive an amount less than net asset value of redeemed shares, Applicants have requested an exemption from section 2(a)(32) to the extent necessary to have shares subject to a CDSL be considered "redeemable securities" for purposes of the Act. In support of their position, Applicants have maintained that, although the imposition of a CDSL, in effect, could cause the shareholder to receive an amount less than the net asset value of his redeemed shares, payment of a CDSL does not prevent a redeeming shareholder from receiving his proportionate share of the fund's current net asset value. Rather, Applicants have argued that payment of a CDSL constitutes only the payment of the same sales load that could have been charged when the shares were purchased.

Section 2(a)(35) defines the term "sales load" to be an amount properly chargeable to sales or promotional expenses that is paid at the time the securities are purchased. Because CDSLs are not charged at the time of purchase, Applicants routinely have requested an exemption from section 2(a)(35). Applicants have maintained that a CDSL, in essence, is a sales load because a CDSL is used to pay expenses relating to sales and promotional activities, and that the basic nature of a CDSL as a sales charge is not changed by the fact that payment is deferred and made contingent upon the occurrence of a certain event.

Section 22(c) of the Act and rule 22c-1 thereunder require that the price of a redeemable security issued by a fund, for purposes of

> sale, redemption and repurchase, be based on the fund's current net asset value. Because a CDSL would cause a redeeming shareholder to receive an amount less than the net asset value of the redeemed shares, Applicants have sought an exemption from this section and rule, arguing that the redemption price of shares subject to a CDSL is based on current net asset value, and that a CDSL imposed at the time shares are redeemed simply is deducted from the redemption price in arriving at the net proceeds payable to the shareholder.
>
> Section 22(d) of the Act requires a mutual fund, its principal underwriter, and any dealer in redeemable securities issued by a fund to sell securities only at a current public offering price described in the fund's prospectus. Because sales loads (i.e., front-end sales loads) have traditionally been a component of the public offering price, section 22(d) has required historically that all investors be charged the same load. Funds seeking to charge different amounts of sales loads to different classes of investors or for different classes of transactions were, therefore, required to seek an exemption from section 22(d). These applications were codified in rule 22d-1 under the Act. . . .
>
> By its terms, rule 22d-1 applies to the sale of redeemable securities "at prices that reflect scheduled variations in, or elimination of, the sales load." Because this language contemplates sales loads paid at the time of purchase, the exemption provided by rule 22d-1 does not extend to scheduled variations in deferred sales loads. Therefore, Applicants seeking to offer scheduled variations in, or elimination of, CDSLs to specified classes of investors, or in connection with specified classes of transactions, have requested exemptions from section 22(d). In seeking these exemptions, Applicants have represented that either the scheduled variations would be imposed subject to the conditions set forth in rule 22d-1 under the Act for scheduled variations in front-end sales loads, or the scheduled variations would satisfy equivalent conditions set forth in the particular application.
>
> The Commission granted the CDSL exemptions under section 6(c) of the Act. . . . Those exemptions were based on several representations. Applicants represented that a CDSL would be more advantageous to shareholders than a front-end sales load because shareholders would have a greater amount of money available for investment at the time of purchase. Applicants also represented that shareholders would not be charged any greater amount as a CDSL than they could have been charged as a front-end sales load. Other representations related to the administration and calculation of CDSLs. . . .

In 1992, the National Association of Securities Dealers (now FINRA) dealt with "asset based securities sales."[1] The NASD proposed this rule and the SEC approved it, effective 1993. As background, mutual funds often have three

1. National Association of Securities Dealers, Inc.; Order Approving Proposed Rule Change Relating to the Limitation of Asset-Based Sales Charges as Imposed by Investment Companies, Exchange Act Rel. No. 30897 (Jul. 7, 1992). The current

components to their distribution-related expenses: (1) a sales load, whether up-front or contingent deferred, (2) an asset-based distribution fee, which is money paid by the fund from its own assets to finance distribution-related expenses (these are typically paid pursuant to a Rule 12b-1 plan adopted by the fund's board, which is described in more detail later in this Chapter), and (3) a shareholder servicing fee which, like the asset-based distribution fee, is paid by the fund from its own assets; however, this fee is paid in consideration of shareholder servicing activities by brokers and other financial intermediaries, and not to compensate such intermediaries for distribution-related services. A fund's adviser also often engages in so-called "revenue sharing" with its distribution partners by making supplemental payments from the adviser's own assets. These supplemental payments have been considered appropriate where the payments are made from the adviser's legitimate profits (in other words, the adviser has not charged an excessive fee to the fund to subsidize these supplemental payments). The NASD noted:

> Under the [NASD] "maximum sales charge rule" . . . no member may offer or sell shares of any open-end investment company or any "single payment" investment plan issued by a unit investment trust registered under the 1940 Act if the public offering price includes a sales charge which is excessive. Under existing rules, the maximum front-end sales charge may not exceed 8.5 percent of the offering price of mutual fund shares. The maximum amount is scaled down in steps to 6.25 percent if investors are not offered one of three additional services or benefits: dividend reinvestment at net asset value, quantity discounts, or rights of accumulation.
>
> II. Rationale for the Proposed Changes to the Maximum Sales Charge Rule
>
> At the time the maximum sales charge rule was adopted, the primary method used by mutual funds to finance sales related expenses was a front-end sales charge deducted from the offering price of mutual fund shares. Consequently, the rule was drafted specifically to address front-end sales charges. Since the adoption of the rule in 1975, the mutual fund industry has devised other methods of assessing sales related charges. These methods include "asset-based sales charges" and "deferred sales charges," which include "contingent deferred sales charges," or "CDSLs." Contingent deferred sales charges are "contingent" since they are paid only on redemptions that occur within a specified period after purchase and may be expressed as a percentage of either the original purchase price or, more typically, the redemption proceeds.
>
> The NASD has applied the existing maximum sales charge rule to contingent deferred sales charges even though such charges do not fit within the literal definition of sales load contained in Section 2(a)(35) of the 1940 Act. The rule has not been applied to asset-based sales charges, however. Such payments are the only type

version of the Rule is NASD Rule 2830, *available at* http://finra.complinet.com/en/display/display_main.html?rbid=2403&element_id=3691.

of mutual fund sales compensation that currently is not subject to NASD regulation. With the advent of these new methods of assessing sales charges on mutual funds, the NASD believed the Rules of Fair Practice should be amended specifically to encompass all sales charges. The NASD desired to take steps to assure a level playing field among all members selling mutual fund shares. Moreover, it believed additional amendments were necessary to prevent circumvention of the existing maximum sales charge rule because it had become possible for funds to use 12b-1 plans, either separately or in combination with initial or deferred sales loads, to charge investors more for distribution than could have been charged as an initial sales load under the existing maximum sales charge rule.

* * *

V. Discussion

The Commission is of the opinion that the proposed rule change carries out the NASD's congressional mandate to prevent excessive sales charges on mutual funds shares. The Commission believes that the proposed rule change appropriately balances the need to ensure that the NASD's rules allow broker-dealers, sales personnel and underwriters to receive reasonable compensation, against the need to ensure that investors are charged reasonable sales loads. While disclosure of the sales loads in the fund's prospectus is critical to an informed investor, disclosure alone in this instance is insufficient to comply with the congressional mandate that the NASD adopt rules to prevent excessive sales loads. Additionally, the Commission believes the amendments will promote fairness by assuring some degree of parity between the sales and sales-promotion expenses permitted of traditional load funds and those allowable to funds that assess finance charges against their assets. . . .

[The Commission concluded that the NASD had the jurisdiction with respect to service fees]. The ability of the NASD, through its rules, to regulate comprehensively mutual fund fees received by members is fully consistent with the statutory mandate of Section 22(b) of the 1940 Act that gives the NASD authority to prohibit excessive sales loads, and with protection of investors and the promotion of just and equitable principles of trade pursuant to Section 15A(b)(6) of the Act.

Section 22(b) of the 1940 Act gives the NASD a specific grant of authority to prohibit excessive sales loads. In addition, Section 15A(b)(6) of the Act requires, in pertinent part, that the Association adopt and amend its rules to promote just and equitable principles of trade, and in general to provide for the protection of investors and the public interest. The requirement that the Association's rules comport with just and equitable principles of trade encompasses the power to provide safeguards against unreasonable rates of commission or other charges.

The Association's proposal would revise its existing regulation of maximum sales charges that may be imposed by investment companies. The revision would extend the current maximum sales charge rule to include asset-based sales charges and tailor the rule's application to different sales charge compensation structures. The purpose of the revised maximum sales charge rule is to create "approximate economic equivalency" as to maximum sales charges for different types of mutual funds. Given the specific mandate of Section 22(b) of the 1940 Act and the requirement of just and equitable principles of trade embodied in Section 15A(b)(6) of the Act, the Commission is of the view that the NASD has authority to adopt rules that ensure overall reasonableness of sales fees received by members.

The Association's proposal would also directly limit members' underwriting and distribution of shares of investment companies that impose or pay service fees in excess of prescribed maximums. These limitations are intended to assure that service fees paid by investors are reasonable. If maximum sales loads are regulated, but service fees are not subject to any maximum limitation, it will be possible for members and investment companies to circumvent the intention of the sales fee rules by imposing or paying increased service fees. Such a result would frustrate the NASD's power to regulate sales charges pursuant to Section 22(b) of the 1940 Act. In addition, the limitations on service fees are consistent with the NASD's authority, pursuant to Section 15A(b)(6), to prevent excessive compensation of members and to assure that fees paid by investors for services are reasonable. Accordingly, the Commission finds the NASD has properly exercised its authority in proposing to limit both sales loads and service fees.

The Commission believes that the maximum asset-based sales charge of .75 of 1 percent per annum of average net assets in Subsection (d)(2)(E) of the proposed rule and the maximum service fee of .25 of 1 percent of a fund's average annual net assets proposed in Subsection (d)(5) should be adequate to finance sales related expenses and to provide compensation for continued service to mutual fund shareholder accounts.

The Commission also has considered the scope of the prohibition on use of the no-load label and finds the NASD's proposal to include a de minimis exception appropriate. To a large degree, the components of financing distribution costs -- sales loads, Rule 12b-1 fees, advisory fees, and underwriting fees -- are all inextricably linked. Given that all funds have distribution costs, tying the no-load label to the "sales charge/no sales charge" distinction may ignore the realities of distribution financing.

Making statistical comparisons, on the other hand, as to whether funds with de minimis 12b-1 charges ("de minimis fee funds") more closely resemble traditional no-load funds or traditional load funds is complicated somewhat by the evolution of the mutual fund industry. Virtually all de minimis fee funds are money market funds, a type of fund that did not exist until 1970. Most traditional load funds are equity funds or bond and income funds; virtually none is a money

> market fund. Accordingly, because expense ratios vary greatly among fund investment objectives, comparing expense ratios of de minimis fee funds to those of traditional load funds is difficult.
>
> Comparing the expense ratios of de minimis fee funds to traditional no-load funds is possible, however, and that comparison supports the NASD's determination to include the de minimis exception. Data submitted by the Investment Company Institute indicates that, for all fund categories analyzed, although de minimis fee funds on average have higher expense ratios than funds without such charges, the difference is relatively small -- between 12 and 24 basis points, depending on fund size and investment objective.
>
> Moreover, there is a significant degree of overlap between the expense ratios of de minimis fee funds (funds with Rule 12b-1 fees of 0.25 percent or less) and traditional no-load funds. For example, the data show that the expense ratios of de minimis fee funds almost all fall within the range of variation for traditional no-load funds in every fund investment objective category. Taxable and tax-free money market funds that have a traditional no-load structure have a mean expense ratio of 0.55 percent; their expense ratios range from 0.01 percent to 1.52 percent. De minimis fee money market funds have a mean expense ratio of 0.72 percent, with expense ratios ranging from 0.13 percent to 1.88 percent. Ninety-nine percent of all de minimis fee money market funds have expense ratios within the range of variation of traditional no-load money market funds. Thus, de minimis fee funds and traditional no-load funds are generally comparable in price. Any differences may be properly addressed by the prospectus fee table, preventing possible investor confusion. Accordingly, the Commission believes that the line drawn by the NASD is reasonable and consistent with its mandate under the Act.

Sales loads in mutual funds usually offered quantity discounts. Thus, if an investor purchased 5,000 shares, the sales load would be lower than if he purchased a lower number of shares. It was discovered in 2003 that brokers would sell investors' shares just below the cut-off point and fail to disclose that the sales load would be far lower if a few more shares were bought. Similarly, investors were not aware that some brokers received benefits from particular funds and advisers would recommend those funds' shares but not others. Unless the investors asked, the brokers, who did not consider themselves fiduciaries, did not disclose.

Concerned that investors in mutual funds lack information about such distribution-related costs and arrangements that pose conflicts of interest for broker-dealers, the Commission proposed, in January 2004, rules 15c2-2 and 15c2-3 under the Exchange Act, and conforming amendments to Rule 10b-10 under the Exchange Act and amendments to Form N-1A. This proposal was not adopted.[1]

---

1. Confirmation Requirements and Point of Sale Disclosure Requirements for Transactions in Certain Mutual Funds and Other Securities, and Other Confirmation Requirement Amendments, and Amendments to the Registration Form for Mutual Funds, Investment Company Act Rel. No. 26341 (Jan. 29, 2004).

Proposed rule 15c2-2 would require a broker, dealer, or municipal securities dealer to make written disclosures regarding "covered securities." The disclosure should be made at or before the completion of the transaction. Disclosure includes the transaction date, the issuer and class of the security, the net asset value, the number of shares, the total dollar amount, the net amount of the investment, any commission received by the broker or dealer, any deferred sales load (if the customer is selling shares or units), and a disclosure that the broker or dealer is not a member of the Securities Investor Protection Corporation ("SIPC").[1] In addition, a customer should be informed about the sales loads, the availability of breakpoints, asset-based sales charges and service fees, the amount earned from the fund complex by the broker, dealer, or municipal securities dealer and any associated person that is a broker, dealer, or municipal securities dealer (and other associated persons of the broker, dealer, or municipal securities dealer if the security is not a proprietary covered security).[2] The amount earned from the fund complex may be disclosed as a percentage of the total net asset value of the securities of the complex sold by the dealer, regarding certain arrangements.[3]

The broker or dealer must also disclose median information and comparison ranges for front-end sales loads, deferred sales loads, annual asset-based sales charges and service fees, dealer concessions or other sales fees, revenue sharing, and portfolio brokerage commissions. The Rule would permit the SEC to exempt a broker or dealer that provides appropriate alternative procedures. The Rule maintains the broker-dealers' obligations under the general antifraud provisions of the federal securities laws, or under any other legal requirements.[4]

Proposed Rule 15c2-3 would require disclosure of the sales load at the time of purchase and an estimate of any asset-based sales charge and asset-based service fees for the year following the purchase (if net asset value does not change). Disclosure would include an estimate of the maximum deferred sales load, if the shares or units are sold within one year, the number of years the deferred sales load may be in effect, and the dealer concession at the time of sale. The broker or dealer must also disclose whether it or any affiliate receives revenue sharing or portfolio brokerage commissions from the fund complex, and disclose certain differential compensation practices. Disclosure must generally be made in writing using Schedule 15D. The customers have a right to terminate orders made before disclosure, and broker-dealers must make and keep records of the disclosure.[5]

---

## Discussion Topics

a. What are the different ways of financing share distribution? Which one would you choose as an investor? As an investor would you ever buy load shares?

---

1. *Id.*
2. *Id.* The broker or dealer must also disclose certain types of differential compensation practices. *Id.*
3. *Id.*
4. *Id.*
5. *Id.*

b. You are counsel to a fund complex that has marketed its funds as "front-end loaded." The managers now would like to convert these funds to a contingent deferred load structure and intend to raise advisory fees, in part to cover distribution expenses. What are the legal issues involved in this plan?

c. Why did advisers devise deferred loads? What would they gain or lose by such a load structure?

d. Do you agree with the justifications of the SEC for permitting such loads? How does the rationale of such loads fit with the rationale of the sections that prohibited the imposition of the load?

e. Should the regulation of loads be delegated to the Financial Industry Regulatory Authority (FINRA), which is a self-regulatory organization? Why should the SEC not directly regulate this area? Are the interests of the SEC and FINRA the same in this area?

f. Do you agree that "disclosure alone . . . is insufficient to comply with the Congressional mandate that the NASD adopt rules to prevent excessive sales bonds"?

g. Why regulate advisory fees and sales loads under different provisions of the Investment Company Act? Would it make sense for the SEC to regulate both sales loads and advisory fees together and subject the aggregate fee to a reasonableness standard? Do the various payments mean different services?

---

## 2. Financing Distribution Using Fund Assets

### a. What "Sells" Investment Company Shares?

The saying "mutual fund shares are not bought but sold" may be true even today. Two elements drive the sale of investment company shares: performance of the investment adviser and sales efforts such as active brokers and advertising. While performance draws investors, sales efforts bring them in as well. Most, if not all advisers' fees, are linked to the amount of assets under management. Because the rise in such assets might be achieved by sales to a greater extent than by performance, and perhaps because redemption and shareholder mobility has increased, the pressure to finance sales of redeemable securities of investment companies has mounted with the years. The initial position of the SEC was that advisers may not use fund assets to finance the sale of fund securities. By definition, the financing might demonstrate that the fee charges were too high. Therefore, advisers were not permitted to use fund assets for distribution expenses. Existing shareholders did not benefit from larger fund asset bases; the adviser did. Instead, these costs should be borne by the purchasing shareholders. This issue has been revisited time and again since the adoption of rule 12b-1 in 1980, which permitted the use of fund assets to finance distribution-related costs, and was most recently revisited in 2010.

### b. Who Should Bear the Distribution Costs? How Should the Costs be Divided?

In 1980, the SEC adopted rule 12b-1, mentioned in the previous releases discussed in this Chapter. The following is a discussion of these "12b-1 fees" in the SEC's release adopting rule12b-1.[1]

> The Commission is adopting a rule to permit open-end management investment companies to bear expenses associated with the distribution of their shares, if such companies comply with certain conditions and procedures. The rule requires that any decision by an open-end management investment company to use its assets to finance distribution be approved by its shareholders and directors, including its disinterested directors.
>
> The rule also contains provisions intended to ensure that the disinterested directors are not dominated nor unduly influenced by management and that the directors are fully informed and exercise reasonable business judgment. The procedures in the rule by which shareholders and directors would approve a plan to use assets for distribution are generally similar to those prescribed by statute for approval of investment advisory contracts. The procedural requirements are somewhat less stringent than they were in the rule as proposed.
>
> * * *
>
> The Commission is adopting certain disclosure and reporting requirements relating to the use of assets for distribution, including a revision of the registration and reporting form for open-end management investment companies.
>
> The Commission is taking these actions because it believes that directors and shareholders of open-end management investment companies should be able to make business judgments to use fund assets for distribution in appropriate cases but that, in view of the investment adviser's conflict of interest with respect to any recommendation to bear distribution expenses and because of uncertainties about whether such companies are likely to benefit from such expenditures, any such exercise of business judgment should be subject to conditions designed to ensure that it is made by persons who are free of undue management influence and have carefully considered all relevant factors.
>
> * * *
>
> The Commission has decided to adopt the rules substantially as proposed in Release No. 10862. In response to the comments, however, the Commission has made certain modifications . . . . [T]he Commission believes there should be some latitude for fund directors to exercise their business judgment to authorize such a use of fund assets. Nevertheless, the Commission still remains generally

1. Bearing of Distribution Expenses by Mutual Funds, Investment Company Act Rel. No. 11414 (Oct. 28, 1980).

concerned about: (1) the conflicts which may exist between the interests of a fund and those of its investment adviser in deciding whether a fund should pay its distribution costs; (2) the likelihood that the fund will benefit from paying for such costs, and (3) the fairness to existing shareholders. Therefore, the Commission believes that any permissive rule in this area must contain substantive standards to protect fund shareholders, guidelines to ensure an orderly process of decision-making by directors, and accountability for exercising the authority to use fund assets for distribution. . . . The Commission and its staff will monitor the operation of the rules closely[.]

* * *

General Requirements

Accepting [certain] recommendations would make evasion of the rule easy. The Commission has historically been concerned with whether funds are paying for distribution in substance and not with the form of particular arrangements. In this connection, it should be noted that section 48(a) of the Act . . . in effect prohibits doing indirectly that which cannot be done directly. Therefore, the Commission believes that the rule should apply to indirect expenses as well as direct expenses.

[T]here can be no precise definition of what types of expenditures constitute indirect use of fund assets. That judgment will have to be made based on the facts and circumstances of each individual case. . . . [F]und directors, particularly the disinterested directors, would bear substantial responsibility for making that judgment. Under sections 15(a) and (c) of the Act they are also responsible for evaluating and deciding whether to approve the advisory contract. In fulfilling these obligations directors of mutual funds would have to give careful scrutiny to any past, present or planned expenditures by the investment adviser for distribution, and determine on the basis of the facts of each particular case whether such expenditures constituted an indirect use of fund assets in violation of their fiduciary obligations under section 36 of the Act and in contravention of the rule. . . .

[After consideration the rule, as adopted, requires only a majority shareholder vote and] subsequent to the adoption of a distribution plan, only modifications which would materially increase the amount of money to be spent need be submitted to the shareholders for approval. Moreover, agreements pursuant to a plan will not be subjected to a shareholder vote. The Commission recognizes that once a distribution plan has been approved in the manner prescribed in the rule, directors should be allowed some discretion to modify agreements with the providers of distribution services as the circumstances change.

*Independence of Directors.* Permitting the use of fund assets for distribution is a major regulatory change for the Commission. . . .

The Commission views a decision to use fund assets for distribution as a particularly difficult business judgment which is complicated by the conflicts of interest which are present. Since rule 12b-1 does not restrict the kinds or amounts of payments which could be made, the role of the disinterested directors in approving such expenditures is crucial. No formal provisions in a rule can insure that directors will make the right decision in every instance; however, the likelihood that a decision will be in the best interests of a fund and its shareholders will be increased if the disinterested directors are genuinely independent of management. Of course, a requirement that the tenure of disinterested directors be independent of management control will not guarantee that disinterested directors will in fact be independent. Nevertheless, experience indicates that such formal independence will breed an atmosphere in which actual independence will develop. The well-documented trend among corporations generally toward director independence (e.g., the increasing number of boards which have independent majorities and majority independent committees, including nominating committees) strongly implies a recognition of the validity of this proposition. Accordingly, the Commission believes that, in order for rule 12b-1 to be effective, disinterested directors must be independent.

The Commission remains concerned that there will be situations in which disinterested directors may not be able to act with complete independence in deciding whether to use fund assets for distribution because of the possibility that the advisers' control over the funds they advise could lead to domination of or undue influence over the disinterested directors. The Commission recognizes that many advisers who control the funds they advise would not attempt to misuse such control over the disinterested directors and that many disinterested directors are fully independent. However, the Commission still believes that it is appropriate to enhance the independence of disinterested directors by adopting the provisions of paragraph (c) as proposed. [Paragraph (c) reflects the previously discussed "Fund Governance Standards."] This belief reflects the cumulative experience of the staff in regulating the mutual fund industry, and for that reason, citations of such cases as *Burks v. Lasker* are not apposite. Whatever *Burks* or *Tannenbaum* may have said about the theoretical role of disinterested directors or about the actual independence of the directors who were involved in those cases, it is the Commission's view that as a general proposition disinterested directors should not be entrusted with a decision on use of fund assets for distribution without receiving the benefit of measures designed to enhance their ability to act independently.

With respect to the argument that paragraph (c) is extra statutory, the Commission acknowledges that there are no identical provisions in the Investment Company Act, although section 15(f) contains provisions of similar import. Nevertheless, the Commission believes that paragraph (c) is a reasonable restriction. That provision does not impose a new regulatory requirement on all investment companies; instead it makes available an exemption from regulation for companies which elect to institute a corporate governance mechanism which, as suggested above, is consistent with salutary developments among corporations of all types.

Factors

In order to avoid the appearance of either unduly constricting the directors' decision making process or of creating a mechanical checklist, the Commission has decided to delete the list of factors from rule 12b-1. However, in order to insure a proper record of the deliberative process, the rule will require preservation of minutes. Since corporate minutes are frequently cryptic, the rule requires explicitly that these minutes set forth the factors the directors considered, together with an explanation of the basis for the decision to use fund assets for distribution.

Although the Commission has decided not to require directors to consider any particular factors, the Commission believes that the factors enumerated in rule 12b-1 would normally be relevant to a determination of whether to use fund assets for distribution. Therefore, it appears that setting forth those factors in this release may provide helpful guidance to directors. The following list of factors is the same as the list contained in proposed rule 12b-1, except for a slight amplification of the fourth factor:

(1) Consider the need for independent counsel or experts to assist the directors in reaching a determination;

(2) Consider the nature of the problems or circumstances which purportedly make implementation or continuation of such a plan necessary or appropriate;

(3) Consider the causes of such problems or circumstances;

(4) Consider the way in which the plan would address these problems or circumstances and how it would be expected to resolve or alleviate them, including the nature and approximate amount of the expenditures; the relationship of such expenditures to the overall cost structure of the fund; the nature of the anticipated benefits, and the time it would take for those benefits to be achieved;

(5) Consider the merits of possible alternative plans;

(6) Consider the interrelationship between the plan and the activities of any other person who finances or has financed distribution of the company's shares, including whether any payments by the company to such other person are made in such a manner as to constitute the indirect financing of distribution by the company;

(7) Consider the possible benefits of the plan to any other person relative to those expected to inure to the company;

(8) Consider the effect of the plan on existing shareholders; and

(9) Consider, in the case of a decision on whether to continue a plan, whether the plan has in fact produced the anticipated benefits for the company and its shareholders.

*Reasonable Business Judgment*

The Commission is adopting the standard of care required of directors in implementing a distribution plan as proposed originally . . . [and] intentionally did not define the relationship between a "reasonable business judgment" and "fiduciary duties" under state law and sections 36(a) and (b) of the Act, nor did it define those director activities that would be consistent with each concept. The Commission did this in recognition that the concepts are constantly evolving and, particularly, that there have been no comprehensive or definitive interpretations of the various fiduciary duty requirements of section 36. Certainly it was not the Commission's intent to assert any such interpretation of its own. Rather, as stated clearly in Release No. 10862, paragraph (e) incorporates directors' existing duties in order to emphasize that formal compliance with the other provisions of the rule will not establish a safe harbor. The Commission believes that the standards for accountability placed on the directors concerning their decision to implement a distribution plan are necessary and are consistent with the standards under the Act and under state law required of fund directors in other decision making contexts.

*Disclosure and Reporting Requirements*

The Commission is adopting the disclosure and reporting requirements substantially as proposed in Release No. 10862 for the reasons stated in that release. As noted above, the few comments that were received on the disclosure and reporting requirements generally supported the concept of full disclosure to investors. Moreover, the Commission continues to believe that it is inappropriate, at this time, to modify the position taken in the Vanguard proceedings that a fund which bears distribution expenses but which does not charge a front-end sales load cannot refer to itself as a "no-load" fund or use equivalent terminology. Instead, the Commission remains of the opinion that it is more appropriate to give further consideration to this issue within the context of the Vanguard proceeding. . . .

In sum, it is important to note several of the features of rule 12b-1, which are touched upon in the SEC's release. First, to use fund assets to pay distribution-related expenses, the fund's board must adopt a written plan describing all material aspects of the proposed financing of distribution. This plan must be approved by the board and the disinterested directors in person — i.e., the same formal procedure required by section 15(c) with respect to advisory contracts and discussed earlier. Moreover, rule 12b-1 describes distribution-related expenses as "any activity which is primarily intended to result in the sale of shares issued by" the fund. This standard is quite broad and thus many boards will include the shareholder servicing fees discussed earlier within the 12b-1 plan they adopt as a prophylactic matter. The 12b-1 plan must also be approved by shareholders if adopted after the fund has been publicly offered. The continuance of a 12b-1 plan must be approved at least annually by the board in the same manner described above.

Second, also similar to section 15(c), directors have a duty to request and evaluate, and any person who is a party to any agreement with the fund relating to its 12b-1 plan has a duty to furnish, such information as may reasonably be necessary to an informed determination of whether such plan should be implemented or continued. Additionally, as alluded to in the SEC's release, the fund's directors must conclude, in the exercise of reasonable business judgment and in light of their fiduciary duties under state law and under sections 36(a) and (b) of the 1940 Act, that there is a reasonable likelihood that the plan will benefit the company and its shareholders.

Third, from an ongoing maintenance standpoint, rule 12b-1 requires directors to review a quarterly report regarding amounts expended under the 12b-1 plan and the purposes for which such expenditures were made. Also, the plan must be terminable at any time by a vote of the board or of shareholders.

Fourth, it is important to understand that agreements relating to a 12b-1 plan — i.e., selling agreements with financial intermediaries who will ultimately be receiving payments pursuant to the plan — are generally subject to the same approval, continuance and termination provisions as the 12b-1 plan itself.

All of these matters are important and have recently been receiving heightened scrutiny by the SEC enforcement staff. For several years, the SEC enforcement staff has been conducting an investigation regarding "payments for distribution in guise" — in other words, payments for distribution-related expenses that are called something else (e.g., "sub-transfer agent fees") and not subject to approval pursuant to rule 12b-1. In September 2015, the SEC brought its first enforcement action under this initiative and imposed civil penalties and disgorgement of $40 million on the offending adviser and its affiliated broker-dealer.[1] Thus, it is incumbent on boards to understand what fees a fund is paying to whom and for what.

---

## Discussion Topics

a. Note that rule 12b-1 does not apply to closed-end funds nor to unit investment trusts. Why is that so? Further, as a matter of policy, compare and contrast the issues that arise when permitting 12b-1 fees as a means of financing distribution (and increasing the advisory fees) as opposed to deferred sales loads.

b. As demonstrated by the case you read in the chapter on advisory fees, some argue that section 36(b) does not provide an effective limit to the use of investment company assets for the sale of the company's shares. Had this fact been demonstrated before the adoption of the rule, would the SEC have recommended its adoption? Could the SEC establish effective limits even under section 36(b)? Can other effective limits be imposed on the use of the rule 12b-1?

c. How would you interpret section 12(b) of the 1940 Act? Were investment companies prohibited from financing the distribution of their shares before the enactment of rule 12b-1? Is the rule permissive or prohibitive?

d. Assuming that the rule is permissive, is the rule justified on the merits? What justifications might you assert? It seems plausible that this rule

1. In the Matter of First Eagle Investment Management, LLC and FEF Distributors, LLC, Investment Company Act Rel. No. 31832 (Sept. 21, 2015).

contributed to the enormous growth of open-end investment companies. It has also contributed to the change in the composition of the board of directors of such companies. Now, a substantial percentage of such companies have a board with more than 50% disinterested directors. The full impact of the rule was not anticipated when it was adopted.

e. Today, advisers often borrow to finance the distribution of their mutual fund shares, in reliance on Rule 12b-1 fees. The difference between the cost of borrowing and the fees generated by increased assets from the sales seems to justify the expenditure. Suppose an investment company declared that it has closed its doors to new investors. Would the adviser be justified in continuing to charge the investment company 12b-1 fees? What if these fees cover previous distribution costs that were financed by the adviser? What if these fees are to be used to provide investors with better and more services? As a judge, how would you determine these issues?

---

### c. Sales by Fund Supermarkets

The following is a 1998 SEC's staff discussion of fund supermarkets.[1] Note that this discussion continues to be relevant given the SEC's focus on what fees paid by funds are or are not for financing distribution costs.

> As you know, fund supermarkets are an increasingly popular means through which investors can buy and redeem shares of mutual funds. As of late last year, approximately $ 79 billion had been invested in mutual funds through no-transaction-fee fund supermarkets, an increase of over 750% during the prior five years.
>
> In a typical fund supermarket, the sponsor of the program -- a broker-dealer or other institution -- makes available various services to a participating fund and its shareholders. The sponsor offers a menu of services including: establishing, maintaining, and processing changes in shareholder accounts; communicating with shareholders; preparing account statements and confirmations; and providing distribution services on behalf of, or with, the fund. For the services that it provides, the sponsor charges the participating fund a fee that is calculated on the basis of the amount of assets of the fund's shareholders that is held through the program. The fee is paid by the fund, its investment adviser, an affiliate of the adviser, or a combination of all three entities. . . .
>
> [A review of fund supermarkets by the Commission's Office of Compliance Inspections and Examinations ("OCIE")] revealed that different funds participating in the programs generally received the same services from program sponsors, although the funds characterized the services differently and paid for those services in different ways. . . .
>
> In the Division's view, payments of fees for participating in fund supermarkets may be made pursuant to or outside of rule 12b-1

1. Investment Company Institute, Corres. (Oct. 30, 1998).

plans, depending on the purpose of the payments and the party making the payment. Whether a fund's payment of part or all of a supermarket fee must be made pursuant to a rule 12b-1 plan depends on an analysis of the purpose for which the payment is made. The determination of the purpose of the payment must be made by the fund's board of directors and requires careful consideration and monitoring.

Fund Supermarkets

* * *

Beginning in [1992], several broker-dealers introduced a new method for investors to purchase and redeem mutual fund shares: the fund supermarket. A fund supermarket is a program offered by a broker-dealer or other financial institution through which its customers may purchase and redeem a variety of funds, with or without paying transaction fees.

The sponsor of a fund supermarket usually charges a fee to the participating fund if the sponsor does not charge transaction fees to its customers. The fee generally ranges from .25% to .40% annually of the average net asset value of the shares of the fund held by the sponsor's customers . . . for permitting the fund to participate in the fund supermarket and for providing the services . . . [which] include certain administrative services to customers who purchase shares of the fund, and certain distribution services for the fund. [These supermarkets are popular with investors and fund managers as well].

The OCIE Examinations

OCIE conducted its examinations of fund supermarkets [because the supermarkets were novel and not reviewed and because participating funds and their assets under management] had grown dramatically. [The OCIE found that funds participated in order to increase sales and benefitted from the administrative services, in many cases, with the approval of the boards. Payment was made through rule 12b-1 charges].* * *

Rule 12b-1 under the Investment Company Act of 1940 permits any open-end management investment company to use its assets to pay broker-dealers and others for providing services that are primarily intended to result in the sale of the fund's shares. The rule was intended, in part, to address the potential conflicts of interest between a fund and its investment adviser that are created when a fund bears its own distribution expenses.

Rule 12b-1 generally requires, among other things, that any payments by a fund in connection with the distribution of its shares must be made pursuant to a written plan, often referred to as a "rule 12b-1 plan," that has been approved by the fund's shareholders and by the fund's board of directors, including a majority of the directors who are not interested persons of the fund and who have no direct or indirect financial interest in the operation of the plan or in any agreements related to the plan ("financially independent directors"). The requirements of the rule are designed to ensure that a fund's financially independent directors are not unduly influenced by management, are fully informed, and are able to exercise reasonable business judgment in determining whether the plan is in the best interests of the fund.

The Commission has taken steps to ensure that funds clearly disclose to investors any fees paid pursuant to rule 12b-1 plans. . . .

Some funds pay a portion of the fund supermarket fee out of their own assets, but not pursuant to a rule 12b-1 plan, and some of their advisers or the advisers' affiliates pay the remainder of the fee. Whether payments of fund supermarket fees must be made pursuant to rule 12b-1 primarily depends on (a) whether the payments are being made for services that are primarily intended to result in the sale of the fund's shares, and (b) whether the fund or another party is making some or all of the payments.

A. Payment of Fees by Funds Pursuant to Rule 12b-1 Plans

When a fund participates in a fund supermarket primarily to sell its shares to investors, at least part of the fee must be considered to be compensation paid to the sponsor for providing distribution services, i.e., services primarily intended to result in the sale of the fund's shares. In such a case, the part of the fee paid for distribution may be paid by the fund only pursuant to a rule 12b-1 plan.

If a fund has adopted a rule 12b-1 plan, then the fund may pay for distribution expenses to the extent permitted under its plan. A fund that pays all of its fund supermarket fee pursuant to a rule 12b-1 plan need not determine which portion of the fee is primarily for distribution services or which portion is primarily for administrative services.

B. Payment of Fees by Funds Outside of Rule 12b-1 Plans

If a fund has not adopted a rule 12b-1 plan, then it cannot use fund assets to pay for services that are primarily intended to result in the sale of the fund's shares. Thus, any portion of the supermarket fee that is primarily for distribution services cannot be paid out of the fund's assets. A fund that has not adopted a rule 12b-1 plan, however, may use its assets to pay a fund supermarket sponsor for services that the fund's board has determined to be non-distribution services.

C. Payment of Fees by Funds' Investment Advisers

If a fund's investment adviser makes distribution related payments out of its own resources, rule 12b-1 generally would not apply because the payments are not being made out of fund assets. Thus, if a fund's investment adviser pays all of the fund supermarket fee, or the portion of the fee that is for services that are primarily intended to result in the sale of fund shares, rule 12b-1 generally would not apply.

Rule 12b-1 could apply, however, in certain cases in which the adviser makes distribution related payments out of its own resources. As the Commission has stated, "an indirect use of fund assets for

> distribution would result if any allowance were made in the investment adviser's fee to provide-[sic] money to finance distribution." Thus, for example, if a fund approved an increase in the advisory fee of its investment adviser so that the adviser could pay for distribution services for the fund, such payments could be made only pursuant to a rule 12b-1 plan. In future examinations, OCIE staff will closely scrutinize any increase in a fund's investment advisory fee that appears to be for the purpose of compensating the fund's investment adviser for paying the fund's supermarket fee.
>
> Role of the Fund's Board of Directors
>
> The board of directors of a fund that participates in a fund supermarket . . . is responsible for determining whether any portion of a fund supermarket fee paid (or to be paid) by the fund is for distribution, i.e., services primarily intended to result in the sale of fund shares. Whether or not any particular payment of a fund supermarket fee by a fund is for distribution services or non-distribution services is primarily a question of fact for the fund's board of directors to determine. This responsibility necessarily entails considering the nature of the services used by the fund or provided to the fund by the supermarket sponsor. The sponsor's characterization of the services that it offers is one factor that the board should consider in making this determination. . . .

### d. The Role of Brokers as Sellers of Fund Shares and as Executors of Fund Trading Activities: Additional Focus on Rule 12b-1

Investment advisers choose the composition and trading of funds' portfolios and their related expenses, including the payment of brokerage commissions to brokers who execute the purchases or sales of securities as agent for the fund. Some of these brokers may also serve as distributors of the fund's shares to investors.

The dual role played by these brokers gives rise to a conflict of interest for the mutual fund adviser. Advisers' fiduciary duty requires them to choose for fund activities brokers that are most skillful, and solely to advance the interests of the fund. Yet, fund advisers have an incentive to increase the size of the funds under their management, which is likely to increase the advisers' management fees.

The Investment Company Act of 1940 provides, in section 12(b), that the assets of a mutual fund cannot be used to pay for the sale or distribution of fund shares in violation of rules adopted by the SEC. The SEC in 1980 adopted rule 12b-1 which permits fund assets to be used to pay for distribution of fund shares under certain conditions. Those conditions include, most notably, approval by the fund's board (including separate approval by the board's independent directors) and by the fund's shareholders of a written plan that sets forth, among other things, the amount of payments to be made to brokers acting as distributors of the fund. The written plan must thereafter be approved annually by the board and its independent directors, and any material changes to the plan must be approved by the fund's shareholders.

In early 2004, the SEC published a proposal, excerpted below, to amend rule 12b-1 to prohibit the use of a fund's brokerage commissions to pay brokers for the distribution of a fund's shares. The proposed amendment was adopted with little change. The following is the SEC's explanation for the proposed amendments.[1]

> Investment companies buy and sell large amounts of securities each year. In 2002 alone, mutual fund securities transactions totaled approximately $ 7.8 trillion. Fund advisers choose which broker or dealer will effect transactions ("executing broker"), and often use commissions from these transactions to reward brokers or dealers for selling fund shares ("selling brokers"). Recently . . . our staff found that the use of brokerage commissions to facilitate the sale of fund shares is widespread among funds that rely on broker-dealers to sell their shares. Selling brokers appear to have significant leverage over funds because the number of distribution channels is limited, and fund complexes compete to seek a prominent position in them. This leverage permits selling brokers to demand additional payments from fund advisers from their own assets ("revenue sharing") or through the direction of fund brokerage. These payments can purchase prominence (or better "shelf space") in an increasingly crowded fund marketplace.
>
> In many cases, meeting the increasing compensation demands of selling brokers has caused funds' distribution-related fees (i.e., sales loads and rule 12b-1 fees) to reach the National Association of Securities Dealers ("NASD") limits (or "caps") on such fees (which we describe below). Fund advisers often use brokerage commissions to generate additional revenue to finance distribution. Brokers have, in turn, based their demands for greater compensation from funds on the apparent availability of these supplemental revenues. As a result, funds have allocated, over time, an increasing share of their brokerage commissions to support distribution. Our staff estimates that brokerage commissions may compose approximately twenty percent of annual expenditures for fund distribution.
>
> A. Current Practices
>
> The broker's cost of executing large, institutional brokerage transactions such as those effected for funds is often substantially less than the commission (or mark-up or mark-down) that funds actually pay on most of their transactions. The adviser to a fund complex, which controls the allocation of fund brokerage, can use the excess of brokerage commissions paid over execution costs to purchase goods or services from the executing broker or third parties. Fund advisers often choose to use excess brokerage commissions to buy a place for the fund in the selling broker's distribution network. The use of excess commissions to pay for distribution costs has resulted in intricate business arrangements between fund advisers and securities firms that sell their shares.

1. Prohibition on the Use of Brokerage Commissions to Finance Distribution, Investment Company Act Rel. No. 26356 (Feb. 24, 2004) (footnotes omitted).

Under the simplest of these arrangements, an adviser directs transactions in fund portfolio securities to a selling broker. The selling broker executes trades on behalf of the fund and credits to the fund a portion of the commission it receives to pay for distribution-related services. If the selling broker lacks the capacity to execute the fund's securities transactions, the adviser may implement a more complicated arrangement. The adviser may select another broker to execute the transaction and require the executing broker to "step out" a portion of its commission to pay the selling broker. Alternatively, the executing broker may retain a portion of the commission as compensation for its execution services and set the remainder aside pending the adviser's designation of the selling brokers to which the remainder will be directed. In an "introducing broker" arrangement, a clearing broker executes the transaction, forwards the entire commission to the selling broker ("introducing broker"), and periodically charges the selling broker for its execution services.

Some fund advisers and selling brokers enter into an agreement that sets forth a target dollar amount of commissions to be paid over a period of time to the selling broker as compensation for distributing fund shares. A typical arrangement covers all of the funds in a complex that are subject to sales or dealer agreements between the selling broker and the funds' principal underwriter. If the funds do not generate the specified dollar amount of commissions during the year, the difference may be paid by the funds' adviser or carried forward into the next year. If the selling broker's overall compensation for distributing the shares of a fund complex falls below agreed-upon levels, the selling broker may reduce its selling efforts for the funds. As described below, these arrangements are covered by rule 12b-1.

B. Current Regulatory Requirements

Fund brokerage is an asset of the fund, and therefore must be used for the fund's benefit. Use of fund assets to pay selling brokers or otherwise finance the sale of fund shares is regulated by rule 12b-1, which we adopted under our authority in section 12(b) of the Act. Section 12(b) makes it unlawful for a fund "to act as a distributor of securities of which it is the issuer, except through an underwriter, in contravention of such rules and regulations" as we prescribe. Section 12(b) was intended to protect funds from bearing excessive sales and promotion expenses. Rule 12b-1 permits funds to use their assets to pay distribution-related costs. In order to rely on rule 12b-1, a fund must adopt "a written plan describing all material aspects of the proposed financing of distribution" that is approved by fund shareholders and fund directors. We included these and other conditions in the rule to address concerns about the conflicts of interest arising from allowing funds to finance distribution.

Rule 12b-1 does not itself limit the amount of distribution costs that a fund can assume, nor does it explicitly address the extent to which fund brokerage can be used to reward brokers for promoting the sale of fund shares. Two NASD rules address these matters.

First, NASD Conduct Rule 2830(d) prohibits NASD members (i.e., broker-dealers) from selling shares of funds that impose excessive sales charges. The rule deems a sales charge to be excessive if it exceeds the rule's caps. A fund's sales load (whether charged at the time of purchase or redemption) may not exceed 8.5 percent of the offering price if the fund does not charge a rule 12b-1 fee. The aggregate sales charges of a fund with a rule 12b-1 fee may not exceed 7.25 percent of the amount invested, and the amount of the asset-based sales charge (the rule 12b-1 fee) may not exceed 0.75 percent per year of the fund's average annual net assets. Under the cap, therefore, an increase in the fund's sales load could reduce the permissible level of payments a selling broker may receive in the form of 12b-1 fees. The NASD designed the rule so that cumulative charges for sales-related expenses, no matter how they are imposed, are subject to equivalent limitations.

Second, NASD Conduct Rule 2830(k), the "Anti-Reciprocal Rule," prohibits NASD members from conditioning their efforts in distributing a fund's shares on the receipt of the fund's brokerage commissions. An exception to the Anti-Reciprocal Rule permits NASD members to sell shares of funds that follow a disclosed policy "of considering sales of their shares as a factor in the selection of broker/dealers to execute portfolio transactions, subject to best execution." Broker-dealers may not, however, condition their promotion or sale of fund shares on the receipt of brokerage commissions from the fund.

We approved this exception to the NASD's rules in 1981, shortly after adopting rule 12b-1. We concluded that, in light of the adoption of rule 12b-1, "it is not inappropriate for investment companies to seek to promote the sale of their shares through the placement of brokerage *without the incurring of any additional expense.*" We recognized the conflicts of interest and stated that we expected fund boards, before adopting a policy permitting the "consideration of the sale of an investment company's shares as a factor in the selection of broker-dealers to execute portfolio transactions, subject to the requirements of best execution," to "carefully weigh the possible advantages to the investment company and its shareholders and the possible abuses that may stem from the adviser's use of portfolio brokerage to encourage the sale of investment company shares."

Because, as noted above, fund brokerage is an asset of the fund, a fund's use of its brokerage to promote the sale of its shares is generally viewed as a payment by the fund and thus subject to rule 12b-1. In approving the exception to the NASD's Anti-Reciprocal Rule in 1981, however, we concluded that the practice of merely *considering* selling brokers' sales efforts when allocating brokerage would be addressed by the NASD rules governing broker-dealers and advisers' fiduciary obligations to seek best execution, rather than by Commission rules governing the use of fund assets for distribution.

Our decision in 1981 to approve the exception to the NASD's Anti-Reciprocal Rule was based on a view that merely factoring sales efforts into the selection of brokers, consistent with the investment adviser's fiduciary duties to the fund, was essentially benign. . . .

Our review of current practices, however, suggests that many arrangements that direct brokerage to reward selling brokers for distribution constitute more than mere allocation of brokerage, and are not consistent with our 1981 rationale for approving the exception to the NASD's Anti-Reciprocal Rule. The use of multiple broker-dealers for execution, step-outs, and other arrangements described above explicitly quantify the value of the distribution component of fund brokerage commissions and belie the notion that fund advisers are merely "considering" the selling efforts of the broker(s) involved. Rather, these arrangements bear all the hallmarks of barter arrangements in which the fund advisers trade brokerage (a fund asset) for sales efforts. Moreover, that brokerage commissions could instead be used to offset other fund costs rebuts the notion that the use of fund brokerage to finance distribution imposes no additional costs on the fund. Foregoing an opportunity to seek lower commission rates, to use brokerage to pay custodial, transfer agency and other fund expenses, or to obtain any available cash rebates, is a real and meaningful cost to fund shareholders.

While the benefits to funds and their shareholders of using fund brokerage to promote the sale of fund shares are unclear, the benefits to fund advisers are clear. . . . An adviser that uses fund assets to promote the sale of fund shares may be able to avoid having to pay fees out of its own pocket ("revenue sharing"). . . . [T]he use of fund brokerage exacerbates the conflicts and complicates efforts to control them because of the practical limitations on the ability of fund directors to monitor and evaluate the motivations behind the selection of brokers to effect portfolio securities transactions.

- We believe that the way brokerage has been used to pay for distribution involves unmanageable conflicts of interest that may harm funds and fund shareholders. . . .
- We are also concerned about the effect of this practice on the relationship between broker-dealers and their customers. Receipt of brokerage commissions by a broker-dealer in exchange for shelf space creates an incentive for the broker to recommend funds that best compensate the broker rather than ones that meet the customer's investment needs. Because of the lack of transparency of brokerage transactions and their value to a broker-dealer, customers may not have appreciated the extent of this conflict. Finally, the direction of valuable fund brokerage to compensate brokers for the sale of fund shares may permit brokers to circumvent the NASD's rules against excessive sales charges, thus undermining the protections afforded fund shareholders by those rules and by section 22(b) of the Act, which authorized them.

A. Proposed Ban on Directed Brokerage

In light of these concerns, we are proposing amendments to rule 12b-1 under the Act to prohibit funds from compensating a

> broker-dealer for promoting or selling fund shares by directing brokerage transactions to that broker. The rule would also prohibit step-out and similar arrangements designed to compensate selling brokers for selling fund shares.
>
> * * *
>
> B. Policies and Procedures
>
> We are also proposing to require that *any* fund (or its adviser) that directs any portfolio securities transactions to a selling broker-dealer implement policies and procedures designed to ensure that its selection of brokers to effect portfolio securities transactions is not influenced by considerations about the sale of fund shares. These procedures must be reasonably designed to prevent; (i) the persons responsible for selecting broker-dealers to effect transactions in fund portfolio securities (*e.g.,* trading desk personnel) from taking broker-dealers' promotional or sales efforts into account in making those decisions; and (ii) the fund, its adviser or principal underwriter, from entering into any agreement under which the fund directs brokerage transactions or revenue generated by those transactions to a broker-dealer to pay for distribution of the fund's shares. The fund's board of directors, including a majority of its independent directors, must approve the policies and procedures. . . .

In September 2004, the Commission adopted these proposed amendments to rule 12b-1. As described above, these amendments govern the use of assets of open-end management investment companies to distribute their shares.[1] The amended rule, as adopted, prohibits funds from paying for the distribution of their shares with brokerage commissions. The amendments are designed to end a practice that poses significant conflicts of interest and may be harmful to funds and fund shareholders.

> Pressures to distribute fund shares (or to avoid making payments for distribution out of their own assets) have caused advisers to direct more fund brokerage (or brokerage dollars) to selling brokers. The directed brokerage has been assigned explicit values, recorded, and traded as part of increasingly intricate arrangements by which fund advisers barter fund brokerage for sales efforts. These arrangements are today far from the benign practice that we approved in 1981 when we allowed funds to merely consider sales in allocating brokerage.
>
> Fund brokerage is an asset of the fund, and its use to pay for distribution expenses implicates rule 12b-1, which regulates the use of fund assets to pay selling brokers or otherwise finance the sale of fund shares. Rule 12b-1 permits funds to use their assets to pay distribution-related costs, subject to certain conditions designed to address concerns about the conflicts of interest arising from allowing funds to finance distribution. In 1981 . . . we concluded that 'it is not inappropriate for investment companies to seek to promote the

1. Prohibition on the Use of Brokerage Commissions to Finance Distribution, Investment Company Act Rel. No. 26591 (Sept. 2, 2004).

sale of their shares through the placement of brokerage without the incurring of any additional expense.'

After reviewing the current directed brokerage practices described above, in February 2004, we proposed to amend rule 12b-1 to prohibit the use of fund brokerage to compensate broker-dealers for selling fund shares. Our proposal was intended to end practices that we concluded were inconsistent with the rationale of our 1981 decision and involved unmanageable conflicts of interest. The NASD also has proposed a corresponding change to its rules. . . .

[We] are adopting the amendments to rule 12b-1 substantially as proposed. We are taking this action because we have concluded that the practice of trading brokerage for sales of fund shares may harm investors in mutual funds in at least four ways:

*Adverse Impact on Best Execution of Fund Transactions.* The decision to use brokerage commissions to pay for distribution poses significant conflicts. Fund advisers, whose compensation is based on the amount of assets held by the fund, have an incentive to promote the sale of fund shares to increase their advisory fees, and to avoid having to pay brokers out of their own pockets for selling fund shares ("revenue sharing"). Competition among fund advisers to secure a prominent place in selling brokers' distribution networks ("shelf space") has created powerful incentives to direct brokerage based on distribution considerations. This can adversely affect decisions on how and where to effect portfolio securities transactions, or how frequently to trade portfolio securities. Because of the practical limitations on the ability of fund directors to actively monitor and evaluate the motivations behind the selection of brokers to effect portfolio securities transactions, we believe that reliance on fund directors to police the use of fund brokerage to promote the sale of fund shares is not sufficient.

*Circumvention of Limits on Distribution Expenses.* Pursuant to section 22(b) of the Investment Company Act, the NASD prohibits its members (*i.e.*, broker-dealers) from selling shares of funds that impose excessive sales loads and other distribution costs directly or indirectly on shareholders. By using these directed brokerage arrangements, fund advisers and brokers are able to circumvent the NASD rules on excessive sales charges, thus undermining the protections afforded fund shareholders by those rules and by section 22(b) of the Act.

*Transparency of Distribution Expenses.* Under our rules, fund investors receive information about fund expenses, including distribution expenses, in a fee table contained in every fund prospectus, which identifies the amount of sales load, as well as "12b-1 fees" that are deducted from fund assets. The practice of trading brokerage for sales efforts involves costs that are built into brokerage commissions, which are treated as capital items rather than expenses. Thus, the practice of directing brokerage for distribution of fund shares diminishes the transparency of fund distribution costs and the ability of an investor or prospective investor to understand the amount of those costs.

*Consequence of Broker Conflicts.* Finally, these practices may corrupt the relationship between broker-dealers and their customers. Receipt of brokerage commissions by a broker-dealer for selling fund shares creates an incentive for the broker to recommend funds that best compensate the broker rather than funds that meet the customer's investment needs. Because of the lack of transparency of brokerage commissions and their value to a broker-dealer, customers are unlikely to appreciate the extent of this conflict.

*A. Ban on Directed Brokerage*

Rule 12b-1(h)(1) prohibits funds from compensating a broker-dealer for promoting or selling fund shares by directing brokerage transactions to that broker. The prohibition applies both to directing transactions to selling brokers, and to indirectly compensating selling brokers by participation in step-out and similar arrangements in which the selling broker receives a portion of the commission. The ban extends to any payment, including any commission, mark-up, mark-down, or other fee (or portion of another fee) received or to be received from the fund's portfolio transactions effected through any broker or dealer. . . .

*B. Policies and Procedures*

The prohibition we adopt today is not intended to compromise best execution. Nevertheless, the fact that a selling broker provides best execution would not cure a violation of the prohibition on funds or their advisers directly or indirectly compensating the broker for promoting fund shares with payments from portfolio transactions. Rule 12b-1(h)(2) permits a fund to use its selling broker to execute transactions in portfolio securities only if the fund or its adviser has implemented policies and procedures designed to ensure that its selection of selling brokers for portfolio securities transactions is not influenced by considerations about the sale of fund shares. These procedures must be approved by the fund's board of directors, including a majority of the independent directors, and must be reasonably designed to prevent: (i) The persons responsible for selecting broker-dealers to effect transactions in fund portfolio securities transactions (*e.g.*, trading desk personnel) from taking into account, in making those decisions, broker-dealers' promotional or sales efforts, and (ii) the fund, its adviser and principal underwriter from entering into any agreement or other understanding under which the fund directs brokerage transactions or revenue generated by those transactions to a broker-dealer to pay for distribution of the fund shares. These procedures must be designed to prevent funds from entering into informal arrangements to direct portfolio securities transactions to a particular broker.

The procedures should be incorporated into each fund's compliance policies and procedures, which each fund is required to adopt by our rule 38a-1. Fund chief compliance officers should assure themselves that the required procedures are in place as well as any others that they believe are reasonably necessary to prevent violation of the prohibition against directing brokerage for sales of fund shares. Compliance officers of broker-distributed funds should monitor the operation of the policies and procedures, and should consider periodic testing of brokerage allocations to determine whether there is a significant correlation between sales and the direction of brokerage that may suggest the existence of informal arrangements in violation of the rule.

---

## Discussion Topics

a. Is there a difference between the Commission's interpretation in 1980 and that of the later date? What can regulators and lawyers learn from the developments in this case for future regulation?

b. Is it practicable to allow a fund to select a broker to execute portfolio trades for the fund so long as the fund has policies and procedures designed to ensure that the selection, as the SEC proposes, "is not influenced by considerations about the sale of fund shares"? How can a fund board adequately monitor or oversee the broker selection process? Today, many large brokerage firms provide services to individuals as well as to large fund portfolio transactions. Would this change affect your opinion?

c. Should the SEC adopt a rule that simply prohibits any broker who effects portfolio trades for a fund from also serving as a distributor of the fund's shares?

d. Usually, the management contracts of funds with their advisers provide for "break points" on the level of management fees as the size of the fund increases. For example, the management fee might be set at 0.75% for the first $100 million of assets in the fund, at 0.70% for the next $100 million of assets, at 0.65% for the next $100 million, and so on.

Accordingly, putting aside other types of fund expenses (such as custody expenses), a fund's expense ratio will decrease as the fund grows larger and will increase as the fund grows smaller. A rational fund shareholder will be more concerned about the level of his fund's expense ratio than about the absolute dollar amounts of a fund's expenses. For example, a fund with $5 billion of assets will likely be a less expensive fund (because it has a lower expense ratio) for its shareholders than a fund with $50 million of assets, even though the $5 billion fund will pay higher dollar amounts in expenses than the smaller fund. What is your opinion regarding this argument? Is it rational?

Has the SEC followed a consistent line of reasoning in evaluating the presence (or absence) of benefits to shareholders flowing from the sale of fund shares? Compare the following comments made by the SEC in this release:

- The 'mere allocation' of brokerage to promote the sale of fund shares could benefit existing shareholders of funds that were in 'net redemption,' that is, fund assets were shrinking and the ratio of fund expenses to fund assets was rising.

- While the benefits to funds and their shareholders of using fund brokerage to promote the sale of fund shares are unclear, the benefits to fund advisers are clear. Fund advisers' compensation is based on a percentage of assets under management. A larger fund typically generates more advisory fees.

e. Should the SEC limit rule 12b-1 to situations in which the fund is experiencing net redemptions?

---

## B. Retail Price Maintenance

Open-end investment companies that issue redeemable securities face a number of problems relating to the distribution of their shares. The companies must continuously sell shares to avoid "net redemptions." Therefore, these companies have traditionally resorted to reliable underwriters. To support the stability of the system, Congress provided underwriters who serve as "principal underwriters" for these funds, special protection against competition in section 22(d). This section provides that investors must be charged a fixed price stated in the prospectus, including distribution costs. Underwriters and brokers who participate in the distribution may receive varying commission amounts, but may not sell the securities at a discount from the fixed price. Thus, only among themselves can brokers bargain and divide the commissions as they wish. In effect, this system eliminates competition among brokers that are not within the underwriters' net. It thus eliminates the secondary market in these redeemable securities, although so long as the securities are redeemable it is unlikely that investors will seek to trade at market prices. Even though section 22(d) has been criticized and reexamined, neither Congress nor the SEC has eliminated it. Instead, the SEC has granted numerous exemptions from the section that culminated later in exemptive rules.

Consider the following release. It proposes an exemptive rule to permit variations in sales loads.[1] The rule was adopted as rule 22d-1.[2]

> Background
>
> Section 22(d) of the Act prohibits a registered investment company and a principal underwriter of or a dealer in its redeemable securities from selling such securities to "any person" except at a current public offering price described in its prospectus. This section effectively prohibits price competition in sales loads on mutual fund shares at the retail level. . . .

---

1. Exemption from Section 22(d) to Permit the Sale of Redeemable Securities at Prices that Reflect Different Sales Loads, Investment Company Act Rel. No. 13183 (Apr. 22, 1983).
2. Exemption from Section 22(d) to Permit the Sale of Redeemable Securities at Prices that Reflect Different Sales Loads, Investment Company Act Rel. No. 14390 (Feb. 22, 1985) (codified at 17 C.F.R. § 270.22d-1 (2015)).

1. Purposes of Section 22(d)

In the years since the enactment of the Act, arguments have been advanced that section 22(d) was intended as a means to prevent three abuses that existed in the distribution of investment company shares prior to 1940. . . .

[The first problem] was riskless trading by insiders and the dilution of fund assets that resulted under the system of backward pricing utilized prior to passage of the Act and for many years thereafter. Under the backward pricing system, the price of a mutual fund share was based upon the fund's net asset value per share determined at the close of the market on the previous day. If the market gained, an investor could purchase fund shares near the end of the day at the price based upon the previous day's valuation, knowing that the net asset value of the shares was greater than the price he was paying, thereby diluting the interests of existing shareholders the transaction could be made riskless by redeeming the shares the following day, before a new (and possibly lower) price reflecting that day's market activity was established. While payment of a sales load made riskless trading impossible, since the sales load would more than offset any profit that could result from one day's increase in the value of a fund's shares, certain insiders and favored customers could often purchase fund shares without paying a sales load. Since the overwhelming majority of open-end funds at the time of the act were load funds, the enactment of section 22(d) greatly reduced the possibility of dilution occurring from such riskless trading practices by requiring all investors to pay the same sales load.

The second purpose which has been suggested for section 22(d) was to avoid disruption in the orderly distribution of mutual fund shares and the development of a secondary market in such shares. [While] authorized dealers who distributed a fund's shares were generally bound by contract with the principal underwriter to charge a single price described in the prospectus. . . . [n]on-contract dealers were able to compete with contractual dealers by paying investors wishing to sell shares a little more than the published redemption price and offering the shares at less than the published sales price. This situation apparently led to a somewhat active secondary market, the so-called "bootleg market," which is said to have resulted in the cancellation of many selling agreements between underwriters and contractual dealers and threatened to undermine the orderly distribution system. Representatives of the industry have contended that an orderly distribution system under the control of the funds facilitates the funds' ability to offer constant redemption of their shares. It has been argued that section 22(d) was intended to preserve such orderly distribution by eliminating competition from non-contract dealers.

The third abuse arguably addressed by section 22(d) was discrimination among investors resulting from a fund charging different prices to different investors. While commentators have differed on whether section 22(d) was intended to address price discrimination, it appears that Congress contemplated that more than one offering price could be charged different investors since it used the phrase "a current public offering price described in the prospectus" rather than "the price." In this regard, the Commission has long viewed volume and group discount and other specified types of discounts as consistent with the purposes of section 22(d). It has granted a large number of exemptions by rule and by order premised on the theory that discrimination is not unjust, and thus the purpose of the section is not violated, if there is a rational basis for the variation in sales load. At the same time, the Commission has expressed concern that retail price maintenance may be unfair when investors requiring different levels of sales efforts must be charged the same sales load.

* * *

[Policy approach to SEC exercise of power]

Over the last few years, the Commission has implemented a policy of reducing its involvement and that of its staff in regulating the decisions of investment companies to the extent that such reduced involvement is consistent with investor protection. The Commission views the decision to establish a pricing system that permits variations in sales loads to be one that is particularly appropriate for management to make. Since rule 22c-1 . . . has eliminated the possibility of dilution resulting from the "riskless trading" practices described earlier, the determination of whether to permit variations in sales loads now involves basically a consideration of marketing factors. Investment companies and their underwriters are in the best position to know and assess such factors.

The Commission further believes that the determination of whether to permit price variations is a business judgment determination in which it is appropriate for the Commission to reduce its involvement because sufficient investor protections are provided elsewhere in the securities laws[.]

* * *

b. Changes in Circumstances

Since enactment of the Act, circumstances have changed so as to diminish substantially several concerns relating to the alleged purposes of section 22(d). . . .

As noted above, the concern of dilution of fund assets arising from "riskless trading" by insiders was addressed by the adoption of rule 22c-1 under the Act . . . which prohibits "backwards pricing" and requires instead "forward pricing" whereby the price of shares is based upon a fund's net asset value per share next determined after receipt of an order for purchase (generally at the close of business on the day of a sale), rather than the previous day. Rule 22c-1, by eliminating the possibility of a purchaser or seller taking advantage of any discrepancy between a fund's current net asset value and a sales price based upon the previous day's net asset value, renders retail price maintenance unnecessary as a method of preventing dilution from riskless insider trading.

The concern of unjust price discrimination among purchasers has been substantially dispelled by the results achieved under Securities Exchange Act rule 19b-3 . . . which, since its adoption in 1975, has prohibited the national securities exchanges' prior practice of requiring their members to charge fixed brokerage commissions. Market experience under rule 19b-3 has shown that commission rates have fallen into rational patterns that reflect the sales costs involved and the services provided.

The concern of maintaining an orderly market in mutual fund shares should be considered in light of industry and regulatory developments. It has been argued since before enactment of the Act that an ongoing continuous sales effort by contractual dealers is necessary to prevent the funds from experiencing net redemptions of their shares, and that a secondary market would undermine the contractual distribution system. The number and size of no-load funds, however (even excluding money market funds), has grown over the years.

In this regard, because of regulatory changes, it is now possible to provide investors with more information through fund advertising. Moreover, as the Commission has relaxed the restrictions against retail price competition by rule and by order, funds have established numerous types of plans whereby fund shares are sold at a greater variety of reduced sales loads. These developments suggest that some mutual funds may find that it is in their best interests either to establish distribution plans that reflect greater price flexibility or to permit the dealers in their shares to negotiate sales loads with investors. In any event, mutual funds and their underwriters would seem to be in a better position than the Commission to make that determination. Under the proposed rule, funds that believe that tail price maintenance is desirable for them could continue it.

* * *

2. The Proposed Rule

The proposed rule provides that a company may adopt a pricing system that includes rates (1) described in a schedule, (2) that are determined by a process of negotiation, or (3) which combine such two methods. This provision is intended to give investment companies maximum flexibility in establishing the pricing of their shares. . . . [Current] rules 22d-1 through 22d-5 permit companies some flexibility, subject to various conditions, to establish certain scheduled variations in sales loads. Proposed rule 22d-6 would expand this flexibility to permit companies to establish any scheduled variation if the company complies with the conditions of the proposed rule. Rule 22d-6 would also provide that companies may permit negotiated sales loads subject to the same conditions, but only in those situations where the sales load is negotiated and agreed to at the time of purchase and not at the time of redemption.

> The conditions under the proposed rule are far more general in their terms than has been the case either in prior rules promulgated under section 22(d) or in individual orders exempting companies from the provisions of section 22(d). This departure reflects the judgment that investment companies should determine what factors are important in determining the best pricing system for their shares. The Commission believes that the proposed rule provides flexibility to registrants without sacrificing appropriate investor protection, and is consistent with the purposes fairly intended by the policy and provisions of the Act, including section 22(d). It does not require mutual funds to sell their shares pursuant to a distribution plan that permits reduced or negotiated sales loads or to change their current distribution system. It is a permissive rule that recognizes that under certain conditions designed to protect investors, mutual funds may unfix the sales loads charged on their redeemable securities. If a fund wishes to introduce now variations or negotiation in its distribution, it would have to comply with the rule's conditions; otherwise, it must continue to sell its securities at uniform prices or seek an order exempting it from section 22(d). . . .

The final adopted rule 22d-1 contains an important difference from the rule as proposed. This SEC did not adopt the proposal to permit negotiated loads, which were opposed by a majority of those commenting on the rule proposal.[1] Thus, rule 22d-1, as adopted, provides only for scheduled variations in sales loads:

> A registered investment company that is the issuer of redeemable securities, a principal underwriter of such securities or a dealer therein shall be exempt from the provisions of section 22(d) to the extent necessary to permit the sale of such securities at prices that reflect scheduled variations in, or elimination of, the sales load. These price schedules may offer such variations in or elimination of the sales load to particular classes of investors or transactions, Provided, That:
>
> > (a) The company, the principal underwriter and dealers in the company's shares apply any scheduled variation uniformly to all offerees in the class specified;
> >
> > (b) The company furnishes to existing shareholders and prospective investors adequate information concerning any scheduled variation, as prescribed in applicable registration statement form requirements;
> >
> > (c) Before making any new sales load variation available to purchasers of the company's shares, the company revises its prospectus and statement of additional information to describe that new variation; and
> >
> > (d) The company advises existing shareholders of any new sales load variation within one year of the date when that

---

1. Exemption from Section 22(d) to Permit the Sale of Redeemable Securities at Prices that Reflect Different Sales Loads, Investment Company Act Rel. No. 14390 (Feb. 22, 1985) (codified at 17 C.F.R. § 270.22d-1 (2015)).

variation is first made available to purchasers of the company's shares.

---

## Discussion Topics

a. Would investors benefit by a secondary market in redeemable fund shares?

b. To the extent that section 22(d) serves as a vehicle to protect against discriminatory practices among investors, it has an analogue in insurance law. State insurance laws generally provide that an insurer may not discriminate among policyholders. Is there more or less of a need for such a provision in the mutual fund context? Does the rule discussed in the previous excerpt water down section 22(d) too much?

---

## Problem

Assume you are advising a client on how to structure a new open-end fund. In particular, your client is looking to access different types of investors and different distribution channels. Your client tells you that this will necessitate offering different options for the financing of distribution costs. You are aware that distribution costs are financed through sales loads and/or asset-based distribution fees, like those approved under Rule 12b-1. Please draft a memo to your client addressing the following:

1. If the fund is structured as a multiple-class fund under rule 18f-3, can the fund charge a different advisory fee to different classes — i.e., perhaps have an institutional class that charges a lower advisory fee than the retail classes in order to attract institutional investors?

2. Assume your client wants an institutional class (large institutions with substantial negotiating power, but who require very little sales effort), a class for retail investors that only have small amounts to invest (but are likely to hold the investment for many years) and a class for retail investors who have a relatively substantial amount to invest (but are more likely to redeem within a year or two). Describe the different methods of financing the distribution cost and how different methods or combinations thereof might be appropriate for these different classes.

3. The factors the board may want to consider in adopting any 12b-1 plan and any terms required in contracts with broker-dealers who receive payments pursuant to the 12b-1 plan.

---

## C. Buying Mutual Fund Shares on Margin

I. Introduction[1]

The Commission today announced the adoption of Rule 11d1-2 (17 C.F.R. 240.11d1-2) under the Exchange Act. The Rule was published for public comment in April, 1984. The Rule has been adopted substantially as proposed. In response to a comment received, however, the Rule has been modified in one respect.

The Rule will exempt any security issued by an open-end management investment company or a unit investment trust registered under the 1940 Act from certain credit restrictions of the Exchange Act provided that the security has been owned for more than thirty days by the security holder. The effect of the Rule, together with the credit regulations of the Board of Governors of the Federal System, is to allow a broker-dealer to extend credit to a customer on fully-paid securities issued by open-end management investment companies or unit investment trusts if the customer purchased the securities held as collateral more than thirty days prior to the extension of credit. The thirty day holding period requirement will not apply to shares acquired as a result of the automatic reinvestment of dividends.

II. Discussion

Background. Section 11(d)(1) of the Exchange Act prohibits a broker-dealer from effecting any transactions in connection with which he directly or indirectly extends or maintains credit or arranges for the extension or maintenance of credit to or for a customer on any security, other than an exempted security, which was part of a new issue in the distribution of which the broker-dealer participated as a member of a selling syndicate or group within thirty days prior to such transaction. Section 11(d)(1) prohibits the extension of credit in connection with the original sale of the security. It also prohibits the security from being used as collateral in connection with other transactions that the broker-dealer may effect for his customers within the stated thirty-day period.

Section 11(d)(1) generally applies to the extension of credit of fund shares by a broker-dealer distributing the fund's shares either as a principal underwriter or as a retailer. In either capacity the broker-dealer is a member of a selling group and the fund shares sold in an original distribution are a "new issue." Since fund shares are continuously in registration, section 11(d)(1) prohibits a broker-dealer engaged in the distribution of the shares of a fund from using those shares as collateral for the initial purchase of other securities on margin, whether or not the prior sale of fund shares occurred within thirty days of the credit transaction. In this regard, fund shares are affected differently by section 11(d)(1) than are shares of other companies which are distributed in discrete offerings that usually last far less than thirty days.

1. Extension of Credit by Broker-Dealers on Investment Company Shares, Investment Company Act Rel. No. 14277 (Dec. 18, 1984) (codified at 17 C.F.R. § 240.11d1-2 (2015)).

* * *

Rule 11d1-2. Rule 11d1-2 exempts from the provisions of section 11(d) (1) mutual funds shares and shares of unit investment trusts sold by a broker-dealer to a customer more than thirty days prior to an extension of credit by the broker-dealer on such shares. The exemption will not be available for the initial sale of fund shares on margin where the purchased shares are to be used as collateral. The Rule will, however, eliminate seemingly unnecessary restrictions upon the use of fund shares for margin purposes that are caused by the fact that the shares are in continuous registration. At the suggestion of the commentators, the proposed rule was changed specifically to provide that fund shares that result from the automatic reinvestment of dividends be exempt from the provisions of section 11(d)(1).

* * *

Several commentators suggested deletion of the thirty day holding period or reexamination of the thirty day holding period at some future time. These commentators believe that the manner in which fund shares are priced, i.e., on the basis of their net asset value and not on the basis of the supply of, or demand for, shares, precludes the possible increase in volatility which the immediate availability of credit otherwise might cause. In addition, commentators stated that the broker-dealer's rule in distributing fund shares did not present the potential for conflicts of interest which section 11(d)(1) was intended to avoid because the broker-dealer has no capital at risk or market exposure from unsold shares. One commentator also noted that the thirty day holding period could present operational and data processing problems for broker-dealers because of the continuous nature of the offering of fund shares. Another commentator, however, stated that it felt that the thirty day holding period was fair. For several reasons, the Commission does not believe that it would be appropriate to eliminate the thirty day holding period without first having some experience with the extension of credit on fund shares. A broker-dealer that has participated in a distribution of securities is generally prohibited by section 11(d)(1) from extending credit on those securities for 30 days after the distribution, and the primary purpose of this rulemaking was to place fund shares and other types of securities on equal regulatory footing. Also fund shares are often sold with the kinds of sales compensation that could lead to the abuse that prompted the Congress to prohibit the use of credit in the sale of new issues of securities. Accordingly, the Commission has retained this 30-day holding period requirement, but will attempt to monitor its effects. . . .

---

## Discussion Topics

a. Should greater flexibility than that provided by Rule 11d1-2 be afforded the extension of credit in the mutual fund context?

b. As a policy matter, should investors be allowed to pay for mutual fund shares with credit cards? With debit cards? What is the difference between these two modes of payment? Do such transactions fall within Section 11(d)(1)?

---

## D. Exchanging Investment Company Shares

The following is the SEC's discussion of section 11 of the Investment Company Act.[1]

> Section 11 was intended to prevent "switching", the practice of inducing security holders of one investment company to exchange their securities for those of a different investment company "solely for the purpose of exacting additional selling charges". Finding that practice to be widespread in the 1930s, Congress provided in section 11(a) that the terms of an offer involving the exchange of mutual fund shares on any basis other than the relative net asset values of the securities to be exchanged should be approved in advance by the Commission or made pursuant to rules adopted by the Commission.
>
> Investors in "fixed trusts", now known as unit investment trusts, were found to be particularly vulnerable to switching operations. In order to earn another sales commission, a UIT sponsor would often pressure unitholders into exchanging their units for those of another of the sponsor's trusts. Therefore, section 11(c) provides that any exchange offer involving UIT securities must be approved in advance by the Commission or comply with whatever rules or regulations the Commission may have prescribed to govern such exchanges.* * *
>
> A. Proposed rule 11a-3
>
> Proposed rule 11a-3 would exempt from section 11(a) certain exchange offers involving mutual fund shares. The proposed rule would limit the recipient of an exchange offer to any person holding a security of the offering fund or of any other fund within the same "family of investment companies". "Family of investment companies" would be defined as "any two or more registered open-end investment companies that have the same investment adviser or principal underwriter and hold themselves out to investors as related companies for purposes of investment and investor services." This approach is consistent with nearly all the exemptive orders, where the two mutual funds involved in an exchange transaction have either an investment adviser or principal underwriter in common.
>
> As in prior exemptive orders, the proposed rule would allow the exchanging security holder to be charged an administrative fee and a sales load under certain conditions. Although prior exemptive orders

---

1. Offers of Exchange Involving Open-End Investment Companies and Unit Investment Trusts, Investment Company Act Rel. No. 15494 (Dec. 23, 1986). The SEC adopted a modified version of the rule. Offers of Exchange Involving Open-End Investment Companies and Unit Investment Trusts, Investment Company Act Rel. No. 17097 (Aug. 3, 1989) (codified as amended at 17 C.F.R. § 270.11a-3 (2015)).

specified the highest administrative fee that a fund could charge for an exchange transaction, the proposed rule would permit a "nominal" administrative fee and would not designate a fixed dollar limit on the amount that could be charged. Any administrative fee or scheduled variation thereof would have to be uniformly applied. The proposed rule would require that the prospectus of the offering company disclose any administrative fee imposed on an exchange transaction for its shares, as well as any fee imposed on its shareholders to acquire shares of any other funds in an exchange transaction. It would also require disclosure of any administrative fee in any sales literature or advertising that describes the exchange offer. The Commission specifically requests comment on whether the provisions in proposed rule 11a-3 with respect to administrative fees are appropriate.

In addition to a nominal administrative fee, an exchanging security holder could be charged a sales load on the acquired security at the time of the exchange or when the acquired security is redeemed or exchanged. At either time, the sales load could not exceed the excess, if any, of the sales load that the exchanging security holder would ordinarily have to pay to purchase the acquired security over the sales load previously paid on the exchanged security (the "sales load differential"). The rule would define "exchanged security" to include the security actually exchanged and any security previously exchanged for that security or for any of its predecessors. Since the Rules of Fair Practice of the National Association of Securities Dealers set the maximum sales load that a fund may charge on a single transaction at 8½% of the offering price, an exchanging shareholder could not be charged a cumulative sales load of more than 8½% of the offering price of the security being acquired. As in shareholder credit for any sales loads previously paid.

Where either no sales load is imposed on the exchange or the sales load imposed is less than the sales load differential, the proposed rule would permit the offering company to require the exchanging shareholder to have held the exchanged security for a minimum period of time prescribed by the offering company and uniformly applied to all offerees of the class specified. The minimum holding period provision found in many exemptive applications, prevents an investor from buying shares of one fund and then immediately exchanging them -- without paying a sales load -- for those of a higher-load fund. The Commission specifically requests comment on whether proposed rule 11a-3 should require a minimum holding period and, if so, whether it should specify the length of the minimum holding period.

The proposed rule would also codify the representations found in the exemptive applications that address exchanges of less than all of a shareholder's shares of a particular fund and exchanges of securities acquired through dividend reinvestment or capital gains distributions. Specifically, the rule would provide that in calculating the sales load differential, when the exchanging shareholder is exchanging less than all shares held of a particular fund, the security upon which the highest sales load was previously paid would be considered to be exchanged first. Any securities acquired through dividend reinvestment or capital gains distributions would be considered to have been sold with a sales load equal to the sales load previously paid on the shares on which the dividend was paid or distribution made.

Where the sales load on the acquired security is deferred, the proposed rule would require that the load be calculated as if the acquired security had been held from the date on which the exchanged security was acquired. This tacking of time formula, which was developed in the exemptive application process, is intended to ensure that an exchanging security holder receives credit for the length of time the exchanged security was held. . . .

---

## Discussion Topics

a. Why was section 11(e) enacted in the first place?

b. Why should the SEC provide exemptions from section 11?

c. What has changed since 1940 that would justify exemptions and reexamination of the prohibition? Presumably, human nature, and the motivations of some sales persons and advisers, have not changed since 1940.

---

# Chapter 12

## *Protection Against Conflicts of Interests*

### A. Introduction: The Nature of Conflicts and the Structure of Fiduciary Law

### 1. What Are Conflicts of Interest and How Are They Resolved?

The answer to these questions is best illustrated by the following. Suppose I give my friend $50 and ask him to buy flowers for me. He agrees. Being a shrewd businessman he goes to the market at the end of the day when the merchants are hard pressed to sell their flowers, and buys a very nice bouquet for $25. He brings me the flowers and I am delighted until I hear that he has made 100% profit on this deal. So I confront him and demand my $25, but he says: "This is my $25."

Since we agreed on the terms of the transaction, we can call the transaction a contract. It is indeed an arrangement to which we both agreed. But what are the legal consequences of this agreement? What branch of law would apply to it? Is it contract law? Not necessarily. Contract law is based on the assumption that each party can fend for itself. If I gave my money to my friend there was an exchange. The money became his money. Yet this transaction can also be classified as agency. As agency, the money I gave my friend remains my money. It was given for one purpose only: to enable him to buy the flowers for me. Whatever money remains after the purchase must be returned to me. My friend is "transparent."[1] His agreement with the flower shop is in effect an agreement between me and the flower shop. Whatever money he did not spend on buying the flowers is mine.

My friend would classify the transaction very differently. He would say that the transaction was a contract for the sale of flowers. The money constituted the price of the flowers. He was not transparent at all. He was indeed the buyer of the flowers and then sold them to me. The money was his from the moment I gave it to him. He owed me flowers, not money. Perhaps by refining the facts, we can find out the true intent of the parties and the legal category to which our transaction belongs.

Note that these legal classifications bring very different results in other circumstances as well. If my friend, on the way to the market, is robbed and loses the money through no fault of his, the legal classification would

1. *See* Tamar Frankel, Fiduciary Law (2010) (Oxford University Press).

determine who bears the loss. If he is an agent — I will bear the loss. If he is a seller — he will bear the loss.

Further, the classification would bring very different remedies for breach. If my friend breaches the contract and does not deliver the flowers, I can sue him for the price I paid, or for the price of the flowers, plus any transaction costs that I may incur, or my lost profits, if any. If my friend found someone who was willing to pay him more than the market price, there are scholars who would justify his breach of promise to me. Such as breach would be "efficient" if I could buy the same flowers at the same price elsewhere. Therefore, he owes no damages and can enjoy the gain. In contrast, if my friend breaches his duties as agent and uses my money for something other than the purpose for which he was entrusted with it, or if he pockets the profits, he will have to account to me for his profits.

Thus, classification may bring very different results. These results are based on very different values and different power relationships. In the contract and efficient contract models, the main purpose of both parties is to maximize their personal profits but refrain from damaging the other. In the second model, trust is the foundation of the relationship, without the need to explicitly say so. When trust is an important consideration in human relationships and financial stability, the agency model will trump the contract model.[1]

When mutual fund investors buy fund shares, they hand over their money to advisers to manage their money for them. The advisers must manage investors' money according to the investors' directions, although the advisers may have very broad discretion. They may not use the investors' money for any other purposes including their own benefit. If advisers do, they must account for their profits and sometimes spend time in prison.

Thus, in fiduciary relationships, a fiduciary undertakes to provide service to entrustors and in order to do that some property or power is transferred from the entrustor to the fiduciary. In all cases, the services require that property or power will be entrusted to the fiduciaries for the purpose of performing and facilitating the service.

In these arrangements, the entrustors are exposed to the risk that the fiduciaries will use the entrustors' property for other than the purposes of the entrustment. If the cost of monitoring and controlling the fiduciaries' performance is too expensive for the entrustors, the law is used to cover the gap and reduce the entrustors' costs and risks. That is especially true if the services of the fiduciaries are socially desirable.

There are numerous other arrangements, all of which involve entrustment of something valuable and obligations of the recipient to act for the benefit of someone else. That is why lawyers, doctors and money managers are

1. In fact, we also have a third contract as follows. In my will, I give my money to a trusted person and ask him after my death to invest the money for the benefit of my small children, pay their support and return the rest to them when they grow up. You can call the arrangement a will or a contract. But you can also call it a trust and describe the transaction in terms of transfer of property for a limited purpose: to manage it for my children under the directions in the will. He may not do with the money what he wishes. If he does, and profits, he must account for the profits.

fiduciaries. The "contract" is an agreement but *contract law* does not apply to it. Fiduciary law applies to it.

### 2. How Is Fiduciary Law Structured?

In fiduciary law, the entrustor has the legal right to rely on the fiduciary to perform his duties well and honestly, that is, to serve effectively and according to the expected expertise, *and* avoid using the entrusted power and property for other than the purpose for which the entrustment was made. Arguably, the law establishes and protects the interests of, and reduces the cost of, the entrustor's supervision over the fiduciary. In fact, often the entrustor cannot supervise the fiduciary. In such cases entrustors do not entrust. Thus the law strengthens the culture of trust in society. Without that trust lawyers, doctors and money managers will have no business. Mistrustful communities are usually poor.

This does not mean that fiduciaries can never use their power to benefit themselves or third parties. It means that the fiduciary can do so but only if the entrustor agrees to the different use or the law permits it. With entrustors' consent there is no violation of fiduciary duties. However, consent to conflict of interest transactions requires a process: the fiduciary must notify the entrustor that a conflict exists and ask for consent. If the entrustor agrees, the legal relationship of the parties might change. The entrustor may not rely on the fiduciary to perform his duties and the relationship may be transformed into a contract model. However, for the entrustor's consent to be binding, the fiduciary must give the entrustor information in order to enable the entrustor to make an informed and independent decision.

### 3. The Investment Company Act

When there are many entrustors, such as shareholders of a corporation, the law establishes a delegate for the shareholders to supervise the fiduciary and give consent to conflicts of interests in which the fiduciary may wish to engage. In corporate law, for example, the directors are empowered to consent to the fiduciaries' conflicts of interest. Under the Investment Company Act the SEC is empowered to consent, and in some cases it has delegated this power to the directors of the investment company.

Conflict of interest transactions are one of the most serious problems involving investors' use of discretionary money managers who have control over investors' funds. Trustees who wish to engage in conflict of interest transactions must obtain the consent of all beneficiaries. Corporate directors who wish to engage in conflict of interest transactions must obtain the consent of a majority of the independent directors, and, in the absence of such independent directors, may be subject to the court's evaluation of the transaction on the merits instead of consent.[1] In the Investment Company Act, it is the SEC, directly or by delegation, that is vested with the power to consent to conflicts of interest of investment company fiduciaries.

---

1. The "business judgment rule," in corporate law, under which the courts maintain a "hands off" attitude towards the directors' decisions, protects directors only to some extent. The rule is usually discussed in the context of the shareholders' demand in a derivative suit and there are relatively few cases on this issue. However, in trust law the trustee may seek the court's approval to conflict of interest transactions.

With the exception of section 15 of the Investment Company Act of 1940, which authorizes disinterested directors and/or a majority of the shareholders to approve the advisory and underwriting contracts, most other conflict of interest transactions are prohibited altogether, exempt by specific statutory provisions or rules and subject to conditions, or allowed by SEC exemptive authority. However, the SEC has delegated to the disinterested directors the power to consent to conflict of interest transactions by the adviser in certain circumstances and under certain conditions.

## B. Section 17 of the Investment Company Act of 1940

We start with a definition of the persons who may not engage in conflict of interest transactions under the 1940 Act. These persons include five groups of affiliates defined in section 2(a)(3) of the 1940 Act, as well as others. The most relevant categories of affiliates in section 2(a)(3) are:

> (A) any person directly or indirectly owning, controlling, or holding with power to vote, 5 per centum or more of the outstanding voting securities of such other person; (B) any person 5 per centum or more of whose outstanding voting securities are directly or indirectly owned, controlled, or held with power to vote, by such other person; (C) any person directly or indirectly controlling, controlled by, or under common control with, such other person; (D) any officer, director, partner, copartner, or employee of such other person; [and] (E) if such other person is an investment company, any investment adviser thereof or any member of an advisory board thereof . . .

Also relevant to the definition of affiliated person in section 2(a)(3) is the definition of "control" in section 2(a)(9):

> "Control" means the power to exercise a controlling influence over the management or policies of a company, unless such power is solely the result of an official position with such company. Any person who owns beneficially, either directly or through one or more controlled companies, more than 25 per centum of the voting securities of a company shall be presumed to control such company. Any person who does not so own more than 25 per centum of the voting securities of any company shall be presumed not to control such company. A natural person shall be presumed not to be a controlled person within the meaning of this title. Any such presumption may be rebutted by evidence, but except as hereinafter provided, shall continue until a determination to the contrary made by the Commission by order either on its own motion or on application by an interested person.

Section 17(a) of the 1940 Act contains a prohibition on conflict of interest transactions that is very broad. It applies not only to affiliates but also to affiliates of affiliates: thirty categories of affiliates altogether. In addition, the prohibition applies to promoters and principal underwriters who are not defined as affiliated persons under section 2(a)(3). The prohibition applies also to these actors' affiliated persons, and adds four categories of persons to the persons who may not engage in conflict of interest transactions.

Thus, also important to an understanding of section 17 of the 1940 Act are the definitions of "principal underwriter" and "promoter," which are contained in sections 2(a)(29) and 2(a)(30) of the 1940 Act:

> (29) "Principal underwriter" of or for any investment company other than a closed-end company, or of any security issued by such a company, means any underwriter who as principal purchases from such company, or pursuant to contract has the right (whether absolute or conditional) from time to time to purchase from such company, any such security for distribution, or who as agent for such company sells or has the right to sell any such security to a dealer or to the public or both, but does not include a dealer who purchases from such company through a principal underwriter acting as agent for such company. "Principal underwriter" of or for a closed-end company or any issuer which is not an investment company, or of any security issued by such a company or issuer, means any underwriter who, in connection with a primary distribution of securities, (A) is in privity of contract with the issuer or an affiliated person of the issuer; (B) acting alone or in concert with one or more other persons, initiates or directs the formation of an underwriting syndicate; or (C) is allowed a rate of gross commission, spread, or other profit greater than the rate allowed another underwriter participating in the distribution.
>
> (30) "Promoter" of a company or a proposed company means a person who, acting alone or in concert with other persons, is initiating or directing, or has within one year initiated or directed, the organization of such company.

Moreover, to be a "principal underwriter," one must first be an "underwriter," which is also defined in the 1940 Act in section 2(a)(40):

> (40) "Underwriter" means any person who has purchased from an issuer with a view to, or sells for an issuer in connection with, the distribution of any security, or participates or has a direct or indirect participation in any such undertaking, or participates or has a participation in the direct or indirect underwriting of any such undertaking; but such term shall not include a person whose interest is limited to a commission from an underwriter or dealer not in excess of the usual and customary distributor's or seller's commission. . . . When the distribution of the securities in respect of which any person is an underwriter is completed such person shall cease to be an underwriter in respect of such securities or the issuer thereof.

The current manner in which open-end and closed-end funds are distributed reflect the practicalities of these definitions. In particular, the only "underwriter" of an open-end fund is typically its "principal underwriter," which is often an affiliate of the fund's investment adviser. This principal underwriter arranges for the sale of fund shares through other broker-dealer firms, and these legions of broker-dealer firms sell open-end fund shares as "dealers" whose "interest is limited to a commission from an underwriter or dealer not in excess of the usual and customary distributor's or seller's commission." In this manner, the broker-dealer firms avoid both underwriter liability under the Securities Act and the reach of section 17 of the 1940 Act (assuming the broker-dealer firm is not affiliated with the fund in some other prohibited manner).

For closed-end funds, which are usually distributed in one initial public offering by a syndicate of underwriters, the scope of "principal underwriters" is much broader given that the entire syndicate is in privity of contract with the fund. However, the section 17 concerns arising from having such a broad swath of principal underwriters usually never come to fruition since principal underwriter status typically ceases before the fund begins any investment operations. Of course, to the extent the closed-end fund conducts additional capital raising activities after its initial public offering, it must be cognizant of these issues.

Additionally, often critical to a section 17 analysis is whether you collapse affiliated persons in a control relationship. For example, assume Company A owns 6% of Company B's voting securities, Company B controls Company C, and Company C owns 6% of Company D's voting securities. Is Company A an affiliated person of an affiliated person of Company D? Company C is an affiliated person of Company D because it owns more than 5% of Company D's voting securities. But do you collapse Company B into Company C because they are in a control relationship? If you do, then Company A, which owns more than 5% of Company B's voting securities, is an affiliated person of an affiliated person of Company D; if you do not, then Company B is the an affiliated person of an affiliated person of Company D (by virtue of the control prong of the definition) and Company A is beyond the reach of section 17. In this regard, the SEC staff has stated that, absent substantial policy reasons, it would not seek to collapse persons in control relationships into a single person.[1] However, this still has the effect of making a "collapsing" determination a detailed facts and circumstances analysis and, as a practical matter, it is often prudent to collapse all entities in a control relationship to evaluate a "worst case" scenario and then conduct further analysis from that point. Additionally, the SEC staff generally takes the view that an investment adviser that creates and sponsors an investment company controls that investment company.

### 1. The Reach of Section 17(a)

Section 17(a) generally makes it unlawful for any affiliated person or promoter of, or any principal underwriter for, a registered investment company, or any affiliated person of such an affiliate, promoter or underwriter, to knowingly purchase or sell securities or other property from or to the registered investment company (except securities of which the investment company is the issuer), or to borrow money from the registered investment company. The following is a description of section 17(a).[2]

> Section 17(a) makes it unlawful for any affiliated person or promoter of, or any principal underwriter for, a registered investment

1. Salomon Brothers Inc., SEC No-Action Letter (May 26, 1995); G. T. Capital Management, Inc., SEC No-Action Letter (Feb. 2, 1996); First Financial Fund, Inc., SEC No-Action Letter (Jun. 5, 1997).

2. Tamar Frankel & Ann Taylor Schwing, The Regulation of Money Managers §§ 14-55 to -56, 14-63 to -65 (2001 & Supp. 2015) (footnotes omitted).

company, or any affiliated person of such an affiliate, promoter or underwriter, to effect certain transactions with the registered investment company or a company controlled by the investment company. To determine whether a company is "controlled" for purposes of section 17(a), the SEC will look through layers of companies; so long as the registered investment company has control, the SEC will apply section 17(a) despite the existence of intervening companies. Section 17(a) prohibits transactions in which one party is an investment company, or a company controlled by the investment company, and at least one of the other parties is (1) an affiliated person of the investment company, or an affiliate of the affiliate, (2) a principal underwriter for the investment company, or an affiliate of the underwriter, or (3) a promoter of the investment company or an affiliate of the promoter. . . .

Section 17(a) is far-reaching. . . . The purpose of the Act could be easily evaded if only affiliates were prohibited from dealing with the investment company, because they could create a personal holding company to buy and sell, or cause their partners or their partnerships to do so. When an investment company owns 32 percent of the voting stock of A Company and B Corporation owns 51 percent of the stock of A Company, since A Company is an affiliate of the investment company, and the B Corporation is an affiliate of A Company, B Corporation is an affiliate of an affiliate of the investment company, and any sale of securities between B Corporation and the investment company is prohibited. Also, if an investment company controls A Company and has a principal underwriter, and the underwriter has a director, the director, being an affiliate, is prohibited from dealing with the controlled A Company. An underwriter of the controlled company, however, is not its affiliate, and a transaction between them is not prohibited. The degree of affiliation is measured from the investment company, not from the controlled company, even though only the controlled company is a party to the transaction, For measuring affiliation, the controlled company is an affiliate of the investment company. . . .

Section 17(a) does not prohibit transactions between two unaffiliated investment companies, but the corporate veil of these companies might be pierced to reach affiliated shareholders. In the opinion of the staff the following transaction fell within section 17(a). An investment company (seller) exchanged its assets with another investment company (buyer) for the buyer's shares. The seller intended to distribute the buyer's shares to the seller's shareholders. Some of the seller's shareholders were affiliates of the *buyer* but not affiliates of the *seller*. The staff deemed the transaction to be sale of assets between the seller and its own affiliates. Had this been a transaction between two affiliated investment companies, it would, of course, have been prohibited by section 17(a). The staff has granted a no-action relief to an acquiring fund allowing it to use the redemption credits of an acquired fund. This relief was granted because the issue was "novel or unusual."

> Section 17(a) does not explicitly prohibit transactions between an investment company and its controlled company; these transactions will always be prohibited because a controlled company is an affiliate by virtue of section 2(a)(3)(C).
>
> A transaction that is a condition to a prohibited sale of securities is also prohibited, even if, standing alone, it is effected between affiliates only and is not subject to section 17(a). For example, in *Small Business Investment Co.,* an investment company (seller) proposed to sell portfolio shares to an unaffiliated operating company (buyer). The buyer would not purchase the stock unless one of the 15 directors of the investment company accepted an employment contract to operate the portfolio company as its president. This director had a unique expertise for the position. The employment agreement included, in addition to salary, the right to purchase from the employer-buyer certain percentages of stock of the portfolio company. The buyer and seller became affiliates of affiliates through the director's relationship to both.

The following case demonstrates the expansive interpretation of section 17(a)(3) (the prohibition on borrowing) by the SEC. To some extent, it reflects the approach to other sections of the 1940 Act as well.[1]

> The order for proceedings alleges that during the period from on or about November 30, 1969 to on or about May 1970, Adviser, an affiliated person of a registered investment company, acting as principal, willfully violated Section 17(a)(3) of the Investment Company Act, and Section 206(1) and (2) of the Advisers Act, and that Sierega & Co. and Sierega willfully aided and abetted such violation by borrowing money or other property from Fund, which Adviser was obligated to repay to Fund and which was not repaid.
>
> Fund's prospectus states that its expenses shall not exceed 1% of the average of its quarterly net assets. Any excess expenses were charged against Adviser as reimbursed expenses due to Fund. The record discloses that Fund had paid expenses in an amount of $30,179 in excess of the stated 1% of the average of its quarterly net assets. On June 8, 1970, when a new management company took over, Fund had a receivable for these excess expenses which it had paid, due from Adviser, for $30,179. This receivable was written off as uncollectible in November 1970.
>
> The management contract created an obligation on the part of Adviser to repay the expenses in excess of 1% of the average net assets. Respondents' failure to settle this obligation had the practical effect of a borrowing, with the Fund extending a non-interest bearing loan to Adviser. Accordingly, respondents' failure to repay the excess expenses was a violation of Section 17(a)(3), which prohibits an affiliated person of a registered investment company from borrowing money from such registered company.

1. In re Sierega Co., Admin. Proc. File No. 3-2971 (Apr. 3, 1973).

One notable statutory exception from section 17(a) is section 17(c), which provides, "Notwithstanding subsection (a), a person may, in the ordinary course of business, sell to or purchase from any company merchandise or may enter into a lessor-lessee relationship with any person and furnish the services incident thereto." This exception has been used to, for example, permit affiliates of a registered investment company to "lease" the investment company's shareholder list in order to market other products to those shareholders.[1]

---

**Discussion Topics**

a. If *Company A* owns 5 percent of the voting securities of an investment company, and the investment company owns 5 percent of the voting securities of *Company B,* would section 17(a) apply to a sale by *Company A* to *Company B?* Would section 17(a) apply if *Company B* is controlled by the investment company?

b. Assume the same facts as above except that the transaction is between *Company A* and *Company C,*in which *Company B* owns 5 percent of the voting securities. Does section 17(a) apply to this transaction?

c. A director of an investment company sold property to a company in which he has 5 percent of the voting securities, or of which he is a director. Is he precluded from the sale? Would your answer change if the director or the company is controlled by the investment company?

d. Does section 17(a) prohibit a transaction between a fully-owned subsidiary of a controlled company and an affiliate of the investment company?

e. Does section 17(a) prohibit a transaction in which *Affiliate A* sells all its assets to *Affiliate B*? What if, as the next step, *Affiliate A* offers its shareholders (including the investment company) the shares of *Affiliate B* in exchange for its own shares? What if the entire transaction is unfair?

f. Please read the definitions of an affiliate and of control. Then determine whether the following arrangement requires an exemption by the SEC under section 17(b) or 17(d) (explained in the following pages) of the 1940 Act.

Bank desires to establish a conduit through which it would sell the loans that Bank originates. For that purpose, Bank establishes a corporation. All common shares of the corporation are held by Bank or its holding company. The corporation is planning to offer preferred shares and those will be sold to the public. Bank will initially transfer to the Corporation loans that it is currently holding and in exchange receive the common stock. Bank intends to continue to transfer loans to the Corporation and expects the Corporation to continue to issue to the Bank additional common stock and

1. Aetna Financial Services, Inc., SEC No-Action Letter (Jan. 3, 1983); Lion Resources Corp., SEC No-Action Letter (Sept. 23, 1982); Capital Preservation Fund, Inc., SEC No-Action Letter (Jan. 5, 1981).

an amount of preferred stock that equals the value of the additional loans that the Bank transfers to the Corporation.

What is the relationship between Bank, its holding company, the Corporation and any of the shareholders of the Corporation? Are the contemplated transactions subject to section 17(a) of the 1940 Act? Do they require an exemption from the SEC? When? At the outset? Every time Bank transfers loans to the Corporation? At the time the Corporation issues shares to Bank or its holding company?

Is this regime for controlling conflict of interest transactions too burdensome? How can you avoid some of the difficulties which this regime imposes? How can Bank persuade the SEC to grant it an exemption covering future transactions, if necessary?

---

## 2. Rule-Based Exemptions from Section 17(a)

As innovations and complexities developed, the broad coverage of section 17(a) imposed a high cost on both the SEC and investment companies for exemptions. Over time, the SEC has provided exemptions first to particular applicants and then by rules to allow certain transactions that would be covered by section 17(a), but do not present issues of overreaching. Two widely-relied-upon exemptions are rule 17a-7 and rule 17a-8.[1]

Rule 17a-7 permits cross-trades between affiliated investment companies (i.e., the investment companies may buy and sell securities from each other). Specifically, rule 17a-7 exempts from section 17(a) the purchase and sale of securities (a) between registered investment companies or separate series of registered investment companies, which are affiliated persons, or affiliated persons of affiliated persons, of each other, (b) between separate series of a registered investment company, or (c) between a registered investment company or a separate series of a registered investment company and a person which is an affiliated person of such registered investment company (or affiliated person of such person) solely by reason of having a common investment adviser or investment advisers which are affiliated persons of each other, common directors, and/or common officers, provided that certain conditions are met:

(a) The transaction must be "a purchase or sale, for no consideration other than cash payment against prompt delivery of a security for which market quotations are readily available";

(b) it must be effected at the current market price;

(c) it must be consistent with the policy of each company or series participating in the transaction;

(d) there is no brokerage commission or fee (except for customary transfer fees);

(e) the board of directors of the company (including a majority of disinterested directors) (1) has adopted procedures for such transactions, reasonably designed to provide that the above

---

1. 17 C.F.R. §§ 270.17a-7, -8 (2015).

conditions have been complied with, pursuant to which such purchase or sale transactions may be effected for the company,, (2) reviews these procedures as necessary, and (3) determines at least quarterly that such transactions during the last quarter were effected in compliance with such procedures;

(f) the board of directors meets the Fund Governance Standards (discussed earlier in this book); and

(g) certain recordkeeping requirements are met.

Chief among these conditions is that the purchase/sale involves securities only for which market quotations are readily available. In other words, funds may not use rule 17a-7 with respect to illiquid or untraded securities.

Rule 17a-8 exempts certain mergers of affiliated investment companies. The release proposing rule 17a-8 in 1979 is excerpted below:[1]

> INTRODUCTION
>
> From time-to-time a registered investment company may determine to enter into a merger transaction with another investment company. This is usually accomplished pursuant to a plan of reorganization under which substantially all of the assets of one investment company are transferred in exchange for shares of the other. The investment company receiving the shares, in turn, distributes them to its shareholders as a liquidating dividend. The number of shares exchanged for the assets of the liquidating investment company typically is determined on the basis of the relative net asset values of the participating investment companies so that the interests of existing shareholders of either investment company are not diluted. However, in some instances, this formula may be adjusted to compensate one investment company for assuming potential liabilities of the other investment company or for extraordinary expenses anticipated as a result of the merger or consolidation. Such an adjustment commonly takes the form of a diminished aggregate value being placed on the assets of the investment company exchanging its assets for shares, thereby effectively raising the price paid for the shares received.
>
> I. MERGERS AND CONSOLIDATIONS OF AFFILIATED REGISTERED INVESTMENT COMPANIES
>
> BACKGROUND
>
> Section 17(a) of the Act [15 U.S.C. 80a-17(a)], generally, prohibits any investment company from selling to or purchasing from an affiliated person of that investment company (or any affiliated person of such a person) any security or other property. By virtue of having in common an investment adviser, directors, and/or officers, investment companies may be considered to be under common control and, therefore, affiliated persons of each other. A merger involving the exchange of substantially all the assets of one investment company for shares of an affiliated investment company may be deemed

1. Mergers and Consolidations Involving Registered Investment Companies, Investment Company Act Rel. No. 10886 (Oct. 2, 1979).

to be a purchase or sale of those assets within the purview of section 17(a) of the Act. . . .

DISCUSSION

. . . When a merger involves investment companies which are affiliated persons exclusively by virtue of having a common investment adviser, directors and/or officers, no person who is responsible for evaluating and approving the terms of the transaction on behalf of the various participating investment companies would have a significant personal financial interest in improperly influencing these terms.

Nonetheless, the Commission recognizes that, while such persons may not always have a significant personal financial interest in the specific terms pursuant to which such a transaction is effected, the investment adviser may have a significant self-interest in the decision whether the affiliated investment companies should participate in a particular merger. Therefore, the Commission believes that an exemptive rulemaking pertaining to such transactions should be conditioned upon the board of directors, including a majority of specified disinterested directors, of each participating investment company making certain determinations to ensure that the interests of the investment companies and their shareholders regarding such a transaction are not compromised. To protect investment company shareholders from bearing the costs of such a transaction where the greater benefit accrues to any other person, the proposed rule also requires the directors to find that no dilution of these shareholders' financial interests will result. These procedures, established in the context of an exemptive rulemaking, would accord with the Act's statutorily mandated procedures for directors to monitor and approve the investment advisory contract relationship.

PROPOSED RULE 17a-8

Proposed rule 17a-8 would exempt from the prohibitions of section 17(a) of the Act a merger or consolidation of registered investment companies which are affiliated persons solely by reason of having a common investment adviser, directors and/or officers, provided that certain conditions are satisfied.

In order to obviate any concern that the transaction would be effected primarily to benefit any person other than the participating investment companies, the proposed rule would require the board of directors of each affiliated investment company participating in the merger or consolidation -- including a majority of the directors who are not interested persons of any participating investment company -- to determine that the transaction (1) is in the best interests of the investment company; and (2) will not result in diluting the financial participation of any investment company shareholder. In making the findings, directors should consider all information which would be material to the determination -- such as the compatibility of the participating companies' investment objectives, policies, restrictions and portfolios, the terms and conditions of the transaction which

> affect the price of the shares to be exchanged, and any other direct or indirect costs to be incurred by the investment company as a result of the transaction. . . .

---

## Discussion Topic

In 2002, the SEC adopted amendments to permit mergers of registered investment companies and unregistered entities, such as a bank collective trust.[1] What issues are presented when an unregistered entity merges with a registered entity?

---

Importantly, the 2002 amendments to Rule 17a-8 also removed the limitations on the manner of affiliation that would entitle a fund to rely on the rule, introduced additional suggestions of topics for the funds' boards to consider in evaluating a merger and required the target fund's shareholders to receive a vote on the merger in certain circumstances:[2]

> The Commission is adopting, as proposed, an amendment to rule 17a-8 to permit affiliated fund mergers regardless of the reasons for the funds' affiliation. The rule will continue to require that each fund's board (including a majority of disinterested directors) determine that the merger is in the best interests of the fund and will not dilute the interests of shareholders. These are critical determinations boards must carefully consider, particularly when the merger involves significant conflicts of interest. Directors must request and evaluate any information reasonably necessary to their determinations, and consider and give appropriate weight to all pertinent factors in making their findings under the rule, and in fulfilling the overall duty of care they owe to the fund's shareholders. In making their determinations, boards should consider, if relevant, the following factors, among others
>
> - Any fees or expenses that will be borne directly or indirectly by the fund in connection with the merger;
> - Any effect of the merger on annual fund operating expenses and shareholder fees and services;
> - Any change in the fund's investment objectives, restrictions, and policies that will result from the merger; and
> - Any direct or indirect federal income tax consequences of the merger to fund shareholders.
>
> We do not intend the list of factors to be exhaustive, and none of the factors would necessarily be determinative. Consideration of these specific factors does not relieve a board of the obligation to consider other relevant factors.
>
> We are also adopting an amendment that requires the acquired

1. Investment Company Mergers, Investment Company Act Rel. No. 25666 (Jul. 18, 2002).
2. *Id.*

> fund, in a merger relying on rule 17a-8, to have the merger approved by its shareholders in certain circumstances. In the Proposing Release we expressed concern that funds were increasingly organized (or reorganized) under state laws that did not require shareholder approval of mergers, which could deny shareholders a voice in an important change in their investment. Most commenters supported requiring acquired companies to obtain shareholder approval, but in light of the costs of proxy solicitations, urged us to limit the requirement. One commenter recommended that we require shareholder approval only when the merger would result in a change that, in a context other than a merger, would require a shareholder vote under the Investment Company Act. We believe such an approach has merit because it would preserve important values embodied in the Investment Company Act while reducing the need for a fund to incur the expense of soliciting proxies when the merger may not raise significant issues for shareholders.
>
> Under rule 17a-8, as we are today amending it, reliance on the rule requires the acquired fund to obtain the approval of a majority of its shareholders in circumstances that we have derived from various provisions of the Act and our rules that specify when a fund must obtain the approval of its shareholders. Under the rule as amended a majority of the shareholders of the acquired fund must approve the merger if-
>
> - Any policy of the acquired fund that under section 13 of the Act could not be changed without a vote of a majority of its outstanding voting securities is materially different from a policy of the acquiring fund;
> - The acquiring fund's advisory contract is materially different from that of the acquired fund, except for the identity of the funds as parties to the contract;
> - After the merger, directors of the acquired fund who are not interested persons of the acquired fund and who were elected by its shareholders will not comprise a majority of the directors of the acquiring fund who are not interested persons of the acquiring fund; or
> - After the merger, the acquiring fund will be authorized to pay charges under a plan that provides for use of fund assets for distribution ("rule 12b-1 plan") that are greater than charges authorized to be paid by the acquired fund under such a plan.

Another important exemptive rule is 17a-6,[1] which exempts transactions between an investment company and certain "portfolio affiliates" or "downstream affiliates" from section 17(a). The rule exempts a transaction between a company (or a company it controls) and a portfolio affiliate of the investment company provided that no (1) officer, director, employee, investment adviser, member of an advisory board, depositor, promoter of, or principal underwriter for the company, (2) person controlling the company, (3) person owning, controlling, or holding with power to vote,

1. 17 C.F.R. § 270.17a-6 (2015).

five percent or more of the outstanding voting securities of the company, (4) person under common control with the company (other than a portfolio affiliate or a fund whose sole interest in the transaction or a party to the transaction is an interest in the portfolio affiliate), or (5) affiliate of the parties in (1) to (4) above (other than the company or a portfolio affiliate of the company) is a party to the transaction or has (or within six months prior to the transaction had, or pursuant to an arrangement will acquire) a financial interest (as defined in the rule) in a party to the transaction other than the investment company.

Rule 17a-6 defines a "portfolio affiliate" as:

> a person that is an affiliated person (or an affiliated person of an affiliated person) of a fund solely because the fund, a fund under common control with the fund, or both: (i) Controls such person (or an affiliated person of such person); or (ii) Owns, controls, or holds with power to vote five percent or more of the outstanding voting securities of such person (or an affiliated person of such person).

In 2002, the SEC proposed amendments to a number of rules, including Rule 17a-6. This proposal is excerpted below. In January 2003, the proposed amendments were adopted.[1]

> Since 1940, the number of persons who are either first-tier or second-tier affiliates of a fund has grown markedly for a number of reasons. First, as funds have grown larger, they are more likely to own positions in excess of five percent of the voting securities of an issuer, creating "portfolio affiliates." Second, many funds today use subadvisers to help manage fund assets, making each subadviser an affiliate of the fund and persons affiliated with each subadviser second-tier affiliates of the fund. Third, most funds are today organized into complexes under the common control of an adviser (or other person), making each fund an affiliated person of all of the other funds in the complex. When multiple funds with subadvisers and portfolio affiliates are under common control, the number of potential first- and second-tier affiliated persons can be quite large.
>
> The growth in the number of first-tier and second-tier affiliates of funds has resulted in an increasing number of persons with whom funds may not enter into transactions or arrangements under the Act. Many of these affiliated persons, however, have neither the ability nor the incentive to take advantage of the fund. . . .
>
> A. Portfolio Affiliates
>
> Rules 17a-6 and 17d-1(d)(5) permit a fund and its portfolio affiliates to engage in principal transactions and enter into joint arrangements that would otherwise be prohibited by section 17(a), or by section 17(d) and rule 17d-1(a). Under the rules, a fund may enter into a principal transaction or a joint arrangement with a portfolio affiliate, or an affiliated person of a portfolio affiliate, as long as certain other affiliated persons of the fund (e.g., the fund's adviser, persons

1. Transactions of Investment Companies with Portfolio and Subadviser Affiliates, Investment Company Act Rel. No. 25888 (Jan. 14, 2003) (footnotes omitted).

controlling the fund, and persons under common control with the fund) ("Prohibited Participants") are not parties to the transaction and do not have a financial interest in a party to the transaction.

1. Second-tier Affiliates

Rules 17a-6 and 17d-1(d)(5) give broad exemptions that permit transactions and arrangements involving a fund and its own portfolio affiliates, but do not extend to identical transactions or arrangements involving portfolio affiliates of funds under common control with the fund. As a result, a fund may be able to enter into a transaction or arrangement with its own portfolio affiliate (a first-tier affiliate), but not with a portfolio affiliate of another fund in the same complex (a second-tier affiliate).

Fund complexes and series companies were relatively uncommon when we amended rules 17a-6 (in 1964) and 17d-1(d)(5) (in 1974) to permit funds to engage in principal transactions and joint arrangements with their portfolio affiliates. Transactions and arrangements between a fund and its second-tier portfolio affiliates do not appear to raise concerns that are different from those raised by transactions and arrangements between a fund and its first-tier portfolio affiliates. Therefore, we are proposing to amend rules 17a-6 and 17d-1 to permit a fund to engage in principal transactions or enter into joint arrangements with its second-tier portfolio affiliates under the same conditions as with first-tier portfolio affiliates.

* * *

2. Financial Interests

As discussed above, our exemptions for transactions or arrangements with portfolio affiliates are unavailable if certain other affiliated persons have a "financial interest" in a party to the transaction (other than the fund). Our rules do not explain what constitutes a "financial interest" in a party. Instead, the rules provide a list of interests that are deemed not to be "financial interests."

We are concerned that the rules, as currently drafted, do not (and cannot) anticipate every remote or minor interest in a party to a transaction, and thus they may prohibit many transactions with portfolio affiliates even though the affiliated person's financial interest is unlikely to present an incentive for overreaching the fund. We are therefore proposing to amend rules 17a-6 and 17d-1(d)(5) to provide that, in addition to the interests currently deemed not to be "financial interests," the term "financial interest" does not include any interest that the fund's board of directors, including a majority of the directors who are not interested persons of the fund, finds to be not material.

We are also proposing to amend our rules to make them consistent with one another with regard to the time period for which a Prohibited Participant's financial interest will result in loss of the rules' exemption. Under the proposed amendments, the exemptions under both rules 17a-6 and 17d-1(d)(5) will be available unless a Prohibited Participant (i) has a financial interest in a party at the time of the fund's participation in the transaction or arrangement, (ii) had a financial interest in a party within the six months preceding the fund's participation, or (iii) will obtain a financial interest in a party pursuant to an arrangement in existence at the time of the fund's participation.

## C. The SEC's Self Limitations on the Use of Exemptive Relief

As noted, Congress granted the SEC exemptive authority under various sections of the Investment Company Act. The SEC may exempt transactions from section 17(a) under section 17(b), as well as under section 6(c). Although Congress did not provide the SEC with detailed guidelines on how to exercise its broad authorities under section 17(b), section 6(c) and other sections of the Investment Company Act, the language of the sections is not identical. For example, under section 6(c) there is no limitation with respect to retroactive exemptions. In contrast, section 17(b) provides the SEC with exemptive power only with respect to "prospective" transactions. Sometimes the SEC would exempt past prohibited transactions under section 17(a) by utilizing Section 6(c). On the other hand, the SEC very rarely uses its power to exempt past violations even under section 6(c).

Another issue involving exemptive power is the degree of proof that an applicant must provide to substantiate the request for exemption. In a 1990 request for exemption, the applicant, Vanguard Municipal Bond Fund, Inc., applied for exemption on the ground that it would provide savings to shareholders.[1] There is, of course, no way to prove that such savings will occur in the future, unless tested, and there is no way to test unless an exemption is granted. The applicant, however, included conditions such as relief of the subject funds from sales loads. Nonetheless, potential conflicts existed and evidence of true savings was by definition missing. The majority of the Commissioners voted for granting exemption over a dissent.

## D. Conflict of Interest in Joint Transactions: Section 17(d) and Rule 17d-1

### 1. The Reach of Section 17(d)

Section 17(d) of the 1940 Act is a "catch-all" provision relating to conflicts of interests when the adviser or its affiliates partner with their investment companies and controlled companies. Such partnership may not be equal in terms of advantages and disadvantages. This section is different from other sections authorizing the Commission to grant exemptions. First, the section is not a self-executing provision; rather, it is an enabling provision authorizing the SEC to prohibit certain activities by rules. Pursuant to this authority, the SEC has promulgated rule 17d-1. Second, the section relates not to direct transactions between the investment company (and its controlled companies) and affiliates and their affiliates. Rather, it relates to parallel and joint transactions in which the investment company and its controlled companies are on one side of the transaction with a third party and the affiliates and their affiliates are also on the same side of the

---

1. Vanguard Municipal Bond Fund, Inc., Investment Company Act Rel. No. 17655 (Aug. 7, 1990).

transaction with a third party. Yet the terms for the affiliates and for the investment company may differ. To exempt from the prohibited conflict of interest, the SEC must find that the terms of the transaction for the investment company are equal to those of the affiliate (the SEC must consider "the extent to which such participation is on a basis different from or less advantageous than that of other participants").[1] Note the difference between the standard in this section and that in section 17(b), under which the SEC may exempt conflict of interest transactions if the terms of the conflict of interest transaction are "reasonable and fair."

Section 17(d) provides:

> It shall be unlawful for any affiliated person of or principal underwriter for a registered investment company (other than a company of the character described in section 12(d)(3) (A) and (B)), or any affiliated person of such a person or principal underwriter, acting as principal to effect any transaction in which such registered company, or a company controlled by such registered company, is a joint or a joint and several participant with such person, principal underwriter, or affiliated person, in contravention of such rules and regulations as the Commission may prescribe for the purpose of limiting or preventing participation by such registered or controlled company on a basis different from or less advantageous than that of such other participant.

One of the first issues that arose in connection with section 17(d) was the interpretation of the term "joint and several." Does it mean that the investment company and affiliates must agree to act together? Does it mean that any parallel action by them toward a third party raises issues under section 17(d)? Suppose the affiliates and the investment company buy shares of IBM at the same time, is this a joint and several transaction? The following case provides some guidelines.[2]

> For the second time this term . . . we are confronted with a close question of interpretation of § 17 of the Investment Company Act of 1940 . . . setting limits on "Transactions of Certain Affiliated Persons and Underwriters." On this occasion we believe the district judge construed the relevant clause, § 17(d), too narrowly, reverse his judgment dismissing the complaint, and direct further appropriate proceedings.
>
> I. Section 17(d), so far as here relevant, provides as follows:
>
>> (d) It shall be unlawful for any affiliated person of or principle [sic] underwriter for a registered investment company (other than a company of the character described in section 80a-12 (d) (3) (A) and (B) of this title), or any affiliated person of such a person or principal underwriter, acting as principal to effect any transaction in which such registered company, or a company controlled by such registered company, is

1. 17 C.F.R. § 270.17d-1(b) (2015).

2. *SEC v. Talley Industries, Inc.*, 399 F.2d 396 (2d Cir. 1968), *cert. denied*, 393 U.S.1015 (1969) (footnotes omitted).

> a joint or a joint and several participant with such person, principal underwriter, or affiliated person, in contravention of such rules and regulations as the Commission may prescribe for the purpose of limiting or preventing participation by such registered or controlled company on a basis different from or less advantageous than that of such other participant.

Defendant Talley Industries, Inc. (hereafter Industries) is an "affiliated person" of defendant American Investors Fund, Inc. (hereafter Fund), a registered investment company, by virtue of Fund's owning 9% of Industries' voting shares, *see* § 2(a) (3) (B). As a result of discussions between Franz G. Talley, president of Industries, a company having a net worth of some $10 million, and Michael Kimelman, a partner in the brokerage firm of M. Kimelman & Co., in which Kimelman advanced General Time Corporation, a much larger corporation, as a candidate for acquisition by a merger with Industries, Talley gave Kimelman an order under which he bought 24,800 shares of General Time for Industries on December 26 and 27, 1967; the price was around $23 or $24 per share. This was only some 1% of the outstanding stock of General Time, a long way from what Talley thought would be needed to afford a prospect of success if he should decide to go forward with an acquisition or merger proposal.

On December 29, 1967, Talley telephoned Fund's office, and . . . spoke to. . . Chestnutt, Jr., president of Fund and of Chestnutt Corporation, its investment adviser. Talley told him that Industries had bought stock in a certain company which he viewed as a possible merger candidate and that he had in mind that Fund also might wish to buy some stock. Chestnutt broke off the conversation to consult his counsel. The latter advised that Fund could follow Talley's suggestion so long as it "maintained complete independence in our acquisition of stock and didn't make any promises or arrangements" as to voting, disposition or otherwise. Chestnutt relayed this to Talley, who accepted Fund's proceeding in this manner. Talley then named the company, saying he thought it a good investment that might become better under a more aggressive management.

He indicated that Industries intended to buy more General Time stock in the market, with an eye toward a merger; Chestnutt got the impression that Talley was thinking of terms that would yield around $45 in Industries securities for each share of General Time. Talley proposed that Kimelman get in touch with Chestnutt; the latter, after telling Talley that 10% of the General Time stock would be his legal limit, said he would study his own data on the company, would like to see Kimelman, and would think the whole thing over. Shortly thereafter Industries bought 42,000 shares of General Time.

Kimelman visited Chestnutt on January 3. Next day Chestnutt determined that Fund should take a position in General Time. He was motivated both by a study of the company's earnings and by a belief that if Industries sought a merger, the stock would rise as a result of that offer or of others it might stimulate. On January 5 Fund placed an order with Kimelman for 205,000 shares, subsequently increased to 210,000, just under Fund's 10% limit, on a "not-held" basis, i.e., with the time of execution at the broker's discretion. Chestnutt reported this to Talley.

Chestnutt maintained close supervision of Kimelman's purchases, insisting that on days when Kimelman had "not held" orders from other customers, shares should be allocated so as not to favor another customer over Fund. Industries was also making some purchases of General Time through Kimelman but at least on one occasion agreed to forego allocation and accept the most expensive shares. By February 15 Fund had acquired 210,000 shares at an average cost of $28.49 per share.

During the first week of January 1968, Talley discussed the situation, including his initial conversation with Chestnutt, with his counsel, who did not mention § 17(d). After some backing and filling unnecessary to recount, Industries resumed purchases of General Time toward the end of January. Talley talked to Chestnutt four or five times during January and reported how many shares he thought "were being acquired by the Kimelmans and himself and his friends and so on." He would give Chestnutt percentage figures of what "we have" and these rather obviously included the holdings of Fund. On February 5 Industries sold 40,000 shares to Donald Harrington, a friend of Talley's, who later increased his holdings to 104,500 shares. Finding that the record date for General Time's annual meeting was March 1, somewhat earlier than he had believed, and that Industries' own holding were only some 52,000 shares, about 2½% of the stock as against the 10% he considered necessary for a meaningful merger proposal, Talley made a special bid on the advice of his investment bankers, Smith, Barney & Co., and against that of Chestnutt who thought this would drive the price up and would not get Industries the amount of stock it wanted. The bid, on February 19, 1968, was for 200,000 shares at 36½. General Time denounced this as "grossly inadequate" and said it had a higher offer, on a tax-free basis, from another company. Only 66,437 shares were acquired.

On the afternoon of February 19, a meeting was held at Smith, Barney & Co. at the instance of the management of General Time. Talley proposed a merger and said "We and our associates own about a third of the stock" — a figure which included Fund's holdings. Later that evening the management sent word to Talley it had decided to fight. Industries, which then owned 118,537 shares, about 5½% of the total, went back into the market and quickly bought another 139,400 shares at prices ranging from 41½ to 43½. This brought its holdings to 257,937 shares, about 12½%, at an average cost of $36.76 per share.

General Time's response was an action in the District Court for the Southern District of New York alleging inter alia a violation of 17(d) of the Investment Company Act and seeking an injunction against the voting of the stock, the obtaining of more, or any merger. Judge Bryan dismissed the action for lack of standing; General Time appealed. Meanwhile Industries selected ten nominees . . . for election as directors at the annual meeting of General Time on April 22, obtained a stockholders list only after litigation in Delaware, and sought to clear its proxy material with the SEC. On March 25 the SEC staff advised that the material would not be cleared unless Industries filed an application for approval of the acquisition of General Time stock by Fund and Industries under Rule 17d-1, which we reproduce in relevant part in the margin. Industries filed such an application, with appropriate disclaimers of the need for doing so; a hearing was set for April 16; and the proxy material was cleared.

General Time then started a new action in the District Court for the Southern District of New York, claiming the proxy material was false and misleading in violation of § 14 of the Securities Exchange Act of 1934. Judge Tyler denied a preliminary injunction on April 11. On the next day Chestnutt was asked whether he would consider an offer for Fund's holdings in General Time from Del Coleman, president of Seeburg Corporation having its headquarters in Illinois. He countered by saying that he would be "down in front of the SEC testifying on the General Time situation next week, probably Tuesday" and might have to reveal anything that was said. Coleman first drew back but then asked whether Chestnutt would entertain a cash offer of $40 a share. Chestnutt replied that he would have to compare this with what anyone else might offer.

April 13 saw the announcement of a plan to merge General Time and Seeburg Corporation, "contingent upon the continuation of General Time's present management." The details appeared on April 15. Chestnutt found the terms "shockingly unattractive"; he thought they would work out at not more than $28 per share of General Time as against a current market of $35. This, according to Chestnutt, was what made him decide to vote Fund's shares for the Committee's nominees and against the management.

The SEC hearings were held April 16, 17, and 18, oral argument was had before the Commission on April 19, and the Commission issued a Memorandum Opinion and Order that afternoon. Concluding that Industries and Fund had entered into and carried out a joint arrangement under 17(d), that application for approval should have been made under Rule 17d-1, and that there was "no warrant for granting retroactive approval of the transactions effected in such violation," the Commission denied the application. It made no direction beyond an assertion in a footnote of its "continuing jurisdiction . . . over any future transfers by Industries of the GTC stock it has acquired. . . ."

On April 22, after a further unsuccessful attempt by General Time to secure an injunction from Judge Tyler, the stockholders met, the ballots were cast, and the meeting was adjourned to May 3 so that the inspectors could count the votes and certify the result. Preliminary reports indicate a victory for Industries' slate, although by a margin considerably less than the shares voted by Fund.

On May 1, the SEC began this action in the District Court for the Southern District of New York. Asserting violation of § 17(d) and Rule 17d-1 by Industries and Fund, the complaint sought temporary and permanent relief enjoining further acquisition of General Time stock, requiring Industries and Fund to withdraw any votes cast at the stockholders' meeting, enjoining the voting of such shares for nominees proposed by Industries or for any merger with Industries, and enjoining future violations by Industries and Fund. The parties agreed that the court should order the trial to be advanced and consolidated with the hearing on the application for a preliminary injunction. . . . After trial Judge Wyatt delivered an opinion directing dismissal of the complaint, this appeal followed, and we have given it expedited treatment. Meanwhile the stockholders' meeting of General Time has been adjourned at first by stipulation and later by a stay issued by this court.

II. The first issue is whether the SEC may lawfully conclude that when an affiliated person and a registered investment company engage in a plan to achieve together a substantial stock position in another company, they can have effected "any transaction in which such registered company . . . is a joint or a joint and several participant" with the affiliate even though there is no legally binding agreement between them; we postpone the related issue whether if that proposition be affirmed, the facts here sufficiently disclose such a plan.

Little purpose would be achieved by tired-eye scrutiny of the word "transaction." This is not a technical term; "transact" means "To prosecute negotiations; to carry on business; to have dealings. . . ." If any investment company and an affiliate agreed that each would buy 20% of the stock of a third company and would not sell without the other's consent, the case would evidently come within § 17(d), and it would be altogether immaterial whether "transaction" was read to refer to each purchase or the entire course of dealing or both. The real issue concerns the phrase "is a joint or a joint and several participant."

We begin by conceding that, on a quick reading, such black-letter words call up an image of situations where there is a considerable degree of common understanding. Industries argues, in a conspicuously able brief, that this conclusion is reinforced by § 12(a)(2) which forbids any registered investment company, in contravention of Commission rules, regulations or orders, "to participate on a joint or a joint and several basis in any trading account in securities" this rather obviously contemplating a situation where definite legal obligations are fixed. Against this, however, § 17(d) must have been intended to reach situations not already covered by § 12(a). Furthermore any idea that § 17(d) is limited to the typical joint venture in which each of the parties has a fractional share is negated by the point that its very bite is to limit or prevent participation by the investment company "on a basis different from or less advantageous than that" of the affiliated person.

We find it hard to believe that a Congress which had declared "that the national public interest and the interest of investors are adversely affected . . . when investment companies are organized, operated, managed, or their portfolio securities are selected, in the interest of directors, officers, investment advisers, depositors, or other affiliated persons thereof . . . rather than in the interest of all classes of such companies' security holders," § 1(b)(2), meant "a joint or a joint and several participant" to be read in light of common law concepts of jointness. The need for a liberal construction in order to effectuate the statutory purpose would be clearer if, for example, Industries had been an affiliate because of its holding of 5% or more of the voting securities of Fund, § 2(a)(3)(A), rather than the reverse. Yet if "joint" embraces a loose kind of combination in cases of the former type where the case for a liberal construction is strong, as held by Judge Nordbye with respect to directors in *SEC v. Midwest Technical Development Corp.* . . . it must also do that here where the case is less so -- and this even though the strict letter of the statutory command is limited to the affiliate. Moreover, Congress could have thought that downstream affiliation also involved some danger that the investment company's stockholders might be put upon for the benefit of other stockholders of the affiliate. "Joint" can mean not only "joined" or "united" but "combined. . . ." The case is thus appropriate for application of the settled principle that when administration of a statute has been confided to a regulatory agency and a statutory term is reasonably capable of the interpretation the agency has given, a court will sustain this even though it might have reached a different conclusion if the issue had arisen otherwise. . . .

Even on that view, however, some element of "combination" is required. Industries forcefully contends this to be negated, particularly by Chestnutt's statement to Talley before Fund had even decided to make purchases of General Time. But here Industries encounters the Commission's decision to the contrary. Passing for the moment the question of the validity of the portion of Rule 17d-1 authorizing the hearing conducted by the SEC, we cannot subscribe to Industries' argument that in any event the administrative proceeding was "without legal significance," so that, as in *SEC v. Frank* . . . the Commission was cast in the district court in the same role as a private litigant as regards factual issues. To be sure the case is not here on a petition to review the SEC's order denying Industries' application for retrospective approval, and the provision of § 43(a) making its findings conclusive if supported by substantial evidence thus is not applicable by its terms. But the principle underlying that rule -- that a factual determination by an agency responsible for the execution of Congressional policy and vested with expertise shall not be disturbed by a court where there is substantial evidence to support it -- applies none the less, and it would be little short of absurd for us to decline to follow the same standard by which a court reviewing the Commission's order would be bound. Cf. *SEC v. Central-Illinois Securities Corp.* . . .

Our summary of the facts shows there was substantial evidence here. While no one has cast doubt on the veracity of Chestnutt's testimony as to his initial conversation with Talley, this did not preclude the Commission's drawing a contrary inference of intention from what the parties actually did. Indeed developments may well have brought Industries and Fund into a "combination" not clearly envisioned by either at the outset; war and the threat of war have always been powerful forgers of alliances. The Commission was justified in using its knowledge of the unspoken customs of the business world to conclude that, after Chestnutt had seen Industries spend over $8,300,000 in acquiring the 205,837 shares purchased in the special offer and on February 21 and 23, he was no longer a completely free agent as to the 210,000 shares Fund had purchased, on Talley's recommendation, for about 70% of that price.

Experienced business men must have known at the outset that such a situation might arise. "An administrative agency with power after hearings to determine on the evidence in adversary proceedings whether violations of statutory commands have occurred may infer within the limits of the inquiry from the proven facts such conclusions as reasonably may be based upon the facts proven. One of the purposes which lead to the creation of such boards is to have decisions based upon evidential facts under the particular statute made by experienced officials with an adequate appreciation of the complexities of the subject which is entrusted to their administration." *Republic Aviation v. NLRB. . . .*

---

## Discussion Topics

a. Is section 17(d) violated if the directors of an investment company that invests in stocks of biotechnical companies invest in such stock in tandem with the company, but sell the stocks before the investment company does?

b. Would it make a difference if the directors bought options on the stock instead of the stock itself?

c. Would it make a difference if the stock was widely traded?

d. What guidelines would you prepare for the directors with respect to their stock purchases?

e. Assume that an investment adviser plans to insure the life of a "star" portfolio manager. May the adviser join the investment company as a beneficiary of the insurance policy?

f. What questions would you ask to determine whether such a joint and several arrangement is permissible? If not, would you ask for a no-action letter or an exemption from the provision?

g. If you were the SEC staff members who deal with such an application, would you grant a no-action letter? Would you impose conditions?

---

## 2. Additional Practical Issues Under Section 17(d) and Rule 17d-1

As mentioned, section 17(d) and rule 17d-1 are quite broad. Rule 17d-1 implements section 17(d), broadly defines a "joint transaction," and makes clear that entering into any such joint transaction generally requires an exemptive order from the SEC:

> (a) No affiliated person of or principal underwriter for any registered investment company (other than a company of the character described in Section 12(d)(3)(A) and (B) of the Act) and no affiliated person of such a person or principal underwriter, acting as principal, shall participate in, or effect any transaction in connection with, any joint enterprise or other joint arrangement or profit-sharing plan in which any such registered company, or a company controlled by such registered company, is a participant, and which is entered into, adopted or modified subsequent to the effective date of this rule, unless an application regarding such joint enterprise, arrangement or profit-sharing plan has been filed with the Commission and has been granted by an order entered prior to the submission of such plan or modification to security holders for approval, or prior to such adoption or modification if not so submitted, except that the provisions of this rule shall not preclude any affiliated person from acting as manager of any underwriting syndicate or other group in which such registered or controlled company is a participant and receiving compensation therefor.
>
> * * *
>
> (c) "Joint enterprise or other joint arrangement or profit-sharing plan" as used in this section shall mean any written or oral plan, contract, authorization or arrangement, or any practice or understanding concerning an enterprise or undertaking whereby a registered investment company or a controlled company thereof and any affiliated person of or a principal underwriter for such registered investment company, or any affiliated person of such a person or principal underwriter, have a joint or a joint and several participation, or share in the profits of such enterprise or undertaking, including, but not limited to, any stock option or stock purchase plan, but shall not include an investment advisory contract subject to Section 15 of the act.

Importantly, however, the SEC staff has recognized that some element of combination or profit motive must generally be present for section 17(d) and rule 17d-1 to apply.[1] Additionally, Rule 17d-1 provides important exemptions that permit transactions that would arguably be joint without

1. *See* SMC Capital, Inc., SEC No-Action Letter (Sept. 5, 1995) (citing *In re Steadman Security Corp.,* 1974-75 Fed. Sec. L. Rep. (CCH) ¶80,038 at 84,848 (Dec. 20, 1974) (rule 17d-1 "is concerned with joint enterprises or joint arrangements that are in the nature of a joint venture, i.e., that involve the element of seeking to realize a profit or gain through the investment of funds."); *SEC v. Talley Industries, Inc.,* 399 F.2d 396, 403 (2d Cir. 1968), *cert. denied,* 393 U.S. 1015 (1969) (while section 17(d) is not limited to the typical joint venture, "some element of 'combination' is required")).

obtaining an exemptive order — namely, joint liability insurance policies (i.e., directors & officers/errors & omissions insurance), an investment adviser's bearing expenses in connection with a merger, consolidation or purchase or sale of substantially all of the assets of a company which involves a registered investment company of which it is an affiliated person, and a conforming exception related to transactions permitted by rule 17a-6.

Through the no-action letter process, the SEC staff has also clarified that aggregation of orders for publicly traded securities among various advisory clients, including registered investment companies, would generally not violate rule 17d-1 subject to a variety of conditions designed to ensure that no advisory client would be favored over another advisory client.[1] Similar conditions also apply with respect to aggregated purchases of privately placed securities; however, significant differences in that context include the necessity of board-approved (including by the disinterested directors) aggregation procedures and that price is the only term that may be negotiated.[2] The SEC staff has also applied rule 17d-1 to service contracts with affiliates — such as contracts for administrative services, custody, transfer agency services, distribution services and the like. The staff has permitted these types of agreement with affiliates, provided that the fund's board (including the disinterested directors) make the following findings:

- the agreement is in the best interest of the fund and its shareholders;
- the services to be performed by the affiliate pursuant to the agreement are required for the operation of the fund;
- the affiliate is capable of providing services the nature and quality of which are at least equal to those provided by others offering the same or similar services; and
- the fees to be charged to the fund by the affiliate for the services it is to provide under the agreement are fair and reasonable in light of the usual and customary charges made by others for services of the same nature and quality.[3]

### E. Conflict of Interest in Agency Transactions: Section 17(e)

Section 17(e) addresses conflicts of interest that arise when an affiliated person (or an affiliated person of an affiliated person) serves as an agent of the investment company or its controlled companies. An agent is a person who has the authority to bind the principal to a legal obligation (without binding himself to such an obligation). Most agent conflicts of interest arise when the affiliated person benefits from acting as agent for the investment company, in the performance of his duties as agent. The section raises two basic questions. First, what kind of activity constitutes a person an agent? Second, what kind of benefits would fall within the prohibition? The following is one of the few decisions and authorities focusing on section 17(e).[4] Note that section 17(e)(1) prohibits an affiliated person of a registered investment company, or any affiliated person of such

1. SMC Capital, Inc., SEC No-Action Letter (Sept. 5, 1995).
2. Massachusetts Mutual Life Ins. Co., SEC No-Action Letter (Jun. 7, 2000).
3. *See, e.g.,* Washington Square Cash Fund, Inc., SEC No-Action Letter (Jul. 9, 1990).
4. *United States v. Deutsch,* 451 F.2d 98 (2d Cir. 1971), *cert. denied,* 404 U.S. 1019 (1972) (footnotes omitted).

person, acting as agent, from accepting from any source any compensation (other than a regular salary or wages from such registered company) for the purchase or sale of any property to or for such registered company or any controlled company thereof, except in the course of such person's business as an underwriter or broker.

> [Deutsch was charged together with co-defendant, Frank D. Mills with knowingly effecting purchases of securities for his personal account and for the accounts of two registered investment companies of which he was an affiliated person, in violation of § 17(d) of the Act, aiding and abetting these crimes, in violation of 18 U.S.C. § 2 (1964), knowingly accepting compensation from the issuer of the securities, while Mills was acting as agent for the registered investment companies, in violation of 15 U.S.C. § 80a-17(e)(1) (1964). Mills pleaded guilty and was fined $7,500.]
>
> During the summer of 1967, Deutsch was executive vice-president and a member of the three-man board of directors of Realty Equities Corporation in New York, a real estate investment company listed on the American Stock Exchange. Realty had been founded by Deutsch and others in 1959. By 1968 it had consolidated assets of $137 million.
>
> In the summer of 1967, Realty anticipated a forthcoming merger in connection with which it needed to raise a substantial amount of capital. Realty decided to finance the merger by a private placement, limited to institutional investors only, of $12 million in promissory notes with warrants attached. . . .
>
> Deutsch was in charge of selling the issue. His initial efforts met with failure. As of December 4, 1967, he had not succeeded in selling a single note. While peddling this issue, however, Deutsch had his first contact with the co-defendant, Frank D. Mills, a contact which resulted in the first sale of Realty notes.
>
> During the summer of 1967 and throughout 1968, Mills was a senior officer of Fidelity Management and Research Company in Boston, and of twelve mutual funds for which it acted as investment adviser. Mills was a member of the six-man investment committee of all the funds, whose aggregate assets exceeded $3.5 billion and whose combined stockholders numbered over 500,000. As such, he participated in the preparation of periodic guidelines listing securities and maximum dollar values which the fund account managers could buy or sell without approval; he also was one of the two men whose approval was needed for any transaction outside the guidelines. Mills was the account manager of one of the funds, the Puritan Fund, and, as such, he had authority to buy or sell up to $2 million in any bond and up to the guideline limits for approved stocks. Mills also was vice president of eight of the funds, including Puritan Fund and Fidelity Trend Fund. It is undisputed that Puritan and Fidelity Trend were registered investment companies and that Mills was an affiliated person of each of them within the meaning of the Act. . . .
>
> Deutsch's first contact with Mills occurred as a result of Deutsch's

attempt, in the summer of 1967, to sell some of the issue to Massachusetts Mutual Life. He told Deutsch that state insurance law barred Massachusetts Life from purchasing that type of security; but a few days later, Chapin recommended the issue to Mills, saying that from what he knew Realty was satisfactory in every way and that if he were interested he should contact Deutsch directly. The first sale of Realty notes ensued.

On December 8, 1967, Mills committed the Puritan Fund to purchase two notes. This first sale appeared to be the shot in the arm that Realty needed. With Mills' permission, Deutsch used Puritan's prestigious name in talking to prospective buyers. As Deutsch testified at trial, this was "a good sales pitch" and "very helpful." The entire offering was soon fully subscribed, and an additional $5 million in notes was authorized. This offering, too, was fully subscribed, with Puritan itself taking an additional $700,000 on June 14, 1968, bringing its investment up to the statutory limit of 10% of the offering. By August 9, 1968, Realty had thus succeeded in borrowing $17 million.

On August 29, 1968, Deutsch again called Chapin who had recently joined Realty's board of directors at Deutsch's invitation. Realty had contracted to repurchase five units from Republic National Life Insurance Company in Texas, one of the original subscribers, and had an option to repurchase seven more, the balance of Republic's interest, at prices which were advantageous in view of an appreciable rise in the market price of Realty stock. Meanwhile, Massachusetts law had changed, and the notes were now permissible purchases for insurance companies. Deutsch was thus able to offer to sell Massachusetts Life some of the Republic National Life units. Deutsch did not disclose the repurchase contract between Realty and Republic National Life. He led Chapin to believe that the seller was Republic National Life and that the price had not yet been negotiated. Deutsch pointed out to Chapin that the exercise price was 15¼ whereas the stock was trading at 32. Chapin said he was interested and asked for more information.

On September 11, Richard Dooley, a Massachusetts Life securities analyst to whom Chapin had referred the matter, told Deutsch that Massachusetts Life was rejecting the offer because of house counsel's opinion that the price was so advantageous it gave the transaction the appearance of being a corporate gift in view of Chapin's interlocking directorships. Deutsch renewed the offer at a higher price, 7¾ premium per warrant instead of 3, saying that it brought the price into line with what he was told was the customary discount. Counsel for Massachusetts Life still thought the price was too advantageous. On September 25, Dooley relayed his company's final rejection.

Sometime between September 23 and September 26, Chapin told Mills about Realty's exceptional offer and suggested that Mills call Deutsch. However, unknown to Chapin, Mills already knew about Deutsch's offer and had taken steps to seize the opportunity for himself. On September 16, five days after the initial rejection by Massachusetts Life, Mills had approached the president of the National Shawmut Bank in Boston for the purpose of borrowing enough cash to buy a unit of the Realty securities for himself.

Mills told the bank that he wanted the transaction kept strictly confidential. To insure confidentiality, Mills asked the bank to make an exception to its general practice and to place the transaction in a nominee account. Shortly after September 24, the bank agreed to lend Mills $572,000 as the entire purchase price of a unit.

On September 30, a few days after the Shawmut Bank agreed to lend Mills the $572,000, the Banque de Paris bought two identical units from Republic National Life at a price per unit of $928,125.

Sometime in early October, Mills took two steps with respect to Realty securities. First, he gave a 50% participation in his private deal with Realty to a real estate investor named Philip Levin. Second, he tried unsuccessfully to interest Richard Smith, the account manager of one-half of Fidelity Trend, to buy two notes for the fund.

On October 15, after his unsuccessful approach to Richard Smith, Mills approached the account manager of the other half of Fidelity Trend, Ross Sherbrooke. Mills said two units would be available for a little over $900,000 per unit, but that there was some urgency and that Sherbrooke had to make up his mind by October 17, after which the notes would no longer be available. Mills did not disclose that he and Levin were about to buy a unit themselves at a substantially lower price. On the same day, Mills told the Shawmut Bank that he was ready to proceed with the loan and would require only half the money since he was buying only half the unit.

Mills undoubtedly was influential in Sherbrooke's decision to buy the Realty notes. Sherbrooke had never heard of Realty before. He looked up the company in standard reference books, asked a Fidelity specialist about it, and a day or so later told Mills he would take the two units. Mills was considerably senior to Sherbrooke. Since Sherbrooke had been on the job for only four months, he may well have been reluctant to reject his senior's suggestion. Sherbrooke at trial conceded that Mills' high opinion of Realty played a "significant role in influencing my judgment. . . ." Mills' and Levin's purchase and Fidelity Trend's purchase closed three days apart. Mills and Levin paid $537,000 for one unit on October 21; Fidelity Trend paid $928,125 per unit for two units -- a total of $1,856,250 -- on October 24.

After his purchase was made, Mills continued to try to conceal the transaction. In violation of the Fidelity group's internal code of ethics, Mills did not report his purchase of the Realty note. Moreover, Mills had not requested advance approval of the transaction from the SEC, in violation of the regulations governing joint and several transactions of an affiliated person such as Mills and a fund such as Fidelity Trend. . . .

Deutsch also tried to conceal the transaction. He insisted that Levin use a nominee. When called before the SEC on November 22,

1968, he falsely testified that the two nominees were "two banks in the United States", when in fact Levin's nominee was Saul and Co. and Mills' nominee was Harris and Co. Deutsch also supplied the SEC with what he said was an office memorandum listing all subscribers and purchasers at resale. With respect to other nominees, this memorandum indicated the real parties in interest in parentheses; but with respect to Mills' and Levin's nominees, the real parties were not indicated.

At trial, the main thrust of Deutsch's defense was that he had agreed to sell a Realty note to Mills in February or March 1968 and that the actual sale the following October was the fulfillment of a promise made at a time when Deutsch had no idea that the notes would be worth so much more than face value.

Deutsch testified that on February 29, 1968, after the closing of the sale of two Realty notes to Puritan, Mills told him he wanted personally to buy a note; that the next day, Deutsch told Realty's president, Morris Karp, about Mills' request and that Karp said it could not be done on original issue, but that Mills could purchase one of the notes on re-sale; and that several weeks later, near the end of March, Deutsch told Mills, "I got approval from Morris that if there is ever a resale you can have it for whatever price we get it for," to which Mills' response was, "Great. You got a deal."

Despite Deutsch's customary practice of making notes on his way home from negotiations, he made none of this commitment. His promise was not reflected in any contemporaneous writing. Moreover, this alleged oral agreement was not binding on Realty. *See N. Y. Uniform Commercial Code. . . .*

CLAIM THAT TRIAL COURT MISINTERPRETED § 17(e)(1) OF THE ACT

The essential issues on this appeal require interpretation of § 17(e)(1) of the Act. . . . While this is the first criminal prosecution under § 17(e)(1), the SEC has had occasion at the administrative level to construe this section of the statute. Prior to the instant case, however, no court, so far as we know, has discussed the intent of Congress in enacting § 17(e)(1).

Unfortunately, the legislative history affords little help. . . . The Senate and House Reports indicate that the Act was designed primarily to correct the abuses of self-dealing which had produced injury to stockholders of investment companies. Four sections of the Act, including § 17, were aimed specifically at insuring the independence of management and its fidelity to stockholders. Congress recognized that its existing laws were inadequate to prevent the abuses of self-dealing. . . . The Act was thus designed in part quite clearly to establish broad standards which would more easily enable the government to convict affiliated persons for self-dealing in the management of investment companies -- an industry the very nature of which made it particularly difficult to gather proof.

Interpretation of the Phrase "Acting as Agent"

Section 17(e)(1), so far as here relevant, provides as follows: "It shall be unlawful for any affiliated person of a registered investment company . . . acting as agent, to accept from any source any compensation . . . for the purchase . . . of any property . . . for such registered company. . . ."

Deutsch does not dispute the fact that Mills was an affiliated person within the meaning of the Act and that Puritan and Fidelity Trend were registered companies. He contends, however, that the trial court misconstrued the phrase "acting as agent." He argues that this phrase makes the violation proscribed by § 17(e)(1) incomplete unless the compensation actually caused a fund to purchase or sell securities. . . .

Section 17(e)(1) does not explicitly make it an element of the offense that the recipient of the compensation take any action as a result thereof. Deutsch argues that the draftsman's use of a verb in the phrase "acting as agent" expresses a Congressional intent to prohibit only gratuities which succeed in influencing the recipient's conduct. We find it hard to believe, however, that a Congress which had recognized that the investment company industry "offer[ed] manifold opportunities for exploitation by unscrupulous managements . . ." meant that an offense was complete only when the affiliated person acted as a result of receiving something of value. Rather, we believe that the more reasonable interpretation is that an offense under § 17(e)(1) is complete when the compensation is delivered and received with the forbidden intent. The objective of § 17(e)(1) is to prevent affiliated persons from having their judgment and fidelity impaired by conflicts of interest. It is clear that, as soon as Mills purchased the Realty note at a reduced price, he was inhibited by a conflict of interest which could easily becloud his judgment to the detriment of the beneficiaries of the funds. The abuse which § 17(e)(1) was designed to prevent -- affiliated persons operating under conflicts of interest -- was complete when Mills received the compensation, even if he never exerted any influence on Realty's behalf. Moreover, to accept Deutsch's construction would emasculate § 17(e)(1). Given the nature of the investment company industry, it would be extremely difficult to prove that the payment of compensation actually caused a particular purchase. It is most unlikely that Congress intended a construction which would rob § 17(e)(1) of its effectiveness. . . .

Our interpretation of the phrase "acting as agent," that it is not necessary to show actual conduct as a result of the compensation, further appears to be consistent with decisions of this Court and of other Courts of Appeals interpreting statutes analogous to § 17(e)(1) which likewise are designed to prevent officials and other "insiders" from operating under conflicts of interest. In *United States v. Irwin* . . . we held that it was not necessary to show actual conduct to prove the unlawful payment of a gratuity to a public official under 18 U.S.C. § 201(f) (1964): "It is not necessary for the Government to show that the gift caused or prompted or in any way affected the happening of the official act. . . ." [T]he First Circuit said that under the anti-kickback statute, 41 U.S.C. § 51 (1964), the crime is "complete upon the acceptance of a bribe regardless of whether or not improper action is thereafter taken. . . ." The section] "is directed not only at dishonor, but also at conduct that tempts dishonor . . ." and "whether he actually gives or withholds instructions . . . is immaterial").

Rejection of Deutsch's construction does not make the phrase "acting as agent" superfluous. It defines a subclass of affiliated persons. Within the statutory scheme of § 17(e), affiliated persons who are acting as brokers may receive limited compensation in connection with portfolio transactions of the registered investment company. 15 U.S.C. § 80a-17(e)(2) (1964). If affiliated persons are not acting as brokers, however, but otherwise are acting as agents of the investment company, they cannot accept compensation in connection with the purchase or sale of securities. While § 17(e) is far from a model of clarity, we believe that an affiliated person is acting as agent within the meaning of § 17(e)(1) in all cases when he is not acting as broker for the investment company. . . . In view of our interpretation of the phrase "acting as agent," we believe that the trial court erred in submitting to the jury the issue of whether Mills was acting as agent. As we have indicated, "acting as agent" does not require a showing that Mills took any action as a result of being compensated. Since Deutsch did not dispute the facts that Mills was an affiliated person and that Mills was not acting as broker, we believe that the government established, as a matter of law, that Mills was acting as agent for the investment companies within the meaning of § 17(e)(1). While the trial court erred in submitting this issue to the jury, it was harmless error, for Deutsch suffered no prejudice. . . .

Deutsch . . . maintains that the phrase [acting as agent] was intended to mean acting as agent for an outsider dealing with the investment company and not as agent for the investment company itself. This contention is without merit. . . .

Requisite Intent Under § 17(e)(1)

Deutsch maintains that the evidence was insufficient to prove that compensation was given with the intent to influence. We find it unnecessary to reach this issue, because we believe that the trial court erred in charging the jury that, in order to convict, they must find that the compensation was given and received with the intent to influence Mills.

The language of § 17(e)(1) makes no mention of intent to influence; the subsection is cast in the familiar "for" terminology of the gratuity statutes . . . where the only intent required is that the payment be given and accepted in appreciation of past, or in anticipation of future, conduct. . . . The trial court's error in charging the jury that intent to influence was a necessary element of the offense did not prejudice Deutsch, for the erroneous charge merely "exacted a higher standard of proof than the law required."

> Claim that there was insufficient evidence to prove compensation
>
> Deutsch argues that the evidence was insufficient to prove the statutory element of compensation. He admits that he sold Mills a note at a substantial discount in October and he does not dispute the trial court's definition of compensation as a "benefit or thing of value [including] being granted an opportunity to purchase securities at a discount price." He claims, however, that he made a commitment to sell one of the notes to Mills in February or March 1968 and that when he made this commitment he had no idea that the Realty note and attached warrant would be so valuable eight or nine months later. He contends that, since compensation must be paid and accepted knowingly and willfully to render him guilty, he did not violate § 17(e)(1) by fulfilling an oral agreement which was made with no intention of selling at a discount price. . . .
>
> [The jury] evidently chose to disbelieve Deutsch's story of a February-March commitment. Deutsch now contends that the issue of compensation should never have gone to the jury, because the government failed to challenge his affirmative defense with directly contradictory proof, and because there was insufficient evidence to prove that the first time Deutsch offered the deal to Mills was in September 1968. These contentions are without merit.
>
> Deutsch's claim that the government was required to offer proof which directly contradicted his testimony about the February-March commitment is frivolous. In *Masciale v. United States* . . . the Supreme Court held that a jury was entitled to disbelieve the defendant's testimony that an informant trapped him into meeting with an undercover agent, notwithstanding the fact that the defendant's testimony was uncontradicted because of the informant's failure to testify. . . . In light of the inherent implausibility that Realty would orally contract, without consideration, to sell a valuable security, at some indefinite time in the future, at an indefinite price, the jury was warranted in disbelieving Deutsch's story. The jury's disbelief is further supported by inconsistencies within Deutsch's own testimony and between his testimony and that of his colleagues. . . . We have considered Deutsch's other claims of error and find them to be without merit. Affirmed.

Recently, the SEC staff has reminded the industry about the prohibitions in section 17(e)(1).[1] As explained by the staff:

> The prohibition in section 17(e)(1) generally applies whenever fund advisory personnel, acting as agent, accept from any source any compensation (other than regular salary or wages from the fund) for the purchase or sale of any property to or for the fund. For example, if a fund's portfolio manager accepts any gifts or entertainment from a broker-dealer for the purchase or sale of the fund's portfolio securities, the portfolio manager has violated section 17(e)(1).

---

1. Acceptance of Gifts or Entertainment by Fund Advisory Personnel — Section 17(e)(1) of the Investment Company Act, IM Guidance Update No. 2015-01 (Feb. 2015).

> The prohibition reflects one of Congress' fundamental policy concerns when it enacted the 1940 Act, expressed in section 1(b)(2) of the 1940 Act — the potential for funds to be managed, or their portfolio securities selected, in the interest of their investment advisers and their affiliates or other persons rather than in the interest of the fund's shareholders.

In giving the industry this reminder, the staff noted several previous cases, including *Deutsch,* which is excerpted above. In particular, the staff noted, "'[A]n affiliated person is acting as agent within the meaning of § 17(e)(1) in all cases when he is not acting as broker for the investment company.' See *United States v. Deutsch,* 451 F.2d 98, 111 (2d Cir. 1971), *cert. denied,* 404 U.S. 1019 (1972)."[1] The staff also noted, "The mere receipt of compensation for the purchase or sale of property to or for a fund is a violation of section 17(e)(1), so that it is not necessary to show that the person receiving the compensation influenced the actions of the fund, or that the fund suffered economic injury. See Deutsch, 451 F.2d at 109-10."[2]

Lastly, in explaining the "for" nexus in section 17(e)(1), the staff noted as follows:[3]

> Because section 17(e)(1) prohibits the receipt of compensation in exchange "for" the purchase or sale of property to or for a fund, courts have found "some nexus must be established between the compensation received and the property bought or sold." See *Decker v. SEC,* 631 F.2d 1380, 1384 (10th Cir. 1980). This provision does not require any proof of any "intent to influence." *Id.* (citing *Deutsch* at 112-13). Further, direct evidence of a nexus will "ordinarily not be available" and "often be disguised by arrangements that are 'facially proper.'" *Id.* at 1385. In part because of this difficulty of proof, "once a conflict of interest is proven, the burden shifts to the party in conflict to prove that he has been faithful to his trust." *Id.* (quoting *Investors Research Corp. v. SEC,* 628 F.2d 168, 175 (D.C. Cir. 1980)). See also generally In the Matter of Robert L. Burns, Advisers Act Release No. 3260 (Aug. 5, 2011), supra note 5, at 9-10.

In giving the industry these reminders, the staff noted in particular the need for compliance policies and procedures around gifts and entertainment, and noted that some funds and advisers may find it appropriate to impose a blanket prohibition, whereas others may find some type of pre-clearance mechanism to be appropriate. The Investment Company Institute has also attempted to clarify the import of this guidance with the SEC staff, and the Investment Company Institute has noted its understanding of the matter based on its discussions with the SEC staff in a memorandum to the industry.[4] In particular, it should be noted that this guidance is not viewed

1. *Id.* at n.3.
2. *Id.* at n.4.
3. *Id.* at n.6.
4. Clarification of the SEC's Recent Guidance on Gifts and Entertainment Paid to Advisory Personnel, Investment Company Institute Memorandum (Jun. 9, 2015).

as expressing a "zero tolerance" policy, and that the *Decker* case, cited above in the SEC staff's guidance, is informative on this point:[1]

> Petitioner argues that the Commission has misinterpreted § 17(e)(1) as a flat prohibition against conflicts of interest. . . . We agree with petitioner that such an interpretation of § 17(e)(1) is too expansive. The Investment Company Act and the Investment Advisers Act were designed, in part, to prevent conflicts of interest from affecting the judgment of investment advisers. [Citations omitted.] The statute prohibits the receipt of compensation in exchange for the purchase or sale of property to or for an investment company. Thus, some nexus must be established between the compensation received and the property bought or sold. Although it need not be shown that there was any 'intent to influence,' [citations omitted] it must be shown, or properly inferable, that compensation was received 'for' the sale or purchase of property.

Moreover, it was noted that a former director of the SEC's Division of Investment Management stated, in a 2005 speech, "There is no doubt that the receipt of *lavish gifts* and entertainment can influence fund personnel's actions, and even tempt fund personnel to take actions that may not be in the best interest of fund investors."[2]

### 1. Treatment of Brokers and Underwriters Under Section 17(e)

Brokers and underwriters could be viewed as agents of the investment companies whose shares they sell and distribute. Nonetheless, section 17(e)(1) treats brokers and underwriters differently than other affiliates that act as agents. That is because investment companies need the services of brokers and underwriters in order to distribute their shares and trade the companies' assets. Therefore, these may become affiliates. Hence, brokers are excluded from the provisions in section 17(e)(1), but are subject to section 17(e)(2), which imposes a limitation on the brokerage fees that affiliated brokers may charge the investment company. It should be noted that underwriters are neither subject to the prohibition in section 17(e)(1) nor to a limitation on the fees that they may charge the investment company. However, section 15(b) of the Investment Company Act, which deals with the contracts that the investment company enters into, prohibits underwriters from acting as such except under a contract approved by the board of directors of the investment company or its shareholders. In addition, sections 36(a) and (b) impose fiduciary duties on underwriters and limitations on their fees. These provisions were designed to protect investment companies from overreaching by underwriters.

In particular, section 17(e)(2) provides:

> It shall be unlawful for any affiliated person of a registered investment company, or any affiliated person of such person —
>
> > (2) acting as broker, in connection with the sale of securities to or by such registered company or any controlled

1. *Id.* (citing *Decker v. SEC,* 631 F.2d 1380 (10th Cir. 1980).
2. *Id.* (citing Remarks before the Mutual Fund Directors Forum Fifth Annual Policy Conference: Critical Issues for Investment Company Directors, by Paul F. Roye (Feb. 17, 2005), *available at* https://www.sec.gov/news/speech/spch021705pfr.htm).

> company thereof, to receive from any source a commission, fee, or other remuneration for effecting such transaction which exceeds (A) the usual and customary broker's commission if the sale is effected on a securities exchange, or (B) 2 per centum of the sales price if the sale is effected in connection with a secondary distribution of such securities, or (C) 1 per centum of the purchase or sale price of such securities if the sale is otherwise effected unless the Commission shall, by rules and regulations or order in the public interest and consistent with the protection of investors, permit a larger commission.

Note the SEC rule concerning broker-dealers, which deals with the "usual and customary" prong contained in section 17(e)(2)(A), above (this rule has since been re-designated as rule 17e-1):[1]

> SUMMARY: The Investment Company Act of 1940, in part, prohibits an affiliated person of a registered investment company who is acting as broker in a securities transaction involving that company from receiving a commission, fee or other remuneration exceeding the usual and customary broker's commission if the purchase or sale is effected on a securities exchange. However, the advent of negotiated commission rates may make it impracticable for an investment company to determine whether brokerage commissions paid to affiliated persons satisfy the statutory standard of a usual and customary broker's commission. Accordingly, the Commission is requesting public comment on a proposed rule which, provided that certain conditions are satisfied, would deem a commission which is fair and reasonable (compared to that received by other brokers in comparable transactions for similar securities on a securities exchange) as not exceeding the usual and customary broker's commission. Among the conditions is a requirement that the transaction be effected pursuant to procedures, established by the investment company's directors, which are reasonably designed to provide remuneration that is reasonable and fair compared to the remuneration received by other persons in connection with similar transactions on a securities exchange during a comparable time period. This proposed rule was prepared by the Division of Investment Management's Investment Company Act Study Group as part of its re-examination of the regulation of investment companies.
>
> * * *
>
> SUPPLEMENTARY INFORMATION: In enacting the Investment Company Act of 1940 ("Act") [15 U.S.C. 80a-1 et seq.], Congress determined that the national public interest and the interest of investors are adversely affected when investment companies are organized, managed, or their portfolio securities are selected in the interest of, among other persons, brokers. Presumably in part to address

1. Agency Transactions by Affiliated Persons on a Securities Exchange, Investment Company Act Rel. No. 10605 (Feb. 27, 1979) (footnotes omitted) (codified as amended at 17 C.F.R. § 270.17e-1 (2015)).

that concern, Congress enacted section 17(e) of the Act [15 U.S.C. 80a-17(e)] which concerns the remuneration that an affiliated person of an investment company and an affiliated person of such person may receive in transactions involving that company.

Section 17(e)(1) of the Act prohibits such an affiliated person acting as agent from accepting any compensation from any source (other than a regular salary or wage from an investment company) for the purchase or sale of property to or for such company or any controlled company thereof, except in the course of such person's business as an underwriter or broker.

Section 17(e)(2) of the Act specifically prohibits such an affiliated person -- acting as broker, in connection with the sale of securities to or by such registered investment company or any controlled company thereof, to receive from any source a commission, fee, or other remuneration for effecting such transaction which exceeds (A) the usual and customary broker's commission if the sale is effected on a securities exchange . . . .

Thus, in effect, section 17(e)(2) limits the compensation which may be received by a person acting in reliance on the exemption for the brokerage business from the prohibitions of section 17(e)(1) of the Act. Congress thereby intended an affiliated broker in executing such transactions to receive only "the ordinary stock exchange brokerage commission."

However, in 1975 the Commission promulgated rule 19b-3 [17 CFR § 240.19b-3] under the Securities Exchange Act of 1934 [15 U.S.C. 78a et seq.], which prohibits the fixing of commission rates by national securities exchanges. Consequently with the advent of fully negotiated -- and therefore fluctuating -- commission rates, it may be impracticable presently to determine the "usual and customary broker's commission" for any particular agency transaction on such a securities exchange.

Accordingly, the Commission proposes adopting rule 17e-2 [17 CFR § 270.17e-2] under the Act to define the conditions under which, if satisfied, an affiliated person could receive a commission, fee, or other remuneration as broker in such a securities transaction which would be deemed not to exceed the "usual and customary broker's commission" for purposes of section 17(e) (2)(A) of the Act. As incorporated in proposed rule 17e-2, these conditions, in part, would require that the investment company's directors, including a majority of its disinterested directors, establish procedures which are reasonably designed to provide that the commission, fee, or other remuneration received by the affiliated broker is reasonable and fair compared to the commission, fee or other remuneration received by other brokers in connection with similar securities in comparable transactions during a comparable period of time.

This standard would allow an affiliated broker to receive no more than the remuneration which would be expected to be received by an unaffiliated broker in a commensurate arm's-length transaction.

> Because of the difficulties inherent in monitoring continuously the reasonableness and fairness of such unfixed commission rates, the Commission believes that the first line of responsibility for determining compliance with proposed rule 17e-2 must be with each investment company's directors. Therefore, proposed rule 17e-2 would require that, at least quarterly, the investment company's directors, including a majority of its disinterested directors, determine whether the transactions effected pursuant to rule 17e-2 have satisfied the procedures established in the guidelines. These requirements are analogous to conditions proposed to be incorporated into rule 10f-3 [17 CFR § 270.10f-3], which exempts the acquisition of securities from certain underwriting syndicates which would otherwise be prohibited under section 10(f) of the Act [15 U.S.C. 80a-10(f)]. Furthermore, they are consistent with the Investment Company Act Study Group's recommendation that enhanced responsibility for management decisions and legal compliance generally should be retained by investment companies' directors.
>
> As in the proposed amendments to rule 10f-3, a copy of the director's guidelines and records pertaining to each such transaction effected in reliance on proposed rule 17e-2 must be maintained by the investment company, pursuant to section 31(a) of the Act [15 U.S.C. 80a-30(a)], so that the Commission may monitor experience with proposed rule 17e-2 through its inspection program. However, unlike the proposed amendments to rule 10f-3, rule 17e-2 would not require that all transactions effected thereunder be indicated in the investment company's quarterly report. Information concerning aggregate brokerage commissions paid by an investment company to any affiliated person or any affiliated person of such person presently must be disclosed in that investment company's prospectuses and in certain proxy statements pertaining to the election of certain directors.

## 2. Duties and Relationships with Auditors

The Sarbanes-Oxley Act of 2002 recognized the possibility of a conflict of interest when the auditor of a company also provides a non-audit service to the company. Consequently, the Act amended section 10A of the Securities Exchange Act to prohibit the auditor of a company from performing certain non-audit services for the company at the same time as the audit. These prohibited services include bookkeeping, other accounting-related services, financial information systems services, broker-dealer services, investment adviser services, and legal and other expert services unrelated to the audit. The reason for the prohibition is that the auditor is required to evaluate and judge the company's financial situation objectively, and sometimes in conflict with the corporation's management's interest. Being beholden to management may create conflicting interests with the auditor's independent judgment. Therefore, the services may not be provided without an exemption from the Public Company Accounting Oversight Board. An auditor may generally perform tax services or other non-audit services not prohibited by the statute only if the services are preapproved by the audit committee of the corporation or its delegate and disclosed to investors.

In addition, an accounting firm may not perform audit services for a company if a chief executive officer, controller, chief financial officer, or chief accounting officer of the company was employed by the accounting firm and participated in an audit of the company during the previous audit year.

## F. Conflict of Interest by Underwriters: Section 10(f)

### 1. Protecting Investment Companies from "Dumping"

The following describes the rationale and structure of section 10(f) of the 1940 Act.[1]

> Section 10(f) of the 1940 Act complements section 17's prohibitions on self-dealings. Section 10(f) prohibits a registered investment company from acquiring any security during an underwriting period when a principal underwriter of that security is any of the listed affiliates, unless (1) the company is itself the issuer of the purchased security, (2) in acquiring the security the company is itself acting as a principal underwriter or (3) the principal underwriter is a section 12(d)(3) company.
>
> The purpose of the section is to prevent investment companies from purchasing securities to advance the interests of their affiliates rather than their own. The SEC may exempt any transactions or classes of transactions from the section by regulations or by orders pursuant to an application, conditionally or unconditionally, when consistent with the protection of investors. As originally proposed, this provision prohibited *affiliates* of investment companies from acting as principal underwriters if the investment company held .5 percent of the issuer's securities.
>
> The final bill reversed the prohibition. The investment company is prohibited from purchasing securities if certain insiders of the investment company are principal underwriters, except by SEC exemption, but the section does not prohibit the insiders from engaging in the underwriting. Section 10(f) must be read in conjunction with the prohibitions on self-dealing in section 17. It is narrower than section 17 in that it deals only with purchase and acquisition of securities, whereas section 17(a) deals also with sales and loans, section 17(d) with transactions furthering a joint enterprise and section 17(e) with brokerage transactions. On the other hand, section 10(f) is wider than section 17 in that it requires no proof of any dealings between an affiliate and the investment company. In subsections (a) and (e) of section 17, there must be proof of direct dealings, and in subsection (d) there must be a showing of joint or joint and several participation. The assumption in section 10(f) is that the interests of the affiliated underwriter in any purchase are sufficient to require examination of the purchase by the investment company. Therefore, the investment company may not acquire publicly distributed securities even from a nonmember of an underwriting group or an unaffiliated person if

1. Tamar Frankel & Ann Taylor Schwing, The Regulation of Money Managers § 14.04 (2001 & Supp. 2015) (footnotes omitted).

one of the listed affiliates or its affiliate is the principal underwriter of these securities. The investment company may, of course, sell these securities.

The prohibition lasts as long as there exists an underwriting or selling syndicate, presumably beginning with formation of the syndicate and ending with its dissolution, after the final accounting among the parties; or perhaps just the exit of the affiliate.

The insiders whose underwriting activities trigger the prohibition are officers, directors, employees, members of the advisory board, or the adviser of the investment company, and persons to whom these insiders are affiliated — namely, any company with interlocking directors, officers or employees with the investment company, any person who controls, is controlled by or is under common control with the insider, and any partner and copartner of the insider, as well as any company in which the insider owns 5 percent of the outstanding voting securities. The list of insiders is smaller than the list of affiliates of the investment company in section 2(a)(3). It excludes persons in control, controlled by or under common control with the investment company, as well as those owning 5 percent or more of the investment company's shares or in which the investment company owns 5 percent or more. It also excludes partners and copartners of the investment company. In addition, the insiders in section 10(f) do not include underwriters and brokers. These persons are not affiliates. If the *principal* underwriter of an issue controls the investment company through ownership of 5 percent or more but has no affiliation with the insiders mentioned in the section, the investment company is not prohibited by section 10(f) from purchasing the securities. Such a transaction may, however, be a violation of section 17(d) as a joint and several transaction.

The danger to investment companies that are controlled directly or indirectly by underwriters is that when the underwriters cannot place all the shares of issuers in the markets, or when the placement of many shares might reduce their market price, it is tempting for such insider underwriters to place the shares into the investment companies that they control as advisers.

## 2. Exemptions Under Section 10(f): Rule 10f-3

The SEC has promulgated rule 10f-3[1] exempting some transactions from the prohibitions in section 10(f). The following is a 1979 rule proposal to extend the exemptive rule to municipal securities, providing a background to the law.[2] The amendments were generally adopted as proposed.[3]

Section 10(f) of the Act . . . provides, in part that:

No registered investment company shall knowingly

1. 17 C.F.R. § 270.10f-3 (2015).
2. Exemption of Acquisition of Securities During the Existence of Underwriting Syndicate, Investment Company Act Rel. No. 10592 (Feb. 13, 1979).
3. Exemption of Acquisition of Securities During the Existence of Underwriting Syndicate, Investment Company Act Rel. No. 10736 (Jun. 14, 1979).

> purchase or otherwise acquire, during the existence of any underwriting or selling syndicate, any security (except a security of which such company is the issuer) a principal underwriter of which is an officer, director, member of an advisory board, investment adviser, or employee of such registered company, or is a person (other than a company of the character described in section 12(d)(3)(A) and (B)) of which any such officer, director, member of an advisory board, investment adviser, or employee is an affiliated person, unless in acquiring such security such registered company is itself acting as a principal underwriter for the issuer.

In 1958, the Commission promulgated rule 10f-3 . . . which permits certain transactions that otherwise would be prohibited by section 10(f) of the Act, subject to compliance with prescribed conditions which are summarized below. The Commission proposes to revise these conditions and to extend the permissive scope of rule 10f-3 to include also certain underwriting of municipal securities.

* * *

Pursuant to its specific rulemaking authority under section 10(f), the Commission has adopted three rules since 1940. The most significant of these rules is rule 10f-3, [which] permits, under certain specified conditions, the purchase of registered securities from underwriting syndicates whose members include affiliated persons of the purchasing investment company . . . when the circumstances would make it unlikely that the purchases are inconsistent with the purposes of section 10(f). The conditions may be substantially summarized as:

(a) the securities to be purchased are (i) part of an issue registered under the Securities Act of 1933 . . . (ii) purchased at not more than the public offering price and within specified time periods, and (iii) offered pursuant to a firm commitment underwriting;

(b) the gross commission, spread or profit to the underwriters remains within certain prescribed percentage limits, depending upon the type of security to be purchased;

(c) the issuer of the securities to be purchased has been in continuous operation for not less than three years;

(d) the amount of securities to be purchased of any class does not exceed certain limits;

(e) the consideration paid by the investment company for the securities so purchased generally must not exceed 3% of such company's total assets;

(f) the securities must not be purchased directly or indirectly from certain affiliated persons, including the company's investment adviser;

(g) the purchase must have been authorized by a resolution of the board of directors or a committee thereof; and

(h) a statement of the transaction, indicating compliance with each of the rule's provisions, must be filed with the Commission within thirty days after such purchase. . . .

* * *

PROPOSED AMENDMENTS TO RULE 10f-3

The proposed amendments to rule 10f-3 have two major purposes. First, they would allow municipal bond funds to purchase securities pursuant to the rule rather than require their applying individually for exemptive orders under section 10(f) of the Act. Second, they would change the role of directors of an investment company in establishing the procedures and terms for such company's purchasing securities from an underwriting syndicate of which an affiliated person is a member.

A. Inclusion of Municipal Securities

Rule 10f-3(a) would be amended, in part, to permit the purchase of municipal securities, as defined in section 3(a)(29) of the Securities Exchange Act of 1934, in addition to securities registered under the Securities Act of 1933, provided that certain revised conditions are met. . . .

B. Enhanced Role of Directors

1. Permissible Underwriting Commission

Subsection (b) of rule 10f-3 presently provides that the gross commission, spread or profit to the principal underwriters not exceed certain fixed percentages of the public offering price, depending upon the type of security acquired (e.g., common or preferred). . . . Provided that appropriate safeguards exist, the Commission believes that the directors, particularly the disinterested directors, of an investment company, rather than the Commission, should be allowed to determine in the first instance the propriety of the gross commission, spread or profit to be received by the underwriters for a particular issue. In this context, the necessary investor protections appear to be provided by the other substantive conditions in the revised proposed rule, and by the directorial review process required by new subsection (h) of the rule. Rule 10f-3(b), therefore, would be revised to require that the commission, spread or profit to be received by such persons in connection with the issuance of the type of securities is reasonable and fair compared to the commission, spread or profit to be received by other persons in connection with the underwriting of comparable securities purchased during that period of time. That determination should be made by the directors in the form of guidelines establishing procedures under which purchases may be made for the investment company. . . .

* * *

4. Approval of Purchase Program by Investment Company Directors

Subsection (g) of rule 10f-3 presently provides that each proposed acquisition of securities under the Rule must be authorized by the bond [sic] of directors of the investment company. That authorization must state that the various conditions of rule 10f-3 were met and were supported by a resolution of a majority of specified directors of the investment company. The language contained in this provision may be somewhat ambiguous and may have created some interpretive problems. Moreover, the procedure that it seems to require appears unduly cumbersome to execute. Although present subsection (g) of rule 10f-3 requires that a majority of certain unaffiliated directors approve each purchase some boards of directors may have believed that they must satisfy themselves only that the technical conditions of subsections (a) through (f) of the rule have been met. In addition, it appears that it is often difficult to obtain the collective approval of these directors prior to the breakup of the syndicate. As a result, investment companies may be foregoing purchases of corporate and municipal securities in the underwriting market and purchasing in the secondary market at a higher cost to their shareholders.

The Commission proposes that rule 10f-3 be revised to require a more substantive review by investment company directors, particularly disinterested directors, of the program under which an investment company proposes to implement such purchases in the primary market. The board should establish guidelines for such transactions under which purchases will be made for the investment company, including the manner of compliance with the conditions of rule 10f-3 and the criteria concerning the commissions, spreads or profits which would be acceptable considering the class of securities to be purchased. The Commission believes that the proposed revision of rule 10f-3 would result in a more responsive rule, enabling investment companies to purchase freely in the underwriting market where appropriate while, at the same time, successfully preventing the abuses to which section 10(f) was directed. . . .

In 2002, the rule expanded the exemption, to "respond to recent changes in the method of offering certain U.S. government securities." In 2003, in conjunction with new rule 17a-10, to facilitate transactions with subadviser affiliates, rule 10f-3 was amended "to deem each series of a series company ('series') and the 'managed portions' of a fund's portfolio ('portion') to be separate registered investment companies for purposes of section 10(f) and rule 10f-3." In 2004, the rule was amended again as part of the investment company governance amendments (i.e., requiring companies relying on the exemptions to meet the Fund Governance Standards discussed earlier in this book). And in 2009 the rule omitted the references to credit ratings.

---

## Discussion Topics

a. Did the SEC change some fundamental policies in amending rule 10f-3? Are the changes justified?

b. What issues led to the amendments? What alternatives were available to address the issues?

---

The following no-action letter demonstrates the impact of section 10(f) in a large investment bank structure.[1]

> [Trust, a registered open-end investment company, offers shares in Funds to the public. GS&Co. is the Funds' principal underwriter. The Funds' Advisers may be deemed affiliated persons of GS&Co.
>
> GS&Co. is also principal underwriter for fixed income securities offerings including (i) co-issuer underwritings and (ii) guarantor underwritings. Co-issuer underwritings involve (a) Co-Issuer A, an established company that has been in operation for at least three years, and (b) Co-Issuer B, a new company that is either a wholly owned subsidiary of Co-Issuer A or under common control with it. Both Co-Issuers are unconditionally responsible for principal and interest on fixed income securities purchased by a Fund.
>
> The guarantor offerings involve fixed income securities guaranteed by Guarantor, an established company that has been in continuous operation for at least three years. Guarantor is unconditionally responsible for principal and interest on fixed income securities purchased by a Fund. The securities are issued by Issuer C, an affiliate of Guarantor that may not have been in operation for three years.
>
> Trust proposes purchases from each type of offering. Trust represents that the securities are registered under the 1933 Act or not required to be registered, and that the transaction will be conducted in accordance with Rule 10f-3 under the 1940 Act except for the requirement that the issuer be in operation for three years.]
>
> [The following is the Staff's discussion:]
>
> . . . Section 10(f) of the 1940 Act was designed primarily to prevent an underwriter from "dumping" otherwise unmarketable securities on a fund in order to benefit the fund's affiliated underwriter. . . .
>
> . . . [The three-year continuous operation requirement of Rule 10f-3] was added, in part, to prevent the purchase of less seasoned securities. . . .
>
> [The applicant contended] that the concerns that rule 10f-3(c)(4) under the 1940 Act . . . that a fund will acquire less seasoned securities from an affiliated underwriter, will not be implicated by the proposed purchases. . . .

1. Goldman Sachs Trust, SEC No-Action Letter (Aug. 19, 2008) (footnotes omitted).

[The staff noted in particular that in each offering Funds had direct recourse against an established company and a co-issuer or guarantor was responsible for the respective payment obligations.] . . .

[The staff granted no-action relief.]

---

<u>Discussion Topics</u>

a. Please draw a chart demonstrating the relationships among the Funds and the other participants in the underwriting and identify the relationships that create a problem under section 10(f) and rule 10f-3.

b. Please identify the proposed activities and the potential problem for the Funds from these activities.

c. What was the solution of the applicant to the problems?

d. What was the applicant's interest in the transactions?

e. Did the solution address all problems posed by the purchase of the securities?

---

## G. Disclosure Regarding Portfolio Managers

Several areas of concern were raised in the year 2004 regarding funds' disclosure about their portfolio managers. First, disclosure that a fund uses a team management approach enables a fund to avoid disclosure about the team members and about turnover in team membership. Second, concerns arose regarding possible conflicts of interest when a portfolio manager oversees a mutual fund as well as other investment vehicles. For example, because hedge fund performance fees tend to be higher than mutual fund fees, managers may give hedge funds preferential treatment in allocating new investment opportunities, or trading-execution priorities, or providing hedge funds with inside information about the mutual fund's portfolio holdings. Third, compensation of fund managers had not been disclosed, and yet their incentives may be affected if the managers receive bonuses linked to the amount of fund assets under management, or if they are rewarded for short-term performance. Finally, some had advocated disclosure of portfolio managers' securities holdings, similar to that required of directors, suggesting that "disclosure of a portfolio manager's holdings in a fund would provide a strong signal of his or her alignment with the interest of fund shareholders."

The SEC addressed these concerns by requiring increased disclosure regarding fund portfolio managers.[1] Amendments to Forms N-1A and N-2 require a fund to identify in its prospectus each member of a "committee, team, or other group of persons associated with . . . an investment adviser" that is "jointly and primarily responsible for the day-to-day management

1. Disclosure Regarding Portfolio Managers of Registered Management Investment Companies, Investment Company Act Rel. No. 26533 (Aug. 23, 2004).

of the [fund]'s portfolio," including a brief description of each person's role in the group, e.g., "lead member."[1]

The fund must disclose in its SAI the number of other accounts managed within each of three categories and their total assets by category. For each category, the fund should disclose the number of accounts in which the advisory fee is performance-based, their total assets, and a description of any conflicts of interests that may arise between managing the fund's investments and managing the investments of the other accounts the portfolio manager manages. The fund would also be required to describe the policies and procedures aimed at addressing such conflicts.[2]

The amendments also require a description of the structure of, and the method used to determine, the portfolio manager's compensation (e.g., salary, bonus, deferred compensation, and retirement plans and arrangements) in the SAI. The information must include compensation received from any source with respect to management of the fund and any other account included by the fund in the disclosure of other accounts. For each type of compensation, the fund must describe the criteria on which it is based (e.g., whether compensation is fixed, whether it is based on pre- or after-tax performance over a certain time period, and whether compensation is based on fund asset value). The fund must clearly disclose any differences between the methods used to determine compensation with respect to the fund as well as other accounts, but need not specify the value of compensation.[3]

The amendments also require a fund to disclose in its SAI the beneficial ownership of securities of its portfolio managers. The information about portfolio managers' ownership of fund securities generally must be provided as of the end of the fund's most recently completed fiscal year.

## H. Conclusion

In practice, not all transactions fall neatly into one of the categories of affiliated transactions. Often, a transaction involves more than one type. Consider the following release.[4] It can serve to review the material in this chapter. Note that the scenario described in this release has since been codified by rule amendments, principally rule 17a-10 and conforming amendments to other relevant rules.

> 1. H&W is [a registered investment adviser, and] an operating division of MLAM, which in turn is owned and controlled by Merrill Lynch & Co., Inc. MLP . . . a registered broker-dealer and a registered investment adviser.
>
> 2. H&W currently serves, and may in the future serve, as one of several investment advisers to certain separate portfolios (the "Portfolios") of registered investment companies that otherwise

1. *Id.* The amendments also amend Form N-3, used by insurance company managed separate accounts, to require similar disclosure. *Id.*
2. *Id.*
3. *Id.*
4. Merrill Lynch Asset Management, L.P., Investment Company Act Rel. No. 22616 (Apr. 14, 1997).

have no affiliation with applicants (the "Unaffiliated Funds"). H&W currently serves as subadviser to certain Portfolios of the following Unaffiliated Funds . . . . Each of the Portfolios is advised by a primary investment adviser ("Primary Adviser") and/or one or more subadvisers in addition to H&W ("Unaffiliated Subadvisers"). The Primary Adviser and Unaffiliated Subadvisers are not affiliated persons of applicants or affiliated persons of such affiliated persons ("second-tier affiliates"). (The portion of each Portfolio that is subadvised by an Unaffiliated Subadviser is an "Unaffiliated Portion.")

3. Applicants request relief only for those Portfolios where H&W manages a discrete portion of the Portfolio and there are one or more Unaffiliated Portions of the same Portfolio managed by Unaffiliated Subadvisers (such Portfolios may also be referred to as "Multi-Managed Portfolios"). In a Multi-Managed Portfolio, each subadviser's contract assigns it responsibility to manage a discrete portion of the Portfolio. Each subadviser is responsible for making independent investment and brokerage allocation decisions based on its own research and credit evaluations. H&W does not serve as subadviser to any Multi-Managed Portfolio in which the Primary Adviser dictates or influences brokerage allocation decisions. Each subadviser to a Multi-Managed Portfolio is compensated based on a percentage of the value of assets allocated to that subadviser.

4. Applicants request that relief be extended to both the Unaffiliated Portion of the Multi-Managed Portfolios of the above Unaffiliated Funds for which H&W currently serves as subadviser, as well as to any other Multi-Managed Portfolio to which H&W may in the future provide investment advisory services and which is operated in a manner consistent with the terms and the conditions of the application. In addition, applicants request that relief be extended to broker-dealers that control, are controlled by, or are under common control with MLP (collectively with MLP, "Affiliated Broker-Dealers"). . . .

Applicants' Legal Analysis:

A. Relief From Section 17(a)

1. Section 17(a) of the Act generally prohibits sales or purchases of securities between a registered investment company and any affiliated person of the company or an affiliate of such affiliated person. Section 2(a)(3) of the Act defines an affiliated person of another person to be any person directly or indirectly controlling, or under control with such person and any investment adviser of an investment company.

2. H&W is an affiliated person of the Portfolios that it subadvises. It is also under common control with the Affiliated Broker-Dealers. Thus, the Affiliated Broker-Dealers would be second-tier affiliates of a Multi-Managed Portfolio managed by H&W as subadviser. As a result, any transactions sought to be effected by the Unaffiliated Subadviser with an Affiliated Broker-Dealer on behalf of a Multi-Managed Portfolio would be subject to the provisions of section

17(a). Applicants seek relief from section 17(a) to exempt principal transactions entered into in the ordinary course of business between the Unaffiliated Portions and an Affiliated Broker-Dealer. The requested exemption would apply only where an Affiliated Broker-Dealer is deemed to be an affiliated person or a second-tier affiliate of a Portfolio solely because H&W is the subadviser to a discrete portion of the assets of that Portfolio.

3. Section 6(c) permits the SEC to exempt any person or transaction from any provision of the Act, if such exemption is necessary or appropriate in the public interest and consistent with the protection of investors and the purposes fairly intended by the policies of the Act.

4. Section 17(b) permits the SEC to grant an order permitting a transaction otherwise prohibited by section 17(a) if it finds that the terms of the proposed transaction are fair and reasonable and do not involve overreaching on the part of any person concerned. For the reasons stated below, applicants believe that the terms of the proposed transactions meet the standards of sections 6(c) and 17(b).

5. Applicants submit that the primary purpose of section 17(a) is to prevent self-dealing. Applicants state that when the person acting on behalf of an investment company has no direct or indirect pecuniary interest in a party to a principal transaction, then the abuses that section 17(a) is designed to prevent are not present. Applicants state that this is the situation in each transaction for which relief is requested because neither the Primary Adviser nor the subadviser to the Unaffiliated Portion are affiliates of H&W or its affiliated persons.

6. Applicants state that each subadviser's contract assigns it responsibility to manage a discrete portion of the Multi-Managed Portfolio. The contracts neither require nor authorize collaboration between or among subadvisers. Each subadviser is responsible for making independent investment and brokerage allocation decisions based on its own research and credit evaluations. Applicants state that H&W does not serve as subadviser to any Portfolio where the Primary Adviser dictates or influences brokerage allocation or investment decisions, or has the contractual right to do so. Applicants submit that in managing a discrete portion of a Portfolio, each subadviser acts for all practical purposes as though it is managing a separate investment company. Further, applicants state that, for each transaction for which relief is requested, the Unaffiliated Subadviser would be dealing with an Affiliated Broker-Dealer that is a competitor of that subadviser. Applicants believe therefore, chat [sic] each such transaction would be the product of arm's length bargaining.

7. In addition, applicants state that the method of compensating subadvisers in the context of a multiple subadviser Portfolio furthers the element of competition among them. Applicants state that subadvisers are paid on the basis of a percentage of the value of the assets allocated to their management. Applicants argue that the execution of a transaction to the disadvantage of the Unaffiliated Portion

of the Portfolio would disadvantage the Unaffiliated Subadviser to the extent that it diminishes the value of the Unaffiliated Portion of the Portfolio, with no countervailing benefit to the Unaffiliated Subadviser. Applicants further submit that the Primary Adviser's power to dismiss subadvisers or to change the portion of a Portfolio allocated to each reinforces a subadviser's incentive to maximize the investment performance of its own portion of the Portfolio.

B. Relief from Section 17(e) and Rule 17e-1

1. Section 17(e)(2)(A) of the Act prohibits an affiliate or a second-tier affiliate of an investment company from acting as broker in connection with the sale of securities to or by the investment company, to receive a commission, fee or other remuneration for effecting such transaction which exceeds the usual and customary broker's commission if the sale is effected on a securities exchange.

2. Rule 17e-1 sets forth the conditions under which an affiliated person or a second-tier affiliate of an investment company may receive a commission, fee, or other remuneration which would not exceed the "usual and customary broker's commission" for purposes of section 17(e)(2)(A). Paragraph (b) of rule 17e-1 requires the investment company's board of directors, including a majority of the disinterested directors, to adopt certain procedures and to determine at least quarterly that all transactions effected in reliance on rule 17e-1 in the preceding quarter were effected in compliance with the company's rule 17e-1 procedures. Rule 17e-1(c) specifies the records that must be maintained by each investment company with respect to any transactions effected pursuant to rule 17e-1.

3. Applicants request relief under section 6(c) to the extent necessary to permit the Unaffiliated Portion of each Portfolio to pay commissions, fees, or other remuneration to an Affiliated Broker-Dealer, acting as broker in the ordinary course of business, in connection with the sale of securities to or by such Unaffiliated Portion of a Portfolio, without complying with the requirements of rule 17e-1(b) and (c) under the Act. In addition, applicants request that such relief extend to transactions in futures contracts and related options as well as securities. For the reasons stated below, applicants believe that the request for relief meets the standards of section 6(c).

4. Applicants state that the transactions for which relief is requested will involve no conflict of interest and that there is no possibility of self-dealing. Applicants submit that the pecuniary interests of the particular Unaffiliated Subadviser are directly aligned with those of the Unaffiliated Portion of the Portfolio and that, therefore, the brokerage commissions, fees, or other remuneration to be paid by the Unaffiliated Portion will be reasonable and fair.

5. Applicants argue that the procedures imposed by rule 17e-1(b) and (c) will be unduly burdensome to the Unaffiliated Funds and the Unaffiliated Subadvisers. Applicants state that H&W and MLP's lack of control over the Unaffiliated Funds makes such procedures unnecessary for the protection of shareholders, since the absence of

a control relationship will ensure that all brokerage transactions will be executed on an arm's length basis, Moreover, applicants submit that even if the Unaffiliated Funds had procedures relating to the selection of an Affiliated Broker-Dealer as broker by the Unaffiliated Subadvisers, compliance with such procedures would be entirely within the control of such Unaffiliated Subadvisers and not within the control of H&W or MLP.

6. In addition, applicants state that it is not uncommon for an Unaffiliated Subadviser to place orders for trades for the respective Unaffiliated Portions of the Portfolio at the same time and with the same broker-dealer as trades for other clients. Applicants submit that since H&W, MLP, and their affiliates are not affiliated with such Unaffiliated Subadvisers or the Unaffiliated Fund (other than by virtue of H&W's subadvisory relationship with the Portfolio), the requirement that such transactions be monitored under rule 17e-1 greatly complicates the compliance process for such Unaffiliated Subadviser and the Unaffiliated Funds.

7. Applicants state that each Unaffiliated Subadviser that selects an Affiliated Broker-Dealer as broker will do so in accordance with the brokerage allocation practices set forth in the prospectus and statement of additional information for the respective Unaffiliated Fund (i.e., subject to best price and execution). In addition, applicants state that each Unaffiliated Subadviser selecting broker-dealers for its Unaffiliated Portion of a Portfolio has an inherent interest in obtaining best price and execution, so as to maximize the Unaffiliated Portion of the Portfolio's potential return. Conversely, applicants submit that such Unaffiliated Subadvisers have no interest in benefiting H&W or its affiliates at the expense of the Unaffiliated Portions of the Portfolios they manage.

C. Relief from Section 10(f) and Rule 10f-3

1. Section 10(f), in relevant part, prohibits a registered investment company from knowingly purchasing or otherwise acquiring during the existence of any underwriting or selling syndicate, any security (except a security of which the company is the issuer) a principal underwriter of which is an officer, director, member of an advisory board, investment adviser, or employee of the company, or an affiliated person of any of the foregoing. Section 10(f) also provides that the SEC may exempt by order any transaction or classes of transactions from any of the provisions of section 10(f), if and to the extent that such exemption is consistent with the protection of investors.

2. Applicants acknowledge that each subadviser to a Multi-Managed Portfolio which has multiple subadvisers, although under contract to manage only a distinct portion of the Portfolio, is an investment adviser to the Portfolio itself, not just the portion of the Portfolio it manages. As such, all purchases of securities by such subadviser on behalf of the Portfolio from an underwriting syndicate a principal underwriter of which is an affiliated person of any of the

Portfolio's other subadvisers, fall within the prohibitions of section 10(f).

3. Applicants request relief pursuant to section 10(f) exempting from the provisions of section 10(f) any purchase of securities by an Unaffiliated Portion of a Multi-Managed Portfolio in the ordinary course of business during the existence of an underwriting or selling syndicate, a principal underwriter of which is an Affiliated Broker-Dealer.

4. Applicants believe that the requested relief meets the standards set forth in section 10(f). Applicants state that section 10(f) was designed to prevent the practice of "dumping" otherwise unmarketable securities on investment companies, either by forcing the investment company to purchase unmarketable securities from the underwriting affiliate itself, or by forcing or encouraging the investment company to purchase such securities from another member of the syndicate. Applicants submit that such abuses are not present in the context of Multi-Managed Portfolios to any greater extent than is the case with a series investment company with unaffiliated subadvisers to separate portfolios. As stated above in the context of sections 17(a) and (e) transactions, in each underwriting transaction that would be subject to the requested relief, the Unaffiliated Subadviser would be dealing, on behalf of the Unaffiliated Portion of the Portfolio, with an Affiliated Broker-Dealer that is a competitor of the Unaffiliated Subadviser in an arm's length arrangement.

5. Rule 10f-3 exempts certain transactions from the prohibitions of section 10(f) if specified conditions are met. Paragraph (d) of rule 10f-3 provides that the amount of securities of any class of an issue to be purchased by the investment company, or by two or more investment companies having the same investment adviser, shall not exceed 4% of the principal amount of the offering of such class or $ 500,000 in principal amount, whichever is greater, but in no event greater than 10% of the principal amount of the offering.

6. Applicants also request exemptive relief pursuant to section 6(c) to the extent necessary so that where a portion of a Portfolio managed by H&W purchases securities in reliance upon rule 10f-3, for purposes of determining H&W's compliance with the percentage limits of rule 10f-3(d), such purchases will not be aggregated with any purchases that might be made by an Unaffiliated Portion of the Portfolio. For the reasons below, applicants believe the requested relief meets the standards of section 6(c).

7. Applicants believe that the restrictions of rule 10f-3 would erect an unnecessary barrier to their purchase of securities in underwritings where there is no conflict of interest present. Applicants state that in order to comply with the restrictions of rule 10f-3(d), it would be necessary for all of the subadvisers to coordinate their securities purchases in underwriting to ensure compliance, which would require communication among them regarding their investment plans. Applicants state that such communication would otherwise

be unnecessary. In addition, applicants submit that it would be contrary to the interests of shareholders to maintain unnecessary barriers to purchases by the Portfolio of securities that conform to its investment objective and policies where there is no reason to fear "dumping" or other self-dealing. Applicants state that H&W would comply with rule 10f-3 with respect to transactions on behalf of the portion of any Multi-Managed Portfolio it subadvises.

Applicants' Conditions:

Applicants agree that any order of the SEC granting the requested relief will be subject to the following conditions:

1. Each Portfolio will be advised by H&W and at least one other Unaffiliated Subadviser and will be operated consistent with the manner described in section I.C. of the application.

2. Neither H&W (except by virtue of H&W serving as subadviser to a discrete portion of a Portfolio of an Unaffiliated Fund) nor the Affiliated Broker-Dealer will be an affiliated person or a second-tier affiliate of any Unaffiliated Subadviser or any officer, director, or employee of the Unaffiliated Fund engaging in the transaction.

3. H&W will not directly or indirectly consult with any Unaffiliated Subadvisers concerning allocation of principal or brokerage transactions.

4. H&W will not participate in any arrangement whereby the amount of its subadvisory fees will be affected by the investment performance of an Unaffiliated Subadviser.

For the Commission, by the Division of Investment Management, pursuant to delegated authority.

---

## Discussion Topics

a. Determine the business arrangements for which the applicant is seeking exemptions. Chart the relationships and functions of the various actors and determine their status as affiliates of the investment companies and their functions. Also determine why the exemptions from sections 17(a), 17(e) and rule 10f-3 are necessary.

b. Why does the applicant resort to section 6(c) as well as 17(b)? Does the applicant list all the transactions from which it seeks an exemption, or does it also seek exemption from future similar transactions?

c. An exemption was granted in the *H&W* case. Would you have granted an exemption? Who may benefit and who may lose from the exemption? Who has the burden of persuasion?

d. Please comment on the following abstract of an article:[1]

1. Alexander Dyck & Luigi Zingales, *Private Benefits of Control: An International Comparison*, 59 THE JOURNAL OF FINANCE 537 (2004).

> We estimate private benefits of control in 39 countries using 393 controlling blocks sales. On average the value of control is 14 percent, but in some countries it can be as low as –4 percent, in others [as] high as +65 percent. As predicted by theory, higher private benefits of control are associated with less developed capital markets, more concentrated ownership, and more privately negotiated privatizations. We also analyze what institutions are most important in curbing private benefits. We find evidence for both legal and extra-legal mechanisms. In a multivariate analysis, however, media pressure and tax enforcement seem to be the dominating factors.

---

## Problem

In practice, affiliation analyses are one of the most important and most complicated tasks of an investment management lawyer. Rarely does outside counsel get a straightforward affiliation question and when you explain the scope of these affiliation rules to private fund lawyers, the reaction is inevitably shock and disbelief. Please consider the following scenario and write a memo to your client analyzing each question. Your client has also asked you to attach a chart depicting the relationships described.

HoldCo is a diversified financial services company that is publicly traded on the NYSE. HoldCo wholly owns RIA, a registered investment adviser, which is investment adviser to Fund A (which it established) and which is sub-adviser to one sleeve of the portfolio of Fund B. Fund B has a primary adviser unaffiliated with RIA and other sleeves of its portfolio are managed by other sub-advisers unaffiliated with RIA. RIA is also general partner and investment adviser to Private Fund C. Private Fund C is a private equity fund and it owns 35% of Company D. Other investors also have stakes in Company D, including Company E, who owns 8% of Company D. Company D also has a strategic investment in Company F, which amounts to a 26% stake in Company F. Company F also happens to own 6% of Company G. The remainder of Company G is owned by Company H. Fund A also happens to own 5.3% of Company I. Company J owns 7% of HoldCo. Mr. K is a director of HoldCo and is also CEO of Company L. Mr. M is a director of Fund A and a director of Company N. HoldCo also owns a 45% stake in JV, which wholly owns BrokerDealer, a registered broker-dealer.

1. Company G wants to sell some miscellaneous investments it owns to Fund A. Is this permitted? What if it were Company H selling Fund A the investments? What if the sale were by Company G to the sleeve of Fund B that RIA manages?

2. A sleeve of Fund B not advised by RIA wants to buy debt securities from BrokerDealer (debt securities are usually traded on a principal, rather than an agency, basis). Is this permitted?

3. BrokerDealer is participating as an underwriter in an IPO. It is a firm commitment underwriting, and standard terms include all underwriters being a party to the underwriting agreement with the issuer. BrokerDealer's commitment is only for 5,000 shares out of

10,000,000. Can Fund A buy shares in the IPO from an underwriter other than BrokerDealer?

4. Company N wants to borrow money from Fund A. Is this permitted? Assume instead that Company N is a broker-dealer that executes portfolio transactions for Fund A on a regular basis, and that Mr. M is instead a candidate to be an independent director of Fund A. Can Mr. M be an independent director of Fund A?

5. Identify and describe at least two other issues raised by these relationships.

# Chapter 13

## *Money Market Funds*

### A. The History of Money Market Funds

Money market funds were invented during a period of high inflation and strict regulation of depository institutions. Regulation Q of the Comptroller of the Currency prohibited banks from offering more than 5¼% on demand deposits. Savings and loan associations were prohibited from offering more than 5½% on their savings accounts. With double digit inflation, depositors were losing the buying power of their dollars. Money market funds offered an alternative to depository institutions' deposits (without government insurance). The offered returns were sufficiently higher to compensate for depositors' cost of changing habits, unknowns, and lack of government insurance. In addition to providing money market fund shareholders with redemption on demand, these funds reduced investors' costs by offering checking privileges. The relatively higher returns that money market funds offered were made possible by investments in money market instruments, bank CDs and government securities and by lower relative costs as compared to those of depository institutions (electronic transfers, savings on real estate branches and reduced regulatory costs). By the time Regulation Q was eliminated and banks were allowed to pay a higher returns on bank deposits, they found depositors satisfied with the services of money market funds and with the low transaction costs that they offered. The world had changed, and depository institutions never recouped the full amount of their deposits. As of year-end 2014, taxable money market funds held about $2.5 trillion in net assets, about 16 percent of total mutual fund net assets.[1]

Although they are equity shares, money market funds shares are described differently. For example, assume that a fund has assets of $1,500, income of $10 and 100 shareholders. In a usual equity fund, each shareholder will receive the notice that he is a proud owner of one share valued at $15 with a return of 10 cents, and together worth $15.10. In a money market fund, however, the shareholder's investment will be described as 15 shares of $1 each and a return of 1 cent on each share, together being $15.10. The same amount is described in a different way. Had the shareholder put

1. Inv. Co. Inst., Investment Company Fact Book 175 Table 3 (55th ed. 2015), *available at* https://www.ici.org/pdf/2015_factbook.pdf.

his money in the bank, he would have received a statement that he owns $15.10, similar to a money market fund.

Two features of money market funds raise problems under the 1940 Act. One feature involves the valuation of the portfolio securities. Money market funds issue redeemable securities which must be sold and redeemed at net asset value. Because the sponsors of the funds wished to offer the funds' shares as alternatives to bank deposits, they offered one share for each dollar of investment. So long as the income on the shares exceeded one dollar, it could be shown as a return on one dollar of investment, similar to a debt security. If the value of the portfolio declined below one dollar per share, however, the equity characteristic of the securities would be discovered. To reduce the possible volatility of this dollar base, the sponsors of money market funds wished to value the portfolios of these funds on an amortized cost basis, rather than at their market value.

Under the amortized cost basis method, funds initially value the debt securities that they hold at cost on the date of purchase, ignoring the market price, even though the value may be affected by changes in the market interest rates and other factors. The longer the remaining maturity date of the securities, the more likely these factors could affect the price of the securities. The use of the amortized cost method may result in overvaluation or undervaluation of the portfolio securities as compared to the market price. Investors in money market funds, which are open-end investment companies, would purchase or redeem shares paying more or less than the actual value of their proportionate share in the current net assets, thus resulting in dilution of the assets and returns of existing shareholders who did not redeem their shares.

Rule 2a-7[1] allows government money market funds (i.e., money market funds that invest virtually all of their assets only in cash, U.S. government securities and repurchase agreements collateralized by U.S. government securities) and retail money market funds (i.e., funds owned by natural persons) to use either the amortized cost method and/or the penny-rounding method, in which the securities are valued at fair market value or amortized cost, and then the current net asset value per share is rounded to the nearest cent. These methods are designed to permit government money market funds and retail money market funds maintain a "stable" net asset value per share of $1.00. Before using either method, the fund's board must make a good faith determination "that it is in the best interests of the fund and its shareholders to maintain a stable net asset value per share or stable price per share, by virtue of either [method], and that the money market fund will continue to use such method only so long as the board of directors believes that it fairly reflects the market-based net asset value per share." As discussed below, however, institutional prime money market funds (i.e., any money market fund that is not a retail fund or a government fund) must "float" their net asset value and may not use the amortized cost method or the penny-rounding method.

1. Money Market Fund Reform; Amendments to Form PF, Investment Company Act Rel. No. 31166 (Jul. 23, 2014).

The second problematic feature of money market funds is the daily distributions of income and capital gains which the funds make to their shareholders. Section 19(b) of the 1940 Act prohibits daily distributions, and section 19(a) requires disclosure of the source of distributions other than income and capital gains. The rationale for the prohibitions of this section was that shareholders might receive distributions of their own investments but believe that these distributions are in fact income. Yet, daily distributions are an essential feature for money market funds. The returns on each share of one dollar must be added to each share. The SEC, recognizing that purchasers are not misled by these distributions into believing that the funds are unusually profitable, granted exemptions from sections 19(a) and (b) of the 1940 Act, even though the distributions may contain return of capital.

The success of money market funds as alternatives to bank deposits has caused their sponsors a major problem. When funds "broke the dollar," i.e., when the net asset value of the shares fell below one dollar, the sponsors feared a "run" on the funds. Runs do not occur as often when investors lose money as when investors' reasonable expectations are not met. Because money market funds look like bank deposits, even though they are in fact equities, investors may expect (regardless of their legal rights) that their invested dollar will always be repaid. Disappointment of this expectation may raise the likelihood of a "run." Hence, when interest rates rose, and the value of portfolio securities fell, the advisers and sponsors of these funds purchased from the funds, at face amount, the securities (usually derivatives) that caused the funds to break the dollar. The advisers' representations and the structure of the instruments created a "market guarantee," even without explicit legal guarantee for these representations.

The SEC has established a rule under section 17(a) for such a repurchase of the losing instruments by a money market fund sponsor. However, there is a question of whether these practices give investors a wrong impression of the funds' invulnerability, and whether, and how, the practice of guaranteeing the funds' dollars should be disclosed. In light of this question, there has been a suggestion of allowing the creation of two classes of shares in money market funds: one redeemable and the other traded in the secondary market. The secondary market price will signal the redeeming shareholders the real valuation of the fund's assets.

In the meantime, the SEC has tightened the conditions under Rule 2a-7 to ensure more liquidity and lower risk in these funds' assets and expand the disclosure concerning their portfolios.

## B. Proposals for Reform and Fundamental Changes in 2014

In light of the financial crisis of 2008, there were various proposals to reform the regulation of money market funds.

> Aside from sponsor support, money market funds largely avoided the financial debacle that struck banks and other financial services firms. That changed when, as the direct result of the failure of Lehman Brothers Holdings Inc. the day before, a large money market fund, Reserve Primary Fund (Primary Fund), saw its NAV drop below $1.00 per share. Primary Fund's losses led investors in other prime money

market funds to question whether their funds might also experience difficulties maintaining a stable NAV. Broader concerns arose about the stability of U.S. and European financial institutions, the credit-worthiness of their debt, and the willingness and wherewithal of the United States and foreign governments to support those institutions. To protect themselves against the possibility of other money market funds' NAVs dropping below $1.00 per share, investors — primarily institutional investors — withdrew about $210 billion from prime money market funds over the next two days. Fanned by a year of dire financial news, government bailouts, and spectacular business failures, a true, broad market panic ensued.

To meet outflows during this period, many money market funds were forced to sell commercial paper and other assets. By the end of that week, the Federal Reserve Board and the U.S. Department of the Treasury, seeking to cope with illiquid markets, stepped in, taking several actions to shore up the money market in general and to calm money market fund investors in particular. The Treasury Department's Temporary Guarantee Program for Money Market Funds (Treasury Guarantee Program), although limited to investors' account balances in participating money market funds as of September 19, 2008, worked well to stem investor concerns. Other programs offered by the Federal Reserve helped to provide necessary liquidity to the marketplace, which has contributed to increased investor confidence in the money market.[1]

The ICI Report made the following recommendations:

Impose for the first time daily and weekly minimum liquidity requirements and require regular stress testing of a money market fund's portfolio.

Tighten the portfolio maturity limit currently applicable to money market funds and add a new portfolio maturity limit.

Raise the credit quality standards under which money market funds operate. This would be accomplished by requiring a "new products" or similar committee; encouraging advisers to follow best practices for determining minimal credit risks; requiring advisers to designate the credit rating agencies their funds will follow to encourage competition among the rating agencies to achieve this designation; and prohibiting investments in "Second Tier Securities."

Address "client risk" by requiring money market fund advisers to adopt "know your client" procedures and requiring them for the first time to disclose client concentrations by type of client and the potential risks, if any, posed by a fund with a client base that is strongly concentrated.

Enhance risk disclosure for investors and the market and require

1. Inv. Co. Inst., Report of the Money Market Working Group Submitted to the Board of the Governors of the Investment Company Institute, Executive Summary, at 3 (Mar. 17, 2009), *available at* http://www.ici.org/pdf/ppr_09_mmwg.pdf.

monthly website disclosure of a money market fund's portfolio holdings.

Assure that when a money market fund proves unable to maintain a stable $1.00 NAV, all of its shareholders are treated fairly. For this purpose, a money market fund's board of directors, or a committee of the board, would be authorized to suspend redemptions and purchases of fund shares temporarily under certain situations, and permanently for funds preparing to liquidate, in order to ensure that all shareholders are treated fairly.

Enhance government oversight of the money market by developing a nonpublic reporting regime for all institutional investors in the money market, including money market funds, and encouraging the SEC staff to monitor higher-than-peer performance of money market funds.

Address market confusion about money market institutional investors that appear to be — but are not — money market funds.[1]

A number of suggestions concerning money market funds have been "floated." One proposal was to impose on money market funds bank regulation. A second proposal was to eliminate the "stable" dollar net asset value format and create a floating net asset value of both a dollar and any return, the way all open-end funds are reporting their share prices. A third possibility was to create a private liquidity facility and a fourth one was mandating a reserve or capital requirements on the funds. The Investment Company Institute inquired into a possible "industry" "liquidity facility" as well, like the FDIC. Another possibility was in kind mandatory redemptions for large redemptions. Yet another possibility was a "two-tiered" system of money market funds, that is, a stable NAV for money market funds subject to greater risk limiting conditions and possible liquidity facility requirements.[2] Even though money market funds have not experienced runs except during 2008, they may pose a systemic risk. These proposals all culminated in a fundamental shift in money market fund regulation, implemented through amendments to rule 2a-7.

The 2014 amendments to rule 2a-7[3] represent a fundamental shift in money market fund regulation. In July 2014 the SEC adopted two money market fund reforms. First, the SEC set a floating net asset value requirement for institutional prime funds, noting that these funds may be more at risk for heavy redemptions since their investors are larger and more sophisticated. Other funds (i.e., retail funds (owned by natural persons) and government funds (investing in cash, government securities, and/or fully collateralized

1. *Id.* at 4.
2. *See* Money Market Fund Reform, Investment Company Act Rel. No. 29132 (Feb. 23, 2010), *available at* http://www.sec.gov/rules/final/2010/ic-29132.pdf and U.S. Sec. & Exch. Comm'n, Speech by SEC Chairman: Statement on Money Market Funds Before the Open Commission Meeting by Chairman Mary Schapiro, *available at* http://www.sec.gov/news/speech/2010/spch012710mls-mmf.htm (Jan. 27, 2010).
3. Money Market Fund Reform; Amendments to Form PF, Investment Company Act Rel. No. 31166 (Jul. 23, 2014).

repurchase agreements) retain the exception to use the amortized cost and/or penny-rounding method.

Second, the SEC provided for liquidity fees and redemption "gates" (*i.e.*, suspensions of redemptions) to discourage or delay redemptions during times of stress. Government money market funds are permitted, but not required, to impose fees and gates. These liquidity fees and gates are subject to detailed parameters set forth in rule 2a-7.

A number of other of other amendments in 2010 and 2014 were generally designed to reduce risk. The 2010 amendments[1] further restricted the amount of lower quality securities a fund can hold and required liquidity buffers, *i.e.*, levels of liquid assets. The amendments also reduced interest rate risk exposure by reducing the average maturity of the portfolio. Finally, the amendments required periodic stress tests of a fund's ability to maintain a stable NAV under certain events, and required enhanced disclosure. The 2014 amendments also tightened diversification requirements, amended stress testing requirements and required enhanced disclosure.

---

## Discussion Topics

a. What is the unique problem posed by money market funds that does not exist in other funds?

b. Which of the choices described above would you support, and why?

c. What is the main danger that a "run" on a money market fund poses for other money market funds? Is there a danger that such a "run" poses for mutual funds that are not money market funds?

---

## C. Regulatory Framework of Rule 2a-7

### 1. Introduction

The SEC started regulating money market funds in the beginning of 1972 by imposing conditions linked to exemptions from market valuation requirements and section 19. Throughout the years the exemptions were codified in rule 2a-7, which is quite complex and different from most other exemptive rules by its high degree of detail.

Because, in form, money market funds look like bank accounts rather than equity shares in an investment pool, their form might be misleading. If they were managed as other mutual funds are, they might be doubly misleading. Therefore, their regulation is designed to reduce the risk of their portfolios so that they might not only look like bank accounts but will be similar to bank accounts in their performance. Consequently, the regulation is more substantive in contrast to that of other investment companies. SEC regulation includes "risk-limiting conditions" on the maturity, quality, and diversification of fund investments. In 1991, the SEC amended Rule 2a-7 to generally require a money market fund to: (1) limit its investment in the

---

1. Money Market Fund Reform, Investment Company Act Rel. No. 29132 (Feb. 23, 2010).

securities of any one issuer to no more than five percent of fund assets; (2) limit investments to securities with "minimal credit risks" and that meet certain rating requirements; and (3) limit investments to securities with a remaining maturity of not more than thirteen months.[1] The references to ratings were eliminated in 2015.[2]

In addition, because of "investor expectations that money market funds are relatively secure investments and that fund investment policies are designed to maintain a stable net asset value,"[3] the SEC amended Rule 2a-7 to prohibit a fund from using the term "money market" or similar terms in its name or holding itself out as a money market fund unless it complies with rule 2a-7 and thus meets rule 2a-7's risk-limiting conditions. Further, so that investors will understand that investments in a money market fund are not risk-free, nor guaranteed by the U.S. government, the SEC required that the cover page of the prospectus disclose that the funds' shares are neither insured nor guaranteed by the U.S. government and state generally that there is no assurance that the funds will be able to maintain a stable net asset value of one dollar per share.

As of various dates in 2010, the SEC imposed under rule 2a-7 tighter requirements applicable to money market funds. This step was taken after the Reserve Primary Fund "broke the dollar" in September 2008, as described above.

Money market funds must maintain a minimum percentage of their assets in cash or highly liquid securities, as previously there was no minimum requirement for liquidity. The daily requirement is 10% of assets in cash or highly liquid and riskless securities. There is a weekly requirement of at least 30% of assets in such liquid assets. There are restrictions on purchasing illiquid securities if, after the purchase, more than 5% of the fund's portfolio will be illiquid securities. "Illiquid" securities are defined as any security that cannot be sold or disposed of within seven calendar days at carrying value.

The funds' assets must meet higher credit quality levels, and there are limitations on holding low-quality securities, as defined. There are limits on buying long term securities. Therefore, funds must establish procedures that will enable them to identify the investors whose redemption requests may pose risks for funds and to anticipate the likelihood of large redemptions.

Money market funds must examine their risk levels with periodic stress tests to determine their ability to maintain a stable NAV per share or minimize principal volatility, as applicable, in the event of shocks, such as interest rate changes, higher redemptions, and changes in credit quality of the portfolio. Rule 2a-7 does not impose one format nor testing at one particular interval. These are left to the board. However, the rule requires

1. Revision to Rules Regarding Money Market Funds, Investment Company Act Rel. No. 18005 (Feb. 20, 1991).

2. Removal of Certain References to Credit Ratings and Amendment to the Issuer Diversification Requirement in the Money Market Fund Rule, Investment Company Act Rel. No. 31828 (Sept. 16, 2015), 80 Fed. Reg. 58,124 (Sept. 25, 2015).

3. Revision to Rules Regarding Money Market Funds, Investment Company Act Rel. No. 17589 (Jul. 17, 1990).

that the board receive the stress testing results at its next regularly scheduled meeting, or more frequently, if appropriate, in light of the results. The rule contains specific items which the report must include. With respect to stress testing, the SEC noted:

> We do not agree with commenters who argued that advisers should not be required to provide an assessment of a fund's ability to withstand events that are reasonably likely to occur within the following year. . . . The rule does not require advisers to predict the future in order to determine which hypothetical events to use in stress testing (and we recognize that advisers will not always be correct in their assessments of which events are reasonably likely to occur within the following year). Instead, the provision is designed to provide to the board some context within which to evaluate the assessment on the magnitude of each hypothetical event that would cause the fund to break the buck.[1]

Historically, money market funds could only hold securities rated in the top two categories by NRSROs (or unrated securities of comparable quality). Even under this standard, funds were required to perform an independent credit analysis of every security that it purchased. Money market funds were also required to designate each year at least four NRSROs whose ratings the fund's board considered to be reliable.

Section 939A of the Dodd-Frank Wall Street Reform and Consumer Protection Act required the SEC, along with all other federal agencies, to remove references to NRSRO credit ratings in its rules and replace such credit rating references with an appropriate standard of creditworthiness.[2] In September 2015, the SEC implemented this mandate with respect to rule 2a-7 and removed the above-described references to credit ratings as a means to define permissible investments for money market funds (i.e., "eligible securities").[3] As amended, rule 2a-7 defines an "eligible security" as:[4]

> a security . . . that the fund's board of directors determines presents minimal credit risks to the fund, which determination must include an analysis of the capacity of the security's issuer or guarantor (including for this paragraph the provider of a conditional demand feature, when applicable) to meet its financial obligations, and such analysis must include, to the extent appropriate, consideration of the following factors with respect to the security's issuer or guarantor:
>
> (A) Financial condition;
>
> (B) Sources of liquidity;

1. Money Market Fund Reform, Investment Company Act Rel. No. 29132 at n. 268 (Feb. 23, 2010).
2. Pub. L. No 111-203, § 939A.
3. Removal of Certain References to Credit Ratings and Amendment to the Issuer Diversification Requirement in the Money Market Fund Rule, Investment Company Act Rel. No. 31828 (Sept. 16, 2015).
4. 17 C.F.R. § 270.2a-7(a)(11), as amended by Investment Company Act Rel. No. 31828 (Sept. 16, 2015).

(C) Ability to react to future market-wide and issuer- or guarantor-specific events, including ability to repay debt in a highly adverse situation; and

(D) Strength of the issuer or guarantor's industry within the economy and relative to economic trends, and issuer or guarantor's competitive position within its industry.

According to the SEC, "In determining whether a security presents minimal credit risks, . . . a board (or its delegate) should consider not just the individual risks of the security, but also the overall impact of adding that security to the fund in light of the fund's other holdings."[1] Moreover, in addition to the codified factors for boards to consider, excerpted above, the SEC also suggests various asset-specific factors boards may wish to consider in the release adopting these amendments to rule 2a-7.[2]

Recent revisions to rule 2a-7 also strengthen the requirements allowing a money market fund to "look through" a repurchase agreement to the underlying collateral securities for diversification purposes. The collateral must be cash items or government securities (the previous requirement was highly rated securities), and the fund must evaluate the creditworthiness of the repurchase counter-party.

New rule 2a-7(h)(10) requires money market funds to post their portfolio holdings on their websites each month and to maintain the information on the fund's website for no less than six months after posting. New rule 30b1-7 requires money market funds to report portfolio information on new Form N-MFP within five business days after the end of each month. This information should include a "shadow" NAV, or a mark-to-market value of the fund's net assets (rather than the "stable" NAV per share certain money market funds are permitted to transact at using the amortized cost and/or penny rounding methods).

Money market funds are required to improve their operations. The funds and their administrators are required to have the ability to process purchases and redemptions electronically at a price other than $1.00 per share, to facilitate share redemptions if a fund were to break the buck.

New rule 22e-3[3] permits a board of a money market fund to suspend redemptions if the fund is about to break the buck and the board decides to liquidate the fund. This process will allow for an orderly liquidation of the fund. The fund will be required to notify the SEC before relying on this rule. (Formerly, the board was required to request an order from the SEC to suspend redemptions.)

Amended rule 17a-9[4] expands the ability of affiliates of money market funds to purchase distressed assets from the funds in order to protect a

1. Removal of Certain References to Credit Ratings and Amendment to the Issuer Diversification Requirement in the Money Market Fund Rule, Investment Company Act Rel. No. 31828 at 17 (Sept. 16, 2015).
2. *Id.* at 22-24; Note to 17 C.F.R. § 270.2a-7(a)(11), as amended by Investment Company Act Rel. No. 31828 (Sept. 16, 2015).
3. 17 C.F.R. § 270.22e-3 (2015).
4. 17 C.F.R. § 270.17a-9 (2015).

fund from losses. The amendment permits such purchases without the need for approval subject to certain conditions. The fund will be required to notify the SEC when it relies on this Rule. (Previously, an affiliate could not purchase securities from the fund before a ratings downgrade or a default of the securities — unless it received individual approval.)

The 2014 amendments provided for liquidity fees and redemption "gates" (i.e., suspensions of redemptions) to discourage or delay redemptions during times of stress. A fund is allowed to impose a *discretionary* liquidity fee on redemptions (up to 2 percent of the value of the redeemed shares) if it has invested less than 30 percent of its total assets in weekly liquid assets. In addition, a fund is required to impose a *default* liquidity fee of 1 percent if it has invested less than 10 percent of its total assets in weekly liquid assets, unless the board determines that it would not be in the best interests of the fund. Similarly, a fund may impose a redemption gate if it has invested less than 30 percent of its total assets in weekly liquid assets. Government money market funds are permitted, but not required, to impose liquidity fees and gates.

European regulators have also focused on money market funds: they required that the primary investment objective of the funds should be to:

- maintain the principal and aim at a return that reflects money market rates;
- invest in money market instruments that their management determines are of "high quality" in terms of credit, maturity of asset class, liquidity and for structured financial instruments, operational and counter-party risk profile;
- invest in securities that have maturity or redemption dates of no more than 397 days;
- provide daily net asset value ("NAV");
- take no direct or indirect exposure to equities, commodities, or derivatives, and limit the use of foreign exchange derivatives to hedging purposes; and
- have either a constant or fluctuating NAV. If the funds have a fluctuating NAV, then somewhat different criteria apply.[1]

---

## 2. Money Market Fund Investments in Derivatives

Derivatives are mechanisms for risk shifting, and legitimate wagers rather than gambling. The difference lies in the subject matter of the agreements, and in the peculiar "split" among the affected parties. An acceptable derivative is an agreement under which if the price of grain rises above a certain level within a certain period, party A will pay the difference to party B, and if the price falls, party B will pay the difference to party A. The same agreement can be made between two parties with respect to the level of interest rates. Such an agreement is useful to both parties. If party A's portfolio contains many loans that pay a fixed interest rate, party A would like, for a small price, to obtain the difference between the fixed rates and

1. Derived from Orrick Financial Market Alert, May 24, 2010.

the future higher rates. Party B's portfolio may contain many loans that pay variable rate, and would like to obtain a "bottom" fixed rate, for a small price.

One of the unique features of derivatives is that they can be designed according to the parties' needs. The United States government could offer treasury bonds that are linked to the cost of living if it finds a party that would back this obligation. That party will have to create a portfolio of instruments that would reflect changes in the cost of living. With the aid of computers that can provide "what if" scenarios and "stress tests" (worst possible scenarios) people have been designing these unique instruments to hedge against risks as well as to speculate that certain events will happen. Herein lies the problem. Hedging against portfolio risks is a socially desirable activity. But speculation might not be, although this is a debatable point. Note that some derivatives such as futures and options have trading markets and rules are in place to reduce the chances that the parties gamble without assets to back their obligations. The regulation of trading in derivatives is now in the making, as their view as securities has overcome their view as personal contracts among specified individuals. Therefore, a board overseeing money market funds (and other investment pools) may add derivatives to its list of items deserving attention.

---

## Problem

Assume you are the general counsel of a medium-sized public company. Your company regularly issues very short term notes, known as commercial paper, to fund its operations and payroll. Your company's commercial paper is rated A-1 by S&P and P-1 by Moody's. You know that the principal purchasers of your commercial paper are money market funds.

Your CEO has heard about the SEC's recent amendments to the money market fund rule (rule 2a-7) under the Investment Company Act, and is wondering how its implementation might impact your company's ability to raise money through the sale of commercial paper. He is, in particular, concerned about the effects of the implementation of a floating NAV for institutional prime funds and the elimination of credit rating references in rule 2a-7, together with the new requirement for money market fund boards of directors to make credit quality determinations. Create a Power Point presentation for your CEO addressing his areas of concern.

---

# Chapter 14

## *Unit Investment Trusts*

### A. Introduction

### 1. Organization of Unit Investment Trusts[1]

Unit investment trusts (UITs) are investment companies within the definition of section 3 of the 1940 Act: they issue securities and invest in securities. The 1940 Act defines a unit investment trust as an "investment company which (A) is organized under a trust indenture, contract of custodianship or agency, or similar instrument, (B) does not have a board of directors, and (C) issues only redeemable securities, each of which represents an undivided interest in a unit of specified securities." As you can see, subparagraph (A) of the definition limits the forms of UITs, in contrast to the definition of a management company, which does not specify any form of organization. Even though the definition in the 1940 Act describes three forms of organization of unit investment trusts, only the trust form is currently used. The two other forms of organization have become obsolete.

UITs are organized like any other trust. The promoter usually assumes the role of a depositor, and hands over to a trustee or custodian the trust "res."[2] An evaluator is selected to value the trust's securities. The trust indenture specifies the functions of the trustee, depositor and evaluator, the UIT's duration (varying in practice between two and thirty years), and distribution of its assets. Unlike the trustor of a private trust, the depositor receives from the trustee participations or units representing pro rata shares in the portfolios, and distributes the units to investors, either alone or by organizing a syndicate of underwriters.

---

1. The materials for this chapter are derived mainly from 4 TAMAR FRANKEL & ANN TAYLOR SCHWING, THE REGULATION OF MONEY MANAGERS § 31.02[A] (2001 & Supp. 2015); Thomas S. Harman, *Emerging Alternatives to Mutual Funds: Unit Investment Trusts and Other Fixed Portfolio Investment Vehicles,* 1987 DUKE L.J. 1045; Division of Investment Management, U. S. Securities and Exchange Commission, Protecting Investors: A Half Century of Investment Company Regulation (1992); and Jay B. Gould & Gerald T. Lins, *Unit Investment Trusts: Structure and Regulation Under the Federal Securities Laws,* 43 BUS. LAW. 1177 (1988).
2. Pursuant to section 14(a) of the 1940 Act, the "res" must be at least $100,000.

The depositor promotes and establishes the trust because he is interested in the income from the sale of the trust's certificates, and sometimes in the additional income from other services which he might render to the trust. For example, the trustee usually administers the trust and keeps custody of its assets. Other services, which either the trustee or the depositor might offer to the trust, include the issuance of certificates to the investors, the receipt of the price for the certificates, reporting to the SEC and to tax and other authorities, and bookkeeping.

## 2. Registration of UITs

Unless exempt, UITs must be registered under the 1940 Act. Section 7(b) provides that "no depositor or trustee of or underwriter for any investment company, organized or otherwise created under the laws of the United States or of a State and not having a board of directors, unless such company is registered under section [8 of this Act] or exempt under section [6 of this Act] shall directly or indirectly — (1) offer for sale, sell, or deliver after sale, by use of the mails or any means or instrumentality of interstate commerce, any security or any interest in a security of which such company is the issuer; or offer for sale, sell, or deliver after sale any such security or interest, having reason to believe that such security or interest will be made the subject of a public offering by use of the mails or any means or instrumentality of interstate commerce; (2) purchase, redeem, or otherwise acquire or attempt to acquire, by use of the mails or any means or instrumentality of interstate commerce, any security or any interest in a security of which such company is the issuer; or (3) sell or purchase for the account of such company, by use of the mails or any means or instrumentality of interstate commerce, any security or interest in a security, by whomever issued."

Section 8(b) of the Act requires the registration form of UITs to provide a general description of the trust and the securities of the trust, the organization, personnel and affiliated persons of the trust, the distribution and redemption of its securities, information concerning the trustee or custodian, and financial and statistical information. For those unit investment trusts, substantially all of whose assets of which are securities issued by another registered investment company, the SEC is authorized in section 8(d) to prescribe a registration statement which eliminates inappropriate duplication of the information in the registration statement under section 8(b) filed by the other investment company.

## 3. Governance of UITs

By definition, unit investment trusts do not have boards of directors. Section 4(2) of the Investment Company Act defines a unit investment trust as "an investment company which . . . (B) does not have a Board of Directors. . . ."

## 4. History of UITs and Distribution of Their Units

UITs were first used as a tool for dividing large denomination securities into securities with smaller denominations to make the securities more affordable to smaller investors, and to reach a larger group of investors. UITs later developed into an investment tool offering small investors liquid units in diversified portfolios, in small denominations, that can be redeemed or resold at net asset value.[1]

Because their portfolios are fixed rather than managed, UITs do not incur advisory fees. Having relatively low turnover of their portfolio securities, UITs bear little brokerage commissions. However, because UITs do not manage their portfolios, their portfolios must consist of less volatile securities with more stable returns, as compared to equity funds. Today, most UITs invest in debt securities, such as municipal bonds and corporate bonds, and some invest in corporate preferred stock. Section 4(2) of the Investment Company Act provides that UITs issue redeemable securities. In the 1930's, UITs issued and distributed their units like open-end investment companies. To avoid "net redemptions," more units were continuously offered to the public, and underwriters acted on a "best efforts" basis. Today, the redemption requirement is achieved in a somewhat different way through a secondary market. When unit holders seek redemption, the sponsors are notified, and they, rather than the UIT, purchase the units from the holders, always at net asset value. When investors seek to buy UITs' units, sponsors resell the units to the new investors. Only when the net asset value of the units does not attract new investors will the sponsors decline to buy, and the UITs will liquidate some of their portfolios to meet the redemption demands.

These secondary markets have changed the UIT units' mode of distribution. UITs no longer make continuous offerings; they usually make one issue. The underwriters — essentially the sponsors — make the initial distribution of the units on a "firm commitment" basis: they acquire the UIT units and resell them to the public. Secondary markets enable UITs to hold portfolios that are not fully liquid, yet provide liquidity to unit holders at net asset value.

### 5. The Main Actors

Four main actors establish and operate UITs: sponsor-depositors, trustees, underwriters, and evaluators.

#### a. Sponsors-Depositors

Sponsors are usually also the depositors of UITs. As sponsors, they organize the UIT and usually act as one of the underwriters. As depositors, they assemble portfolios of securities that they deposit with trustees and receive from the trustees units representing a pro rata share in the portfolios. These units are distributed to the public. Sponsors profit from a number of sources, including: (i) the difference between the price of the securities that they deposit and the amount they charge for the securities to the public; (ii) distribution charges of the units issued by the UITs; (iii) sales loads they charge to new investors who purchase UIT units in the secondary markets; and (iv) fees from serving as evaluators of the UIT's portfolios.

#### b. Trustees

UIT trustees usually have little discretion. They hold the legal title to the UIT assets, create and issue the UIT units, and serve as custodians and administrators. They are responsible for collecting and distributing the

1. Thomas S. Harman, *Emerging Alternatives to Mutual Funds: Unit Investment Trusts and Other Fixed Portfolio Investment Vehicles,* 1987 Duke L.J. 1045.

income on the UITs' portfolios and reporting annually to unit holders about interest received, amounts actually distributed, a list of the securities remaining in the UITs as required in the trust indentures, keeping the books and records, and maintaining them for inspection. If trust assets contain voting securities, trustees deliver the proxies to the depositors and vote the shares as directed by the depositors.

Trustees gain from annual fees measured by the size of the UITs' assets, and from using the monies held on behalf of the UITs in noninterest-bearing accounts for future distributions to unit holders. Most UITs employ as trustees a small number of large banks and a few UITs employ subsidiaries of their sponsors. The banks bestow prestige on the UITs to gain the public's trust.

### c. Underwriters

The units which trustees issue to sponsors-depositors representing pro rata shares in the UITs' assets distributed to the public are distributed by underwriters. These underwriters usually include the sponsors-depositors. The underwriters act on a firm commitment basis — they purchase the units and resell them. Firm commitment involves for the underwriters the risks that investors will decline to purchase the units at the offering price, either reducing or even eliminating the "spread" for the underwriters. Therefore, these underwriters receive concessions (fees) that are higher than the concessions for best efforts underwriting. In a best efforts underwriting arrangement, underwriters do not purchase the issued securities or units, but promise to do their best to place the securities. The risk that the units would not be distributed in full is borne by the issuer. Hence, best efforts underwriting is compensated by lower concessions. Yet, in this case the sponsor is likely to bear the risk. In the past, units of UITs were distributed by the "best efforts" method if the sponsor and the underwriters were not one and the same party. As noted, today UITs are distributed by the method of firm commitment underwriting.

### d. Evaluators

Because UITs' portfolios are not always very liquid, evaluators value the UITs' portfolios for the purpose of establishing the redemption and secondary market prices of UITs' units. In addition, evaluators may prepare the list of portfolio securities that should be sold in order to meet the UITs' redemption requirements, if demand in the secondary markets would not suffice to cover redemption demands.

The 1940 Act does not require evaluators to be independent from the sponsors and, in fact, sponsors or their affiliates serve as evaluators. Evaluators typically receive either a fixed annual fee or a fixed fee per evaluation.

---

## Discussion Topics

a. Why would investors prefer unit investment trust units to shares of open-end investment companies, or the reverse?

b. What other forms of investment companies can have a fixed portfolio? Can a closed-end investment company and an open-end investment company have a fixed portfolio? If so, why don't companies with fixed portfolios usually register as closed-end companies?

c. Should the Investment Company Act require that the evaluator of a trust portfolio be independent of the trustee or sponsor?

d. Review the definition of a UIT. Can a UIT invest in futures contracts?

e. As we saw in Chapter 5, some fixed portfolio investment vehicles have obtained exemptive relief from the entire 1940 Act under rule 3a-7. Are these vehicles UITs? Why were they exempt?

---

## B. Regulation of UITs

The main 1940 Act provision that regulates UITs is section 26. This section regulates the terms of the trust indenture or similar documents under which UITs can be established. In this way, Congress addressed some of the problems that it found regarding UITs. Notice the differences and the similarities between the regulation of open-end investment companies and UITs, and how these relate to the structures of each form of an investment company. Under their applicable definitions, UITs and open-end investment companies issue redeemable securities. Therefore, the provisions of the 1940 Act relating to redemption, including valuation and timing of the valuations, apply equally to both. In addition, because both forms of investment companies must continuously sell their securities to avoid net redemptions, they both employ "principal underwriters" and the provisions applicable to such underwriters apply in both cases.

In contrast, open-end investment companies are management companies, while UITs are not. Therefore, the regulation of the portfolio management functions relating to open-end investment companies (and closed-end investment companies) does not apply to UITs. Because investors in UITs have no voting powers and no ability to remove their sponsor or trustee, except in very egregious circumstances, section 26(a) establishes standards of behavior for both parties, especially regarding the charges they can make.

### 1. Charges to UITs

In the 1940 Hearings, Congress found that depositors could gain from charges that were not clearly disclosed to the public.[1] Hence, section 26 sets forth that UITs may be subject only to the charges and collections allowed

---

1. Thomas S. Harman, *Emerging Alternatives to Mutual Funds: Unit Investment Trusts and Other Fixed Portfolio Investment Vehicles,* 1987 DUKE L.J. 1045. Sponsors gained from: sales charges from buyers of the units in the secondary markets; compensation for providing portfolio supervisory services, use of cash paid that sponsors collect before the date of settlement for the purchase of units; difference between the price of the deposited portfolio securities and the price the depositors charged the trust and added brokerage commission at a high level of odd-lot brokerage premiums, and rounding up the price of the portfolio; double-charges of sales load on the spread and on the differential between the odd-lot and the round-lot brokerage commission, on dividend accumulations, before the distribution date, in reality

under section 26(a)(2)(A), (B), and (C). These are limited to the trustee's fees for services and reimbursement for expenses, if provided for in the governing instrument and the trustee is not otherwise paid, for services or expenses actually performed or incurred, and exclude any payment to the depositor, a principal underwriter, or an affiliated person or agent of either (other than a reasonable fee for bookkeeping and other administrative services normally performed by the trustee or custodian, as permitted by the SEC).

### 2. Protection of UITs' Assets

Another main concern of Congress with respect to UITs was to protect their assets against embezzlement. Section 26(a)(1) of the 1940 Act therefore provides:

> No principal underwriter for or depositor of a registered unit investment trust shall sell . . . any security of which such trust is the issuer . . . unless the trust indenture, agreement of custodianship, or other instrument pursuant to which such security is issued [1] designates one or more trustees or custodians, [2] each of which is a bank, [3] and provides that each such trustee or custodian [4] shall have at all times an aggregate capital, surplus, and undivided profits of a specified minimum amount, which shall not be less than $500,000.

The financial and regulatory qualifications stated in section 26(a)(1) are also required of trustees and custodians of other investment companies.[1]

### 3. Orphan UITs

One of the recurrent problems of UIT investors was the UITs' abandonment by the trustees and depositors. Investors in abandoned UITs ("orphan trusts") remained locked into the trusts and at the same time did not have the care that their assets needed. Therefore, section 26(a)(3) requires that the constitutional documents under which UITs are established provide that "the trustee or custodian shall not resign until either (A) the trust has been completely liquidated and the proceeds of the liquidation distributed to the security holders of the trust, or (B) a successor trustee or custodian, having the qualifications prescribed in [section 26(a)(1)], has been designated and has accepted such trusteeship or custodianship."

### 4. Substitution of UITs' Assets

In 1970, Congress amended section 26 by providing that "[i]t shall be unlawful for any depositor or trustee of a registered unit investment trust holding the security of a single issuer to substitute another security for such security unless the Commission shall have approved such substitution. The Commission shall issue an order approving such substitution if the evidence establishes that it is consistent with the protection of investors and the purposes fairly intend[ed] by the policy and provisions of this [Act]."

Congress recognized that when UITs invest in the securities of only one issuer, the requirement in section 26(a)(4)(B) that the shareholder be notified of any substitution of the securities of the trust is insufficient to protect

---

charging investors for on money due to them, and sometimes management fees, as well as other charges.

1. *See* section 17(f), 15 U.S.C. § 80a-17(f).

the shareholders. If unit holders are dissatisfied with the substitution, they can only redeem their shares and purchase the securities of another unit investment trust or the securities of an open-end investment company. These measures, however, are likely to involve transaction costs, including new sales load charges. To close this gap in shareholder protection section 26(c) provides that the trustee and depositor of this type of unit investment trust may not substitute the underlying security of the trust without the SEC's approval.

In addition, the constitutional documents must provide that the depositor, or agent for the depositor, will, within five days from the day on which a security was deposited with the trustee in substitution for another security, mail to the unit holders a notice of substitution, identify the eliminated security and the substituted security, and specify the shares of the unit holder which were affected by the substitution.

### 5. Affiliated Transactions

Section 17 of the 1940 Act regulates all investment companies' affiliated transactions. In the case of UITs, these transactions would include transactions between UITs and their sponsors or principal underwriters. Section 17 excepts from its coverage the one type of affiliated transaction most likely to occur with a UIT. While section 17(a)(1) prohibits affiliated persons of an investment company from knowingly selling any security or other property to the company, section 17(a)(1)(C) excepts such a transaction from the provisions of section 17 if the sale involves only securities deposited by sponsors with trustees of UITs. Because UITs have fixed portfolios and would rarely purchase or sell securities after they are organized, section 17(a)(1)(C) makes the prohibitions of section 17(a) largely inapplicable to all but occasional elimination or substitution in which UIT depositors are involved as buyers or sellers (but not as redeemers) of UITs' units.

---

**Discussion Topic**

Consider a University Faculty Loan Trust organized for the purpose of acquiring certain loans from the United States Department of Education in connection with the federal government's pilot loan asset sale program. The Trust is registered as a closed-end investment company but has a fixed portfolio, except for certain limited powers of substitution. The trustees of the Trust wish to continue to purchase loans from its promoter, the Department of Education, which may be considered an affiliated person. The Trust agreed to retain an independent evaluator to determine the fairness of the consideration paid for the loans.

Should the Trust seek relief from some or all of the provisions of the Act?

---

### 6. Minimum Size of UITs

Section 14(a)(2) of the 1940 Act exempts from the minimum capital requirement investment companies that had a net worth of at least

$100,000 at the time they made a public offering. This exemption is still important today for UITs organized in a series form because they may rely on the offerings of the other series within the UIT, if a prior series qualified under section 14(a)(2).

In addition, Rule 14a-3[1] exempts from the minimum capital requirements UITs holding at least $100,000 of certain portfolio securities at the beginning of their unit offering, provided that, if the net worth falls below $100,000 within 90 days after the effective registration statement, or if the UITs fail to become on-going concerns, each unit purchaser will receive his pro rata share of the UIT's net worth, and all sales charges paid on the purchase of UIT units. Further, if the sponsors or underwriters effect redemption of unsold units and thereby reduce the UIT's net worth to less than forty percent of the principal amount of the securities initially deposited in the trust, the sponsor must terminate the UIT and distribute its assets, and the sales charges (upon demand of unit holders).

### 7. Switching of UIT Units

Because their compensation came mainly from sales of UIT units, sponsors-depositors pressured investors to exchange their units for new UIT units or mutual funds which the sponsors created. Such pressures resulted from threats that the UITs will be eliminated at investors' loss, and promises of benefits from the exchanges. In fact, such exchanges depleted the trusts and caused excessive sales load payments to investors. Hence, under section 11(c) of the 1940 Act, the exchange of unit investment trust securities for the securities of any other investment company is prohibited without the SEC's approval.

---

**Discussion Topics**

a. Under what circumstance would it be beneficial for an investor in one UIT to switch to another UIT?

b. Should the SEC pass a rule that would exempt UITs from the prohibition of section 11(c) if the exchanges of the units do not involve any charges?

---

### 8. Distribution of UITs' Securities

Like open-end investment companies, UITs issue redeemable securities. Therefore, the provisions of the 1940 Act applicable to redeemable securities apply to units of UITs. These units may not be sold except at net asset value and pursuant to other requirements as to sales load, as provided in section 22(a), (b), (c), (d) and (e) of the 1940 Act,[2] and in rule 22c-1.

1. 17 C.F.R. § 270.14a-3 (2015).

2. If UITs sell their units by installments or sell the underlying portfolio securities by installments, the units constitute periodic payment plan certificates and are regulated by section 27, in addition to the other provisions of the 1940 Act. To the extent that UITs continuously offer their securities to the public, the special provisions with respect to the registration of these units and with respect to the

Because some portfolios of UITs are illiquid, sponsors have developed secondary over-the-counter markets for UIT units, offering investors the unit values and then reselling the units to new investors. Over-the-counter markets usually publish two prices: the price at which sellers are ready to sell (offer) and the price which buyers are willing to pay (bid). Most securities trade on the bid side. Hence for over 10 years most major UIT sponsors have used the bid side for their secondary market activities, and the unitholders were willing to accept the price and did not care whether their units are redeemed by the trust or repurchased by the trust sponsor.

Even though UIT units are designed to reflect and distribute a pro rata share of the UITs' portfolios, the business realities of UITs lead to necessary adjustments. For example, payments under the portfolio securities are not necessarily distributed immediately upon receipt because investors are not interested in "dribbled" payments. Rather, payments are accumulated and distributed on specified dates. In addition, trustees usually undertake to pay investors on the specified dates even though issuers of the portfolio securities have not yet made payments. The following enforcement proceedings respecting Merrill Lynch demonstrate the difficulties of both creating perfect pass-throughs for UITs, avoiding redemptions through secondary markets, and at the same time accurately establishing the net asset value of the UIT portfolios.

We have dealt with the issues concerning redemptions and valuation of fund securities. The following is an example of such issues in the context of UITs. In 1993, the SEC instituted proceedings against Merrill Lynch, Pierce, Fenner & Smith, Inc. on the basis of the following facts.[1]

> Since in or about January 1972, Merrill Lynch's UIT division acted as lead sponsor for over 2,500 series of UITs. These UITs had a face amount of approximately $88 billion, approximately $45 billion of which remains outstanding. All of the UITs sponsored by Merrill Lynch issue redeemable securities and are registered with the Commission as investment companies pursuant to Section 8(a) of the Investment Company Act. . . .
>
> [During the relevant period], the trust indentures provided that, if a UIT had not received sufficient funds to make a monthly distribution, the trustee was required to advance to the UIT, without interest, sufficient funds to make the distribution. In order to minimize these situations, the trust indentures authorize the trustees to delay the commencement of monthly distributions until approximately ninety days after the deposit of securities into a UIT's portfolio. This delay permitted the UITs to accrue interest without distributing that interest to unitholders, and thereby eliminated some of the cash flow problems faced by the UITs. This accrued, but undistributed, interest is known as "lag. . . ."
>
> [During that time, Merrill Lynch operated a secondary market for

advertising of the units apply to them. Today, however, most UITs have developed secondary markets for their units.

1. Merrill Lynch, Pierce, Fenner & Smith Inc., Investment Company Act Rel. No. 19425 (Apr. 22, 1993).

most of the UITs that it sponsored. Merrill Lynch was required by Rule 22c-1 to purchase and sell units in the secondary market at a price based on the current net asset value of the units. The net asset value consists of the principal value of the UIT's portfolio securities, and the accrued interest on the portfolio securities, cash on hand, and all other assets of the UIT, less accrued fees, expenses and taxes.] Merrill Lynch computed the accrued interest value for secondary market trading from a pre-determined formula that relied upon expected accruals from the bonds in the portfolio with certain adjustments. . . .

During the relevant period, according to the trust indentures, unitholders had the option to tender units for redemption to the trustees. Merrill Lynch, however, had the right to purchase units tendered by unitholders to the trustees for redemption, and, during the relevant period, always exercised that right. As a result, only Merrill Lynch redeemed units to the trustees; it did so when it was unable to resell in the secondary market. Units redeemed to the trustees were valued on the lower bid side of the market with respect to their principal value. The trustees, not Merrill Lynch, calculated the interest value paid to Merrill Lynch when units were redeemed.

[I]n calculating prices for secondary market transactions, Merrill Lynch did not properly account for lag. When bonds were called, sold, or matured from the UITs' portfolios, the UIT was paid all of the accrued interest on that bond, including the portion of accrued interest attributable to lag. Merrill Lynch incorrectly accounted for the transactions in the formula it used to calculate accrued interest as if the lag attributable to those bonds had been included in the periodic distributions made to unitholders by the trustees. In fact, these amounts had not been distributed and the cash remained in the UITs' accounts.

As a result, discrepancies grew between the accrued interest as calculated and recorded on Merrill Lynch's books and the actual cash income in the accounts of the 570 UITs from whose portfolios bonds had been called, sold, or matured. The problem did not affect Merrill Lynch's approximately 1,900 other UITs, because insignificant amounts of bonds or no bonds had been called, sold, or matured from their portfolios or for other reasons.

Merrill Lynch paid individual secondary market sellers in the affected UITs less than they were entitled to receive, because Merrill Lynch calculated the trade price based on its own, incorrect formula. By utilizing this incorrect pricing formula, Merrill Lynch's NAV or trade price calculation for secondary market transactions did not include all cash on hand in the affected UITs. This caused Merrill Lynch to underpay unitholders when it purchased units from them in the secondary market and to undercharge unitholders when it sold units to them in the secondary market. This contravened the provision of the UITs' prospectuses that NAV would include all cash on hand. . . .

The number of UITs affected by this pricing error increased over time, as more UITs had bonds removed from their portfolios as a result of calls, sales, or maturities. Likewise, the size of the error in particular UITs increased as additional securities were removed from the UITs' portfolios and the lag attributable to those securities accumulated in the UITs' income accounts. The average error was $3.84 per unit; one of the affected UITs, however, had a pricing error amounting to approximately twenty dollars per unit. . . .

In or about April 1985, managers in Merrill Lynch's UIT division became aware that Merrill Lynch was accounting for lag incorrectly. Thereafter, when a bond was called, sold, or matured, Merrill Lynch no longer adjusted its records as if the lag attributable to that bond had been distributed. At that time, however, Merrill Lynch did not take adequate steps to ascertain the full scope of the problem. Merrill Lynch did not adjust its records to reflect the cash that had accumulated in the affected UITs in prior years when bonds had been called, sold, or matured. As a result, from in or about April 1985 through in or about September 1987, Merrill Lynch continued to underpay unitholders of the affected UITs in secondary market transactions. . . .

In December 1987, Merrill Lynch brought its records into agreement with the trustees' records by requesting the trustees to distribute a certain amount of the accumulated cash lag held by the UITs to unitholders as of September 25, 1987. Following this distribution, Merrill Lynch began using the trustees' records, rather than Merrill Lynch's records to calculate accrued interest. . . .

Merrill Lynch benefitted financially from the [calculation] practices . . . when it redeemed units of the affected trusts. The trustees calculated the redemption price based on their own records, which correctly reflected that [lag] had not been distributed. Accordingly, on redemptions, Merrill Lynch received a pro rata share of cash in the UITs' accounts that it had not included in the price paid to selling unitholders in the secondary market. . . .

Merrill Lynch's underpayments to selling unitholders reduced the losses that Merrill Lynch otherwise would have incurred on unit redemptions. Before September 1987, Merrill Lynch represented in its UITs' prospectuses that it intended to purchase units in the secondary market priced on the offer side of the market and redeem units to the trustees on the lower, bid side of the market. As a result of this practice, Merrill Lynch usually lost money on unit redemptions. The underpayments to unitholders reduced the difference between the sale and redemption prices and, accordingly, reduced Merrill Lynch's losses on the transactions. . . .

Merrill Lynch, in its Offer of Settlement, consents to the issuance of a cease-and-desist order against it and undertakes to compensate affected unitholders and to pay disgorgement, if necessary, plus prejudgment interest, and further undertakes as follows:

Merrill Lynch undertakes to compensate unitholders who, from January 1, 1972 through trade date September 18, 1987, sold units of the 570 affected UITs to Merrill Lynch or any of its co-sponsors at a price below NAV as a result of the violation alleged in the Order. . . .

As to all payments . . . Merrill Lynch undertakes to pay interest on the amount of such compensation due from the date of the sale to the date of the compensation payment. . . .

Merrill Lynch undertakes, within thirty days of the issuance of the Order, to establish and submit to the Commission written procedures for identifying all eligible unitholders and determining the amount of compensation due to each eligible unitholder (including the determination of any permissible setoffs and interest). . . .

Merrill Lynch undertakes to retain, within thirty days of the issuance of the Order, a Special Review Person, not unacceptable to the Commission's staff, to review Merrill Lynch's compliance with the Undertakings. . . .

---

## Discussion Topics

a. Did Merrill Lynch benefit from the error in calculating the net asset value of the UIT units? If so, how did it benefit?

b. Who was harmed by the error? Was the UIT, as such, harmed by the error?

c. What caused the decision to establish a "lag"? Was this justifiable?

d. Although the bonds issued by such municipalities as New York City are liquid, many other municipal tax-exempt securities are not as liquid because their issues are small and their issuers are small local communities. Yet the definition of unit investment trusts requires that they offer redeemable securities. What is the classification of a unit investment trust that does not offer redeemable securities, and how should such a UIT be regulated? How can a unit investment trust ensure redemptions even if its portfolio is not liquid? Is there any legal limit on the duration of the trust?

e. How can sponsors or depositors help maintain the redeemability of the trust certificates? If a sponsor wishes to create a secondary market in the trust certificates, are there limits on the sale price of unit investment trust certificates?

---

### 9. Dividend Distributions

Section 19 and rule 19b-1[1] regulate the disclosure and frequency of investment companies' distributions of dividends and long-term capital gains. The purpose of these provisions is to prevent investment companies from creating a misleading impression of success by making frequent distributions. Rule 19b-1 makes an exception for unit investment trusts which obtain dividends from "regulated investment companies." These trusts may receive distributions from various portfolio securities more

1. 17 C.F.R. § 270.19b-1 (2015).

frequently than once a year. Had the trusts been forced to adhere to the rule, they would have had to keep and accumulate the payments which they had received. The rule permits the unit investment trust, in such circumstances, to distribute within a reasonable time after receipt, to their own shareholders, the payments that they had obtained on their portfolio securities. Rule 19b-1 exempts UITs from the rule's prohibition if the capital gains rose substantially independently of actions by the UITs' sponsors or trustees.

## C. 1940 Act Regulation Which Does Not Apply to UITs

Many of the provisions of the 1940 Act that apply to management companies, such as sections 10 (qualifying directors), 15 (regulating advisory contracts), 16 (dealing with election of directors), 18 (dealing with voting rights, and applying only to management companies) and 20 (governing proxy statements) do not apply to UITs because UITs have no advisers or board of directors, or voting shareholders. Because a UIT is essentially an entity that holds a fixed portfolio, the provision of the 1940 Act regulating an investment company's transactions with its affiliates is rarely relevant. The nature of the UIT is also reflected in the required periodic reporting to the SEC. Unlike open-end investment companies which must file semi-annual reports with the SEC, UITs must file reports annually.

# Chapter 15

## *Closed-End Investment Companies*

### A. Use and Nature of Closed-End Investment Companies[1]

Closed-end investment companies are management companies, namely, investment companies other than unit investment trusts and face-amount certificate companies. They are similar to open-end investment companies in that both types have advisers that actively manage their portfolios. In this respect, they differ from unit investment trusts that do not have a board of directors or managed portfolios. Unlike open-end investment companies and unit investment trusts, closed-end investment companies do not offer or issue redeemable securities.

In some cases, a closed-end company's structure is used to hold long-term investments or illiquid securities that cannot back the redemption requirements to which open-end companies are subject. This can be seen, for example, in closed-end funds that invest in a portfolio of hedge funds, or in so-called "senior loans." In other cases, however, a closed-end company structure is used for relatively ordinary investments, such as equities, debt and municipal bonds. In both cases, however, closed-end companies cannot be left without management. Additionally, the closed-end structure is often used for products marketed to investors seeking a regular periodic income stream. In this regard, closed-end companies often pursue fixed-income based strategies, including municipal bond strategies, equity strategies with a dividend focus, or seek to enhance distributable income through portfolio management techniques, such as writing options.

Because closed-end investment companies do not issue redeemable securities, they do not typically offer their securities to the public continuously in order to avoid "net redemptions." Hence, their relationship to their underwriters is usually similar to an operating company's relationship with its underwriter. Usually operating companies also do not offer their securities to the public continuously. This situation is in contrast to the greater dependence of open-end companies and unit investment trusts that offer redeemable securities and need to engage in public distribution

1. This material is extrapolated mainly from 4 TAMAR FRANKEL & ANN TAYLOR SCHWING, THE REGULATION OF MONEY MANAGERS (Mutual Funds and Advisers) § 31.01[B] (2001 & Supp. 2015).

of their securities continuously. Therefore, the 1940 Act does not regulate closed-end investment companies' distribution, advertising, or the pricing of their securities in the same way as it does with open-end investment companies.

Though closed-end funds do not issue redeemable securities, some offering structures are considered a hybrid of the open-end and closed-end fund structure. Some closed-end funds do continuously offer their shares and will institute certain mechanisms to buy back shares from investors that approximates the redeemability offered by an open-end fund. These repurchases are typically accomplished through periodic tender offers pursuant to the Securities Exchange Act of 1934, or pursuant to repurchase offers under rule 23c-3 of the 1940 Act (which are like tender offers, but with a simpler set of rules conditioned on the fund having a fundamental policy of conducting such repurchases). Often the liquidity offered to investors through these mechanisms is no more frequent than once per quarter.

Nonetheless, closed-end investment companies are subject to a set of potential abuses, perhaps because the controlling persons of such companies are not as subject to the shareholders' pressure by redemption or to market prices of the companies' shares. In particular, investors in these companies can be subject to discriminate treatment, dilution of their equity, or sale and repurchase of their shares at unfair prices. The 1940 Act regulates closed-end investment companies with respect to the issuance, sale, and repurchase of the companies' securities. These issues are addressed in Section 23 of the 1940 Act.

Certain provisions of the 1940 Act apply to both open-end and closed-end companies, but they regulate conduct differently, depending on the type of company. For example, in contrast to the prohibition on the issuance of senior securities by open-end companies, under Section 18 closed-end investment companies may have a class of debt securities and a class of preferred stock. However, even this exception is not as broad as the freedom of corporations generally.

The provisions of the 1940 Act that apply to management companies and to companies that have a board of directors apply to closed-end investment companies.[1] Management companies, including closed-end investment companies, must comply with section 17(f) of the 1940 Act regulating the custody of their assets, and section 17(g) requiring bonding of officers and employees having access to the companies' assets. Management companies must also select their independent accountants and controllers in compliance with the procedures set forth in section 32(a) and (b) of the 1940 Act. The 1940 Act's provisions, applicable to all investment companies, are, of course, applicable also to closed-end investment companies.

Closed-end funds' shares are typically traded on a national securities exchange, such as the New York Stock Exchange, and thus their shares are

1. These provisions include section 7(a) (registration of investment companies with boards of directors), section 10(a), (b), and (c) (the boards' composition), section 16(a) (prohibiting persons from serving as directors unless elected by the companies' shareholders), section 10(h) (management companies not having a board of directors).

also usually registered under the Securities Exchange Act of 1934. This is the manner in which most closed-end fund investors are provided with liquidity for their investment (as opposed to open-end funds, which redeem their shares on demand). Because closed-end funds are typically exchange-traded, closed-end funds must additionally comply with the listing standards applicable to companies traded on the relevant exchange (such as a requirement to hold an annual shareholder meeting, and to have an audit committee that meets certain standards).

---

## Discussion Topic

Please review the distinctions between closed-end and open-end investment companies discussed in Chapter 3. What is the status of a management investment company that plans an annual offering to purchase its security holders' securities at a fair, but undeterminable price? Is it an open-end investment company or a closed-end investment company?

---

## B. Distribution of Closed-End Fund Shares and the Puzzle of Closed-End Investment Companies: Their Shares Sell at a Discount from Their Net Asset Value

Closed-end funds typically trade on a national securities exchange. This means that their shares have two prices: (1) the market value based on exchange trading, and (2) the net asset value, which is the value of the fund's portfolio. Traditionally, closed-end fund shares sold at a discount of 15% to 20% from the net asset value that they represented.[1] Then the mid-1980s:

> saw an explosion in the number of initial public offerings: Lee, Shleifer, and Thaler estimated that a fifteen percentage point narrowing in the closed-end fund discount carries with it an increase in the rate of IPOs of 300 per year. . . . .
>
> The closed-end fund discount as a measure of small investor sentiment does not reflect superior information, but instead overenthusiasm (or over pessimism) on the part of small investors. [It could be novelty of new funds or 'celebrity managers'. The funds increased in the 1920s. They were sold as easy to manage portfolios of common stocks for dividends and capital gains. Many were structured as pyramids].
>
> * * *
>
> The emergence of discounts puzzled the community of closed-end fund promoters and brokers. Keane's Investment Trust Monthly Magazine, for example, served as a source of information and a trade journal for those interested in closed-end funds in the early 1930s.

---

1. J. Bradford De Long & Andrei Shleifer, *Closed-End Fund Discounts*, J. PORTFOLIO MGT., Jan. 1992, at 46.

> Its columnists repeatedly show surprise and puzzlement at the existence of continued discounts from net asset values.
>
> * * *
>
> As in the 1930s, discounts have been the rule. The average fund sells at a premium for a four-year period in the late 1960s and early 1970s, and comes close to selling at a premium during the bull market of the mid-1980s.
>
> * * *
>
> Why do closed-end funds typically sell for a discount? We think that discounts are the rule rather than the exception because since 1929 investors have been aware that investments in closed-end funds carry an extra source of risk. Investors face the normal risk that the portfolio of the fund might perform badly. They also face the abnormal risk that investors in the future might like funds less, and so lead funds to sell at an even greater discount in the future. Investors have proven willing to bear this additional source of risk inherent in closed-end funds only if they are offered a higher average return as well. This higher return on average can be provided only if closed-end funds typically sell at discounts. . . .

---

## Discussion Topics

a. Does the issue of the discount of closed-end fund shares pose a problem that needs to be addressed by regulation?

b. Compare and contrast the distribution practices of an open-end with a closed-end company. Compare and contrast the role of the underwriter in each of these distributions.

---

## C. Proposed Solutions to the Discount Problem

### 1. Interval Funds and Tender Offer Funds

As one solution to the closed-end fund discount problem, the SEC has allowed the creation of interval funds. Interval funds are closed-end funds that offer shareholders periodic repurchases of their shares at the net asset value of their portfolios (e.g., above the market price).[1] The solution of interval funds is based on the assumption that supply and demand affect stock prices. This assumption contradicts the efficient markets hypothesis, which has been one of the lasting theories regarding the markets. The hope is that if investors know they will be able to tender their shares to the fund at net asset value, shareholders will not fear losses due to deeper discounts,

1. Since the decision of whether to repurchase the shares is vested in the board of directors of the fund, the shares are not redeemable pursuant to section 2(a)(32) of the 1940 Act. Thus, although this arrangement looks like a partial redemption, it is not because the repurchase decision is made not by the shareholders but by the companies' managers.

demand for the funds' shares will increase and share prices will rise.[1] The jury is still out on whether interval funds can resolve or reduce the discount problem. Rule 23c-3 under the 1940 Act, which was briefly referenced in the introduction to this chapter, allows the establishment of interval funds.

The SEC adopted rule 23c-3[2] to allow "closed-end management investment companies (including business development companies) to make repurchase offers to shareholders at net asset value, either at periodic intervals pursuant to a fundamental policy, or on a discretionary basis not more frequently than once every two years."[3] Note that the repurchases must be made pursuant to a fundamental policy of the fund — i.e., a policy that cannot be changed without a vote of the fund's shareholders. However, these repurchases did not solve the problem. As we shall see later, exchange-traded funds (ETFs), which were differently structured, resolved the problem, although they created some of their own.

A related type of closed-end fund, which predated interval funds and Rule 23c-3, is the closed-end tender offer fund. This type of structure functions similarly to an interval fund; however, repurchases are made pursuant to tender offers compliant with the issuer tender offer rule under the Securities Exchange Act of 1934 (i.e., rule 13e-4), and are not made pursuant to a fundamental policy of the fund. Often, the fund's offering documents will state an intention to commence tender offers at periodic intervals. Unlike rule 23c-3, these tender offers can offer to repurchase shares at below net asset value, which is done from time to time. Many closed-end funds that commence regular tender offers, however, are closed-end funds that do not trade on an exchange, and thus use tender offers as a means to provide shareholders with liquidity for their investment. In this sense, the tender offer mechanism does not really function as a discount management technique. Some closed-end funds that trade on an exchange, however, do attempt to use tender offers as a discount management technique.

Repurchases of closed-end funds' shares are discussed in more detail below.

## 2. Conversion into Open-End Companies

Attempts to resolve the discount problem of a closed-end fund's shares included conversion of the fund to an open-end company. In an effort to attract investors, many closed-end sponsors have held out the possibility of converting to an open-end fund at some future date. Complaints concerning these pressures led the SEC staff to issue a comment letter.[4] The staff noted the complaints and its concerns. Funds that have described their effort to

1. In essence, the efficient market hypothesis proposes that stock prices represent the incorporation of all available information. Therefore, stock prices are always "right." A weaker version of the theory suggests that stock prices represent all publicly available information, and to that extent there is no possibility of picking better stock. These theories lead to the conclusion that supply and demand do not affect stock prices, or at least not significantly.

2. 17 C.F.R. § 270.23c-3 (2015).

3. Repurchase Offers by Closed-End Management Investment Companies, Investment Company Act Rel. No. 19399 (Apr. 7, 1993).

4. Investment Company Institute, SEC No-Action Letter (Feb. 15, 1996).

minimize the discounts at which their shares traded from their net asset values have also committed to consider and/or to conduct tender offers. That would allow the shareholders to receive the pro rata share of the value of the fund's assets (if the tender offer is conducted at net asset value) rather than the lower market value. Investors believed that the repurchases would be effected only to find out that the fund's board of directors changed its mind, and that the fund's disclosures could have allowed this change of mind by "vague references."

The staff responded by contacting the Investment Company Institute, conducting a close review of closed-end funds' registration statements, focusing "on the clarity and prominence of disclosure regarding these actions," and alerted examiners of the funds to this issue. Some materials were also sent to the brokers' self-regulatory organization.

---

## Discussion Topics

a. Suppose a closed-end investment company offers its shares to the public and states that it will "open-end" the fund within 6 months, if, in the opinion of the directors, such a step would be beneficial to the company and its shareholders. At the end of the 6 months the board of directors determines not to "open-end" the fund, on the ground that it is not in the best interests of the fund and its shareholders. A class of shareholders sues the board and the fund, seeking damages (the value of the discount) or specific performance (open-end the fund). What are the grounds for this claim? How likely is it to succeed? Should it succeed? Should the law be amended in this area?

b. How do a closed-end investment company's tender offers at a fixed price dilute the existing shareholder's equity? Do they always do so? Do the provisions regulating tender offers of closed-end investment companies' shares parallel the provisions regulating the repurchase of investment companies' shares?

---

## 3. Repurchase of Closed-End Fund Shares[1]

> Open-end and closed-end companies are subject to many of the same key provisions of the Act. . . . Nevertheless, the fact that open-end shareholders have redemption rights and closed-end shareholders do not leads to many differences in the regulatory treatment of open-end and closed-end companies under the Act.
>
> * * *
>
> Section 22 of the Act imposes specific requirements governing the pricing and redemption of open-end shares. Different requirements apply to non-redeemable shares of closed-end companies

1. Division of Investment Management, U.S. Securities and Exchange Commission, Protecting Investors: A Half Century of Investment Company Regulation 422-423, 425-428 (1992) (citations omitted).

under section 23, which permits closed-end companies to repurchase their shares from investors on the open market (after notice to shareholders), pursuant to tender offers, or in compliance with Commission rules or orders.

* * *

Background

The Treatment of Open-End and Closed-End Investment Companies Under the Act: The Historical Context

The Act's delineation of the closed-end and open-end categories responded to the characteristics of the investment company industry in the decades preceding the Act and sought to correct certain abuses and problems. Closed-end companies became prominent during the 1920's, when new issues quickly sold out at large premiums over net asset value. The stock market crash of 1929 virtually eliminated the market for new public offerings of closed-end securities, however, and closed-end shares began trading in the secondary market at prices below net asset value. Open-end companies, relatively unknown before the crash, quickly became popular because they offered protection from discounts by committing to redeem investors' shares at net asset value.

Although the open-end company was a fairly new form of investment vehicle in 1940, the Commission's Study on Investment Trusts and Investment Companies (the "Investment Trust Study") documented extensive abuses in the operations of both open-end and closed-end investment companies. Not surprisingly, abuses were often related to practices that gave preferential treatment to investment company insiders and affiliates. Three areas in particular provided substantial opportunity for abuse. Closed-end companies had aggressively repurchased their shares in response to discounts, often manipulating the market for shares in ways that benefited management and insiders to the detriment of selling shareholders. Similarly, open-end companies had engaged in questionable pricing and distribution practices in connection with their ongoing sales and redemptions procedures. Finally, complex capital structures, particularly in closed-end companies, had resulted in dangerous leveraging effects that threatened the viability of many investment companies. These abuses, and the provisions of the Investment Company Act and rules that address them, are discussed more fully below.

Repurchases of Closed-End Shares

The condition of the market during the 1920's and 1930's provided powerful incentives for closed-end companies to engage in extensive repurchase operations. While repurchasing of shares is not, in itself, an abusive practice, certain strategies used by closed-end companies during the period of 1927-1935 resulted in market manipulation and harm to public shareholders.

Before the crash, it was not unusual for sponsors of closed-end companies to instigate repurchases for the purpose of influencing the market to aid in the distribution of new shares. Repurchases could support or increase the market price, creating an appearance that the value of the shares was steady or rising, and enhancing the value of the sponsors' own holdings.

After the crash, repurchases often were made for different reasons. As the price of closed-end shares fell to a discount, repurchases at discount prices became a source of book profits for closed-end companies. Many times, however, the profits were made at the expense of selling shareholders who had no way of knowing the extent of the discount and, therefore, the extent to which they were liquidating their shares at prices that did not reflect their true value. This was possible because closed-end companies did not disclose the net asset value of their shares. In addition, because some companies made purchases on the open market without informing investors, investors could not determine the extent to which the market was being driven by the company's management.

Other abuses occurred. Some closed-end companies would repurchase securities from insiders in private purchases, sometimes at a premium or in blocks that could not have been sold at the prevailing market price because of the size of the purchase. Some companies would repurchase from certain shareholders to establish control or remove opposition to management. Finally, repurchases were used in various ways in connection with mergers, consolidations, and acquisitions. Some companies, for example, made repurchases to manipulate the market values of securities involved in exchanges.

In response to these abuses, Congress enacted section 23 of the Investment Company Act. Section 23(c) restricts repurchases of closed-end company shares, limiting them to purchases (1) on a national securities exchange or other market designated by the commission (after adequate notice to all shareholders); (2) pursuant to tenders open to all security holders; or (3) in such other circumstances as the Commission permits by rule or order. Section 23 also regulates additional sales of common stock by closed-end companies after the initial offering is completed. Section 23(b) generally prohibits such sales at prices below net asset value, except (1) in connection with an offering to holders of one or more classes of capital stock; (2) with the consent of a majority of the holders of common stock; (3) upon conversion of a convertible security in accordance with its terms; (4) upon the exercise of any warrant issued in accordance with the provisions of section 18(d); or (5) under such other circumstances as the Commission may permit by rule or order. These provisions are aimed at protecting existing shareholders from the effects of sales of new shares that would unfairly dilute their holdings. . . .

### 4. Other Issues in Discount Management

Closed-end funds have attempted to address discounts through various other techniques, both at their own volition and in response to pressure from investors. One common method used is a "discount management program," which is in effect a tender offer program. In essence, the fund commits to commence a tender offer for some percentage of its shares either at net asset value, or at a slight discount to net asset value, if the discount exceeds some threshold over a period of time.

Another strategy some closed-end funds use is to hire a broker-dealer to provide "secondary market support services." These services basically involve educating the trading community about the fund in an effort to keep the fund's profile high and views of it positive and thus, theoretically, reduce the discount. There are several broker-dealer firms that specialize in this kind of service for closed-end funds.

More recently, in IPOs closed-end funds have imposed a limited term on themselves, after which the fund will terminate and distribute its net assets. The theory here is that because investors know they will be entitled to the fund's net asset value at a date certain it will help the fund trade closer to net asset value during its life.

### 5. Additional Capital Raising Activities

Section 23(b) of the 1940 Act provides that closed-end funds cannot sell their shares at a price below net asset value, exclusive of any sales load, subject to certain exceptions. The most relevant of these exceptions include (1) in connection with an offering to the holders of one or more classes of its capital stock, and (2) with the consent of a majority of its common stockholders. Because closed-end funds so frequently trade at discounts, it makes raising additional assets after the closed-end fund's IPO difficult, if not at times impossible.

Without using these exceptions, closed-end funds trading at a premium (which are few and far between) have found it advantageous to engage in "at-the-market" offerings of their common shares. In this type of an offering, a closed-end fund issues shares at their market price into normal trading volume. As indicated in section 23(b), these transactions can only take place if the market price is at a premium to net asset value equal to or greater than the sales load charged by the broker-dealer running the at-the-market program. These programs are established under Rule 415 of the Securities Act, and have been helped along by SEC staff no-action relief that permits closed-end funds to use the applicable portion of Rule 415 permitting "at-the-market" offerings.[1]

Another strategy closed-end funds use to raise additional assets is a rights offering. In a rights offering, the fund distributes "rights" to its existing shareholders that entitle them to subscribe for a particular number of common shares. These types of offerings rely on the exception with respect to offerings to the holders of one or more classes of its capital stock and are also subject to compliance with various SEC staff positions.

## D. Capital Structure of Closed-End Investment Companies[2]

Section 18 gives a closed-end investment company more flexibility to issue senior securities than is given to open-end companies. While an open-

1. Nuveen Virginia Premium Income Municipal Fund, SEC No-Action Letter (Oct. 6, 2006); Pilgrim America Prime Rate Trust, SEC No-Action Letter (May 1, 1998).

2. This material is extrapolated from 3 Tamar Frankel & Ann Taylor Schwing, The Regulation of Money Managers § 21.05[C] (2001 & Supp. 2015).

end company is generally prohibited from issuing senior securities, such issuance is permitted as to closed-end companies.

Closed-end funds may issue both preferred stock and debt securities. With respect to preferred stock, such preferred stock must have an asset coverage ratio of 200% (i.e., for every dollar of liquidation preference of the preferred stock, the fund must have $2 of assets) and must contain certain terms that are designed to protect the preferred shareholders. These terms include requiring that two of the fund's directors be elected exclusively by the preferred shareholders, and requiring the preferred shareholders, voting as a separate class, to approve certain investment policy changes and any plan of reorganization "adversely affecting" such preferred shareholders. Moreover, if preferred dividends are in arrears for more than two years, the preferred must be entitled to elect a majority of the board until such arrears have been paid or otherwise provided for. With respect to asset coverage, asset coverage must be met upon initial issuance and in the event the fund wishes to declare any dividend on, or repurchase, the fund's common shares.[1] These protective provisions arise out of the abuses found in the investment company industry that led to the enactment of the 1940 Act.

With respect to debt securities, such debt securities must have an asset coverage ratio of 300% (i.e., for every dollar or debt the fund must have $3 of assets). Debt securities also have a similar prohibition on dividends (to both common and preferred shareholders) in the event asset coverage is not maintained (though asset coverage for debt must only be 200% in order to declare preferred share dividends). Debt holders, however, do not have a general right to elect directors akin to the right granted to preferred shareholders; however, a right to elect a majority of the board arises should asset coverage for such debt securities drop below 100% for twelve consecutive months. Importantly, however, bank debt is only subject to the 300% asset coverage requirement and not the other protective provisions.

Section 18(c) makes it unlawful for a "closed-end investment company to issue or sell any senior security representing indebtedness if immediately thereafter such company will have outstanding more than one class of senior security representing indebtedness, or to issue or sell any senior security which is a stock if immediately thereafter such company will have outstanding more than one class of senior security which is stock. . . ." This section generally permits one class of common, one class of preferred, and one class of debt securities for closed-end funds.

There are however, four exceptions to the limitation on the number of classes of securities. First, any class of senior security representing indebtedness or senior security which is stock may be issued in one or more

1. This, in effect, requires asset coverage to be maintained nearly continuously since many closed-end funds pursue a strategy of seeking current income for common shareholders, and thus seek to make monthly or quarterly distributions. Additionally, to the extent a fund does not make a distribution of substantially all of its net investment company taxable income on an annual basis, it will lose its pass-through tax treatment as a "regulated investment company" under the Internal Revenue Code — a pressure which also keeps closed-end funds focused on asset coverage requirements.

series, provided that no series has preference or priority over any other series upon the distribution of assets, or in respect of payment of interest or dividends. Presumably, the term "priority" means priority in case of default or liquidation. This exception is meant to provide for, e.g., different series of debt with different interest rates. The second exception from the limitation of section 18(c) concerns promissory notes or other evidence of indebtedness issued in consideration, extension, or renewal, of a loan made by a bank or another person, privately arranged and not intended to be publicly distributed.[1] The third exception appears in section 18(g), defining senior security. A privately placed debt security as described above, "issued for a loan which is for temporary purposes only and is in an amount not exceeding 5 per centum of the value of the total assets of the issuer at the time when the loan is made," is not a senior security. The fourth exception from the limits on the number of classes of senior securities representing indebtedness concerns small business investment companies licensed to do business under the Small Business Investment Act of 1958.

From a practical perspective, many closed-end funds rely on leverage — i.e., the issuance of preferred shares or debt — to enhance their common share returns. This is because the marketing of closed-end funds is very "yield-centric" — i.e., the selling point is income and leverage can enhance such income in rising markets (conversely, leverage magnifies losses in declining markets). Over the years, the form of this leverage has varied. For many years, closed-end funds leveraged their common shares through public issuances of auction rate preferred securities. These were preferred securities that paid a dividend based on short term interest rates, which dividend was reset at periodic auctions (usually weekly or monthly). During the 2008 financial crisis, these auctions stopped functioning and, as a practical matter, made the continued use of this form of leverage impractical (though a small handful of funds continue to have auction rate preferred shares outstanding). More recently, closed-end funds have leveraged with bank debt, other leveraged borrowing transactions such as reverse repurchase agreements or tender option bonds (a special kind of securitization vehicle meant to leverage municipal bond portfolios), or with new forms of preferred equity — usually taking the form of single-holder bank owned preferred, or privately placed preferred shares that trade in the qualified institutional buyer market.

---

## Discussion Topic

What justifies a different treatment under the Investment Company Act of the capital structure of closed-end companies and open-end companies?

1. This exception, however, is not an absolute. A closed-end fund may not have unsecured public debt alongside secured private bank debt. *See* In the Matter of Israel Dev. Corp., Investment Company Act Rel. No. 3214 (Mar. 16, 1961).

---

## Problem

Your client is the adviser to a closed-end fund. In the time since the 2008 financial crisis, financing for purposes of leveraging the fund's portfolio has been hard to come by on acceptable terms. Thus, your client has been at the forefront of innovating different methods of obtaining leverage and combining them. The fund currently has a secured bank credit facility and one class of preferred shares outstanding. The bank credit facility carries a variable interest rate that currently amounts to 1.75% per annum and the preferred shares pay a fixed dividend of 5% per annum with an obligation to redeem all preferred shares at their liquidation preference of $25,000 per share in 5 years (i.e., the preferred has a fixed term and is not perpetual).

Your client would like to do the following:

1. Issue to the public 10-year unsecured notes carrying a fixed interest rate of 2.00%;

2. Issue more preferred shares, but make them perpetual preferred carrying a variable dividend rate reset in quarterly remarketings and a $50,000 liquidation preference.

Please write your client a memo analyzing whether this proposal is permissible under the 1940 Act. If some aspect of this proposal is not permissible, discuss how your client might modify the fund's existing or proposed financing arrangements to comply with the 1940 Act. Also discuss any other aspects of the 1940 Act, particularly section 18, that would bear on your client's proposal.

---

# Chapter 16

## *Exchange-Traded Funds*

Exchange-traded funds (ETFs) resolved the discount issue that has plagued closed-end funds, discussed in Chapter 15, and provided an alternative type of liquidity for investors in open-end funds through market trading rather than redemptions. In the case of open-end funds, redemptions offer investors a fixed price once a day, and the price is not known until after the order is placed. Yet, in volatile markets investors want the flexibility to trade shares far more often and quicker.

ETFs have characteristics of both open-end and closed-end funds.[1] ETFs are structured as open-end funds or unit investment trusts. ETFs issue shares in blocks (e.g., of 50,000 shares) called "Creation Units," which are purchased by "Authorized Participants," generally broker-dealers, and are generally purchased "in-kind" with a "basket" of securities that reflect the ETF's portfolio. These purchasers in turn may split the Creation Units and sell the shares in the secondary market. Unlike open-end funds, ETF's shares are not fully redeemable. Investors can sell Creation Units back to the ETF (generally Authorized Participants that purchased shares on the market), but ETFs generally give them the underlying securities instead of cash (a redemption "in-kind," rather than in cash).

Most ETFs are "index-based" ETFs that attempt to track the performance of a stock index (e.g., the S&P 500) and generally invest in those companies' securities. "Leveraged" or "inverse" ETFs attempt to obtain a multiple (or the inverse or a multiple of the inverse) of the index. "Actively-managed" ETFs allow an investment adviser to buy and sell portfolio securities without reference to an index. The first ETF was introduced in 1993;[2] the first actively-managed ETFs received SEC exemptive relief in early 2008.[3] At

1. Derived generally from U.S. Sec. & Exch. Comm'n, Exchange-Traded Funds (last modified Nov. 8, 2013), *available at* http://www.sec.gov/answers/etf.htm; Ofc. Of Investor Education & Advocacy, SEC, Investor Bulletin: Exchange-Traded Funds (ETFs) (2012), *available at* http://www.sec.gov/investor/alerts/etfs.pdf.
2. Investment Company Institute, Investment Company Fact Book 58 (55th ed. 2015), *available at* https://www.ici.org/pdf/2015_factbook.pdf.
3. *Id.* at 59.

the end of 2014 there were 1,411 ETFs in the U.S. with nearly $2.0 trillion in assets under management.[1]

Index-based ETFs differ from index funds, which are open-end funds whose portfolios track stock indexes, in that ETF's shares are not fully redeemable; however, arguably this is advantageous as ETFs need not maintain cash for redemption demands but may invest the cash at a higher yield. In addition, ETF investors also have the advantage of knowing the share price at the time of order, as with closed-end funds. However, as ETFs involve brokers, investors must pay a trading commission.[2]

Unlike mutual funds, ETF shares are traded on an exchange and at market prices that may include a premium or discount from the net asset value (NAV) of the fund shares (*i.e.*, the net value of the ETF's assets divided by the number of shares at the end of the day). An "intraday" NAV is calculated and updated frequently during the day based on the estimated net value of the assets. The market price may trade at a premium or discount from NAV because of changes in the value of the assets and in the demand for the ETF.

In 1993, Standard & Poor's introduced the first successful ETF, Standard and Poor's Depository Receipts (SPDRs, pronounced "spiders").[3] This attempt proved successful, not only to overcome the problem of the share discounts of closed-end funds, but also to provide investors with liquidity and price information throughout their trading time. SPDRs' portfolio closely reflected the S&P 500 index, allowing investors to "play the market with a single investment."[4] SPDRs, structured as a unit investment trust, required exemptions from several sections of the 1940 Act: (1) section 4(2)[5] (the definition of unit investment trust, requiring issuance of only redeemable securities); (2) section 14(a)[6] (requiring a $100,000 initial investment; applicants represented that they would generally comply with the investor protections of the rule 14a-3 exemption for a trust investing in "eligible trust securities");[7] and (3) section 17(a)[8] (generally prohibiting an affiliate from purchasing/selling property to/from an investment company, which provision would arguably prohibit redemption of Creation Units by an affiliate). "The exemption for SPDR is justified on the grounds that the affiliate will receive for its [C]reation [U]nits a pro rata share of the portfolio, and that measure is sufficiently ascertainable to preclude discretionary redemption. Whether a similar structure should be allowed for managed portfolios is an open question."[9]

---

1. *Id.* at 60.
2. 4 Tamar Frankel & Ann Taylor Schwing, The Regulation of Money Managers § 31.01[C], at 31-26 to -27 (2001 & Supp. 2015).
3. 4 Tamar Frankel & Ann Taylor Schwing, The Regulation of Money Managers § 31.01[C], at 31-25 (2001 & Supp. 2015).
4. Jack Sirard, *Spiders Climb Web of Investment Popularity,* Sacramento Bee, Mar. 18, 1993, at F1.
5. 15 U.S.C. § 80a-4(2).
6. 15 U.S.C. § 80a-14(a).
7. 17 C.F.R. § 270.14a-3 (2015).
8. 15 U.S.C. § 80a-17(a).
9. 4 Tamar Frankel & Ann Taylor Schwing, The Regulation of Money Managers § 31.01[C], at 31-27 ((2001 & Supp. 2015).

## A. Issues Under Section 22(d) and Rule 22c-1

Because they are a hybrid of unit investment trusts and closed-end funds, ETFs structured as open-end funds raise issues under section 22(d) and rule 22c-1 of the 1940 Act.[1] Section 22(d) and rule 22c-1 are intended to prevent discrimination among shareholders in buying and selling shares. ETFs involve secondary market transactions at negotiated prices rather than at a pro rata share value, reflected in the portfolio (as redemption would). Investors purchasing shares on the market are at a disadvantage compared to Authorized Participants, who may also purchase and redeem shares with the ETF and therefore take advantage of differences between market price and NAV.[2]

To reduce these investor concerns, ETFs are designed with an arbitrage mechanism intended to keep the market price close to NAV.[3] Authorized Participants, who can both trade with the ETF at NAV and trade on the market, have an incentive to "arbitrage" or take advantage of a premium or discount. For example, if the shares are trading at a discount, arbitrageurs will purchase a Creation Unit of ETF shares and redeem them with the ETF for the underlying securities, to be sold at a profit.[4] As a result of arbitrage, the market price is expected to approach NAV and investors will be able to purchase ETF shares at a price close to NAV. This mechanism enables institutional investors and other arbitrageurs to trade in ETF shares in the secondary market and engage in purchases and redemptions with the fund, helping to keep the trading of the shares at a small discount or premium.[5]

Arbitrage is dependent on the transparency of the ETF's portfolio. If arbitrageurs know what securities are in the portfolio, they can trade based on a comparison of the market value of the ETF shares and the value of the securities in the portfolio.[6] With *index-based* ETFs, the index provides transparency, as index providers publically release some information about the index,[7] possibly including the methodology used to determine the index, although the specific component securities may or may not be released.

In this regard, the SEC has granted exemptive relief to *actively managed* ETFs that are fully transparent, i.e., that disclose their holdings of portfolio securities and other assets daily.[8] However, this required disclosure would reveal the fund's trades to other fund managers.[9]

1. 15 U.S.C. § 80a-22(d) (2012); 17 C.F.R. § 270.22c-1 (2015).
2. Exchange-Traded Funds, Investment Company Act Rel. No. 28193 (Mar. 11, 2008), 73 Fed. Reg. 14,618, 14,624 (Mar. 18, 2008).
3. *Id.* at 14,622.
4. 4 Tamar Frankel & Ann Taylor Schwing, The Regulation of Money Managers § 31.01[C], at 31-26 (2001 & Supp. 2015).
5. Exchange-Traded Funds, Investment Company Act Rel. No. 28193 (Mar. 11, 2008), 73 Fed. Reg. 14,618, 14,623 (Mar. 18, 2008).
6. *Id.* at 14,620.
7. *Id.* at 14,620 n.27.
8. *Id.* at 14,621; *id.* at 14,620 (citing orders).
9. Daisy Maxey, *SEC Will Maintain Open Veil On ETFs,* Wall St. J., Oct. 23, 2014, at C1, LEXIS, News Library, WSJ File.

Therefore, fund creators and managers sought to design actively-managed ETFs that use another mechanism to minimize trading at discounts or premiums without full transparency. Fund companies proposed a structure involving a "blind trust" mechanism for "creation unit" purchases and in-kind redemptions to avoid disclosure of the portfolio securities, and dissemination of the "intraday indicative value" of the ETF by a third-party exchange every 15 seconds. The SEC expressed preliminary views that these mechanisms are not adequate for exemptive relief.[1]

However, in December 2014 the SEC granted relief to actively managed non-transparent exchange-traded managed funds (ETMFs), described as a hybrid of a traditional ETF and a traditional mutual fund. The fund would use "NAV-based trading," in which shares will trade at NAV plus or minus a premium/discount which may vary during the day. However, the final trade price would be NAV at the end of the day plus or minus the locked-in premium/discount. The applicants contended that the NAV-based trading would result in narrow premiums.[2] Subsequently the SEC has granted relief to other ETMFs.[3]

---

## B. Advantages and Disadvantages for Investors

> ETFs use a novel pricing mechanism that harnesses the utility of arbitrage to provide investors with accuracy, efficiency, tax advantages, and a range of investment choices, while insulating investors from many of the structural problems associated with mutual funds. Despite these advantages, critics decry their brokerage fees and vulnerability to harmful short-term trading. This article argues that the mutual fund industry and its recent spate of dramatic scandals contributed to the emergence of ETFs and concludes that mutual funds offer vivid warnings of the conflicts of interest that may come to afflict the ETF industry as it continues to grow.
>
> One of the great successes of the ETF industry has been the ability to create a market-rather than a regulatory or litigated-solution to much of the mutual fund difficulties. Nevertheless, ETFs are not free from their own possible conflicts of interest. One particular source of vulnerability involves the stock lending plans, whereby ETFs lend their stocks to other market participants in exchange for a fee. Since many ETFs hold themselves out as vehicles for tracking a benchmark, their sponsors are under no affirmative duty to boost returns with

1. Spruce ETF Trust, Investment Company Act Rel. No. 31301 (Oct. 21, 2014); Precidian ETFs Trust, Investment Company Act Rel. No. 31300 (Oct. 21, 2014).
2. Eaton Vance Mgmt., Investment Company Act Rel. No. 31333 (Nov. 6, 2014) (application); Investment Company Act Rel. No. 31361 (Dec. 10, 2014) (order).
3. Hartford Funds NextShares Trust, Investment Company Act Rel. No. 31576 (Apr. 23, 2015) (application); Investment Company Act Rel. No. 31607 (May 19, 2015) (order); Gabelli ETMF Trust, Investment Company Act Rel. No. 31575 (Apr. 23, 2015) (application); Investment Company Act Rel. No. 31608 (May 19, 2015) (order); American Beacon NextShares Trust, Investment Company Act Rel. No. 31498 (Mar. 6, 2015) (application); Investment Company Act Rel. No. 31542 (Apr. 1, 2015) (order).

the proceeds of these stock lending plans. Competitive market forces may encourage ETF sponsors to use the proceeds to increase fund returns, but the mutual fund precedent demonstrates that market forces may not succeed in disciplining investment advisers who choose to direct such proceeds directly into their own pockets.

Another possible pitfall for ETFs may be the dystopia predicted by Bogle. If, as he fears, investors saving for retirement do in fact manage to hurt themselves and their savings by aggressively trading their accounts in and out of ETFs, the ETF may be discredited as a savings vehicle.[1]

---

**Discussion Topics**

a. What are the pluses and minuses of the ETF structure for investors? Who else benefits from the structure? What are the effects of ETFs on the investment advisers, the portfolio managers, the holders of "creation units," the brokers, and any other actor?

b. What are the effects of ETFs on the financial system and on the markets in particular?

c. Please focus on the investment strategy. Was the disclosure of this strategy adequate?

d. What other alternative structure could be used to give investors the proposed investment strategy?

e. Could individuals engage in this strategy? Why did they not do that?

f. Should this type of ETF be allowed, and if so, on what conditions?

---

## C. ETFs' Use of Derivatives; Leveraged and Inverse ETFs

The use of derivatives by ETFs arguably raises unique investor protection issues under the 1940 Act.

"Leveraged" and "inverse" ETFs attempt to achieve performance results through swaps, futures, and other derivatives. Leveraged ETFs attempt to deliver a multiple of the performance of the index. Inverse ETFs attempt to deliver the opposite of the performance. Leveraged inverse ETFs attempt to deliver a multiple of the opposite of the performance. [2]

Leveraged and inverse ETFs generally "reset" daily; *i.e.,* they attempt to achieve their objectives on a daily basis. Consequently, their results over a period of time may vary greatly from a multiple of or the inverse of the results of the index over the period. For example, a leveraged ETF may fall

1. William A. Birdthistle, *The Fortunes and Foibles of Exchange-Traded Funds: A Positive Market Response to the Problems of Mutual Funds*, 33 Del. J. Corp. L. 69 (2008).
2. U.S. Sec. & Exch. Comm'n, Leveraged and Inverse ETFs: Specialized Products with Extra Risks for Buy-and-Hold Investors (last modified Aug. 18, 2009), *available at* http://www.sec.gov/investor/pubs/leveragedetfs-alert.htm.

during a period when the index gains, or it may fall more than a multiple of the fall of the index during the period. [1]

In *Rafton v. Rydex Series Funds,*[2] the trustees of trusts that invested in a fund sued the fund and related entities under the Securities Act of 1933, alleging faulty disclosure regarding the fund shares. The opinion described the fund as follows:

> The Fund [was] an "exchange-traded fund" ("ETF"), designed to track a benchmark: the *inverse* price movements of the 30-Year U.S. Treasury Bond ("Long Treasury Bond"). As an 'inverse' fund, the Fund was designed to produce investment returns that are the opposite of the performance of the underlying benchmark, i.e., when the price of the benchmark decreases, the price of the fund should increase by the same percentage. . . . According to Plaintiffs, most inverse funds are designed to track a benchmark on a daily basis and reset daily. . . . Unlike a traditional index fund, the Fund's objective is to perform, on a daily basis, exactly opposite its benchmark, the Long Treasury Bond. As its primary investment strategy, the Fund enters into short sales and swap transactions, and engages in futures and options transactions. On a day-to-day basis, the Fund holds U.S. Government securities or cash equivalents to collateralize its short sales and derivative positions. With this daily re-setting, such funds are subject to a "mathematical compounding effect" that leads a fund's price to deviate from the inverse movement of the benchmark for periods beyond a single day. . . . In a two-day example, if a benchmark index starts at 100 and closes at 101 on the first day, and goes back down to close at 100 on the second day, the benchmark is even over the two-day period, but the Fund (assuming it also started at 100 and has met its daily goal) will have actually lost value over the same two-day period. In this example, the calculation for the Fund is: 100 (start), 99 (end of day one, dropping 1% from 100 to 99 as benchmark increased 1% from 100 to 101), 99.98 (end of day two, increasing 0.99% from 99 to 99.98 as benchmark decreased 0.99% from 101 to 100). The compounding effect is more pronounced in periods of high volatility, in which the benchmark moves up and down in greater amounts. . . . Plaintiff's central allegation is that, because of this compounding effect, inverse funds are not appropriate for investors seeking to hold the investment for longer than a single day. . . .
>
> According to Plaintiff, each of the Registration Statements contained substantially similar untrue statements of material fact and/or omitted material facts, as "investors holding Fund shares during the Class period lost money even though the benchmark price of the U.S. Treasury Long Bond fell--precisely the type of period during which investors would have expected to make money." For example, Plaintiffs allege that between March 20, 2008 and February 22,

1. *Id.*

2. *Rafton v. Rydex Series Funds,* No. 10-CV-01171-LHK, 2011 U.S. Dist. LEXIS 707, Fed. Sec. L. Rep. (CCH) ¶96,024 (D.C. Cal. Jan. 5, 2011) (Citations omitted).

2010, the price of the U.S. Treasury Long Bond fell by 4.91%, but the Fund price did not increase and instead also fell by 11.29%.

---

## Discussion Topics

a. What was the justification for permitting ETFs? Was the Rydex Fund envisioned then?

b. Why did the fund design develop? Who benefitted from it?

c. Why did sophisticated trustees that manage very large assets invest in these funds? What was the trustees' mandate? What enticed them to invest? Would you, as trustee, have invested in this fund?

d. The claim in the above case was based on a violation of the Securities Act of 1933, alleging that the disclosure regarding the fund shares was faulty. How would you have advised the issuers to describe the fund shares?

---

The SEC staff has expressed concerns about the use of derivatives by ETFs and other investment companies and said that it was conducting a review of such use, including whether:

- current market practices involving derivatives are consistent with the leverage, concentration and diversification provisions of the Investment Company Act;
- funds that rely substantially upon derivatives, particularly those that seek to provide leveraged returns, maintain and implement adequate risk management and other procedures in light of the nature and volume of the fund's derivatives transactions;
- fund boards of directors are providing appropriate oversight of the use of derivatives by funds;
- existing rules sufficiently address matters such as the proper procedure for a fund's pricing and liquidity determinations regarding its derivatives holdings;
- existing prospectus disclosures adequately address the particular risks created by derivatives; and
- funds' derivative activities should be subject to special reporting requirements.[1]

The staff also said that it would "defer consideration of exemptive requests under the Investment Company Act to permit ETFs that would make significant investments in derivatives" with respect to both actively-managed and leveraged ETFs.[2]

Similarly, in a concept release, the SEC requested comment on issues regarding use of derivatives by ETFs and other investment companies, including:

1. U.S. Sec. & Exch. Comm'n, SEC Staff Evaluating the Use of Derivatives by Funds (Mar. 25, 2010), *available at* http://www.sec.gov/news/press/2010/2010-45.htm.
2. *Id.*

- The attendant costs, benefits and risks;
- The application of the 1940 Act's prohibitions and restrictions on senior securities and leverage;
- The application of the 1940 Act's prohibition on investments in securities-related issuers;
- The application of the 1940 Act's provisions concerning portfolio diversification and concentration; and
- The application of the 1940 Act's provisions governing valuation of funds' assets.[1]

Subsequently, the staff announced that it would no longer defer consideration of such requests for actively-managed ETFs that make use of derivatives provided that they include representations that (i) "the ETF's board periodically will review and approve the ETF's use of derivatives and how the ETF's investment adviser assesses and manages risk with respect to the ETF's use of derivatives"; and (ii) "the ETF's disclosure of its use of derivatives in its offering documents and periodic reports is consistent with relevant Commission and staff guidance."[2] The staff position applies only to actively-managed ETFs and not leveraged ETFs.[3]

---

**Discussion Questions**

a. Do ETFs use derivatives in the same way as other investment companies?

b. Does their use of derivatives present unique investor protection issues?

---

### D. Affiliated Index Providers

Where the index provider (*i.e.*, the compiler of the underlying index) is an affiliate of the ETF or the adviser, there are conflict of interest issues. First, the index provider may have incentive to manipulate the index. Second, employees of the index provider may be able to trade on advance knowledge of changes in the index.[4]

1. Use of Derivatives by Investment Companies Under the Investment Company Act of 1940, Investment Company Act Rel. No. 29776 (Aug. 31, 2011), 76 Fed. Reg. 55,237, 55,239-40 (Sept. 7, 2011).
2. Office of Exemptive Applications/Office of Investment Company Regulation, Corres. (Dec. 6, 2012). In the no-action letter, the SEC staff granted no-action relief to ETFs relying on 18 prior exemptive orders including a representation that "no actively-managed ETF relying on the relief would invest in options contracts, futures contracts or swap agreements," allowing them to invest in these derivatives provided that they comply with the above representations.
3. Norm Champ, Director, Division of Investment Management, U.S. Securities & Exchange Commission, Remarks to the ALI CLE 2012 Conference on Investment Adviser Regulation: Legal and Compliance Forum on Institutional Advisory Services (Dec. 6, 2012), *available at* http://www.sec.gov/news/speech/2012/spch120612nc.htm.
4. *E.g.,* Highland Funds I, Investment Company Act Rel. Nos. 31579/31646 (2015).

Consequently, early exemptive orders for ETFs with affiliated index providers included representations regarding transparency of the index and other policies and procedures. Transparency of the index was established through public disclosure of the index methodology. The other policies and procedures included (i) "firewalls" between the index provider and advisory personnel managing the fund; (ii) a representation that the index methodology would not change without advance public notice limitations, and a limitation on how frequently the index could be reconstituted; and (iii) appointment of an independent entity as "Calculation Agent" to calculate and reconstitute the index.[1]

Subsequently, after the SEC began issuing exemptive orders for actively-managed ETFs, applicants obtained exemptions for ETFs with affiliated index providers with representations regarding full portfolio transparency and without representations for the other policies and procedures. The applicants analogized to actively-managed ETFs and argued that the conflict of interest issues are similar (i.e., the portfolio managers have advance knowledge of portfolio changes) and adequately addressed by full portfolio transparency.[2] Applicants also analogized to the potential conflicts of interest where an adviser manages two or more funds, and argued that the 1940 Act and Advisers Act have adequate protections in that situation.[3]

Similarly, in a proposed rule release, the SEC stated its belief that the representations in the early exemptive orders were not necessary as existing requirements should be sufficient to protect against abuse of nonpublic inside information, and funds can implement appropriate procedures to address circumstances that can lead to abuse.[4]

---

1. *Id.* (citing WisdomTree Investments Inc., Investment Company Act Rel. Nos. 27324/27391 (2006); IndexIQ ETF Trust, Investment Company Act Rel. Nos. 28638/28653 (2009); Van Eck Assocs. Corp., Investment Company Act Rel. Nos. 29455/29490 (2010); Guggenheim Funds Investment Advisors, LLC, Investment Company Act Rel. Nos. 30560/30598 (2013)).
2. *E.g., id.*
3. *Id.* (citing 17 C.F.R. § 270.17j-1 (2015) (prohibiting certain personal investment activities of investment company personnel; requiring fund, its adviser, and its underwriter to adopt code of ethics); 15 U.S.C. § 80b-4a (requiring adviser to adopt policies and procedures regarding prevention of misuse of public information) ; 17 C.F.R. § 275.204A-1 (2015) (requiring adviser to adopt code of ethics); 17 C.F.R. § 275.206(4)-7 (2015) (requiring adviser to adopt compliance procedures and practices)).
4. Exchange-Traded Funds, Investment Company Act Rel. No. 28193 (Mar. 11, 2008), 73 Fed. Reg. 14,618, 14,626-27 (Mar. 18, 2008) (citing 17 C.F.R. § 270.38a-1 (2015) (requiring investment company to adopt policies and procedures to prevent violations of securities laws); 17 C.F.R. § 240.17j-1 (2015); 15 U.S.C. § 80b-4a; 15 U.S.C. § 78*o*(g) (requiring a broker-dealer to adopt policies and procedures to prevent misuse of material nonpublic information by broker-dealer or associated person); NYSE, NYSE MKT Rules, Rule 1000A, Commentary .02(b)(1) (last amended May 14, 2012) (if index is maintained by broker-dealer or fund advisor, requiring "fire wall" around personnel with information on changes to the index and requiring that index be calculated by third party not a broker-dealer or fund advisor), *available at* http://wallstreet.cch.com/MKTtools/PlatformViewer.asp?SelectedNode=chp_1_7&manual=/MKT/rules/mkt-rules/). Proposed Rule 6c-11, which would have exempted certain ETFs without exemptive orders, was not adopted.

## F. Exchange Listing Standards

As ETFs are traded on securities exchanges, some ETFs raise issues under the listing standards of the exchanges.[1] An exchange is required to file proposed rule changes with the SEC for approval.[2] The listing and trading of a new derivative securities product by an exchange is not deemed a proposed rule change provided that the SEC has approved listing standards for a product class that would include the product and other conditions are met.[3] The exchanges have listing standards for ETFs that are based on, or represent, an index or portfolio of securities.[4] However, actively-managed ETFs require the exchanges to file for approval.[5]

To list an actively-managed ETF, or an ETF that does not meet the existing listing standards, an exchange must file a proposed rule change on Form 19b-4.[6] In determining whether to approve a Form 19b-4 request, the SEC looks to a number of factors including (1) the effectiveness of an arbitrage mechanism, to minimize the difference between the trade price and net asset value,[7] and (2) the liquidity of the underlying securities.[8]

---

1. For an overview of this issue, *see* Benjamin J. Haskin, James R. Burns, & James E. Doench, *Exchange Listing of ETFs: Key Concerns in the 19b-4 Process,* Inv. Law., Mar. 2015, at 12.
2. 15 U.S.C. § 78s(b); *see* 17 C.F.R. § 240.19b-4 (2015) (governing filings with respect to proposed rule changes).
3. 17 C.F.R. § 240.19b-4(e) (2015).
4. *E.g.,* NYSE, NYSE Arca Equities Rules, Rule 5.2(j)(3), *available at* http://nysearcarules.nyse.com/PCXtools/PlatformViewer.asp?SelectedNode=chp 1 1&manual=/PCX/pcxe/pcxe-rules/ (listing standards for "investment company units").
5. E.g., NYSE, NYSE Arca Equities Rules, Rule 8.600, *available at* http://nysearcarules.nyse.com/PCXtools/PlatformViewer.asp?SelectedNode=chp 1 1&manual=/PCX/pcxe/pcxe-rules/ (listing standards for "managed fund shares"); *id.* Commentary .01 (requiring filing for approval).
6. 17 C.F.R. § 240.19b-4(b)(1) (2015) (requiring filing on Form 19b-4); Form 19b-4, *available at* http://www.sec.gov/about/forms/form19b-4.pdf.
7. *E.g.*, Exchange Act Rel. No. 73424 (2014).
8. *E.g.,* Exchange Rel. No. 73706 (2014). Other factors include: (3) product complexity, i.e., whether the product would be understood by investors and other market participants, (4) the adequacy of the exchange's trade surveillance program, (5) a potentially risky investment strategy, and (6) the effect of the ETF on the prices of the underlying investments. *See* Benjamin J. Haskin, James R. Burns, & James E. Doench, *Exchange Listing of ETFs: Key Concerns in the 19b-4 Process,* Inv. Law., Mar. 2015, at 12, 14-15 (summarizing factors).

# Chapter 17

## Variable Insurance Products

### A. The History and Structure of Variable Insurance Products[1]

#### 1. Variable Annuities

A conventional annuity is an insurance company's obligation to pay the annuitant a fixed amount over a specified period and usually throughout the life of the annuitant or other persons. A buyer can pay for an annuity in one payment or in installments. When the buyer pays in installments, the payment of the annuity starts only after the price has been paid in full. Therefore, in such a case the annuity contract has two distinct periods: the "pay-in" period, during which the contract-holder makes installment payments on the annuity, and the "pay-out" period, during which the insurance company pays the annuity, unless the contract-holder chooses another option. The insurance company invests the annuity payments, subject to insurance regulation, which is usually conservative. At the end of 1960s, however, when the securities markets had shaken off the memories of the 1930s, insurance companies sought to offer annuitants investments in the securities markets. They then designed variable annuities, that is, annuities that were invested in the stock market.

The variable annuity is a retirement plan that offers insurance against unexpected longevity, together with investment opportunities and some tax benefits. Payments under this annuity vary with the investment performance of a fund; hence, the name "variable," in contrast to "fixed," annuity. A variable annuity is classified as both insurance and investment. This discussion focuses on the insurance aspect of the annuity and on its security aspect since it combines both.

There are many definitions for insurance. But its fundamental features are identical. Basically, it is a scheme for the pooling and distribution of risk. A life insurance covers the risk that a person might die early before that person accumulated sufficient assets for his or her dependents. If each of 10,000 persons has a risk of loss of earning of $100,000 upon death, and the probability is that 1 percent, namely 100, of the group will die in any given year, then payment of $10,000,000 will be sufficient to cover the loss

1. Derived from 1 Tamar Frankel & Ann Taylor Schwing, The Regulation of Money Managers, §§ 5-139 to -143, 5-155 to -158 (2001 & Supp. 2015).

due to early death. If each member of the group pays $1,000, each member is assured that, in the event of death, the designated beneficiary will receive $100,000. An individual who stays alive loses the $1,000 paid. This sum will go to cover the payments for those who died.

The converse scheme works in annuities. Individuals cannot divide their savings to last throughout their lifetime, since they do not know how long they will live. But if they pool their savings with 10,000 other persons, and each contributes $1,000 to a pool of $10,000,000, then, if it is known that 25 percent of the contract-holders will die each year, payments can be divided into four years. Those who live longer will obtain the payments of those who died sooner.

In order to constitute insurance, there must be risk of loss, the risk must be assumed by the insurer, the technique which the insurer must use is pooling and distribution, and the main purpose of the insurance contract must be protection; in life insurance it is protection of the insured's dependents or of those having an interest in the insured's life.

Variable annuities are based on the same insurance principles. However, whereas conventional annuities credit contract-holders with a fixed rate of return, all or some of the payments in variable annuities are linked to the investment performance of a separate fund invested in securities at the risk of the contract-holders. The insurance company invests the net installment payments — the reserves funding the variable annuities — in securities instead of in conservative investments, and contract-holders benefit from successful investments and suffer from investment losses. In the pay-in period, contract-holders in fact purchase units in a separate fund that invests in the securities. The more units purchased, the more money is invested. The value of units corresponds to the value of the underlying securities in the fund. During this period, there is no difference between the separate account funding the annuities and an investment company. In the pay-out period, an insurance feature is involved. No contract-holder has a claim to a proportionate share in the reserves. Contract-holders may obtain more or less than they paid in. In this respect, the reserves resemble insurance reserves, not assets of an investment company. But annuity payments are linked to the investment performance of the reserves.

When a contract-holder retires after all installment payments have been paid, the value of these contributions is determined. In a variable annuity with a variable feature during the pay-in period, the number of units that the contract-holder had accumulated is multiplied by the value of each unit. The value of each unit is determined by the proportionate value of the underlying securities in the account. Having determined the cash available to the contract-holder, the amount of annuity that can be purchased can be calculated and expressed in a specified number of dollars payable periodically. This amount is then converted into a number of units of the same value. From then on, the contract-holder receives periodic payments calculated according to the current value of this fixed number of units. The annuity payment varies with the value of the units, which in the case of a variable pay-out option varies with the value of the underlying securities.

The essence of the difference between fixed and variable annuities is that variable annuities are linked to the value of investment company shares, managed by the insurance company for the contract-holders' benefit, and at the contract-holders' risk. Conventional annuities are credited with a fixed percentage return that the insurance company pays whether or not the investment of the reserves produced this amount.

### 2. Variable Life Insurance Contracts

Variable life insurance contracts were a natural sequel to variable annuities. Variable annuities educated insurance companies and annuitants to "think variable." The companies became acquainted with the reality of securities regulation and with the potential source of profit from investment management services. Their actuaries went to work to construct a truly variable life insurance contract offering conventional policies and investment company shares combined: a contract that would pay not only a fixed-dollar amount but also the value of a number of shares of an investment company, whichever amount is higher, at the time when payment is due. The best of both worlds.

Variations on the main theme of a variable life insurance contract are many. All these contracts have a few basic features in common. Some features were influenced by the desire of the industry to be free of securities regulation and, in the case of contracts funded by separate accounts, exempt from some of the provisions of the 1940 Act by the conditions imposed by the SEC. Some of these very same features were also prompted by the industry desire to preserve the most valuable aspect of conventional insurance policies, namely, security and certainty. A variable life insurance contract is an insurance policy that links some of the payments under the policy to the investment performance of a fund invested and reinvested in securities, at least partially at the risk of the contract-holder. In some respects, the contract is identical to a conventional life insurance policy. In other respects, the contract is similar to a share in an investment company. On its insurance side, the contract is based on a life insurance model, in that death benefits and premiums are calculated on the basis of the age, health, and sometimes sex of the insured. The premiums are pooled (reserves) and obligations under the policies are paid from the reserves. Calculation of the premiums follows a conventional level premium policy. In the early years of the contract, the insurance company collects premiums in excess of the cost of insurance. This excess is in fact advanced by the contract-holder to cover the insurance cost in later years, when premiums will not be sufficient. As to all these features, a variable life insurance contract is like a conventional life insurance policy.

The contract differs from a conventional policy with respect to the investments of the reserves and excess payments and the bearers of the investment risks. In a conventional policy, regardless of the investment results of the premiums, the policyholders' beneficiaries receive a fixed amount. The insurance company profits if its investments bring higher returns. Its investments, however, are regulated. The arrangement with respect to variable life insurance contracts is different. Reserves and excess payments are allocated to a separate account and invested and reinvested in securities, and contract-holders take a substantial portion of the investment risk. The separate account's investment profits or losses are reflected in the payments under the contracts. The payments, however, are not directly proportional to the investment results, and the relationship between investment performance and contract payments may differ. Under some contracts, the payment will fluctuate more than under others, depending on the design and formula used.

## B. The Status of Variable Financial Instruments as Securities

Variable financial instruments present two issues under federal securities laws: First, are they securities; and second, is the separate account which funds them an investment company. Here we deal with the first issue. *SEC v. Variable Life Insurance Company of America*[1] shows that it is not helpful to pose the issue by asking whether these instruments are insurance or investment. They include features of both. The issue is, therefore, what problems they pose and what regulations would reduce these problems. The answer is that both regulatory systems apply, and are adjusted. The following is part of the opinion of Justice Douglas and concurring opinions of Justices Brennan and Stewart.

> Opinion: Mr. Justice Douglas delivered the opinion of the Court.
>
> Respondents are regulated under the insurance laws of the District of Columbia and several other States. It is argued that fact brings into play the provisions of the McCarran-Ferguson Act . . . which provides that "No Act of Congress shall be construed to invalidate, impair or supersede any law enacted by any State for the purpose of regulating the business of insurance. . . ." It is said that the conditions under which that law is applicable are satisfied here. The District of Columbia and some of the States are "regulating" these annuity contracts and, if the Commission is right, the Federal Acts would at least to a degree "supersede" the state regulations since the Federal Acts prescribe their own peculiar requirements. Moreover, "insurance" or "annuity" contracts are exempt from the Securities Act when "subject to the supervision of the insurance commissioner . . . of any State. . . ." Respondents are also exempt from the Investment Company Act if they are "organized as an insurance company, whose primary and predominant business activity is the writing of insurance . . . and which is subject to supervision by the insurance commissioner . . . of a State. . . ." While the term "security" as defined in the Securities Act is broad enough to include any "annuity" contract, and the term "investment company" as defined in the Investment Company Act would embrace an "insurance company," the scheme of the exemptions lifts *pro tanto* the requirements of those two Federal Acts to the extent that respondents are actually regulated by the States as insurance companies, *if indeed they are such.* The question common to the exemption provisions of the Securities Act and the Investment Company Act and to § 2 (b) of the McCarran-Ferguson Act is whether respondents are issuing contracts of insurance. . . .

1. *SEC v. Variable Annuity Life Insurance Co. of America,* 359 U.S. 65 (1959) (footnotes omitted).

While all the States regulate "annuities" under their "insurance" laws, traditionally and customarily they have been fixed annuities, offering the annuitant specified and definite amounts beginning with a certain year of his or her life. The standards for investment of funds underlying these annuities have been conservative. The variable annuity introduced two new features. First, premiums collected are invested to a greater degree in common stocks and other equities. Second, benefit payments vary with the success of the investment policy. The first variable annuity apparently appeared in this country about 1952 when New York created the College Retirement Equities Fund to provide annuities for teachers. It came into existence as a result of a search for a device that would avoid paying annuitants in depreciated dollars. The theory was that returns from investments in common stocks would over the long run tend to compensate for the mounting inflation. The holder of a variable annuity cannot look forward to a fixed monthly or yearly amount in his advancing years. It may be greater or less, depending on the wisdom of the investment policy. . . .

The difficulty is that, absent some guarantee of fixed income, the variable annuity places all the investment risks on the annuitant, none on the company. The holder gets only a *pro rata* share of what the portfolio of equity interests reflects — which may be a lot, a little, or nothing. We realize that life insurance is an evolving institution. Common knowledge tells us that the forms have greatly changed even in a generation. And we would not undertake to freeze the concepts of "insurance" or "annuity" into the mold they fitted when these Federal Acts were passed. But we conclude that the concept of "insurance" involves some investment risk-taking on the part of the company. The risk of mortality, assumed here, gives these variable annuities an aspect of insurance. Yet it is apparent, not real; superficial, not substantial. In hard reality the issuer of a variable annuity that has no element of a fixed return assumes no true risk in the insurance sense. It is no answer to say that the risk of declining returns in times of depression is the reciprocal of the fixed-dollar annuitant's risk of loss of purchasing power when prices are high and gain of purchasing power when they are low. We deal with a more conventional concept of risk-bearing when we speak of "insurance. . . ." For in common understanding "insurance" involves a guarantee that at least some fraction of the benefits will be payable in fixed amounts. . . . The companies that issue these annuities take the risk of failure. But they guarantee nothing to the annuitant except an interest in a portfolio of common stocks or other equities — an interest that has a ceiling but no floor. There is no true underwriting of risks, the one earmark of insurance as it has commonly been conceived of in popular understanding and usage. Reversed.

Concur: Mr. Justice Brennan with whom Mr. Justice Stewart joins, concurring.

I join the opinion and judgment of the Court. However, there are additional reasons which lead me to the Court's result, and since the nature of this case lends it to rather extended treatment, I will express these reasons separately.

*First.* The facts of this case are quite complex, but the basic problem involved is much more simple. . . . [The case involves the coverage of] the Securities Act of 1933 and the Investment Company Act of 1940. These Acts were specifically drawn to exclude any "insurance policy" and any "annuity contract" (Securities Act § 3 (a)(8)) and any "insurance company" (Investment Company Act § 3 (c)(3)) from their coverage. These exclusions were to take effect where the issuer of the policy or contract was subject to the supervision of the state "insurance commissioner, bank commissioner, or any agency or officer performing like functions" . . . or where a company classifiable as an "insurance company" was "subject to supervision by the insurance commissioner or a similar official or agency of a State. . . ." The exclusions left these contracts and companies to the sole control of such state officials. Except for these exclusions, there is little doubt that these contracts and the companies issuing them would be subject to the Federal Acts.

Why these exclusions? They could not have been made out of some general desire on the part of Congress to avoid any concurrent regulation by both the Federal Government and the States of investments or companies subject to the two Acts. On the contrary, § 18 of the Securities Act and § 50 of the Investment Company Act preserve generally the jurisdiction of state officials over their subject matter; the former in terms of "the jurisdiction of the securities commission (or any agency or office performing like functions) of any State" and the latter in terms of "the jurisdiction of any other commission, board, agency, or officer of . . . any State or political subdivision." Conversely, of course, however adequately State Securities Commissioners might regulate an investment, it was not for that reason to be freed from federal regulation. Concurrent regulation, then, was contemplated by the Acts as a quite generally prevailing matter. Nor is it rational to assume that Congress thought that *any* business whatsoever regulated by a specific class of officials, the State Insurance Commissioners, would be for that reason so perfectly conducted and regulated that all the protections of the Federal Acts would be unnecessary. This approach of personally selective deference to the state administrators is hardly to be attributed to Congress. The point must have been that there then was a form of "investment" known as insurance (including "annuity contracts") which did not present very squarely the sort of problems that the Securities Act and the Investment Company Act were devised to deal with, and which were, in many details, subject to a form of state regulation of a sort which made the federal regulation even less relevant.

At this time, of course, the sort of "variable annuity" contract with which we are concerned in this case did not exist. When Congress made the exclusions provided for in the Acts, it did not make them with the "variable annuity" contract before it. Of course, the point is not that if the insurance industry seeks to retain its exemption, it must limit itself to the forms of policies and contracts in effect in 1933 and 1940. But if a brand-new form of investment arrangement emerges which is labeled "insurance" or "annuity" by its promoters, the functional distinction that Congress set up in 1933 and 1940 must be examined to test whether the contract falls within the sort of investment form that Congress was then willing to leave exclusively to the State Insurance Commissioners. In that inquiry, an analysis of the regulatory and protective purposes of the Federal Acts and of state insurance regulation as it then existed becomes relevant.

At the core of the 1933 Act are the requirements of a registration statement and prospectus to be used in connection with the issuance of "securities" — that term being very broadly defined. Detailed schedules, set forth in the Act, list the material that the registration statement and the prospectus are to contain. The emphasis is on disclosure; the philosophy of the Act is that full disclosure of the details of the enterprise in which the investor is to put his money should be made so that he can intelligently appraise the risks involved.

The regulation of life insurance and annuities by the States proceeded, and still proceeds, on entirely different principles. It seems as paternalistic as the Securities Act of 1933 was keyed to free, informed choice. Prescribed contract clauses are ordained legislatively or administratively. Solvency and the adequacy of reserves to meet the company's obligations are supervised by the establishment of permissible categories of investments and through official examination. The system does not depend on disclosure to the public, and, once given this form of regulation and the nature of the "product," it might be difficult in the case of the traditional life insurance or annuity contract to see what the purpose of it would be. . . .

*Second.* Much bewilderment could be engendered by this case if the issue were whether the contracts in question were "really" insurance or "really" securities — one or the other. It is rather meaningless to view the problem as one of pigeonholing these contracts in one category or the other. Obviously they have elements of conventional insurance, even apart from the fixed-dollar term life insurance and the disability waiver of premium insurance sold with some of these contracts (both of which are quite incidental to the main undertaking). They patently contain a significant annuity feature (unless one defines an annuity as a contract necessarily providing fixed-sum payments), and the granting of annuities has been considered part of the business of life insurance. Of course, some urge that even the traditional annuity has few "insurance" features and is basically a form of investment. . . . But the point is that, even though these contracts contain, for what they are worth, features of traditional annuity contracts, administering them also involves a very substantial and in fact predominant element of the business of an investment company, and that in a way totally foreign to the business of a traditional life insurance and annuity company, as traditionally regulated by state law. This is what leads to the conclusion that it is not within the intent of the 1933 and 1940 statutes to exempt them.

The individual deferred variable annuity contract of respondent Variable Annuity Life Insurance Company (VALIC) gives a basis for exploration of this. A sample contract, given in evidence in the District Court, is one issued to a 35-year-old male, providing for his making 30 annual payments of $1,000 each. Of this, $39.60 is the consideration for an undertaking by the company by which payment of the annual $1,000 is waived in the event of disability. Of the remaining $960.40, designated the "basic annuity premium," specified percentages are used to credit to the account of the investor certain "accumulation units." Of the first year's "basic annuity premium," less than 45% is so used; for the next 4 years, the percentage is in the approximate range of 85% to 87%; for years 6 through 10, the figure is 89%, and for the remainder of the 30-year pay-in period it is 92%. Declining term life insurance in a fixed-dollar amount, beginning at five times the annual "basic annuity premium" the first year and declining through a period of 5 years to nil, is provided as a benefit over and above the "accumulation units" credited to the account of the investor. The contract is said to build up a "cash value" as the investor's payment "buys" further accumulation units, but while the value is one which can and would be finally settled by the payment of dollars, the obligation owed by the company to the investor is not one owed to him in dollar terms. It is one which is measured only in terms of "units" — the petitioners suggest a resemblance to "shares" — in a portfolio. The units are established by an arbitrary computation which has the effect of dividing the company's investment assets as of a starting day into a number of units, and assigning to each unit its share of the over-all market value — though the division is not in fact made. Then monthly the value of the units is recomputed. This is done, broadly, by taking into account all interest and dividends paid on the company's portfolio and all realized capital gains and losses, with relevant income taxes, together with all unrealized capital shrinkage and increase, less a monthly surcharge of 0.15% (1.8% per annum) of asset value. New dollars from investors which "buy" units buy them at the new rate, thus preventing dilution, and those investors who draw down their accumulated units receive cash for them at such rate.

The contract uses insurance terminology throughout and many of the common features of life insurance and annuity policies are operative in regard to it at this "pay-in" stage. . . . And very certainly the commitment of the company eventually to disburse the accumulated values on a life annuity basis once the pay-in period is over is present throughout this period. But what the investor is participating in during this period, despite its acknowledged "insurance" features, is something quite similar to a conventional open-end management investment company, under a periodic investment plan. . . . In this sort of operation, examination by state insurance officials to determine the adequacy of reserves and solvency becomes less and less meaningful. The disclosure policy of the Securities Act of 1933 becomes, by comparison, more and more relevant. And the detailed protections of the 1940 legislation — disclosure of investment policy, regulation of changes of that policy, of capital structure, conflicts of interest, investment advisers — all become relevant in an acute way here. These are the basic protections that Congress intended investors to have when they put their money into the hands of an investment trust; there is no adequate substitute for them in the traditional regulatory controls administered by state insurance departments, because these controls are not relevant to the specific regulatory problems of an investment trust.

The same conclusions follow from a consideration of the next stage of this contract. . . .

The effect of this is that the investor, during the pay-out period, is in almost every way as much a participant in something equivalent to an investment trust as before. . . .

Accordingly, while these contracts contain insurance features, they contain to a very substantial degree elements of investment contracts as administered by equity investment trusts. They contain these elements in a way different in kind from the way that insurance and annuity policies did when Congress wrote the exemptions for them in the 1933 Act and the 1940 Act. Since Congress was intending a broad coverage in both these remedial Acts and since these contracts present regulatory problems of the very sort that Congress was attempting to solve by them, I conclude that Congress did not intend to exclude contracts like these by reason of the "insurance" exemptions.

*Third.* The respondents contend that a reversal of the judgment will put them out of business. The reason given is that if the Investment Company Act of 1940 applies to them, they are probably categorizable under it as open-end management companies, and it is declared unlawful by § 18 of the Act for an open-end company to have outstanding any "senior security," that is, any security senior to any other class of securities. These companies have capital stock, and the contracts in question would be securities senior to the stock. If one assumes that this is correct, there is of course the possibility that the SEC might use its broad dispensing powers in this regard, and, in any event, the whole point would be of no concern at all if the contracts in question were issued by mutual companies. But in the final analysis, it is not decisive of the issues here that a holding that these contracts are subject to the Federal Acts might require some modification in the business of issuing them. Since these contracts are in fact covered by the Acts, there can be no reason why their issuers should be able to carry on the investment business in a way which Congress has forbidden.

Similarly, it may be conceded freely that this form of investment contract may be one of great potential benefit to the public. So, of course, may be orthodox open-end investment trusts, and they clearly are regulated by federal law. In short, notions that this form of arrangement is a desirable one and that it might be well to allow it to exist for a while immune from federal regulation are not relevant to the matter for decision. Congress regulates by general statutes. The passage of a federal regulatory statute is a delicate balancing of many national legislative interests and political forces. Congress need not go through the initial travail of re-enacting its general regulatory scheme every time a new form of enterprise is introduced, if that new form falls within the scheme's coverage. If there is deemed wise any adjustment of the regulatory scheme in the light of new developments in the subject matter to which it extends, Congress may make it.

Mr. Justice Harlan, whom Mr. Justice Frankfurter, Mr. Justice Clark and Mr. Justice Whittaker join, dissenting.

Variable annuity policies are a recent development in the insurance business designed to meet inflationary trends in the economy by substituting for annuity payments in fixed-dollar amounts payments in fluctuating amounts, measured ultimately by the company's success in investing the premium payments received from annuitants. One of the early pioneers in this field was Teachers Insurance and Annuity Association, a New York regulated life insurance organization engaged in selling annuities to college personnel. The Association in 1950 made exhaustive studies into the feasibility and soundness of variable annuities. Two years later, it incorporated College Retirement Equities Fund, a companion company under joint management with Teachers Insurance, which, subject to regulation under the New York Insurance Law, commenced offering such annuity contracts in the teaching profession. The first life insurance company to offer such contracts generally appears to have been the Participating Annuity Life Insurance Company, which since 1954 has been selling variable annuity policies under the supervision of the Arkansas insurance authorities. VALIC and EALIC [Equity Annuity Life Insurance Company] entered the field in 1955 and 1956 respectively.

The characteristics of a typical variable annuity contract have been adumbrated by the majority it is sufficient to note here that, as the majority concludes, as the two lower courts found, and as the SEC itself recognizes, it may fairly be said that variable annuity contracts contain both "insurance" and "securities" features. It is certainly beyond question that the "mortality" aspect of these annuities — that is the assumption by the company of the entire risk of longevity — involves nothing other than classic insurance concepts and procedures, and I do not understand how that feature can be said to be "not substantial," determining as it does, apart from options, the commencement and duration of annuity payments to the policyholder. On the other hand it cannot be denied that the investment policies underlying these annuities, and the stake of the annuitants in their success or failure, place the insurance company in a position closely resembling that of a company issuing certificates in a periodic payment investment plan. Even so, analysis by fragmentization is at best a hazardous business, and in this instance has, in my opinion, led the Court to unsound legal conclusions. It is important to keep in mind that these are not cases where the label "annuity" has simply been attached to a securities scheme, or where the offering companies are traveling under false colors, in an effort to avoid federal regulation. The *bona fides* of this new development in the field of insurance is beyond dispute.

The Court's holding that these two companies are subject to SEC regulation stems from its preoccupation with a constricted "color matching" approach to the construction of the relevant federal statutes which fails to take adequate account of the historic congressional policy of leaving regulation of the business of insurance entirely to the States. It would be carrying coals to Newcastle to re-examine here the history of that policy which was fully canvassed in the several opinions of the Justices in *United States v. South-Eastern Underwriters Assn* . . . and which was again implicitly recognized by this Court as recently as last Term when, in *Federal Trade Comm'n v. National Casualty Co.* . . . we declined to give a niggardly construction to the McCarran Act. Suffice it to say that in consequence of this Court's decision 90 years ago in *Paul v. Virginia* . . . and the many cases following it, there had come to be "widespread doubt" prior to the time the Securities and Investment Company Acts were passed "that the Federal Government could enter the field [of insurance regulation] at all. . . ."

I can find nothing in the history of the Securities Act of 1933 which savors in the slightest degree of a purpose to depart from or dilute this traditional federal "hands off" policy respecting insurance regulation. On the contrary, the exemption of insurance from that Act, which is couched in the broadest terms, reflected not merely adherence to tradition but also compliance with a supposed command of the Constitution. . . .

Similarly, I can find nothing in the history of the Investment Company Act of 1940 which points in any way to a change in federal policy on this score. Here tradition, perhaps more than constitutional doubt, explains the exemption of insurance companies from the Act. In hearings before the House Committee, Commissioner Healy of the SEC discussed the "face-amount installment certificates" issued by certain investment companies and often "sold on the basis of the comparison with savings bank deposits and insurance policies." The major factor appearing to distinguish these investment companies from insurance companies for purposes of federal control was the strict state regulation present over insurance policies but absent over investment certificates. . . . Likewise, in the Senate debates, preservation of state regulation over insurance companies appears as the crucial factor distinguishing them from investment trusts. . . . Stating that "the bill has nothing to do with the regulation of insurance companies," Senator Byrnes went on to say: "The platforms of both political parties have urged supervision of insurance by the several States, but not regulation by the Federal Government. . . ."

> In 1944, this Court removed the supposed constitutional basis for exemption of insurance by holding, in *United States v. South-Eastern Underwriters Assn., supra,* that the business of insurance was subject to federal regulation under the commerce power. Congress was quick to respond. It forthwith enacted the McCarran Act . . . which on its face demonstrates the purpose "broadly to give support to the existing and future state systems for regulating and taxing the business of insurance" . . . and "to assure that existing state power to regulate insurance would continue. . . ." Thus, rather than encouraging Congress to enter the field of insurance, the *South-Eastern* decision spurred reiteration of its undeviating policy of abstention.
>
> In this framework of history the course for us in these cases seems to me plain. We should decline to admit the SEC into this traditionally state regulatory domain.
>
> Admittedly the variable annuity was not in the picture when the Securities and Investment Company Acts were passed. . . . This, however, should not be allowed to obscure the fact that Congress intended when it enacted these statutes to leave the future regulation of the business of insurance wholly with the States. . . .
>
> It is asserted that state regulation, as it existed when the Securities and Investment Company Acts were passed, was inadequate to protect annuitants against the risks inherent in the variable annuity and that therefore such contracts should be considered within the orbit of SEC regulation. The Court is agreed that we should not "freeze" the concept of insurance as it then existed. By the same token we should not proceed on the assumption that the thrust of state regulation is frozen. As the insurance business develops new concepts the States adjust and develop their controls. This is in the tradition of state regulation and federal abstention. If the innovation of federal control is nevertheless to be desired, it is for the Congress, not this Court, to effect. I would affirm.

---

## Discussion Topics

a. How did the majority, the concurring opinion and the dissent approach the issue? Could you map out their approaches and the system by which they interpreted the statutes?

b. To what extent did the majority, concurring and dissent examine the nature of the variable annuity contract? On which part of the contract did they focus?

c. Facing any new complex hybrid financial instrument, which approach would you take? What questions would you ask?

---

## C. The Status of "Mixed" Contracts as Securities

Not all insurance contracts fall neatly into classification as a fixed contract or a variable contract. Some of the newer contracts combine features of both in ways that are more difficult to classify. One of the newcomers has caused considerable controversy regarding its regulation under the federal securities laws. Consider the following decision by Chief Judge Sentelle that dealt with an index annuity. Petitioners challenged Rule 151A under the Securities Act, which provided that fixed index annuities issued by an insurance corporation are not annuity contracts exempt from federal regulation. The opinion described fixed index annuities as follows:[1]

> A traditional fixed annuity is a contract issued by a life insurance company, under which the purchaser makes a series of premium payments to the insurer in exchange for a series of periodic payments from the insurer to the purchaser at agreed upon later dates. In a fixed annuity, the insurance company guarantees that the purchaser will earn a minimum rate of interest over time. Fixed annuities are subject to state insurance law regulation, and are exempt from federal securities laws. State insurance laws governing fixed annuity contracts require insurance companies to guarantee a minimum of the contract value after any costs and charges are applied. These state laws generally require the minimum guarantee be at least 87.5 percent of the premiums paid, accumulated at an annual interest rate of 1 to 3 percent. The laws also generally impose disclosure and suitability requirements, which vary from state to state.
>
> A fixed index annuity (FIA) is a hybrid financial product that combines some of the benefits of fixed annuities with the added earning potential of a security. Like traditional fixed annuities, FIAs are subject to state insurance laws, under which insurance companies must guarantee the same 87.5 percent of purchase payments. Unlike traditional fixed annuities, however, the purchaser's rate of return is not based upon a guaranteed interest rate. In FIAs the insurance company credits the purchaser with a return that is based on the performance of a securities index, such as the Dow Jones Industrial Average, Nasdaq 100 Index, or Standard & Poor's 500 Index. Depending on the performance of the securities index to which a particular FIA is tied, the return on an FIA might be much higher or lower than the guaranteed rate of return offered by a traditional fixed annuity. Due to the fact that the purchaser's actual return is linked to the performance of a securities index, however, the purchaser's return cannot be calculated until the end of the crediting period. Insurance companies typically apply an annual crediting period; that is, the index-linked interest of an FIA is typically calculated on an annual basis after each one-year period ends.
>
> B. While this is the first case in which we have had occasion to address the § 3(a)(8) annuity exemption as it regards FIAs, the Supreme Court has offered guidance on the scope of the exemption. . . . [T]he Supreme Court considered whether a variable annuity fell within the

1. *American Equity Investment Life Insurance Co. v. SEC,* 572 F.3d 923 (D.C. Cir. 2009) (footnotes and citations omitted), *amended by, vacated by, in part, on rehearing at* 2010 U.S. App. LEXIS 14249 (D.C. Cir. Jul. 12, 2010). Reprinted as amended at 2010 U.S. App. LEXIS 14257 (D.C. Cir., Jul. 12, 2010).

§ 3(a)(8) exemption. . . . The Court explained that a variable annuity did not fall within the § 3(a)(8) exemption because it placed "all the investment risks on the [purchaser], none on the company. . . ." In *United Benefit*, the Court concluded that another product similar to a variable annuity called a "Flexible Fund Annuity" was not exempt under § 3(a)(8) of the Act. A Flexible Fund functioned in much the same way as a variable annuity. Most notably, the purchaser paid premiums into a separate account that was primarily invested in common stocks, with the object of producing capital gains as well as an interest return. Unlike the variable annuity in *VALIC*, however, the insurer guaranteed that the purchaser would receive a percentage of his premiums back. This percentage gradually increased from 50 percent of net premiums in the first year to 100 percent after 10 years. United Benefit argued that, under *VALIC*, the existence *vel non* of substantial investment risk by the insurer ultimately determined whether a product fell within the § 3(a)(8) exemption.

The Court disagreed that *VALIC* should be interpreted so narrowly. Rather, the critical inquiry under § 3(a)(8) was whether the product at issue "'involve[d] considerations of investment not present in the conventional contract of insurance.'" In concluding that the Flexible Fund did not fall within § 3(a)(8), the Court relied significantly on the fact that the Flexible Fund "appeal[ed] to the purchaser not on the usual insurance basis of stability and security but on the prospect of 'growth' through sound investment management." Though the Court acknowledged that the "guarantee of cash value based on net premiums reduces substantially the investment risk of the contract holder," it reasoned further that "the assumption of an investment risk [by the insurer] cannot by itself create an insurance provision under the federal definition." The Court recognized that a "basic difference" exists between "a contract which to some degree is insured and a contract of insurance." In the case of the Flexible Fund, the insurer's assumption of risk was minimal. The insurer was "obligated to produce no more than the guaranteed minimum at maturity, and this amount is substantially less than that guaranteed by the same premiums in a conventional deferred annuity contract."

C. Since the Court's decisions in *VALIC* and *United Benefit*, the SEC has engaged in rulemaking to address the newer financial products that have entered the market. In the mid-1980s, the SEC promulgated Rule 151 in response to the creation of a new hybrid financial product called a guaranteed investment contract. Guaranteed investment contracts are like traditional fixed annuities, in that they promise a return at a guaranteed rate of return for the life of the contract. In some guaranteed investment contracts, however, the insurer may agree to periodically pay the purchaser an additional discretionary amount above the already guaranteed return amount. Rule 151 provided that, under certain conditions, a guaranteed investment contract would qualify for the § 3(a)(8) exemption notwithstanding an insurer's ability to pay a discretionary amount to the purchaser. Under Rule 151, a contract falls within the § 3(a)(8) exemption if:

(1) The annuity or optional annuity contract is issued by a corporation (the *insurer*) subject to the supervision of the insurance commissioner, bank commissioner, or any agency or officer performing like functions, of any State or Territory of the United States or the District of Columbia;

(2) The insurer assumes the investment risk under the contract as prescribed in paragraph (b) of this section; and

(3) The contract is not marketed primarily as an investment.

Though the SEC considered excluding from the Rule 151 safe harbor any product in which an issuer calculates the rate of any excess return by reference to an index, it concluded that an issuer may reference an index to set the excess return rate, but only if the rate is set *before* each crediting period begins and remains in effect for at least one year.

In the mid-1990s, insurance companies began marketing FIAs. The SEC did not take any regulatory action with respect to FIAs until 2007. By this time, the sales volume of FIAs had increased to $ 24.8 billion; indexed annuity assets totaled $ 123 billion. A total of 322 FIAs were being offered by 58 insurance companies. Having grown increasingly concerned that these FIAs were not being sold through registered broker-dealers and were not registered with the SEC despite their tie-in to a securities market, the SEC proposed Rule 151A. Rule 151A provides that a contract that is regulated as an annuity under state insurance law is not an "annuity contract" under § 3(a)(8) of the Act if:

(1) The contract specifies that amounts payable by the issuer under the contract are calculated at or after the end of one or more specified crediting periods, in whole or in part, by reference to the performance during the crediting period or periods of a security, including a group or index of securities; and

(2) Amounts payable by the issuer under the contract are more likely than not to exceed the amounts guaranteed under the contract.

By redefining an "annuity contract" to exclude FIAs, the Commission sought to ensure that purchasers of FIAs would be entitled to the full protection of the federal securities laws, including disclosure, antifraud, and sales practice protections.

To support this new rule, the SEC first noted that the Securities Act did not define "annuity contract," and that FIAs were not in existence at the time the "annuity contract" exemption in the Securities Act was enacted. Without express statutory guidance, the Commission looked to the reasoning set forth in the Supreme Court's decisions in *VALIC* and *United Benefit* to assess whether FIAs were the type of financial product that Congress would have been willing to leave to state insurance regulation.

The SEC began its analysis by considering the level of risk associated with FIAs. Citing *VALIC*, the Commission reasoned that "Congress intended to include in the insurance exemption only those policies and contracts that include a 'true underwriting of risks' and 'investment risk-taking' by the insurer. . . ." The annuities that were offered at the time of the enactment of the § 3(a)(8) exemption were fixed annuities that generally involved no investment risk to the purchaser. Therefore, the SEC reasoned, Congress was willing to offer a securities law exemption to these types of no risk products because, by their nature, they did not raise the kinds of problems or risks that the federal securities laws were intended to address. . . . Additionally, the state insurance laws in existence could adequately deal with any issues that might arise from such low risk insurance products. On the other hand, the SEC explained, "[i]ndividuals who purchase [FIAs] are exposed to a significant investment risk--*i.e.*, the volatility of the underlying securities index. . . ." At the time an FIA is purchased, the purchaser "assumes the risk of an uncertain and fluctuating financial instrument, in exchange for participation in future securities-linked returns. . . ." Unlike the guaranteed, fixed return offered by a traditional fixed annuity, the SEC asserted that an FIA's return was neither known nor guaranteed. The SEC acknowledged that "indexed annuities contracts provide some protection against the risk of loss," but determined that these provisions did not adequately transfer the investment risk from the purchaser to the insurer. Because the value of the purchaser's investment was entirely dependent upon an unknown and fluctuating securities index, the assumption of a guaranteed minimum percentage of the FIA, though giving FIAs an outward aspect of insurance, was a superficial and unsubstantial offset of the purchaser's risk. Therefore, the SEC reasoned that an FIA's value is much like that of a security, as the value of each product depends on the performance of the market. This securities-like investment risk, the SEC explained, was the exact type of investment risk that the Securities Act was created to address.

Though the SEC set forth in Rule 151 that the manner in which a product was marketed factored into the SEC's determination of whether it constituted an annuity contract under § 3(a)(8), the SEC opted not to include such an element in Rule 151A. The SEC noted that the performance of an FIA is obviously associated with the performance of a securities index, given the nature of the product. Moreover, the SEC noted that the Supreme Court in *VALIC* did not consider how the variable annuity was marketed in determining whether it fell within § 3(a)(8)'s exemption. For these reasons, the SEC felt that inclusion of a marketing element in Rule 151A was unnecessary.

The SEC supplemented its analysis of Rule 151A by undertaking a consideration of the rule's promotion of efficiency, competition, and capital formation, as is required by § 2(b) of the Act for certain SEC rulemakings.

* * *

The Court cited the SEC's consideration of how the rule would promote these objectives. First, Rule 151A would promote efficiency, extending the benefits of disclosure and sales practice protections of the federal securities laws to FIAs so that investors could make more informed investment decisions. Second, investors' informed investment decisions would increase competition between issuers of FIAs. Third, increased efficiency under Rule 151A would promote capital formation.

> Petitioners argue that Rule 151A is in conflict with the text of § 3(a)(8), the aforementioned decisions of the Court, and the text of the SEC's prior rule, Rule 151 [and] that the SEC failed to undertake properly its statutory responsibility to consider Rule 151A's effect on efficiency, competition, and capital formation, pursuant to § 2(b) of the Act. We will address each argument in turn.
>
> When an agency is given express authority to execute and enforce its enabling statute and to prescribe such rules and regulations as are or may be necessary to carry out provisions of the statute, courts must apply a two-step analysis in reviewing the agency's interpretation of the statute under *Chevron U.S.A. Inc. v. Natural Res. Def. Council, Inc.* Section 19(a) of the Act bestows upon the SEC the power to define terms and make rules to that effect. 15 U.S.C. § 77s(a). Rule 151A, which interprets the term "annuity contract" in § 3(a)(8) of the Act is clearly such a rule.
>
> Under *Chevron*, we first determine whether the statute being interpreted is ambiguous. If "Congress has directly spoken to the precise question at issue . . . [then] that is the end of the matter; for the court, as well as the agency, must give effect to the unambiguously expressed intent of Congress." On the other hand, if the court determines that the statute is either "silent or ambiguous with respect to the specific issue," then *Chevron* Step One is satisfied. Here, *Chevron* Step One is satisfied because the Act is ambiguous, or at the very least silent, on whether the term "annuity contract" encompasses all forms of contracts that may be described as annuities. Indeed, the analyses in the Supreme Court's decisions in *VALIC* and *United Benefit* confirm this ambiguity. Had the statute been unambiguous, the Court need not have undertaken such an exhaustive inquiry in determining whether the two products at issue in those cases were annuities under § 3(a)(8) of the Act.
>
> Petitioners nevertheless argue that the Court's decisions in *VALIC* and *United Benefit* establish that an "annuity" falls outside of § 3(a)(8) only if it is subject to the insurer's investment management, and not subject to state insurance laws. Given the absence of these two elements, petitioners assert, § 3(a)(8) clearly governs FIAs because FIAs are not subject to the insurer's investment management and are governed by a panoply of state insurance laws. Petitioners' argument misses the mark because it interprets *VALIC* and *United Benefit* too restrictively.
>
> Nothing in those cases indicated that the Court's determination whether the § 3(a)(8) exemption applies to particular contracts

depends on the investment management of the issuer and the applicability of state insurance regulation. Rather, the Court embraced a broader approach in its § 3(a)(8) analysis. The Court clearly indicated in both *VALIC* and *United Benefit* that the § 3(a)(8) exemption applied to products that "did not present very squarely the sort of problems that the Securities Act . . . [was] devised to deal with, and which were, in many details, subject to a form of state regulation of a sort which made the federal regulation even less relevant." The Court therefore focused its § 3(a)(8) analysis on whether the product at issue "involve[d] considerations of investment not present in the conventional contract of insurance." Though an insurer's investment management actions associated with a product may be relevant to determining whether that product is an annuity, this is not the only relevant characteristic. Petitioners' reliance on the existence of state law regulation governing FIAs is also too limited. The Court recognized in *United Benefit* that it had "conclusively rejected" in *VALIC* the argument that the existence of adequate state regulation was the basis for the § 3(a)(8) exemption. Therefore, the fact that FIAs are subject to state insurance regulation does not, without more, place them within the § 3(a)(8) exemption. Accordingly, the language of § 3(a)(8) does not unambiguously include FIAs within the § 3(a)(8) exemption. In light of the fact that the statute is ambiguous with respect to the term "annuity contract," we reiterate that *Chevron* Step One is satisfied.

We must next determine whether the SEC's rule is a reasonable interpretation of the statute. The SEC's rule will satisfy Step Two of the *Chevron* analysis so long as it meets this requirement. It is irrelevant that this court might have reached a different--or better--conclusion than the SEC.

In this case, the SEC has adopted an interpretation that is based in reason. By their nature, FIAs "appeal to the purchaser not on the usual insurance basis of stability and security but on the prospect of 'growth' through sound investment management." An FIA is akin to an annuity contract with respect to its pay-in and guaranteed minimum value of purchase payment features. The interest return rate of an FIA, however, is decidedly more like a security in that the index-based return of an FIA is not known until the end of a crediting cycle, as the rate is based on the actual performance of a specified securities index during that period. Similar to an investor in securities, a purchaser of an FIA knows the level of annual return he will receive once the year is concluded and the index's value is compared with its value at the beginning of the year. In FIAs, as in securities, there is a variability in the potential return that results in a risk to the purchaser. By contrast, an annuity contract falling under Rule 151's exemption avoids this variability by guaranteeing the interest rate ahead of time. As these characteristics show, FIAs "involve considerations of investment not present in the conventional contract of insurance." Accordingly, the SEC's interpretation that an FIA does not constitute an "annuity contract" under § 3(a)(8) of the Act was reasonable.

Petitioners assert that the SEC based its analysis of Rule 151A on an "insupportable definition of investment risk." The SEC determined that a purchaser bears sufficient risk to treat a product as a security when "[a]mounts payable by the issuer under the contract are more likely than not to *exceed* the amounts guaranteed under the contract. . . ." In petitioners' view, investment risk exists only where the purchaser of a security faces the possibility of a loss of principal. Petitioners' view is certainly a defensible one. However, that is not sufficient to establish that the SEC's rule is arbitrary or capricious. As the SEC points out, comparing two slightly different annuity products--one with a 5 percent interest rate guaranteed ahead of time; one with an interest rate that could be between 1 and 10 percent determined at the end of the year--the second product is riskier than the first product because its potential return could be lower than the rate of return from the first product, even though it guarantees a minimum return rate of at least 1 percent. Moreover, the SEC has also been consistent in its position on investment risk. When it adopted Rule 151, which provided a safe harbor to certain types of annuity contracts including those that based interest payments on an investment index, the SEC noted that it was allowing products involving investment indices with the caveat that such index-based interest rates be calculated in advance of the upcoming year. This, the SEC said, would minimize the investment risk exposure of the purchaser. We cannot hold that this interpretation is unreasonable.

Petitioners' argument that the SEC failed to balance the investment risks assumed by the insurer against those assumed by the purchaser misses the mark. To the contrary, the SEC considered the risk to insurers, and weighed that risk against the risk to the FIA customer in determining whether the product is an annuity or security. . . . The SEC concluded in its adopting release that annuities were those products that included a "true underwriting of risks" and "investment risk-taking" by the insurer, with more minimal risk exposure to the purchaser. . . . In traditional fixed annuities, "the insurer bears the investment risk under the contract. . . ." FIAs did not fall within this term because insurers offering FIAs left a more than minimal risk upon the purchaser. Rule 151A appears to be the SEC's means of ensuring greater protection for consumers exposed to greater risk when insurers are exposed to less risk than normal. Indeed, the rule "sets forth a test" to distinguish between those contracts where the insurer bears more risk by paying a fixed amount, and those in which the purchaser bears more risk because he will receive a variable amount that is dependent upon fluctuating stock market prices. . . . Such an approach, in light of this risk assessment, is reasonable. Petitioners' argument that the SEC's adoption of Rule 151A was in error because it allegedly failed to consider and balance the investment risks of the insurer and purchaser fails.

Petitioners' further argument that the SEC failed to account for marketing in considering whether a product is a security, though raising a closer issue, does not demonstrate that the SEC's adoption of

Rule 151A is unreasonable. Admittedly, the Supreme Court in *United Benefit* recognized that marketing is another significant factor in determining whether a state-regulated insurance contract is entitled to be exempt under § 3(a)(8). The SEC echoed this point when it enacted Rule 151 by stating that a product issued by a state-regulated insurance company falls within the § 3(a)(8) exemption if (1) the insurer assumes the investment risk of the contract and (2) "*[t]he contract is not marketed primarily as an investment.*" Nevertheless, the SEC's conclusion that an analysis of marketing was unnecessary for FIAs because "[i]t would be inconsistent with the character of such an indexed annuity, and potentially misleading, to market the annuity without placing significant emphasis on the securities-linked return and the related risks" is not unreasonable.

At the outset, the Supreme Court never held in either *VALIC* or *United Benefit* that marketing was an essential characteristic in assessing whether a product falls within the § 3(a)(8) exemption. Rather, as discussed above, the Court focused its inquiry on whether the product exhibited "considerations of investment not present in the conventional contract of insurance." The fact that the Court considered how Flexible Funds were marketed only shows that that inquiry was relevant to Flexible Funds. It does not establish that the SEC must undertake a complete marketing analysis of FIAs in order to make a proper § 3(a)(8) determination. Regardless of that fact, the SEC did consider marketing of FIAs, and ultimately deemed the inclusion of this factor to be unnecessary. Again, we cannot say that the SEC's decision was unreasonable. Indeed, the key characteristic of FIAs is that they offer a wide range of potential yearly return interest rates based on the performance of a securities index. This potential for a greater rate of return is what makes FIAs potentially more enticing than those exempt annuities that guarantee an interest rate ahead of time but at a lower rate. As we have noted above, this key distinction between these two products shows that FIAs are more like securities from a risk perspective than other annuity contracts. Where, as here, the essential characteristic of the product bestows upon those product obvious securities-like qualities, it is reasonable to assume that any marketing of the product would correspondingly be securities-related. It was also therefore reasonable for the SEC to find that the structure of FIAs--in particular the potential of securities-linked returns-is itself an implicit marketing tool aimed at consumers who wish to participate to some extent in the securities market, and that the rule need not contain an additional explicit prong addressed to marketing. Indeed, this is in line with much of the analysis in *United Benefit.* The SEC's reasoning therefore was not in error.

Contrary to petitioners' arguments, Rule 151A does not conflict with Rule 151. Petitioners assert that Rule 151's adopting release states that annuity contracts that have interest rates tied to a securities index can fall within the Rule 151 safe harbor so long as the rate of interest to be credited is not modified more frequently than once a year. They argue that FIAs fall within Rule 151's safe harbor because the interest rate tied to the securities index is only determined once a year. This argument fails, however, because it ignores an express statement in the same portion of the adopting release of Rule 151 which states that annuity contracts that have interest rates tied to a securities index can fall within the Rule 151 safe harbor if the rate tied to the securities index is calculated prospectively. FIAs, however, do not calculate their rates of return tied to securities indices prospectively; their rates are calculated retroactively once the year is complete. Rule 151A is premised on this very distinction, and is therefore not in contradiction with Rule 151.

For these reasons, we hold that the SEC's interpretation of "annuity contract" was reasonable and *Chevron* Step Two is satisfied.

B. Even though the SEC's interpretation of "annuity contract" was reasonable, petitioners argue that the SEC contravened § 2(b) of the Act because it failed to consider the efficiency, competition, and capital formation effects of the new Rule 151A. Section 2(b) of the Act states that, for every rulemaking in which the SEC "is required to consider or determine whether an action is necessary or appropriate in the public interest, the Commission shall also consider, in addition to the protection of investors, whether the action will promote efficiency, competition, and capital formation." Petitioners argue that the costs of implementing Rule 151A are too burdensome and that the imposition of additional regulations would be inefficient. They also contend that the SEC failed to properly assess the existence of abuses of FIAs before applying securities regulations on the issuers of those products. The SEC counters that it properly rejected petitioners' concerns regarding duplicative regulation because the Supreme Court's decisions in *VALIC* and *United Benefit* made clear that state regulatory approaches to new products are not conclusive in a § 3(a)(8) analysis. In any event, the SEC argues that the challenges to its efficiency, competition, and capital formation analysis under § 2(b) fail because the SEC was not required to undertake such an analysis when it promulgated Rule 151A.

At the outset, we must reject the SEC's argument that no error occurred because the SEC was not required by the Securities Act to conduct a § 2(b) analysis. "The grounds upon which an administrative order must be judged are those upon which the record discloses that its action was based." The SEC conducted a § 2(b) analysis when it issued the rule with no assertion that it was not required to do so. Therefore, the SEC must defend its analysis before the court upon the basis it employed in adopting that analysis.

We now turn to the merits of the SEC's § 2(b) analysis. We review the analysis under the statutory standard set by the Administrative Procedure Act. 5 U.S.C. § 706. The APA requires the court to set aside agency action that is "arbitrary, capricious, an abuse of discretion, or otherwise not in accordance with law." We hold that the Commission's consideration of the effect of Rule 151A on efficiency, competition, and capital formation was arbitrary and capricious. The SEC purports to have analyzed the effect of the rule on competition, but does not disclose a reasoned basis for its conclusion that Rule 151A would increase competition. The SEC concluded that enacting the rule would resolve the present uncertainty prevailing over the legal status of FIAs. The SEC reasoned that the rule "will bring about clarity in what has been an uncertain area of law." The SEC explained that this newfound "clarity" brought about by the rule would

> enhance competition because insurers who may have been reluctant to issue indexed annuities, while their status was uncertain, may decide to enter the market. Similarly, registered broker-dealers who currently may be unwilling to sell unregistered indexed annuities because of their uncertain regulatory status may become willing to sell indexed annuities that are registered, thereby increasing competition among distributors of indexed annuities.

This reasoning is flawed. The lack of clarity resulting from the "uncertain legal status" of the financial product is only another way of saying that there was not a regulation in place prior to the adoption of Rule 151A determining the status of those products under the annuity exemption of § 3(a)(8). The SEC cannot justify the adoption of a particular rule based solely on the assertion that the existence of a rule provides greater clarity to an area that remained unclear in the absence of any rule. Whatever rule the SEC chose to adopt could equally be said to make the previously unregulated market clearer than it would be without that adoption. Moreover, the fact that federal regulation of FIAs would bring "clarity" to this area of the law is not helpful in assessing the effect Rule 151A has on competition. Again, creating a rule that resolves the "uncertain legal status" of FIAs might be said to improve competition. But that conclusion could be asserted regardless of whether the rule deems FIAs to fall within the SEC's regulatory reach or outside of it. Indeed, the SEC would achieve a similar clarity if it declined outright to regulate FIAs. Section 2(b) does not ask for an analysis of whether *any* rule would have an effect on competition. Rather, it asks for an analysis of whether the *specific rule* will promote efficiency, competition, and capital formation. The SEC's reasoning with respect to competition supports at most the conclusion that any SEC action in this area could promote competition, but does not establish Rule 151A's effect on competition. Section 2(b) requires more than this.

The SEC's competition analysis also fails because the SEC did not make any finding on the existing level of competition in the marketplace under the state law regime. The SEC asserted competition would increase based upon its expectation that Rule 151A would require fuller public disclosure of the terms of FIAs and thereby increase price transparency. The SEC could not accurately assess any potential increase or decrease in competition, however, because it did not assess the baseline level of price transparency and information disclosure under state law. The SEC nevertheless argues that it is not required to conduct such a detailed § 2(b) analysis because doing so would contravene the Supreme Court's reasoning in *United*

*Benefit* and *VALIC*. According to the Commission, these two cases established that adequate state regulation is not relevant to whether a product qualifies for a § 3(a)(8) exemption. Therefore, the SEC argues, it was reasonable to conclude that state regulation, "no matter how strong," could not "substitute for the federal securities law protections that apply to instruments that are regulated as securities." The SEC's reliance on *VALIC* and *United Benefit* is misplaced. The SEC's obligations under § 2(b) are distinct from the questions posed in *VALIC* and *United Benefit*. Those cases addressed whether a particular product fell within the § 3(a)(8) exemption; § 2(b) imposes on the SEC an obligation to consider the economic implications of certain rules it proposes. Accordingly, the SEC's § 2(b) analysis is arbitrary and capricious because it failed to consider the extent of the existing competition in its analysis.

The Commission's efficiency analysis is similarly arbitrary and capricious. The SEC concluded that Rule 151A would promote efficiency because the required disclosures under the rule would enable investors to make more informed investment decisions about purchasing indexed annuities. The SEC advanced further that the rule's sales practice protections would enable sellers to promote more suitable recommendations to investors; this, in turn, would lead to investors making even better informed decisions, which would offer greater efficiency. As with its analysis of competition, however, the SEC's analysis is incomplete because it fails to determine whether, under the existing regime, sufficient protections existed to enable investors to make informed investment decisions and sellers to make suitable recommendations to investors. The SEC's failure to analyze the efficiency of the existing state law regime renders arbitrary and capricious the SEC's judgment that applying federal securities law would increase efficiency.

Finally, the SEC's flawed efficiency analysis also renders its capital formation analysis arbitrary and capricious. The SEC's conclusion that Rule 151A would promote capital formation was based significantly on the flawed presumption that the enhanced investor protections under Rule 151A would increase market efficiency. This analysis fails with the failure of its underlying premise.

Having determined that the SEC's § 2(b) analysis is lacking, we grant the petitions insofar as they assert that the SEC failed properly to consider the effect of the rule upon efficiency, competition, and capital formation.

* * *

We therefore order that Rule 151A be vacated.

---

**Discussion Topics:**

a. How different is a mortality risk from an investment risk?

b. Whose investment risk is involved in this case?

c. Why should the way in which a contract is marketed determine its status under the federal securities laws?

d. What aspects of the index annuities posed a problem for the issuer?

e. Is the rule adequate in light of the fact that state laws are not uniform in regulating insurance?

f. Evaluate the requirement in section 2(b). Does it make sense to impose on the SEC the requirement to evaluate the efficiency and cost of a regulation? Is there any requirement to determine the lack of efficiency when no rule exists? If not, why not?

---

## D. The Status of Separate Accounts as Investment Companies

The *Prudential* case held that separate accounts which offer variable products are within the definition of investment companies. What are the differences between insurance regulation and 1940 Act regulation? Essentially, the 1940 Act is designed to protect the interests of investors in their relationship with the adviser and other fiduciaries that serve them. Insurance laws are designed to protect policyholders by ensuring the safety and soundness of the insurance company that has undertaken to pay them certain amounts under certain conditions. Presumably, if the insurance company is profitable and careful in its investments and operations, it would be able to meet its long-term obligations to the policyholders. Therefore, insurance laws do not aim at reducing the income of insurance companies, while the 1940 Act aims at creating an environment in which investors will receive fees comparable to those negotiated at arm's length.

The following no-action letter highlights the approaches that insurance companies are taking in creating separate accounts and the conceptual morass involved in the insurance company — investment company debate. What useful guidelines are available to provide a clearer roadmap to answer the issues involved?

On December 20, 1995, the SEC staff granted a no-action letter to Equitable Life Assurance Society of the United States (Equitable Life) for amending certain annuity contracts that contain a market value adjustment feature.[1] The amendment would provide for legal insulation of the non-unitized separate accounts ("Accounts") that support Equitable Life's liabilities under the MVA Contracts, and Equitable Life does not intend to register the Accounts pursuant to the Investment Company Act of 1940.

> *I. Operation of the MVA Contracts*
>
> **A. MVA Contract Guarantees**
>
> The holder of an MVA Contract may elect one or more of several "Guarantee Periods" offered by Equitable Life. A Guarantee Period is a period of time with a specified expiration date ("Expiration Date") during which Equitable Life will credit a guaranteed rate ("Guaranteed Rate") of interest to amounts allocated by the holder

---

1. The Equitable Life Assurance Society of the United States, SEC No-Action Letter (Dec. 22, 1995).

to that Guarantee Period. For each business day, Equitable Life establishes a Guaranteed Rate of interest for each Guarantee Period. The Guaranteed Rate established for a specified Guarantee Period and business day applies to all amounts newly allocated to that Guarantee Period on that day and continues in effect as to such amounts so long as they remain allocated to that Guarantee Period. This results in an amount credited to the holder at the Expiration Date ("Maturity Value") that is guaranteed by Equitable Life and is mathematically determinable in advance.

The Guaranteed Rate established for a Guarantee Period each business day is in large part based on then-current yields for zero coupon corporate securities with approximately the same maturity as that Guarantee Period, less a "spread" established by Equitable Life. Neither the return earned by assets in the Accounts nor any realized or unrealized gains or losses in the Accounts' assets are considered by Equitable Life in setting Guaranteed Rates. Rather, such rates are based on considerations that are solely prospective in nature.

**B. MVA Contract "Market Value Adjustment"**

Subject to certain restrictions, the holder of an MVA Contract may withdraw or transfer his or her interest allocated to a Guarantee Period prior to the Expiration Date. In the event of such a premature withdrawal or transfer, the value of the holder's interest on the withdrawal or transfer date ("Annuity Account Value") is the then present value of the Maturity Value. The discount rate used to compute the Annuity Account Value is generally the Guaranteed Rate applicable on the withdrawal or transfer date to new allocations made to that same Guarantee Period (i.e., the Guarantee Period having the same Expiration Date). As a result, on any business day prior to the Expiration Date, the amount that a holder may withdraw or transfer from a Guarantee Period having a given Maturity Value is generally the same as the amount that would need to be allocated to that Guarantee Period on that date to provide that same Maturity Value. This precludes holders from seeking to profit by withdrawing funds earning a particular Guaranteed Rate from a Guarantee Period and simultaneously reallocating those funds to the same Guarantee Period at a time when Equitable Life is offering a higher Guaranteed Rate.

If the Guaranteed Rates for a Guarantee Period are different at the time a holder allocates monies to the Guarantee Period and the time he or she makes a premature surrender or withdrawal, the holder's Annuity Account Value on surrender or withdrawal will be different from the "Guaranteed Period Amount," which is the amount the holder originally allocated to the Guarantee Period, plus interest accumulated to the surrender or withdrawal date at the Guaranteed Rate applicable at the time of the original allocation. The difference between the Annuity Account Value and the Guaranteed Period Amount is the "market value adjustment." The market value adjustment results from any difference between the Guaranteed Rates for a Guarantee Period at the time the holder of an MVA Contract allocates monies to the Guarantee Period and the time he or she makes a premature surrender or withdrawal. The amount of the market value adjustment is not determined by the market value of any assets or class of assets, including assets maintained in the Accounts, or any index, except to the extent that Equitable Life's daily establishment of Guaranteed Rates takes account of certain then-current market rates of interest.

*II. Background and Business Purposes of Non-Unitized Separate Accounts*

The Request Letter represents that insurers generally have maintained assets supporting market value adjustment contracts in non-unitized separate accounts primarily to permit such assets to be valued on a market value basis, rather than an amortized cost basis, for purposes of state insurance law requirements. Equitable Life believes that valuation of assets and liabilities associated with MVA Contracts on a market value basis, rather than an amortized cost basis, results in a more timely and direct reflection of market value adjustment contract operations in statutory financial statements. Equitable Life also believes that use of a non-unitized separate account facilitates the establishment and monitoring of specific investment policies appropriate to the assets supporting the MVA Contracts.

In establishing the Accounts, Equitable Life was motivated primarily by the foregoing considerations. If the MVA Contracts are amended to provide for legal insulation of the Accounts, the holders of MVA Contracts will, in the event of Equitable Life's liquidation under circumstances where it could not pay all of its insurance obligations, have a priority claim to the portion of the related Account's assets covered by the insulation provision, while retaining the right to share in the general assets of Equitable Life to the extent of any deficiency in amounts available from the Account. Legal insulation for the Accounts would therefore serve the additional purpose of providing the holders of MVA Contracts with enhanced assurance that, in the event of Equitable Life's liquidation under circumstances where it could not pay all of its insurance obligations, sufficient assets will be available to satisfy Equitable Life's obligations with respect to the MVA Contracts. Equitable Life believes that this additional protection may enhance its competitive position with respect to the sale of MVA Contracts.

*III. Account Investment Experience is Not Passed Through to the Holders of MVA Contracts*

Amounts received by the holders of MVA Contracts upon maturity do not depend upon the investment experience of the Accounts. As described above, upon the Expiration Date of a Guarantee Period, the holder of an MVA Contract receives the amount originally allocated to the Guarantee Period, plus interest accumulated to the Expiration Date at the Guaranteed Rate. This amount, which is guaranteed by Equitable Life and is mathematically determinable in advance, is not affected by the investment experience of the related Account.

Nor do amounts received by the holders of MVA Contracts upon premature withdrawal or surrender depend upon the investment experience of the Accounts. The amount of any market value adjustment results from and depends on the difference between the Guaranteed Rates for a Guarantee Period at the time the holder of an MVA Contract allocates monies to the Guarantee Period and the time he or she makes a premature surrender or withdrawal. In setting Guaranteed Rates, Equitable Life does not consider the investment performance of the related Account.

The assets maintained in the Accounts are the property of Equitable Life and are managed as a part of its business. Like assets supporting traditional insurance products other than the MVA Contracts, Account assets are managed with the ultimate objective of generating a return to Equitable Life that, after payment of all obligations to holders of MVA Contracts, covers expenses and provides a profit to Equitable Life. To the extent these efforts are successful, Equitable Life retains the resulting profit. To the extent they are unsuccessful, Equitable Life bears the resulting loss.

*IV. Obligations of Equitable Life*

When the holder of an MVA Contract holds his or her interest to the Expiration Date, Equitable Life is obligated, without regard to the value of Account assets, to pay the full amount allocated to the Guarantee Period, plus accumulated interest at the Guaranteed Rate, as in the case of fixed insurance products. Equitable Life is also obligated, without regard to the value of Account assets, to pay the Annuity Account Value to a holder who makes a premature withdrawal or surrender. So long as Equitable Life is not liquidated under circumstances where it could not pay all of its insurance obligations, holders of MVA Contracts have no claim against the Accounts. Moreover, even in the event of Equitable Life's liquidation under circumstances where it could not pay all of its insurance obligations, the holder of an MVA Contract has a claim against the related Account's assets and against Equitable Life that is measured not by the value of the Account's assets or the Account's investment performance over any period of time, but by a mathematical formula based on Guaranteed Rates.

State insurance laws require life insurance companies periodically to value their assets and liabilities according to prescribed accounting principles. These laws require that the insurer maintain an excess of such "statutory assets" over "statutory liabilities" of at least a prescribed amount — i.e., a minimum amount of statutory capital and surplus. The minimum capital and surplus required of Equitable Life in its domiciliary state of New York is $2 million. As a practical matter, Equitable Life has statutory capital and surplus far in excess of that amount — approximately $2 billion at September 30, 1995. Under New York law, providing legal insulation for a separate account does not affect the computation of (or the required minimum amount of) an insurer's statutory capital and surplus.

New York state has adopted regulations applicable to market value adjustment contracts and the non-unitized separate accounts that fund them. Under New York law, Equitable Life is required to value the assets and contract liabilities of the Accounts at least annually. In addition, the law imposes on Equitable Life an ongoing requirement to maintain Account assets at least equal to the Account's contract liabilities, and procedures must be maintained to assure that this requirement is satisfied. If the liabilities exceed the assets, Equitable Life is required immediately to transfer sufficient assets into the Account to remedy the shortfall. On the other hand, whenever the value of an Account's assets exceeds the value of the Account's contract liabilities, state law permits Equitable Life to transfer the surplus to its general account. Holders of MVA Contracts have no claim upon or interest in such transferred assets, except that such assets are part of Equitable Life's general account. Equitable Life represents that the value of the assets maintained in each Account will at all times at least equal the amount of that Account's contract liabilities, both determined as required by New York law.

Providing legal insulation for the Accounts will not change the New York insurance law requirements as to contributing, withdrawing, and maintaining Account assets; nor will it change Equitable Life's practices in these regards.

*V. Marketing the MVA Contracts*

Equitable Life will take steps to ensure that its marketing program and materials refer to the Accounts as pools of assets that provide an additional measure of assurance that the holders of MVA Contracts will receive full payment and not as investment vehicles in whose performance the holders of MVA Contracts will have any interest.

*VI. Conclusion*

In *Hartford Life Insurance Company* (pub. avail. Oct. 29, 1984) ("*Hartford*"), we indicated that we would not recommend enforcement action against an insurance company that established a non-unitized separate account to support its liabilities under annuity contracts that contain a "market value adjustment" feature without registration of the account under the Investment Company Act. We believe that legal insulation of the account alone should not alter the *Hartford* conclusion. We have therefore reconsidered the *Travelers* and *Fortis* letters and have determined that the position taken in those letters regarding legally insulated non-unitized separate accounts supporting annuity contracts that contain a "market value adjustment" feature no longer represents the views of the Division. A non-unitized separate account that supports an annuity contract that contains a "market value adjustment" feature is not an issuer for purposes of section 3(a) of the Investment Company Act solely because the separate account is legally insulated. Legal insulation provides an additional protection for the holder of such a contract, which does not change the fact that the insurance company is obligated to pay the holder an amount that is mathematically determinable and not dependent on the investment experience of the account.

Based on the representations in the Request Letter, and without necessarily agreeing with your legal analysis, the staff would not recommend enforcement action against Equitable Life if the MVA Contracts are amended to provide for legal insulation of the Accounts without registration of the Accounts pursuant to the Investment Company Act. Our conclusion is based in particular on the representations that:

(1) a holder of an MVA Contract receives an amount upon maturity that is mathematically determinable in advance and is not affected by the investment experience of the related Account;

(2) a holder of an MVA Contract who makes a premature withdrawal or surrender receives an amount adjusted by a mathematical formula based on changes in guaranteed interest rates and not based on the investment experience of the related Account;

(3) Equitable Life is obligated to pay all amounts due to the holder of an MVA Contract without regard to the value of the related Account's assets, and Equitable Life retains the profits and bears the losses from Account operations;

(4) Equitable Life is obligated under state law to maintain Account assets at least equal to the related contract liabilities and immediately to transfer to an Account sufficient assets to remedy any shortfall, and Equitable Life represents that the value of the assets in each Account will at all times at least equal the amount of that Account's contract liabilities;

(5) whenever the value of an Account's assets exceeds the value of the Account's contract liabilities, state law permits Equitable Life to transfer the surplus to its general account, and the holders of MVA Contracts have no claim upon or interest in such transferred assets, except that such assets are part of Equitable Life's general account;

(6) Equitable Life established, and proposes to provide for legal insulation of, the Accounts for business purposes unrelated to any attempt to pass through investment experience of the Accounts; and

(7) Equitable Life will take steps to ensure that its marketing program and materials refer to the Accounts as pools of assets that provide an additional measure of assurance that the holders of MVA Contracts will receive full payment and not as investment vehicles in whose performance the holders of MVA Contracts will have any interest.[1]

## E. 1940 Act Regulation of Variable Financial Instruments

The recent history of periodic payment plans in relation to variable insurance products is described in the following excerpt of a 1992 SEC staff report.[2]

1. *Id.* (footnotes omitted).
2. Division of Investment Management, U.S. Securities & Exchange Commission, Protecting Investors: A Half Century of Investment Company Regulation 390-402 (1992).

### A. The Nature of the Products and Sponsors

Variable insurance contracts fall within the definition of periodic payment plans because they are contracts "providing for a series of periodic payments by the holder, and representing an undivided interest in certain specified securities or in a unit or fund of securities purchased wholly or partly with the proceeds of such payments. . . ." Despite this superficial resemblance, variable contracts differ fundamentally from the periodic payment plan contemplated by Congress: in terms of the benefits contract owners receive; the services the sponsors provide; the capital structure of the sponsor companies; and the extent of state regulation. These differences highlight the inappropriateness of the current statutory framework as applied to variable insurance and provide a basis for understanding the difficulties such issuers face.

First, in terms of the benefits contract owners receive, the differences are significant enough to justify different pricing and distribution requirements. . . . [while] periodic payment plans are no more than a means of purchasing securities by installment. In the early stages of plan participation, an investor receives little more than the opportunity to pay excessive sales loads on initial payments. Because a relatively small portion of early payments is actually invested, there is the certainty of severe economic harm if payments are not continued. Variable insurance, on the other hand, offers a combination of insurance and investment in one product for which there is no obvious substitute.

Variable life contracts provide immediate benefits to a contract owner in the form of full insurance protection after the first premium payment. Although a relatively high percentage of initial payments is subject to charge deductions . . . [v]ariable annuities also typically offer benefits in the form of death benefit protection during the contract's pay-in phase and rights to select annuity pay-out options at rates established when the contract is purchased.

Second, there are significant differences in the administrative services provided to contract owners that may warrant a more flexible approach for regulating variable contract charges. The periodic payment plan, because it is nothing more than a means of purchasing securities by installment, requires a plan trustee or sponsor to perform relatively simple administrative tasks. Therefore, the often illusory services for which such sponsors were paid out of trust assets before 1940 necessitated the restrictions of section 26(a)(2)(C) and the at cost limits of rule 26a-1. A variable insurance sponsor, on the other hand, provides a wider array of services in administering a variable contract. An insurer must make a significant commitment of capital to develop and maintain very elaborate systems that can handle a variety of contract features and monitor the panoply of insurance, tax, and securities law requirements that apply to the contracts. These services have real market value. . . .

A third important distinction between the periodic payment plan and variable insurance relates to the capital structure of the sponsor companies. Periodic payment plan sponsors historically were thinly capitalized entities . . . . Therefore, when trusts were "orphaned" and liquidated, a not infrequent occurrence in the pre-Investment Company Act era, some investors did not receive the services for which they had already paid. Moreover, despite successful judgments, these investors could not recover damages from the thinly capitalized sponsors. . . . Because the average insurance company has a stronger capital base than the typical plan sponsor, and because a separate account is an integral part of an insurance company with little chance of being "orphaned," a less paternalistic structure for variable insurance regulation may be more suitable. . . .

Finally, the presence of state insurance law as an additional layer of regulation for the insurance industry distinguishes variable insurance from periodic payment plans and argues in favor of a more flexible approach for regulating variable contract charges. . . . While the Division does not recommend a full exemption from Investment Company Act regulation for variable insurance issuers, the presence of state insurance law suggests that a more flexible approach to charge regulation would be appropriate.

**B. The Investment Charge — Insurance Charge Dilemma**

Regulation of variable products under the system established for periodic payment plans presents a formidable challenge: the Commission must enforce the rigid controls placed on charges levied by the plans, and, at the same time, attempt to separate the insurance features of variable contracts from their investment features and regulate only the latter. Efforts to regulate some charges, but not others, may be ineffectual because issuers may compensate for restrictions on regulated charges by increasing unregulated charges and using the proceeds for regulated purposes. These problems argue in favor of a regulatory approach that explicitly grants the Commission jurisdiction over all contract charges.

The Commission's experience with mortality and expense risk charges is illustrative. The insurance industry contends that mortality and expense risk charges are insurance charges properly subject to state regulation and outside the Commission's jurisdiction. The Commission, on the other hand, is concerned that an insurer may use the proceeds of mortality and expense risk charges to pay for distribution, an activity that is properly within the Commission's domain. In fact, mortality and expense risk charges may be used to cover insurance-related expenses or may be profit, depending upon the ultimate wisdom of the actuarial projections that shape the contract. If the actual mortality and expense experience under a contract is consistent with or better than the original projections of the pricing actuary, the insurer makes a profit on the charge. If actual experience differs and mortality or expense losses exceed original projections, the risk charge is needed to pay "insurance" costs. Many insurers anticipate, however, that the entire risk charge deduction will not be needed to pay contingent mortality costs or administrative expenses under the contracts.

Beginning in 1980, the Commission interpreted the Investment Company Act to require insurers to obtain exemptions from sections 26(a)(2) and 27(c)(2) to deduct the so-called risk charges from the assets of the separate account. The volume of these applications led to proposed rule 26a-3, proposed in 1984 and reproposed in 1987 but never adopted. . . . In the mid-1980's, the Division took the position that it would not support exemptions from the Act for risk charges that exceeded specified levels. The Division's search for an appropriate standard for mortality and expense risk charges was suspended when the Investment Company Act Study began.

**C. Problems With Variable Life Insurance — Industry Concerns**

The insurance industry claims that the application of sections 26 and 27 of the Investment Company Act to variable life insurance has created enormous pricing and distribution problems for insurers. Under current regulation, an insurer may not price its contracts in a way that adequately reflects the heavy capital expenditure needed to establish and maintain a variable insurance operation. In addition, an insurer may not distribute its variable life contracts on an equal basis with fixed-dollar contracts unless it undertakes an extra burden on its capital and surplus. Accordingly, variable life insurance has had modest growth, both in terms of product development and in terms of the number of insurers offering the product.

Many commenters asserted that the current statutory emphasis on regulation of individual charges is inappropriate for variable insurance because it inhibits product development. . . .

By restricting individual contract charges, current Investment Company Act regulation forces the creation of inappropriately priced contracts. An insurer may not arrive at the combination of assumptions that best suits its objectives and that may produce the best value for contract owners. In addition, the industry has indicated that it is difficult for companies to adapt existing fixed-dollar contract design to a variable contract form because of the restrictions of sections 26 and 27. These sections, which are more restrictive than state law, cause an insurer to make costly changes to its administrative systems in reproducing fixed-dollar designs.

The lack of pricing flexibility in variable life insurance is exacerbated by the stringent limits placed on specific charges. In particular, most commenters were critical of the requirement that an insurer must perform the administrative services under a variable life contract at cost. Unlike periodic payment plans where sponsors incur very little capital expenses, the operation of variable life insurance requires a heavy capital outlay. An insurer must develop elaborate administrative systems to handle the far more complex variable life contract. In addition, such systems must be capable of monitoring compliance with a variety of securities, insurance, and tax law provisions. An insurer would not be willing to invest heavily in variable life insurance if it perceived any competitive disadvantage in doing so. The more liberal state law pricing provisions that apply to fixed-dollar life insurance create such a disadvantage. Therefore, unless Investment Company Act regulation provides comparable flexibility to issuers of variable life insurance, many insurers would continue to emphasize fixed-dollar products.

Another major concern expressed by commenters was the belief that the refund requirements of section 27(d) and rules 6e-2 and 6e-3(T) create a marketing bias against the sale of variable life insurance. Under these provisions, an insurer is required to return (or may not deduct more than) certain prescribed sales load amounts if an excess-loaded contract is surrendered during the first twenty-four contract months. . . .

The effect of the refund requirements on a variable life issuer's capital and surplus may be best illustrated by example. Assume that an insurer pays an agent that sells a scheduled premium variable life contract a commission equal to fifty-five percent of the first year annual premium, the same rate it pays for selling a comparable fixed-dollar life contract. Consistent with industry practice, the insurer finances a portion of this commission, together with other issuance expenses, from its capital and surplus. If the contract is surrendered after six months, the insurer may assess a sales load of only thirty percent of the first year annual premium. The company, therefore, will incur a loss of twenty-five percent on the contract, unless it can recapture commissions from the selling agent, a difficult task to accomplish. Under a fixed-dollar contract, by contrast, an insurer may recover a higher portion of its unamortized issuance expenses because of the more liberal state refund (nonforfeiture) requirements. To minimize its loss, the variable life issuer can pursue one of two basic courses. First, it can establish a higher annual premium and, by applying a lower commission rate, effectively pay the agent the same amount that is paid for selling the fixed-dollar contract; alternatively, it can pay the agent a commission equal to the effective current maximum limit of thirty percent. Under either option, however, the variable life issuer would be at a competitive disadvantage. Because the fixed-dollar contract is a close substitute for the variable life contract, the two contracts must have reasonably competitive prices. In addition, an agent would not have an incentive to sell a variable life contract paying a commission of thirty percent when that agent can earn a higher commission for selling a comparable fixed-dollar contract.

The net effect of current pricing and distribution problems has been to make the offering of variable life insurance riskier than the sale of fixed-dollar contracts. Not many insurers appear willing to undertake additional risk of offering variable life insurance, particularly when they can sell certain interest-sensitive, fixed-dollar life contracts that are relatively close substitutes for variable life insurance and avoid regulation under the federal securities laws. As a result, variable life insurance has not realized its growth potential. The few insurers that have entered the marketplace are the larger companies that have a strong capital base capable of withstanding the additional strain on their capital and surplus, and smaller insurers that are committed to the product.

### D. Problems with Variable Annuities — How Much Is the "Insurance" Worth?

Related to the problem of the uses to which the proceeds of risk charges may be applied is the question of the extent to which there exists a justifiable basis for deducting mortality and expense risk charges during a variable annuity's pay-in phase. Insurers assert that it is appropriate to deduct risk charges because the variable annuity offers important insurance benefits: annuity options at pre-established rates, death benefit protection during the pay-in phase, and expense guarantees. In support of this assertion, insurers make representations regarding the reasonableness of risk charges. However, the Division has had a difficult time in determining whether and to what extent these insurance benefits contain value.

Notwithstanding the questionable worth of a variable annuity's insurance benefits, the Division believes that the contract does offer some insurance protection, and that an issuer should be permitted to assess a reasonable fee for underwriting these risks. Accordingly, the Division does not recommend prohibiting such charges. At the same time, the Division does not believe the Commission should continue to expend resources in trying to affix a reasonable value to mortality and expense risk charges individually; rather, any attempt to assess the reasonableness of risk charges should be part of a larger effort to determine the overall reasonableness of aggregate interest charges. The history of the rulemaking effort for rule 26a-3 illustrates the futility of retaining an individualized approach to charge regulation, under which limits are established for investment-related charges but not for insurance-related charges. The aggregate approach to charge regulation the Division is recommending would improve the Commission's role in regulating variable contracts and avoid most of the regulatory problems we have identified.

### IV. Recommendation

The Division believes that variable insurance issuers should have the same ability as mutual funds to set product charges as long as the charges are plainly disclosed and not excessive. Accordingly, the Division recommends that the Commission propose amendments to the Investment Company Act to exempt variable insurance contracts from the charge restrictions in sections 26 and 27, and instead require aggregate charges under variable contracts to be reasonable. Under the Division's proposal, the Commission would be given explicit authority to adopt rules establishing guidelines for this standard.

The Division's proposal would eliminate most of the current charge limits for variable contract issuers:

There would be no direct limit on the amount of administrative charges under a variable insurance contract. Rather, administrative charges would be regulated as a component of aggregate charges.

> Insurance-related charges, such as mortality and expense risk charges and cost of insurance, would be subject to the federalsecurities [sic] laws as components of aggregate charges. Risk charges would no longer be subject to *de facto* limits.
>
> The limits of section 27 would not apply to sales charges, but sales charges would be subject to the reasonableness requirement for aggregate charges and any guidelines established by Commission rules. There would be no refund, conversion, or free-look requirements under the Investment Company Act, although state law typically provides similar provisions. There would be no "stair step" requirements.
>
> Variable annuity sales charges would still be subject to section 22(b) and NASD [now FINRA] rules. Although there are no current NASD [now FINRA] limits pertaining to variable life insurance sales charges, the Commission and NASD [now FINRA] would retain authority under section 22(b) to promulgate standards for sales loads under those contracts.
>
> In conjunction with the proposed increased flexibility in pricing, the Division expects to give priority to the development of a registration form for variable life insurance and standardized illustrations of benefits and expenses for variable insurance contracts to be used in prospectuses and supplemental sales literature. Improved disclosure would foster competition, particularly in variable life insurance, because it would assist contract owners in comparing the relative costs and benefits of competitive contracts. . . .

## F. Variable Annuities and Section 27 of the Investment Company Act of 1940: Sales Charges of Periodic Payment Plans

Periodic payment plans (purchase of fund shares by installment) were popular in the 1960s, but are almost extinct today. These plans offered investors the opportunity to buy investment company shares in installments. Many problems resulted from these plans. Probably the most notable was that many purchasers ceased payments early on and found that they lost their payments in the front end load paid to the sales persons. As a result, the Investment Company Act regulates periodic payment plans under section 27.

Section 27's main application was to variable insurance products that the SEC analogized to periodic payment plans. In 1996, however, Congress expressly mandated that section 27 would not apply to variable insurance products. This legislation removed pricing design issues from the securities regulation of variable products and left the focus on disclosure and sales practices issues.[1]

---

1. Today, in 2016, this section has little use and will not be discussed further. However, if mutual fund shares will again be sold in installments, this section ought to be kept in mind. For the history and analysis of section 27 and periodic payment plans, see 4 TAMAR FRANKEL & ANN TAYLOR SCHWING, THE REGULATION OF MONEY MANAGERS (Mutual Funds and Advisers) ch. 28 (2001 & Supp. 2015).

# Chapter 18

## *Ethics Issues*

### A. The Investment Management Profession

Ethics issues accompany us through life. Among others, lawyers and investment managers face these issues frequently. This chapter covers five situations raising ethical issues. One situation relates to the duty of lawyers if the client violates the law in contradiction of the lawyers' advice. The second closely-related situation deals with the responsibility of lawyers to disclose the clients' misdeeds notwithstanding the duty of confidentiality to their clients. The third situation concerns the responsibility and liabilities of in-house counsel, and the fourth situation focuses on the behavior of lawyers engaged in activities that do not involve lawyers' services, for example, as compliance officers in a financial services company. The fifth situation concerns ethical issues of a lawyer's client, such as an investment manager or fund director may face, when these clients seek an outside lawyer's advice.

Ethics raises a number of difficulties. One is the difficulty, yet the need, of defining the nature of ethics. Lawyers must recognize ethical issues when they see them because law involves some but not all of the ethical issues. It is hard to draw the line-difference between law and ethics, in part because the difference may be one of enforcement. Ethical behavior is enforced by the actors' internal compunction, by social pressure, by religious beliefs and perhaps by upbringing and psychological make-up. One does what is right even if there are no police around.[1] Another is a law-abiding citizen if one does what is right when the police are around.

A second view of ethics relates to coercion and giving. Doing something good voluntarily is more ethical than doing something that we are required to do. Although law may not require good actions, it may nod its approval of them. The third view of ethics relates to expected rewards. Doing the right thing without expecting benefits except from doing the good act itself constitutes a higher level of ethical behavior. The fourth view involves the hard case when actors are faced with conflicts between obligations owed to different parties, including society, and especially when our own interests

1. *See* Tamar Frankel, Trust and Honesty, America's Business Culture at a Crossroad, Ch. 2 (2006).

align us with those of some of the parties. Lawyers and investment managers may face such conflicts.

In addition, one should consider the impact of various actions or omissions on society, and the ability of lawyers to prevent social harm. Thus, when lawyers are aware of violations (whether of clients or third parties) that pose substantial harm not only to other individuals but also to the financial system, their ethical behavior may be judged by standards that are stricter than those that do not involve such harms. When the financial system is threatened, for example, in the case of the 2008 bubble and the sub-prime mortgages securitization disaster, the ethical behavior of lawyers may require a higher standard.

When an organization is the subject of ethical behavior because outside enforcement is very costly or undermines the benefits of independent organizations, an important issue of organizational culture arises. A culture, like a habit, is a condition that induces automatic behavior. Therefore, a more efficient enforcement of the rules is by installing a culture of obeying the rules.[1] Once SEC rules are followed for a period, they induce a culture of legal actions. Lawyers can contribute to the establishment of a culture of honesty and trust.

Thus, many of the questions discussed in this Course involve unresolved issues posed for lawyers and the extent to which they should play the role of enforcing the law and its policies. This issue arises when the lawyers are aware of the clients' plans or tendency to violate the law, or to start the slippery slope towards violations. This issue raises further concern when lawyers are aware that clients have already violated the law. On these issues the SEC, the courts and the bar associations have adopted different views.

One explanation for the fluctuating importance and enforcement of ethical behavior may be our fluctuating values regarding the interests and rights of the strong and knowledgeable versus the weaker individuals, and rights and duties of the individual versus society, and the evaluation of the future versus the present. We approve ethical behavior for its contribution to social well-being: to the social order as well as to particular members of society. These contributions create a pattern of mutual help that leads to social security and trust, and lower enforcement and maintenance costs. One explanation for downgrading the value of ethical behavior is that contribution to others may not bring immediate benefits and satisfactions to oneself, and undermines the drive for self-help and competition that is crucial to society's well-being. When we emphasize the self rather than the community, self-reliance and competition rather than reliance on others and trust, the value of ethics falls and the value of these other values rise. Can these seemingly contradictory values be reconciled? Should they be reconciled?

Enforcement of our obligations to others cannot be completely left to the law. Ethics is an additional means of enforcing such obligations to others. Therefore, arguably, the law and ethics complement each other.

---

1. *See id.*

The first topic of inquiry is the securities lawyer. An overriding issue in the securities area is whether a securities lawyer is subject to a higher ethical standard than a lawyer serving in other areas of law practice, and if so, why? Is it because the attorney is providing services to a regulated profession? Or is it because the attorney has special entry into the practice of the law regulating this industry, a semi-monopoly to practice, if you will?

Like all lawyers, securities lawyers are regulated by the rules of the bar, the courts before whom they appear, and by state laws. In addition, they are also regulated by the SEC. The SEC asserts jurisdiction over lawyers, accountants, and other professionals that appear before it (directly or indirectly, by preparing documents to be filed with the SEC) by virtue of Rule 102(e) of the SEC Rules of Practice.[1] The SEC does not purport to regulate these professionals, but asserts authority to disqualify them from appearing before it. This disqualification amounts to serious sanctions because the practice of disqualified securities lawyers becomes far more limited. The authority of the SEC to disqualify has been debated, especially if the SEC requires lawyers to act in a proactive way, when they become aware that their clients have violated the securities laws. The bar has taken a far more limited view.

The SEC has not brought many cases against lawyers under section 2(e) (now 102(e)). It did bring claims against lawyers on violations of the substantive securities acts, such as insider trading. Nonetheless, the *Altman* case, discussed later in this chapter, is a recent case that stands out.

A difficult issue arises in connection with lawyers' responsibility for securities violations of their clients.[2] In this case, Carter and Johnson were partners in the law firm of Brown, Wood, Ivey, Mitchell & Petty ("Brown, Wood") since 1954 and 1967 respectively. Both practiced in the areas of general corporate and securities law. The SEC instituted Rule 2(e) proceedings against them for aiding and abetting securities law violations by their client, National Telephone Co. (NTC), and for their own improper professional conduct.

In 1974, NTC's business required heavy infusion of capital that put NTC in a precarious cash flow position. Yet the company's public posture remained optimistic. There were two forms of aiding and abetting allegations against Carter and Johnson. Initially, Carter and Johnson participated in the drafting

1. Rule 102(e)(1) [17 C.F.R. § 201.102(e)(1)(2015)] provides in part: "The Commission may . . . deny, temporarily or permanently, the privilege of appearing or practicing before it in any way to any person who is found by the Commission after notice of and opportunity for hearing in the matter . . . to have engaged in unethical or improper professional conduct. . . ." *See* Ted J. Fiflis, *Choice of Federal or State Law for Attorneys' Professional Responsibility in Securities Matters,* 56 N.Y.U. L. Rev. 1236 (1981); Simon M. Lorne, *The Corporate and Securities Adviser, The Public Interest, and Professional Ethics,* 76 Mich. L. Rev. 423 (1978); Lewis D. Lowenfels, *Expanding Public Responsibilities of Securities Lawyers: An Analysis of the New Trend in Standard of Care and Priorities of Duties,* 74 Colum. L.Rev. 412 (1974); Theodore Sonde, *The Responsibility of Professionals Under the Federal Securities Laws — Some Observations,* 68 N.W. U. L.Rev. 1 (1973). James C. Cox et al., Securities Regulation 1178 (1991); *see generally id.* at 1021-1024, 1160-1185.

2. William R. Carter, Exchange Act Rel. No. 17597 (Feb. 28, 1981).

of a press release and a Form 8-K that omitted material information about a plan to which NTC had agreed in order to obtain additional financing from a consortium of banks. The plan, when triggered, would have required NTC to wind down its existing business. The company's press release and Form 8-K referred to the plan, but did not explain its nature or the likelihood that it would have to be implemented in the near future.

The second aiding and abetting claim involved Carter and Johnson's inaction in the face of subsequent nondisclosures by NTC, which were made, or not made, under the direction of Sheldon L. Hart, NTC's chief executive officer and controlling stockholder. Hart insisted that the plan not be made public, and Carter and Johnson acquiesced. Further, despite an agreement that Carter and Johnson review NTC's public releases, NTC mailed its stockholders a glowing report about second quarter performance, while falsely representing to a Brown, Wood attorney that Carter and Johnson approved the report.

In March 1975, the banks' counsel informed Carter and Johnson of events that triggered the plan, and the two lawyers strongly recommended that Hart publicly disclose the plan and its impact on NTC. Ignoring their advice, NTC prepared an 8-K form that did not mention the plan. While Carter and Johnson, with increasing exasperation, continued to urge Hart to disclose the plan, Hart brazenly asked them to prepare a legal opinion for the banks that disclosure of the plan was unnecessary. Johnson was incredulous at this request and finally approached the board of directors. Hart's relationship with NTC's outside directors soured and he resigned in May 1975.

Carter and Johnson appealed an administrative law judge decision finding them liable under the predecessor to Rule 102(e) of the SEC Rules of Practice.

The Commission reversed the decision, partly on the ground that "certain concepts of proper ethical and professional conduct were not sufficiently developed, at the time of the conduct here at issue, to permit a finding that either respondent breached applicable ethical or professional standards." However, it stated that it was "giving notice of an interpretation . . . of the term 'unethical or improper professional conduct.'"

The SEC addressed "the professional obligations of the lawyer who gives essentially correct disclosure advice to a client that does not follow that advice and as a result violates the federal securities laws":

> While precise standards have not yet emerged, it is fair to say that there exists considerable acceptance of the proposition that a lawyer must, in order to discharge his professional responsibilities, make all efforts within reason to persuade his client to avoid or terminate proposed illegal action. Such efforts could include, where appropriate, notification to the board of directors of a corporate client. . . .
>
> We are mindful that, when a lawyer represents a corporate client, the client — and the entity to which he owes his allegiance — is the corporation itself and not management or any other individual connected with the corporation. Moreover, the lawyer should try to "insure that decisions of his client are made only after the client has

been informed of relevant considerations." These unexceptionable principles take on a special coloration when a lawyer becomes aware that one or more specific members of a corporate client's management is deciding not to follow his disclosure advice, especially if he knows that those in control, such as the board of directors, may not have participated in or been aware of that decision. Moreover, it is well established that no lawyer, even in the most zealous pursuit of his client's interests, is privileged to assist his client in conduct the lawyer knows to be illegal. The application of these recognized principles to the special road of the securities lawyer giving disclosure advice, however, is not a simple task.

The securities lawyer who is an active participant in a company's ongoing disclosure program will ordinarily draft and revise disclosure documents, comment on them and file them with the Commission. He is often involved on an intimate, day-to-day basis in the judgments that determine what will be disclosed and what will be withheld from the public markets. When a lawyer serving in such a capacity concludes that his client's disclosures are not adequate to comply with the law, and so advises his client, he is "aware," in a literal sense, of a continuing violation of the securities laws. On the other hand, the lawyer is only an adviser, and the final judgment — and, indeed, responsibility — as to what course of conduct is to be taken must lie with the client. Moreover, disclosure issues often present difficult choices between multiple shades of gray, and while a lawyer's judgment may be to draw the disclosure obligation more broadly than his client, both parties recognize the degree of uncertainty involved.

The problems of professional conduct that arise in this relationship are well-illustrated by the facts of this case. In rejecting Brown, Wood's advice to include the assumptions underlying its projections in its 1974 Annual Report, in declining to issue two draft stockholders letters offered by respondents and in ignoring the numerous more informal urgings by both respondents and Socha to make disclosure, Hart and Lurie [another officer] indicated that they were inclined to resist any public pronouncements that were at odds with the rapid growth which had been projected and reported for the company.

If the record ended there, we would be hesitant to suggest that any unprofessional conduct might be involved. Hart and Lurie were, in effect, pressing the company's lawyers hard for the minimum disclosure required by law. That fact alone is not an appropriate basis for a finding that a lawyer must resign or take some extraordinary action. Such a finding would inevitably drive a wedge between reporting companies and their outside lawyers; the more sophisticated members of management would soon realize that there is nothing to gain in consulting outside lawyers.

However, much more was involved in this case. In sending out a patently misleading letter to stockholders on December 23 in contravention of [the] plain and express advice to clear all such disclosure with Brown, Wood, in deceiving respondents about Johnson's approval of the company's quarterly report to its stockholders in early December and in dissembling in response to respondents' questions about the implementation of the LMP [Leare Maintenance Plan], the company's management erected a wall between National and its outside lawyers — a wall apparently designed to keep out good legal advice in conflict with management's improper disclosure plans.

Any ambiguity in the situation plainly evaporated in late April and early May of 1975 when [the issuer's President] first asked Johnson for a legal opinion flatly contrary to the express disclosure advice Johnson had given Hart only five days earlier, and when Lurie soon thereafter prohibited Kay from delivering a copy of the company's April 1975 [Form] 8-K to Brown, Wood.

These actions reveal a conscious desire on the part of National's management no longer to look to Brown, Wood for independent disclosure advice, but rather to embrace the firm within Hart's fraud and use it as a shield to avoid the pressures exerted by the banks toward disclosure. Such a role is a perversion of the normal lawyer-client relationship, and no lawyer may claim that, in these circumstance, [sic] he need do no more than stubbornly continue to suggest disclosure when he knows his suggestions are falling on deaf ears. . . .

When a lawyer with significant responsibilities in the effectuation of a company's compliance with the disclosure requirements of the federal securities laws becomes aware that his client is engaged in a substantial and continuing failure to satisfy those disclosure requirements, his continued participation violates professional standards unless he takes prompt steps to end the client's noncompliance. The Commission has determined that this interpretation will be applicable only to conduct occurring after the date of [the Carter and Johnson] opinion.

We do not imply that a lawyer is obliged, at the risk of being held to have violated Rule 2(e), to seek to correct every isolated disclosure action or inaction which he believes to be at variance with applicable disclosure standards, although there may be isolated disclosure failures that are so serious that their correction becomes a matter of primary professional concern. It is also clear, however, that a lawyer is not privileged to unthinkingly permit himself to be co-opted into an ongoing fraud and cast as a dupe or a shield for a wrongdoing client.

Initially, counseling accurate disclosure is sufficient, even if his advice is not accepted. But there comes a point at which a reasonable lawyer must conclude that his advice is not being followed, or even sought in good faith, and that his client is involved in a continuing course of violating the securities laws. At this critical juncture, the lawyer must take further, more affirmative steps in order to avoid the inference that he has been co-opted, willingly or unwillingly, into the scheme of non-disclosure.

The lawyer is in the best position to choose his next step. Resignation is one option, although we recognize that other considerations, including the protection of the client against foreseeable prejudice,

> must be taken into account in the case of withdrawal. A direct approach to the board of directors or one or more individual directors or officers may be appropriate; or he may choose to try to enlist the aid of other members of the firm's management. What is required, in short, is some prompt action that leads to the conclusion that the lawyer is engaged in efforts to correct the underlying problem, rather than having capitulated to the desires of a strong-willed, but misguided client.
>
> Some have argued that resignation is the only permissible course when a client chooses not to comply with disclosure advice. We do not agree. Premature resignation serves neither the end of an effective lawyer-client relationship nor, in most cases, the effective administration of the securities laws. The lawyer's continued interaction with his client will ordinarily hold the greatest promise of corrective action. So long as a lawyer is acting in good faith and exerting reasonable efforts to prevent violations of the law by his client, his professional obligations have been met. In general, the best result is that which promotes the continued, strong-minded and independent participation by the lawyer.
>
> We recognize, however, that the "best result" is not always obtainable, and that there may occur situations where the lawyer must conclude that the misconduct is so extreme or irretrievable, or the involvement of his client's management and board of directors in the misconduct is so thoroughgoing and pervasive that any action short of resignation would be futile. We would anticipate that cases where a lawyer has no choice but to resign would be rare and of an egregious nature.

In November 8, 1996, SEC Commissioner Norman S. Johnson spoke before the American Bar Association, Federal Securities Law Committee, concerning "Suits Against Lawyers."[1]

In this talk, the Commissioner Johnson noted the SEC's policy of reluctance to use Rule 102(e). He recognized the role of securities lawyers in the system of securities regulation, which is based on disclosure, and the assistance of the securities bar to reduce the SEC's workload.

The Commissioner noted a preference for actions against lawyers in an SEC-initiated injunctive proceeding in a federal court, as an independent federal court is better suited to "separate illegal conduct from ethical advocacy." Such actions are often brought as aiding and abetting actions. In addition, the SEC can bring administrative cease-and-desist actions against lawyers.

The Commissioner read *Carter and Johnson* for the standard that suits against lawyers should "allow even negligence, as necessary to accomplish the Commission's larger purposes." Quoting the opinion:

---

1. Norman S. Johnson, Commissioner, U.S. Securities and Exchange Commission, Suits Against Lawyers, Speech Before the American Bar Association Federal Securities Law Committee (Nov. 8, 1996), *available at* http://www.sec.gov/ news/ speech/ speecharchive/1996/ spch137.txt.

> If a securities lawyer is to bring his best independent judgment to bear on a disclosure problem, he must have the freedom to make innocent—or even, in certain cases, careless mistakes without fear of legal liability or loss of the ability to practice before the Commission. Concern about his own liability may alter the balance of his judgment in one direction as surely as an unseemly obeisance to the wishes of his client can do so in the other.

In cease and desist actions, the SEC should not "penalize good faith though negligent conduct — the instance where the lawyer commits an innocent mistake, or is used to help perpetrate a fraud despite using best efforts to ascertain the truth." Consequently, this authority should be "limited to those situations where the attorney's conduct was so egregious that he could properly be deemed a principal actor."

The Commissioner also agreed with the SEC's policy of bringing only "derivative" Rule 102(e) proceedings (i.e., another violation is involved), and said that in a Rule 102(e) proceeding "the Commission must make a facts and circumstances determination before it seeks to disqualify that person from continued practice before it." The Commissioner noted a preference for referring conduct involving ethical or professional responsibility issues to state disciplinary bodies.

---

## Discussion Topics

a. In what respect is the *Carter and Johnson* case about ethical behavior? In what respect is the case about professional behavior, and what is the difference between the two, if any?

b. What exactly should the lawyers have done in *Carter and Johnson*? Whom should they have approached when their immediate client ignored their legal advice? Are they required to inform the SEC?

c. Why should lawyers be put in a position as enforcers of the securities acts? Why should their burden be heavier than that of attorneys who represent accused persons in criminal cases?

d. Is resignation an equally viable option of an in-house counsel as it is for an outside counsel?

e. Do you agree with the position of Commissioner Johnson? Should Rule 102(e) be erased from the books, not only from enforcement?

f. Is it right for a Commissioner of the SEC to explicitly state that it should not be enforced? What is the Commissioner's duty regarding Rule 102(e)? Where do the "practical" and the "theoretical" conflict?

---

## 1. Introduction

Two recent SEC opinions demonstrate the light touch of the SEC's supervision of unethical conduct. One opinion mentions but does not apply the SEC's Rule of Practice 102(e).[1] The second opinion, on appeal from a self-regulatory organization action, holds that "unethical conduct" by securities professionals violated New York Stock Exchange Rule 476(a)(6) (now Rule 2010 of FINRA), regardless of absent bad faith. It is suggested that this Rule is based on a long standing self-regulatory rule of broker-dealers that prohibits "conduct inconsistent with just and equitable principles of trade." Another source of this rule may be the SEC "shingle theory." The question is whether FINRA or any other self-regulatory system can regulate lawyers. Arguably, these decisions could be read to support SRO action against lawyers and compliance professionals subject to SRO jurisdiction where their allegedly unethical conduct violates industry norms and professional standards. In the past, however, the SEC generally has been reluctant to employ its conduct rule prohibiting unethical conduct by attorneys practicing before the SEC primarily because such actions might deter lawyers from counseling clients in need of advice.

The SEC has continued to exercise restraint in applying section 102(e), absent evidence that an attorney has engaged in a substantive violation of the federal securities laws. Only in one case has the SEC used solely the provisions of Rule 102(e)(1) to discipline an attorney. This was a unique case concerning alleged obstruction of an SEC administrative hearing by a lawyer charged with attempting to extort a payment from the respondent in exchange for his client's not making herself available to testify against the respondent.

### 2. The *Altman* case

The *Altman* case was decided first by Chief ALJ Brenda Murray on January 14, 2009 after a contested hearing. The ALJ found that Altman, while representing a witness in an SEC administrative hearing against her former employer, violated Rule 102(e) and certain canons of the New York State Code of Professional Responsibility and Disciplinary Rules when he knowingly contacted counsel for her employer and attempted to obtain benefit for his client at the expense of hindering a proceeding by the Commission. Thus, Altman's conduct was deceptive and fraudulent. According to the decision, Altman held telephone conversations with the respondent's counsel to resolve financial issues on behalf of his client, after learning that she would be called by the SEC Enforcement staff to testify against the respondent. Altman intimated that his client's availability and memory might be affected favorably toward the respondent if her outstanding financial issues were resolved. Respondent's counsel rejected the overtures and secretly recorded the conversations. When the SEC's Division called Altman's client as a witness, the respondent's counsel presented the tapes at the SEC proceeding and successfully impeached the witness. The SEC then sued Altman alleging his conduct violated Rule 102(e). After a hearing, the ALJ rejected Altman's arguments with regard to the enforceability of Rule

1. These materials were derived from Ethical Responsibilities of Legal and Compliance Professionals: Recent SEC and FINRA Cases Involving Lawyers and Compliance Professionals prepared by Anne C. Flannery, partner, and Alice L. McCarthy, associate resident in the New York office of Morgan, Lewis & Bockius LLP. Copyright 2009, Morgan, Lewis & Bockius LLP.

102(e) and ordered that he be suspended from practice before the SEC for 9 months.

Before *Altman,* the SEC had not brought enforcement proceedings against an attorney on the grounds of unethical behavior for many years. Just six months before the *Altman* ALJ decision, the SEC strongly signaled its reluctance to use Rule 102(e) absent conduct that violated the federal securities laws in a case on appeal where the attorney respondent was not even charged with a violation of Rule 102(e) (this case is discussed below).[1]

### 3. The *Monson* and *Rasch* Cases Indicating Possible Rule 102(e) Applicability

The SEC refused to reverse an ALJ's dismissal against an attorney in a case based on negligent drafting of a market timing agreement. This draft resulted in a violation of rule 22c-1 by a broker-dealer client, because the terms of the final agreement allowed clients to enter late trades, after the close, and still receive that day's NAV. Such trades were contrary to rule 22c-1 under the Investment Company Act. The SEC separately sued and obtained judgments and settlements against the firm, its CEO and its head of Operations. The lawyer contested the charges and, after a hearing, the ALJ dismissed all the charges against him. The Division appealed the dismissal to the SEC which reviewed the case de novo, affirming the dismissal.[2]

Attorney Monson was not charged under Rule 102(e). On appeal to the full Securities and Exchange Commission, the staff argued that Monson's lack of knowledge that his acts or omissions would contribute to a violation of rule 22c-1 was not dispositive of whether he should be found to have contributed to his firm's violation of the pricing rule. In essence, the Division argued that Monson should be sanctioned because his actions as an attorney fell short of the professional standards to which he was subject, a rationale that sounded a lot like the principles underlying Rule 102(e). The three SEC Commissioners who signed the Opinion seemed reluctant to draw that conclusion.

The Opinion rejected the Division's rationale and concluded that there was insufficient evidence that Monson had acted negligently in drafting the agreement. The SEC did not find that the circumstances surrounding certain changes in the agreement (allowing the client to place late trades) "necessarily should have alerted Monson, given his background and responsibilities, to the need for inquiry."[3] Consequently, the SEC dismissed the charges. However, notwithstanding its review of the evidence and conclusion that the Division had failed to prove even negligent conduct by Monson, the Opinion went to great lengths to preserve but refrain from applying the principles behind Rule 102(e). Although Monson was not charged under Rule 102(e), the Commissioners presumably felt compelled to both defend and caution against the Rule's application. In doing so, the

1. *See* In the Matter of Scott G. Monson, Investment Company Act Rel. No. 28323 (Jun. 30, 2008).
2. Investment Company Act Rel. No. 28323, 2008 SEC LEXIS 1503 at *1-4 (Jun. 30, 2008) (Only three Commissioners participated in the decision: Chairman Cox and Commissioners Atkins and Casey.).
3. *Id.*

Opinion reviewed the controversy stemming from the SEC's 1981 decision in Carter, its subsequent adoption of Rule 102(e) and its concern that the Rule not be invoked in such as a way as to chill a lawyer's advocacy or a client's decision to consult counsel when confronted with difficult problems.

Yet, notwithstanding the fact that the rule was not relevant to the issues the three Commissioners focused on the rule. That they defended their restraint is worth consideration. Although quite lengthy, *Monson's* spirited warnings about invoking Rule 102(e) are noteworthy, especially as a backdrop to their consideration of the "J&E Rule" discussed below a few months later. The Commissioners noted:

> Over twenty-five years ago, in William R. Carter, we recognized particular concerns attendant to disciplining lawyers based on faulty legal advice and noted a distinction between actions with scienter and those without scienter. We held that, to sanction a lawyer pursuant to former Rule of Practice 2(e) for having aided and abetted a securities law violation, the Commission had to show "that respondents were aware or knew that their role was part of an activity that was improper or illegal." In confirming this "intent requirement" for aiding and abetting, we emphasized the "[s]ignificant public benefits [that] flow from the effective performance of the securities lawyer's role." We also recognized that, "[i]n the course of rendering securities law advice, the lawyer is called upon to make difficult judgments, often under great pressure and in areas where the legal signposts are far apart and only faintly discernible." We expressed concern that, to the extent lawyers exercising their professional judgment are excessively motivated by "fear of legal liability or loss of the ability to practice before the Commission," clients may well decide not to consult lawyers on difficult issues.
>
> Given these considerations, we eschewed a standard that would expose an attorney to professional discipline "merely because his advice, followed by the client, is ultimately determined to be wrong." The intent requirement, we said, is crucial to an allegation of wrongdoing by a lawyer because it "provides the basis for distinguishing between those professionals who may be appropriately considered as subjects of professional discipline and those who, acting in good faith, have merely made errors of judgment or have been careless." These Commissioners noted that the historically the Commission exercised restraint in the use of the rule against attorneys. . . .
>
> Concerns about the scope of liability that have motivated our restraint with respect to Rule 102(e) actions against lawyers similarly are present in litigated administrative enforcement actions such as this case alleging that a lawyer caused another person's violation of the securities laws. The charges against Monson as framed by the Division — that Monson departed from professional standards of competence in rendering private legal advice to their clients — raise the same risks we identified in *Carter* and other proceedings: an encroachment by the Commission on regulation of attorney conduct historically performed by the states; interference with lawyers'

> ability to provide unbiased, independent legal advice regarding the securities laws; and chilled advocacy on behalf of clients in proceedings before the Commission. As far as we are aware, we have not sanctioned attorneys in litigated enforcement proceedings based on alleged negligent acts or omissions they may have committed in providing non-public legal advice to clients."[1]

In 2009, two lawyers were charged with operating a "legal opinion mill."[2] Whether the SEC's long tradition regarding unethical and negligent behavior by lawyers will continue remains to be seen.

In the *Rasch* case, the lawyers' firm named "144 Opinions Inc." together with their principal who was not a lawyer served promoters by issuing fraudulent legal opinions for a "pump-and-dump" scheme. Thus, they violated the federal securities laws. Rasch and his associate allegedly executed at least 24 legal opinion letters concerning the removal of restrictive legends on certificates representing over 22 million shares of an issuer called Mobile Ready Entertainment Corp. ("Mobile Ready"). According to the SEC, they cited to non-existent documents and misrepresented material facts. Allegedly, these false and misleading statements were drafted by the non-lawyer who owned "144 Opinions Inc." These opinions were then executed by Rasch and his associate, inducing the transfer agent for Mobile Ready to remove the restrictive legends and permitting the illegal sale of over 22 million shares of Mobile Ready in violation of the registration provisions of the federal securities laws. The SEC does not allege in this case unethical conduct under Rule 102(e). But the activities of these attorneys seem to fall within 102(e).

### 4. FINRA Rule 2010 and Conduct Inconsistent with Just and Equitable Principles of Trade: The *Heath* case.[3]

In 2009, another case determined by FINRA points to the possible applicability of Rule 102(e). FINRA Rule 2010[4] suggests it views an SRO's authority to police unethical professional behavior to be on stronger ground than Rule 102(e). The status of this decision is far from clear. According to the SEC opinion, Heath was an investment banker who, in the course of completing a banking assignment at the firm he was leaving, disclosed the deal he was working on to his future colleague at his new bank, in circumstances where Heath understood the latter would keep the information confidential. Instead, the individual contacted Heath's client and sought a role for himself and his own bank. Both Heath and his "tippee" were fired and Heath's offer of employment at the new firm was rescinded. The NYSE (prior to its merger with the NASD into FINRA) brought an action

1. In the Matter of Scott G. Monson, Investment Company Act Rel. No. 28323 (Jun. 30, 2008).
2. *SEC v. Rasch,* No. 09-cv-1190 (N.D. Ga. filed May 5, 2009).
3. *In the Matter of the Application of Thomas W. Heath, III,* 2009 SEC LEXIS 14 (Jan. 9, 2009), *appeal docketed,* No. 09-0825 (2d Cir. Mar. 3, 2009).
4. FINRA Rule 2010: "[a] member, in the conduct of business, shall observe high standards of commercial honor and just and equitable principles of trade." Correspondingly, NYSE Rule 476(a)(6) calls for the imposition of sanctions upon any individual or entity that is found guilty of "failing to observe high standards of commercial honor and just and equitable principles of trade."

against Heath for violating the "J&E Rule." After a hearing, Heath was found to have violated the J&E Rule and fined $100,000. He appealed and the SEC affirmed the violation and the $100,000 fine. Heath appealed to the Second Circuit.

Although Heath was an investment banker and not a lawyer, the SEC resorted to Rule 102(e) by analogy, noting that the FINRA Rule "is grounded in an explicit and long standing statutory mandate." It may be that this decision applies to lawyers as well. Perhaps the SEC prefers to shift the burden of enforcement in this area to an SRO.

The SEC's ringing endorsement of the J&E Rule to police unethical conduct therefore raises a question about its potential use to police the ethical responsibilities of, and potential conflicts of interest relating to, broker-dealer legal and compliance personnel. It also raises the question whether the SEC, if presented with the same facts as those in *Monson* or *Rasch* on appeal in an SRO case, would sustain a charge under the FINRA Rule.

---

**Discussion Topics**

a. How do you explain the SEC's reluctance to regulate the ethical conduct of attorneys who appear before it? Is the explanation that the SEC is concerned with the relationship among the attorneys and their clients convincing? What other explanation can there be?

b. Should the rules of ethics that apply to broker-dealers be applied to attorneys? Are attorneys different from brokers? And if so, how?

c. What is unique about the *Altman* case?

---

## B. Responsibility of Lawyers to Disclose Clients' Misdeeds

The material above focuses on what a lawyer should do when his advice to the client is not followed by the client and results in securities laws violations. This section deals with a different aspect of lawyers' involvement in clients' violations of the law.

In 1992, after the failure of Charles Keating's Lincoln Savings & Loan Association, the Office of Thrift Supervision (OTS) brought an action against Kaye Scholer, seeking, among other things, to recover at least $275 million from Kaye Scholer to reimburse the Federal Insurance Fund for losses incurred by Lincoln. Pursuant to its powers over "institution affiliated parties," which includes attorneys, appraisers and accountants, OTS issued an "asset freeze order" against Kaye Scholer's assets. The order was based on the law firm's breach of professional responsibility, among others. The asset freeze order led to a hasty settlement within less than a week. The settlement included Kaye Scholer's agreement to pay the government $41 million. Needless to say, the asset freeze order had quite a chilling impact on the profession. The following is summary of the decision in the *Kaye Scholer* case.[1]

1. The formal cite of this case: Peter M. Fishbein, OTS AP9219 (no date in original).

ACC/Lincoln retained Kaye Scholer on the legality of an issue although it had no bank regulatory expertise. Kaye Scholer learned that ACC/Lincoln had created backdated consents of its board in order to claim reliance on a "grandfather clause." Kaye Scholer also opined in a memorandum to ACC/Lincoln that certain of its direct investments were grandfathered, knowing that the relevant documents were backdated and, under state law and the corporate documents, not effective before the effective date of the rule. ACC/Lincoln relied on the opinion.

In addition, Kaye Scholer learned from ACC/Lincoln's independent auditor, Arthur Andersen, that ACC/Lincoln's financial condition was risky and that its financial statements may not adequately reflect the risks. Arthur Andersen resigned as auditor. However, Kaye Scholer subsequently transmitted a Form 8-K stating that the resignation "was not the result of any concern by AA [Arthur Andersen] with [ACC/Lincoln's] operations . . . or asset/ liability management. . . ."

Further, Kaye Scholer prepared and submitted responses to two FHLBB examinations for ACC/Lincoln. It interviewed employees and reviewed documents and learned material facts relevant to ACC/Lincoln's material violations but did not advise ACC/Lincoln to disclose, and did not disclose, many such facts, thereby making false and misleading representations to the FHLBB. Kaye Scholer also "knowingly and recklessly" omitted material facts and made misrepresentations in its representations to the FHLBB, thereby aiding and abetting ACC/Lincoln's concealment of facts.

These facts included facts material to ACC/Lincoln's: (a) income and net worth, (b) loan underwriting and documentation, (c) reporting of certain transactions as loans instead of joint ventures, (d) claims that the direct investments were properly grandfathered, and (e) participation in financing of a limited partnership which financing violated regulatory prohibitions on affiliate transactions and conflict of interest transactions, including also participation in SEC filings failing to disclose relevant facts material to these transactions.

Finally, Kaye Scholer violated its fiduciary duties to ACC/Lincoln and engaged in "unethical and improper professional conduct." It (a) failed to advise Lincoln's board that ACC Chairman Keating and others were not acting in Lincoln's best interests, and acted on behalf of Lincoln while representing both Lincoln and ACC, (b) knew of accounting irregularities and other risks, (c) knew that officers/directors of ACC/Lincoln were not fulfilling their fiduciary duties to depositors and the deposit insurance fund and violating federal regulations but did not advise them accordingly, and (d) knew that ACC and Lincoln had adverse interests and knew it could not adequately represent both but continued joint representation.

---

## Discussion Topics

a. Although the OTS sued on behalf of Lincoln Savings, it did not claim as a successor. Rather, the OTS's claim was based on the law firm's responsibility to the public and not just its client. In the wake of the *Kaye Scholer* case, regulators in industries other than banking and finance are looking at what the OTS did, trying to fashion similar actions to target lawyers as potential deep-pocket defendants. An example of this is a state insurance commissioner's professional liability suit against a large New Orleans law firm.[1]

b. Compare the behavior of counsel in the *Kaye Scholer* case with that of counsel in the *Carter & Johnson* case. How does it differ and how is it similar?

---

## C. In-House Counsel

Many securities lawyers serve as in-house counsel. In this role, they become part of the organization, participating actively in business decisions. To what extent is the position of such a lawyer different from the position of lawyers in private practice? Note the following materials.[2]

> For Attorneys who represent private and public businesses in an in-house capacity, the Rules of Professional Conduct under which they and all other lawyers must abide take on a different kind of meaning. For much of the bar, the rules represent a sweeping mandate for professional responsibility presented in a generalized context. But for in-house counsel and lawyers in a few other select areas of practice, the rules actually "get personal." They instruct almost on a one-to-one level, providing specific examples of appropriate action under established parameters.
>
> Following a lengthy discussion, in-house attorneys from across Pennsylvania who gathered recently to discuss the application — and effectiveness — of the so-called custom-made rules drew a common conclusion: while *their* rules talk in specifics, they aren't necessarily any easier to follow.
>
> Though many of the conduct rules apply to in-house counsel, the rule that most in-house attorneys deem the principle [sic] rule for their practice is Rule 1.13 governing lawyers representing organizations. Broken down into several parts, the rule states that lawyers who represent an organization have a duty to that organization, not to its individual officers and agents. It goes on to outline a lawyer's obligation when confronted with an illegality within the organization.
>
> "You as in-house counsel are obligated to act in the best interest of the organization," attorney Joel R. Burcat, a planner of the in-house counsel Continuing Legal Education session, told lawyers at the Pennsylvania Bar Association's Midyear Meeting in Baltimore Nov. 3.
>
> "This means you must do what is necessary to minimize the disruption to the organization, to minimize reviewing information outside of the organization and by going to the highest level of the organization if necessary — sometimes even to the board of directors if that

---

1. *See* Gerald J. Buchwald, *InHouse Target,* NAT'L L.J., Nov. 15, 1993, at S1.
2. Mark A. Tarasiewicz, *Rules of Conduct Get Personal, Specific Examples Cited for In-House Lawyers,* LEGAL INTELLIGENCER, Nov. 22, 1993, at 9.

is absolutely necessary — to seek to get the organization to act in a manner that is consistent with the law." Using a video vignette as a backdrop, Jeffrey Norton, in-house counsel at Philadelphia Electric Co., and Brian Addison, in-house counsel at the Hershey Co., provided role playing to illustrate the proper course of action. In the situation, a young lawyer for a hypothetical metal manufacturing company is presented with information from one of the company's engineers that one of its alloys used to build bridges has a latent defect that surfaces in a sub-zero-degree environment. According to Addison, such a situation is not uncommon, and it targets some key aspects of the rules. "Under Rule 1.2, a lawyer is required to abide by the client's decisions concerning objective representation — this is a mandatory dictate," Addison said.

"But another rule that is likely to come up [in this situation] is the rule on client confidentiality. Rule 1.6(a) provides that a lawyer shall not reveal information relating to the representation of the client. This is clearly a broader dictate than the familiar attorney-client privilege."

Addison also pointed to the application of Rule 1.6(c), which states that a lawyer may reveal discretionary information to the extent that he or she believes it necessary to, among other things, prevent criminal activity likely to result in substantial financial injury, bodily harm or death.

"The general principle is fairly absolute that the lawyer shall abide by client confidentiality, but it is not completely absolute," he said. "There are exceptions to that rule."

Speaking on the issue of what can happen when an attorney fails to report to regulators a potentially explosive situation, Constance Foster, former Pennsylvania insurance commissioner, recounted the story of the New York law firm Kaye Scholer Fierman Hays & Handler, which, on March 6, 1992, was sued by the Office of Thrift Supervision for $275 million over the firm's representation of the failed Lincoln Savings and Loan Association.

Six days later, the lawsuit was settled for $ 41 million, and heavy restrictions were placed on two Kaye Scholer partners. "Even though this was outside counsel, this [situation] is absolutely applicable to in-house counsel," Foster said. "People talk about regulated industries and that lawyers who work in regulated industries have perhaps stricter rules of ethics, [but] I would assert in today's environment that probably everybody is a regulated industry in some aspect or another. There's probably no business today which in some respect does not have to report to a regulator."

In the *Kaye Scholer* case, Foster said, the OTS argued in its complaint that the lawyers involved actually become more than lawyers and made themselves agents of the corporation. The OTS alleged that Kaye Scholer failed to give the regulator important information, and that the firm and its lawyers were in a conflict of interest because they represented Charles Keating, the holding company, the banks and their respective employees all at the same time. "The

> *Kaye Scholer* case raises some very crucial and important questions about the role of the attorney when it comes to dealing with regulated industry," Foster said. She explained that the standards of conduct for such lawyers are often enhanced in the context of statutory provisions. What the OTS was saying is that there are statutory concerns and duties which may be of a higher degree than what you may find under your normal ethical code," Foster said. "This case is a solemn reminder to all of us about just how significant your duty is to disclose, report and pursue possible criminal and other kinds of wrongdoing in your corporation."

* * *

In certain contexts, an in-house lawyer may be deemed to be a "supervisor" for purposes of the securities laws, thereby imposing liability on the lawyer for failure to supervise. This point was made clear in the following SEC proceeding against John Gutfreund. In *Gutfreund*, the head of the government trading desk at Salomon Brothers Inc. submitted a false bid to the U.S. Treasury and subsequently committed two other federal securities violations. Salomon's chief legal officer learned of the false bid submission later that year. In this excerpt, the SEC sets forth what it believes the appropriate steps that the chief legal officer should have taken.[1]

> Employees of brokerage firms who have legal or compliance responsibilities do not become "supervisors" for purposes of Sections 15(b)(4)(E) and 15(b)(6) solely because they occupy those positions. Rather, determining if a particular person is a "supervisor" depends on whether, under the facts and circumstances of a particular case, that person has a requisite degree of responsibility, ability or authority to affect the conduct of the employee whose behavior is at issue.[2*] Thus, persons occupying positions in the legal or compliance departments of broker-dealers have been found by the Commission to be "supervisors" for purposes of Sections 15(b)(4)(E) and 15(b)(6) under certain circumstances.
>
> In this case, serious misconduct involving a senior official of a brokerage firm was brought to the attention of the firm's chief legal officer. That individual was informed of the misconduct by other members of senior management in order to obtain his advice and guidance, and to involve him as part of management's collective response to the problem. Moreover, in other instances of misconduct, that individual had directed the firm's response and had made recommendations concerning appropriate disciplinary action, and management had relied on him to perform those tasks.

1. John H. Gutfreund, Exchange Act Rel. No. 31554 (Dec. 3, 1992).

2*. Although it did not represent an opinion of the Commission, the concurring opinion in Arthur James Huff, Exchange Act Release No. 29017 (March 28, 1991), is consistent with this principle. The operative portion of that opinion, Part VI, explains that in each situation a person's actual responsibilities and authority, rather than, for example, his or her "line" or "nonline" status, will determine whether he or she is a "supervisor" for purposes of Sections 15(b)(4)(E) and (6).

> Given the role and influence within the firm of a person in a position such as Feuerstein's and the factual circumstances of this case, such a person shares in the responsibility to take appropriate action to respond to the misconduct. Under those circumstances, we believe that such a person becomes a "supervisor" for purposes of Sections 15(b)(4)(E) and 15(b)(6). As a result, that person is responsible, along with the other supervisors, for taking reasonable and appropriate action. It is not sufficient for one in such a position to be a mere bystander to the events that occurred.

The SEC then elaborated on the responsibilities of such a person:

> Once a person in Feuerstein's position becomes involved in formulating management's response to the problem, he or she is obligated to take affirmative steps to ensure that appropriate action is taken to address the misconduct. For example, such a person could direct or monitor an investigation of the conduct at issue, make appropriate recommendations for limiting the activities of the employee or for the institution of appropriate procedures, reasonably designed to prevent and detect future misconduct, and verify that his or her recommendations, or acceptable alternatives, are implemented. If such a person takes appropriate steps but management fails to act and that person knows or has reason to know of that failure, he or she should consider what additional steps are appropriate to address the matter. These steps may include disclosure of the matter to the entity's board of directors, resignation from the firm, or disclosure to regulatory authorities.[1*]
>
> These responsibilities cannot be avoided simply because the person did not previously have direct supervisory responsibility for any of the activities of the employee. Once such a person has supervisory obligations by virtue of the circumstances of a particular situation, he must either discharge those responsibilities or know that others are taking appropriate action.

---

## Discussion Topics

a. Do you agree with the SEC's position? Was Feuerstein acting in a compliance capacity? Was he in the supervisory chain of the trading desk?

b. Under what circumstances, if any, would it be appropriate to subject outside counsel to liability as a supervisor?

c. As general counsel of a large corporation, is it possible not to be involved in the management of the entire enterprise? What about being involved in the establishment of a new subsidiary in China or another part of the world? Once established, what are the duties of the general counsel?

---

1*. Of course, in the case of an attorney, the applicable Code of Professional Responsibility and the Canons of Ethics may bear upon what course of conduct that individual may properly pursue.

## D. Behavior of Lawyers Engaged in Occupations Other than Lawyering

If an attorney is engaged in an occupation other than lawyering, how should that attorney represent himself to the public? May the attorney still demonstrate his capacity as a lawyer? To whom and under what circumstances? These issues arise in the financial services enterprises where lawyers hold positions involving the business side or compliance side of the operations. The following is an example of the issues.[1]

The Kansas Bar Association's ethics advisory service responds to inquiries from Kansas lawyers concerning proposed conduct. The following is the Committee's opinion, based upon a review of the disciplinary rules, model rules of professional responsibility and conduct, and applicable case law. The opinion does not grant immunity from legal or disciplinary proceedings.

> **Facts.** An attorney is employed fulltime as the "Trust and Financial Services Marketing Director" of a bank. The attorney's legal work and research opinions are for the bank pertaining to her work at the bank. The attorney's business card identifies the person, names the bank and gives the attorney's title, but does not indicate that such person also is a licensed attorney. The attorney is responsible for business development of the bank's financial services which include trusts, estates, investments, discount brokerage, annuities, mutual funds and retirement plans. The lawyer works directly with employers for the adoption agreements and summary plan documents for profit-sharing and 401K plans when the bank is the trustee. The legal documents for such work are not drafted by the lawyer or the bank. If legal work is needed by the bank customers, they acquire it through private counsel. Third party organizations supply the bank with retirement plan documents. In addition, the bank has invested in the attorney's continuing education to receive additional licenses, e.g., stockbroker's and life insurance agent licenses. The attorney indicates that when she calls on potential customers for the bank, the customers are more willing to talk about financial and business matters if they know she is also an attorney.
>
> Question: 1. May the attorney in conversations disclose to prospective clients her attorney status? 2. May the attorney list on her business card or separate bank station[e]ry that this marketing officer also is an attorney at law?
>
> Analysis. Lawyers may not make false or misleading statements about the lawyer or lawyer's services. The rule applies to all "communications," including advertising; however, the mode of communication does not matter. "Whatever means are used to make known a lawyer's services, statements about them should be truthful."
>
> The requesting lawyer is not providing private legal services. She is a bank employee. Lawyers with an active license to practice law, however, are subject to the Model Rules of Professional Conduct. . . .

1. Kansas Formal and Informal Opinions No. 93-07, Nat'l Rep. Legal Ethics (Univ. Pub. Am.) KS Opinions: 63 (Jul. 15, 1993).

Lawyers licensed to practice law are not precluded from non-legal business activities. Many are employed by businesses. They remain subject to the Model Rules. MRPC 5.4(b) precludes lawyers from forming business arrangements with nonlawyers if any of the activities of the partnership consist of the practice of law. Lawyers cannot split "legal fees" with nonlawyers except in limited circumstances not pertinent here. . . .

In March, 1988, the Model Rules of Professional Conduct replaced the older canons. Lawyers employed by other non-law firm businesses cannot perform legal services for third parties for which the attorney's employer benefits. While employers can determine general business policies and directions, so long as a lawyer has an active license to practice law on matters regarding a lawyer's truthfulness with others and professional judgment, an employer cannot direct the lawyer's independence and judgment.

The banking industry, because of its vulnerability to regulatory action by federal and state regulators and litigation from disgruntled customers, generally takes special pains that its lawyer-employees not provide legal services or advice to bank customers. To the extent a lawyer-employee is giving legal advice or services, it would violate MRPC 5.5(b) which prohibits assisting nonlawyers in activities which constitute the unauthorized practice of law. It would also constitute improper business entity relations with nonlawyers, along with possible non-lawyer fee splitting problems. Such practices also raise corporate malpractice issues about the lawyer-employee's independent judgment on behalf of the bank's customer-client. We view the banking industry's temperance in this arena as quite proper.

Since 1988 several U.S. Supreme Court cases interpreting the Model Rules have been decided. In the advertising area, MRPC 7.3 regulating direct contact with prospective clients by targeted mail was held to be a constitutional exercise of commercial free speech, and states could regulate only false or misleading activities of that nature. MRPC 7.3 applies to "lawyers" soliciting "professional employment." It is not limited to lawyers seeking legal service employment.

MRPC 7.3 regulates advertising and solicitation. The Rule is construed that a lawyer who goes on inactive status or works in a different profession or business can still state on business cards that he or she is a lawyer and may list degrees but may not "hold himself out as a lawyer." However, several opinions indicate that it is not false or misleading for lawyers to list on business cards the phrase "J.D." The restrictions of the Model Code date back to a more restrictive climate regarding lawyer advertising. Generally, today's Model Rules are more permissive in that they do not prohibit a lawyer from stating on a letterhead or by other means of communication that the lawyer is also qualified in a different professional field. Jurisdictions with the more modern view indicate lawyers may indicate on letterhead and other advertising "all professional licenses and academic degrees," or that a lawyer is both a CPA and certified financial planner. MRPC 7.4 does not appear to apply since it discusses dissemination of information about various "fields of law" within a "law practice." Inquiring counsel does not maintain such a practice.

MRPC 7.3's former restrictions on soliciting are getting weaker by the moment. Not only has the Supreme Court allowed lawyers to solicit using direct mail (and presumably use of appropriate letterheads and business cards), but it now has decided that CPAs who directly solicit business clients are not bound by the broad prophylactic rules against direct solicitation by the legal community.

In *Edenfield v. Fane*, the Supreme Court ruled that direct nonsolicitation rules for CPAs were unconstitutionally overbroad infringements on commercial speech. The theory is that CPAs seek sophisticated business clients and the business client is in a position to accept or deny the direct solicitation far better than a person who has just lost a loved one in an accident about which a personal injury attorney might inquire. Banning all direct solicitation by CPAs, as Florida did, is inconsistent with the state's proper regulatory role in conjunction with the First Amendment.

Since the inquiring attorney for this opinion is a bank marketing director who solicits the business and financial community for projects on which other bank employees process, *Edenfield* may have application. Bank customers of the type she is seeking are generally business clients. While the Model Rules do apply to her if she discloses on letterhead or business cards her attorney status, does *Edenfield's* liberalized view of attorney-solicitation limits under MRPC 7.3 apply?

We think so. In making the anti-solicitation restriction that was the subject of *Edenfield*, the Florida Board of Accountancy had relied on several U.S. Supreme Court cases allowing prophylactic "blanket bans" on direct lawyer solicitation. *Edenfield* indicates the reliance may be misplaced, and that key Supreme Court attorney-discipline decisions like *Ohralik v. Ohio Bar Association* should be limited to the facts and such cases do not stand for the proposition that "all personal solicitation is without First Amendment protection," or that "blanket bans on personal solicitation by all types of professionals are constitutional in all circumstances."

In *Ohralik*, Ohio disciplined a lawyer who directly solicited business from two young accident victims in their hospital room. Justice Kennedy wrote for the *Edenfield* majority:

"Because 'the distinctions, historical and functional, between professions, may require consideration of quite different factors'. . . the constitutionality of a ban on personal solicitation will depend on the identity of the parties and the precise circumstances of the solicitation. . . . *Ohralik's* holding was narrow and depended upon certain 'unique features of in-person solicitation by lawyers' that were present in the circumstances of that case. . . .'"

"*Ohralik* . . . held only that a State Bar 'constitutionally may discipline a lawyer for soliciting clients in person, for pecuniary gain, under circumstances likely to pose dangers that the State has a right to prevent. . . .'"

"The engagements Fane seeks are also long-term in nature; to the extent he engages in unpleasant, high pressure sales tactics, he can impair rather than improve his chances of obtaining an engagement or establishing a satisfactory professional relation. The importance of repeat business and referrals gives the CPA a strong incentive to act in a responsible and decorous manner when soliciting business. . . . The ban on attorney solicitation in *Ohralik* was prophylactic in the sense that it prohibited conduct conducive to fraud and overreaching at the outset, rather than punishing the misconduct after it occurred."

In a related advertising case, a Florida lawyer ethics rule requiring lawyers to wait 30 days before sending targeted direct mail solicitation letters to victims of accidents or disasters unconstitutionally restricted lawyer free speech rights. While based on an equal protection basis (personal injury lawyer restrictions versus all other lawyers), *McHenry* again shows that blanket banning of certain solicitation and advertising rules are suspect.

Obviously, *Edenfield* has not been directly applied to lawyer solicitation of business clients, but we think *Edenfield's* facts and conclusions analogous to the questions posed here. Many lawyers are also CPAs. Many lawyers, like inquiring counsel, work solely within and desire to built [sic] rapport with the business community. Generally a lawyer-CPA, whether practicing as a lawyer or in a CPA firm, seeks similar types of business clients. At the least it would appear *Edenfield* requires that direct solicitation of business clients by lawyers for falsehoods or misrepresentations must be reviewed on a case by case basis to see if improper solicitation has occurred. Use of the business cards and individualized letterhead are simply a means of solicitation. If a letter is used for introductory purposes, *Shapero* and *McHenry* may apply. If a business card is used in personal solicitations, *Edenfield* may be applicable.

Further, we note that inquiring counsel is not in the private practice of law, and will not be soliciting private practice clients. The work she does for clients of the bank is not intended to be the subject of litigation; indeed, any legal work she does is directly for the bank and its officers and employees. Her motive for inclusion of the "attorney at law" notation on her bank business card and separate bank letterhead is not private pecuniary gain, but rather to give her a professional status and visibility on behalf of her employer. On behalf of the bank's financial services division, she is seeking to communicate her degree and learned abilities to the same sort of "sophisticated business clients" as did CPA Fane.

**OPINION**

Given the emerging trend in lawyer solicitation cases by the U.S. Supreme Court and the commentary of applicable Model Rules, we believe that the inclusion of "attorney at law" on a bank lawyer-employee's individualized bank letterhead and business cards for the limited purpose of enhancing her status within the business community in which she exclusively works does not violate the Model Rules.

---

**Discussion Topics**

a. Financial services firms generally have large compliance departments. Some of these departments, charged with instilling and monitoring procedures to ensure compliance with relevant laws, work as part of the firm's law department and some are independent of the law department. Naturally, lawyers are often recruited to work in the compliance departments. What impact does this decision have on lawyers who work in a compliance department that is attached to the firm's law department? What if the compliance department is unattached?

b. Are communications between a client and an attorney acting in a compliance capacity subject to the attorney-client privilege?

c. What is the status of lawyers whose main occupation is administrative but who work part-time at providing legal advice?

d. Should a lawyer engaged in non-legal business be subject to the rule of ethics applicable to lawyers? Should a lawyer engaged in non-legal business be allowed to describe himself as a lawyer? In what respect is ethics involved in these issues?

It should be remembered that a lawyer who engages in other than lawyerly activities may be subject to the regulation of such activity. The staff of the SEC declined to grant no-action relief from section 15(a) of the Securities Exchange Act, regulating brokers, to a law firm that assists a corporation in obtaining financing. The assistance consisted of soliciting firms to purchase its securities. The firm's compensation was based on a percentage of financing obtained. The staff noted that "transaction-based compensation in connection with [purchase or sale of securities] is a hallmark of broker-dealer activity."[1] If your activities look like those of a broker and you are paid as brokers do, you are subject to a brokers' regulation.

---

## E. Investment Managers' Ethical Issues

### 1. Investment by Portfolio Managers

This section deals with ethical issues involving non-lawyer investment managers. These issues may be presented to the attorney as adviser for an investment manager client. Similar issues are raised in section 17(j) of the 1940 Act. Usually portfolio managers love their profession and sometimes are obsessed with trading and with predicting markets' movements. Portfolio managers of large funds generally have at their disposal the best research tools and large databases available to help them make investment decisions for their funds. They study the materials long and hard. These research tools can be costly, in terms of acquisition and on-going service.

1. Brumberg, Mackey & Wall, P.L.C., Corres. (May 17, 2010).

Portfolio managers use the research tools for the benefit of the funds, as well as for their own investment purposes. In fact, so do any experts who acquire added information while working and creating. Portfolio managers do not always follow the advice and investment decisions they offer to clients and managed pools of investors. That is because the purposes and investment policies of their clients and funds do not always fit those of the managers. Therefore, this is one of the arguments for allowing portfolio managers to make personal investments other than their clients' investments. Thus, there are two main arguments for allowing portfolio managers and brokers to invest for their own accounts and to make different investments than those recommended for clients: the managers' and brokers' insatiable drive to trade and their different investment policies and circumstances.

Yet, trading for their own accounts brings to the fore conflicts of interest. Not only do the managers and brokers benefit from information that belongs to the investors, but they may also benefit from information of the very trades they make for their clients. They may invest before they invest for the clients or after, depending on their own predictions as to the effect of their decisions for the clients might be on the markets.

Yet, one can imagine a portfolio manager who feels entitled to some benefits from his work apart from salary and bonuses. After all, it is he who contributes to the investors' wealth while the investors do not do a thing but give him the money to manage. Consequently, some managers may view investors as unjustly enriched, at the managers' expense. That view justifies some adjustment of the benefit — at the expense of the clients.

---

**Discussion Topics**

a. Following the strict principles of fiduciary law, should portfolio managers be allowed to use the research tools of the funds for their own benefit? What are the reasons for allowing managers to do so? How difficult would it be to enforce a full prohibition on the use of these tools?

b. Is it right for portfolio managers to trade for their own account? What are the ethical issues involved in doing so? Should they trade for the account of their family and friends? Should they be prohibited from doing so by law?

c. Do these issues relate to ethics? Should these questions be settled among the portfolio managers and the fund directors? Or should they be settled among the managers and their clients? Or should portfolio managers be expected to refrain from trading even if the law or the clients do not prohibit such trading? Or only if clients expressly permit them to trade? Why are these questions an issue in the first place?

---

## 2. "Social Investing"

Social investing is an issue that arises from time to time with different levels of intensity. This issue may be viewed as involving ethical principles. There is a real question of whether avoiding investments in liquor, tobacco or weapon productions or avoiding investments in countries which are controlled by dictators, even at the expense of higher returns, is ethical. If the owners of the investments express their preferences against such investments, no question arises. If the fiduciary managers make the decision, a question arises whether they have the right to make such decisions, whether the decisions are for the benefit of the clients even if the returns on the investments are the same. The difficult issues arise when ethical principles conflict when doing good is not compatible with doing well. Here is a discussion on the issue.[1]

> For those who like precise moral slide rules to guide action, application of ethical principles to the social investment area may prove disappointing. The chief contribution lies precisely in the ethician's insistence that pension fund managers operate in two cities — the city of economic fact and the city of moral values. To act as though each operated with its own rules or, even worse, that each is at war with the other, is to blur reality. Pension fund managers who are expected to have competence in judging what investment areas promise solid financial returns should be equally competent in determining what ethical judgment promises substantial social returns. While the relationship may be marked by tension and uncertainties, the important thing to recognize is that the relationship exists — and that social investments are not necessarily riskier than financial investing.
>
> Since every pension fund represents a portfolio whose total assets are both economic and ethical, investments must be made to seek total returns. Total returns, so defined, involve policy making which blends the moral geometry to a financial geometry. That it is possible to perform ethically while doing well financially is a moral to be drawn from the Dreyfus Third Century Fund, a money market fund that examines a company's regard for consumer protection, its commitment to an affirmative-action philosophy as shown by the hiring record, its concern for the physical environment, and sensitivity to its neighbors [sic] needs. The result? By a substantial margin Dreyfus was ahead of the average stock performance in 1980-81. Where we now stand in this blending process between the financial and moral geometries can best be answered by experts themselves: how many trustees, how many legislators, how many regulators engaged in pension fund operations recognize their roles as moral geometers in America? If the thesis of this paper is correct, the question will become the center of critical debate during this decade — even as corporate social responsibilities and corporate governance were the lively issues of the last two decades.

---

__Discussion Topic__

What are the conflicting principles in the case of social investing? How is the issue being solved these days? How should it be resolved?

---

1. Clarence C. Walton, Pension Funds and Social Investments, A Tale of Two Cities in Social Investing 37-38 (Dan M. McGill ed., 1984).

### 3. Relation to Two or More Clients

How should an adviser treat more than one client? Suppose an adviser has two client accounts. One account holds about $200,000 and the other $50,000. He charges both accounts one percent of the amounts under management. Should the adviser spend the same amount of time and attention on both accounts? Should he use the information and analysis he received in connection with the large account to manage the smaller account? Should he charge the smaller account more? If the smaller account happened to be performing better than the larger account, may the adviser move some of the better performing assets from the smaller account to the larger account to make both profitable (although that would render the smaller account less profitable than it would otherwise)? What guidelines should the adviser follow? Wherefrom would he derive these guidelines? Are the clients' expectations relevant here? What are the expectations of these two clients?

The issues and questions are not unique to advisers and money managers. Lawyers face the issue when relating to clients with conflicting interests. Trustees face the same issue when they serve both income beneficiaries — those who receive the income from the estate's assets, and remaindermen — those who will receive the remainder of the estate after the income beneficiaries die. Risky investments benefit the income beneficiaries while conservative investments benefit the remaindermen.

All these cases involve fiduciaries. In all cases, there are a few guidelines that might be helpful. One guide is the implicit or explicit expectations and consents of the beneficiaries, or clients, or "entrustors" as all of them can be called. No reasonable client of a lawyer expects the lawyer to commit as much time if a huge amount of money is involved as compared to a very small amount. In the case of a trust, the trustor's intentions and the way he dealt with the beneficiaries before his death may provide a signal for the trustees. Sometimes the majority of the shareholders or the explicit public policy of the investment company may guide the advisers and their portfolio managers. And sometimes congressional policies may guide the fiduciary.

## F. Issues Regarding Fund Directors

The following problem raises difficult ethical questions, regardless of the law. It deals with a case which we covered in discussing fund governance.[1]

As a shareholder in a mutual fund, you expect the fund's directors to look out for your interests, first and foremost. But if the fund company pays a director $100,000, will he still do so? What if he is paid a package worth $400,000? We noted the *Strougo* case in the Chapter dealing with governance. However, in the wake of the 2008 crash, the pressure on allowing shareholders to have a say with respect to the management's compensation has grown. One form of possible pressure is to allow shareholders to voice their opinion with respect to advisers' fees and portfolio managers' compensation. The shareholders can do that by receiving information

1. Carole Gould, *Who's Watching Out for the Shareholders?* N.Y. TIMES, Jun. 8, 1997, § 3 (Money & Business), at 6.

about the management's compensation. More intrusive reaction allows investors to express their opinion about the compensation by filling a box or responding to a comment in the shareholder proposals.

---

## Discussion Topics

a. Should a director refuse to sit on more than one (or a few) board(s)? Or should the director ask whether the law prohibits multiple directorships and be content with the answer that the law does not prohibit them? Should that decision be made by the director or by his lawyer, or both?

b. How should a director decide whether director payments or his director status inhibit his free decision and exercise of his duties?

c. If a director is pressed hard by the adviser or its counsel to approve a certain course of action, what questions should the director ask of himself? What questions should the director ask his lawyer? Are these the same questions?

d. Having gone through the Course materials, what are the main policies underlying the regulation of investment advisers and investment companies? What aspect, if any, of the federal regulation did you find helpful to achieve the policies? What should be the regulatory role of state regulation on this subject?

e. Would you invest in the shares of a mutual fund? Would you like to become a general counsel, or a compliance officer of a mutual fund, or of a hedge fund?

---

# *Epilogue*

With the crash of 2008 came numerous proposals on mending the financial system. After proposals by the Administration, House, and Senate, in June 2010, the House passed a financial reform proposal that had been negotiated by a conference committee.[1] Not many suggestions focused on mutual funds. After all, apart from money market fund issues, there were no problems in the fund area. Nonetheless, there are two interesting suggestions that involve mutual funds in different ways. One suggestion is by Professor Laurence J. Kotlikoff, in his recent book JIMMY STEWART IS DEAD.[2] In this book, he offers the mutual fund model as a model for banks. Investors who desire no risk at no return can invest in banks for that sort of investment. The more risk they are willing to take, the more return they will receive, just as shareholders in mutual funds do.

The other proposal that involves mutual funds goes to the opposite extreme. In that proposal, mutual funds and the Investment Company Act would disappear and what remains is an offer of shares with simple structures by money managers, presumably the issuers. There is no regulation of investors' pooled assets and no board of directors. The business of the issuer is financial management, but that is no different than the business of an issuer that is engaged in producing shoes. Both ideas share one feature: Both emphasize simplicity. Kotlikoff emphasizes simplicity of structure. The other proposal emphasizes simplicity of the offered security. Both reduce regulation. Both reduce complexity. Even though it is unclear to what extent either banks or mutual funds will change form, the two proposals raised attention because of their similar purpose: to simplify financial structures and products. To that extent, they are both prescient and convincing.

Another trend that might affect investment managers and their funds is the disagreements among the members of Congress. The most interesting proposal is to delegate to the Securities and Exchange Commission the decision of whether brokers should be subject to fiduciary duties.[3] This issue

1. Dodd-Frank Wall Street Reform and Consumer Protection Act, H.R. 4173 (passed by House Jun. 30, 2010). The bill was signed into law. Dodd-Frank Wall Street Reform and Consumer Protection Act, Pub. L. No. 111-203, 2010 U.S.C.C.A.N. (124 Stat.) 1376, *codified in scattered sections of* U.S.C.

2. L.J. KOTLIKOFF, JIMMY STEWART IS DEAD (2010).

3. Dodd-Frank Wall Street Reform and Consumer Protection Act, Pub. L. No. 111-203, § 913(g), 2010 U.S.C.C.A.N. (124 Stat.) 1376, 1828, *codified at* 15 U.S.C. § 78*o*(k) (authorizing SEC to adopt rules providing that a broker or dealer has a fiduciary

was unresolved among the House and Senate. The Senate was adamant at not imposing fiduciary duties on brokers who say "trust me." And the House did not retreat altogether from its position.[1] To some extent, the Commission has been subject to very great pressures by both parties, and the issue has not been fully resolved as of October 2015.

A development worthy of note is the agreement of Democratic Congressman Frank (then a Representative from Massachusetts) and Republican Senator Brown (then a Senator from Massachusetts) to exempt mutual funds, most of which are based in Massachusetts. Apart from the explanations that both parties sought the support of the financial giants in Massachusetts, there may be a justification for granting exemptions to institutions that remained more "clear" than others during the "Great Temptation" period. Thus, it may be that the fact that these large institutions gained exemption on the merit and relief from costly regulation is a signal to others to follow suit.[2] Perhaps exemptions should be offered as rewards to institutions that withstood temptations, controlled risks, and maintained services.

---

duty "when providing personalized investment advice to a retail customer"); *id.* § 913(b), 2010 U.S.C.C.A.N. (124 Stat.) at 1824-25 (requiring SEC to study issue); *id.* § 913(c), 2010 U.S.C.C.A.N. (124 Stat.) at 1825-27 (listing considerations in conducting study). The SEC staff study recommended a uniform fiduciary standard. SEC, Study on Investment Advisers and Broker-Dealers As Required by Section 913 of the Dodd-Frank Wall Street Reform and Consumer Protection Act (2011), *available at* http://www.sec.gov/news/studies/2011/913studyfinal.pdf.

1. *See, e.g.,* Financial Reform May Include Fiduciary Standard, FFS Blog, Jun. 25, 2010, LEXIS, News Library, Curnws File (noting that previous House version would have required imposing fiduciary duties on brokers; previous Senate version would have required only that SEC study the issue).

2. *See, e.g.,* Meredith Shiner, *Volcker Rule Backers Praise Bill,* Politico.com, Jun. 25, 2010, LEXIS, News Library, Curnws File (quoting statement by Congressman Frank that "mutual funds, which have not been engaged in volatility . . . not be treated exactly the same as Goldman Sachs or people with greater volatility").

# *Tables of Authorities*

**Investment Advisers Act**



**United States Public Laws**

**Bills**



**United States Code of Federal Regulations**

**Exchange Act Releases**



**Investment Company Act Releases**

**Investment Advisers Act Releases**

**Federal Register**

**Table of Cases and Enforcement Actions**

**Litigation Releases**



**Correspondence**

**Division of Investment Management Guidance Updates**



**SEC Press Releases**



**Hearings, Testimony, Speeches and Letters**

_____, Institutional Investors Full Disclosure Act: Hearings on S. 2234 and S. 2683 Before the Subcomm. on Sec. of the S. Comm. on Banking, Hous. & Urban Affairs, 93d Cong. 19, 20 —179

Atkins, Paul S., Examining the Dangers of the FSOC's Designation Process and Its Impact on the U.S. Financial System: Hearing on H.R. 4387 Before the H. Comm. on Fin. Serv. 113 Cong. 60-69 (2014) (statement of Paul S. Atkins, CEO, Patomak Global Partners) —5, 6

Barbash, Barry P., Keynote Address, "This Year in Funds: The Responsibilities of Prosperity," Dec. 3, 1996 —229

Breeden, Richard C., Chairman, Securities and Exchange Commission, to The Honorable John D. Dingell, Chairman, House Committee on Energy and Commerce, (Apr. 15, 1992) —298

Breeden, Richard C., Chairman, U.S. Securities and Exchange Commission, Concerning Proposed Revisions to Rules Governing Bank Common Trust Funds Before the Subcomm. on Telecommunications and Finance of the Comm. on Energy and Commerce, 101st Cong. (1990). —121

Champ, Norm, Director, Div. of Investment Management, SEC, Remarks to the ALI CLE 2012 Conference on Investment Adviser Regulation: Legal and Compliance Forum on Institutional Advisory Services (Dec. 6, 2012), sec.gov/news/speech/2012/spch120612nc.htm —476

Examining the Dangers of the FSOC's Designation Process and its Impact of the U.S. Financial System: Hearing on H.R. 4387 Before the H. Comm. On Fin. Serv. 113 Cong. (Memorandum to members of the Comm. On Fin. Serv. From FSC Comm. Maj. Staff) —4

Johnson, Norman S., Commissioner, U.S. Securities and Exchange Commission, Suits Against Lawyers, Speech Before the American Bar Association Federal Securities Law Committee (Nov. 8, 1996), http://www.sec.gov/ news/speech/ speecharchive/1996/ spch137.txt. —521

Jones, David B., Senior Vice President, Fidelity Management & Research Co. & Eric D. Roiter, Senior Vice President and General Counsel, Fidelity Management & Research Co. 8-9 (Jun. 4, 2004), http://www.sec.gov/rules/proposed/s71104/fidelity060404.pdf —274

Jones, David B., Senior Vice President, Product Strategy & Communications, Fidelity Management & Research Co. & Eric D. Roiter, Senior Vice President and General Counsel, Fidelity Management & Research Co. (Mar. 2, 2004), http://www.sec.gov/rules/concept/s72903/fidelity03022004.htm —181

McNabb III, F. William, Examining the Dangers of the FSOC's Designation Process and Its Impact on the U.S. Financial System: Hearing on H.R. 4387 Before the H. Comm. on Fin. Serv. 113 Cong. 73-87 (2014) —6

Mutual Fund Directors as Investor Advocates, Remarks by Chairman Arthur Levitt, U.S. Securities and Exchange Commission, The Second Annual Symposium for Mutual Fund Trustees and Directors, Washington, D.C., Apr. 11, 1995 —249

Risks That Hedge Funds Pose to the Banking System: Hearing Before the House Comm. on Banking, Finance and Urban Affairs, 103d Cong. 144 (1994) —149

### U.S. House of Representatives

H.R. Rep. No. 76-2639, Investment Trust Study, Investment Company Act of 1940 and Investment Advisers Act of 1940 —11

H.R. Rep. No. 89-2337, Report of the SEC on the Public Policy Implications of Investment Company Growth, (1966) —201, 205, 216

H.R. Rep. No. 113-1800, Small Business Credit Availability Act (rev. Jun. 30, 2014) —111

### U.S. Senate

S. Rep. No. 293, Report of the Senate Committee on Banking, Housing and Urban Affairs, to accompany S.1815, 104th Cong. 20 (Jun. 26, 1996) —53, 301

## Books and Treatises

_____, Inv. Co. Inst., Investment Company Fact Book (55th ed. 2015), https://www.ici.org/pdf/2015_factbook.pdf —431, 469, 470

_____, Restatement (Second) of Agency (1958) —49

_____, Restatement (Third) of Agency (2006) —49

_____, The Financial Services Revolution, Understanding the Changing Role of Banks, Mutual Funds, and Insurance Companies (Clifford E. Kirsch ed., 1997) —142

Cox, James C. et al., Securities Regulation (1991) —517

Ervin, Susan C., Commodity Pools: Collective Investment Funds Under the Futures Regulatory Framework (1998) —147

Frankel, Tamar and Ann Taylor Schwing, The Regulation of Money Managers (2001 & Supp. 2015) —8, 19, 20, 21, 50, 51, 123, 124, 125, 198, 252, 257, 294, 382, 415, 443, 457, 465, 470, 471, 479, 513

Frankel, Tamar and Mark Fagan, Law and the Financial System (2009) —1

Frankel, Tamar, Fiduciary Law (2010) —29, 201, 377

Frankel, Tamar, Fiduciary Law (2011) —49

Frankel, Tamar, Securitization: Structured Financing, Financial Asset Pools, and Asset-Backed Securities (Ann Taylor Schwing ed., 2d ed. 2005) —7, 130, 135, 139, 141

Frankel, Tamar, The Ponzi Scheme Puzzle (2012) (Oxford University Press) —43

Frankel, Tamar, Trust and Honesty, America's Business Culture at a Crossroad (2006) —515, 516

Galbraith, John Kenneth, The Great Crash, 1929 (1988) —10, 11

Hagstrom, Jr., Robert G., The Warren Buffett Way: Investment Strategies of the World's Greatest Investor (1994) —112

Helm, Robert W., Offshore Investment Funds, appearing in The Financial Services Revolution, Understanding the Changing Role of Banks, Mutual Funds, and Insurance Companies (Clifford E. Kirsch ed., 1997) —142

Kirsch, Clifford E., Investment Adviser Regulation, A Step-by-Step Guide to Compliance and the Law (1996) —173

Kirsch, Clifford E., Investment Adviser Regulation, A Step-by-Step Guide to Compliance and the Law (1998) —59, 62, 301, 303

Kirsch, Clifford E., Investment Adviser Regulation: A Step-By_Step Guide to Compliance and the Law (PLI 2010) —56

Kotlikoff, L.J., Jimmy Stewart Is Dead (2010) —543

Lemke, Thomas P., & Gerald T. Lins, Regulation of Investment Advisers (2015) —9
Lowenstein, Roger, Buffett: The Making of an American Capitalist (1995) —112
Sorkin, Andrew Ross, Too Big to Fail (2009) —4
Stern, Gary H. & Ron J. Feldman,Too Big To Fail (Brookings Institution Press 2003) —4
Walter, Ingo, The Secret Money Market (1990) —143
Wright, Gregory S., et al, The Securities Enforcement Manual (2d ed. 2007) —27

**Articles, Notes and Comments**

_____, Charles Schwab Corp. Managed Accounts, http://www.aboutschwab.com/about/ facts/managed-accounts.html —51
_____, Clarification of the SEC's Recent Guidance on Gifts and Entertainment Paid to Advisory Personnel, Investment Company Institute Memorandum (Jun. 9, 2015). —410
_____, Financial Reform May Include Fiduciary Standard, FFS Blog, June 25, 2010, LEXIS, News Library, Curnws File —544
_____, International Association of Financial Engineers Investor Risk Comm., Valuation Concepts for Investment Companies and Financial Institutions and their Stakeholders, Jun. 8, 2004 —261, 262
_____, Investment Company Institute, Re: Proposed Rules Relating to Selective Disclosure and Insider Trading (Apr. 27, 2000), at http://www.ici.org/policy/comments/ci.00_SEC_REGFD_COM.print —332
_____, Kansas Formal and Informal Opinions No. 93-07, Nat'l Rep. Legal Ethics (Univ. Pub. Am.) KS OPINIONS: 63 (Jul. 15, 1993) —533
_____, Orrick Financial Market Alert, May 24, 2010 —440
_____, U.S. Dep't of the Treas., Fact Sheet: Administration's Regulatory Reform Agenda Moves Forward: Legislation for Strengthening Investor Protection (July 10, 2009), http://www.treas.gov/press/releases/tg205.htm —46
Astarita, Mark J., The Wells Notice in SEC and NASD Investigations: Could It Possibly Be a Good Thing? (2010), http//www.seclaw.com/docs/wellsnotice.htm —28
Birdthistle, William A., The Fortunes and Foibles of Exchange-Traded Funds: A Positive Market Response to the Problems of Mutual Funds, 33 Del. J. Corp. L. 69 (2008) —473
Bogle, John C., Founder and Former Chairman, The Vanguard Group, The Mutual Fund Industry 60 Years Later: For Better or Worse?, http://www.vanguard.com/ bogle_site/sp20050102.htm —205
Buchwald, Gerald J., InHouse Target, Nat'l L. J., Nov. 15, 1993 —529
CFTC Division of Economic Analysis, Survey of Commodity Pool Operators in Futures Markets with an Analysis of Interday Position Changes (1991) —150
Comment, Investment Company Act of 1940, 50 Yale L.J. 440 (1941) —17
Cutler, Stephen M., Remarks Before Investment Company Institute. Securities Law Developments Conference (Dec. 6, 2001) —74

Dyck, Alexander & Luigi Zingales, Private Benefits of Control: An International Comparison, 59 The Journal of Finance 537 (2004) —428

Fiflis, Ted J., Choice of Federal or State Law for Attorneys' Professional Responsibility in Securities Matters, 56 N.Y.U. L. Rev. 1236 (1981) —517

Frankel, Tamar, Papers on a Fiduciary Duty for Broker-Dealers: The Regulation of Brokers, Dealers, Advisers, and Financial Planners, 30 Rev. Banking & Fin. L. 123 (2010) —47

Frankel, Tamar, Professor of Law, Boston University School of Law, to Securities and Exchange Commission, Mutual Funds as Shareholders of Corporate America: Should Funds Be Required to Disclose Their Voting Record? (2002) —314

Frankel, Tamar, Should Funds and Investment Advisers Establish a Self-Regulatory Organization? In The Financial Services Revolution, Understanding the Changing Role of Banks. Mutual funds, and Insurance Companies (Clifford E. Kirsch ed. 1997) —31

Frankel, Tamar, The Delaware Business Trust Act Failure as the New Corporate Law, 23 Cardozo L. Rev. 325 (2001) —240

Frankel, Tamar, The Jurisprudence of the Securities and Exchange Commission New Rule 206(4)-7 (2004) —81

Gould, Jay B. & Gerald T. Lins, Unit Investment Trusts: Structure and Regulation Under the Federal Securities Laws, 43 Bus. Law. 1177 (1988) —443

Harman, Thomas S., Emerging Alternatives to Mutual Funds: Unit Investment Trusts and Other Fixed Portfolio Investment Vehicles, 1987 Duke L.J. 1045 —443, 445, 447

Haskin, Benjamin J., James R. Burns, & James E. Doench, Exchange Listing of ETFs: Key Concerns in the 19b-4 Process, Inv. Law., Mar. 2015 —478

Hunt, Isaac C. Jr., Commissioner, U.S. Securities and Exchange Commission, 1997 Investment Adviser Conference, Investment Company Institute Washington, D.C. (Jun. 16, 1997) —176

Jaretzki, Alfred Jr., The Investment Company Act of 1940, 26 Wash. U. L.Q. 303 (1941) —17

Johnsen, D. Bruce, Property Rights to Investment Research: The Agency Costs of Soft Dollar Brokerage, 11 Yale J. Reg. 75 (1994) —67

Jones, David B., Senior Vice President, Product Strategy & Communications, Fidelity Management & Research Co. & Eric D. Roiter, Senior Vice President and General Counsel, Fidelity Management & Research Co. (Mar. 2, 2004) —181

Livingston, Miles & Edward S. O'Neal, Mutual Fund Brokerage Commissions, 19 J. Fin. Res. 273 (1996) —67

Lorne, Simon M., The Corporate and Securities Adviser, The Public Interest, and Professional Ethics, 76 Mich. L. Rev. 423 (1978) —517

Lowenfels, Lewis D., Expanding Public Responsibilities of Securities Lawyers: An Analysis of the New Trend in Standard of Care and Priorities of Duties, 74 Colum. L. Rev. 412 (1974) —517

**Newspapers and Magazines**

**The Atlantic**



**Business Wire**



**Canadian Business**



**C-Span, National Cable Satellite Corporation**



**The Financial Times**



**Journal of Portfolio Management**



**Legal Intelligencer**



**The New York Times**

### Reuters

Adler, Lynn, BDCs Step Closer to New Legislation, More Leverage, REUTERS, Nov. 19, 2015, http://www.reuters.com/article/2015/11/19/us-bdc-legislation-idUSKCN0T82DW20151119?feedType=RSS&feedName=PersonalFinance#eA4tp2q9FzMOjmMQ.97 —111

### Sacramento Bee

Sirard, Jack, Spiders Climb Web of Investment Popularity, Sacramento Bee, Mar. 18, 1993 —470

### Wall Street Journal

Franecki, David, Pension Trustees Pressed to Quit Tobacco, Wall St. J., Jul. 7, 1997 —319

Lauricella, Tom & Strasburg, Jenny, SEC Probes Cancelled Trades: Regulators Looking Into Role "Quote Stuffing" May Have Played in Flash Crash, Wall St. J., Sept. 2, 2010 —52

Maxey, Daisy, SEC Will Maintain Open Veil On ETFs, Wall St. J., Oct. 23, 2014 —471

Mullins, Brody, Family Trusts Lobby to Avoid New Rules, Wall St. J., Oct. 21, 2009 —71

Salwen, Kevin G. & Cohen, Laurie P., Getting Tough: SEC Under Breeden Takes a Harder Line on Securities Crime, Wall St. J. May 10, 1990 —26

## Investment Company Institute Memorandum

Clarification of the SEC's Recent Guidance on Gifts and Entertainment Paid to Advisory Personnel, Investment Company Institute Memorandum (Jun. 9, 2015) —410, 411

## Law Firm Memos

Ethical Responsibilities of Legal and Compliance Professionals: Recent SEC and FINRA Cases Involving Lawyers and Compliance Professionals prepared by Anne C. Flannery, partner, and Alice L. McCarthy, associate resident in the New York office of Morgan, Lewis & Bockius LLP. Copyright 2009, Morgan, Lewis & Bockius LLP —523

Memorandum of Simona Suh, Certain Hedge Fund Trading Practices, NY-7563-A (Apr. 10, 2006) —43

## Internet Links

### The Atlantic Monthly Group

Deutsche Bank Also 'Victimized' Goldman 'Victim', The Atlantic (April 26, 2010), http://www.theatlantic.com/business/archive/2010/04/deutsche-bank-also-victimized-goldman-victim/39471/ —41

### Charles Schwab Corp.

Charles Schwab Corp. Managed Accounts, http://www.aboutschwab.com/about/facts/managed-accounts.html —51

### Congressional Budget Office

Cost Estimate: H.R. 1800, Small Business Credit Availability Act (rev. Jun. 30, 2014), http://www.cbo.gov/sites/default/files/cbofiles/attachments/hr1800revised.pdf —111

### C-Span, National Cable Satellite Corporation

Securities and Exchange Commission: Wall Street Journal CFO Network Conference, C-SPAN (Jun. 25, 2013), www.c-spanvideo.org/program/313430-10. —27

### Federal Deposit Insurance Corporation

FDIC Trust Examination Manual, Appendix D: Securities Law, http:/www.fdic.gov/regulations/examinations/trustmanual/appendix_d/appendix_d. html —68, 69, 70

### The Financial Times

Definition of too big to fail, http://lexicon.ft.com/Term?term=too-big-to-fail —3

### FindLaw, Thomson Reuters

State v. Canary Capital Partners (N.Y. Sup. Ct. Sept. 3, 2003), http://news.findlaw.com/nytimes/docs/nys/nyscanary90303cmp.pdf —263

### Financial Industry Regulatory Authority, Inc.

NASD Rule 2830, http://finra.complinet.com/en/display/display_main.html?rbid=2403&element_id=3691 —341

### Investment Company Institute

Investment Company Fact Book (55th ed. 2015), https://www.ici.org/pdf/2015_factbook.pdf —431, 469,470

Proposed Rules Relating to Selective Disclosure and Insider Trading (Apr. 27, 2000), http://www.ici.org/policy/comments/ci.00_SEC_REGFD_COM.print —332

Report of the Money Market Working Group Submitted to the Board of the Governors of the Investment Company Institute, Executive Summary, (Mar. 17, 2009), http://www.ici.org/pdf/ppr_09_mmwg.pdf —434, 435, 477

### Jim Hamilton Blogspot

Jim Hamilton's World of Securities Regulation, Dec. 22, 2010 President Signs Legislation Modernizing Federal Tax Code Treatment of SEC-Regulated Investment Companies, http://jimhamiltonblogspot.com/2010/12/ president-signslegislationmodernizing.html —31

### New York Stock Exchange

NYSE Arca Equities Rules, Rule 5.2(j)(3), http://nysearcarules.nyse.com/PCXtools/PlatformViewer.asp?SelectedNode=chp_1_1&manual=/PCX/pcxe/pcxe-rules/ —478

NYSE Arca Equities Rules, Rule 8.600, http://nysearcarules.nyse.com/PCXtools/PlatformViewer.asp?SelectedNode=chp_1_1&manual=/PCX/pcxe/pcxe-rules/ —478

NYSE MKT Rules, Rule 1000A, Commentary .02(b)(1), http://wallstreet.cch.com/MKTtools/PlatformViewer.asp?SelectedNode=chp_1_7&manual=/MKT/rules/mkt-rules/ —477

### The New York Times

A Wall Street Scapegoat Goes Down, The New York Times (Aug. 2, 2013), http://takingnote.blogs.nytimes.com/2013/08/02/another-scapegoat-goes-down/?ref=fabricetourre&_r=0 —41

Trich, Teresa, NY Times, http://takingnote.blogs.nytimes.com/2013/08/02/another-scapegoat-goes-down/?ref=fabricetourre&_r=0, A Wall Street Scapegoat Goes Down, The New York Times (Aug. 2, 2013) —41

### North American Securities Administrators Association

Form ADV, Part 1B, http://www.nasaa.org/wp-content/uploads/2012/10/Form-ADV-Part-1B.pdf —56

### Notre Dame Law Review

Farina, Richard H., John P. Freeman & James Webster, Mutual Fund Industry: A Legal Survey, 44 Notre Dame L. Rev. 732 (1969), http://scholarship.law.nd.edu/ndlr/vol44/iss5/5 —277

### Reuters

Adler, Lynn, BDCs Step Closer to New Legislation, More Leverage, REUTERS, Nov. 19, 2015, http://www.reuters.com/article/2015/11/19/us-bdc-legislation-idUSKCN0T82DW20151119?feedType=RSS&feedName=PersonalFinance#eA4tp2q9FzMOjmMQ.97 —111

### Securities and Exchange Commission

Carey, Paul R., Commissioner, Securities & Exchange Commission, Remarks to the Investment Company Institute Procedures Conference, http://www.sec.gov/news/speech/speecharchive/1999/spch335.htm —322

Champ, Norm, Director, Division of Investment Management, U.S. Securities & Exchange Commission, Remarks to the ALI CLE 2012 Conference on Investment Adviser Regulation (Dec. 6, 2012), http://www.sec.gov/news/speech/2012/spch120612nc.htm —476

Comments of David B. Jones, Senior Vice President, Fidelity Management & Research Co. & Eric D. Roiter, Senior Vice President and General Counsel, Fidelity Management & Research Co. 8-9 (June 4, 2004), http://www.sec.gov/rules/proposed/s71104/fidelity060404.pdf —274

Comments of David B. Jones, Senior Vice President, Product Strategy & Communications, Fidelity Management & Research Co. & Eric D. Roiter, Senior Vice President and General Counsel, Fidelity Management & Research Co. (Mar. 2, 2004), http://www.sec.gov/rules/concept/s72903/fidelity03022004.htm —181

Cybersecurity Guidance, IM Guidance Update, No. 2015-02 (Apr. 2015), http://www.sec.gov/investment/im-guidance-2015-02.pdf —22

Division of Investment Management, Securities and Exchange Commission, Report on Mutual Fund Fees and Expenses (Dec. 2000), http://www.sec.gov/ news/studies/feestudy.htm —233

Donohue, Andrew J., Director, Division of Investment Management, Securities and Exchange Commission, Investment Company Act of 1940: Regulatory Gap between Paradigm and Reality? http://www.sec.gov/news/speech/2009/spch041709ajd.htm —286

Exchange-Traded Funds (last modified Nov. 8, 2013), http://www.sec.gov/answers/etf.htm —469

SEC Staff Evaluating the Use of Derivatives by Funds (Mar. 25, 2010), http://www.sec.gov/news/press/2010/2010-45.htm —475

Study on Investment Advisers and Broker-Dealers As Required by Section 913 of the Dodd-Frank Wall Street Reform and Consumer Protection Act (2011), http://www.sec.gov/news/studies/2011/913studyfinal.pdf —47, 544

Suh, Simona, Memorandum of, Certain Hedge Fund Trading Practices, NY-7563-A (Apr. 10, 2006), http://www.sec.gov/news/studies/2009/oig-509/exhibit-0344.pdf —43

### Securities Law Home Page

Astarita, Mark J., The Wells Notice in SEC and NASD Investigations: Could It Possibly Be a Good Thing? (2010), http//www.seclaw.com/docs/wellsnotice.htm —28

### U. S. Department of the Treasury

U.S. Dep't of the Treas., Fact Sheet: Administration's Regulatory Reform Agenda Moves Forward: Legislation for Strengthening Investor Protection (July 10, 2009), http://www.treas.gov/press/releases/tg205.htm —46

www.ingramcontent.com/pod-product-compliance
Lightning Source LLC
LaVergne TN
LVHW082013200926
848481LV00010B/2854
* 9 7 8 1 8 8 8 2 1 5 6 0 1 *